AMERICA'S ROAD TO EMP

New Approaches to International History

Series Editor: Thomas Zeiler, Professor of American Diplomatic History, University of Colorado Boulder, USA

Series Editorial Board
Anthony Adamthwaite, University of California at Berkeley (USA)
Kathleen Burk, University College London (UK)
Louis Clerc, University of Turku (Finland)
Petra Goedde, Temple University (USA)
Francine McKenzie, University of Western Ontario (Canada)
Lien-Hang Nguyen, University of Kentucky (USA)
Jason Parker, Texas A&M University (USA)
Glenda Sluga, University of Sydney (Australia)

New Approaches to International History covers international history during the modern period and across the globe. The series incorporates new developments in the field, such as the cultural turn and transnationalism, as well as the classical high politics of state-centric policymaking and diplomatic relations. Written with upper level undergraduate and postgraduate students in mind, texts in the series provide an accessible overview of international diplomatic and transnational issues, events and actors.

Published
Decolonization and the Cold War, edited by Leslie James and Elisabeth Leake (2015)
Cold War Summits, Chris Tudda (2015)
The United Nations in International History, Amy Sayward (2017)
Latin American Nationalism, James F. Siekmeier (2017)
The History of United States Cultural Diplomacy, Michael L. Krenn (2017)
International Cooperation in the Early 20th Century, Daniel Gorman (2017)
Women and Gender in International History, Karen Garner (2018)
International Development, Corinna Unger (2018)
The Environment and International History, Scott Kaufman (2018)
Scandinavia and the Great Powers in the First World War, Michael Jonas (2019)
Canada and the World since 1867, Asa McKercher (2019)
The First Age of Industrial Globalization, Maartje Abbenhuis and Gordon Morrell (2019)
Europe's Cold War Relations, Federico Romero, Kiran Klaus Patel, Ulrich Krotz (2019)
United States Relations with China and Iran, Osamah F. Khalil (2019)
Public Opinion and Twentieth-Century Diplomacy, Daniel Hucker (2020)
Globalizing the US Presidency, Cyrus Schayegh (2020)
The International LGBT Rights Movement, Laura Belmonte (2021)
American-Iranian Dialogues, Matthew Shannon (2021)

Forthcoming
Reconstructing the Postwar World, Francine McKenzie
Global War, Global Catastrophe, Maartje Abbenhuis and Ismee Tames
China and the United States since 1949, Elizabeth Ingleson
Activism Across Borders: Causes, Campaigns and Conflicts in Europe since 1870, Daniel Laqua

SERIES EDITOR PREFACE

New Approaches to International History takes the entire world as its stage for exploring the history of diplomacy, broadly conceived theoretically and thematically, and writ large across the span of the globe, during the modern period. This series goes beyond the single goal of explaining encounters in the world. Our aspiration is that these books provide both an introduction for researchers new to a topic, and supplemental and essential reading in classrooms. Thus, *New Approaches* serves a dual purpose that is unique from other large-scale treatments of international history; it applies to scholarly agendas and pedagogy. In addition, it does so against the backdrop of a century of enormous change, conflict, and progress that informed global history but also continues to reflect on our own times.

The series offers the old and new diplomatic history to address a range of topics that shaped the twentieth century. Engaging in international history (including but not especially focusing on global or world history), these books will appeal to a range of scholars and teachers situated in the humanities and social sciences, including those in history, international relations, cultural studies, politics, and economics. We have in mind scholars, both novice and veteran, who require an entrée into a topic, trend, or technique that can benefit their own research or education into a new field of study by crossing boundaries in a variety of ways.

By its broad and inclusive coverage, *New Approaches to International History* is also unique because it makes accessible to students current research, methodology, and themes. Incorporating cutting-edge scholarship that reflects trends in international history, as well as addressing the classical high politics of state-centric policymaking and diplomatic relations, these books are designed to bring alive the myriad of approaches for digestion by advanced undergraduates and graduate students. In preparation for the *New Approaches* series, Bloomsbury surveyed courses and faculty around the world to gauge interest and reveal core themes of relevance for their classroom use. The polling yielded a host of topics, from war and peace to the environment; from empire to economic integration; and from migration to nuclear arms. The effort proved that there is a much-needed place for studies that connect scholars and students alike to international history, and books that are especially relevant to the teaching missions of faculty around the world.

We hope readers find this series to be appealing, challenging, and thought-provoking. Whether the history is viewed through older or newer lenses, *New Approaches to International History* allows students to peer into the modern period's complex relations among nations, people, and events to draw their own conclusions about the tumultuous, interconnected past.

Thomas Zeiler, University of Colorado Boulder, USA

AMERICA'S ROAD TO EMPIRE

FOREIGN POLICY FROM INDEPENDENCE TO WORLD WAR ONE

Piero Gleijeses

BLOOMSBURY ACADEMIC
LONDON • NEW YORK • OXFORD • NEW DELHI • SYDNEY

BLOOMSBURY ACADEMIC
Bloomsbury Publishing Plc
50 Bedford Square, London, WC1B 3DP, UK
1385 Broadway, New York, NY 10018, USA
29 Earlsfort Terrace, Dublin 2, Ireland

BLOOMSBURY, BLOOMSBURY ACADEMIC and the Diana logo are trademarks
of Bloomsbury Publishing Plc

First published in Great Britain 2022

Cover design: Terry Woodley
Series design: Catherine Wood
Cover image: Cartoon by Joseph Keppler titled *It's 'Up To' Them*,
published November 20, 1901, in Puck magazine. Retrieved from the Library of Congress,
https://www.loc.gov/item/2010651486.

A catalogue record for this book is available from the British Library.

Library of Congress Cataloging-in-Publication Data
Names: Gleijeses, Piero, author.
Title: America's road to empire : foreign policy from independence to World War One / Piero Gleijeses.
Description: London ; New York : Bloomsbury Academic, 2021. | Series: New approaches to international history
| Includes bibliographical references and index. |
Identifiers: LCCN 2021005070 (print) | LCCN 2021005071 (ebook) | ISBN 9781350028678 (hardback) |
ISBN 9781350028685 (paperback) | ISBN 9781350028661 (ebook) | ISBN 9781350028692 (epub)
Subjects: LCSH: Imperialism. | United States–Foreign relations–1783–1865. | United States–Foreign
relations–1865–1921. | United States–Territorial expansion. | United States–Colonial question.
Classification: LCC E183.7 .G553 2021 (print) | LCC E183.7 (ebook) | DDC 327.73009/034—dc23
LC record available at https://lccn.loc.gov/2021005070
LC ebook record available at https://lccn.loc.gov/2021005071

ISBN: HB: 978-1-3500-2867-8
        PB: 978-1-3500-2868-5
        ePDF: 978-1-3500-2866-1
        eBook: 978-1-3500-2869-2

Series: New Approaches to International History

Typeset by RefineCatch Limited, Bungay, Suffolk
Printed and bound in Great Britain

To find out more about our authors and books visit www.bloomsbury.com
and sign up for our newsletters.

To Setsuko Ono

CONTENTS

FIGURES

MAPS

Maps

ABBREVIATIONS

AA	Auswärtiges Amt
AAE	Archive des Affaires Etrangères, Paris
AHN	Archivo Histórico Nacional, Madrid
AMAE	Archivo del Ministerio de Asuntos Exteriores, Madrid
AHR	*American Historical Review*
AN, MRREE	Archivo Nacional, Ministerio de Relaciones Exteriores, San José, Costa Rica
Annals	*The Debates and Proceedings in the Congress of the United States*
BA	Bundesarchiv, Auswärtiges Amt, Berlin
c	container
CG	*Congressional Globe*
CP	Correspondence Politique
DOS	United States Department of State
FRUS	United States, Department of State, *Foreign Relations of the United States*
GPO	Government Printing Office
HAHR	*Hispanic American Historical Review*
JAH	*Journal of American History*
JLAS	*Journal of Latin American Studies*
JNH	*Journal of Negro History*
MAH	Archivo Histórico Genaro Estrada de la Secretaría de Relaciones Exteriores, Mexico City
NA	National Archives, College Park, MD
LOC	Library of Congress, Washington DC
NAR	*North American Review*
NYH	New York *Herald*
NWR	*Niles' Weekly Register*
PA	Bundesarchiv, Politisches Archiv
PAH	Syrett, Harold, ed. *The Papers of Alexander Hamilton*, 27 vols. (New York: Columbia University Press, 1961–87)

Abbreviations

PBF	Labaree, Leonard et al., eds. *The Papers of Benjamin Franklin*, 43 vols. (New Haven, CT: Yale University Press, 1959–2018)
PHC	Hopkins, James et al., eds. *The Papers of Henry Clay*, 11 vols. (Lexington: University of Kentucky Press, 1959–92)
PHR	*Pacific Historical Review*
PJM: SSS	Brugger, Robert et al., eds. *The Papers of James Madison, Secretary of State Series*, 11 vols. to date (Charlottesville: University of Virginia Press, 1986–)
PJMO	Preston, Daniel, ed. *The Papers of James Monroe*, 6 vols. (Westport, CT: Greenwood, 2003–17)
PGW: PS	Twohuig, Dorothy et al., eds. *The Papers of George Washington: Presidential Series*, 21 vols. (Charlottesville: University of Virginia Press, 1987–2016)
PTJ	Bond, Julian et al., eds. *The Papers of Thomas Jefferson*, 43 vols. to date (Princeton, NJ: Princeton University Press, 1950–)
PTJ:RS	Looney, Jefferson et al., eds. *The Papers of Thomas Jefferson, Retirement Series*, 14 vols. to date (Charlottesville: University of Virginia Press, 2004–)
PWW	Link, Arthur, ed. *The Papers of Woodrow Wilson*, 69 vols. (Princeton, NJ: Princeton University Press, 1966–96)
RG	Record Group
SDDF	State Department Decimal File
TNA	The National Archives of the UK

PROLOGUE

Twelve years before he became president, Woodrow Wilson wrote about US foreign policy: "When issues of our own interest arose, we have been selfish ... We have shown ourselves kin to all the world, when it came to pushing an advantage."

Kin to all the world? What about American exceptionalism, that special moral compass that made the foreign policy of the United States unlike that of all other powers, past and present? What about the City on the Hill?

The debate over the very nature of the United States and its foreign policy rages to this day. Different interpretations clash; different narratives of the same past emerge.

Look at the birth of the nation. Americans celebrate the Revolution, when the people of the Thirteen Colonies overthrew British rule and created a Republic. Herein lie the roots of America's anticolonialism—the United States is the product of the first successful revolution against a colonial power in modern history.

But does that narrative reflect the truth, all the truth? Americans celebrate a revolution that brought no radical social transformation: the great slaveholding planters, the mighty merchants, and the successful lawyers remained on top. If a revolution was attempted during the American war of independence, it was that of the enslaved Blacks in the South. The British soldiers who crisscrossed the southern states, home to ninety percent of African Americans, offered freedom to "any negro, the property of a rebel," who sought their protection, regardless of gender or age. But with the victory of the American colonists, black freedom was defeated. This paradox is illustrated by the Franco-American victory at Yorktown, celebrated in US history books as a triumph of freedom. Thousands of runaways had joined the British troops. When the British surrendered, the runaways' masters descended on Yorktown to hunt down their human chattel. Many recovered their property—among them George Washington (two slaves) and Thomas Jefferson (five).

The American War of Independence was an anticolonial war. Janus-like, it was also something else: the rebels were fighting for independence, against the British; and also for empire, against the Native Americans.

In 1787, the Continental Congress did something unprecedented, truly revolutionary. It stipulated that, in the western lands ceded by England, new states would be created as soon as they had the requisite number of inhabitants, and these new states would become members of the federal union with the same rights as the original thirteen. These were the admirable foundations of what Jefferson called the empire of liberty. This empire, however, was for whites only. As Jefferson asserted, white Americans could not "contemplate with satisfaction either blot or mixture on that surface."

As the empire expanded, seizing the lands of Native Americans and Mexicans, it remained a white man's empire. It is impossible, when looking at the first 150 years of US foreign policy, to talk about "America." There were white Americans and there were the others: Blacks, Native Americans, Mexican Americans, Asians … the pariahs. The vaunted American melting pot was for whites only. The Statue of Liberty bears a plaque with Emma Lazarus's stirring words, but Lady Liberty faces eastward, toward white Europe, correctly reflecting the immigrants white Americans sought from the earliest days of the Republic. For those who came from Asia there was San Francisco's Angel Island, with its forbidding message: you are not welcome, we don't want you.

America's Road to Empire explores the first 150 years of the foreign policy of the United States. It seeks to assess the nature of this foreign policy, its motivations, and the elements that triggered the extraordinary expansion of the United States. It also examines the foreign threats the young nation faced. And here we come to another paradox: Americans at the time, and later historians, have spoken eloquently about the threat posed by European powers—France, Britain, Germany—but it was in fact the absence of a foreign threat that made the US situation exceptional in the century that preceded the First World War. European powers, on the other hand, had to live in uneasy proximity with each other. Geography made sure that none could aspire to more than relative security. But the United States, surrounded by weak neighbors, could develop and grow in a world without serious external threats. In the words of historian Nancy Mitchell, Americans came to believe "that they deserve absolute security, the security geography blessed them with and ruthlessness secured … because they are the last best hope for humankind, the bastion of freedom." This had a hidden cost: it spurred intolerance and the tendency to exaggerate threats, and to confront them with violence. This may help explain the extraordinary exchange that took place in March 1915, when Secretary of State William Jennings Bryan told President Wilson: "There seems to be some sympathetic cooperation between the French and German interests in Haiti. There are some indications that their plans include taking advantage of Mole St. Nicholas [a potential a naval base]." Wilson was alarmed: "The whole matter has a most sinister appearance," he responded. At first sight, the two men's alarm may seem plausible: after all, many historians have written that there was a German threat to the Western Hemisphere in the years preceding the First World War. But at that very moment, as the Great War raged in Europe, Germans and French were slaughtering one another in an existential battle for survival.

Any serious study of US foreign policy must focus not only on the actions of the United States but also on the actions of the countries with which it interacted. This means: multi-archival research. Accordingly, *America's Road to Empire* relies on documents from the US, British, French, Spanish, German, Mexican, and Costa Rican archives, as well as on the most authoritative secondary sources and the press in English, French, Spanish, German and, occasionally, in Russian, Portuguese and Italian.

ACKNOWLEDGMENTS

Setsuko Ono has stimulated me along my journey with her probing and frank comments, and she has inspired me with her intelligence, her courage, and her art. Her sculptures adorn Havana, Washington, Baltimore, Tokyo, and Shibukawa. The paintings that she exhibited in Havana, Washington, Venice, and London express with exquisite sensitivity her longing for a more just world. They challenge me to be relentless in seeking the truth in my chosen field.

The Johns Hopkins School of Advanced International Studies (SAIS), where I teach, has a library staff that is always helpful and gracious, and it has a star, Jenny Kusmik, a superb research librarian, who performed miracles, tracking down even the most outlandish publications for me.

Excellent historians have read chapters of this manuscript and given me the benefit of their comments: Kerry Abel, Carl Benn, Jonathan Dull, Paul Gilje, Oliver Gliech, Donald Hickey, Thomas Hietala, Alan Knight, Paul Kramer, Erika Lee, Robert May, Gary Nash, Jeffrey Ostler, Peter Onuf, Theda Perdue, Alan Taylor, and Ana Zuley Zúñiga Jiménez. Two SAIS students—Emmanuel Vassor and Isabel Migoya Iroso—helped me greatly, as did Starr Lee, the coordinator of the American Foreign Policy department.

Judy Tither is the best copy editor I have ever had. Working with her was a pleasure.

I owe a great debt to three special people: my dear friend Isaac Cohen, a profound intellectual with a towering knowledge of Latin America, and Gloria León and Jorge Risquet, whom I considered my siblings. For thirty years Gloria and Risquet were my constant companions and they helped me grow as a human being. I remember them every day.

Dr. Marwa Adi has protected my eyesight—a challenging task—for over a decade. She has now been joined by Dr. Lauren Taney. I am very fortunate to have two ophthalmologists who combine exceptional skill with grace and dedication.

Professor Nancy Mitchell is the most gifted historian I know and a superlative stylist. She generously took the time to read and improve my manuscript. Her constructive criticism—raising questions and pointing to weaknesses in my arguments—drove me to distraction and forced me to probe deeper. *America's Road to Empire* is a much better book because of her, and I cannot thank her enough.

CHAPTER 1
INDEPENDENCE

Only one of the world's great powers played a critical role in the Thirteen Colonies' struggle against the mother country: France, which was thirsting for revenge against Britain after a lost war. France, which had the second strongest fleet in the world and a colonial empire in the Caribbean.

Compared to mighty France, the infant United States was like a Third World country. But the Americans were not intimidated. What is striking is how demanding they were and how obliging were the French. The French king and his aides had no sympathy for the American rebels, but they decided to help them even before being asked. When they joined the war against Britain their paramount aim was the independence of the United States. Their aid would prove crucial to the success of the revolt. This surprising Franco-American minuet forms the heart of this chapter.

Quebec

France and Britain had competed for empire in North America for nearly a century. When the Seven Years' War began in 1756, France had a colony in Canada (Quebec), another in the lower Mississippi Valley, and it claimed the entire watershed of the Mississippi, where it held a string of tiny forts and settlements. Spain, which entered the Seven Years' War as an ally of France, had a colony east of the Mississippi—the peninsula of Florida and the panhandle all the way to the Mississippi north of New Orleans. But when the war ended in 1763, France lost its empire on the North American continent. It surrendered Quebec and its possessions east of the Mississippi (except the Isle d'Orleans, a substantial area that included New Orleans) to the victor, Britain, and it ceded the Isle d'Orleans and its territory west of the Mississippi to its ally Spain to compensate it for the loss of Florida to Britain [Map 1]. Suddenly, with the collapse of the French empire in North America, the Thirteen Colonies no longer shared a border with a powerful neighbor.[1]

This removed a key factor that had bound the Americans to the mother country: fear of France. It was as if the cement holding the bricks together had disappeared from a wall. The wall still stood, but it had become unstable. The French hoped that this signaled that the Thirteen Colonies would break free of Britain, a prospect that delighted them because they were convinced that the source of Britain's might was its commerce and navy, both of which depended on its colonial empire, increasingly centered in the Thirteen Colonies. Longing for the day the colonies would be independent, Louis XV's principal minister, the duke of Choiseul, sent secret agents to North America in the wake of the Seven Years' War to observe the colonial scene, and he also sought information from French diplomats in London. "Monsieur Durand [the French chargé in London] . . . is extremely curious to inform himself in the affairs of America," Benjamin Franklin wrote to his son in 1767; he "has desired to have all my political writings, invited me to dine with him, was very inquisitive, treated me with great civility, makes me visits, &c. I fancy that intriguing nation [France] would like very well to meddle on occasion, and blow up the coals between Britain and her colonies; but I hope we shall give them no opportunity." In fact, opportunity beckoned.[2]

The gathering storm

In 1760 the Thirteen Colonies had a population of approximately 1,300,000 whites and 300,000 Blacks, almost all of whom were enslaved. (The population of England, Wales, and Scotland together was about 8 million.)[3] Slavery existed in all the colonies but was concentrated in the South. The standard of living of white Americans was the highest in the world, and white American men enjoyed political freedoms that residents of Britain— or any other country—lacked; most adult white males could vote, and the colonies enjoyed a large degree of self-government.

Britain emerged from the Seven Years' War victorious but burdened with a public debt of £130 million, "a colossal sum, greater by a fifth than the annual output of the nation's economy."[4] Victory entailed still more expenses: the government planned to station fifteen regiments (approximately 7,500 soldiers) in North America to secure the vast territories it had just acquired. Seven of the fifteen regiments would be deployed in Quebec; four in Florida, which London divided into East Florida (the peninsula) and West Florida (the panhandle all the way to the Mississippi north of New Orleans); and the remaining four would be dispersed between the Appalachians and the Mississippi—a great Indian revolt that broke out in the summer of 1763 confirmed to the British the wisdom of this deployment.[5]

In March 1765, Parliament imposed a tax on the American colonies: the Stamp Act required that stamps be affixed to several articles, including legal documents and newspapers. Prominent Americans would be appointed stamp distributors, a lucrative position. The proceeds of the tax would be spent in the Thirteen Colonies to procure supplies for the new regiments.

From the British point of view, the Stamp Act made sense. It would ease the financial burden of maintaining troops in North America. But for the colonists it made sense to oppose it. Accepting the act would set a dangerous precedent. Until then, only the colonial legislatures had the power to impose internal taxes (external taxes were custom duties, set by the British government). Americans argued that a fundamental right of the English was not to be taxed without consent, expressed by their representatives; since the colonies were not represented in the British parliament, it could not impose taxes on them. As Virginia's legislature declared, taxation by Parliament "must necessarily establish this melancholy truth, that the inhabitants of the colonies are slaves of Britons."[6]

Many Americans had been irritated with the British government before the Stamp Act was approved. Colonists eager to move into Indian territory had been angered by the royal proclamation of October 7, 1763, reserving the vast area from the Appalachians to the Mississippi River for the Indians. Members of the colonial elite, like George Washington, who wanted to acquire large tracts of Indian land to sell to settlers, were also aggrieved. Furthermore, the British, in search of revenue, had begun cracking down on smuggling—a time honored American profession.

The British government had expected the colonists to grumble at the Stamp Act, but to comply with it. Instead, riots broke out. They began in Boston in August 1765 and gradually extended to the other colonies. The ire of the Sons of Liberty—as the protesters called themselves—was directed against three groups: those who had been appointed stamp distributors, those who were accused of supporting the Stamp Act, and those who believed that it should be obeyed because it was the law, even though they opposed it. The Sons of Liberty "seized private mail, restricted the freedom of the press, and terrorized their enemies without mercy," write Edmund and Helen Morgan, the two leading authorities on the act. The riots fed on impunity: when the rioters razed the houses of stamp distributors or forced them to flee for their lives, no one was punished. This was the irony: it was dangerous to be a loyal subject of the crown; it was safe to be a rioter. It was easy to rally a mob to oppose taxation when rioters went unpunished. And they could act with impunity for a simple reason: the governors had no troops. The few thousand British regulars in North America were spread through the territories acquired in 1763 from France and Spain. In February 1766, the governor of New York reported that he had only 160 men and that "nothing at present but a superior force [would] bring the people to a sense of their duty."[7]

It was members of the elite of American society who roiled up the protesters to the Stamp Act. Merchants, lawyers, and plantation owners "may have appeared seldom enough in the actual work of destruction," the Morgans note, "but that they directed the show from behind the scenes is suggested by every surviving piece of evidence." This mattered, because they galvanized the anger of the poor against the British Government and deflected it from themselves. They did so by claiming that the Stamp Act was the thin edge of the onslaught: if the colonists submitted, they would be crushed by taxes and American freedom would be smothered.[8]

This would be a keynote of the American War of Independence, and the reason why it did not turn into a social revolution: the people's fury would be directed against the distant metropole rather than the local upper class. The war brought no radical social transformation: the great slaveholding planters, the mighty merchants, and the successful lawyers remained on top. Chattel slavery remained the lot of the overwhelming majority of African Americans. And white women, despite their contribution to the cause of independence, remained "in a state of submissive dependence."[9]

In 1765, while the lower classes rioted, the elites organized a boycott of British goods. Violence was directed against those merchants who did not join the boycott; violence with impunity—a potent combination. The boycott was effective. In London, British merchants pleaded with Parliament to repeal the Stamp Act, and in February 1776 the government gave in.

After this painful experience, the British authorities had two plausible paths forward: use force in the Thirteen Colonies to reestablish their authority, which meant deploying thousands of soldiers there; or return to the *status quo* of before the Seven Years' War, which meant foregoing taxes, going easy on smuggling, and simply enjoying the profits of trade with the Americans. It is understandable that London resisted the first option: at home it faced a very strained financial situation, and abroad it confronted a Franco-Spanish alliance eager for revenge. But what made no sense is that it chose a third approach, one that was unworkable: it continued to challenge the Americans, but it did not bolster its ability to enforce its demands. In 1767, Parliament passed the Townshend Acts, which levied import duties on paper, paints, glass, lead, and tea shipped to the colonies. Chancellor of the Exchequer Charles Townshend had told Parliament that the goal of these duties was to raise revenue; therefore, the Americans claimed, they were taxes. Worse, Townshend had said that more duties might follow. The cycle resumed: the colonists boycotted British goods, the Sons of Liberty rioted, and the authorities did not respond.[10] On only one occasion did British soldiers use deadly force against rioters: in Boston, on March 5, 1770, a mob threatened a small party of British soldiers who finally opened fire; five Americans died.[11]

The following month, the British government again capitulated and repealed most of the Townshend duties, maintaining, however, the duty on tea to uphold the principle of Parliament's sovereignty. This meant that the British East India Company had to pay a heavy duty on its tea in Britain and then, in America, had to pay the Townshend duty. As a result, Americans smuggled cheaper tea from Holland.

An uneasy calm returned to the colonies. Mobs harassed—with impunity—British customs officials who sought to curb smuggling. Even when Rhode Islanders in June 1772 set fire to a British Customs schooner, London did not respond. "There is scarcely a case on record of a serious attempt on the part of a British government to punish attacks on those whose duty was to enforce the laws of trade," two scholars note.[12] Meanwhile, land speculators and settlers seethed at British constraints: in 1768 British officials on the frontier had bullied the Indians into ceding vast areas, but the Americans wanted more. George Washington, Thomas Jefferson, Patrick Henry, and dozens of other Virginia leaders "had engaged in a land rush of amazing proportions," historian Gary Nash writes.[13] The great southern planters had yet another grievance: they were mired in ever mounting debt to the British merchants who bought their crops and sold them the luxury products they craved. They could have reduced their "extravagant consumption," but this they were not willing to do. Instead, they gorged on credit and blamed their British creditors for their plight. Of the £4,000,000 owed by Americans to British merchants at the outset of the War of Independence, half was owed by Virginia's planters, among them Thomas Jefferson and George Washington. This explains, Washington's biographer Ron Chernow remarks, "why rich Virginia planters ... formed a hotbed of revolutionary ferment."[14]

The British government had no desire to embark on a major confrontation with the Americans and paid little attention to the Thirteen Colonies, focusing instead on what seemed more urgent matters in Europe, in India, and at home. Throughout 1773, a careful historian writes, "America was never mentioned once in any of the scores of letters that passed to and from between [Prime Minister] Lord North and [king] George III."[15] They were in for a rude awakening.

To help the East India Company, which was on the brink of bankruptcy, in March 1773 Parliament slashed the heavy duty imposed on tea at British ports before transshipment to America, but maintained the Townshend duty. This meant that the company could sell its tea in the colonies at a lower price than Dutch tea, which threatened to put the smugglers—some of the most important merchants of Philadelphia, New York, and Boston—out of business. They countered with a call to principle: merchants must refuse to sell the cheaper tea because to do so meant accepting the Townshend duty and therefore Parliament's right to tax Americans. Many colonists agreed. Once again violence ensued: those merchants who had agreed to sell British tea were intimidated, and they all gave in, except in Charleston and Boston. Three British ships laden with tea waited in Boston's harbor for their cargo to be unloaded, but on December 16 a large group of Bostonians decided that it was time to act.[16]

The story of the Boston Tea Party is well known: that same evening, small groups of men "roughly disguised as Indians, in most cases with no more than a dub of paint and with an old blanket wrapped around them," boarded the ships. They dumped the tea into the harbor while an approving crowd watched from the shore.[17]

This time Britain reacted. In March 1774 Parliament passed the first of four "Coercive Acts": no ships would be allowed in the port of Boston—except those bringing food and fuel for the inhabitants—until the city had compensated the East India Company for the spoiled tea. The second Coercive Act, in May, abrogated key provisions of the charter of Massachusetts, restricting the colonists' rights. Two more Coercive Acts followed, further tightening London's grip on the colony. "The Americans have tarred and feathered your subjects," Prime Minister North told the House of Commons, "burnt your ships, denied obedience to your laws and authority; yet so clement and so forbearing has our conduct been, that it is incumbent on us now to take a different course."[18]

It was too late. For the Americans, the years between the Stamp Act riots and the Boston Tea Party had witnessed the waning of the foreign threat—the cement that had bound them to mother England. "Protection and obedience are reciprocal," the former Chancellor of the Exchequer George Grenville had told Parliament in early 1766. "Great Britain protects America; America is bound to yield obedience."[19] But here was the rub: the French empire in North America had dissolved so Americans no longer needed Britain's protection. Against this backdrop the British, with their taxes and their failure to protect law-abiding, loyal colonists, had projected an image of both malevolence and weakness—a deadly combination. The Boston Tea Party and the Coercive Acts set up a confrontation that could be resolved only if one side capitulated, and that was increasingly unlikely. While British troops occupied Boston, the first Continental Congress met in Philadelphia from September 5 to October 26, 1774, attended by representatives of all the colonies except Georgia, to devise a response to the Coercive Acts. The Congress approved a trade embargo against Britain, and set up an "association" to enforce it. "Terror was employed," when necessary, "as speech was controlled, the newspapers censored, and dissent crushed."[20] Throughout the colonies, militia units were organized, and the loyalists—perhaps 20 percent of the population—repressed. By the time the second Continental Congress assembled in Philadelphia in May 1775, blood had been shed at Lexington and Concord. In June, the congress created the Continental Army. Its initial nucleus was the New England militia that was besieging the British in Boston. In August, King George III declared that the colonies were "in open and avowed rebellion."[21]

With each month, support for independence grew. The British continued to display weakness: their foray to Lexington and Concord had been a failure, and their assault on Bunker Hill in June a Pyrrhic victory; in March 1776 they ignominiously withdrew from Boston.

The British islands in the Caribbean did not follow the example of the Thirteen Colonies. The reason was simple: they needed British protection. From whom? Possibly the French, who retained their Caribbean possessions. But the people whom the whites living on those islands feared were the enslaved black men and women who greatly outnumbered them. In 1775, there were fewer than 50,000 whites and more than 400,000 Blacks on the islands. (In the Thirteen Colonies Blacks were only one fifth of a population of two and half million.) The nightmare of slave revolts haunted the whites of the British Caribbean, and they welcomed the presence of British troops. Fear kept them loyal.[22]

A similar fear gripped the white men and women of the southern half of the Thirteen Colonies, where almost all the enslaved lived, but it had the opposite impact: it drove them away from Britain. In late 1775, Lord Dunmore, the British governor of Virginia, had promised that any of the rebels' slaves who were "able and willing to bear arms" and join his troops would be granted freedom, and he began to create a regiment of runaways. Dunmore's actions were misunderstood as an assault on slavery and they struck terror in the slaveholding South and beyond. Edward Rutledge, a prominent member of the Continental Congress from South Carolina, wrote that Dunmore's declaration did "more effectually ... work an eternal separation between Great Britain and the Colonies than any other expedient which could possibly have been thought of."[23] The quip of English essayist Samuel Johnson—"How is it that we hear the loudest yelps for liberty among the drivers of negroes?"[24]—was grounded in reality. Slaveowners flocked to the rebel standards.

As the momentum toward independence accelerated, Americans looked abroad for support. In March 1776, a few days before the British evacuated Boston, Congress voted to send a Connecticut merchant, Silas Deane, to Paris to buy military and other supplies on credit from the French government and to inquire whether, if the colonies declared their independence, France would "enter into any treaty or alliance with them, for commerce or defence or both?"[25] By the time Deane arrived in Paris on July 6, France's King Louis XVI had already decided to help the Americans.

France and the rebel colonies

Louis XVI was twenty years old when he ascended the throne in 1774. Intelligent, but indecisive and insecure, he sought a mentor and selected the Count de Maurepas, an old and experienced courtier. "I am the king, but I am just twenty years old," Louis wrote to Maurepas. "I don't think that I have acquired all the knowledge I will need."[26] He flanked Maurepas with two able and strong personalities, Robert Turgot, Baron de l'Aulne, as finance minister, and Charles Gravier, Count de Vergennes, as foreign minister. Both men wanted to enhance the greatness of France, but their strategies clashed. For Turgot, the imperative was to reform the country's finances; he looked inward and opposed foreign adventures. Vergennes believed that France could resume its rightful position in world affairs only by weakening the nation that had humbled it. In a December 1774 memorandum to Louis XVI, Vergennes suggested that war against Britain was inevitable. Across the Channel he saw "a nation restless and greedy, more jealous of the prosperity of its neighbors than awake to its own happiness, powerfully armed and ready to strike on the instant."[27]

In this ineluctable war against Britain, France would have a natural ally: Spain, which was no longer a great military power, but still had a respectable fleet. Sealed in 1761, the Family Compact between the two Bourbon powers was, for Vergennes, "the cornerstone of France's system,"[28] a belief Louis XVI shared. Under no circumstances should France fight Britain alone; only united could the two Bourbon fleets hope to defeat the Royal Navy. In Charles III Spain had an intelligent and reform-minded king, and its fleet was third in the world.

Vergennes' December 1774 memorandum only alluded to the unrest in the Thirteen Colonies, but soon he began attributing ever increasing importance to America. This was not due to sympathy for the rebels, but to his conviction that British power would be crippled if the colonies broke free. "Trade with the colonies is London's most lucrative and most reliable source of revenue," he wrote. "If it were to dry up the impact would be terrible."[29]

Vergennes believed that rebellion in the Thirteen Colonies could be spurred by assuring the colonists that France was sympathetic to their cause. He instructed Achard de Bonvouloir, the secret agent he sent to North America in the summer of 1775, to hint at the possibility of French aid. To avoid provoking London, Bonvouloir was not, however, to speak in the name of the French government.[30] In December 1775, he appeared in Philadelphia under a false identity—as a merchant from Antwerp, with good, but ill-defined contacts at the French court.

Bonvouloir's report, which reached Vergennes on February 27, 1776, was encouraging on every point. The Americans were powerful and ready to die rather than continue to submit to British rule. They were amicably disposed toward France, eager to develop contacts, and convinced that its support would be crucial.[31] The report was, Jonathan Dull, a leading authority on the period, notes, "the catalyst for a major shift in the French position toward the American war."[32]

On March 1, 1776, Vergennes sent a note to the Spanish foreign minister, the Marquis de Grimaldi, asking whether Spain would be willing to join France in providing secret assistance to the Americans. Then, without waiting for a reply, on March 12, Vergennes presented his "Considérations" to Louis XVI, in which he suggested that "it made sense to give the insurgents secret assistance in arms and money." France should also, he urged, embark on a program of naval rearmament. The king, noted a confidant of Maurepas, "asked his ministers to present their views [on Vergennes' suggestions] in writing, so that they could discuss them in the Council of State."[33] Besides Vergennes, this select group included only four men: Maurepas, Turgot, Navy minister Antoine de Sartine, and war minister Claude-Louis, Count de Saint-Germain. The debate on France's American policy had begun.

"America was in fashion," writes a leading biographer of Louis XVI. "Books of geography, travel accounts, articles in the journals—all elaborating on Rousseau's theme of the 'noble savage'—repeatedly praised . . . the New World." With one exception, however, the members of the Council of State had no sympathy for the American rebels. Vergennes, the prime mover of the policy of secret aid, was a deeply conservative man, "a man of the Ancien Regime from head to toe," with "a visceral repugnance . . . for the idea of revolt.'" Maurepas, Navy minister Sartine, and war minister Saint Germain shared Vergennes's antipathy for rebellious colonists. As did the king, who considered helping the Americans morally wrong. Aiding them, he explained, went against "my heart and my beliefs."[34]

The one member of the council who sympathized with the American rebels, Turgot, a man of progressive views, was, ironically, the only one who opposed extending aid to them. He believed that it would lead to war against Britain and that a war would be "the worst of all evils" because of the disastrous financial condition of the country. He argued that France should "help the colonists acquire arms and even money through trade, but remain neutral and decline to give them direct aid."[35]

While Louis hesitated, a positive Spanish reply reached Versailles. "It is in our interest that the colonists' rebellion continue," the Spanish foreign minister, Grimaldi, acknowledged, "And we must hope that they and the British exhaust each other."[36] Spain had many reasons to wish ill to the British—their occupation of Gibraltar and Minorca, their encroachment in Spanish America, and, more recently, the loss of Florida.

Encouraged by the almost unanimous Council of State and by the support of Spain, Louis XVI took two closely-related decisions: in late April he ordered strengthening the navy; then, on May 2, he approved one million French *livres* (almost $6 million in 2021 dollars) in secret aid to the rebels.[37] The decision was taken eight weeks before the arrival of Silas Deane; that is, well before the Americans asked for help.

Money that France desperately needed for internal recovery would be lavished on armaments, and more funds would be diverted to support the rich Americans. Louis had unwittingly taken the first step toward war and the scaffold.

The diplomacy of "a new age"?

Silas Deane's March 1776 instructions to seek French aid were soon outdated. On July 4, the Continental Congress proclaimed the independence of the United States. It could now openly seek foreign alliances. On September 17, it approved a Model Treaty to be proposed to France. The treaty stipulated that the commerce of each party would receive the same privileges as given to nationals, and established liberal principles for neutral trade in case of war: neutral ships had the right to carry the goods of a belligerent as long as they were not contraband (known as "free ships, free goods"); contraband items were narrowly defined and excluded food and naval stores; neutrals could trade between the ports of a belligerent.

The treaty's political clauses stipulated that the king of France would never attempt to acquire any part of British North America (including his lost colonies) and would recognize the Americans' right to "sole, exclusive, undivided and perpetual possession" of all these territories. In the instructions prepared for the three commissioners who would negotiate with the French, the Continental Congress promised that if the Franco-American treaty triggered a British declaration of war on France (an outcome that was inevitable, because French recognition of American independence would be an intolerable insult for London), the United States would not conclude a separate peace with Britain without notifying France six months in advance. The task of the commissioners was to persuade France to sign the treaty and thus provoke war between Britain and France. In order to better nudge the French, the instructions urged the commissioners to indulge in a little blackmail: they should "press for the immediate and explicit declaration of France in our favor, upon a suggestion that a re-union with Great Britain may be the consequence of a delay."[38]

The Americans "entered European diplomacy as heralds of a new age," writes George Herring, a prominent US historian.[39] In fact, while the Model Treaty introduced liberal economic principles, its territorial and political clauses reeked of age-old power politics. The Americans wanted to bring France into the war but refused to offer anything in return. They staked out an empire for themselves in which France would renounce all ambitions.

In Paris, the three commissioners, Benjamin Franklin, Silas Deane, and Arthur Lee, were hard at work. On January 5, 1777, they asked Vergennes to provide eight armed ships of the line (the largest battleships of the time) and a large quantity of military supplies under convoy, arguing disingenuously that "As other princes of Europe are lending or hiring their troops to Britain against America, it is apprehended that France may . . . afford our independent states the same kind of aid, without giving Britain any just cause of complaint." They dangled their threat: "unless some powerful aid is given us," the American people might "find themselves reduced to the necessity of ending the war by an accommodation."[40]

Meanwhile, the defeats of the Continental Army from August through November 1776 had brought Congress to a more realistic position. As British General William Howe's victorious army advanced in New Jersey, a dejected George Washington and his dwindling force had fled across the Delaware River. On December 12, Congress had authorized the commissioners to offer the Bourbon powers an alliance if this was the price of bringing them into the war.

Upon receiving these new instructions, the commissioners raised the stakes. Deane addressed a note to Vergennes on March 18, 1777, outlining a grandiose plan, if France joined the war: "It is proposed that the conquest of Canada [Quebec], Nova Scotia, Newfoundland, St. Johns, the Floridas, Bermuda, Bahama and all the West India islands now in possession of Britain be attempted by the joint force of France and the United States." American warships would come to the aid of France if it sought to conquer the British West Indies; Congress would also provide supplies "to the amount of two million of dollars [c. $49 million]." The rewards would be bountiful: France would acquire all the British Caribbean possessions while the United States—thirteen rebel colonies whose independence no state had acknowledged and whose survival was doubtful—would receive "the rest," that is, all the British possessions in North America.

Spain, too, would be rewarded if it joined the war. Madrid had strained relations with Portugal, a British ally that had closed its ports to American ships. As part of its own fight for independence, the United States suggested the destruction of Portugal: "It is also proposed by the Congress that in case Spain shall enter with France into the said war, the United States will, if thereto required, declare war against Portugal . . . and will continue the said war for the total conquest of that Kingdom, to be added to the Dominions of Spain."[41]

On April 7, Franklin augmented the spoils promised to Spain: the United States would help Spain acquire Pensacola, the capital of British-held West Florida, on the condition that "the inhabitants of the United States shall have the free navigation of the Mississippi and the use of the harbor of Pensacola."[42]

It is true that Franklin "emphasized by the simplicity of his dress that he was the representative of a new and uncorrupted world."[43] But while the Commissioners' attire was striking, their notes of March 18 and April 7, 1777 were laughable, because their promises so far outstripped the rebels' capabilities. Vergennes understood this: "I have several letters from these gentlemen," he wrote to Spain's ambassador to Versailles. "Quite simply, they are urging us to wage war on their behalf."[44]

The Americans' bombast equaled their greed. They sought desperately needed French help, but they could not resist insisting that Quebec, Nova Scotia, and the other morsels be added to the still unborn American empire, all territories that had expressed no desire to be freed, and that could be conquered only with the assistance of the French. When in 1775 they had sought to conquer Quebec, the attempt had ended in disaster.

However overblown their promises, however greedy their demands, the Americans had a powerful trump: the French government believed that the independence of the United States would cripple British power and was, therefore, a vital French interest. This is why it went to great lengths to help the Americans. When the commissioners presented their note of January 5, 1777, Vergennes refused the proposed treaty, as well as the demand for eight ships of the line, explaining gently that such measures would amount to an open act of war against Britain; but he offered two million French *livres* (c. $12 million), of which 500,000 were disbursed immediately.[45]

This set a pattern. Vergennes received the commissioners but did not grant them an official audience; he communicated with them but no written note bore his signature. This fig-leaf allowed the French to claim to be neutral in the Anglo-American conflict despite the fact that ships laden with military supplies left France for the rebel colonies and American privateers used French ports.[46] Meanwhile, the French navy was being strengthened at a furious pace.

Then, on December 4, came news of the great American victory at Saratoga.

Louis XVI's choice

Saratoga was crucial in bringing France into the war, writes George Herring, because it provided "a convincing and long-sought indication that the Americans could succeed with external assistance."[47] The meager results of the British campaign in Pennsylvania in the fall of 1777 deepened this impression of American strength.

Nevertheless, Louis hesitated. The king's council was divided: Vergennes and Navy minister Sartine urged war, but they were opposed by the ministers of finance and of war.[48] The most influential minister, Maurepas, had serious reservations. His fears were paraphrased by a friend, the abbé de Véri: "Why should I rush to join a war when it is impossible to foresee its length and its consequences? ... Is our fleet, even if joined by Spain, equal to Britain's? ... Are our finances able ... to bear the cost?"[49]

It was a key tenet of France's policy to avoid war against Britain unless Spain was at its side. On December 6, Louis approved a memorandum authorizing conversations with the commissioners for the conclusion of a treaty with the United States with a significant proviso: "His Majesty ... expressly reserves the right not to conclude any agreement without the participation of the Spanish king."[50]

The Spanish considered Britain and its rebel colonies "equally dangerous enemies."[51] They rightly discounted the Americans' professions of friendship and worried that an independent United States might be even more aggressive than Britain toward Spain's North American possessions. On December 31, Madrid's reply to what was in fact a proposal for war against Britain (the sure consequence of a treaty with the Americans) reached Versailles. It was negative.[52] Nonetheless, a week later Louis approved a memorandum drafted by Vergennes, stating that France would seek forthwith to conclude a treaty with the United States.[53] In so doing he accepted a serious risk: the British Navy was stronger than the French. Historian Jonathan Dull argues that "given the advantage of surprise" France could begin war with a fleet at "near parity" with the British.[54] But the French launched no surprise attacks. In mid-March, they made public their recognition of the United States. Then they waited. They wanted Britain to fire the first shot so that it would appear to be the aggressor to the European governments. On June 17, 1778, British warships opened fire on a French frigate.

Maurepas later remarked, "without Mr. Franklin's threats ..., we would not have concluded a treaty with the United States."[55] What, then, was the role of Franklin and his fellow commissioners in pushing France to war?

In London, on December 10, 1777, the British prime minister, Lord North, had adjourned Parliament to gain time to formulate a strategy to deal with the Americans; it was expected that after the Christmas recess he would offer them generous peace terms, short of independence. Then, on December 15 and 16 an American loyalist, Paul

Wentworth, sent by the British government, met in Paris with Deane; a few days later another British envoy, James Hutton, met with Franklin, who also spoke with Wentworth. At the same time, letters from London crossed the channel to Paris. The British were sounding out the American commissioners to explore whether there could be reconciliation short of independence.

Franklin and Deane reported the British overtures to Vergennes. They used the British soundings to apply pressure on him, hinting broadly that French indecisiveness could force the rebels to accept the British offer. "If I can judge the American attitude from the statements of the commissioners," Vergennes wrote on December 13 to France's ambassador in Madrid, "I think that the Americans would prefer an alliance with the two crowns [France and Spain] to reconciliation with Britain, but the commissioners clearly convey the impression that if they do not soon receive considerable assistance, they might be forced by their people to approach the nation they fear most [Britain]."[56]

There are two possibilities. The first, that Vergennes did not believe the commissioners' threat of Anglo-American reconciliation, but appropriated it to push Louis to war. However, in the weeks that followed the news of Saratoga, Vergennes repeatedly referred to the possibility of Anglo-American reconciliation. As two scholars point out, if Vergennes "was acting a part, he never dropped the mask"—not in his communications with the King or Maurepas, and not even in his private letters to his protégé, Armand de Montmorin, who was the French ambassador to Spain.[57]

The more credible explanation is that the commissioners' thinly veiled blackmail— help us or we will turn to Britain—alarmed Vergennes. The Americans' victory at Saratoga in October 1777, coupled with the expected peace offensive of the North government, had shaken his confidence: would the rebels continue to fight, given enticing British concessions? Vergennes knew very little about the Americans. His major source of information was the American commissioners. And the commissioners—Franklin foremost—skillfully exploited his fears, while the British government unwittingly fanned them. Franklin, John Hardman writes, "ran rings round Vergennes."[58]

The Franco-American alliance

On February 6, 1778, the French and the Americans signed a commercial treaty and a "Treaty of Alliance, Eventual and Defensive."[59] On April 30, the Continental Congress received the two treaties; four days later it ratified them unanimously.

France had sought no privileges in the commercial treaty, and the two countries granted each other most-favored-nation status. The Treaty of Alliance, the only such treaty ratified by the United States until NATO in 1949, specified that if war broke out between France and Britain before the Anglo-American war ended—which all sides fully expected—neither party would sign a separate peace with Britain, and they would "not lay down their arms until the independence of the United States shall have been formally or tacitly assured by the treaty or treaties that shall terminate the war."

The alliance foresaw the possibility of territorial aggrandizement by both parties. France would be free to seize the British colonies in the Caribbean, but it renounced, "forever," all designs on North America east of the Mississippi, with the sole exception of the Isle d'Orleans which it had ceded to Spain after the Seven Years' War. France could acquire the Isle d'Orleans and land west of the Mississippi—but only at the expense of Spain, something that in 1778 seemed little short of absurd, given the alliance between the two Bourbon thrones.

The French public celebrated their government's recognition of the United States, as well as the coming war with Britain. "An informal coalition," Jonathan Dull writes, had developed in favor of war, "which combined intellectuals supporting American independence for ideological reasons, noblemen urging war out of Anglophobia and a desire for military employment, and businessmen who saw in both war and American independence the potential for profit."[60] Sympathy for the American rebels played only a minor role. The driving force was the desire for revenge over Britain.

French policy, however, was based on a fallacy: that the independence of the Thirteen Colonies would cripple Britain. This fallacy explains why Versailles provided secret aid to the rebels; why it joined the war; and why it did not drive a hard bargain from the Americans. The independence of the United States, Versailles believed, "would deal British commerce an irreparable loss."[61]

The poverty of the American war effort

"The French alliance, let it never be forgotten, brought independence," Samuel Flagg Bemis, a renowned US historian, declared.[62] By the time the alliance was signed on February 6, 1778, the Americans' patriotic fervor had long ebbed. It had crested in the first half of 1776, when the British had seemed impotent, but then a British armada arrived with 32,000 soldiers, and the hard times began.

Soon, the rebels would be fighting two wars: one, for independence, against the British; and another, for empire, against the Indians. Approximately 90,000 Native Americans lived in the territory that became the United States. Only too aware of the colonists' insatiable hunger for their land, most of the Indians sided with the British. Their participation in the war "was guided by their own interests, which remained the security of their families, their land, their culture and way of life," historian Armstrong Starkey remarks.[63] This war was a conflict of extreme violence. Both sides killed and scalped women, children, and men. Yet Indian culture provided a glimmer of humanity: whites taken captive might be spared and adopted by Indian families. American frontiersmen did not adopt Indians. "Murder, gradually and inexorably, became the dominant American Indian policy," Richard White writes.[64]

However bloody, the war against the Indians was a sideshow, compared with the rebels' main effort, against the British. Two of the most distinctive features of American society compromised the rebels' chances of victory. First, by the standards of the day the white population of the Thirteen Colonies was prosperous, and people who had an adequate livelihood were reluctant to risk their lives and economic well-being to fight against the British. Second, America's white population enjoyed the most democratic society in the western world. An authority on the war, John Shy, notes that "if Americans fought, it could be only because they wanted to fight—they were not Russian peasants" who could be marched off to the battlefield like cattle.[65] Nor could the rebels be compelled to pay taxes. These "negative" characteristics—relative freedom and prosperity—might have been offset by the desire to defend cherished religious beliefs threatened by an intolerant foe or by fervent nationalism. But the religious considerations that hardened the Dutch in their struggle against Spain in the latter half of the sixteenth century were absent in the American rebels' fight against Britain. Nor could these same rebels experience the patriotism that in 1848 would make the people of Venice, remembering proud centuries of independence, rise against the Austrian empire. The bitter and unexpected frustrations that followed the facile enthusiasm of early 1776 eroded the nascent American nationalism. In the words of Don Higginbotham, "Americans seemed more independent-minded than they were independence-minded."[66]

By 1778, the United States was in a state of financial collapse caused, to some extent, by Congress' impotence, and far more by the population's refusal to pay taxes. The Continental Army was unable to pay its soldiers and fewer men volunteered to fight. As the army's size shrank its composition changed. The yeomen farmers and men "of the middling sort" who had made up the bulk of the rebel army that besieged the British in Boston in late 1775 were largely gone. The new recruits came from the poorest sector of society. Also included in the ranks were large numbers of convicted criminals and Tories pardoned on condition that they enlist.[67]

What about African Americans?[68] When Washington reached the Continental Army outside Boston, he found free blacks from New England among the troops; he wanted to dismiss them, but he did not because he lacked sufficient white soldiers. Following his lead, Congress allowed free blacks to enlist. In 1778, first Rhode Island, then Connecticut and Massachusetts, began recruiting enslaved men, offering them freedom at the end of the war, and their masters compensation. "Desperate to recruit more manpower," Ron Chernow writes, Washington "gave his stamp of approval" to these northern states. But he balked when it came to southern enslaved men, and he refused to endorse the plan of one of his most trusted aides, South Carolinian John Laurens, who urged that Georgia and South Carolina, threatened by British invasion, enlist 5,000 enslaved men, compensating their masters. Among the southern states, only Maryland dared allow slave enlistments. While Virginia and North Carolina accepted free blacks (a tiny portion of their black population), Georgia and South Carolina refused to enlist a single Black, despite the British onslaught. A despondent Laurens wrote to Washington that rationality had been "drowned by the howlings of a triple-headed monster, in which prejudice, avarice and pusillanimity were united."[69]

No one can doubt the patriotism of George Washington or Thomas Jefferson. And yet Washington, who bitterly complained that he had too few soldiers, not only refused to endorse Laurens' plan, but he also failed to use his immense prestige to persuade the Virginia legislature to allow the enlistment of the enslaved. Likewise, Thomas Jefferson.

The sage of Monticello was the governor of Virginia when the state staggered under the blows of several thousand British regulars. He lamented the ineptitude of the militia, "of whom, . . . [he] wailed, 'there is not a single man who has ever seen the face of an enemy,'"[70] but he supported the legislature's refusal to recruit the enslaved. Laurens' "triple-headed monster" howled at both Washington and Jefferson.

African Americans made up between 6 and 13 percent of the Continental Army, which is impressive if we remember that the rebels refused to tap the largest reservoir of black manpower—enslaved southerners. They fought with grit. The First Connecticut regiment, which was largely black, became one of the best units of the Continental Army.[71]

An unknown number of African Americans also fought valiantly on the British side, but the British commanders wasted an opportunity to augment their troops significantly because most runaways were put to work as laborers rather than trained as soldiers.[72] This is understandable: while slavery was on the wane in England, hundreds of thousands of enslaved people toiled in the British Caribbean, and most British officers, many of them slaveowners, preferred to see Blacks with shovels, not guns.

In 1775, before the colonies had declared independence, the British governor of Virginia, Dunmore, had offered freedom only to those slaves of rebels who were willing and able to fight, but in 1779, as the British prepared to shift their major military effort to the southern colonies, where most of the enslaved lived, they adopted a bolder policy promising freedom to "any negro, the property of a rebel, who may take refuge with any part of this army," regardless of gender or age.[73] They largely kept this promise as they fought in the South from 1780–2. However, slaves of rebels who were not runaways but were taken from their masters' plantations often remained enslaved; those who fled loyalists were usually returned to their owners. It was, in short, a soiled record. But with all its flaws and contradictions, it differed from that of the rebels on one key point: the rebels freed only the enslaved who served in the Continental Army, while the British offered freedom to a far large number of enslaved people. Estimates of the number of southern slaves who fled to freedom vary wildly, from 20,000 to 100,000. One thing, however, is certain: for African Americans in the South the British flag represented the dream of liberty and the American, the certainty of continued enslavement.

The French role

From 1776 through 1782, the Continental Congress received from Versailles 45,000,000 *livres* in subsidies and loans, that is, over $152 million in 2021 dollars.[74] French weapons and money prevented a rebel collapse. Moreover, France's entry into the war meant that the British were no longer able to concentrate their efforts on the Thirteen Colonies. They had to worry about the defense of the home islands, as well as fight the French in new theaters, foremost in the West Indies, but also as far away as India. Urged on by France, Spain joined the war in 1779. Its contribution was critical: the Spanish blockaded Gibraltar, forcing the Royal Navy to divert naval expeditions to resupply the garrison. In the spring of 1781, this delayed the dispatch of British naval reinforcements to the Western Hemisphere and made possible French naval superiority at Yorktown, Virginia.[75]

The French fleet prevented the Earl of Cornwallis, whose troops had wreaked havoc in the South, from evacuating Yorktown. He had about 8,300 men but he faced 7,800 French and 5,800 Continentals. There were also 3,000 Virginia militia, but many "had little or no training."[76] Lacking food and subjected to violent artillery bombardments, the British surrendered on October 18, 1781.

Yorktown was above all a French victory. The French contribution went beyond the indispensable supply of ships and troops. On September 6, 1781, as Washington prepared to march his soldiers through Philadelphia to Yorktown, he implored the Continental Congress: "I [am] entreating you in the warmest terms to send on a month's pay at least with all the expedition possible. I wish it to come on the wings of speed." The previous January, detachments of the Continental Army had mutinied over lack of pay, and Washington feared another mutiny. Congress was bankrupt; the French gave the money.[77]

The plan of the campaign, too, was French, even though Washington never publicly acknowledged it. His eyes riveted on New York, he had been reluctant to consider a major effort in Virginia. It was the French commander, the Count de Rochambeau, who persuaded him. Once the American and French armies reached Yorktown, Washington, who lacked experience in siege warfare, had the good sense not to interfere: "Each day's labors were worked out in the early morning conferences attended by Washington, Rochambeau, and the heads of the artillery and the engineers. Although titularly commander-in-chief, Washington could only listen and agree."[78]

African Americans were present at Yorktown, on both sides. There were perhaps 1,000 Blacks in the Continental Army units at Yorktown. An aide-de-camp to Rochambeau noted in his diary, "Three-quarters of the Rhode Island regiment consists of Negroes, and that regiment is the most neatly dressed, the best under arms, and the most precise in the maneuvers."[79]

The British forces at Yorktown included hundreds of black soldiers as well as several thousand African Americans laborers and camp followers. Reporting that the British had crossed the James River on their way to Yorktown, a Virginian wrote, "Our negroes flock fast to them."[80] When the British surrendered, the runaways' masters descended on Yorktown to hunt down their human chattel. They had the assistance of the governor of Virginia, Thomas Nelson, who "made it an immediate high priority to track down as many fugitives as could be found." Washington ordered that all captured runaways be delivered to a designated officer until claimed. Advertisements were placed in southern newspapers. Many masters were thus able to recover some of their property—among them Washington himself (two slaves) and Jefferson (five).[81]

Perhaps, as historian Alan Gilbert writes, there was a true revolution within the American War of Independence—a revolution of the enslaved Blacks in the South, made possible by the presence of the British troops.[82] But with the rebels' victory black freedom was defeated.

The fate of slavery exemplifies the extent and the limits of social change brought about by the War of Independence. In 1780, the fledgling United States had a population of 2,780,000, including 575,000 Blacks, almost all of whom were enslaved. By the end of the war, Vermont and Massachusetts had abolished slavery. Pennsylvania approved a law in 1780 that would gradually abolish it, and in the aftermath of the war all the New England states followed suit. But fewer than 23,000 Blacks lived in New England and Pennsylvania in 1780. In New York and New Jersey, where the enslaved population was larger and economically more important, laws for the gradual abolition of slavery were passed only in 1799 and 1804 respectively.[83] These were important changes, but the War of Independence left chattel slavery virtually untouched in the South, where 90 percent of African Americans lived.

Peace

Three months before Yorktown, in June 1781, Congress had sent peremptory instructions to the commissioners in Paris: "You are to make the most candid and confidential communications upon all subjects to the ministers of our generous ally, the king of France; to undertake nothing in the negotiations for peace or truce without their knowledge and concurrence; and ultimately to govern yourselves by their advice and opinion."[84] Congress had consented to this humiliating stipulation, which had been demanded by Vergennes, in the justified belief that the rebel cause was near collapse and only continuing French aid could save it.

The commissioners who were negotiating a peace settlement with the British in Paris in the fall of 1782 disregarded these instructions. They were fortunate because Vergennes, who was busy trying to hammer out a peace treaty with Britain that Spain would accept, had no objection to the Americans negotiating on their own; and a government had come to power in London, led by the Earl of Shelburne, eager to pry the Americans from the French alliance and to set the basis for a future close relationship with the United States. Shelburne was willing to pay a high price for this. Therefore, in the negotiations with the American commissioners the British abandoned their demand for the restoration of property of loyalists that had been confiscated. Furthermore, in the preliminary peace treaty signed on November 30, 1782, they granted the United States the entire area between the Appalachians and the Mississippi, south of the Great Lakes and north of Florida, without making any provision on behalf of their Indian allies[85] [Map 2]. At a meeting with Shawnee Indians a US military officer gloated: "Your Fathers the English have made peace with us for themselves, but forgot you, their children, who fought with them, and neglected you like bastards."[86] The cession of the Northwest—the immense territory that included present day Ohio, Indiana, Illinois, Michigan, Wisconsin, and Minnesota east of the Mississippi— was particularly striking because the Indians and the British were still in control of most of it, and in 1781 and 1782 the Indians had inflicted costly defeats on the Americans. Britain ceded to the United States "the very lands that the Indians had just successfully defended," historian Randolph Downes writes. "The vanquished had become the victors."[87]

It was only after the peace preliminaries had been signed that the American commissioners informed the French. This embittered Vergennes. "If their present behavior foretells the future," he wrote, "the Americans will reward us poorly for what we have done for them."[88] Vergennes would have preferred that the British retain the Northwest: he knew that in language, religion, and political institutions the Americans were far closer to Britain than to France, and he thought that the continued British presence in the Northwest would inflame the Americans' fear of Britain and guard against an Anglo-American rapprochement. But he accepted the *fait accompli*, and he continued to support the Americans. In late 1782, France, although financially exhausted, lent more money to its irresponsible American ally, prompting Franklin to note: "Our people certainly ought to do more for themselves. It is absurd the pretending to be lovers of liberty while they grudge paying for the defence of it."[89]

Franklin deserves the praise that has been showered on him. "Without his presence in Paris throughout that tumultuous time, the French would never have been as supportive of the American Revolution as they were," writes Gordon Wood. "Franklin's genius was to understand how the French saw him and to exploit that image on behalf of the American cause."[90] Alone among the American commissioners, he was able to forge a good relationship with Vergennes. Franklin was helped by his immense prestige that had preceded him before he reached France. But even more, by his exquisite sense of realpolitik: whereas John Adams indignantly demanded that the French treat him as an equal, Franklin had no hesitation in showing the necessary deference—he assuaged the French to better fleece them. His skill "in negotiating loan after loan," Jonathan Dull concludes, "helped keep Congress from total bankruptcy and the American army from disintegrating."[91]

The United States under the Articles of Confederation

Hoping to gain the Americans' goodwill, Shelburne had conceded a great deal in the peace treaty. The British public decried the abandonment of the Loyalists and the surrender of the Northwest, and Shelburne was ousted in February 1783. In July, an Order-in-Council (British government decree) declared that American trade with British colonies had to be carried in British ships, as was the rule for all foreign countries. A few weeks earlier a book by a member of the British Parliament, Lord Sheffield, had argued that Britain had no need to make concessions to the Americans to retain their trade: Americans had no industries, while Britain had the best in the world; Americans needed to buy on credit, and British merchants, unlike their European rivals, could provide it. Sheffield's book was a great success: "it revived his fellow countrymen's self-confidence, so rudely shaken by the loss of the best part of the Empire."[92]

It is impossible to say which government, British or American, first violated the peace treaty. They both did, from the beginning. The Americans contravened two key points. The first: the states of the Confederation, particularly in the South, obstructed British merchants from recovering the prewar debts owed them by Americans. Secondly, the treaty had provided amnesty for the loyalists. The Americans, however, were not generous winners: they persecuted and attacked loyalists, particularly in the South.[93] (About 60,000 loyalists escaped with the British; they took 15,000 of the enslaved with them.[94])

The Americans, too, had their grievances: the peace treaty had stipulated that Britain would evacuate the United States "without carrying away any Negroes or other property of the American inhabitants." But the British commander-in-chief in North America, General Guy Carleton, had refused to deliver the runaways who were with his troops in New York. When George Washington met with Carleton in May 1783 to demand their return, Carleton rebuffed him, asserting that the runaways who had reached the British lines before November 30, 1782, when the preliminary peace treaty had been signed, had become free. Carleton was violating the treaty, but London backed him. The king himself expressed "His Royal Approbation" of Carleton's stance. There are no reliable figures, but several thousand African Americans departed with the British as free people. (A few thousand more had been evacuated as free people from Savannah and Charleston in 1782, and many more as slaves of loyalists.)[95]

The British also refused to evacuate eight posts in the Northwest, including Detroit. An anomalous situation developed: the Northwest was legally part of the United States, but most of it was controlled by Indian tribes who had fought on Britain's side during the war, and British troops remained in the territory. The British began repairing their relations with the Indians, whom they had betrayed in the peace treaty, supplying them with provisions and ammunition.[96] They were not pursuing a long-term strategy; they stayed because they could do so at virtually no cost. Eventually, some British officials began dreaming of an Indian buffer state in the Northwest, but the ambiguous *status quo* was acceptable to London.

Beginning in May 1785, John Adams was the US minister to Britain. An honest man, he understood that his countrymen were violating the peace treaty by failing to pay their debts, but as the US envoy he justified this by saying that the British had failed to pay for the enslaved who had left with them. He demanded that Britain evacuate the posts in the Northwest, but the British justified their continuing presence by the Americans' failure to pay their debts and by their treatment of the Loyalists. It was a stalemate.

Unsurprisingly, most Britons did not like the Americans and did not respect the United States, with its puny army of 700 soldiers, no navy (the last warship of the Continental Navy was sold in 1785), and no money. When the Continental Congress sent John Adams to London, Whitehall did not reciprocate. British officials treated Adams courteously enough—with "dry decency and cold civility," he reported[97]—but they had no interest in negotiating with him. Adams' main goal was to conclude a commercial treaty that would give American ships the right to trade with the British West Indies, which before the war had been the destination of more than half the tonnage owned by the Thirteen Colonies.[98] But he hit a wall. Frustrated, he told Jefferson, the US minister to Versailles, that if the British continued to be unreasonable, the United States should establish "still closer and stronger connections with France."[99] Jefferson was eager for Franco-American trade to increase, but there was not much he could do. As Sheffield had predicted, the bulk of American trade remained with Britain even though no treaty of commerce was concluded.

The Confederation had strained relations with its other European neighbor, Spain. It demanded the right to navigate the Mississippi through Spanish territory all the way to the Gulf of Mexico, and disputed the northern border of Spanish West Florida, but it lacked the strength to impose its will. The Spaniards allowed Americans from the fledgling settlements in the future states of Kentucky and Tennessee to navigate the Mississippi through Spanish territory, but only as a privilege, not as a right.

The impotence of the Confederation was a key reason for the Constitutional Convention that led in 1789 to the establishment of the federal union with George Washington as its first president.

"The First of Men"[100]

George Washington belonged by birth to the planter class, but it was his marriage to Martha Curtis, "probably the wealthiest widow in Virginia," that propelled him to the highest rank of Virginia's society. In June 1775, he was chosen by the Continental Congress to lead the rebel army, because unity demanded a southern commander for what was then a New England army; because Virginia was the most populous and wealthy of the Thirteen Colonies; and because his creditable service during the Seven Years' War made him the most qualified Virginian candidate. However, Washington had never commanded a large force. As one of his foremost biographers writes, as commander of the Continental Army he demonstrated that "he was not, by any standard, a military genius." His repeated blunders endangered the survival of the army.[101]

According to a sympathetic scholar, "Washington's errors, significantly, were concentrated in the first half of the war, when he was a learner in command of learners."[102] This is true, but after June 1778 he fought no major battles. He led the American troops at Yorktown, but the plan of the campaign was French.

Washington was, however, a great leader of men. This Virginia planter, who had traveled little beyond the commonwealth before the war, became "the first meaningful symbol of national unity."[103] He did something "unprecedented," Chernow writes, "by cobbling together a creditable fighting force from the poor, the young, the black, and the downtrodden."[104] Laboring indefatigably at the head of the Continental Army, he dealt with Congress and the States with patience and diplomacy. He was ambitious, but his ambition was harnessed by a stern and unflagging sense of duty. No financial or moral scandal marred his record, and his refusal to accept any payment for his services stood in stark contrast to the rampant profiteering of many rebel leaders. He towered over his generals who, throughout the war, squabbled over rank and status.

By 1780, Washington had become the unchallenged leader of the army, and the most powerful and respected figure in America, while the Continental Congress had sunk in public esteem and effectiveness. But he never wavered in his conviction that the army, and its commander-in-chief, were subordinate to civilian authority. He consistently lent his formidable prestige to a discredited congress, his respectful attitude a counterpoint to the tantrums of his generals, and he squashed any thoughts of military coup among his subordinates. "Having now finished the work assigned to me," Washington told the Continental Congress on December 23, 1783, "I here offer my commission, and take my leave of all the enjoyments of public life." He returned to Mount Vernon without asking for any privilege or favor. It was, Joseph Ellis writes, "the greatest exit in American history."[105] It was a most precious service to the infant nation he had defended, and an invaluable legacy for future generations. This was the true genius of George Washington.

CHAPTER 2
THE FEDERALIST ERA

The ratification of the constitution in 1788 launched the United States on a grand experiment. This former British colony, now a republic, was the most democratic country in the world—for white men; approximately two thirds of them could vote.[1] The 1790 census indicated that the white population of the United States was 3,172,006. Slightly fewer than 100,000 Native Americans lived within the territory claimed by the United States. There were also 697,681 black slaves and 59,466 free blacks. Virginia was the most populous state, with 748,000 inhabitants, followed by Pennsylvania with 434,000. Except for Massachusetts and Vermont (which joined the union in 1791) slavery existed in every state, but 94 percent of the enslaved people were concentrated in the South and in Kentucky, which became a state in 1792.[2] Without ever using the word, the constitution protected slavery: it gave slaveowners the right to capture their fugitive slaves anywhere in the country; it forbade Congress from outlawing the international slave trade for twenty years; and it counted each enslaved person as three-fifths of a free person for the purpose of apportioning members of the House of Representatives.

Although bankrupt and largely impotent, the Confederation had done something unprecedented, truly revolutionary. It had stipulated that in the western lands ceded by England to the United States new states would be created, as soon as they had the requisite number of inhabitants, that would become members of the federal union with the same rights as the original thirteen states. "Thus the parameters of America's empire for liberty were established," a historian writes. "Voluntarily constituted, democratically governed, it was an empire with an extraordinary capacity to reap the benefits of its citizens' energies." This was, however, an empire of liberty for white men. Non-whites would be enslaved or marginalized.[3]

Could such an extensive country endure? An axiom of eighteenth-century political theory was that republics were fragile, liable to be fractured by internal dissent. Montesquieu had argued that "In an extensive republic the public good is sacrificed to a thousand private views."[4] Did history's lesson apply to the United States? In 1796, in his Farewell Address, George Washington asked: "Is there a doubt whether a common government can embrace so large a sphere? . . . It is well worth a fair and full experiment."[5] Yet while American leaders wondered whether their country could remain united, "a remarkable feature of the young United States," Reginald Horsman writes, "was the degree to which there was confidence in the future continental destiny of the American people."[6] White Americans, who were multiplying to a degree unprecedented in human history (from 1,300,000 in 1760 to more than 3 million thirty years later), expected to spread over North America and possibly also the Southern Hemisphere, whether as one republic or as sister republics.

In the early 1790s, two loose groups began to take shape: the Republicans, led by Thomas Jefferson and his loyal lieutenant James Madison, and the Federalists, led by Alexander Hamilton. The Republicans' stronghold was the South and their leaders were great slaveholding planters, men like Jefferson, whom the Federalists dubbed the "Generalissimo," and Madison, whom they called the "General."[7] The Federalists' stronghold, on the other hand, was New England; many of their leaders owned no slaves and some, like Hamilton and John Adams, abhorred slavery. As a group, however, they were not hostile to the institution. Just as there were Republicans in New England, so too there were Federalists in the South.

Contrary to the allegations of Jefferson and his friends, the Federalists were sincere republicans, not monarchists in disguise, but they were not democrats—indeed, they boasted that they were the enemies of democracy, which they saw as a dangerous monster. Hamilton and his friends did not trust the masses, whom they considered prey to base instincts and the wiles of demagogues. They were convinced that class struggle was inevitable: "the jealousy of the rich is a passion in the poor which can always be appealed to with success in every question," they warned. Whereas Jefferson saw a future in which virtuous yeomen farmers would happily follow the lead of the landed elites, all working together for a greater destiny, the Federalists were profoundly pessimistic (the rich were few, the poor were many) and sought protection in restricted suffrage based on property qualifications and in "temperate liberty."[8]

Jeffersonians and Hamiltonians held sharply differing views of how America should develop, economically and socially. The chasm separating them was magnified by their clash over foreign policy. The United States in the 1790s had few connections with the wider world. In 1784, the first American merchant ship reached Canton (Guangzhou), the gateway for trade with China; other US ships were trading with British India. This was America's toehold in Asia. With the major exception of the slave ships that hugged the west coast of Africa, Americans had no contacts with that continent other than strained relations with the Barbary states (Morocco, Algiers, Tunis, and Tripoli). In the Western Hemisphere, the Spanish and Portuguese colonies were virtually closed to American trade. For the United States in the 1790s, the "world" meant Europe and the European colonies in North America and the Caribbean.

Europe was at war. In July 1789, the French Revolution had erupted; it steadily radicalized, leading to the proclamation of the Republic in September 1792 and the execution of King Louis XVI in January 1793. France had been at war with Austria and Prussia since April 1792, and in February 1793 it declared war on Britain and Holland; a month later on Spain. The French republic had formidable advantages over its enemies. The other European powers had small professional armies, but with the Revolution every Frenchman became a citizen, and the French government imposed conscription. France was the European country with the largest population—25 million in 1789—and by 1794 it fielded an army of 700,000. What they lacked in professionalism, the French made up for in revolutionary zeal. Soon, great generals emerged, foremost Napoleon. One after the other, the European powers made peace with France. All except Britain.

This is the world the United States faced in the 1790s. To appreciate the situation of the American leaders, it is useful to compare them with the leaders of the African countries that became independent in the 1960s. These Africans, too, faced a bipolar world. Some, full of resentment toward their former colonial masters, looked east, toward Moscow; others looked toward the former colonial powers, because they preferred their political institutions to those of the Soviet Union and understood that only the West could provide the economic resources they so desperately needed.

So it was for the United States in the 1790s. Americans faced what was essentially a bipolar world—France and Britain—and they had to decide which of the two superpowers would be more beneficial, or more dangerous, for their country as they launched their great fragile experiment. Washington's two most important advisers, Secretary of State Thomas Jefferson and Treasury Secretary Alexander Hamilton, held opposite views on this key question.

This chapter focuses on the presidencies of George Washington and John Adams. It discusses US relations with Britain, France, and Spain, as well as with the aggregate of small powers that stood on the path of US expansion: the Indian tribes that lived east of the Mississippi on land white Americans coveted.

The world of Thomas Jefferson

"Those who labor in the earth," Jefferson rhapsodized in 1785, "are the chosen people of God" and the only sure guardians of American liberty.[9] Farming, he believed, produced citizens who would be the pillars of a virtuous republic. He dreamed of a society composed of small farmers who would escape the horrors of manufacturing he had seen in Europe: hordes of propertyless laborers mired in poverty and ignorance, dependent on the whims of their employers. Jefferson's "sobering contact with the landless poor in Europe made him all the more anxious to prevent the development of a similar class in Europe."[10] The United States, he argued, had enough land to create a society of yeomen farmers, and as the population grew it could expand its farms over North and South America. American farmers would export their surplus abroad and import the industrial goods they needed, avoiding the ills of manufacturing and urbanization.

However utopian Jefferson's vision, however dim his understanding of economics, his conception of the rights of white American men was generous. Jefferson believed in expanding the franchise for white men, he trusted their common sense and he was an ardent advocate of public education, which would make them better citizens. On the other hand, he thought that the "sole purpose" of a white woman "was to take care of the man in her life, her children, and the home,"[11] and his vision did not extend to African Americans, male or female.

There were white southerners who believed that slavery was wrong and who acted on their beliefs. In 1791, George Washington's neighbor, Robert Carter, began freeing his 509 slaves, about twenty-five a year, until by 1812 all were free. "I have for some time past," he wrote, "been convinced that to retain them in slavery is contrary to the true principles of religion and justice."[12] As other Virginians freed some of their slaves the state's free black population grew from 12,766 in 1790 to 20,124 in 1800 (out of a total black population of 367,000).[13]

Like Carter, Jefferson knew that slavery was a crime against humanity. He wrote in the *Notes on the State of Virginia*: "The whole commerce between master and slave is a perpetual exercise of the most boisterous passions, the most unremitting despotism on the one part, and degrading submissions on the other.... The man must be a prodigy who can retain his manners and morals undepraved by such circumstances."[14]

Jefferson took two steps against slavery: in 1783, his draft of a new constitution for Virginia provided for the freedom of all children born of the enslaved after the year 1800; and in 1784, at the Continental Congress, he chaired a committee that proposed excluding slavery from the western territories after 1800. These two measures, both of which were defeated, represent "the high-water mark of his reform zeal."[15]

Perhaps Jefferson truly "abhorred slavery," as two eminent historians, Stanley Elkins and Eric McKitrick, write.[16] If so, he bore the burden with fortitude. When he died in 1826, he owned about 200 slaves, including his enslaved concubine, Sally Hemings and their children, but in his lifetime he freed only three slaves (and five more in his will).[17] To emancipate his slaves would have undercut his popularity in the South, the base of his political power, and made it impossible to maintain his lavish lifestyle. Jefferson lived well above his means. "A chronic acquirer," David McCullough writes, "Jefferson is not known to have denied himself anything he wished in the way of material possessions or comforts."[18]

Jefferson, who had been the US minister to Versailles since 1784, left France in October 1789, a few weeks after the fall of the Bastille ushered in the promise of a democratic future. But his Francophilia had been rock solid even when France had been an absolute monarchy. He was grateful for France's aid during the War of Independence, he treasured the years he had spent in Paris, and he had close friendships with several Frenchmen. The cement that bound him to France, however, was hatred of Britain. "The correspondence of Jefferson and Madison all during the Confederation period bristles with hatred for England and all things British," Elkins and McKitrick write.[19] Not only had Britain fought against American independence, but after the war it refused the treat the United States as an equal.

Not all Americans were hostile to Britain. John Adams, who experienced British arrogance at first hand as minister in London, did not hate Britain. But Adams' New England had suffered little during the War of Independence and could be proud of the performance of its militia; Virginia, on the other hand, had endured harsh British raids and its militia had behaved poorly. Jefferson had been Virginia's wartime governor from 1779 to 1781, and his performance had been mediocre. Furthermore, during the war more than thirty of his slaves had joined the British, and British troops had raided his beloved Monticello, forcing him to flee.

Unlike Jefferson, Hamilton was of humble origins: the illegitimate son of a poor woman, born and raised in the British Caribbean, he was "able to escape his fate as a 'groveling' clerk"[20] on the island of St. Croix because his employer and other local businessmen recognized his extraordinary talents and sent him to New York to obtain an education. He was at King's College (now Columbia University) when the War of Independence began.

Unlike Jefferson, Hamilton could recall with pride his service during the war—he had been one of Washington's most valued aides, and he had fought bravely at Yorktown. In 1780 he married Elizabeth Schuyler, who belonged to one of the most prominent families in the state of New York. When peace returned he became a very successful lawyer in New York City. But he yearned for public service and for a stronger United States. He was, with Madison, the prime mover behind the summoning of the Constitutional Convention and the principal author of the *Federalist Papers*.[21]

While Jefferson loathed Britain, Hamilton believed that only Britain could help transform the United States into a powerful country. Like many African leaders who in the 1960s understood that economic development could be fostered only by the West, so Hamilton understood that French goods were inferior to British, and France's ability to provide credit and capital was sorely limited; British political institutions, he believed, were far preferable to those of France. He was no British client; like Jefferson he was a fierce nationalist who believed he was putting his country's interests first.

Washington's first term

Washington could not have chosen two more brilliant minds for his cabinet than Jefferson and Hamilton; nor could he have chosen a more ill-assorted pair. As treasury secretary, Hamilton set to work with extraordinary energy and skill formulating the administration's economic program—funding the Revolutionary debt, assuming the state debts, creating a national bank, and adopting excise taxes. He clashed with Secretary of State Jefferson and with Madison, who led Jefferson's friends in the House of Representatives. Hamilton won most of these battles, to the benefit of the United States but to the dismay of the two Virginians. Hamilton, they believed, favored northern bankers and industrialists over the agrarian South, the rich and powerful over the common man, and they were incensed that he sought to strengthen the authority of the federal government over the states. This was not a simple disagreement about economic policy. Hamilton's program, they believed, was a deadly threat. America's soul, and its future, were at stake. It was around these domestic issues that the two inchoate groups— the Federalists, led by Hamilton, and the Republicans, led by Jefferson—began to crystalize into political parties.

Foreign policy intervened in two ways during Washington's first term. Tensions with Britain festered due to Britain's failure to evacuate the posts in the Northwest, to pay compensation for the enslaved people who had left with the British troops, and to sign a commercial treaty with the United States. In April 1789, during the first session of Congress, Madison introduced proposals to retaliate by penalizing British trade. It was the opening salvo of a debate over policy toward Britain that would rage for two decades. Jefferson and Madison believed that the British were so dependent on American trade that commercial sanctions would force them to concede to the Americans' demands. Hamilton disagreed: Britain would retaliate, he argued, precipitating a trade war that would grievously wound the United States. Hamilton was right. As Jerald Combs, an authority of the period, writes, US sanctions would have led to "a commercial war that would have threatened the entire financial structure of the infant American nation."[22]

The other way that foreign policy intruded was more insidious: it exacerbated the divisions between Republicans and Federalists. For Jefferson and his friends, Hamilton and his cohorts were the fifth column of the hated British monarchy. They saw France and the United States as sister republics in a world dominated by monarchies. Jefferson told his French friend, the Marquis de Lafayette, in June 1792, "While you are exterminating the monster aristocracy ... a contrary tendency is discovered in some here. A sect [led by Hamilton] has shewn itself among us, who declare they espouse our new constitution ... only as a step to an English constitution." Jefferson was unfazed by the massacres of September 1792 in Paris, when more than 1,200 prisoners were killed. "The liberty of the whole earth was depending on the issue of the contest," he wrote in January 1793, "rather than it should have failed, I would have seen half the earth desolated." And he repeatedly stressed the link between events in France and in the United States: "There are in the U.S. some characters ... hostile to France and fondly looking to England as the staff of their hopes." Their goal was to restore the monarchy. "The successes of Republicanism in France have given the coup de grace to their prospects and I hope to their projects."[23] In fact, the threat existed only in the fevered minds of Jefferson and his supporters. They were haunted by their hatred of England.

The Federalists, on the other hand, were haunted by their fear of revolutionary France. They saw England as the bastion that stood between the French hordes and the United States, and they saw the Jeffersonians as France's fifth column who would bring the horrors of the French Revolution to their country. As John Miller writes, "the Federalists felt the hot breath of the 'canaille' [rabble] upon their necks."[24] These twin fears of fifth columns help explain the extraordinary violence of the public debate in the United States in the 1790s, comparable only to the debates of the 1850s and the McCarthy era.

In October 1791, George Hammond, the first minister sent by Britain to the United States, arrived in Philadelphia, the provisional capital until 1800, when the new federal capital would be established on the banks of the Potomac. Hammond was instructed to negotiate the disputes between the two countries and report back to London. But Jefferson told Hammond that there was nothing to negotiate: the United States had fulfilled its part of the peace treaty. All that was left was for Britain to honor its pledges: pay compensation for the slaves and evacuate the forts.[25] The impasse continued.

War in the Ohio Valley

The British presence in the Ohio Valley and the Great Lakes region gave the Indians who lived there hope that they were not alone against the United States. In 1787, Congress had created the Northwest Territory [Map 3]. When Washington assumed the presidency,

US relations with the tribes of the Ohio Valley were explosive. Many of these Indians enjoyed a material standard "equal to, and often above, that of American frontier families," a careful scholar notes. They lived in villages that resembled those of white American settlers, raised cattle and other livestock, and cultivated cornfields and orchards. They considered the Ohio River the border between white America and their domain, but settlers and land speculators were moving into their lands. Increasingly, there were armed clashes between Indians and settlers, and raiding parties of Indians and Kentuckians crossed the Ohio River in both directions.[26] US officials knew that the settlers bore a heavy responsibility for these clashes. "It is in the highest degree mortifying to find that the bulk of the frontier inhabitants consider the killing of Indians in time of peace to be no crime," Washington's principal negotiator with the Native Americans, Timothy Pickering, wrote to the president, adding that the frontier settlers were "far more savage and revengeful than the Indians." The governor of the Northwest Territory, General Arthur St. Clair, noted that "Though we hear much of the injuries and depredations that are committed by the Indians against the whites, there is too much reason to believe that at least equal if not greater injuries are done to the Indians by the frontier settlers of which we hear very little."[27]

President Washington considered himself a just man. He urged Congress to bring civilization to the Indians through agriculture, spinning and weaving, but he also believed that "the gradual extension of our settlements will as certainly cause the savage as the wolf to retire; both being beasts of prey, tho' they differ in shape."[28] He wanted to acquire Indian land peacefully, by purchase, but he believed that if the Indians refused to sell on reasonable terms—as unilaterally defined by him—then the United States had the right to use whatever force might be necessary to wrest it from them.

The Indians were well aware that when the Americans invited them to negotiate they were in fact demanding their land. They had also learned that they could not trust the word of an American. "Indians have been so often deceived by White people," Pickering told Washington, "that *White Man* is, among many of them, but another name for *Liar*."[29] The Shawnees, the Miamis and other tribes in the Ohio Valley began forging a loose alliance to resist the Americans' land hunger. His patience exhausted, in September 1790 Washington sent General Josiah Harmar with 1,450 men into the heartland of the Miamis to "punish" the Indians "for their hostile depredations . . . and for their refusing to treat with the United States when invited thereto."[30] Because the US army had only 1,200 men—Americans mistrusted a standing army and recoiled at the expense—the bulk of Harmar's force was militia from Kentucky and Pennsylvania.

The expedition was a fiasco. Harmar torched several deserted Indian towns in northeastern Indiana, but two of his columns were mauled by the Indians and he withdrew in haste, having lost almost 200 dead. The following year Washington tried again, sending General St. Clair into Indian territory. St. Clair's force of over 1,400 men was routed on November 4, 1791, by about 1,000 Native Americans near the headwaters of the Wabash River in west central Ohio (present day Fort Recovery). Indian casualties were fewer than one hundred; American casualties were about 900, including 600 dead— the largest number of Americans ever killed by Indians in a single battle.[31]

As many Americans suspected, the British were assisting the Indians. Whitehall wanted them to serve as a barrier against the Americans, protecting the fledgling loyalist settlements in Upper Canada, the new province carved out of southwestern Quebec in August 1791. Whitehall's instructions to the British officials in Canada were contradictory: help the Indians unite against the American threat, but observe strict neutrality in the conflict; provide the Indians with food, supplies and ammunition—but reduce expenditures. The governor-general of Canada, and above all the lieutenant-governor of Upper Canada, tended to bend their instructions to favor the Indians, as did the members of the Indian Department of Upper Canada, who implemented the policy on the ground. These men lived in close contact with the Indians; some had married Indian women. They empathized with the Indians' plight, rather than viewing them as mere pawns of British policy. They had assisted the Indians against Harmar and St. Clair with arms and intelligence, and several had participated in the fighting.[32]

After St. Clair's defeat, President Washington and Secretary of War Henry Knox began organizing a much more powerful expedition. This time they would rely on regular troops. In March 1792, at their insistence, Congress increased the size of the army from 1,216 to 5,280 men.[33] One of the best generals of the War of Independence, Anthony Wayne, was chosen to lead the force that would invade the Indian country.

Washington's second term

Soon after Washington began his second term in March 1793, Americans learned that the French king, Louis XVI, had been executed, and that the French Republic had declared war on Britain and Spain. As Europe plunged into war, was the United States still bound by its treaty of alliance with France? No, argued Hamilton: the 1778 treaties had been concluded when France was a monarchy; given the execution of Louis XVI and the proclamation of the republic, the alliance should be regarded as "temporarily and provisionally suspended." Jefferson sharply disagreed: the treaties had been between the two nations and were still in force. Washington sided with Jefferson. But on one fundamental issue Hamilton and Jefferson agreed: both wanted the United States to remain neutral in the European war. (The treaty of alliance stipulated that each party was obligated to intervene only if the other had been attacked—and France had declared war on England.) In late April 1793, Washington issued a proclamation stating that the United States would follow "a conduct friendly and impartial toward the belligerent powers" and that Americans were prohibited from "aiding or abetting hostilities." At Jefferson's request, the word "neutrality" was omitted from the proclamation.[34]

This omission reflected Jefferson's ambivalence. He wanted to help France, and initially was sympathetic to the plans of the newly arrived French minister, Edmond Genet, to recruit American frontiersmen to participate in raids on Spanish and British possessions in North America. However, Jefferson also wanted to use neutrality as a lever to pry from Britain "the *broadest privileges* of neutral nations" for American maritime trade. And he did not want to do anything that could weaken support for the Republicans at home. Therefore, when Genet repeatedly defied Washington by insisting on France's right to arm privateers in US ports to maraud British shipping and when he threatened to appeal over the president's head to the American people, Jefferson agreed with Hamilton that the Frenchman should be recalled. "I saw the necessity of quitting a wreck which could not but sink all who should cling to it," he told Madison.[35]

The most serious clash between Jefferson and Hamilton exploded over relations with Britain. War with France meant that the Royal Navy had to find thousands of additional sailors to man its ships. It resorted to impressment—compulsory naval service—as it had in every war in the eighteenth century. It did not claim the right to impress foreign seamen, but it did claim the right to search foreign vessels in British ports and on the high seas, and remove all British subjects. Americans were vulnerable: in the early years after independence it was difficult to distinguish an American from an Englishman and therefore US citizens were sometimes impressed; furthermore, British naval officers, eager to replenish their crews, willfully made "mistakes" when searching American ships and seized American sailors claiming that they were British subjects. Impressment, writes Scott Jackson, author of the best study on the subject, was "a running sore" in Anglo-American relations, particularly when the Royal Navy found it difficult to recruit men. In 1793–4, the first two years of Britain's war against France, recruitment for the navy proceeded relatively easily; therefore, few Americans were impressed. This changed in 1795.[36]

Tensions also escalated over trade. The Royal Navy sought to prevent trade between France and its colonies, and to deny the French key imports, including food. As the British swept the merchant ships of France and its clients from the seas, the American merchant marine, and carrying trade, expanded to fill the breach. Before the war, the French government had required that trade between its West Indian colonies and the metropole be carried exclusively in French ships, but when the war began it opened that trade to the Americans. Jefferson's prophesy that during a European war the United States would "become the carriers for all parties" and "fatten on the follies of the old [world]"[37] was coming true. But the British intervened, citing a rule they had first invented during the Seven Years' War (hence the name, the Rule of 1756): trade closed to a neutral in peacetime could not be opened in wartime. This meant that regardless of what Paris might say, London decreed that American ships could not trade between the French Caribbean and France.

Americans and British clashed also over the status of a belligerent's goods on a neutral ship: the British claimed that they could be legally confiscated, but the Americans argued that "free ships make free goods." There was also the question of contraband—goods legally subject to seizure even if they belonged to a neutral party. The American definition was very narrow: weapons and implements of war; for the British, contraband was anything that would enable their enemies "to carry on the war against us," including food.[38] This dispute gained substance in June 1793: France was suffering from a shortage of grain and flour, and Britain declared wheat, flour, and cornmeal to be contraband.

Finally, while Americans and British agreed that ships that sought to breach a legal blockade could be seized and their cargo confiscated, they disagreed on what made a blockade legal: for the Americans to be legal a blockade had to be effective, with enough ships to enforce it; but the British, when it suited them, called paper blockades—mere declarations unbacked by sufficient naval forces—legal.

Punishing Britain?

When the third US Congress convened in late 1793, the Republicans launched a two-pronged assault on Britain. First, on December 16, Jefferson presented his report on American foreign trade to Congress; lashing out at Britain, he recommended the adoption of discriminatory duties against it.[39] This was Jefferson's valedictory as secretary of state. A man who shrank from open confrontation, he was tired of wrangling with Hamilton. He stepped down on December 31, 1793 and withdrew to Monticello, where he would busy himself with plans to build a magnificent mansion, while from Philadelphia Madison led the Republican opposition to Hamilton. It was Madison who in January 1794 launched the second prong of the Republican onslaught, proposing to the House discriminatory duties against British ships and merchandise. The Federalists countered that the British would surely retaliate and a commercial war would hurt the United States far more than Britain, because Americans were more dependent on British trade than the other way around. The Republicans, the Federalists warned, were leading the country to war against Britain.[40] Republicans and Federalists were evenly balanced in both chambers, but almost half of the members belonged to neither group.[41] The debate was ongoing when in early March 1794, Americans learned that the Royal Navy was seizing American ships that were in the carrying trade between France and its Caribbean colonies.

A few days later came even more alarming news. Throughout 1793, British officials in Canada had anxiously followed the preparations of General Wayne as he molded his recruits into a well-trained force for the offensive against the Indians in the Ohio Valley. These officials feared that the United States would enter the European war on France's side and attack Canada. As their anxiety grew, so did their reliance on the Indians to shield the colony. On February 10, 1794, the Governor-General of Canada, Lord Dorchester, told a delegation of Indian chiefs. "I shall not be surprised if we are at war with them [the United States] in the course of the present year; and, if so, a line must be drawn by the [Indian] warriors."[42] A copy of the speech found its way to the United States. On March 26, 1794, it was printed in the *Gazette of the United States*. The British, the Americans believed, were calling the Indians to arms.

This, and the Royal Navy's seizure of American ships, annealed Americans' suspicions of Britain into fury. Over the Federalists' opposition, on April 21, 1794, the House approved, fifty-eight to thirty-eight, a bill to prohibit trade with Britain as of November 1 unless it made restitution for the ships and cargoes it had seized and evacuated the posts in the Northwest. In the Senate, only the vote of Vice President John Adams defeated the measure.[43]

The Federalists were no British proxies. They were "shocked, betrayed and embittered" at the British actions;[44] they wanted Whitehall to compensate American shippers and evacuate the forts. But they opposed an embargo that, they believed, would cripple the US economy. Aware that war with England might be inevitable, they urged Congress to raise an army of 20,000 men and appropriate money for coastal fortifications, but they also wanted to give peace one last chance. Therefore, they convinced President Washington to send a special envoy to London to try to negotiate the disputes between the two countries. The president chose John Jay, the Federalist Chief Justice of the Supreme Court. On May 12, Jay left for London. If he failed, economic warfare, and probably war, would be unavoidable.

During his first term, Washington had sought, without success, to reconcile Jefferson and Hamilton, pleading with both to work together on behalf of the American people. He had continued to hope to narrow the divide between Jeffersonians and Hamiltonians after his reelection, and had sought to remain above the warring factions. To show his impartiality when he sent Jay to London, he replaced the US minister to Paris, the Federalist Gouverneur Morris, with James Monroe, an ardent Francophile, a Republican, and close disciple of Jefferson,[45] but the Republicans were still dissatisfied. Washington's decision to send Jay to London had blunted their onslaught, "impeding all legislative measures for extorting redress from G.B. [Great Britain]," Madison groused.[46]

The Jay Treaty[47]

The British did not want to go to war against the United States. They were in the throes of a deadly struggle with revolutionary France. On the continent, their key allies—Austria, Prussia, and Spain—were being mauled by the French armies; at sea, French privateers were assailing British shipping. Trade with the United States was valuable, and if war broke out American privateers would add to the perils British merchantmen faced. Therefore, Prime Minister William Pitt and his colleagues were willing to make concessions to the Americans, but only as long as these did not affect their ability to fight the French. "There is not the slightest doubt," Charles Ritcheson writes, "that Britain would have gone to war with the United States rather than acquiesce in the Jeffersonian view of neutral rights."[48] Jay understood this. He made concessions where vital British interests were at stake. The treaty Jay signed on November 19, 1794, did not mention the carrying trade or impressment (which was not yet a serious problem). It implicitly abandoned the principle of "free ships, free goods" by accepting Britain's right to confiscate enemy property aboard American ships; and it conceded that food "and other articles not generally contraband" could be treated as contraband (but would not be confiscated, rather purchased "with a reasonable mercantile profit" for the owner). These concessions violated the spirit of the 1778 treaty of commerce with France, which had specifically recognized the principle "free ships, free goods" and had excluded foodstuffs from the contraband list. Furthermore, Jay's treaty forbade the United States from discriminating against British trade for twelve years—thus surrendering a weapon the Republicans greatly valued.

The major British concession was to agree to evacuate the posts in the Northwest by June 1, 1796. Furthermore, Jay secured formal approval of American trade with British India. This trade, Bradford Perkins writes, "became an important source of wealth" for the United States.[49] The British West Indies, however, were opened to American ships under such restrictive conditions that when the US Senate debated the treaty, the article was immediately rejected at the request of the Federalists themselves.

The treaty established three joint commissions to arbitrate three contentious issues: the pre-war debts owed by Americans to British merchants; the compensation owed to American shippers for illegal seizures by the Royal Navy; and the boundary between New England and Quebec. There would be no commission, however, to compensate American slaveowners for the humans they had lost to the British during the war.

Given the imbalance of power between the two countries, Jay could not have obtained better terms. The concessions he made, however distasteful to American pride, did not affect vital US interests—American trade continued to grow. Between 1795 and 1800, the value of American exports to Britain tripled (from $6 million to $19 million), and the total value of US exports increased from $48 million to $71 million.[50]

What would have happened if the negotiations had failed? The British would have remained in the forts. And if the Republicans had resorted to their weapon of choice— commercial retaliation—London would have responded by seizing more American ships. The growing tension might have led to war. The Republicans did not seek war but, unlike the Federalists, neither did they fear it. True, the United States had neither an army nor a navy, but American privateers could attack British shipping, and the militia could defend the country from British invasion. The Republicans were unfazed by the disastrous experience of the Harmar and St. Clair expeditions against the Indians, and they whitewashed the militia's performance during the War of Independence. Furthermore, they believed that France had Britain on the ropes. The French had overrun Belgium, Holland, and the Rhineland. They had chased the British troops off the continent and had defeated the armies of Austria, Prussia, and Spain. Jefferson and his cohorts were emboldened by the hope that France would invade Britain. "If I could see them [the French] now at peace with the rest of their continent," Jefferson wrote in April 1795, "I should have little doubt of dining with [French general Jean Charles] Pichegru in London next autumn."[51] Given the disarray of the French Navy, plagued by the indiscipline of the crews and the purges of officers, a French general could have dined in London only if brought as a prisoner of war.[52]

Fallen timbers

While Jay was in London, the situation in the Ohio Valley changed dramatically. In July 1794, General Wayne began his long-awaited offensive, penetrating deep into Indian country with 2,000 regulars and 1,500 Kentucky militia; on August 20, he defeated a force of 1,000 Indians at Fallen Timbers, in Ohio, twenty miles upriver from Lake Erie. Not far from the battlefield was Fort Miami, a British post with a small garrison of

Redcoats. In their hour of need, many Indians fled toward it, but the British commander, fearing a clash with Wayne's army, had closed the gates. "The Indians instantly understood the full meaning of this symbolic act of British isolation," a historian writes. "In spite of a decade of promises and encouragement, the inflammatory Dorchester speech, ... the tons of supplies and powder sent from [the British post at] Detroit, and the continual assurances of assistance, the British at the moment of crisis were abandoning the tribes."[53] Soon, the Indians suffered another devastating blow: while the text of the Jay Treaty was not published until July 1795, the Canadian authorities had learned by late 1794 that it stipulated that the posts would be evacuated, and this knowledge spread to the officials of the Indian Department, and from them to the Indians. The British were leaving. On August 3, 1795, at Fort Greenville (Ohio), the representatives of the tribes agreed to a treaty granting the United States most of what is today the state of Ohio. More than territory was at stake. The British evacuation of the forts meant that the United States would be the dominant white power in the Northwest Territory. For the French and the British, the Indians had been junior partners—hunters of valuable pelts and military auxiliaries in war. For the Americans, the Indians were "unwanted squatters—obstacles to civilized progress."[54] Obstacles, that is, to their appetite for land.

The debate on the Jay Treaty

In the United States, opposition to the Jay Treaty was in full swing before anyone had seen the document or had a firm idea of its terms. For the Republicans it was folly to expect that Jay, a Federalist, could negotiate a treaty with Britain that served the interests of the United States. But perhaps even more ominous was the possibility that Jay might succeed. What then? The prospect of a successful negotiation troubled James Monroe, the US minister to France and a close ally of Jefferson and Madison. Imagine, he wrote to Madison in December 1794, that the British, facing an existential threat from France, decided to appease the United States. Imagine, he insisted, that they agreed to evacuate the forts, offered compensation for seizures at sea, accepted free trade, and ceded Canada. These concessions—all due to France's might—would be presented as a great victory of the Federalists and help them tighten their grip over the American people. "The impudence of the British faction would become intolerable," Monroe anguished.[55]

During the negotiations, Jay had sent only infrequent and spare information to President Washington, Secretary of State Edmund Randolph, and Hamilton.[56] Because of the vagaries of transatlantic crossings it was not until March 7, 1795, that Washington received a copy of the treaty. The president had hoped for better terms. While waiting for the Senate to meet in special session on June 8, he kept the treaty under wraps. He was certain, a perceptive biographer writes, that if the text became public, "controversy would during the three-month interim reach such heights that the Senate might be prevented from achieving a dispassionate decision—or even a decision."[57] (Secrecy was possible because the British government did not submit the treaty to parliament until November 1795.)[58] When the special session opened, Washington forwarded the document to the

Senate without offering any guidance. Perhaps he did not want to interfere in the Senate's deliberations, consistent with his understanding of the constitution; perhaps he had not yet made up his own mind about the treaty.

After deliberating in secret for more than two weeks, the Senate approved the treaty on June 24, 1795 with barely the requisite two-thirds: twenty votes in favor, ten against. Washington was finally ready to make the treaty public, but the *Aurora*, a leading Republican newspaper, beat him to the punch, thanks to a copy provided by a Republican senator. The *Aurora* thundered: "One would have imagined that Americans would turn with loathing from the embrace of a foreign tyrant [the British king] to whom Nero and Caligula were but diminutive butchers, and who has perpetrated every outrage on this country which weakness can suffer, or villainy can inflict."[59] The Republicans castigated the treaty's silence on impressment (which by 1795 had become a serious problem), its clause on the pre-revolutionary debts, and, in Madison's words, its "very extraordinary abandonment of the compensation due for the Negroes."[60] But the treaty's capital sin was that it drew the United States closer to Britain and opened a rift with France. "This infamous act," Jefferson raged, "is really nothing more than a treaty of alliance between England and the Anglomen of this country against the legislature and people of the United States."[61] The Republicans organized meetings throughout the country to condemn the treaty, and the Republican press lashed out against it.

Finally, on August 14, Washington signed the treaty. Until that moment he had made no public statement about it. Some Republicans attacked him with fury, others more cautiously—Washington was still a venerated figure.[62]

Hamilton had resigned as secretary of the treasury in January 1795 to return to private practice as a lawyer in New York, but he remained passionately committed to public affairs. He led the charge in favor of the treaty, writing twenty-eight articles, from July 22 through November 11. He labeled the Republicans' claims that Britain was weak and that Jay should have obtained better terms as "the chimeras of over-heated imaginations."[63] He argued that the treaty safeguarded the essential interests of the United States and pleaded for patience and caution. America was "the embryo of a great empire," but needed time to grow. "If we can avoid war for ten or twelve years more, we shall then have acquired a maturity which will make it [war] no more than a common calamity and will authorize us on [in] our national discussions to take a higher and more imposing tone."[64]

Hamilton "is really a colossus to the anti-republican party," Jefferson wrote to Madison. "In truth, when he comes forward, there is nobody but yourself who can meet him . . . For God's sake, take up your pen."[65] But Madison demurred. Of course, Jefferson could have written the articles himself, but he preferred to let others be bruised in the public debate. He bared his feelings in his private correspondence. "The aspect of our politics has wonderfully changed since you left us," he wrote to his Italian friend Philip Mazzei in April 1796. "An Anglican, monarchical and aristocratical party has sprung up, whose avowed object is to draw over us the substance as they have already done the forms of the British government. . . . It would give you a fever were I to name to you the apostates who have gone over to these heresies, men who were Samsons in the field and Solomons in the council, but who have had their heads shorn by the harlot England."[66]

The reference to Washington was unmistakable. Unfortunately for Jefferson, Mazzei was indiscreet and shared the letter with friends, and eventually it was printed first in a Paris newspaper and then, in May 1797, in the New York *Minerva*, a Federalist paper. Jefferson was in a quandary. To deny authorship would expose him as a liar; but to acknowledge it, he told Madison, would antagonize "all those with whom ... [Washington's] character is still popular, that is to say nine tenths of the people of the US."[67] He remained silent.

The US House of Representatives and the Jay Treaty

Having lost the battle in the Senate, the Republicans turned to the House, which had to appropriate funds for the joint commissions established by the treaty. At the opening of the Fourth Congress, in December 1795, they enjoyed a small majority over the Federalists, but many representatives remained independent, though their number had decreased because the battle over the Jay Treaty had increased party cohesion.[68] Madison argued that before voting on funding, the House had to review the treaty. On March 25, 1796, the representatives approved, sixty-two to thirty-seven, a request for all the documents bearing on Jay's negotiations. A week later, Washington sent a "defiant reply,"[69] stating that he would not provide the documents because the treaty-making power lay entirely with the Senate and the Executive. The battle was joined. On April 15, Madison urged the House to refuse to appropriate the funds and proposed that the treaty be renegotiated.[70]

Washington's support for the treaty, however, had given pause to many. As time had passed, the benefits of the treaty had become increasingly apparent. Without it, the British would not evacuate the posts in the northwest; British seizures of American ships at sea would increase; war might ensue. Furthermore, in early March, goods news had arrived from Madrid. Spain—hard-pressed in Europe—had signed a treaty that agreed to the United States' longstanding demands.

France's declaration of war on Spain, in March 1793, had forced Madrid into an uneasy alliance with its traditional enemy, Britain. But reeling under the blows of the French troops, the Spaniards concluded a separate peace with Paris in July 1795. They feared, however, that Britain might respond to their breach of the alliance by attacking Spanish possessions in the Western Hemisphere and that the United States, having settled its difficulties with England through the Jay Treaty, would seize the opportunity to join in the assault on Spanish lands. Therefore, Madrid hastened to appease the Americans: in October 1795, the Pinckney Treaty (also known as Treaty of San Lorenzo) resolved, in America's favor, the festering conflicts between the two countries. It set the border of the Spanish colony of West Florida at the 31st parallel, as the United States demanded, and granted US citizens both the right to navigate the Mississippi through Spanish territory and the right of deposit at New Orleans [Map 2]. "We gave them everything they wanted," lamented one of Spain's foremost historians, and received nothing in return, beyond the hope that the United States would refrain from attacking Spain.[71]

The Pinckney Treaty, which the US Senate ratified unanimously, added to the drive to implement the Jay Treaty. Many Americans feared that if there was a break between the United States and Britain—the likely consequence of a rejection of the Jay Treaty—Spain might renege on the one-sided concessions of the Pinckney Treaty. On April 30, 1796, by a fifty-one to forty-eight vote, the House appropriated the funds for the joint commissions. The battle was not yet over: the presidential elections were approaching, and the Republicans made the Jay Treaty a major campaign issue.

Choosing Washington's successor

These were the country's first contested presidential elections. (In 1788 and 1792, Washington had run unopposed.) In each state the voters would select presidential electors who, on the appointed day, would choose two names, without indicating who should be president and who vice president. The Federalist candidates were Vice President John Adams of Massachusetts and Thomas Pinckney from South Carolina. The Republican candidates were Jefferson and Aaron Burr of New York. The American economy was prosperous. The Jay Treaty had assured peace with England, and Hamilton's financial program "was working wonders."[72] The Federal assumption of the state debts had allowed the states to cut their taxes, and war in Europe was creating markets for American farmers and opportunities for American trade and shippers. The campaign did not focus on economic issues, but instead on the more emotional issues of relations with France and Britain, and the virtues and sins of the two main contenders: Jefferson, the Republicans argued, was "a steadfast friend to the rights of the people," Adams the "advocate for the hereditary power and distinction."[73] The Federalists responded in kind.

Having decided not to run, Washington prepared, with Hamilton's assistance, a farewell address to the American people. Published on September 19, it included a principle that would be a keynote of US foreign policy until the creation of NATO in 1949. "Europe," the president said, "must be engaged in frequent controversies, the causes of which are essentially foreign to our concerns … It is our true policy to steer clear of permanent alliances with any part of the foreign world." He also warned against "permanent inveterate antipathies against particular nations and passionate attachments for others."[74] Despite its statesmanlike language, the address was in fact a partisan document directed against the Republicans' passionate attachment to France. Not surprisingly, it was condemned by the Republicans and praised by the Federalists.

As if to add substance to Washington's warning against the "insidious wiles of foreign influence,"[75] the French openly intervened in the presidential campaign. The Directory (the five-man council that had ruled France since mid-1795) deemed the Jay Treaty a betrayal of the Franco-American alliance, a view shared by the US minister in Paris, James Monroe. Upon learning that the House had bowed to Washington's will, the Directory announced that France would no longer respect the liberal interpretation of neutral rights stipulated by the 1778 treaty of commerce with the United States. French ships began to seize American merchant vessels that carried British goods.[76]

The French minister to the United States, Pierre Adet, believed that most Americans loved France, and that even those who didn't were awed by the power of the French Republic. This was, indeed, the message blared by many Republicans. "The fall of proud England [is] unavoidable," the *Aurora* asserted in October 1796.[77] Should the Americans fail to elect Jefferson, they would face the wrath of France: "The moment . . . of retribution is approaching," a correspondent warned in the same issue. "If we wish to shun the impending danger of war with a nation [France] whose victorious armies shake Europe to its center, let us elect only such as are tried friends to the dignity and the independence of America."[78]

Therefore, Adet can be forgiven for believing that he could influence the elections. In two broadsides published in the American press on October 31 and November 19, 1796, he threatened, albeit subtly, that France would use force against the United States unless Jefferson were elected. A Federalist newspaper responded: "If the choice of a President of the United States is to depend on any act of a foreign nation, farewell to your liberties and independence."[79]

On December 7, the electors cast their ballots. The Federalist, Adams, won with seventy-one votes. The vagaries of the constitution meant that the Republican, Jefferson, the runner-up with sixty-eight votes, would be Adams' vice president.

On March 4, 1797, John Adams was inaugurated second president of the United States. The *Aurora* celebrated Washington's departure with words that reflected the feelings of many Republican leaders, but that few dared utter publically because Washington remained popular. "The man who is the source of all the misfortunes of our country," the *Aurora* wrote, "is this day reduced to a level with his fellow-citizens, and is no longer possessed of power to multiply evils upon the United States. If ever there was a period for rejoicing, this is the moment—every heart, in unison with the freedom and happiness of the people, ought to beat high with exultation that the name of Washington from this day ceases to give a currency to political iniquity and to legalize corruption."[80] This distorted caricature of George Washington was not unlike that drawn by Jefferson in his letter to Mazzei.

Although highly intelligent, George Washington was not an original thinker, nor did he have the brilliance of Jefferson and Hamilton; he was, however, a sober and realistic leader who had ably navigated the young American nation through the tempest unleashed by the Anglo-French war as well as the battle between Jefferson and Hamilton. That Washington increasingly sided with Hamilton in foreign policy was because he had concluded that the course advocated by Hamilton best served the interests of the United States. By supporting the Jay Treaty Washington courageously challenged the Republican leaders; it was, Joseph Ellis writes, "his most besieged and finest hour."[81]

As one of his shrewdest biographers, Ron Chernow, remarks, Washington "forged the executive branch of the federal government ... and set a benchmark for fairness, efficiency, and integrity that future administrations would aspire to match."[82] This was his towering contribution, and for this he owed no debt to Hamilton or any other adviser.

Chernow laments, however, that in the Farewell Address the president did not mention slavery; this was, he writes, the "most flagrant omission." But what should Washington have said? Like Jefferson, he was a great slaveowner; he privately condemned slavery but he freed not one slave during his lifetime. Chernow himself suggests the reason: Washington's "profligate spending and . . . baronial lifestyle."[83] What, then, could he have said in his Farewell Address? Silence was prudent.

Some will object that one should not judge Washington with the mindset of the twenty-first century. This is true, but it is also true that Washington understood that slavery was wrong. And in the years after the War of Independence hundreds of Virginians manumitted at least some of their slaves. But not Washington.

The presidency of John Adams[84]

The Directory was true to its word: the American people were punished for not electing Jefferson as president. Four days after taking office, Adams learned that France had expelled the newly appointed US minister, Charles Cotesworth Pinckney. Moreover, French interference with American shipping intensified.

On May 16, 1797, Adams addressed a special session of Congress. He had sharp words for the Directory's "indignities" against the United States. He would make "a fresh attempt at negotiation" with France, but Congress must adopt "effectual measures of defense"[85]— sound advice because the United States had only a tiny army and no navy, except for three frigates that were still under construction. The Republicans responded by calling Adams a warmonger. For the next four years Vice President Jefferson would be busy, behind the scenes, leading the opposition to the government he served.

The Federalists outnumbered the Republicans in both chambers of Congress, but party discipline was still very loose. This helps explain why Adams' pleas for military preparedness fared so badly. Congress rejected all military appropriations except the funds needed to put the three frigates in service.[86] It adjourned on July 8, after approving the dispatch of a three-man mission to France to negotiate the differences between the two countries.

Meanwhile, Jefferson was engaging in personal diplomacy behind Adams' back. Britain's allies in Europe had made peace with France, on France's terms: Prussia, Holland and Spain in 1795, and Austria in 1797; Spain had changed sides and joined France in the war against Britain, as had Holland. In Haiti, France's richest colony, the British army had been decimated by black rebels. In Ireland, revolt against British rule brewed. After three very difficult years of war, the French Navy had regained some of the strength it had possessed before the Revolution and had been reinforced by the Spanish and Dutch navies. In early 1797, the Directory began planning an invasion of England. Naval mutinies, financial troubles, and radical agitation sapped Britain's strength in the first half of the year and gave hope to London's enemies, on both sides of the Atlantic. "The wise Jefferson," French Consul General Philippe Létombe reported in June 1797, wanted the Directory to invade Britain and dictate a peace in London that would assure "the repose and happiness of the world." Clearly, Jefferson combined an unrealistic image of the Directory with a stunning disregard for the balance of power. "The best anchor of our hope is an invasion of England," he told his son-in-law; "if they [the French] republicanize that country, all will be safe with us."[87]

The three American envoys arrived in Paris in early October 1797. French Foreign Minister Charles-Maurice Talleyrand was in no hurry to negotiate with them. Before their arrival he had told the Directory "that a complete break with the United States would have serious consequences whereas our current relationship, half friendly, half hostile, is advantageous to us because our colonies continue to get supplies from the Americans while our privateers continue to enrich themselves by capturing their ships."[88] The envoys' first reports, which did not reach Philadelphia until March 4, 1798, relayed a tale of woes. Talleyrand had received them on October 8—for fifteen minutes. Over the following weeks they had been visited by Talleyrand's emissaries who had said that the Directory had been offended by Adams' unfriendly remarks in his address to Congress. Before negotiations could begin the envoys must disavow Adams' offensive words, pay a hefty bribe to Talleyrand, and agree to extend a large loan to the Directory. It would be very dangerous, the emissaries warned, for a weak country like the United States to defy France.[89] The Directory did not seek war with the United States; it did not even deliberately seek to insult the Americans; in fact, it paid very little attention to the United States. It simply treated the envoys with the contempt and arrogance it reserved for lesser powers.

For two weeks Adams, a choleric and impulsive man, struggled with how to respond. At times he was belligerent. "In my opinion," he jotted down, the French actions "demand on the part of Congress an immediate declaration of war."[90] But the message he sent to Congress, on March 19, 1798, was restrained. He simply said that the mission to France had failed, despite the US envoys' best efforts, and he reiterated his demand for military appropriations to strengthen the country's defenses.[91]

The Republicans exploded in insults—not against France for treating the United States with such contempt, but against Adams. Adams' message, Jefferson told Madison, was "insane."[92] Suspecting that the president was manipulating the facts to paint France as the aggressor, the Republicans in Congress demanded that he hand over all the envoys' reports. Adams promptly complied, withholding only the names of Talleyrand's emissaries, identifying them simply as "X", "Y", "Z." A wave of outrage swept across the United States.

Congress sprang into action, preparing the country for war. It appropriated funds for fifteen frigates and many smaller warships; it created a Department of the Navy and a Marine Corps; it increased the army beyond what even Adams considered necessary; and it imposed an embargo on trade with France and its colonies. It also approved the Alien and Sedition Acts—repressive measures against a free press and foreigners that Adams had not demanded, but did not resist.

The Republicans strenuously opposed these measures but, as Jefferson lamented, the shock of the XYZ dispatches caused many "wavering characters" to go over "to the war measures."[93] Talleyrand was a knave, Jefferson conceded, but there was "not the smallest ground to believe" that the Directory knew about his treatment of the American envoys.[94] In any case, the real villain was Adams, who had offended the French with his May 1797 message to Congress accusing the Directory of inflicting "indignities" on the United States—that message, Jefferson repeated time and again, was "the only obstacle to accommodation and the real cause of war, if war takes place."[95] The Alien and Sedition Acts confirmed Jefferson's belief that the Federalists had created a foreign crisis in order to curtail freedom at home. The Republicans must seek to adjourn Congress as quickly as possible, he urged Madison in late March. "To do nothing, and to gain time, is everything with us." Time would allow the American people to understand that the Republicans were their true friends; time would also allow a French "descent" on Britain. Jefferson was confident that the British were on the verge of defeat. "If we could but gain this season, we should be saved," he said. "The affairs of Europe"—the French invasion of Britain—"would of themselves relieve us."[96]

The Quasi War

There is no precise date for the beginning of the Quasi War. The French had begun attacking American merchant vessels in mid-1796, after the US House approved funds to implement the Jay Treaty, and they intensified their attacks after the election of Adams. Of approximately 5,000 American vessels involved in foreign trade in 1797, the leading authority on the Quasi War writes, more than 300 were captured by French warships and privateers (at least 280 of them in the Caribbean).[97] American merchants and shipowners continued to run the risk of capture because the profits of a successful trip were extremely high.

Finally in the spring of 1798, the first US frigates were put at sea. Their number increased as American shipyards worked at full speed and merchant vessels were converted into warships to fight the French. They were joined by American privateers. The clash with the French, historian Alexander DeConde writes, "was a quasi-war. It was a limited war that American fought only at sea and under self-imposed restrictions." These constraints, which stipulated that neither US warships nor privateers could attack unarmed French ships, had been imposed by Congress: the Republicans had vehemently argued that without them the United States would be engaged in open war with France, and they had convinced enough moderate Federalists to vote with them. In any case, those self-imposed rules were largely moot because there were very few French merchant ships left to attack: the Royal Navy "had practically swept French commerce from the seas."[98]

Through the spring and summer of 1798, American anger against France spiked and many Federalists called for a formal declaration of war. "What Adams thought through all this he did not record," an astute biographer writes. "By all signs, however, he was still of two minds in addressing the crisis." At times he seemed to favor a declaration of war, and his wife—his closest confidante—certainly did, berating Congress for its failure to act: "Why, when we have the thing, should we boggle at the name?" she wrote to her sister.[99] By the fall, however, the war fever had abated. The cabinet—hardline Federalists—advised Adams that a declaration of war would be "inexpedient," given the mood of the country; but to avoid further humiliation no more envoys should be sent to France.[100]

The Quasi War continued. In what historian Bradford Perkins has called "the first rapprochement," a modicum of collaboration developed between the United States and Britain against the common enemy. The British government readily granted export licenses to allow the sale of arms to the United States (and on one occasion made a gift of cannons for harbor defenses); indeed, Perkins writes, "an overwhelming proportion of the guns with which American vessels fought or menaced the French were acquired in Great Britain."[101] The Royal Navy gave convoy protection to American merchant ships, allowing the fledgling US Navy to concentrate its efforts in the Caribbean, where it hunted the French privateers, "little ships that were difficult for the frigates and converted merchantmen of the [US] navy to catch."[102] With the Dutch Navy defeated by the British at the battle of Camperdown in October 1797 and the Spaniards largely ineffectual, by early 1798, the Directory had abandoned the hope of an invasion of England and concentrated its efforts in the Mediterranean. Because the Royal Navy dominated the Atlantic, only rarely did a French warship venture to the Caribbean. For the French Navy the Quasi War was, at most, a footnote, a view shared by French naval historians who simply ignore it.[103]

Suddenly, on February 18, 1799, Adams acted. Without warning anyone,[104] he told Congress that he had nominated the American minister to Holland, William Vans Murray, "to be minister plenipotentiary of the United States to the French Republic."[105] In other words, he wanted to resume the negotiations without waiting for the Directory to act first. The Republicans celebrated, while the Federalists split. Some supported the president's decision; others were furious.

Why had Adams reconsidered? Beginning in the fall of 1798 he had been told by people he trusted—and, through intermediaries, by Talleyrand himself—that France was willing to enter serious negotiations. The Directory had no desire to continue an unnecessary war; but it would not deign to send an envoy to the United States to negotiate.

Domestic considerations may have influenced Adams. In 1798, popular revulsion against France's treatment of the American envoys had hurt the Republicans, France's friends. However, military preparations were expensive and the requisite taxes unpopular. Adams was particularly disturbed by the growth of the army which seemed to him excessive—whatever danger might have existed of a French invasion had disappeared with the British victory over the French fleet at Aboukir in August 1798. Furthermore, at Washington's insistence, Hamilton, who in 1796 had schemed to prevent Adams' election to the presidency, had been placed in effective command of the army. Peace with France would cut the army to size, saving money and defanging Hamilton.

Meanwhile the Quasi War was slackening. On the high seas, the Royal Navy was protecting American ships, and in the Caribbean US warships, aided by the British Navy, had curbed the French privateers. During 1799, the number of American merchant ships lost in the Caribbean fell by almost two-thirds.[106]

Adams' bold decision to send Murray to France was followed by inaction: it took eight months for the president to issue the final instructions for the mission, which had been expanded to three envoys. There were reasons for the delay. In his February 18, 1779, message to Congress, Adams had said that Murray would not go to France without "direct and unequivocal assurances" that he would be received with all the honors due to a representative of the United States.[107] Talleyrand had swiftly complied, but transatlantic crossings took time, and Adams did not receive the assurances until early August. Then Secretary of State Timothy Pickering, who opposed the mission, dragged his feet in preparing the envoys' instructions. In late August, news arrived that the Directory might be overthrown at any moment. Wouldn't it be wiser to wait? While these are plausible explanations for the delay, it is also possible that Adams was having second thoughts.

But in mid-October Adams suddenly announced that the mission must depart by November 1. On November 3, two of its members sailed for France (the third, Murray, was waiting in Holland). By the time the three met in Paris, the Directory had been overthrown and Napoleon had become the all-powerful First Consul of the French Republic. In December, the new government revoked the punitive measures taken against American shipping and reestablished the liberal trade rules of the 1778 commercial treaty between France and the United States. However, the Quasi War in the Caribbean continued.[108]

The negotiations began in April 1800. Napoleon had an additional incentive to end the hostilities: he was planning a French empire in North America and the Caribbean and wanted American economic cooperation. But he was not willing to pay a price for peace. The American negotiators could not obtain compensation for French spoliations of American shipping during the Quasi War. In October 1800, a treaty between France and the United States (the convention of Mortefontaine) simply stipulated that the issue would be revisited at a future time.

Adams' term was drawing to a close. Within a few weeks the electors would decide whether to give him a second term. His years in office, like Washington's, had been plagued by the bitter struggle between Republicans and Federalists. The battle had begun over domestic policy in 1790–1 as Jefferson and Madison opposed Hamilton's economic program.

At first, foreign policy played only a minor role in the conflict; Hamilton and Jefferson disagreed about the merits and wisdom of commercial retaliation against Britain. France was not yet a cause of dissension. The initial reaction of Hamilton and his friends to the French Revolution was sympathetic. But as the revolution grew more radical their attitude changed to distaste, and by 1792 it had turned into horror. Jefferson and his friends, on the other hand, celebrated the establishment of the French republic. Nonetheless, domestic politics—the battle over Hamilton's economic program—was still the overriding source of division between the two emerging political parties.

The clash over foreign policy did not explode until 1793, as France and England plunged into war. Hamiltonians and Jeffersonians—Federalists and Republicans—agreed that foreign trade was of fundamental importance for the United States, but they vehemently disagreed about how to respond to the constraints imposed by Britain on neutral trade. Jefferson believed that the United States had the right to fatten on the follies of the old world, as he famously said, and he argued that the US government had to force Britain to bow to the US definition of neutral rights. Hamilton, however, asserted that the United States had to compromise with the British, because the Royal Navy had the power to cripple American foreign trade.

This crucial foreign policy difference was exacerbated by other factors that poisoned the debate: Jefferson and his followers hated Britain, while the Hamiltonians loathed the French Revolution. For the Republicans, noble France challenged British tyranny; for the Federalists, powerful Britain shielded the United States—and civilization—from the ignoble French Revolution. Add to this the Jeffersonians' belief that Hamilton and his cohorts were the fifth column of the British, and the Hamiltonians' belief that the Jefferson and his followers were the tools of the French. For both sides the very existence of the American Republic seemed at stake.

While Republicans and Federalists tore into each other over foreign trade, they had no major disagreements about territorial expansion. Both applauded the Pinckney Treaty, with the concessions it wrested from Spain. Both supported the Indian policy of the Washington administration, which was marked by war against Native Americans and the forced acquisition of Indian lands.

John Adams was stubborn, and he did not work well with Congress or even with his own party. But it is unlikely that a more able politician would have achieved better results in the crisis with France. Despite occasional wavering he acted with dignity and intelligence—opposing an unnecessary war and seeking negotiations, while trying to lift his country out of its defenseless state. Adams's acceptance of the Alien and Sedition Acts is a stain on his record, but Woodrow Wilson would allow far worse sins against civil liberties during the First World War, and he has been extolled as a great idealist.

When the presidential electors cast their vote on December 3, 1800, Jefferson had defeated Adams by eight votes, seventy-three to sixty-five (the other Republican candidate, Aaron Burr, also received seventy-three votes, ensuring that this time, unlike 1796, president and vice president would belong to the same party). There were many reasons Adams lost: the Federalist Party was rent by bitter infighting; people were tired of the war taxes, and many worried about the Federalists' assault on civil liberties. But it was slavery that made it possible for Jefferson, the great slaveowner, to defeat Adams, a man who owned no slaves.

The three-fifths clause of the US constitution, the sordid bargain that the South had extorted at the constitutional convention, favored those states that had many slaves—the more the better—because it stipulated that an enslaved person would count as three-fifths of a free person when determining the number of a state's seats in the House. According to the 1800 census, the population of the United States was 4,306,446 whites, 108,395 free people of color (none could vote), and 893,602 enslaved people, overwhelmingly in the South.[109] These slaves gave the southern states fourteen additional representatives in the House and therefore in the Electoral College. Jefferson "swept the South's extra electors, 12–2," and these votes assured his victory.[110] Jefferson and Burr, a Federalist newspaper wrote in January 1801, will "ride into the Temple of Liberty upon the shoulders of slaves."[111]

CHAPTER 3
THE LOUISIANA PURCHASE

For Thomas Jefferson and his supporters, the election of 1800 was a revolution. It would undo the evils the Federalists had foisted on the United States: an authoritarian, aristocratic government; a large military; a massive national debt; high taxes. "In the Jeffersonian scripture, debt and taxes were public evils of the first magnitude," a historian notes.[1] The paramount concern of the new administration was to eradicate the national debt of $83 million in sixteen years and to repeal the country's internal taxes in four. This would be achieved by running a small, frugal government and slashing the military budget. The Republicans intended to dismantle the navy that the Federalists had built. They viewed a standing army with distaste and suspicion; the first line of defense for a virtuous republic would be the citizen soldier; there would be time to expand the army if war approached. "A well-disciplined militia [is] our best reliance in peace and for the first moments of war," Jefferson asserted in his first inaugural address.[2] The international situation was propitious. In October 1800, the convention of Mortefontaine had ended America's Quasi War with France, and by early 1801, the European war seemed to be drawing to a close. Peace would eliminate the disputes over neutral rights that had roiled US relations with Britain. Moreover, Napoleon's November 1799 coup, heralding the establishment of a military dictatorship in Paris, signaled the end, for Jefferson, of America's special relationship with Republican France.

Presidents Washington and Adams had managed unruly cabinets. Washington's inner circle had included two men of exceptional talent—Thomas Jefferson and Alexander Hamilton—but they had been at each other's throats. President Jefferson had a far easier task. His two key advisers throughout his presidency—his close friend James Madison as secretary of state and Treasury Secretary Albert Gallatin—were not only men of outstanding intelligence and loyalty, but they worked well with each other.[3] In Congress, the Republicans had a two-seat edge in the senate (17–15) and a large majority in the House (68–38).[4]

During the presidency of John Adams, the Quasi War with France had led to the United States' rapprochement with Britain. During Jefferson's first term another crisis with France, far more dangerous than the Quasi War—Napoleon's attempt to create a colonial empire in North America—would force the Anglophobe Jefferson to contemplate an alliance with Britain. While Jefferson wrangled with Napoleon, the United States was at war in the distant Mediterranean.[5]

"To the Shores of Tripoli"[6]

In the eighteenth-century, corsairs (privateers) from the Barbary States of North Africa—Morocco, Algiers, Tunis, and Tripoli—attacked the ships of Christian states that refused to pay tribute. American trade with the Mediterranean had become important in the decades before the War of Independence and the Royal Navy had protected the colonists' ships. After the war, the US government turned to France for protection—to no avail— and then to Britain, also in vain. The Mediterranean became dangerous for American ships, and several were captured by the corsairs, their crews enslaved.

In the second half of the 1790s, the United States began paying tribute to the Barbary states. Presidents Washington and Adams believed that this was cheaper than fighting a war. Jefferson disagreed. He had written to Adams in 1786, "it would be best to effect a peace thro' the medium of war." This would "procure us respect in Europe," and it would be cheaper in the long term than the continuing draining of tribute.[7] This would be tested as soon as Jefferson became president. In October 1800, the Bashaw (ruler) of Tripoli, Yusuf Karamanli, had issued an ultimatum to the United States, threatening war unless the tribute were increased. Having inherited from Adams a respectable fleet manned by sailors battle-hardened from the Quasi War, Jefferson accepted the challenge. In the spring of 1801, he sent three frigates and a schooner to the Mediterranean. He believed that they would easily defeat the Tripolitans' motley fleet. Jefferson's decision illustrates an important point that would be a keynote of his presidency: he was not a pacifist; he was determined to avoid war against powerful states, but was ready to use force against those whom he considered weaker than the United States.

Contrary to Jefferson's expectations, the war against Tripoli dragged on for four years. It is a colorful story. There was the disaster of the frigate *Philadelphia* which in October 1803 ran aground off the harbor of Tripoli and was captured with its crew of 307 by the Tripolitans. There was the bold raid of Lieutenant Stephen Decatur who sailed into the harbor of Tripoli, killed the Tripolitan guards aboard the *Philadelphia* without the loss of a single American, and set the ship ablaze. (The American crew was no longer on the ship and remained captive.) And there was the march of William Eaton from Egypt across the Libyan desert toward Tripoli to effect regime change: with him were the Bashaw Yusuf's older brother Hamet, eight US marines, and several hundred mercenaries and men loyal to Hamet. In April 1805, they captured the coastal city of Derne, halfway between Egypt and Tripoli. And there they stopped. Eaton's advance, and the tight blockade of Tripoli by a large US squadron that included almost the entire US Navy, convinced Yusuf that it was time to negotiate. In June 1805, he signed a peace treaty with the US consul general in Algiers. It was, as Francis Cogliano points out in his careful analysis, "a qualified success" for Jefferson.[8] The United States would no longer pay tribute to Tripoli—but it paid a $60,000 ransom (*c.* $1,335,000) for the sailors of the *Philadelphia*, and it continued to pay tribute to the other Barbary states.

Jefferson had hoped that the war would impress the Europeans with the resolve of the United States, but with rare exceptions (notably Decatur's raid into the port of Tripoli) the Europeans paid scant attention to the conflict. Tripoli was the weakest of the Barbary states, it had only one vessel of more than twenty guns, and yet it took the United States four years to force Yusuf to compromise.

Americans quarreled about Jefferson as a war leader—brilliant, according to the Republicans, inept said the Federalists—but they celebrated the exploits of their sailors.

This patriotic fervor, however, did not save the Navy: as soon as the war was over the administration dismantled or sold most of the ships to reduce expenses.

Louisiana

While the American fleet battled the Tripolitans in the Mediterranean, the people of the United States cheered stunning news: in April 1803, the Jefferson administration had bought the immense territory of Louisiana from France, doubling the size of the United States. Unfortunately, Napoleon left no clear explanation as to why he decided to sell the colony and, therefore, historians disagree about it. Their explanations tend to emphasize one of three factors: Jefferson's diplomacy, the prospect of war against Britain, or the black rebels of Haiti. The most heated disagreements revolve around the significance of the role played by Thomas Jefferson.

Most American historians emphasize the importance of Jefferson's diplomacy in Napoleon's calculations, praising the persuasive powers of the president and Secretary of State Madison. Alexander DeConde, who has written the standard account of the Louisiana purchase, credits Jefferson's balance of procrastination, threats, and military preparedness with intimidating Napoleon out of Louisiana. Walter LaFeber, one of the most eminent US historians, asserts that "Jefferson and Madison devised a brilliant series of policies that finally forced Napoleon to sell not only New Orleans but most of the area between the Mississippi and the Rocky Mountains." The most recent scholarly analysis of the Louisiana purchase concludes that "Jefferson played a weak hand very well. . . . He demonstrated a willingness to use force and occasional duplicity to complement his diplomacy."[9]

French historians, on the other hand, tend to be dismissive of Jefferson's policy. Thus Thierry Lentz, one of the foremost French authorities on Napoleon, lists many reasons for Napoleon's decision to sell Louisiana: "naval weakness, underestimation of the blacks' desire for freedom, errors of the [French] military commanders [in the Caribbean], delay in taking possession of Louisiana and, finally, the renewal of war with Britain." Lentz does not even mention Jefferson—Gallic bias or a sober assessment of the facts?[10]

Napoleon's dream

Louisiana had been a French colony when Britain and France went to war in 1756. The French saw it as a vast wilderness of little economic value. For them it was important not in itself but as part of a grandiose plan to create a French empire in North America that would hem in the Thirteen Colonies between the Appalachian Mountains and the Atlantic.

But in 1763, the dream was dashed when France lost Canada and eastern Louisiana to England. Western Louisiana, therefore, lost its value and the French ceded it to their ally,

Spain. For Spain, western Louisiana (henceforth Louisiana) was important as a buffer separating the greedy Anglo-Saxons from the mines of Mexico.

The allure of a French empire in the New World did not die. When Napoleon's dreams of empire in India were quashed by the British fleet at Aboukir in August 1798, he turned to the Western Hemisphere. In the secret treaty of San Ildefonso of October 1, 1800, King Charles IV of Spain agreed to return Louisiana to France in exchange for the creation of a sizeable kingdom in Italy for his son-in-law. The deal was less one-sided than it might appear. Spain, a decaying power, feared the threat posed by the United States, a rival even more dangerous than Britain had been, as the Americans' rapacity would not be restrained by European politics. In French hands, Louisiana would be a far more effective shield protecting Mexico from the United States than anything Spain could provide [Map 4].

For Napoleon, Louisiana would be part of a French empire in the Western Hemisphere that would include French Guiana, the French West Indies, as well as Florida (East and West). The two Floridas belonged to Spain and were not included in the Treaty of San Ildefonso, but Napoleon hoped to acquire them. They would give France the entire coastline of the Gulf of Mexico east of the Mississippi.

The economic engine of this empire would be Haiti. Haiti, DeConde explains, was "the keystone of an arch that would bind his [Napoleon's] whole colonial system together."[11] In 1789, when the French revolution began, Haiti was France's richest colony, the world's leading producer of coffee and sugar. The planters devoted its soil to those highly profitable crops, and they imported basic necessities such as food, timber, and draft animals, mainly from the United States; Haiti was the Americans' major commercial partner after Britain. More than 500,000 people dwelt on its tiny surface: 35,000–40,000 whites, some 28,000 free people of color and at least 450,000 slaves. (By comparison, in 1790 the United States had 3,930,000 inhabitants.)

The Haitian Revolution

In Napoleon's plans, Louisiana would supply Haiti with timber and foodstuffs. He faced, however, a challenge: in 1791 the enslaved people of Haiti had revolted, and the French had been unable to defeat the insurrection. In 1793, the Spaniards and the British had invaded, eager to seize the lucrative prize. Then, on February 4, 1794, the French Republic—the France of Robespierre and of the Terror—abolished slavery throughout the French empire and extended full citizenship to the former slaves. The Haitian rebels rallied to the flag of the French Republic. It was as French citizens that in 1794 they defeated the Spaniards and then fought off the far more powerful British. Finally, in 1798, the British departed, bloodied, and the former slaves, led by Toussaint Louverture, were in control, although they nominally acknowledged the sovereignty of France.[12]

Under Toussaint, the Haitian economy began to recover from the ravages of the war. Haiti was unique: a multiracial society ruled by a black man in which upper class whites intermingled with the black elite and where intermarriage was legal. This terrified the slaveowners of the US South and of the British colonies in the Caribbean, where slavery continued to thrive. The multiracial moment in Haiti, however, would not last: Napoleon was determined to restore French rule.

The creation of a French empire in the Western Hemisphere required peace with the British, whose navy ruled the waves. On October 1, 1801, Paris and London signed Peace Preliminaries.

Napoleon did not wait for the conclusion of the formal peace, signed at Amiens on March 27, 1802, before sending an expedition to Haiti to reconquer the colony. For the British, the return of white rule—even if French—was welcome. Prime Minister Henry Addington told Napoleon's envoy that "the interest of our two governments ... is absolutely identical: it is to destroy Jacobinism, and that of the Blacks above all."[13] The British press agreed. "The erection of a Negro republic in the West Indies, consisting of half a million of souls, and connected but nominally with France, would be extremely dangerous to the British possessions in that quarter," the London *Times* noted. With the exception of *Cobbett's Annual Register*, no major British newspaper criticized the government's decision to welcome Napoleon's conquest of Haiti. Prophetically, however, the *Morning Post and Gazetteer*, recalling how miserably the British troops had fared against the Haitians a few years earlier, warned that it would be "almost impossible" for Napoleon's soldiers to subdue the Haitians by force.[14]

Jefferson and Haiti

Trade between the United States and Haiti had continued after the outbreak of the Haitian Revolution, but it had been threatened in 1798 when the US Congress, as part of the Quasi War, had imposed the trade embargo on France and its colonies. (Haiti was still legally a French colony.) Toussaint had sent an aide to Philadelphia with a letter to President Adams urging that Haiti be excluded from the embargo. "Americans will find protection and welcome in the ports of St. Domingue [Haiti]," he wrote.[15]

The administration had responded positively. It was motivated by economic interests—trade with Haiti was "so beneficial to the U.S.," Secretary of State Timothy Pickering wrote—as well as by the desire to widen the gulf between Toussaint and France. Ethical considerations also may have played a role. Adams considered slavery immoral, and Pickering was impressed by Toussaint, whom he called "amiable and respectable."[16] In January 1799, the Federalist majority in the House of Representatives approved, against the Jeffersonians' bitter opposition, a bill that allowed Adams to exclude Haiti from the embargo. Jefferson deplored the decision to trade with the "rebellious Negroes under Toussaint." He feared that "black crews" from Haiti would stir trouble in the southern states.[17]

Two years later, Jefferson became president of the United States, and in July 1801, the French chargé in Washington, Louis-André Pichon, asked him if it would be possible to strike an agreement so that France could conquer Haiti more quickly. According to Pichon, Jefferson replied: "That would present no difficulty; but in order that this concert may be complete and effective you must first make peace with England. Then nothing would be easier [for the United States] than to furnish your army and fleet with everything needed to reduce Toussaint to starvation."[18]

Even Jefferson's two leading biographers, both of whom admire the president deeply, concede that he may have "promised too much to Pichon," and that "he appears to have gone further than was wise or necessary."[19] Jefferson's warm response to Pichon can be explained in part by his sympathy for France and by strategic considerations—French control of Haiti would be a counterpoint to the dominance of the Caribbean by Britain, which Jefferson considered a danger to the United States. However, by July 1801 the president had been told by his diplomats in Europe that it was likely that Napoleon had acquired or would soon acquire Louisiana from Spain, which meant that France would take over New Orleans, the hub of trade for the western half of the United States. In the 1795 Pinckney Treaty, the Washington administration had extracted from Madrid two fundamental rights: US citizens could navigate the Mississippi to the Gulf and they had the "right of deposit," meaning that they could store goods at New Orleans without paying customs duties. Not surprisingly, Jefferson and his associates preferred that New Orleans belong to weak and decadent Spain rather than to powerful and aggressive France. "We fear that Spain is ceding Louisiana to France, an inauspicious circumstance to us," Jefferson wrote to his son-in-law in May 1801. Two weeks later he told his friend James Monroe, governor of Virginia, "There is considerable reason to apprehend that Spain cedes Louisiana and the Floridas to France. It is a policy very unwise to both, and very ominous to us."[20]

Therefore, in July 1801, Jefferson should have understood that Napoleon's Haitian venture was part of a larger imperial project that threatened the security of the United States. National interest should have led him to oppose Napoleon's plans to reconquer Haiti. But slavery clouded Jefferson's judgment. Jefferson knew that slavery was a crime. "I tremble for my country [Virginia] when I reflect that God is just," he wrote in the *Notes on the State of Virginia*. He was haunted by a "nagging fear" that the enslaved would rebel, a biographer remarks, because he believed "that an intolerable wrong was being inflicted upon men, women and children." Jefferson lamented, "We have the wolf by the ears; and we can neither hold him, nor safely let him go."[21]

Haiti was a wolf that had broken free; there, enslaved people had won their liberty by killing their masters. Jefferson inveighed against Toussaint and his "cannibals."[22] He told Madison, "If this combustion can be introduced among us under any veil whatever, we have to fear it." The discovery of a vast network of enslaved people planning a revolt in Virginia in August 1800 heightened his fear. "It is unquestionably the most serious and formidable conspiracy we have ever known of the kind," Monroe told Jefferson.[23] Twenty-five enslaved people were tried, sentenced to death, and hanged. "The accused have exhibited a spirit which, if it becomes general, must deluge the Southern country with blood," a prominent Virginian warned. "They manifested a sense of their rights, and a thirst for revenge which portend the most unhappy consequences."[24] Like many southerners, Jefferson believed that the plot had been inspired by the slave revolution in Haiti.[25]

Therefore, in July 1801, when Pichon inquired about US help to crush Toussaint, Jefferson responded like the slave owner and leader of the slave-owning South that he was. He welcomed the French reconquest of Haiti, telling the chargé, "Doesn't the example [of Toussaint] present the greatest danger for two thirds of the [United] States?"[26]

Geopolitics, however, would force him to reconsider. In November 1801, the US minister to Britain, Rufus King, sent Secretary of State Madison irrefutable evidence that Napoleon had acquired Louisiana from Spain. Soon, an armada of almost 20,000 soldiers left France for Haiti. The troops, the US minister in Paris, Robert Livingston, reported, would "proceed to Louisiana" after establishing control over Haiti.[27] Clearly, Haiti and Louisiana were part of a master plan of French empire and Haiti was the United States' first line of defense: as Madison noted, "a protracted and expensive war" in Haiti would "form a very powerful obstacle to the execution of the [Louisiana] project."[28]

Jefferson's response

Jefferson's attitude changed. He no longer welcomed the French conquest of Haiti. According to DeConde's highly regarded *This Affair of Louisiana*, Jefferson "took anti-French action by stepping up aid to the [Haitian] rebels." LaFeber agrees. "Madison sent secret help" to the Haitians, he writes. But DeConde offers no source for his assertion, and LaFeber's only source is DeConde.[29] Nor do they provide any information about the timing or the nature of the aid. This is understandable: the Jefferson administration never gave any assistance to the Haitians.

What Jefferson did do was refuse to help the French reconquer the colony. He would not lend them money for their cash-strapped troops in Haiti, and he did not prevent American merchants from trading with the Haitian rebels, as the French demanded.[30] (Jefferson could have urged Congress to approve an embargo on trade with the rebels, but this would have made neither commercial nor political sense, since by then he knew that Napoleon had acquired Louisiana.)

Jefferson was willing to see Louisiana west of the Mississippi in French hands, although he would have much preferred to have the weak Spaniards there. But he wanted New Orleans, and he hoped to persuade France to sell it. And he wanted the Floridas. He was unsure whether the Floridas had been included in Madrid's cession of Louisiana to France; if yes, then he would purchase them from France; if not, he would persuade Napoleon, who had leverage over the Spanish government, to force Madrid to sell them to the United States.[31]

The administration's diplomatic offensive to obtain these territories unfolded on two fronts: Jefferson and Madison with Pichon in Washington,[32] and Livingston, the US minister to France, with Foreign Minister Talleyrand in Paris. Meanwhile the situation in Louisiana remained unchanged: the Spaniards continued to govern the colony and no French troops had appeared: they were too busy fighting the Haitians.

Jefferson and Madison sought to pressure Napoleon by raising the twin specters of war with the United States and of an Anglo-American alliance. Both these threats were wielded with particular eloquence in Jefferson's April 18, 1802 letter to Livingston: "There is in the globe one single spot, the possessor of which is our natural and habitual enemy. It is New Orleans, through which the produce of three-eighths of our territory must pass to market ... it [is] impossible that France and the United States can continue long friends when they meet in so irritable a position.... From that moment [when France takes possession of New Orleans] we must marry ourselves to the British fleet and nation." If the French insisted on keeping Louisiana, they should cede New Orleans and the Floridas to the United States. "This would certainly in a great degree remove the causes of jarring and irritation between us."[33]

The other prong of Jefferson's diplomatic offensive was directed at enlisting British support in a possible war against France. But, as Robert Tucker and David Hendrickson conclude, these efforts were "half-hearted and without real significance. Given the outlook of the Republicans, this was understandable ... an alliance with Great Britain represented for Jefferson and his political associates something approaching a state of mortal sin."[34]

Even if Jefferson had not loathed the British, even if he had seriously sought their help, he had nothing to offer them. Whitehall welcomed Napoleon's acquisition of Louisiana because it would drive a wedge between France and the United States. British foreign secretary Lord Hawkesbury told the House of Commons in May 1802 that since "the possession of Louisiana [is] now rendering France the natural rival of America, every maxim of sound policy will incline her [America] to cultivate a more intimate connection with this country."[35] The London *Times* agreed: "It has been our opinion from the first that the assent of the British cabinet to this act of Spain [the cession of Louisiana to France] is founded on superior policy ... by bringing the restless power of France to her [the United States'] very back, we shall be relieved from our anxious and active vigilance, as the Americans will be fully employed in attending to the designs of their new, ambitious and enterprising neighbours."[36] As long as the British were at peace with France, they had no reason to be seduced by Jefferson's diplomatic offensive.

Jefferson's real audience, however, was France. He wanted to scare the French with the prospect of a US alliance with Britain. The British understood this. "I have certainly of late found Mr. Livingston more than usually cordial," the British ambassador in Paris remarked. "American policy will be to play off such an appearance of cordiality and concert with Great Britain, as a demonstration against the Government [of France]."[37]

Jefferson's and Madison's threats worried French chargé Pichon, who repeatedly warned Talleyrand that the occupation of Louisiana would have a disastrous effect on France's relations with the United States. "Mr. Jefferson ... believes that our acquisition of Louisiana is a serious political mistake on our part," he wrote to Talleyrand, "which will lead, as soon as Europe is at war, to a break between us and the United States and an alliance between them and England."[38] There is no record of Napoleon's reaction to Pichon's reports, if he read them, but it is clear that Talleyrand was not impressed: he consistently opposed the sale of Louisiana to the United States.[39]

Livingston was very active in Paris. Trying to persuade Napoleon to sell New Orleans and the Floridas to the United States, as Jefferson demanded, he brandished the stick and the carrot, despite being almost deaf and speaking very little French. "He petitioned, begged, cajoled, threatened, and even tried to bribe the Bonapartes."[40] But Talleyrand kept him at arms' length. "I can get him to tell me nothing," Livingston groused.[41] After several months the Frenchman finally acknowledged that his government had indeed acquired Louisiana from Spain but he refused to say whether the purchase included the Floridas. (It did not, as Livingston reported time and again.) Realizing that he was making no headway, Livingston adopted a two-track policy: he told Madison that while continuing to communicate with Talleyrand he had also begun to address "unofficially ... the only man who is supposed to have some sort of influence" over Napoleon, his older brother Joseph.[42] This strategy was not effective: Joseph bitterly opposed the sale of Louisiana to the United States, as did his brother Lucien, another favored target of Livingston. In other words, the US strategy of threats and blandishments failed to move Talleyrand, Joseph and Lucien.[43] There is no reason to assume that it was more successful with Napoleon.

News of the cession of Louisiana to France had begun to circulate in the United States in the summer of 1801. The Federalist press had warned of the dangers that the arrival of "such intriguing and ambitious neighbours" posed for the United States. "It is presumed that American trade will be severely restricted and that the U. States will have little to expect from France on the score of commercial favors," the *Gazette of the United States* warned.[44] But until late 1802 not even the Federalist press made Louisiana a major issue, nor had the US Congress. Any sense of urgency was allayed by the fact that no French troops had arrived in Louisiana, which continued to be defended by a handful of Spanish soldiers.

This complacency ended in October 1802, when the Spanish Intendant in New Orleans, Juan Ventura Morales, revoked the Americans' right of deposit. (The Intendant was the senior official in charge of the customs administration and was independent of the colony's governor.) Suddenly, Americans paid attention. They suspected that Morales had acted at Napoleon's behest, and this stoked their anger and anxiety. The Republican press sought to reassure the public. It stressed that the decision to repeal the right of deposit had been taken by Morales "without orders" from his government and would soon be revoked by Madrid;[45] it published letters from the French and Spanish ministers in Washington to that effect;[46] and it lambasted the "advocates of war and its terrible calamities"—that is, the Federalists.[47] The latter were on the offensive. They had found an issue that could embarrass Jefferson. "Will our dignified president and his wisely chosen ministers," the *Gazette of the United States* inquired, "continue calm spectators of contemplated encroachments on our important western boundary? Will they remain passive until the great key to the navigation of the Mississippi is possessed by the-all grasping hands of the First Consul [Napoleon]; until he acquires the power to dictate law to the settlers on the banks of those rivers which flow into the Atlantic by the mouth of the Mississippi; until he has completed his arrangements to dismember the United States of America by embarrassing the settlers west of the Allegheny mountains in the vortex of his insatiable ambition?"[48]

The president, however, believed Pichon's and the Spanish minister's assurances that the Intendant had acted on his own and that the crisis would be resolved quickly. "We have the best grounded presumptions that the suspension of the right of deposit will be immediately removed," Jefferson wrote in January 1803.[49] But could he trust that Napoleon would respect US rights once French troops had occupied Louisiana?

According to historian Mary Adams in an oft-cited article, Jefferson began to make "important preparations" for war against France. "The Mississippi frontier was seething with the movement of troops, officers, munitions, supplies, and the building of fortifications," she writes. "In the spring of 1803 he [Jefferson] was ready for a showdown." But when Mary Adams details Jefferson's "important preparations" for "a showdown," it is striking how puny they were. She explains that the gravity of the crisis spurred the administration "to accelerate the mail" from Natchez near the border of West Florida to Washington, to strengthen military posts along the frontier, and to move companies of soldiers toward the Mississippi border. This might sound dramatic, but such was the anti-British paranoia of the president and his aides that they dispersed their paltry forces in order to counter a non-existent British threat. In Mary Adams' words, "great care was being taken to protect the northern frontier as well. . . . The federal government believed that the British had designs for extending their domain into the Mississippi Valley and such expansion had to be prevented at all cost."[50]

To erect a barrier against French influence, Jefferson sought to replace the Indians with white settlers along the eastern bank of the Mississippi. He told the governors of the Mississippi and Indiana territories that in order "to be prepared against the occupation of Louisiana by a powerful and enterprising people it is important that . . . we bend our whole views to the purchase and settlement of the country on the Mississippi from its mouth to its northern regions."[51] The policy made sense as a long-term measure, but in the short term it had no practical effect beyond despoiling the Indians of their land. While Jefferson did not tell the officials to cheat and bully the Indians to hand over their land, how else could they acquire it as quickly as he demanded?

Jefferson's "important preparations" were, therefore, to speed up the mail, strengthen US forts, remove the Indians from the shores of the Mississippi, and station small, widely dispersed, groups of soldiers at the border. He did not increase the size of the army. In fact, in early 1802, he asked Congress to reduce the army to a ceiling of 3,289 from the previous ceiling of 5,438. As Dumas Malone remarks, "The reports of the American military establishment which the representatives of foreign governments sent home could not have been expected to overawe European chancelleries or strengthen the hands of American negotiators."[52]

To reassure the people of the western states and territories, who depended on the port of New Orleans, in January 1803 Jefferson nominated James Monroe—who enjoyed great popularity in the West—envoy extraordinary and minister plenipotentiary to join Livingston in Paris to help persuade the French to sell New Orleans and the Floridas (if Spain had ceded the latter to France).

On April 8, 1803, the same day that Monroe's ship reached Le Havre, Jefferson decided, with the support of the majority of his cabinet, that if Napoleon obstructed US navigation of the Mississippi, Livingston and Monroe would be instructed to enter into discussion with the British government about an alliance "on the ground that war [against France] is inevitable."[53] Unlike the previous year, in the spring of 1803 the British would have welcomed a US alliance because war against France loomed. For the Americans, a British alliance would mean that the Royal Navy would prevent the French from landing soldiers in Louisiana. If, however, Napoleon did not inhibit US navigation rights and denied only the right of deposit, then the envoys should request further instructions from Washington. "The Jeffersonian leadership ... [had] made its decision on alliance and war," DeConde writes.[54] It seemed a momentous step, particularly given Jefferson's pronounced Anglophobia. The point, however, was moot because Napoleon had decided to maintain the Americans' rights in Louisiana, including the right of deposit.[55]

The absence of French troops in Louisiana—a keynote of the Louisiana affair—had two causes. The Spanish king, Charles IV, was a French client and an admirer of Napoleon, but he was not a puppet; he waited until October 1802 before signing the documents that officially transferred Louisiana to France because Napoleon had not yet fulfilled his end of the bargain—withdrawing his troops from the Italian Kingdom of Etruria, which he had created for Charles' son-in-law. The second reason for the delay was Haiti, a much more formidable problem. Napoleon had expected that some of the troops he sent to Haiti would, after the colony's pacification, proceed to Louisiana.[56] And he had thought that the pacification of the colony would require only a few months. He was sorely mistaken.

Jefferson's "cannibals"

In November 1801, Napoleon had issued a proclamation to the Haitians pledging that "regardless of your origins and skin color you are all French; you are all free and equal." He called for them to rally behind General Victor-Emmanuel Leclerc, who was coming to protect them "against your enemies and against the enemies of the Republic."[57] When Leclerc and his army of 19,500 soldiers arrived in Haiti in February 1802, several Haitian generals were deluded by these promises and defected with their soldiers to Leclerc's army. By April 1802, Leclerc commanded 7,000 Haitian soldiers—almost a third of Toussaint's regular army.[58] Initially, Toussaint and his troops had fought back, but in May 1802, in a surprising reversal, the Haitian leader accepted an amnesty. His generals followed his example and were incorporated, with their troops, in Leclerc's army. They helped Leclerc hunt down those rebel bands that still resisted French rule. It seemed that Napoleon had been right that French rule in Haiti could be quickly reestablished.

The abrupt arrest and deportation of Toussaint to France in early June was a signal to many Haitians that the French could not be trusted. Their sense of betrayal deepened with the news of the French law of May 20, 1802, which maintained slavery and the slave trade in every French colony except Haiti, Guadeloupe, and Guiana. In early August 1802, the news spread that despite the law the French commander in Guadeloupe, General Antoine Richepanse, had reestablished slavery there. Leclerc despaired: "I implored you, Citizen Consul," he wrote to Napoleon on August 6, "not to do anything that could cause them [the Haitians] to fear the loss of their freedom until I had established myself. I was fast approaching that moment." Three days later Leclerc lamented, "The decrees of General Richepanse are known here and they have damaged us greatly. The one that reestablishes slavery was issued three months too soon, and it will cost our army . . . in Haiti many lives." The revolt against the French in Haiti grew. The rebels "die with incredible fanaticism, they laugh at death, and so do the women," Leclerc reported.[59] They were fighting for freedom in the most literal sense of the word. "Do not even think about reestablishing slavery here in the near future," Leclerc urged the Secretary of the Navy, Denis Decrès.[60]

Meanwhile, another enemy had surfaced: yellow fever. It decimated Leclerc's ranks and killed Leclerc himself on November 2, 1802. The fever was a scourge for the French, but it is likely that they exaggerated the number of its victims. In the words of two leading historians of the war the French generals "embroidered the facts," attributing many of their dead to yellow fever in order to downplay their losses to the black enemy.[61] A flagrant example of this "embroidery" is given by one of Leclerc's generals, Pamphile de Lacroix, in his memoirs. After describing the March 1802 siege of the fortress of Crête-à-Pierrot, where the French lost 2,000 men and the Haitians only 500, Lacroix wrote: "Our losses had been so heavy that they pained General Leclerc very much; he urged us . . . to doctor them as he himself did in his official reports."[62]

Sometimes historians follow one another like lemmings. Thomas Ott, author of a generally good history of the Haitian revolution, argued in 1973 that in the months following Leclerc's death the French troops in Haiti, bolstered by thousands of reinforcements sent by Napoleon, were gaining the upper hand against the rebels. "By early April [1803] the French were in their strongest position since the surrender of Toussaint," Ott writes. General Donatien de Rochambeau, who had replaced Leclerc, "probably had more troops than Leclerc's original expedition, a portion of his forces were immunized against yellow fever, and most of the key coastal cities were still under French control." Other historians have followed Ott's lead, even though he offered no evidence.[63] But the reports written at the time by French officers tell a different story, as do those historians who have sifted through the relevant documents in the French archives and in Haiti.

In October 1802, the Haitian generals who had been fighting under Leclerc deserted to join the revolt against him. Over the next few months, most of the Haitian troops that had rallied to Leclerc—and had come to constitute the bulk of his army—defected to the rebels who had coalesced under the leadership of the very able Jean-Jacques Dessalines, who had been one of Toussaint's top generals. In April 1803, the admiral who commanded the French fleet in Haiti wrote, "We fight with difficulty against men who are becoming ever more dangerous because every day they grow more bold and are better trained. . . . Throughout this vast colony, we control only the towns, and we cannot leave them . . . without placing ourselves in danger."[64] The French difficulties were compounded by the fact that unlike the troops that had accompanied Leclerc, the 11,561 soldiers who reached Rochambeau by April 1803 did not belong to first class units. Their performance on the battlefield reflected this. Thrown into battle upon their arrival, they suffered heavy losses. On April 14, 1803, Rochambeau wrote to Napoleon, "A large part of the South is in revolt, as well as most of the West and almost the entire North."[65] That month he tried to reconquer the South, but his offensive—"his most ambitious operation to date"[66]—was a costly failure. Rochambeau himself uncharacteristically acknowledged that he had lost "many good men."[67] A French naval officer who participated in the fighting described in his memoirs how desperate the situation of the French troops had become.[68] The French "fly before the undisciplined slaves," an American woman wrote from Haiti to US Vice President Aaron Burr.[69]

Haiti was Napoleon's first defeat; 36,800 of the 43,800 soldiers he sent there paid with their lives. In addition, at least 6,000 French sailors died.[70] A French captain who served in Haiti under both Leclerc and Rochambeau wrote the epitaph of the campaign in his diary: the French, he said, despised the Haitians "because of the color of their skin." They failed to understand "that nowhere in the world could one find soldiers who were more brave, more committed, more undaunted by death … and more able to endure suffering. … We have been cruelly punished for our arrogance."[71]

Was Napoleon aware that the French situation in Haiti was desperate and did this contribute to his decision to sell Louisiana? In early 1803, he still seemed committed to the conquest of Haiti; he sent reinforcements to the colony and wrote to Rochambeau on February 4: "Nothing interests the nation more than the island [sic] of Haiti."[72] Yet the fact that he did not send troops of the first rank (which were available) may suggest that his determination was waning. There are no references to Haiti in his correspondence after February 5, except for a March 18 note instructing Navy Secretary Decrès to send to Rochambeau 2,747 soldiers whose departure had been delayed due to the lack of transports.[73] Furthermore, if Napoleon had still wanted to conquer Haiti, the timing of the war with Britain—a war he could have postponed—is surprising: the war, which began on May 18, 1803, meant that Rochambeau could no longer be helped.

Britain

Most French historians assert that the British bear primary responsibility for the outbreak of hostilities. "England refused to accept a France that was powerful on the continent," writes Jean Tulard, a leading authority on the Napoleonic era.[74]

But when the British had agreed to the Peace of Amiens they had implicitly accepted French hegemony in Western Europe. What they could not accept was a France that was "aggressive, threatening, spreading constantly beyond its borders."[75] After Amiens, Napoleon had continued to expand. In Italy, he had annexed Piedmont and the island of Elba, and he had tightened French control over two client states, the Ligurian and Italian republics; he had also occupied Switzerland, a restive client, and he maintained French troops in the Netherlands, in violation of France's 1801 peace treaty with Austria. When Lord Whitworth, the British ambassador in Paris, sought in February 1803 to discuss these French actions, Napoleon dismissed them as "bagatelles."[76] The only issue he wanted to address was Malta, which the British continued to occupy in violation of the Treaty of Amiens.

The signs of renewed French interest in Egypt, Napoleon's refusal to negotiate a commercial treaty with Britain, and the size of the French army—almost half a million men—added to the tension between the two countries. The British were open to negotiations: they wanted Napoleon to withdraw his troops from Holland and agree to their control of Malta for ten years; in return, they would accept French troops in Switzerland and all the gains France had made in Italy after the Peace of Amiens. There was in Paris a strong peace party, led by Napoleon's brother Joseph and Talleyrand, that urged Napoleon to reach an agreement with the British even if it meant allowing them to keep Malta. Napoleon, however, "did not want to cede anything . . . he wanted, instead, to control the entire European continent," explains Thierry Lentz.[77] Napoleon rejected the British proposals. He was not seeking war with Britain, but his continuing expansion in Western Europe and his intransigence made war inevitable. On May 12, 1803, Lord Whitworth left Paris. Six days later, war began.

The decision to sell

It is unknown when exactly Napoleon decided to sell Louisiana to the United States. Talleyrand was the first to be told, on April 7, 1803.[78] He disagreed with the decision. On April 10, Napoleon summoned Navy Secretary Decrès and Treasury Secretary François Barbé-Marbois, and informed them of his decision. Barbé-Marbois writes in his memoirs that Napoleon told them: "The English . . . have twenty warships in the Gulf of Mexico, they sail over those seas as sovereigns, while our affairs in Haiti have been growing worse every day since the death of Leclerc. The conquest of Louisiana would be easy [for the British] if they bothered to land troops there. I don't have a moment to lose in putting it out of their reach. . . . I think of ceding it to the United States . . . I believe that French interests and even commerce will be better served with Louisiana in the hands of that growing power than if I should attempt to keep it."[79]

Once Napoleon had decided that France could not keep Louisiana, it made sense to offer it to the US government. The only alternative would have been to return it to Spain. Politically, that made no sense. Spain was a French client and Napoleon did not need to court Madrid's goodwill; the United States, instead, was an important neutral. Financially, too, it made no sense. Napoleon needed money for the war against Britain. Napoleon could (and did) extort a war subsidy from Spain; but the only way to get money from the United States was by selling it Louisiana.[80]

On April 11, 1803, the day after receiving Napoleon's instructions, Barbé-Marbois told Livingston that France was willing to sell Louisiana to the United States. Livingston and Monroe had been instructed to buy New Orleans and the Floridas. When they asked whether the territory they were being offered included the Floridas, Barbé-Marbois "purposely clothed the matter of Louisiana's boundaries in a fog," DeConde writes.[81] An honest answer, that the Floridas were not included, would have diminished the value of the territory for the Americans and could have affected the price they were willing to pay. The fog, however, was not thick: Monroe reported on April 19 that Barbé-Marbois had told him that Napoleon had promised "his support of our claim to the Floridas with Spain," thus making it clear that Spain owned them.[82] Nonetheless, after the treaty of purchase had been signed on April 30, 1803—the United States agreed to pay $15 million (c. $351 million) for the territory—the two American envoys exultantly, if disingenuously, wrote to Madison that "on a thorough examination of the subject, we consider it incontrovertible that W. Florida is comprised in the cession of Louisiana. . . . Hence the acquisition becomes of proportionally greater value to the United States."[83]

Why Napoleon sold Louisiana

The purchase of Louisiana was a triumph for the United States. But what role did the US president play in Napoleon's decision to sell the colony? It is easy to determine what Jefferson did not do: he did not give any help to the Haitians in their fight against Napoleon, contrary to what renowned US historians have asserted; he did not prepare the United States for war; and he did not take any military steps to intimidate Napoleon. In fairness, given the military impotence of the United States, there was very little Jefferson could have done, as long as France was at peace with Britain. But what he did was risible: he lowered the ceiling of the army from 5,438 to 3,289 men. As for Jefferson's "important preparations" for "a showdown"—speeding up the mail, moving small groups of soldiers along the border, strengthening forts—they were, at best, a show of American weakness.

Did Jefferson's threats and blandishments succeed in intimidating Napoleon *despite* the lack of military preparations? Here we come to a formidable obstacle, for nowhere did Napoleon explain in writing why he sold Louisiana. But there is other evidence. We know that Jefferson and his aides—who had no direct access to Napoleon—failed to convince the three main targets of their efforts: Foreign Minister Talleyrand and Napoleon's brothers Joseph and Lucien. All three opposed the sale of Louisiana. Why would the Americans have been more successful with Napoleon? For the French ruler, the United States was a distant country with a village for a capital, a weak fleet, virtually no army, and no warlike traditions: the Americans' performance in their war of independence had been less than stellar. As Thierry Lentz writes, "in this France that understood power almost entirely through battlefield victories, the military strength of the United States made people smile."[84]

There is one more clue: the memoirs of Barbé-Marbois, the man who negotiated the sale of Louisiana to the Americans. Napoleon told him, he writes, that "the conquest of Louisiana would be easy" for the British and that "our affairs in Haiti have been growing worse every day since the death of Leclerc." Nowhere did Napoleon mention the United States as a reason to sell Louisiana.

In other words, there is no evidence that Jefferson's diplomacy played any role. The clues indicate instead that Jefferson was irrelevant to Napoleon's decision to sell Louisiana.

Britain, however, was crucial. War with Britain meant that Louisiana would be lost to France because there were no French troops to defend it. Why was the colony undefended?

Napoleon had wanted to give Louisiana "a degree of strength which will permit him to abandon it without fear in time of war," Navy Secretary Decrès said, "so that its enemies may be forced to the greatest sacrifices merely in attempting an attack on it."[85] But the French troops never arrived. They went instead to Haiti. And they died there. If Black resistance in Haiti had collapsed quickly, as Napoleon had expected, there would have been thousands of French soldiers in Louisiana by the spring of 1803, when war with Britain threatened.

The Haitian debacle stripped Louisiana of its value for the French. As Barbé-Marbois wrote, "Louisiana had been destined to supply the other colonies [Haiti] with provisions, cattle, and wood and as Haiti was lost to France, the importance of Louisiana was also diminished." His words are echoed by Jean Tulard: "Failure in Haiti made the occupation of Louisiana worthless."[86]

Haiti's role, therefore, was decisive. By defeating Napoleon, the people whom Jefferson deemed "cannibals" made it possible for him to acquire Louisiana and achieve his "greatest triumph."

An empire of liberty

The Louisiana Purchase, by doubling the size of the United States, raised anew questions about whether republican institutions were capable of governing a vast territory. Jefferson believed that it was only a matter of time before white Americans spread over the entire continent. He had written in 1786 that "Our confederacy must be viewed as the nest from which all America, North and South, is to be peopled." And he said as much in a November 1801 letter to Monroe who had asked him for advice about the areas in which freed Negroes from the South could be settled. Jefferson replied that they should settle neither in North America nor in South America: "However our present interests may restrain us within our own limits, it is impossible not to look forward to distant times when our rapid multiplication will expand itself beyond those limits, and cover the whole northern, if not the southern continent with a people speaking the same language, governed in similar forms, and by similar laws; nor can we contemplate with satisfaction either blot or mixture on that surface."[87] Expansion meant that there would be enough land for the multiplying Anglo-Saxon population; this would foster the blossoming of communities of healthy yeoman farmers, instead of the hordes of landless laborers crowded into factories in the towns and cities of Europe. America would be, in Jefferson's words, an "empire of liberty."[88] Jefferson had not determined whether there would be one United States encompassing the entire area of freedom, or several sister republics. After acquiring Louisiana, he wrote in January 1804: "whether we remain in one confederacy, or form into Atlantic and Mississippi confederacies, I believe not very important to the happiness of either part. Those of the Western confederacy will be as much our children and descendants as those of the Eastern." He did not, however, consider separation inevitable. In his second inaugural he asked, rhetorically: "who can limit the extent to which the federative principle may operate effectively?"[89]

While Jefferson referred on several occasions to sister republics, he never defined the idea precisely. "It was one of his many ideas that tantalized, in part because it remained largely unexplained."[90] Furthermore, it is impossible to know how sincere his willingness to accept sister republics was, because it was never tested. But one thing is clear: Jefferson's "empire of liberty" was for white people only; he did not want "either blot or mixture." He never explained what would happen to these blots and mixtures as white America expanded.

Looking back

As a leading biographer of Jefferson writes, the Louisiana Purchase "made the President ten feet tall in the public eye, his re-election a foregone conclusion."[91] He had doubled the size of the United States without firing a shot. The American economy was strong, foreign trade was growing, and increased customs receipts produced the surpluses that made possible the steady reduction of the national debt even though the country's internal taxes had been repealed in 1802. The war between Britain and France, which began in May 1803, brought American shippers great benefits. As the Royal Navy swept the merchant vessels of the French and their clients from the seas, the Americans stepped into the breach. American carrying trade increased dramatically as did the shipbuilding industry and trades associated with it.

Unlike his two predecessors, President Jefferson cultivated an image of simplicity. His dislike of pomp was legendary. The secretary of the British legation, Augustus Foster, described how Jefferson received the British minister, Anthony Merry: "He is dressed and looks extremely like a very plain farmer, and wears his slippers down to the heels."[92] Stuffy European diplomats were shocked. For his admirers, and they were legion, Jefferson was the epitome of virtue, the symbol of the new country, a beacon of democracy in contrast to old Europe. And yet, in one fundamental aspect, Jefferson was akin to the great Lords of Russia: like them, he owned hundreds of human beings who toiled on his estates, complete with his enslaved concubine, Sally Hemings, thirty years his junior. But white Americans did not focus on the plight of black slaves, and rumors of Jefferson's slave concubine were dismissed as lies spread by the Federalists. Jefferson "appealed deeply to American citizens," historian Bradford Perkins writes, and "attracted the blind, even excessive, loyalty of many Americans."[93]

The president's popularity was reflected in the elections of 1804. Jefferson defeated the federalist candidate by a crushing 162 electoral votes to fourteen, winning fifteen of the seventeen states. In Congress, the Republicans outnumbered the Federalists by a 114–28 margin in the House and 27–7 in the Senate.[94]

A few months before Jefferson's electoral triumph his nemesis was killed in a duel. Alexander Hamilton had played a far more important and constructive role than Jefferson during Washington's presidency, setting the foundations of the country's economy and helping steady its foreign policy. Men of outstanding intelligence, sincere patriots, superb writers, ambitious and charismatic, Hamilton and Jefferson were in many ways a study in contrasts. Where Jefferson trusted the masses, Hamilton distrusted them; where Jefferson was secretive, pushing his friends into battle, Hamilton was outspoken and led from the front. A warm and generous person, Hamilton was the rare white American who believed that the "natural faculties [of Blacks] are probably as good as ours."[95] But his role as statesman largely ended when Washington left the presidency. Consumed by a growing and increasingly irrational hatred of John Adams, he squandered his talents trying to prevent the latter's reelection—hurting in the process not only Adams, but also the party he had created and his own prestige. By the time Jefferson became president, Hamilton was, politically, a much-diminished figure. But he remained to the end a sincere nationalist. He approved the Louisiana Purchase. However, while most of his countrymen celebrated the genius of Thomas Jefferson for wresting the territory from Napoleon, Hamilton extolled "the courage and stubborn resistance" of the Haitians, who had foiled Napoleon's plan.[96]

In 1804, Hamilton fervently and loudly opposed the candidacy of Vice President Burr for New York governor, suspecting him of conniving with Federalists plotting to pull New England and New York out of the Union. After losing the election, Burr challenged Hamilton to a duel. He accepted, was mortally wounded, and died on July 12, 1804. Hamilton's biographer Ron Chernow provides the epitaph of his extraordinary life: "No other founder articulated such a clear and prescient vision of America's future political, military, and economic strength or crafted such ingenious mechanisms to hold the nation together."[97]

CHAPTER 4
JEFFERSON'S SECOND TERM

The collapse of the Peace of Amiens in May 1803 hurled Europe into another decade of war that ended only with Napoleon's defeat in 1815. On one side stood a coalition of states dominated by France, on the other Britain, at times with allies, but often alone.

There were in 1803 five great states in Europe: the two superpowers, France and Britain; Austria, the dominant power of Central Europe; Russia; and Prussia, the junior of the five. In December 1805, at Austerlitz, Napoleon defeated the Austrian and Russian armies. The following October, he crushed the Prussians. Then he marched again against the Russians, who had withdrawn to the eastern border of Prussia. Again, he won. In July 1807, Napoleon and the Tsar signed the Peace of Tilsit. The Tsar agreed to join the Continental System, which sought to strangle the British economy by closing the European continent to British trade, and he stood by as Napoleon imposed a draconian peace on Russia's ally, Prussia. Prussia lost half its territory and became a French vassal. A new French satellite was created from lands carved from eastern Prussia: the Duchy of Warsaw, on Russia's border, garrisoned by French troops.

The Peace of Amiens had acknowledged France's hegemony over Western Europe; after Tilsit, Napoleon dominated Europe all the way to the Russian border. He seemed unstoppable, but for one country, Britain. The sea, and only the sea, protected Britain from invasion and conquest. The British believed that they were the last defense of Europe and civilization from tyranny.

The struggle between the French and the British was the backdrop of Jefferson's second term. While the world's greatest powers were locked in a titanic struggle across the Atlantic, Jefferson was absorbed by the United States' maritime dispute with Britain and, to a lesser degree, by his obsessive attempts to acquire the Floridas.

The Floridas

Florida was divided into East and West. The former was the peninsula, and the latter, "West Florida," was the northern coast of the Gulf of Mexico from the Apalachicola River all the way to the Mississippi, excluding New Orleans [Map 4]. West Florida had a population of a few thousand souls—Native Americans, Europeans, white Americans, and their black enslaved people. For Spain, it was important as a geographical barrier protecting the Gulf of Mexico from the Americans.

But President Jefferson wanted West Florida for the United States—particularly its western stretch from the Perdido River to the Mississippi—because it would provide unfettered access to the sea for the people of the Mississippi Territory (the future states of Alabama and Mississippi). Jefferson's desire was understandable. What was extraordinary was his claim that the United States was already the rightful owner of half of West Florida. He managed to convince himself (or at least to argue) that the Louisiana Purchase had included it, despite formidable evidence to the contrary. "The acknowledgment of our right to the Perdido is a *sine qua non*," he reminded Madison.[1] Dumas Malone, Jefferson's eminent and sympathetic biographer, explained:

> Convinced as he had long been that possession of West Florida was necessary for the security and future well-being of his country, Jefferson was predisposed to approve any contention that gave promise of hastening what he regarded as inevitable consummation. While at Monticello in August and September [1803], availing himself not only of the communications of Livingston and Monroe but also of the facilities of his extensive library, he prepared with his own hands a memoir on the limits and bounds of Louisiana.... His written argument ... was wholly independent of the expressed opinions of the Spanish and the French.... Accordingly, he arrived at the gratifying judgement that the United States was entitled to demand and Spain was bound to deliver the country as far east as the Perdido.[2]

If, as Malone claims, Jefferson relied on "the communications of Livingston and Monroe," he did so in a most selective way. Livingston had reported in April 1802 that the Floridas were part of Spain's Louisiana cession to France, but he soon changed his mind. "I have every reason to believe that the Floridas are not included," he wrote to Madison on September 1, 1802. Over the next several months he consistently repeated that "Florida is not ... included in the cession." As late as May 12, 1803, after the sale of Louisiana to the United States, he told Madison that the territory did not include the Floridas. Then, suddenly he reversed himself: on May 20, he wrote to Madison that West Florida was part of Louisiana.[3] Monroe, too, underwent a conversion: on May 18, 1803, he believed that West Florida belonged to Spain. Five days later he changed his mind.[4]

Jefferson paid attention to the opinions of Livingston and Monroe only when they confirmed what he wanted to believe. And he overlooked the reports of the US minister to Spain, Charles Pinckney, who consistently said that the Floridas were not included in Spain's Louisiana cession to France.[5] By cherry-picking the assertions of his advisers the president was able to assert that the Gulf Coast from the Mississippi to the Perdido belonged to the United States and, as Malone writes, "in his own mind it appears never afterwards to have been shaken."[6]

This certitude made it possible for Jefferson to transform the victim into the aggressor. If West Florida (to the Perdido River) was part of the Louisiana Purchase and if Spain refused to cede it, then Spain was in the wrong and Jefferson was morally justified to bribe, threaten, and even wage war to recover what—in his mind—rightfully belonged to his country.

Jefferson first tried diplomacy. Since Spain was a French client, he sent Monroe to Paris to seek French assistance. In April 1803, French Treasury Secretary Barbé-Marbois had told Monroe that Napoleon had promised "his support of our claim to the Floridas with Spain,"[7] but the French reneged on this promise. In December 1804, a week after Spain had joined France in the war against England, Foreign Minister Talleyrand formally told Monroe that West Florida was not part of the Louisiana Purchase. Worse, France guaranteed that "colonies seized in the course of the current war would be returned to Spain,"[8] which suggested that if the United States annexed West Florida, Napoleon would help Spain recover it. Emboldened by French support, the Spaniards refused to surrender West Florida to the United States. Jefferson was indignant: "We want nothing of hers," he wrote to his minister to Spain in April 1805, "but she has met our advances with jealousy, secret malice and ill-faith."[9] And so he shifted gears. The United States would seize West Florida and forge an alliance with England to deter any French response in support of Spain. "I think we should take into consideration," he told Madison in August 1805, "whether we ought not immediately to propose to England an eventual treaty of alliance." The treaty, he explained, "should be provisional only, to come into force *on the event of our being engaged in war with either France or Spain*, during the present war in Europe. In that event we should make common cause and England should stipulate not to make peace without our obtaining the objects for which we go to war." These objects were expansive: "the rightful boundaries of Louisiana"—that is, Texas and West Florida—as well as East Florida (the peninsula) as "indemnification" for the claims of US citizens against Spain.[10] (These were claims for attacks by Spanish privateers against American shipping during the Quasi War, and for Spain's failure to protect American ships from French seizures in Spanish waters.[11])

Jefferson's Anglophobia was such that he could contemplate only a one-sided alliance in which England received nothing beyond the honor of fighting for the United States. This is what Madison sought gently to make Jefferson understand. He pointed out that Jefferson's plan demanded much of England and offered nothing in return. The British would not be interested, "unless indeed some positive advantages were yielded on our part. . . . No such advantage as yet occurs, as would be admissible to us and satisfactory to her." For Jefferson, however, such an advantage existed: "Whatever ill humor may at times have been expressed against us by individuals of that country, the first wish of every Englishman's heart is to see us once more fighting by their sides against France; nor could the king or his ministers do an act so popular as to enter into alliance with us."[12] This was a stunning assessment of the British mood, completely divorced from reality. While Madison and Treasury Secretary Gallatin sought to dissuade Jefferson,[13] the British hardened their position on neutral rights, stoking Jefferson's fury. And yet he continued to mull over his plan—so eager was he to acquire the Floridas. As late as October 11, 1805, he told Madison that the most pressing question for the administration was to decide "Whether we shall enter into a provisional alliance with England to come into force only in the event that *during the present war* we become engaged in war *with France?*"[14]

Twelve days later, Jefferson received a letter from John Armstrong, the US minister in France, informing him that Napoleon would help the United States acquire both Floridas—if, the letter implied, Napoleon received a bribe. Jefferson made a complete volte face. He told Madison that he would "make another effort for peaceful settlement" with Spain.[15] On December 6, he sent a secret message to Congress in which he described the tension between the United States and Spain, and stated that France was willing to help bring about a settlement satisfactory to the United States. He noted that this would require money but did not specify the amount or provide any other information, leaving the matter to the "wisdom" of Congress.[16] This "subtle language of indirection" was characteristic of Jefferson's dealings with Congress, one of his leading biographers, Merrill Peterson, explains. In the 1790s, Jefferson and his followers had criticized President Washington's concentration of diplomatic power in the hands of the executive as a violation of the constitution. Consistent with Republican doctrine, as President Jefferson acknowledged the principle of legislature's superiority over the executive, which had been violated by the alleged monarchical propensities of the Federalists. Therefore, in his communications with Congress "recommendations were suggestions and demands were veiled in obscurity." In fact, however, as the unchallenged head of the Republican Party, which controlled Congress, Jefferson wielded executive authority over the legislature. "The long arm of the president," Peterson writes, "reached out, often through the cabinet, to Capitol Hill. Leaders of both houses of Congress were the President's lieutenants."[17]

In private conversations with key congressional leaders both Jefferson and Gallatin, who was his point man in the negotiations, revealed that they wanted Congress to appropriate $2 million (c. $44.5 million). In February 1806, Congress obliged; the money, it stated, would serve to defray "any extraordinary expenses which may be incurred in the intercourse between the United States and foreign nations." The "extraordinary expenses" were understood to be the bribe for Napoleon.[18]

To court French goodwill, the administration supported a bill introduced by Senator George Logan (R-PA) prohibiting American trade with Haiti, France's rebel colony. The last French troops had ignominiously abandoned the country in late 1803, and the rebel leader Dessalines had proclaimed Haiti's independence on January 1, 1804. The French, who continued to claim Haiti as their colony, had been demanding that the United States impose an embargo on trade with Haiti. Jefferson, given his hostility toward the land of the rebellious Blacks, was sympathetic to the demand. "We are called on by a nation friendly to us to put a stop to this infamous and nefarious traffic," Representative John Eppes, who was Jefferson's son-in-law, told the House in February 1806. "Let us pass the bill at once." From across the political divide a Federalist offered a different viewpoint in a letter to the president. The Haitians were being punished because they had "a skin not coloured like ours," and in order to satisfy "the *insolent demand*" of the French. The bill, if approved, would bring disgrace to the Congress of the United States, he told Jefferson, but "chiefly on You ... on whose will the measure is known to depend." Undeterred, the Jeffersonian majority in Congress approved the Logan Act and Jefferson signed it into law on February 28, 1806.[19]

A few days later, Madison sent Jefferson's instructions to Minister Armstrong in Paris. The president wanted East and West Florida; on Texas (where the US claim was as spurious as that to West Florida) he was willing to compromise: "Although it may not be amiss to urge the claim of the United States to the Rio Bravo [Rio Grande]," Madison told Armstrong, the administration would accept a border that included only half of Texas. The United States would pay Spain $5 million (c. $111 million) but, Madison added, not until Spain had satisfied the claims of US citizens which amounted to "not less than four millions of dollars." In other words, only a pittance would remain for Spain as payment for East Florida and the eastern section of West Florida (east of the Perdido) that even the administration acknowledged was not part of the Louisiana Purchase.[20]

Jefferson was optimistic that Napoleon would force Madrid to do his bidding. "From Paris we may expect now daily to hear something," he wrote in July 1806.[21] But months passed, and Napoleon failed to apply pressure on the Spaniards, who did not budge. Jefferson grew exasperated. In April 1807, he complained to his minister in Madrid, "Never did a nation act towards another with more perfidy and injustice than Spain has constantly practiced against us. And if we have kept our hands off her till now, it has been purely out of respect for France and from the value we set on the friendship of France. We expect therefore from the friendship of the emperor that he will either compel Spain to do us justice, or abandon her to us." The president then descended into idle bluster against Spain: "We ask but one month to be in possession of the city of Mexico."[22] Madrid's crime? It refused to be robbed of one of its colonies by the United States.

Napoleon paid no attention to the American president's demands. When Jefferson stepped down in 1809, the Floridas were still Spanish. His attempts to acquire them highlight key traits of Jefferson's foreign policy: his capacity to delude himself; his overestimation of US power (the British government, he asserted, could do nothing "so popular as to enter into alliance with us"); his territorial greed (he wanted not only the Floridas, but also half of Texas). The disconnect between his purported idealism and his deeds would also be the keynote of his policy toward Native Americans.

Words . . . and deeds

"Among the first generation of American statesmen," historian Francis Prucha writes, "Thomas Jefferson was surely the most important theorizer about aborigines."[23] Jefferson theorized that unlike Blacks, Indians could become the equal of whites through acculturation. The federal government would help them abandon hunting in favor of agriculture and animal husbandry. As they became farmers, they would need less land; they would sell their excess land to the federal government to defray the cost of agricultural implements and to satisfy their growing economic needs. Their land holdings would shrink and finally, once acculturated, they would be integrated into white society with equal rights, and the Indian problem would be solved. It would be a gradual, slow process.

Throughout his presidency, Jefferson proclaimed these high-minded precepts. "When you have property, you will want laws and magistrates to protect your property and persons. . . . You will find that our laws are good for this purpose. You will wish to live under them," he told a delegation of Delawares in December 1808. His words soared.

"You will unite yourselves with us . . . and form one people with us, and we shall all be Americans. You will mix with us by marriage. Your blood will run in our veins and will spread with us over this great land."[24]

Jefferson's rhetoric bore little relationship to his actions. In late 1802, he instructed the governors of the Mississippi and Indiana territories to acquire Indian land along the eastern bank of the Mississippi as quickly as possible in order to create a barrier against French influence. He did not change his instructions after he had purchased Louisiana, ending any French threat. Historian Jeffrey Ostler writes that like President Washington, Jefferson "did not believe that Native nations . . . could legitimately say no when presented with terms the United States defined as reasonable. Should Indians be indisposed to sell, their disposition would have to change." During Jefferson's presidency, US officials concluded thirty-two treaties with the Indians acquiring roughly 200,000 square miles of territory using high-pressure tactics: they bribed and threatened chiefs, struck deals with groups and individuals who had no claim to represent their tribe, used liquor to "mellow" Indians in the negotiations. They got the land at rock bottom prices. As another respected historian writes, "Nearly all the treaties provoked Indian outrage and protest."[25] But Jefferson constructed a different reality: "We continue to receive proofs of the growing attachment of our Indian neighbors," he told Congress in December 1806, and, two years later, as Indian anger swelled, "the attachment of the Indian tribes is gaining strength daily."[26] More soberly, he instructed the governors of Indiana and Michigan territories to warn tribal leaders that "if ever we are constrained to lift the hatchet against any tribe, we will never lay it down till that tribe is exterminated, or driven beyond the Mississippi." The threat of genocidal war was real, Ostler concludes. "It was an official statement of a policy for dealing with Indians who refused to accept U.S. terms of dispossession."[27]

Relations with Native Americans were, however, a minor matter when compared with the issues that dominated Jefferson's second term: neutral rights and impressment.

The maritime quarrel

After war between Britain and France resumed in May 1803, the Royal Navy seized the merchant vessels of France and its clients, and America's carrying trade reaped the benefit. There was a hitch, however: the more the carrying trade grew, the greater America's need for experienced sailors, and the most qualified pool of sailors was British. But the Royal Navy also needed sailors because of the war, and since it could not match the pay and conditions offered by American shippers, it resorted to impressment. Once again, British warships stopped American merchant ships on the high seas to search for British sailors, inflaming American public opinion and angering US officials.[28] The anger was tempered, however, by the spectacular growth of the country's trade which mushroomed from $55.8 million in 1803 to $95.6 million in 1805. In July 1804, the US minister to England, James Monroe, wrote to Madison that "our commerce never enjoyed in any war as much freedom, and indeed favor from this govt [Britain], as it now does."[29] The British had softened the Rule of 1756—that trade closed to neutrals in time of peace was also closed in time of war—with the doctrine of the "broken voyage." The rule of 1756 forbade an American shipper to take a cargo from, for example, Guadeloupe (a French colony) to France in time of war, because Paris had not allowed it in time of peace. The doctrine of "broken voyage" introduced a vital loophole: the shipper could first take the cargo from Guadeloupe to Charleston, South Carolina (allowed by France in time of peace), pay duties, and then take it to France without violating the Rule of 1756—in other words, the cargo had become a US export. As a result, by 1805 the carrying trade represented more than half of total US exports.[30]

British shippers resented the growth of the American merchant fleet. Furthermore, as a rising chorus of Britons pointed out, the American carrying trade was helping their enemy, France. In May 1805, a British Admiralty Court intervened. In the *Essex* decision, it stipulated that henceforth "broken voyage" would require not only transshipment and the full payment of duties, but the American shipper also would have to prove that his original intent had been to terminate the voyage in an American port. The decision, Bradford Perkins writes, reflected Britain's "determination to step up the pace of war against Napoleon."[31]

Through the summer and early fall of 1805, the Jefferson administration's response to the *Essex* decision and the captures of American ships that ensued was restrained: this was when Jefferson was contemplating an alliance with Britain that would give him the Floridas. However, by the time Congress convened, in early December, that idea had been discarded and Jefferson was eager to punish the British for the *Essex* decision. It was tempting to ban British imports—a hallowed weapon in the Republican arsenal—but retaliation had to be tempered with realism: having repealed the internal taxes, the administration relied solely on land sales and import duties. Import duties on British goods brought the government almost half its yearly revenues ($5.4 million of a total of $12 million). Therefore, Jefferson and Madison settled on half a loaf. With their encouragement in April 1806, the Republican majority in Congress passed a selective Non-Importation Act against Britain to go into effect on November 15: it barred goods that could be acquired from other countries or made at home—roughly half of the imports from Britain. (With the exception of maverick senator John Quincy Adams [MA], the son of former President John Adams, all the Federalists opposed the bill.)

The delay from April to November gave Jefferson time to open negotiations with London on maritime issues. He held the threat of the Non-Importation Act in his back pocket, as a lever to pry concessions from the British.

Madison's instructions to the two American negotiators, James Monroe, who was the US minister in London, and William Pinkney, a prominent Baltimore lawyer, "were largely an exercise in wishful thinking," writes Donald Hickey, author of the best analysis of the negotiations.[32] The Americans sought a long list of concessions on neutral rights capped by two *sine qua non*: Britain must repudiate both impressment and the *Essex* decision. The United States offered nothing in return beyond the promise that it would not enforce the Non-Importation Act.[33]

In the negotiations, which began in August 1806, Monroe and Pinkney understood what Jefferson could not—or would not—acknowledge: that for Britain, Monroe told the president, "the very existence of the country depended on an adherence to its maritime pretensions."[34] Without impressment, the Royal Navy would be unable to man its ships. "The demands for men have been beyond all imagination," the Admiralty reported in early 1806, "and the want of them hampers every operation considerably."[35]

Therefore, Monroe and Pinkney abandoned Jefferson's *sine qua non* on impressment and on December 31, 1806, signed a treaty quite similar to that signed by Jay twelve years earlier. On the carrying trade, the British made an important concession: they retracted the *Essex* decision. They also made concessions on contraband and blockades. In return, the United States agreed to the most favored nation clause, which meant that it could not enact punitive measures, such as nonimportation, against Britain that did not apply to all other nations as well. The treaty did not mention impressment. (In a separate note, the British promised to exercise "the greatest caution" when searching for British seamen on American ships, and to afford "immediate and prompt redress" to any American mistakenly impressed.[36])

In early March 1807, Jefferson received a copy of the treaty, and he rejected it out of hand, even refusing to submit it to the Senate for consideration. The president, with the full support of the cabinet, was determined to denounce any treaty "not securing us against impressment."[37]

For Jefferson, a fundamental principle was at stake. As long as the British asserted the right to search American ships for British subjects, mistakes would be made and American seamen impressed—even if the Admiralty exercised "the greatest caution." Accepting impressment, Madison wrote to Monroe and Pinkney, "would violate both a moral and political duty of the government to our citizens."[38] It would also hurt Jefferson politically—American attitudes on impressment had hardened.

But this is only part of the story. As Paul Gilje writes, "There was more to the Republican administration's failure to settle the question of impressment than met the public eye."[39] This became clear as Jefferson and Madison explored ways to make it possible for London to forego impressment. On April 3, the president and the cabinet agreed "to propose to Great Britain not to employ any of her seamen, on her stipulating not to impress from our ships."[40] But a few days later Treasury Secretary Gallatin reported that the number of British seamen in the American merchant marine was "larger than we had estimated" and "an engagement on our part to employ no British sailors would materially injure our navigation." Despite Britain's restrictive practices on neutral rights, "Our tonnage employed in foreign trade has increased since 1803 at a rate of about 70,000 tons a year," Gallatin wrote, "equal to an increase of 8,400 sailors for two years, and I would estimate that British sailors have supplied from one-half to two-thirds of that increase." Jefferson reconsidered: "Mr. Gallatin's estimate of the number of foreign seamen in our employ," he told Madison, "renders it prudent, I think, to suspend all propositions respecting our non-employment of them."[41] In other words, it was not in America's interest to renounce the service of British sailors even though it exposed American seamen to the risk of impressment.

On May 20, 1807, Madison sent new instructions to Monroe that reiterated that Britain had to abandon impressment. The administration was simply trying to gain time.

"As long as negotiation can be honorably protracted," Madison explained, "it is a resource to be preferred, under existing circumstances, to the peremptory alternative of improper concessions or inevitable collisions."[42] Meanwhile the partial Non-Importation Act against Britain, approved by Congress in April 1806, remained suspended.

The *Chesapeake* affair

Procrastination was not as prudent a strategy as the administration had hoped. The officers of the Royal Navy were determined to replenish their crews, depleted by death and desertion; they resented the Americans' insistence on profiting from the war, and had no time for American sensitivities. Their ships hugged the US coast in order to search American merchant ships leaving or entering port. "It may easily be conceived," the British minister to the United States, David Erskine, told Foreign Secretary George Canning, "to be highly grating to the feelings of an independent nation to perceive that their whole coast is watched as closely as if it was blockaded, and every ship coming in or going out of their harbours examined rigorously in sight of the shore by British squadrons stationed within their waters."[43]

Against this backdrop, the attack on the frigate *Chesapeake* occurred. Several sailors—British and American—had deserted from two British warships and enlisted on the *USS Chesapeake*, docked at Norfolk. They strutted in the streets of Norfolk and one of them openly insulted a British officer. Since the beginning of the war with France in 1793, it had been unofficial British policy not to search US warships (this had been violated on only two occasions), but on his own initiative the head of the British North American station, Vice Admiral George Berkeley ordered the captains of the ships under his command to stop the *Chesapeake* if they encountered it outside the territorial waters of the United States and search it for the deserters. Accordingly, on June 22, the British frigate *Leopard* hailed the *Chesapeake* ten miles off the coast of Virginia, and demanded to search it. This being refused, the *Leopard* opened fire, killing three American sailors, wounding eighteen and forcing the US captain to submit to the British demands. After arresting four deserters (one British and three Americans) the *Leopard* allowed the *Chesapeake* to limp back to Norfolk.[44]

News of the attack infuriated Americans. Many favored war. As did Jefferson. "War can never come at a better time for us," he told his secretary of the Navy.[45] Napoleon had defeated the Russians and the European continent was closed to British trade. London was on the ropes. However, the American merchant fleet was at sea, vulnerable to British capture. "We should procrastinate 3 or 4 months," Jefferson wrote in early July, "were it only to give time to our merchants to get in their vessels, property and seamen, which are the identical materials with which the war is to be carried on." Furthermore, the country was utterly unprepared for war. Gallatin had warned Jefferson in September 1805 that "an efficient navy ... would have a favorable effect on our foreign relations. . . . so long as we have none we must perpetually be liable to injuries and insults, particularly from the belligerent powers, when there is a war in Europe." Jefferson, however, had done nothing.[46]

He had come to the presidency, in March 1801, determined to gut the Navy. The war against Tripoli had bought the service a reprieve, but once the war was over the axe had fallen. As the US frigates returned from the Mediterranean they were taken out of service. By 1807 only two remained. Jefferson had focused instead on another kind of vessel, gunboats: small craft, fifty to seventy feet in length, armed with one or two guns; they were designed for coastal defense, being too fragile for rough seas, and were cheap to build and to operate, requiring crews of only twenty to thirty men. By 1807, approximately sixty had been built. The United States had a coast guard, not a blue water navy.[47]

Nor did it have an army. The administration had been bent on saving money. Furthermore, Republican orthodoxy mistrusted a standing army and relied on the citizen-soldier. In March 1802, at the administration's request, Congress had reduced the army, which had been set by law at 5,438, to 3,289.[48] Jefferson was unperturbed: military preparations were "adequate to the present state and prospect of things," he wrote in April 1806.[49]

Soon after the *Chesapeake* incident Jefferson recalled Congress—only it could declare war—to a special October session. In the intervening months he would prepare the country for war: the militia would be reorganized and equipped, and more gunboats would be built. The president and his cabinet discussed a possible invasion of Canada to be carried out by 10,300 militiamen and 200 regulars.[50] Jefferson was also contemplating attacking Spanish possessions. "I had rather have war against Spain than not, if we go to war against England," he told Madison in August. This would enable the United States to finally acquire the Floridas and, "probably," Cuba as well. He shared his warlike dreams with the French minister, Louis-Marie Turreau. (By acquiring Canada and the Floridas, he explained, "We will no longer have any difficulty with our neighbors.") Turreau was not impressed: he noted that given US unpreparedness, "the administration has nothing to gain from a war . . . and could lose everything."[51]

In London, Monroe was still trying to settle the *Chesapeake* incident. The British acknowledged that the Royal Navy did not have the right to search the warships of neutrals and apologized for the "unauthorized act," offering compensation to the families of the seamen killed during the attack.[52] It was not enough: Jefferson demanded that England renounce impressment.[53] War loomed.

The embargo

When Congress convened on October 26, 1807, the bellicose mood had abated in the country and the United States was still not ready for war. "Essential preparations are in some points hardly commenced, in every respect incomplete," Gallatin warned.[54] The Navy had only two frigates, the army was still capped at 3,289 men, and the condition of the militia, Secretary of War Henry Dearborn said, was "really deplorable throughout the Union."[55] The cabinet pleaded with Jefferson to delay. Reluctantly, the president agreed. The Annual Message that he sent Congress on October 27 listed a litany of British offenses but not a word about a response—and certainly no recommendation for war. Jefferson was bitter. He wrote to his son-in-law that the lawmakers were "extremely disposed for peace" and would choose economic retaliation for the violation of the *Chesapeake* over war.[56] Equally bitter was the French minister. Eager to see war between the United States and England, Turreau ridiculed the Americans, "a people with no idea of glory, greatness, justice . . . willing to endure all kinds of humiliations just so they can satisfy their loathsome greed."[57]

Meanwhile, Congress had to decide what to do about the Non-Importation Act against Britain that it had approved in April 1806. The act, which had been repeatedly suspended, was scheduled to come into effect on December 14, 1807, unless Congress suspended it again. The Republican majority was waiting for a sign from the president, but Jefferson offered no guidance. Congress did nothing, and the act, which barred half of British imports, went into effect on December 14.[58]

That same day dispatches from the US minister in Paris reached Washington. Armstrong reported that France had begun to enforce against American ships a year-old decree that had ordered the confiscation of any vessel trading with Britain or stopping at British ports. (Until then the act had almost never been applied to American ships.) From London, Jefferson learned that in November the British cabinet had approved sweeping Orders-in-Council that forbade neutral ships from trading with any country from which the British flag was excluded, unless they called first at a British port and got a British license. Until that moment American foreign trade had continued to thrive, despite the *Essex* decision, and exports had grown from $95.6 million in 1805 to $108.3 million in 1807.[59] But with these new regulations Paris and London were placing the United States in a vise: if American ships traded with the French they were liable to be confiscated by the British, and if they traded with the British they were liable to be confiscated by the French. Of course, since the Royal Navy dominated the Atlantic, those American vessels that traded with the British were in little danger.

At last, Jefferson acted. On December 17, he convened the cabinet to discuss a special message to Congress. The message was cryptic. It spoke of "the great and increasing dangers with which our vessels, our seamen, and merchandise are threatened on the high seas and elsewhere," and recommended "an inhibition of the departure of our vessels from the ports of the United States," in order "to keep in safety these essential resources." Was this embargo a preparation for war? Or was it an attempt to prevent war? How long would it last? There is no record of the cabinet meeting, only a note written by Gallatin the next day, observing that the policy was "doubtful" and "hastily adopted."[60]

On December 18, the cryptic presidential message was presented to Congress. The Jeffersonian majority sprang into action. Pushing aside the Federalists' demands for reflection and discussion, the Senate approved (twenty-two to six) an embargo bill that day; the House followed suit three days later (eighty-two to forty-four).[61] Jefferson signed the bill on December 22. It prohibited American vessels from sailing to foreign ports; it forbade all US exports by sea, whatever the nationality of the vessel carrying them; it did not affect imports, however, by foreign vessels; it did not include penalties for noncompliance and it did not specify a termination date. In the winter and spring of 1808, and again in January 1809, Congress approved Enforcement Acts to tighten the embargo: they introduced penalties for evasion that became progressively more onerous, and prohibited exports by land.

Jefferson's intentions when he proposed the embargo in December 1807 are still a riddle. The embargo was "salutary," he wrote in early January 1808, because "it postpones war, gives time and the benefits of events which that may produce." "Time," he added a few days later, "prepares us for defense; time may produce peace in Europe that removes the ground of difference with England until another European war," when the United States would have grown stronger.[62] But if Jefferson believed in the possibility of peace between France and England in the foreseeable future, he was naive. As for preparing the United States for war, it was not until late February 1808 that Jefferson asked Congress to triple the size of the army, adding 6,000 men to its previous ceiling of 3,289. Recruitment proceeded slowly. By the end of the year the army had grown to only 5,700 men.[63]

In addition to its professed goal of safeguarding American ships and sailors from British and French depredations, the embargo sought to apply pressure on the two warring empires by depriving them of American products; the importance of American exports, particularly for Britain, was a hallowed article of the Republican credo. This is why Jefferson embargoed American exports even if carried in foreign vessels and forbade exports by land.

Jefferson called the embargo a "great weapon" of economic coercion.[64] While the measure was directed against both superpowers, its primary target, Jefferson told the French minister, was Britain, which depended far more than France on American exports. And for once Jefferson's aims were not overblown: he did not seek to force the British to renounce impressment, or even to abandon the Rule of 1756, which prohibited the carrying trade. He sought only the repeal of the Orders-in-Council of November 1807 which forbade neutral ships from trading with any country from which British ships were excluded.[65] Over time, Britain might have been willing to negotiate this issue because its dependence on American trade was real. That dependence was lessened, however, by Napoleon's occupation of Portugal in late 1807 and Spain the following spring; their Latin American colonies responded by opening their trade to British merchants, and in 1808 this compensated for the loss of the US market.[66]

If the embargo's aim was reasonable, its design and implementation were faulty. It allowed foreign countries to continue selling to Americans, provided they did it on their own ships. This was a godsend for the British: before the embargo 30 percent of their exports went to the United States. The Non-Importation Act that went into effect in December 1807 banned only some British exports and Jefferson rejected Gallatin's proposal that it be broadened to include all British goods.[67] Perhaps, as Gordon Wood suggests, fiscal considerations played a role in Jefferson's restraint: "the federal government was so dependent on customs duties on its imports that cutting off all imports would have bankrupted it."[68] Whatever the reason, it meant that legal British imports in 1808 were approximately 50 percent of the previous year's value; and thanks to the embargo, which kept American ships at home, they all arrived only in British bottoms.

From the outset, Jefferson seems to have believed that the embargo should last no more than a year, because the ban on trade would cause hardship at home and the people's support would wane. His tentative deadline, he told Madison in March, was late 1808, when Congress would reconvene and would decide "whether war must be declared."[69] Here lies another riddle of the embargo: how could Jefferson imagine that a few months would suffice to force the British to repeal the Orders-in-Council? And would the United States be more prepared to fight a war in the wake of the embargo?

For the embargo to have a chance of success, Jefferson, the most popular political leader in the United States, would have needed to commit all his prestige to persuade Americans to endure the hardship it caused. But he didn't. Instead, he was silent, as he had been in 1795 during the debate on the Jay Treaty. He did not address the American people or Congress to explain why the sacrifice was necessary. Even biographers sympathetic to Jefferson criticize his inaction. "He betrayed his own principles of leadership," Merrill Peterson writes, "and contributed to the bewilderment and confusion surrounding the embargo." Dumas Malone agrees: "Far from seeking to rally his countrymen around his own person, he followed the general policy of keeping as much out of sight as possible."[70]

Although Jefferson anticipated that Americans would grow weary of the embargo, he was surprised by the ferocity of the opposition. So was Madison, whose wife wrote to in August 1808 that "the President and M[adison] have been greatly perplexed at the remonstrances from so many towns to remove the embargo . . . and the evading it."[71]

Throughout the life of the embargo, American ships laden with American products flouted the law, silently departing the United States for Europe, or leaving openly with forged papers pretending to sail to a port in the United States. The heroic efforts of Gallatin, who as secretary of the treasury had the task of enforcing the embargo, curbed the number of violations at sea. More difficult was the situation along the borders of New York and New England, where smugglers supplied the British in Canada and fought skirmishes with customs officers and the militia, reinforced on two occasions by the army. In late July 1808, Gallatin warned Jefferson that the embargo could be enforced only through "arbitrary powers" that were both "dangerous and odious." Congress, Jefferson replied, "must legalize all *means* which may be necessary to obtain its *end*."[72] Under Jefferson, the champion of state rights, the apostle of liberty, the federal government became increasingly oppressive. As Leonard Levy has written, in its efforts to root out the violators of the embargo, the administration trampled civil liberties. It rendered "meaningless" the protection against self-incrimination; it made "a farce" of the right to trial by jury; and it "abolished" the freedom from unreasonable searches and seizures.[73]

The Non-Importation Act, which ran concurrently with the embargo, stimulated the development of domestic manufactures. But the embargo prostrated American shipping and both it and the Non-Importation Act slashed the government's revenues, which depended almost entirely on customs duties. Workers in maritime industries suffered the most, but farmers shared in the pain, because the ban on exports glutted the domestic market and lowered prices. The price of imported goods rose as did unemployment, while wages fell. If Jefferson thought the embargo would give the United States time to prepare for war, he was sorely mistaken. As Francis Cogliano points out, the United States "was less prepared as a result of the embargo than it had been at its beginning."[74]

In August 1808, Gallatin, who more than anyone else had his hand on the pulse of the nation, warned Jefferson that the embargo "threatens to destroy the Republican interest," and if it was not lifted before October, there was a serious risk that "we will lose the Presidential election"[75] (in which Madison was the party's candidate to succeed Jefferson). Three months later, in his November annual message to Congress, Jefferson announced that the embargo had failed. "It will rest with the wisdom of Congress," he said, to determine the course to be adopted next. Gallatin and Madison pleaded with the president to offer leadership and propose "some precise and distinct course" to Congress.[76] But Jefferson demurred. "I think it is fair to leave to those who are to act on them the decisions they prefer, being myself but a spectator," he explained. As a biographer writes, "Jefferson practically abdicated responsibility for policy in the last four months of his presidency."[77] He was longing for the haven of Monticello, and he was keen to disassociate himself from a discredited policy. He left his supporters in Congress leaderless. In February 1809, Congress voted to repeal the embargo and replace it with a non-intercourse act that forbade trade with Britain and France while opening it to the rest of the world. "I thought Congress had taken their ground firmly for continuing *their* embargo till June, and then war," Jefferson wrote to his son-in-law, conveniently forgetting that it was *his* embargo.[78]

Assessing Jefferson

Thomas Jefferson was exceedingly intelligent, a superb writer, and a charismatic leader. He gained the affection of a majority of white Americans and the unswerving loyalty of the leaders of the Republican Party. His collaboration with Madison was close and important: Madison tempered Jefferson's impulsiveness and added depth and nuance to his decision-making. Jefferson also relied on Gallatin, but not as much as he did on Madison, which was unfortunate, because, as Gordon Wood writes, Gallatin possessed "a sophisticated understanding of how economies worked, an understanding not shared by Jefferson or Madison."[79]

Jefferson's great foreign policy success, the Louisiana Purchase, occurred during his first term. It was, however, good fortune—the impending war between Britain and France, and the heroism of the Haitians—that handed him this plum; his exertions were irrelevant to Napoleon's decision to sell the colony. His second term was consumed by maritime issues. He wanted the United States to be treated by the superpowers as an equal, and he stubbornly refused to understand that this was not realistic. He demanded that Britain respect American rights, as he conceived them, but his arrogance and Anglophobia blinded him to the irrationality of his demands. Engaged in a brutal war with France, Britain was not going to accept Jefferson's interpretation of neutral rights. The American president demanded that the Royal Navy, desperate for sailors, renounce impressment, but he was not willing to pledge, in return, that American shippers would no longer hire British sailors.

What made Jefferson's demands risible, at least in the eyes of the Europeans, was the inattention to military power that characterized his policy. His motto seemed to be, talk loudly and carry a small stick. Jefferson believed that the United States wielded a very big stick—the threat of economic retaliation—but when he made good on the threat with the embargo, he failed to clarify his goals, develop a viable strategy, or sell it to the American people.

France and Britain behaved like thugs toward lesser powers, such as the United States. But so did Jefferson: he dealt with Spain as the British and French dealt with him. He would have invaded Florida had he not feared Napoleon's wrath. On the one occasion, in August 1805, in which he contemplated defying France in order to annex the Floridas and Texas, he wanted British support—without, however, offering London anything in return. Jefferson's inflated sense of the power of the United States warped his foreign policy.

What about Jeffersonian idealism? His words soar, and Americans tend to remember his phrases, articulating the country's ideals. However, there is a disconnect between Jefferson's words and his actions. Slavery is the most glaring example. In private letters and in the *Notes on the State of Virginia*—intended for a small readership of friends—Jefferson expressed his loathing for the institution with searing eloquence. Yet, in his lifetime he freed only three of the hundreds of enslaved people he owned, and in his will he would free only another five.

The same disconnect exists when it comes to Jefferson's foreign policy. If we focus on the policy, rather than the rhetoric, where is Jefferson's idealism? Jefferson loathed Haiti's black rebels and wanted to see the fledgling Haitian state crushed because he feared the example Haiti's successful revolt would set for the enslaved people of the US South. And while he expressed his sympathy for Native Americans with moving words, his relentless pursuit of their land could be achieved only through fraud and violence.

These may seem details. To judge Jefferson by Haitians and Native Americans—how parochial! But by what standards should we judge the idealism of his foreign policy? By his policy toward Europe? His attempts to wrest the Floridas from Spain by whatever means—war, bribery and threats—had no traces of idealism. His clashes with Alexander Hamilton over relations with France and England were motivated not by idealism but by his intransigent assertion of US neutral rights and his dogged antipathy to Britain. The embargo revealed his failure of moral courage to take the lead in defense of the measure, as well as his disregard for civil liberties.

Jefferson's idealism resides in his words, not his deeds. He had no special respect for the rights of the weak and no principled opposition to the use of force—but he had the gift of enveloping his actions in the purest rhetoric.

CHAPTER 5
THE WAR OF 1812

James Madison, a shy, uncharismatic man, was not the Republican Party's unanimous choice for the presidency in 1808. During Jefferson's first term, anti-Federalist fervor had galvanized the Republicans, but in the wake of the 1804 elections, the Federalists seemed on the road to extinction and the Republicans grew more fractious. The failure of the embargo also diluted their cohesion. As did demography. In 1790, when the first census was taken, Virginia was the most populous state of the Union, with 748,000 people, and it also had the most white inhabitants; by 1810, its population had risen to 985,000, but that of New York had skyrocketed from 340,000 to 959,000, with 360,000 more white inhabitants than Virginia.[1] In 1808, many Republicans in the northern states believed that it was time to replace the Virginia dynasty with a New Yorker, namely Jefferson's Vice President George Clinton. Although Madison easily won the presidential elections, the Clintonian opposition would remain a thorn in his side throughout his presidency.

Jefferson's cabinet had worked harmoniously and had included two outstanding advisers, Madison and Gallatin. Gallatin continued as Madison's secretary of the treasury, his most able and closest adviser, but the other cabinet posts went to men chosen to appease various factions within the party. (The situation improved in 1811, when James Monroe became secretary of state, replacing Robert Smith, who was both incompetent and disloyal.)

Whereas Jefferson had come to power in favorable international circumstances, Madison was saddled with British and French restrictions on American commerce as well as the failed embargo. (Paris prohibited neutrals from trading with Britain, and the Orders-in-Council allowed neutrals to trade with French-controlled Europe only after procuring a British license.) Congress had replaced the embargo with the Non-Intercourse Act, which prohibited all trade with the British and French empires and opened it to the rest of the world. If enforced, the act would have spelled disaster for American foreign trade because Britain and France were the destination of 85 percent of American exports.[2] But it was obvious that the act was unenforceable: once a ship had left the United States, there was no way US officials could prevent it from going to Britain or France. Therefore, American foreign trade blossomed, and the US economy revived. In May 1810, Congress tired of the farce and repealed the Non-Intercourse Act, but to retain a shred of leverage it added a proviso: if either the French or the British lifted their restrictions on American commerce, the United States would, within three months, impose non-intercourse against the other if it did not follow suit.[3] It was a sober acceptance of the facts that were deeply humiliating for the United States.

Napoleon saw an opportunity. In August 1810, the French foreign minister announced that restrictions on American trade would be lifted on November 1, 1810 "if, as a

consequence of this declaration the English shall revoke their Orders-in-Council ... or
... the United States ... shall cause its rights to be respected by the English."[4] Napoleon's
decision was part of his strategy to strangle Britain economically: he hoped that in the
likely case that the British would refuse to repeal the Orders-in-Council the United
States would reimpose non-intercourse on Britain and possibly even drift into war with
the former metropole.

Madison, who was keenly aware of the impotence of the United States, jumped at
Napoleon's offer. On November 2, he proclaimed that the French had lifted their
restrictions against American vessels, and gave Britain three months to repeal its Orders-
in-Council. Arguing that the French claim to have lifted their restrictions was a cheap
ploy, London refused. In response, the US Congress in February 1811 banned all British
imports, but having learned the lesson of the embargo, it did not prohibit US exports to
Britain. Madison signed the bill on March 2. Napoleon, who had expected a full embargo,
was disappointed. "The failure of the Americans to cut off both legs of the British trade,"
Peter Hill writes, "did hand Napoleon a convenient pretext for continuing to detain
American shipping."[5]

Furthermore, the French sought to shut down the United States' new, important
export market: in the Iberian Peninsula the tens of thousands of British soldiers who
were fighting the French desperately needed food. US exports of grain and flour to the
peninsula grew dramatically—from $2 million in 1807 to $12 million in 1811. The
British were happy to receive the precious food their troops needed.[6] Napoleon, however,
did not appreciate the Americans feeding his enemies, and the French began attacking,
and even setting afire American ships *en route* to British held ports in Spain and Portugal.
Louis Sérurier, the French minister in Washington, was despondent: "The news arrives
that several ships have been set ablaze, and the Federalists are escalating their attacks on
France." Republicans, too, were furious. Some even called for war against both Britain
and France, "but people realize," Sérurier wrote, "the absurdity of waging a war against
both powers."[7] While the Republicans' talk of war against France was bluster, the demand
for war against Britain was growing. The wounds of the war of independence were still
festering, and new injuries had been inflicted by the impressment of American sailors,
the disputes over neutral rights, and the arrogance of British naval commanders.
Furthermore, unlike the French, the British possessed territories that bordered the
United States, and from there they spread their influence among the Indian tribes of the
Ohio Valley and the Great Lakes.[8]

Canada

At Jefferson's urging, the United States had embarked in 1803 on a campaign to buy
Indian land as quickly as possible. This policy, based on cheating and intimidation,
provoked growing anger among the Indians. In the Ohio Valley, two Shawnee brothers—
Tecumseh and Tenskwatawa (the Prophet), a spiritual leader—sought to forge a Pan-
Indian movement to confront the American threat. Tecumseh, Governor William Henry

Harrison of Indiana Territory wrote in 1811, was "one of those uncommon geniuses, which spring up occasionally to produce revolutions and overturn the established order of things."[9] The brothers had for many years advocated peace, but in 1809 a fraudulent treaty imposed by Harrison "exhausted what remained of [their] patience."[10]

Into this volatile mix came the British. After the Jay Treaty, the British authorities had neglected the Indians of the Ohio Valley and the Great Lakes region. But in 1807, the *Chesapeake* incident raised the specter of war with the United States. In that case, Britain, in its life and death struggle with Napoleon, would be unable to send reinforcements to defend Canada. Therefore, the Indians became a crucial first line of defense. British officials in Canada began showering them with professions of friendship and offered them supplies and some weapons. They were treading a difficult line: London did not want to incite an Indian revolt, but they did want the Indians to be ready to fight against the United States if the US government declared war. For their part, the Indians had not forgotten Britain's betrayal in 1794. In conversations with Matthew Elliott, a senior agent of the British Indian department, Tecumseh "spoke a great deal about the fact that at Fallen Timbers the British fort had been shut against the Indians, and he reminded Elliott how many chiefs fell because of that event."[11]

Tecumseh and other chiefs knew that the British were using them, but the Americans' depredations were increasing and only England could help them. In November 1811, Governor Harrison led a mixed force of regulars and militia against Prophetstown, the town of Tecumseh and Tenskwatawa in western Indiana, where Indians from several tribes, attracted by the brothers' message, lived. An inconclusive battle ensued. American casualties were higher than the Indians', but the Indians withdrew and Harrison's men torched Prophetstown. A spasm of violence followed. Although Tecumseh sought to restrain his followers and avoid premature war with the United States, in the first six months of 1812 some forty-six American settlers were killed by warriors from groups that had fought at Prophetstown. (Only eight or nine settlers had been killed in the previous twenty months.)[12] Overlooking the key reason for this spike in violence—their own greed and racism—white Americans blamed it on the Indians' innate savagery and the intrigues hatched by the British authorities in Canada. The conquest of Canada, Congressman Felix Grundy (R-TN) proclaimed, would stop the British from encouraging "the ruthless savage to tomahawk our women and children."[13]

British North America consisted of Upper Canada (present day southern Ontario), Lower Canada (present day southern Quebec), the five maritime colonies (New Brunswick, Nova Scotia, the islands of Prince Edward and Cape Breton, and Newfoundland), and a vast western domain under the nominal control of the Hudson's Bay Company. There are no reliable population figures (the first censuses were in the 1830s), but it is likely that the two Canadas and the maritime provinces had a total population of 500,000 people compared with the 7 million in the United States. Lower and Upper Canada were defended by 6,000 British regulars.[14] Upper Canada, with a population of little more than 60,000, seemed particularly vulnerable. Many of its inhabitants were the families of loyalists who had fled the United States; others were recent American immigrants attracted by the allure of cheap land. In Lower Canada, the majority population was French. The maritime colonies were ethnically diverse; they were protected by the Royal Navy and also by personal and economic ties with New England, which opposed war with Britain and therefore provided a buffer.

In the spring of 1812, British officials in Canada feared that war was imminent and that Canada would be the inevitable theater—where else could the Americans fight the British? The US Navy could not hope to defeat the British at sea. From Quebec City, in May 1812, the governor-in-chief of British North America, General George Prevost, sent a long report to London, describing the almost defenseless state of the two Canadian provinces which, he rightly surmised, would be the immediate target of the expected US offensive. "If the Americans are determined to attack Canada," he concluded, "it would be in vain the general should flatter himself with the hope of making an effective defense . . . unless powerfully assisted from home."[15]

Americans knew that Britain, hard pressed in Europe, would not be able to send reinforcements to protect the colony. "The acquisition of Canada this year as far as the neighborhood of Quebec will be a mere matter of marching," Jefferson famously wrote in August 1812, "and will give us experience for the attack on Halifax the next, and the final expulsion of England from the American continent."[16] But while the annexation of Canada was desirable, it was not why the United States contemplated war. Nor was impressment, which had poisoned Anglo-American relations—some 10,000 Americans had been impressed since 1793—but was "virtually ignored" by the administration in its negotiations with the British. Its focus instead was on Britain's refusal to repeal the Orders-in-Council.[17]

Through 1811, the administration engaged in desultory talks with the British, demanding the repeal of the orders. Without success. The craven behavior of the United States since the *Chesapeake* incident in 1807 had convinced the British government that the United States lacked the strength and the resolve to confront Britain. There was in England, Horsman writes, strong anti-American sentiment, "which was based on the patriotic fervor of the war against France, a commercial jealousy of the United States, and a hearty dislike of the former colonists."[18] However, in 1810, a commercial depression struck England, increasing the importance of the America market for British manufacturers. Through 1811, the demand in Britain for a repeal of the Orders-in-Council grew, but the government did not budge. Meanwhile, in the United States, vocal factions within the Republican Party were criticizing Madison for his passivity and demanding a more resolute policy against Britain, though rarely did they offer constructive suggestions.

In his November 5, 1811, Annual Message to Congress, misleadingly named the War Hawk Congress, Madison urged the legislators to take measures of military preparedness. But Congress did very little to prepare the country to fight. This was due to a mixture of ideological blinkers—Republicans (who outnumbered Federalists in Congress three to one) disliked standing armies and trusted the militia; of avarice—increased armaments meant higher taxes; and of weak presidential leadership. In early 1812, Congress raised the cap of the army from 9,300 to 35,000 but it did not appropriate the funds necessary to make enlistment financially attractive. By June 1, 1812, the army had only 12,000 men.

As for the Navy, the United States had only five frigates in service, one fewer than when it had gone to war against Tripoli.[19]

The administration counted on the war in Europe to offset American weakness. "It is said that we are not prepared for war and ought therefore not to declare it," the semi-official *National Intelligencer* wrote in April 1812. But, it reminded its readers, Britain was on the ropes. "Where are her troops? ... The war [against France] in the [Iberian] peninsula ... requires strong [British] armies to support it. She [Britain] maintains an army in Sicily; another in India; and a strong force in Ireland, and along her own coast and in the West Indies. Can anyone believe that, under such circumstances, the British government could be so infatuated, or rather mad, as to send troops here for the purpose of invasion?"[20]

Americans were also aware of Napoleon's preparations to invade Russia. They predicted a quick French victory and therefore the total isolation of Britain. In vain did the Federalists warn that a French victory over Britain would be very dangerous for the United States because Napoleon aspired to universal empire. The Republicans dismissed the warning; they were fixated on striking Britain when it was weak. "They saw the struggle," Donald Hickey writes, "as a second war of independence—a contest that would vindicate American sovereignty."[21] Many Republicans, particularly in the south and the west, also believed that the British Orders-in-Council were ruining America's overseas trade.

On June 1, 1812, Madison sent a message to Congress recommending a declaration of war against Britain. The vote was relatively close: seventy-nine to forty-nine in the House on June 4, 1812 and nineteen to thirteen in the Senate on June 17. The forty-two Federalist members of congress were joined in opposition by twenty Republicans motivated by a host of reasons:[22] the awareness that the country was unprepared for war, the belief that negotiations with England were still possible, the distrust in the administration's ability to lead the country through war, and the realization that war meant taxes.

In England, the Orders-in-Council were under attack from an overwhelming majority of businessmen and a growing portion of the press. Parliament was swamped with petitions demanding repeal. Finally, the government gave in. On June 23, 1812, it announced that it had decided to exempt American ships from the Orders-in-Council.[23]

Why had the British conceded in June 1812 what they had refused in 1808? On both occasions, the American demand had been the same: the repeal of the Orders-in-Council that constrained US trade. There were, however, important differences: first, timing: in 1808, Napoleon's invasion of Spain had opened the Spanish American markets to British trade, whereas in 1810, economic depression had struck England. Second, in 1808, the Non-Importation Act against British goods had been partial; in 1811, it was total.

Thus, it was the importance of the American market, "far more than any fears of the military and naval consequences of a war," that led to the British change of heart, writes Bradford Perkins.[24] The repeal of the Orders-in-Council removed the administration's major grievance. Scholars agree that if the decision had been made a couple of months earlier, "it most likely would have averted war."[25] However, news of the repeal of the orders did not reach Washington until August 13. And by then it was too late.

War on the Canadian frontier

Madison signed the declaration of war on June 18, 1812.[26] For the next eighteen months, the Americans launched uncoordinated offensives in three directions: toward Montreal; across the Niagara frontier into the central part of Upper Canada; and from Detroit into the western end of Upper Canada [Map 5]. In 1812, they suffered a string of defeats even though they faced forces that were inferior in numbers: a handful of British regulars, Canadian militia, and Indian warriors. (The Indians "appreciably affected the final outcome" of many battles, a historian writes, "either by inducing a terrible psychological fear on the enemy ... or by fighting with a passionate intensity."[27]) Only in 1813 did the Americans score some successes: in April, 1,700 American soldiers on fourteen ships crossed Lake Ontario, and for a week they occupied the capital of Upper Canada, York, a town of 700 people. (They sullied their victory by their behavior: they set fire to the public buildings, looted private homes, robbed the church, and destroyed the press of the town's only newspaper. No one was punished.[28]) More importantly, on September 10, the American and the British flotillas on Lake Erie clashed, and the Americans won, gaining control of the lake; in the wake of that victory, the former governor of Indiana territory, General Harrison, crossed from Detroit into Upper Canada with 3,500 men, mainly Kentucky militia, and routed a force of about 1,000 British and Indians on October 5. In this battle, "the only real resistance was put up by the Indians," Reginald Horsman notes. "They fought with all the bravery and desperation induced by their long sufferings." Tecumseh died fighting—"a more sagacious or more a gallant warrior does not I believe exist," the British military commander in Upper Canada wrote. After the battle the Kentuckians returned home, taking with them patches of Tecumseh's skin as souvenirs; left with a diminished army, Harrison decided not to advance further.[29] As the 1813 campaign ended, the United States had gained control only of Lake Erie and a sliver of Upper Canada.

The reasons these results were so meager are obvious: the militia performed poorly; military leadership was deficient (particularly in 1812); and the army was understrength: it never reached the levels authorized by Congress, in part because a soldier's pay was lower than that of an unskilled laborer.

At sea, the situation was different. The US Navy had only a few frigates, but they were superbly built and manned by first-rate crews. On three occasions, in the first six months of the war, American and British frigates clashed in one-on-one combat, and on each occasion the Americans won. Meanwhile, swarms of American privateers inflicted heavy losses on British merchant shipping. However, in 1813, the Royal Navy added warships to its North American station and it became difficult for American ships to leave port. In the only other duel between an American and a British frigate, in June 1813, the British were victorious. American privateers continued their successful attacks against British merchant vessels, but the tightening British blockade of US ports and the strict enforcement of the convoy system for British merchantmen meant that fewer privateers were at sea and fewer prizes were available. By the end of the war, American privateers had captured close to 2,000 British ships; however, the most authoritative study of the subject concludes, the British merchant fleet "totaled 21,449 vessels, making the loss of less than 10 percent of it more annoying and embarrassing than worrisome."[30]

In late 1813, alarming news reached the United States: after his disastrous retreat from Russia, Napoleon had held his own in central Germany against the Russians and their allies. But in October 1813, he was defeated at the battle of Leipzig. Napoleon's rampage was over. In early 1814, the allied armies entered France. On April 11, Napoleon abdicated. Britain could now turn its attention to the United States.

The Americans knew that British reinforcements would soon arrive, and they hoped to occupy part of Canada before then. That would put them in a good bargaining position if negotiations ensued. They chose to attack across the Niagara border into Upper Canada. After initial success, the offensive faltered.

The first British reinforcements reached Canada in late June, and more followed in the next two months. "We are this day blessed with a sight which has not been paralleled here since the conquest of the country," a resident of Quebec wrote to the London *Times* in early August: British ships carrying the veterans who had defeated Napoleon—"complete brigades removed from the banks of the Garonne [in France] to the St. Lawrence, with the whole materiel of an army in the field … Such troops, carrying with them such recollections, never [before have] landed in America."[31] For the first time since the war began, the British could take the offensive. In September 1814, 2,500 British soldiers occupied eastern Maine without meeting serious resistance. But this was a sideshow. London had a more ambitious plan: it urged the governor of British North America, General Prevost, to go further. "I am bound in fairness to apprize you," the secretary of state for war and the colonies, Henry Bathurst, wrote to Prevost, "that if you shall allow the present campaign to close without having undertaken offensive measures against the enemy, you will very seriously disappoint the expectations of the Prince Regent and of the country."[32] Accordingly, on August 31, Prevost launched an offensive along the western shore of Lake Champlain to seize Plattsburgh, a commercial town of about 3,000 people twenty-five miles south of the border. His troops—10,000 men, nearly all veterans of the campaigns against Napoleon—advanced along poor roads meeting scant resistance. They were poised to attack Plattsburgh when, on September 11, the American flotilla on Lake Champlain defeated the British flotilla. Immediately, Prevost ordered his troops to retreat to Canada. Prevost was not an inspiring leader, but the decision to withdraw made sense: American control of the lake meant that he could rely for supplies only on a tenuous land line that the enemy could easily sever.[33]

Therefore, the 1814 campaign along the Canadian border was a draw: the American offensive on the Niagara front had failed, but so had Prevost's offensive along Lake Champlain. There was, however, another front, hundreds of miles south.

War on the Chesapeake

British naval forces had begun raiding the rich Chesapeake Bay region in the spring of 1813. "You are not to look at the permanent occupation of any place," Bathurst instructed the commander of the 2,300 soldiers assigned to the operation. His task was "to harass the enemy" with hit and run attacks.[34] The raids, which continued through August, exposed the weakness of the local militia and the absence of US troops. This made the Chesapeake a tempting target for the next British campaign, in 1814, particularly if reinforcements arrived from Europe.

Vice Admiral Alexander Cochrane, the commander of the Royal Navy in North America, expected to receive upward of 15,000 troops and drew his plans accordingly, writing to Bathurst in July 1814 that when the reinforcements arrived he would capture Washington or Baltimore. "I have it much at heart," he added, to give the Americans "a complete drubbing."[35]

The reinforcements arrived, but in far smaller numbers than promised—fewer than 3,000 men, led by a very able general, Robert Ross. Despite Napoleon's defeat, London was reluctant to withdraw troops from Europe precipitously, and it saw the Chesapeake as a diversion from the main war in Canada. In mid-August Cochrane, Ross, and his troops arrived at Chesapeake Bay, where Rear Admiral George Cockburn had been operating since March with a small force, meeting very little resistance. On August 19, the entire British force—about 4,500 soldiers and marines without artillery or cavalry— landed at the small port town of Benedict, Maryland, unopposed. They were led by Ross, and Cockburn accompanied the general. Their arrival caused "terror" in Washington, the French minister, Louis Sérurier, reported, as the inhabitants began to realize, "too late," that within days the city could fall into the enemy's hands.[36] However, Madison "still thought it unlikely," a biographer writes, that "the British would come as far as Washington without cavalry and artillery and with as few as four thousand troops."[37]

The first target of the British, after they landed at Benedict, was the best American force on the Chesapeake, Joshua Barney's flotilla of seventeen gunboats, which had taken shelter from the Royal Navy on the upper Patuxent river [Map 5]. On August 22, as the British troops closed in, Barney blew up his gunboats and withdrew on land with his 400 sailors. For the British, the moment of decision had arrived: would they move on to Washington or withdraw? When he had expected to have more than 15,000 men Cochrane had intended to seize Washington, but Ross had fewer than 5,000 men. Cochrane, who had remained on his flagship, sent a message to Cockburn, saying that "the sooner the army get back [to the ships] the better."[38] The final decision, however, belonged to Ross, who commanded the troops. Ross hesitated, but Cockburn, who had been raiding the Chesapeake area since March, convinced Ross that they should move against Washington because the Americans would mount no serious resistance. He was right. Two days later, at the village of Bladensburg, five miles from the US capital, the British clashed with more than 6,000 Americans, mainly raw militia, who panicked and "fled shamefully," as Sérurier reported. From the village where she had sought refuge, Margaret Smith, the wife of the editor of the *National Intelligencer*, empathized with "our poor broken militia ... Every hour the poor wearied and terrified creatures are passing by the door ... Our men look pale and feeble but more with affright then fatigue—they had thrown away their muskets and blankets."[39] Madison, his cabinet, members of Congress and many prominent citizens fled Washington before the British arrived. As the government in the capital vanished, mobs of residents looted houses that had been deserted.

After defeating the Americans at Bladensburg, Ross let his troops rest "for a short time" before they resumed the advance, reaching Washington "at eight o' clock that night [August 24]."[40] There was no resistance. Ross, Cockburn, and a group of officers entered the White House where they found, Ross noted in his journal, "a table laid with forty covers," with food and beverages waiting ("all the cabinet and several military men and strangers were expected," Madison's black valet remembered). "The fare ... which was intended for *Jonathan* [the Americans]," Ross continued, "was voraciously devoured by *John Bull* [the British]; and the health of the Prince Regent and success of His Majesty's arms by sea and land was drunk in the best wines."[41]

During their brief occupation of the capital—less than twenty-four hours—the British respected private property and the lives and dignity of Washington's citizens. Rear Admiral Cockburn "and all his officers and soldiers were perfectly polite to the citizens," Margaret Smith wrote to her sister after returning to Washington. "He bade them complain of any soldiers that committed the least disorder and had several severely punished for very slight offenses."[42] Cockburn's one act of petty revenge was to order the ransacking of the offices of the *National Intelligencer*, which had consistently demonized him. As historian Donald Hickey remarks, "the paper's owners took this surprisingly well." When the *National Intelligencer* resumed publication, it praised the British: "No houses were half as much plundered by the enemy as by the knavish wretches about town who profited of the general distress."[43]

Washington's public buildings fared less well: the British set fire to the White House, the Capitol, the Treasury, and the building housing the War and State departments. Americans were indignant, and in England some were also critical, but most approved it as just retribution for the Americans' plundering of York in 1813.[44]

The British left Washington in the evening of August 25—to stay longer, with only 4,000 men, would have made no sense. In his report to Foreign Minister Talleyrand, Sérurier remarked that "with this bold action the British delivered an insult to the federal government and exposed its weakness to all Europe ... But the truth, Monseigneur, is that the temporary occupation of Washington has absolutely no military significance."[45] The British had one final, tentative goal: Baltimore, the third largest city of the United States, with about 40,000 inhabitants (five times the population of Washington). But after probing Baltimore's defenses they concluded that an attack would be too costly, and they withdrew to their ships. Vice Admiral Cochrane sailed to Halifax with the bulk of the troops, and Cockburn went to Bermuda.

For the British, the war with the United States—a war they had not sought—was a sideshow, dwarfed by the existential struggle against Napoleon. In 1812 and 1813, their overriding goal had been to defend Canada. In 1814, Napoleon's defeat allowed Britain to breathe and contemplate taking the offensive against the United States, but no strategy emerged. Thus, Secretary of War Bathurst expected General Prevost to take the offensive against the Americans, but did not suggest any plan of action. And in the Chesapeake campaign, Admiral Cochrane and General Ross were left to their own devices with a small force that was able to inflict largely symbolic damage. The attention of the British government was still riveted on Europe.

African Americans and the war

Necessity had forced white America to accept black soldiers during the war of independence. When peace returned, African Americans were excluded from the army and the militia. The prohibition remained in effect during the war of 1812. However, during the Chesapeake campaign "some desperate recruiting officers," Alan Taylor writes, "overlooked the restriction to enlist a few mixed-race men." By late 1814, state officials in New York and Philadelphia, fearing a British attack, were considering allowing Blacks to serve in the militia, and some officials in Washington were contemplating letting them join the army. But the war ended before any change took place.[46] The War of Independence would be the only time until the Civil War when African Americans were allowed to serve in the army, and the only time until the Korean War when they were not confined to segregated units.

The US Navy, unlike the army and the militia, accepted Blacks, although not as officers. Joshua Barney's flotilla of seventeen gunboats included free Blacks and, since recruitment lagged, enslaved men "apparently placed aboard by their masters in return for their pay."[47] On August 22, 1814, after blowing up his gunboats, Barney led his 400 sailors to join the American forces at Bladensburg. According to Madison's black valet, the president had asked Barney immediately before the battle if the "'negroes would not run on the approach of the British.' Barney replied, 'No Sir ... they will die by their guns first.'"[48] Perhaps the story is apocryphal, but the London *Times* reported that at Bladensburg, Barney's men mounted a "severe and desperate" resistance, and Sérurier wrote that they "Lived up ... to their reputation."[49] The all-white militia, on the other hand, "ran like sheep chased by dogs."[50]

More African Americans fought on the side of the British than with the Americans. When the Royal Navy began raiding the shores of the Chesapeake in early 1813, the white residents worried that the slaves might take advantage of the turmoil to revolt and that the British might arm them. The specter of the Haitian Revolution haunted them. "We have two enemies to contend with," the mayor of Richmond lamented in September 1813, "the one open and declared; the other nurtured in our very bosoms! Sly, secret, and insidious: in our families, at our elbows, listening with eager attention; and sedulously marking all that is going forward. They know where our strength lies; and where and in what point we may be most easily assailed. The standard of revolt is unfurled. And whenever practicable, those deluded creatures, regardless to consequences, have flocked to it and enrolled into military bands. We perhaps may have a sanguinary set of desperadoes to contend with."[51]

London's instructions to the British commanders when the Chesapeake campaign began in 1813 had been firm: "You will on no account give encouragement to any disposition which may be manifested by the Negroes against their masters." Nor should they encourage the flight of large numbers of slaves; they should merely recruit a few male runaways to serve as guides for the raiding parties. These runaways would immediately be given their freedom. [52]

The instructions were firm, but unrealistic. Short of using force it was impossible to limit the number of runaways to a chosen few. Soon hundreds crowded the British ships, including women and children. Making virtue out of necessity, the Admirals and their officers in the North American station began pressing London for a change of policy that would allow them to encourage the enslaved to escape. They pointed out that the flight of large numbers would disrupt the economy of the region and force the militia to focus on internal control rather than fighting the British.

There was another reason as well: sympathy for the enslaved. Even though in the British Isles slavery no longer existed, Britain was a slaveholding empire: there were more than 700,000 enslaved people in the British Caribbean. But in the Chesapeake Bay, in 1813, British naval officers began to warm up to their role as liberators. They convinced their government to modify its stance. When the 1814 campaign began, it became British policy to encourage all enslaved to flee to the British lines. Under the British flag they would be free.

Fugitive slaves proved to be excellent guides, who enabled the British to operate in unfamiliar territory, but many enslaved men were eager to fight against their American masters. Rear Admiral Cockburn organized them in a special unit of Colonial Marines. They trained on Tangier Island, in the southern Chesapeake Bay, which the British had occupied. Cockburn wrote that the prospect of their former slaves fighting under the British flag excited "the most general and undisguised alarm" among the Virginians: "they expect Blacky will have no mercy on them and they know that he understands bush fighting and the locality of the woods as well as themselves, and can perhaps play at hide and seek in them even better." On May 29, 1814, the Colonial Marines fought their first battle. "Their conduct was marked by great spirit and vivacity, and perfect obedience," the British officer who led the operation reported.[53] By the end of the Chesapeake campaign, in September 1814, their number had grown to 300, and they had participated in all the major British operations. They had consistently fought, Cockburn said, with "zeal and bravery."[54]

Approximately 3,400 enslaved people fled to the British forces. Scores were killed by the Virginia and Maryland militia as they tried to escape and many more were captured. Fear of slave flight and of slave revolts forced Maryland and Virginia to concentrate their efforts on internal security, rather than fighting the British.

The Battle of New Orleans

During the fall of 1814, while thousands of British reinforcements arrived from Europe, Admiral Cochrane was busy planning a winter campaign against the Gulf Coast. His target was New Orleans, the capital of Louisiana (which had become a state in 1812). New Orleans was the seventh largest city of the United States, with a population of over 20,000 people, more than half of them Blacks. It was also the port for the trade of the western half of the United States and, US officials feared, the demographics of Louisiana made it a vulnerable target. According to the 1810 census, the state had only 77,000 inhabitants, including 34,600 enslaved and 7,400 free people of color. More than half of the whites were French and Spaniards who had been living in the territory before Jefferson acquired it. Would they fight if the British attacked? "I do believe that there is not one person in twenty throughout this state that is friendly to the United States, or who would take up arms in its defence," General Thomas Flournoy, the commander of the Seventh Military District, which included Louisiana, told the secretary of war in January 1814.[55] And even if the whites were willing to fight the British, would they be too distracted by the "enemy within"? The perennial fear of a slave uprising was exacerbated by a revolt three years earlier when as many as 500 enslaved people had rebelled and marched towards New Orleans, forty miles to the south, until a hastily gathered militia had routed them. Approximately one hundred enslaved people died in battle or were executed after capture.[56]

To defend New Orleans, the Madison administration turned to Andrew Jackson, the senior general of the Tennessee militia, who had gained fame by defeating the Creeks in Mississippi Territory in early 1814 and had been rewarded with an appointment as major general in the US army, replacing Flournoy at the head of the Seventh Military District. Aware that he might face a large British force, Jackson called up volunteers from Kentucky, Tennessee, and Mississippi Territory to rendezvous at New Orleans, but he worried that they would arrive too late [Map 5]. There was in New Orleans a small militia unit of free people of color, the only non-white militia unit in the United States. A vestige of Spanish rule in Louisiana, it was resented by many local whites and was kept under strict limits: only four companies of sixty-four men each, under a white commander. Unsure of the loyalty of the white population of Louisiana, Jackson decided to enlist as many free African Americans as were willing to join. On September 21, he issued a proclamation "To The Free Coloured Inhabitants of Louisiana," urging them to join him "in the glorious struggle for national rights in which our country is engaged." In a second proclamation on December 18, Jackson pledged: "The President of the United States shall be informed of your conduct on this occasion, and the voice of the representatives of the American nation shall applaud your valour, as your general now praises your ardor."[57]

Six days later, after four months of negotiations, American and British representatives signed the peace treaty in the Belgian city of Ghent. The war was over, but it would be weeks before the news reached North America. In the interval, Jackson defeated the British as they assaulted New Orleans on January 8, 1815. This was the one great US land victory of the war, the result of foolhardy British tactics: they attacked headlong against entrenched American positions and were decimated by American fire. That day the British lost over 2,000 men; seventy-one Americans were killed or wounded.[58] Among the defenders were 430 free African Americans. "The killed and wounded on our part were chiefly of the New Orleans colored regiment, who were so anxious for glory that they could not be prevented from advancing over our breastworks and exposing themselves," a white American wrote. "They fought like desperadoes and deserve distinguished praise."[59]

Two days after the New Orleans debacle, British Rear Admiral Cockburn descended with 1,000 soldiers on Cumberland Island, the largest of the Sea Islands that dot the coast of Georgia, opposite to the town of St. Mary's. He then seized St. Mary's and raided other Sea Islands and the seacoast. His attacks were part of Cochrane's grand strategy: a diversion to preoccupy US forces in the southeast while the main British force conquered New Orleans. In what must have been a vision from hell for Georgia planters, half of Cockburn's force were black men: 365 Colonial Marines as well as two companies of the 2d West India regiment, a black corps based in the Bahamas. Panic spread among the planters. Jackson's triumph at New Orleans had stripped Cockburn's raid of military significance, but in human terms this was one of the most successful British operations of the war. By the time Cockburn's force departed in mid-March, after the admiral had received official confirmation of the peace treaty between Britain and the United States, 1,700 slaves had fled to the British. They all left with them, as free people.[60]

The Peace Treaty

At Ghent, on December 24, 1814, British and Americans had agreed to a peace without victors—the treaty stipulated the territorial *status quo ante* and said nothing about impressment or neutral rights. US officials were delighted. They were eager to end the war which had gone so badly for them. The Madison administration was bankrupt, and there was no money to enlarge the army; the country was riven by dissension and in New England there were rumblings of disunion. Among Americans, confidence in the administration was at its nadir.

The British had gone to Ghent hoping to acquire some American territory, particularly in Maine, to improve land communications between Halifax and Quebec, but this would have required a major military effort at a time when the British people were tired of war and its associated taxes. Furthermore, in Europe new problems were emerging; in particular, Whitehall feared the ambitions of the Tsar which might lead, the prime minister, Lord Liverpool, wrote, to "a renewal of the war in Europe." Why continue fighting the Americans? As Liverpool noted, "no additional frontier that you could possibly expect to obtain would add to the security of Canada."[61]

Deciding that their vital interests lay not in a chunk of Maine, but in the European balance of power, the British chose peace. This set the pattern. For the next eight decades—until London began actively courting US goodwill through a series of unilateral concessions—the British treated the United States as a strong regional power. If vital interests were at stake they would fight. But while US vital interests were in North America, British vital interests were in Europe and India.

The war: a balance sheet

Even though the Treaty of Ghent simply reestablished the territorial *status quo ante*, the war brought tangible benefits to the United States. First, in West Florida, a Spanish colony: in 1813, the Madison administration had occupied the area around Mobile, claiming that the territory was part of the Louisiana Purchase. The Treaty of Ghent said nothing about Mobile, leaving the Americans in possession of it. Furthermore, the war helped crush Indian resistance east of the Mississippi. Tecumseh had been killed and the Indian coalition he had created had scattered. During the war, the Indian contribution to the British defense of Upper Canada had been decisive: "It was at least doubtful whether without the cooperation of the Indians ... this province would have been preserved to the empire," the Lieutenant Governor of Upper Canada noted.[62] But once the war ended, British officials made it clear to the Indians that they could no longer count on any British support against the Americans; the officials offered instead a few gifts. Little Crow, a Dakota chief, exclaimed, "After we have fought for you, endured many hardships, ... and awakened the vengeance of our powerful neighbors, you make a peace for yourselves, leaving us to obtain such terms as we can. You no longer need our services; you offer us these goods to pay us for having deserted us. But no, we will not take them; we hold them and yourselves in equal contempt."[63] Never again would the British interfere south of the Canadian border. Never again would the Indians represent a military threat to the United States.

In the South, too, the war obliterated whatever military power the Indians still had. The "Red Sticks," a part of the Creek confederacy—the most powerful Indian nation in the South—had risen against the United States in 1813. They had counted on British help, but in 1813, the British were in no position to offer any assistance, and by the time they could, in late 1814, the Red Sticks had been crushed. Andrew Jackson imposed a staggering territorial cession—about half of their territory—on the entire Creek confederacy in August 1814 at the Treaty of Fort Jackson.[64]

Article IX of the Treaty of Ghent—inserted at the insistence of the British—required that the United States end hostilities against the Indians and agree "forthwith to restore to such tribes ... all possessions ... which they have enjoyed or been entitled to in 1811 previous to such hostilities." This nullified the territorial cessions of the Treaty of Fort Jackson. When Secretary of War Monroe notified Jackson of this fact, the latter paid no heed. "He simply decided that whatever the secretary of war intended by his instructions, they did not apply to his treaty," Jackson's leading biographer, Robert Remini, writes. "Despite repeated protests by the Creek chiefs, he continued expelling the Indians from their land. And nobody stopped him.... The administration itself approved expansion. It wanted the Indian removed."[65]

The British averted their eyes. "England sold out," notes Remini. "The Indians were sacrificed to a greater need," rapprochement with the United States.[66] It took time for the Indians to understand the depth of Britain's betrayal. They continued pleading with the British minister in Washington and the government in London, alerting British officials that the United States was violating the Treaty of Ghent. A sympathetic British officer arranged the trip of a prominent Creek chief, Hidlis Hadio, to London in 1815; after several months in the British capital, Hadio was told that the Creeks' grievances against the United States had been presented to the Prince Regent and that, "in proof of the part which he takes in the happiness" of the Creek nation, the Prince Regent urged the Creeks "to return to their habits of friendly intercourse with their neighbors of the United States of America." After lingering for more than a year in London, Hadio was given by the British government £100 and a few presents, and was shipped back home.[67] When another Creek chief arrived in London in 1818, the British government promptly sent him home, instructing naval commanders "not to grant a passage in future" to any Native American chief seeking to reach Britain.[68]

The legacy of the war

For the Americans, despite a few brilliant moments, the war of 1812 was an inglorious affair. As a leading historian of the conflict, Donald Hickey, writes: "Many of the nation's military leaders were incompetent, and enlistments in the army and navy lagged behind need"—in 1814 the army's authorized strength was 62,500 but its actual strength was 40,000. The government was forced to rely on the militia, which was "costly and inefficient."[69] It was difficult to fund war loans, the soldiers' pay was often six months late, and extensive smuggling helped feed the British troops in Canada. The state of the nation's finances was chaotic and deteriorating. In December 1814, the secretary of the treasury reported that the government needed $56 million—three times the national revenue—to fund the war for another year. "Only loans could bridge the gap, but investors had lost confidence in the administration."[70]

Those few free Blacks who were allowed to fight for the United States distinguished themselves at New Orleans and, in sharp contrast to their white countrymen, at Bladensburg. Many more had volunteered to fight when Baltimore, Philadelphia, and New York had seemed threatened. When they were rebuffed, they had volunteered for labor battalions to build defenses against a British attack. Perhaps some were moved by love for the country that oppressed them. Some must have hoped that by showing their courage, their patriotism, they might gain the respect of the white majority and their oppression might be lessened. If this was their hope, they were sadly mistaken.

Amid the relief of the peace and the surge of pride for Jackson's victory at New Orleans, white Americans quickly forgot the humiliations and the defeats of the war. Its memory morphed into yet another example of American exceptionalism. The *Richmond Enquirer* asserted in February 1815, "We have waged a war which has covered us with glory." Forgotten was the fact that the British had been tied down in Europe fighting Napoleon. "We have been able to encounter, without allies, the most powerful of nations," a member of Congress boasted, "and to terminate the war with a memorable triumph."[71]

In the glow of imagined glory, the fortunes of the Republican Party swelled while the Federalist Party, which had opposed the war, collapsed. The elections of 1816 brought to the presidency James Monroe, another scion of the Virginia dynasty, an intelligent but not brilliant man. In the 1790s, Monroe had been a wild man in foreign policy matters—as minister to France in 1794–6 he had embraced the French government, openly criticized his own president, and accused Jay of having been bribed by the British. But during the following decade he had matured, performing a creditable job as US minister to Britain. During the war of 1812, he served Madison well, first as secretary of state, then as secretary of war. As president, he would be flanked by two men of superior ability and intellect—Secretary of War John Calhoun and Secretary of State John Quincy Adams. In his foreign policy, Monroe would prove cautious and inclined to follow the advice of his brilliant secretary of state.[72]

The war left an enduring legacy of Anglophobia in the United States. Alan Taylor writes that in 1815 "the British withdrew from American shores but not from American nightmares . . . The very real (but carefully limited) British use of black troops during the war became multiplied to monstrous proportions in the American imagination." As did the British alliance with the Indians. The Indians had perpetrated atrocities against American soldiers and civilians. However, as Hickey points out, Americans had "reciprocated in kind, rarely taking warriors as prisoners, sometimes slaying women and children, and often appropriating human trophies to celebrate success on the battlefield."[73]

Nevertheless, relations between the British and the American governments gradually improved. Peace in Europe meant that impressment and neutral rights no longer poisoned bilateral relations, and Whitehall sought to strengthen ties with the United States. The British silence at the US violation of the Treaty of Ghent was followed by the settlement of festering issues. The first was the Rush-Bagot Agreement of April 1817 which limited naval armaments of both parties on the Great Lakes. "It was," Samuel Flagg Bemis noted, "the first instance of reciprocal naval disarmament in the history of international relations."[74]

By the time the agreement was signed, another problem was on the way to resolution: compensation for fugitive slaves. About 5,000 runaways had left the United States with the British, as free people. Britain agreed to submit the matter to the arbitration of the Tsar, who in 1822 found in favor of the United States. London bowed to the verdict and paid $1,204,960 (c. $27 million) in compensation.[75]

Spanish Florida

Ever since the Louisiana Purchase, the United States had sought to annex the Floridas. Jefferson had failed, but Madison had been more successful, seizing Baton Rouge in 1810 and Mobile three years later. The Spaniards had been too weak to resist. Thus, by 1813, the United States had grabbed the half of West Florida that it claimed as part of the Louisiana Purchase. Madison wanted more. Once the war with Britain was over, he began badgering the Spaniards to surrender not only the remainder of West Florida, but also East Florida. Spain resisted, trusting that the Americans would not use force for fear of provoking Spain's European allies, especially Britain, the dominant power in the Caribbean. This fear did indeed restrain both Madison and, for a time, Monroe.[76]

The situation on the border between the United States and Spanish Florida (East Florida and what remained under Spanish control in West Florida) grew increasingly tense. For over a century, the colony had been a haven for fugitive slaves from Georgia and South Carolina. Some were re-enslaved by the Seminoles—the name given by whites to all the Indians who lived in Florida—but Seminole slavery was much less harsh than chattel slavery in the United States. Other runaways were welcomed as free people and set up their own villages, living in harmony with their Indian neighbors.

The Treaty of Fort Jackson in August 1814 forced the Creeks to cede land in southern Georgia and Alabama and brought the white frontier much closer to the Seminoles. While more than 1,000 Red Sticks (those Creeks who had fought against the United States in 1813–14) fled to Florida, full of hatred for the Americans, a tide of white settlers moved into the former Creek lands; they were a lawless rabble—the "worst part of our citizens," Secretary of War William Crawford remarked.[77] The frontier was in turmoil. There were raids into Florida by Americans to seize Blacks as well as cattle belonging to the Seminoles, who were expert in animal husbandry; the US troops in Georgia made no effort to stop these raids. And there were raids by the Seminoles and Red Sticks across the border in retaliation, harassing settlers in the ceded Creek lands. The Spaniards were impotent spectators. There were only three Spanish settlements in Florida—Pensacola (the capital, with approximately 1,000 people), the village of St. Augustine, and the fort of St. Marks—garrisoned by 300 poorly armed Spanish soldiers.

In Spanish hands, Florida represented a double threat to the United States: the remote danger that the British might decide to seize the colony, and the real danger that it was a haven for runaway slaves. Even though there were fewer than 1,000 fugitive enslaved people in Florida, slaveowners were very sensitive about the security of their human chattel and the presence of armed runaways in Florida was their ultimate nightmare.

In late December 1817, Secretary of War Calhoun ordered Andrew Jackson, the senior officer of the Southern District, to invade Florida to subdue the Seminoles. Jackson was "authorized," Calhoun told the governor of Alabama Territory, "to conduct the war as he thought best."[78]

Jackson empathized with his fellow slaveowners' concerns. "Throughout the campaign the General showed a lively interest in the problem of runaway slaves," Remini writes. "This was not simply an Indian war, but a war against defiant blacks. Runaway slaves, he said, needed to be punished severely."[79]

In March 1818, Jackson invaded Florida with approximately 3,500 men. It was an overwhelming force: the entire Seminole population did not exceed 5,000. Seminoles and Blacks fled at the approach of the Americans, fighting only rearguard actions to enable their families to escape. Jackson killed fewer than one hundred Seminoles and Blacks, but he left behind a trail of desolation, burning their villages, seizing their livestock, and destroying their food stocks. Turning to the Spaniards, huddled in their three settlements, Jackson seized St. Marks and Pensacola. The Spaniards, hopelessly outnumbered, surrendered without a fight. By late May, the campaign was over. The Monroe administration had not ordered Jackson to attack the Spanish settlements. President Monroe's instructions had been a model of ambiguity, saying that the "movement [against the Seminoles] will bring you on a theatre when possibly you may have other services to perform. This is not a time for you to think of repose. Great interests are at issue, and until our course is carried through triumphantly . . . you ought not to withdraw your active support from it."[80] As historian William Weeks argues, "Given Jackson's reputation for not shirking conflict, the omission of direct orders not to seize Spanish posts is perhaps the strongest proof that the administration wanted benefits of a Jackson rampage in Florida without having to shoulder the blame for sanctioning aggression against another country."[81]

The benefits were obvious: Jackson had invaded Florida, humiliated the Spaniards, and no European power had raised a finger on Spain's behalf. Not even Britain. "Either England does not consider Florida important," the Spanish foreign minister lamented, "or does not care about how its interests will be threatened by having it in US hands"[82] The Spanish ambassador reported from London that Foreign Secretary Castlereagh had responded to the invasion with "generalities" and "indifference."[83] Britain was focusing, instead, on the negotiations with the Monroe administration about compensation for slaves who had fled to the British during the War of 1812 and about the border between the United States and British North America.

Spain had no choice but to capitulate. In February 1819, the Spanish minister in Washington and Secretary of State John Quincy Adams signed a treaty that ceded all Florida to the United States and fixed the border between the two countries at the Sabine, Red, and Arkansas rivers, that is at the Louisiana-Texas border and thence westward to the Pacific Ocean along the 42nd parallel (the northern border of California). In exchange, the United States renounced what Adams called its "mere color of claim"[84] to Texas (claimed by Jefferson as part of the Louisiana purchase) and agreed to pay $5 million (c. $102 million)—not to Spain, but to compensate US citizens who had claims against Spain. It was a one-sided bargain sealed at gunpoint.

Given the terms, it is understandable that the Spanish king, Ferdinand VII, refused to ratify the treaty. His defiance could not last long, however, lest the Americans invade Florida again. The Russian and French governments urged Ferdinand to accept the inevitable. "One must understand," the French ambassador in Madrid insisted, "that the United States will be the master of Florida even if the treaty is not ratified; that the president [Monroe] would not be able to resist the violent desire of a people over whom the government has only very limited authority."[85] Ferdinand signed the treaty on October 24, 1820. The exchange of ratifications took place in Washington on February 22, 1821. "I dare to assure Your Excellency," the Spanish chargé in Washington had warned his foreign minister, that the Americans' "ferocious hatred of us will not diminish even if the King agrees to every concession and sacrifice they are demanding from us . . . [It will endure] as long as Spain owns even a foot of land north of the isthmus of Panama."[86] He was prophetic. Only the loss of Cuba to the United States, in 1898, introduced a new spirit of amity in US relations with Spain.

The first three decades

The United States had grown since Washington assumed the presidency in 1789. It had grown in population, from 3,929,214 in 1790 to 9,638,453 in 1820 (including 1,538,022 enslaved people and 232,634 free Blacks).[87] It had doubled in size, with the acquisition of Louisiana and the Floridas. And its economy had expanded. The years 1793–1807 had been a time of "unparalleled prosperity."[88] They had also witnessed dramatic transformation in the South with the invention of the cotton gin. Cotton, which had been a minor crop in 1790, had become the United States' major export, and had deepened the dependence on and exploitation of enslaved people. The demand for slaves to toil in the new cotton plantations soared. Maryland and Virginia basked in their new role as slave exporters: "I consider a woman who brings a child every two years," Jefferson wrote in 1820, "as more valuable than the best man on the farm."[89]

The domestic politics of the United States had survived a tumultuous period in the 1790s with the creation of the country's first party system and the bitter fights between Republicans and Federalists. While the enmity had persisted, the Federalists had been weakened during Jefferson's presidency and collapsed after the war of 1812. For all practical purposes, only one party remained after 1815, the Republicans.

From the Washington through the Madison administrations three European countries had been important for the United States: the two superpowers, Britain and France; and Spain—an object of contempt and greed for the Americans. Relations with Russia and Prussia were friendly, but distant.

What about Latin America? For commercial and security reasons, in the 1790s Haiti had been far more important to the United States than all of South America. During the presidency of Jefferson, Haiti remained significant as an economic partner and an object of concern, and Cuba surged as a major trading partner and object of desire. South America and Mexico were still marginal—but early in the Madison presidency a new development brought them to US attention: the revolt against Spanish rule, spreading south of the Rio Grande.

CHAPTER 6

THE LIMITS OF SYMPATHY: THE UNITED STATES AND THE INDEPENDENCE OF SPANISH AMERICA

In 1808, Napoleon overthrew the Spanish dynasty and installed his brother Joseph on the throne in Madrid. With the French troops occupying the country the Spaniards rose in revolt and a bloody war of independence began.

The collapse of the Spanish state had a ripple effect in Madrid's colonies across the Atlantic. By 1810, revolts erupted in the province of La Plata (Buenos Aires), in *Tierra Firme* (Venezuela and Colombia), and in Mexico. There were virtually no Spanish troops in the La Plata region and Madrid's power swiftly collapsed there and in neighboring Paraguay and Uruguay. In *Tierra Firme*, however, the Spaniards were able to fight back: war engulfed Venezuela and Colombia.[1]

The revolts in La Plata and in *Tierra Firme* were led by the native elite, with the lower classes serving as cannon fodder. But the leaders of the revolt that broke out in Mexico in 1810 were from the lower class, and they demanded both independence and social reform. The Mexican elites chose to defend their privileges rather than to seek independence, so they sided with the Spanish authorities. The rebels were crushed. The Spanish continued to govern Mexico, as well as Central America, Ecuador, Peru, Chile and Bolivia, while the war continued in Venezuela and Colombia.

In the wake of Napoleon's abdication in 1814, an exhausted Spain attempted to restore its rule in the Western Hemisphere. In 1815, 10,000 Spanish soldiers crossed the ocean— this was all Spain could spare. They went to *Tierra Firme*. At first, they scored important successes, but soon the rebels, led by Simón Bolívar, a white Venezuelan aristocrat who was a gifted general, began to gain the upper hand. The war was still raging when, in 1821, Bolívar became president of Gran Colombia, which united Venezuela, Colombia and the recently liberated Ecuador.

In the southern cone, too, Spain lost ground: in 1817, a small Argentine army crossed the Andes into Chile and defeated the few Spanish troops there. In Mexico, as well, Spanish rule collapsed, this time without war: liberals seized power in Madrid in 1820 promising social reforms. It was more than the Church, the upper class, and the Spanish authorities in Mexico could tolerate. They united in proclaiming the country's independence in 1821. Central America followed, first as part of the Mexican empire, then as the United Provinces of Central America.

By 1823, Bolívar had expelled the Spanish from Gran Colombia and the following year his troops defeated them in Peru, Madrid's last stronghold in South America. The wars of independence of Spanish America were over. Only Cuba and Puerto Rico remained under Spanish rule.

Portugal, too, lost its empire in South America, but without bloodshed, as its giant colony, Brazil, separated peacefully from the mother country in 1822. Besides Spain, the only colonial empire of any significance that remained in the Western Hemisphere was England's in North America, the Caribbean and Central America; France ruled over a few Caribbean islands and had a toehold in South America. Dutch, Danes, and Swedes owned tiny fragments. And there was Haiti, the land of the formerly enslaved who had killed their masters. After defeating Napoleon's troops in 1803, the Haitians had proclaimed independence. Proud, unbending, they represented a threat in a hemisphere dominated by slaveholders. No foreign government recognized their independence.

"You are the greatest benefactor on the earth"[2]

Three countries helped the Spanish Americans in their long struggle for independence: the United States, Britain, and Haiti, the pariah. The Haitian government alone provided the rebels direct aid. This aid was crucial because it was given when the rebels' fortunes were at their nadir. "You are the greatest benefactor on the earth," Bolívar wrote to Haitian president Alexandre Pétion. "One day America will proclaim you her Liberator."[3]

Bolívar had fled to Jamaica, a British colony, in May 1815, as Spanish troops reconquered Venezuela and Colombia. Convinced that London was sympathetic to the rebel cause, he had gone to Jamaica certain that aid would materialize. "Had I a glimmer of hope that [Spanish] America might triumph unaided," he wrote as he arrived in Kingston, "no one would be more eager than I to serve my country without subjecting it to the humiliation of seeking foreign help . . . I come to seek aid . . . If necessary I would go to the Pole; and if all remain insensitive to the voice of humanity, I will have fulfilled my duty, however in vain, and I will return to die fighting in my fatherland."[4]

It was an icy Britain that Bolívar encountered in Jamaica. The rebels' defeats had convinced the British government that Spain would hold onto its colonies. Bolívar penned letter after letter to officials in London—and received no reply. He sought a meeting with the island's governor—and was rebuffed. He tried to borrow funds from local merchants—and was refused.

As weeks passed, Bolívar's situation in Jamaica became increasingly pitiable. To survive, he sold his few possessions. That he did not starve and had a roof over his head was only because British friends lent him small sums of money. These friends, whose generosity he never forgot, were his sole source of hope in the hostile atmosphere of Jamaica.

Despite the humiliations and disappointments, Bolívar lingered in Jamaica, at times in profound despair, nurturing thoughts of suicide, "because death is preferable to so dishonorable a life."[5] Finally, he had to accept that his quest there was hopeless. On December 19, 1815, he sailed to Haiti, where President Pétion received him warmly. Pétion's country, devastated by its long war of independence and unable to count on any foreign support, granted him the aid the British had refused. He received no loans from Haiti—only gifts: 6,000 rifles, a ship with twenty cannons and a few smaller vessels, an undisclosed amount of money, and a printing press. In return, Pétion asked only that slavery be abolished in the lands Bolívar would liberate.

In April 1816, a small fleet left Haiti for the island of Margarita, off Venezuela, which had been chosen as the first step in the reconquest of *Tierra Firme*. Three hundred men accompanied Bolívar—of these, approximately thirty were Haitians.

The expedition ended in disaster and once again Bolívar had to flee. This time, he did not hesitate. In September 1816, Bolívar returned to Haiti. Once more he sought the aid of Pétion—"the most magnanimous republican leader of the New World."[6] Once more he was welcomed, receiving money and weapons. A second expedition left Haiti in December 1816. For Bolívar, it was to be the beginning of a triumphant military campaign that would end eight years later, with the Spaniards' defeats at Junín and Ayacucho in Peru. Bolívar would never again set foot on Haitian soil, but in letters he openly acknowledged his immense debt and his gratitude to the Haitians. He, the white aristocrat, wrote to the former slave Pétion: "Your Excellency is destined to overshadow the memory of the great Washington, building, as you are, the most illustrious career in the face of overwhelming obstacles." And he pledged: "Haiti will not remain isolated among her sisters. The liberality and the principles of Haiti will be found among all the regions of the New World."[7]

Bolívar, however, soon forgot his debt to Haiti, just as so many historians also erase Haiti's contribution to Spanish American independence, waxing eloquent, instead, on the importance of the United States and Britain.

The United States, Britain, and Spanish America

Until 1815, both the United States and Britain were absorbed by far more urgent matters than the fate of Spanish America: the British were fighting Napoleon, and the Americans, Britain.[8]

After peace returned in 1815, Spanish American independence became "one of the most popular causes of its time" in the United States, historian Caitlin Fitz argues in a detailed study. Fitz draws this conclusion from the toasts Americans made on the Fourth of July. "Between 1816 and 1825," she writes, "well over half of July Fourth celebrations included toasts to the [Spanish American] rebel movements." Furthermore, she cites what she calls the "Bolivar baby boom": many babies born in the United States in those years were named Bolívar.[9]

There were many reasons US citizens would sympathize with the rebels: Spain had long been an object of hatred and contempt; independence might mean increased trade with the United States as well as the prospect of a significant loss of European influence in the hemisphere. Fitz argues that there was more: ordinary people in the United States "took republicanism's southward spread as a compliment to themselves, seeing it as proof that their own ideals really were universal. The cause of Latin America became the cause of the United States." When celebrating Spanish American rebels, US citizens "were celebrating themselves, and like Narcissus [who fell in love with his own reflection], they were so riveted they could barely look away. They were blithely unaware that the object of their affection was an image, an illusion."[10]

There is a disconnect. While US citizens were raising their glasses to the Spanish American rebels, Bolívar was in Haiti, imploring Pétion for help. It is a telling indication of Bolívar's opinion of the United States that he never considered asking the US government for the aid denied him by the British. Instead, he "complained of Washington's empty professions of sympathy."[11] This begs the question, beyond 4th of July toasts and the "Bolivar baby boom" how, exactly, did US citizens express their support for the Spanish American rebels? And what about the US government? How important was its contribution to the independence of Spanish America?

As early as July 1815, just a few months after the conclusion of the war with Britain, the Madison administration demonstrated sympathy for the Spanish American rebels by decreeing that their ships should be treated on the same basis as other foreign ships in the ports of the United States—thus granting the rebels belligerent rights. The following year the administration sold gunpowder to the Venezuelans on credit.[12] This was the first, and the last time that the United States offered a loan or a grant to the insurgents.

Sentimental attachment to the rebels did not lead the people of the United States to open their wallets. In US newspapers of the early 1820s there were frequent references to collections of funds for the Greeks, fighting for independence against the Ottoman empire, but none for the Spanish American rebels.[13] Very few US citizens joined the rebel armies. Perhaps the United States' greatest assistance to the cause was provided by the sailors and shipowners who volunteered to join the fight as privateers attacking Spanish ships. They were spurred by economic hardship: the return of peace, in 1815, had idled many US ships that had been profitably employed in privateering against the British. "Their crews," a US historian has written, "lounged about the docks—restless, discontented, and ready for almost any new venture."[14] Therefore, the war to the south provided welcome opportunities.

US merchants, too, were eager to contribute to the cause of freedom—as long as the rebels were able to pay, preferably in cash. Not surprisingly did Simón Bolívar refer to the "arithmetic" neutrality of the United States.[15] Still, when they could pay, the Spanish Americans received military and other supplies that were of great importance to their cause.

What of the British contribution? Whereas for the United States Spain was a traditional enemy, for Britain it was an ally. Therefore, to reassure the Spaniards, the British authorities enacted a "formidable array of laws and orders"[16] that made it almost impossible for British subjects to render any assistance to the Spanish American rebels. The British government then demurely averted its eyes as the laws were systematically violated. Whitehall was motivated not by sympathy for the rebels, but by the desire to ensure that Britain acquire the lion's share of trade with the newly independent states.

Since their resources were greater than those of their US counterparts, British merchants extended more generous credits to the rebels, as long, of course, as they were confident that they would be repaid. (They gave no loans in 1815 and 1816, when the rebel cause was at its nadir.) They were, in fact, the rebels' greatest suppliers. As early as

1822, moreover, Gran Colombia, Chile and Peru floated their first bond issues in the British market.[17]

Other Britons sought employment in the rebel forces. The end of the Napoleonic wars led to an economic crisis and high unemployment in the British Isles, and to a drastic contraction of the British army. Therefore, beginning in late 1817, after Bolívar's prospects had improved, several thousand volunteers left Britain to enlist in his army.

Once in South America many deserted; others proved to be undisciplined, arrogant, and inept. But many were brave and fought with skill. They made a difference. The British volunteers played an important role in several battles. Thus, Bolívar's official communiqué of the great rebel victory at Carabobo (Venezuela) in June 1821 praised "the valiant British battalion" which "has distinguished itself among so many valiant ones."[18] It was an Englishman, General William Miller, who commanded the rebel cavalry at the battle of Ayacucho (Peru) in December 1824.

A handful of volunteers from the United States and many more from Britain served in the rebel navies. Particularly important was their contribution to the Chilean Navy: by 1823, seventeen US citizens and 113 Britons had served as officers.[19]

In 1822, the United States was the first country to recognize the independence of the Spanish American states, three years before any European government. Samuel Flagg Bemis deemed this "the greatest assistance rendered by any foreign power to the independence of Latin America."[20]

Was it? It brought no material benefit to the rebels. The US government still refused to provide any loans, US merchants still held to their "arithmetic" neutrality, and US volunteers still shunned the rebel armies. It is difficult to see how recognition facilitated the victories Bolívar achieved over the next two years—victories that ended with the destruction of Spanish power in South America. Nor did US recognition influence the behavior of the European powers, except possibly Britain, which viewed the United States as a rival for the favor of the new states. Whitehall recognized the Spanish American states in 1825. Perhaps in the absence of US recognition it would have waited longer. But here, too, the same point applies: British recognition had no impact on the course of the war.

The Monroe Doctrine

Nor did the Monroe Doctrine of December 1823 affect the independence struggle in Spanish America. The seeds of the doctrine were sown in Europe. In the summer of 1823, it was no secret that the French government, with the support of Russia, was considering sending troops to Spanish America to help Madrid defeat the rebels. This worried London. It was in Britain's interest that the Spanish American countries become independent because this would mean open markets for British trade and investment. In August 1823, British Foreign Secretary George Canning made a surprising offer to the US minister, Richard Rush: he proposed a joint declaration in which London and Washington would state their opposition to the intervention of any power to help Spain against the rebellious colonies, and would also pledge that neither Britain nor the United States would take over any part of the Spanish empire in the Western Hemisphere.

Britain did not need US assistance: the Royal Navy ruled the waves. On October 1, 1823, Canning quietly summoned the French ambassador, the Prince of Polignac. His message was clear: French military intervention in Spanish America would lead "without doubt" to war with Britain.[21] The French government knew that it could not challenge the Royal Navy, and on October 12 Polignac secretly pledged that France "abjured . . . any desire of acting against the colonies by force of arms."[22] Statesmen in Washington were unaware of these conversations, and they were still anxiously considering Rush's dispatch about Canning's proposal for a joint declaration.

President Monroe consulted his cabinet as well as Jefferson and Madison. Jefferson disliked Canning's "self-denial" principle because he desired Spanish American territory—"I candidly confess that I have ever looked on Cuba as the most interesting addition which could ever be made to our system of states," he wrote; but he urged acceptance as the best way to frustrate the plans of France: with Britain "on our side we need not fear the whole world."[23] Madison too urged acceptance, as did Secretary of War John Calhoun. Monroe was hesitant. Secretary of State John Quincy Adams advised refusal. He surmised that Canning's motivation in proposing the joint declaration must have been "to obtain some public pledge from the government of the United States . . . against the acquisition to the United States themselves of any part of the Spanish-American possessions." By joining Britain "in her proposed declaration," he jotted in his diary, "we give her a substantial and perhaps inconvenient pledge against ourselves, and really obtain nothing in return."[24] He believed that France and Russia would not invade, but if they tried, Britain would oppose them and "would be victorious by her command of the sea."[25]

Adams won the argument. Instead of accepting Canning's offer, the president, in close collaboration with Adams, included two key points in his December 1823 Annual Message to Congress. He asserted that the hemisphere was closed to colonization and, therefore, to the extension of Europe's political system.[26] The "Monroe Doctrine" was born. It was welcomed by many Spanish American leaders who understood it—erroneously—as a promise that the United States would come to their assistance against Spain or other European powers.[27]

It was also well received by the British press. The London *Times* praised Monroe's words. "For us," *The Times* wrote, "it is a source of satisfaction that the . . . government of the United States has spoken out unequivocally to the world. . . . From the similarity of the position occupied by Great Britain and the United States in reference to what was Spanish America, it is difficult to calculate on any but an identity of measures." The leading opposition paper, the *Morning Chronicle*, agreed.[28] Canning, however, was not pleased. Britain was competing with the United States for the hearts and minds—and the trade—of the Spanish Americans, and he feared that they would see Monroe's words as fulsome support for their independence. In the wake of Monroe's message, Canning leaked the contents of the Polignac memorandum to Spanish American officials to let them know that they had the Royal Navy to thank for France's restraint, not James Monroe.[29]

Canning need not have worried. Spanish American leaders were soon disabused of the illusion that Monroe's message signaled that the United States would help them against Spain. However, beyond its ephemeral propaganda value, Monroe's statement carried a lasting message. As Richard Van Alstyne has remarked, the Monroe Doctrine was "assimilated into the catechism of American nationalism ... the United States shall be the only colonizing power and the sole directing power in both North and South America. This is imperialism preached in the grand manner ... The Monroe Doctrine is really an official declaration fencing in the 'western hemisphere' as a United States sphere of influence."[30]

Some Spanish American leaders understood this. Diego Portales, Chile's great statesman, warned, "Let us not escape from one domination only to fall under the sway of another! We must distrust those gentlemen who voice heartfelt approval of our Liberators, but who have not helped us in any way."[31] Bolívar agreed, wholeheartedly.

As the prospect of victory grew closer, Bolívar was tormented by the weakness of the Spanish American states. They needed help, and they needed protection—"against Spain, against the Holy Alliance [Russia, Prussia and Austria], and against anarchy."[32] It was to Britain that he turned. Only the British could provide the capital, the trade, and the protection that Spanish America needed. "Our American federation cannot survive without the protection of England," he wrote in June 1825.[33]

In Britain, Bolívar hoped he could find a protector; in the United States, he saw peril. Britain, he believed, did not threaten the territorial integrity of Spanish America—but the United States did. The United States, unlike Britain, lacked capital to develop Spanish America. What it had was dynamism, greed, and ambition. "There is at the head of this great continent," Bolívar warned, "a very powerful country, very rich, very warlike, and capable of anything."[34]

Territorial expansion had been the drumbeat of the United States from its outset. Americans may have toasted the Spanish American rebels and named their children after Bolívar, but they wanted Spanish American land. The countries closest to the United States—Mexico and Cuba—were most imperiled.

US feelings toward the Mexicans were not neighborly. "[They] look upon us ... as inferiors," warned the Mexican minister in Washington. "In time they will become our sworn enemies."[35] Antipathy was bred by propinquity and fueled by greed: the United States wanted Texas, which was Mexican territory. President John Quincy Adams (1825–9) pestered Mexico to sell it territory; and his successor, Andrew Jackson, persisted, in his heavy-handed way.

Cuba

In the late eighteenth century, an economic revolution began transforming the Spanish colony of Cuba from a cattle economy with a few thousand slaves into a great producer of coffee and sugar, requiring the importation of hundreds of thousands of enslaved people from Africa. By the early nineteenth century, the country had become a great economic prize. Its riches and its strategic position made it very tempting for the United States. The US desire to annex Cuba had deep roots.

Having acquired a window on the Gulf of Mexico with the Louisiana Purchase, Jefferson cast his gaze toward the island. In 1809, he counseled President Madison to make a deal with Napoleon, whose armies occupied Spain: France would give Cuba to the United States and in return receive a free hand in South America. Curiously, Jefferson asserted that "Cuba can be defended without a navy."[36]

During the administrations of Jefferson, Madison, and Monroe, the appetite for Cuba transcended sectional divisions. Southern and Northern statesmen united in greed. Secretary of State Adams' 1823 remarks to the US minister in Madrid illuminated both his and Monroe's dreams: "Cuba, almost in sight of our shores, from a multitude of considerations has become an object of transcendent importance to the commercial and political interests of our Union ... It is scarcely possible to resist the conviction that the annexation of Cuba to our federal republic will be indispensable to the continuance and integrity of the Union itself."[37] US dreams clashed, however, with the sea that encircled the island—the sea and the British fleet. London had made it clear that it would not tolerate Cuba's annexation to the United States.

If the United States could not have Cuba immediately, then it would wait; time was on its side. In Adams' words, "there are laws of political as well as physical gravitation; and if an apple severed by the tempest from its native tree cannot choose but to fall to the ground, Cuba, forcibly disjoined from its own unnatural connection with Spain and incapable of self-support, can gravitate only towards the North American Union, which by the same law of nature cannot cast her off from its bosom."[38]

Through the administrations of Jefferson, Madison, and Monroe, no US official or congressman expressed any sympathy for those Cubans who sought the independence of their country. But early in the presidency of Monroe's successor, John Quincy Adams, a threat arose. Gran Colombia and Mexico were contemplating an expedition to liberate Cuba and Puerto Rico. The moment seemed propitious: in 1824 Bolívar's armies had crushed the Spaniards in Peru and a few months later the Spanish troops in Upper Peru (Bolivia) had capitulated. Spanish rule had ended throughout the hemisphere except for Cuba and Puerto Rico. But Spain stubbornly dreamed of reconquest. Its warships attacked the vessels of its former colonies and Spanish troops occupied a Mexican fortress. By freeing Cuba and Puerto Rico, Gran Colombia and Mexico would deprive Madrid of the bases from which to harass them.[39]

The Adams administration reacted with alarm. In May 1825, Secretary of State Henry Clay warned that the expedition had a good chance of success because "a large portion of the inhabitants of the islands is predisposed to a separation from Spain," and would eagerly join the liberators.[40]

US officials opposed the independence of Cuba because they feared that it might become a second Haiti: the enslaved multitudes might take advantage of the turmoil to seize power. They also feared that France or Britain might seek to dominate the island. But one wonders whether another consideration was not paramount: the independence movement in Cuba had strong democratic tendencies; it advocated both the abolition of slavery and equal rights for Blacks and whites.[41] Had such a Cuban republic emerged, it would have bitterly resisted annexation to the United States, where the Blacks were enslaved chattel or free outcasts. Therefore, in the United States Southerners and Northerners, friends and foes of President Adams agreed that Cuba must remain under Spanish rule until the United States was able to seize the island, or, to paraphrase Adams, until the fruit was ripe.

To avert the danger that Spain might lose Cuba, the Adams administration turned to Europe. It sought to persuade Ferdinand of Spain to recognize the independence of Mexico and Colombia so that they would have little incentive to free Cuba. It also urged Russia, France, and Britain to apply pressure on Ferdinand. But France and Russia remained aloof, while Britain countered with an unwelcome proposal: France, Britain, and the United States should pledge that they had no designs on the island.[42]

The administration also turned to Gran Colombia and Mexico. First it reasoned—to no avail. Then it urged, and finally it threatened: the United States had "too much at stake in the fortunes of Cuba," Secretary of State Clay warned Colombia and Mexico, "to see with indifference" an invasion of the island, and it would employ "all the means necessary" to protect its interests, "even at the hazard of losing the friendship, greatly as they value it, of Mexico and Colombia."[43]

The Panama Congress

While the Cuban issue was at the forefront of the worries of the US government, Bolívar was at the peak of his power. Having liberated Venezuela, Colombia, Ecuador, Peru, and Bolivia, he worried about the future. He planned a congress of the independent republics of Spanish America that would meet in Panama to coordinate policy toward the rest of the world and, ideally, move toward confederation. Two other important items on the agenda were the expedition to free Cuba and Puerto Rico and the place of Haiti among the nations of the Western Hemisphere. (Despite Bolívar's encomiums to Pétion, no Spanish American country had recognized Haiti.)

Bolívar had not intended to invite the United States to the congress, but he relented at the insistence of other Spanish American leaders. Upon receiving the invitation, President Adams asked the US congress in December 1825 to confirm two envoys he had selected for the mission and to appropriate the necessary funds. He expected swift approval.

The storm broke out against the fallout of the divisive presidential election of 1824. In that election, Andrew Jackson had received a plurality of electoral votes, followed by Adams, William Crawford, and Clay. Therefore, the House had to choose among the top three. Clay, with votes to distribute, became the kingmaker. "I seemed to be the favorite of everybody. Describing my situation to a distant friend, I said to him, 'I am enjoying, whilst alive, the posthumous honors which are usually awarded to the venerated dead.'"[44] But as soon as Clay endorsed Adams, who then won the contingent election in the House becoming president elect, the lovefest ended. "The oil," he observed, was "instantly transformed into vinegar."[45] His subsequent appointment by Adams as secretary of state aroused a whirlwind of accusations that there had been a quid pro quo—"secret conclaves" had been held, and "cabals" had been entered "to impair the pure principles of our republican institutions . . . [and] to prostrate the fundamental maxim which maintains the supremacy of the people's will," Andrew Jackson thundered.[46] Adams' presidency would be dominated by the cry against "the corrupt bargain," and the contest for the next presidential election began "within a matter of weeks—nay, days—" of his election.[47] An opposition movement coalesced around Jackson, and Adams' support in Congress eroded.

The debate about the Panama Congress that opened in the US House and the Senate in early 1826 was not memorable for its intellectual heft, its originality, or its wit. But it was the most lengthy debate on US policy toward Spanish America during the region's wars of independence and it revealed the attitudes of the US legislators toward the newly independent countries.

"We are about to violate the maxim of the father of this country," cried out those who opposed going to Panama. "General Washington . . . warned us against the dangers of entangling alliances."[48] They accused Adams of planning to join an "American confederacy."[49] Those who favored attending the Congress countered by praising Washington's admonition with equal fervor and by pointing out, quite correctly, that Adams had pledged that "a cardinal principle of this [Panama] mission . . . was that our ministers are to do nothing, and settle nothing, which can compromise the neutrality of the United States."[50]

The issue that gripped the US Congress' attention was Cuba. Far more was said about it than about the rest of Latin America combined. The debate did not proceed along sectional lines. Northerners and Southerners, friends and foes of the administration, agreed that a Colombian and Mexican invasion of the island could not be tolerated. Cuba had to remain under Spanish rule.

What fueled the debate was domestic politics: could Adams be trusted? Those who supported the president were confident that his administration was "doing all that can be done to prevent the independence of Cuba."[51] Therefore, Adams should be allowed to send delegates to the Panama Congress, where they would tell Mexico and Gran Colombia to stay away from Cuba. Those who opposed Adams countered that there was no need to go to Panama: "this is a question which we cannot safely commit to negotiation," they asserted;[52] the administration should tell "the new states directly and without any disguise that we could not, and would not, permit those islands [Cuba and Puerto Rico] to be disturbed."[53]

The debate over Haiti unfolded along similar lines. Of the many speakers who addressed Haiti, not one advocated establishing diplomatic relations. The limits of the debate were best expressed in an exchange between two southern representatives: "I appeal to every southern member to join with me in protesting against even a preliminary discussion of this topic at Panama," implored John Forsyth of Georgia, who opposed participation. Edward Livingston of Louisiana retorted that the United States should go to Panama "as a probable means of preventing the recognition of Hayti by the South American states."[54]

What divided the legislators was far less than what united them, and it was partisan bitterness that explains the venom of the debate. Neither side expressed any kinship with the Latin Americans. It was not an uplifting debate, one in which ideas or ideals clashed. Finally, on March 14, 1826, the senate confirmed Adams' two envoys by a 27–17 vote, and on April 22, the House appropriated the necessary funds. "The mission to Panama has been very ungraciously sent," remarked a US diplomat.[55] "This first and only victory of the administration in Congress proved an empty one," Samuel Flagg Bemis wrote.[56] One envoy died *en route*, and by the time the other was ready to depart for Panama the Congress had adjourned. But their presence had not been necessary: Gran Colombia and Mexico never launched an expedition to liberate Cuba and Puerto Rico, and the islands remained under Spanish rule, as the United States wished. Nor did the Spanish Americans recognize Haiti, another failure that was highly satisfying for the United States.

A reckoning

Of the three countries that rendered assistance to the Spanish American rebels, Britain comes first in material terms, and Haiti comes first for the generosity of its contribution and its timing. US sympathy for Spanish American independence was, in contrast, shallow and warped by territorial greed.

Bolívar recognized the danger that the United States represented for his region. The United States, he wrote, was "destined by Providence to plague [Spanish] America with miseries in the name of liberty."[57] He invited the Adams administration to the Panama Congress reluctantly because he saw no community of interests between Spanish America and the United States. Whereas Monroe wanted to fence off the Western Hemisphere from Europe, letting the United States dominate the countries to its south, Bolívar wanted to fence off Spanish American from the United States and he looked toward England for help. Unlike the United States, England had no territorial ambitions in Spanish America; unlike the United States, it had the capital necessary to help develop Spanish America. Bolívar and Monroe, therefore, had opposite conceptions of inter-American relations. "Bolívar was in fact the originator of the Pan-American idea," a British official wrote in 1916, but his Panamericanism excluded the United States.[58] Panamericanism, as it developed by the early 1900s, represented Monroe's victory and Bolívar's defeat.

Following the end of the Spanish-American wars of independence, the US public lost interest in the region. When US citizens thought about the Spanish Americans they forgot about freedom fighters seeking to overthrow European rule and thought instead of non-white, backward people. By the late 1820s, with the exception of Cuba, where US economic influence was paramount, US trade with Latin America was very modest, and British trade and investment were dominant. The British could offer cheap manufactured goods and abundant investment capital. They also had an excellent diplomatic and consular service able to foster both the political and economic interests of their country. The US government lacked a professional foreign service and showed little interest in Latin America, except Cuba which it wanted to annex and Mexico, whose province of Texas it coveted. These dreams, however, would have to wait. White Americans turned their attention to the Indians living east of the Mississippi.

CHAPTER 7
INDIAN REMOVAL: A "SICKENING MASS OF PUTREFACTION"

Ever since the creation of the United States, the white American empire had expanded in two ways. At times by annexing territories beyond its borders and, constantly, by pushing the white frontier into the lands of the Indian tribes who lived within the official limits of the United States.

As William McLoughlin, an authority on the Cherokees, has noted, the War of 1812 "unleashed raging hatred of the Indians and irresistible demands for Indian land."[1] The war also crippled the Indians' ability to resist: their fighting power had been broken and British support had evaporated. The Indians were at the mercy of the United States. They had "ceased to be an object of terror," Secretary of War John Calhoun told the House of Representatives in 1818. "The time seems to have arrived when our policy toward them should undergo an important change."[2]

That change materialized at the very end of President Monroe's second term, in January 1825, when in a special message to Congress he abandoned the rhetoric of integration and urged instead the removal of the Indian tribes east of the Mississippi to the west. This, he asserted, was "of very high importance to our Union." The Indians, too, would benefit: removal would not only shield them "from impending ruin, but promote their welfare and happiness."[3] Monroe forwarded to Congress a report from the Office of Indian Affairs of the War Department stating that approximately 110,000 Indians lived east of the Mississippi. Of these, 2,500 were in New England, more than 40,000 were in the northwest (the former Northwest Territory—Ohio, Indiana, Illinois, Wisconsin, Michigan, and a sliver of Minnesota), and the largest group, 60,000, was in the South.[4] (The report undercounted the Indians, particularly those in the South; for example, there were approximately 16,000 Cherokees, not 9,000, as the report stated.[5])

What threatened the Native Americans with "impending ruin" was white violence. The Indians who lived east of the Mississippi had painfully learned about the overwhelming power of the United States. They no longer attacked white settlers who intruded into their territory—instead they appealed to the federal government to keep the intruders away, and signed treaties with the United States ceding land in exchange for promises of protection that were not kept. While whites called them savages—the justification for removing them—Native Americans had built stable communities with diversified economies that combined hunting, farming, and animal husbandry. Contrary to the myth of the vanishing Indian, Jeffrey Ostler writes, they were not disappearing; instead, their numbers were growing, from about 90,000 on the eve of the American War of Independence to more than 120,000 in the early 1820s, despite the losses caused by wars with the United States and the migration of several thousand to the trans-Mississippi West.[6]

In his message, Monroe proposed that the Indians exchange their lands east of the Mississippi for territory in the unorganized public domain west of the river, that is, beyond the states and territories of the United States. He said that removal should be voluntary, but it required naivete not to realize that if the Indians received arable land west of the Mississippi, white settlers would arrive to claim it, and the problem would be repeated again, and again, and again.

Monroe's successor, John Quincy Adams (1825–9), had no sympathy for the Indians. He hoped that they would emigrate west of the Mississippi, but he recognized that they "had perfect right on their side in refusing to remove."[7] But would Adams protect the Indians from the land-grabbing of their white neighbors, as he was bound by treaties to do? The answer emerged in relation to the fraudulent treaty the Monroe administration, at Georgia's behest, had imposed on the Creeks in February 1825, less than a month before Adams' inauguration. In this treaty, a Creek chief had traded all the Creek land in Georgia and two-thirds of the Creek land in Alabama to the United States for land west of the Mississippi and a hefty bribe. The National Council of the Creeks, which was the nation's true representative body, protested vehemently, calling the treaty a "national calamity." Adams and Secretary of War James Barbour were aware that the treaty was fraudulent. Adams was willing to ask the Senate to repudiate it—an unprecedented action in the fraught history of US—Indian relations, where fraudulent treaties abounded—but only if Georgia was satisfied with a substitute. The administration, therefore, began pressuring the Creek National Council to make concessions that would appease Georgia. Finally, in January 1826, the National Council signed the Treaty of Washington, whereby the Creek nation surrendered its lands in Georgia but was allowed to retain its holdings in Alabama. (The whites of Alabama, who were far fewer than those of Georgia, were not yet pressing as vigorously as the Georgians for Indian land.) The new treaty guaranteed that the US government would ensure that the Creeks retain their remaining land. It was soon discovered, however, that the Office of Indian Affairs had made a cartographical error, and a narrow strip of Georgia had been left in the Creeks' possession. Georgia clamored that the Creeks must cede every inch of land in the state and threatened to use force. The Adams administration pressured the Creeks to comply, and they finally did, in the Treaty of Fort Mitchell in November 1827.[8] Adams did not shield the Indians from the Americans' land hunger.

The election of Andrew Jackson in November 1828 brought to the presidency a man who placed Indian removal at the top of his legislative agenda. In his first Annual Message, in December 1829, Jackson recommended that land west of the Mississippi be set aside for the Indians. They could refuse to emigrate, he said, "but they should be distinctly informed that if they remain within the limits of the states they must be subject to their laws."[9] The London *Times* remarked:

> General Jackson speaks with elaborate, and even somewhat ostentatious, sympathy of the wretchedness to which the long-suffering Indian race have been reduced by the tyranny of their white destroyers. The redress, however, which the President proposes ... does not consist of ... even a fragment of those wide regions from

which the unfortunate aborigines have actually, by force or fraud, been extruded; but he recommends that they shall henceforth be relegated to an ample district "westward" of the Mississippi, which is to be formally "guaranteed" to them. Guaranteed! ... This panacea for the Indian sufferings is but a repetition of the system which occasioned them—namely, yet another banishment from lands whereon they have peaceably subsisted.[10]

Jackson's message about Indian removal provoked an intense national debate. It was a sectional debate, pitting the South and the Northwest against New England and the Middle Atlantic states, which had already got rid of most of the Indians. It was also a moral debate about the nature of the United States. And it was a partisan debate, arraying the followers of Jackson against his political enemies. American reform organizations launched a powerful public campaign against removal. Denominational periodicals, which enjoyed a far larger readership than secular periodicals, spearheaded the opposition. Women joined the fray. Catharine Beecher, the head of a private girls' school in Hartford, Connecticut, initiated the first national petition drive by women. Her "Circular Addressed To Benevolent Ladies of the U. States" urged women to make their voices heard. "Have not the females of this country some duties devolving upon them in relation to this helpless race?" she asked. Women "are protected from the blinding influence of party spirit and the asperities of political violence. They have nothing to do with any struggle for power, nor any right to dictate the decision of those that rule over them. But they may feel for the distressed." The response, Beecher wrote, "exceeded our most sanguine expectations." In the span of two years (1830–1) petitions signed by almost 1,500 women from seven northern states flooded Congress. It was the first national women's petition campaign in US history. Jackson's supporters criticized the women for entering into a man's world and depicted the men who supported their petition drive as effeminate.[11]

Jackson's removal message referred to all the Indians living east of the Mississippi, but the debate centered on the Cherokees, who were, as two leading historians, Theda Perdue and Michael Green, write, "widely understood to be the most 'civilized' Indians in the United States," and who enjoyed the fulsome support of Christian missionaries.[12]

The Cherokees

In the seventeenth century, the Cherokees occupied a vast area in the southern Appalachians. Their villages were clustered in the valleys of upcountry South Carolina, western North Carolina, eastern Tennessee, northern Georgia and northeastern Alabama, and their hunting grounds extended far and wide. This territory contracted steadily through the eighteenth century with land cessions to the colonists. In the American War of Independence, the Cherokees sided with the British, and the American rebels invaded their territory, wreaking havoc. "No quarter was given on either side: men, women and children were shot, hacked, scalped, burned, and taken captive," McLoughlin writes. In the peace treaty ending the War of Independence, the British deserted their Indian allies, which meant that the American frontierspeople were free to vent their full wrath on the Indians. Defeated, the Cherokees signed the Treaty of Hopewell in 1785 with the US government. Nevertheless, the militias of Virginia, North Carolina, and Georgia continued to invade Cherokee territory until 1794. After one such incursion, a Cherokee headman lamented that his people were "now like wolves, ranging about the woods to get something to eat. Nothing to be seen in our towns but bones, weeds, and grass." The Cherokee population, 20,000 at the beginning of the century, had fallen to fewer than 10,000.[13]

The three decades that followed the return of peace in 1794 saw the transformation of the Cherokees from a hunting to an agrarian society. The United States provided them with tools such as agricultural implements and spinning wheels. It also guaranteed to protect Cherokee territory from white invaders. Therefore, when white squatters encroached on their lands, the Cherokees turned to the federal government. The response, however, was to urge them to cede more land—and they did, time and again. Through all these years, despite provocations, the Cherokees held fast to one rule: they could not afford to fight the United States. When the United States and Britain went to war in 1812, the Cherokees remained neutral. But when a faction of the Creeks—the Red Sticks—rose against the Americans in August 1813, the Cherokees decided that they had to demonstrate their loyalty to the United States or risk the Americans' wrath: 500 Cherokee warriors joined Andrew Jackson against the Red Sticks.[14] They fought well, earning Jackson's praise. His words, however, were poor recompense. When the Tennessee militia had marched through Cherokee country to join Jackson, it had indulged, a US official reported, in "plunder and prodigal, unnecessary and wanton destruction of property."[15]

In August 1814, the Treaty of Fort Jackson forced the Creeks to cede 2.2 million acres in northern Alabama to the United States in retribution for the Red Sticks' revolt; this was land that was also claimed by the Cherokees who sent a delegation to Washington to argue their case. Its members were, the *National Intelligencer* noted, "men of cultivated understandings, were nearly all officers of the Cherokee forces which served under General Jackson during the late war, and have distinguished themselves as well by their bravery as by their attachment to the United States."[16] President Madison recognized that the Cherokees' claim to the land was just, and in March 1816, the United States signed two treaties with the delegation: the first returned the land in Alabama to the Cherokees and granted them $25,500 (c. $475,000) for the damages inflicted by the Tennessee militia; in the second, the Cherokees agreed to sell the 97,000 acres they owned in South Carolina to the United States for $5,000.[17]

Jackson was furious that the land was restored to the Indians. He also considered the payment of an indemnity to the Cherokees for spoliation an insult to his troops. "No confidence can be placed in the honesty of an Indian," he thundered.[18] The Madison administration capitulated to Jackson's pressure, telling the Cherokees that they would have to give up their land in Alabama, despite the treaty they had just signed, and be content with a modest financial compensation. Further cessions were imposed on the Cherokees in 1817 and 1819. The US position, as expressed by Secretary of War Calhoun, was straightforward: if the Cherokees wanted to avoid total removal, they had to cede land.

Seeking to escape the whites' relentless pressure and urged on by the US government, approximately 3,000 Cherokees emigrated to Arkansas in the first two decades of the century. But the determination of those who remained grew stronger. After 1822, they firmly resisted Washington's insistent demands for additional cessions. "Brothers," the Cherokee National Council told US treaty commissioners in October 1823, "it is the fixed and unalterable determination of this nation never again to cede *one foot* of land."[19] The Cherokee nation occupied 6,000 of the 59,425 square miles of the territory claimed by Georgia, and it was there that most Cherokees lived; it also possessed 11,000 square miles in North Carolina, Tennessee, and Alabama combined. The government of Georgia, with the full support of the white population, led the onslaught against the Cherokees.

It was in the 1820s that the seeds sown in the 1790s blossomed. The Cherokees had become agriculturalists, like their white neighbors. Most Cherokees were subsistence farmers who lived in modest log cabins. "Part of their simple style of life," McLoughlin explains, "resulted from their holding onto the older values of Cherokee culture—community, sharing, harmony."[20] There was also a growing group of artisans and mechanics. And there was a Cherokee upper class—many of them mixed-bloods—who had embraced private property and capitalism. This elite, many of whom were slave owners, challenged the traditional Cherokee way of life. The iron bond that united the Cherokees, mixed blood and full blood, subsistence farmer and planter, was the desperate yearning to remain on their land, not to be deported across the Mississippi.

In 1821, after years of effort, a Cherokee, Sequoyah, developed a written form of the oral Cherokee language. "According to the prevailing standards of ethnology," McLoughlin writes, the Cherokees "had crossed the great dividing line between primitive (pre-literate) and a civilized (literate) society." Most Cherokees did not speak English, and probably only 10 percent could write it, but by the mid-1820s a majority (or a large minority—estimates vary) could read and write Cherokee. "Letters in Cherokee are passing in all directions," a missionary who lived among the Cherokees wrote in 1825, and nothing was "in so great demand as pens, ink and paper."[21] They were the first North American Indians to have a written language.

The Cherokee population was growing; a census conducted in 1809 had cited a population of 12,395 Cherokees, 583 black slaves and 341 whites married to Cherokees. The 1824 census gave a population of 16,060 Cherokees, 1,277 black slaves and 215 whites.[22]

A few missionaries had been proselytizing among the Cherokees since 1801, but their presence increased dramatically after the American Board of Commissioners for Foreign Missions, an influential interdenominational missionary society headquartered in Boston, decided in 1816 to focus on the tribe. The Cherokee leaders welcomed the missionaries. By the late 1820s the number of Cherokee Christians was still small—approximately 6 percent of the population—but the missionaries had established schools and provided technical assistance that helped develop crafts and improve agricultural techniques. Above all, the missionaries made it possible for the Cherokees to build a network of support in the Northeast against the onslaught from their Georgian neighbors.[23]

Northern sympathy for the Cherokees had limits, however. The American Board had opened a mission school for young men at Cornwall, Connecticut. Among the students were two brilliant young Cherokees, John Ridge and Elias Boudinot. In 1824, Ridge married a local white woman, and the trustees of the school condemned the marriage. A year later, Boudinot also got engaged to a local white woman, Harriet Gold. The school issued a special report to express its "unqualified disapprobation of *such connections*" and branded the conduct of those who had allowed the courtship "criminal."[24] The good people of Cornwall burned the couple in effigy while the church bells tolled a death knell. The following year, Boudinot married Harriet Gold, and the American Board closed the school, never to reopen.

The Cherokees' economic development was paralleled by a growing centralization in their government, to better resist the Americans' relentless quest for land. In 1827, they adopted a constitution modeled on that of the United States. It established a bicameral General Council elected every two years, a Principal Chief elected for a four-year term, a judiciary, and the equivalent of the Bill of Rights. The constitution, McLoughlin writes, "was obviously designed ... to demonstrate to the world that politically—as a nation— the Cherokees were now fully civilized and republicanized and that they were fully capable of self-government according to the same kinds of laws and legal system that white Americans adopted in a Western territory prior to statehood." The document also defined the territorial boundaries of the Cherokee nation and said that these boundaries, which were "solemnly guaranteed" by the treaties with the United States, "shall forever hereafter remain inalterably the same."[25]

The constitution provoked fury in Georgia. It gave the lie to the proposition that the Cherokees were half-savages who could not belong in white, civilized society. The more acculturated the Cherokees became, the more eager were the Georgians to expel them. "[Secretary of War] Calhoun thinks that the problem arises from the great progress of the Cherokees in civilization," John Quincy Adams jotted in his diary in 1824. "They are now within the limits of Georgia fifteen thousand, and increasing in equal proportion with the whites; all cultivators with a representative government, judicial courts, ... schools, and permanent property." Their leaders "write their own state papers, and reason as logically as most white diplomatists."[26] With mounting anger, the Georgians reminded the federal government that in 1802 in exchange for Georgia ceding its western lands (Alabama and Mississippi) to the United States, President Jefferson had pledged that the federal government would remove all Indians from Georgia "as soon as the same can be peacefully obtained on reasonable terms." (Jefferson overlooked the fact that the United States had guaranteed to these same Indians the right to remain in the territory.)

In February 1828, the first issue of the *Cherokee Phoenix* was published in New Echota, the Cherokee capital, in northern Georgia. Edited by Elias Boudinot (the Cherokee who had been schooled in Cornwall), and written in both English and Cherokee, this weekly newspaper was a powerful link between the nation and the outside world; copies were sent to missionary societies throughout the United States and to many important newspapers. Initially, the *Cherokee Phoenix* included articles about international affairs and culture—for instance, about the war between Greece and Turkey, about the Nile River, and about the "Zaporovian Cossacks."[27] By 1829, however, the paper was dominated by the removal crisis. It reprinted the racist statements of the governor of Georgia and President Jackson, but also, in issue after issue, articles from various US newspapers supporting the Cherokee cause. When the congressional debate on Indian Removal began in April 1830, the Cherokees were able to follow the insults, slander, and threats of their tormentors through the very good coverage of the *Cherokee Phoenix*. Reports on European affairs and articles about culture became rare, as page after page of the newspaper was filled with news of the tribe's desperate struggle to survive.

The Cherokees were active participants in the national debate over removal. Alone among the Indian nations their voice could be heard throughout the United States, thanks to their newspaper. In measured, yet forthright tones they pointed out the hypocrisy of the Jackson administration. "'You are too near to my white children—there will always be difficulties between you and them—go to the west where I can protect you,' is the language of our political father [Jackson] to us," the *Cherokee Phoenix* wrote in February 1830.

> But, in the name of common sense, we ask, who makes the difficulties? . . . Troubles are made for us by the very government which has pledged itself, and which ought, by every consideration of honor and justice, to protect us. It has encouraged its lawless citizens to intrude upon our lands, to insult and to abuse us; and when any difficulty occurs as a natural consequence of its remissness to do right, it is manufactured into an argument why we should leave our firesides, give up our lands to our invaders, and shelter ourselves . . . in the desolate prairies of the west. It is said that *humanity* to the inhabitants of the frontiers requires the removal of the Cherokees. But we again put it to the good sense of the public—who have the best claim to be protected from savages, the frontier whites or the Cherokees? . . . Does not humanity to the Cherokees require that the laws of the U.S., which were enacted expressly for their defence and that of other Indian tribes, should be executed? That the President should be just to his red, as well as his white children?[28]

The debate in Congress

The Removal Bill was drafted by the Indian Affairs Committees of the House and the Senate with the active guidance of Jackson. It authorized the president to negotiate with the Indian tribes for their removal to unorganized federal territory west of the Mississippi in exchange for their land east of the river. The federal government would compensate the Indians for improvements on the land they ceded, it would bear the cost of their removal until they had reached their destination, and it would provide their subsistence for a year after they had arrived, to give them time to plant crops. Supporters of the bill insisted that its sole purpose was to provide federal assistance to those tribes that wanted to emigrate, and that removal would be voluntary. The real issue, however, was not whether the federal government would use force to compel the Indians to leave, but whether, if they did not leave, it would protect them from their white neighbors, who saw Jackson's election as a green light to push the Indians out. New Jersey Senator Theodore Frelinghuysen presented an amendment designed to test the administration's true intentions: "Provided always, that until the said tribes or nations shall choose to remove . . . they shall be protected in their present possessions, and in the enjoyment of all their rights of territory and government, as heretofore exercised and enjoyed, from all interruptions and encroachments."[29] The amendment was defeated, twenty-seven to twenty. The sectional nature of the debate was obvious: the South voted against eighteen to nil, whereas New England voted in favor eleven to one.

On April 24, the Senate approved the Removal Bill, by a vote of twenty-eight to nineteen. "The glory is departed," the *Connecticut Observer* lamented. "If the House of Representatives concur with the Senate, the world will know just what confidence to place in treaties with the United States." The debate in the House had not yet begun. There, wrote the *American Spectator*, at issue will be "whether the one hundred and sixty treaties which we have made with the Indians *mean* anything, or whether they are a mere *farce*. . . . If this nation is incapable of being bound by treaties, let it be known."[30]

On May 26, 1830, the House approved the Removal Bill, 102 to ninety-seven. Some representatives voted against the bill because they were appalled by its injustice and they feared that Jackson, a notorious Indian fighter, would use brutal force to push the Indians out. Others had more practical motivations: aware that there was strong opposition to the bill in states like Pennsylvania and New York that would be crucial for the next presidential elections, members of the fledgling National Republican party voted against it, even though they had never before expressed any interest in Indian rights. (Most National Republicans were supporters of John Quincy Adams and Clay, united by opposition to Jackson and support of protective tariffs and federally funded internal improvements.) Fourteen congressmen from Pennsylvania who were part of the large, unwieldy Jackson coalition feared offending the Quakers and voted against the bill; three others failed to vote.[31] Many other representatives were concerned about the cost of removal. Those from states, particularly in New England, that had already rid themselves of Indians wondered, why they should foot the bill to solve a southern problem.

Ethnic cleansing

The Removal Bill became law on May 28, 1830. While virtually all Indians were slated for removal, Jackson's priority was the southern tribes. They represented the greatest concentration of Indians, the Cherokees were the *cause célèbre* of the Removal debate, and no state was as impatient as Georgia to cleanse its land.

Jackson wanted removal to be conducted humanely. But he also wanted it to be swift. Above all, he wanted to cut costs, to save taxpayers' money and prove wrong those critics who claimed that removal would be expensive. Congress had appropriated "the absurdly small sum of $500,000 (c. $14.2 million) to carry out the provisions of the law," historian Claudio Saunt notes, and the commissary general of the Office of Indian Affairs urged his agents to use "the most rigid economy" in handling removal.[32] The government issued contracts for food and transportation to the lowest bidders. The contractors, therefore, skimped on the quantity and the quality of the supplies they provided. Thus, the superintendent of Chickasaw removal wrote that the corn was "mildewed. A part of the corn was weevil-eaten. Some of the corn was so much injured that horses would not eat it . . . The pork was so bad that Dr. Walker told me that, if the emigrants continued to eat it, it would kill them all off. It gave those who eat it a diarrhea, and it was always my opinion that many of our poor people died in consequence of it." The removal treaties promised medicine and doctors to emigrants, but medical care during the long, arduous trek was minimal.[33]

The 18,000 Choctaws in Mississippi were the first southern tribe to sign a removal treaty. They had sought to conciliate the United States by sending warriors to fight under Jackson against the Red Sticks in 1813–14, and again at New Orleans in late 1814. They had become successful cattle farmers. But they were Indians. They could remain in Mississippi, Jackson's Secretary of War John Eaton told them, but they would be subjected to the laws of the state, which stipulated that an Indian could not testify in court against a white man. They would receive no protection from the federal government. "Wretchedness and distress will be yours," Eaton insisted. In September 1830, the Choctaws signed the removal treaty demanded of them. Plagued by disease, lack of food, exhaustion, they died in droves on the road to Oklahoma and in the following months.[34] Their former neighbors, the 4,000 Chickasaws, were able to delay the inevitable, but there was never any doubt that they would comply; they left in 1837. The other three great southern tribes, the 23,000 Creeks, the 16,000 Cherokees, and the 5,000 Seminoles proved less easy to intimidate.

Having been forced out of Georgia, the Creeks wanted to stay in what was left of their ancestral domain in Alabama. Following the Removal Act, whites moved into Creek territory. The Creeks protested to Secretary of War Eaton. "We are weak and . . . [whites] daily rob us of our property." They reminded the secretary that the US government had pledged to protect them and their land. But Eaton replied that there was nothing the administration could do; the Creeks had to leave for a new home beyond the Mississippi. They had no powerful white friends who could plead their cause—their welcome of the missionaries had been lukewarm. In despair, in March 1832, they signed a treaty which, as Michael Green writes, marked "the end of the recognized existence" of the Creek nation east of the Mississippi. The Creek National Council ceded to the United States all the nation's land in Alabama. In return, the Creeks received a tract in Oklahoma and each Creek family was granted a plot of land in Alabama (just 40 percent of the 5,200,000 acres the nation was ceding). The treaty stipulated that those who chose to stay would be subject to the laws of Alabama, and they would be protected from white intrusion by the federal government. Emigration to Oklahoma would be voluntary, and the United States would provide food for the emigrants during their journey and for a year after their arrival.[35]

But there were no emigrants. The Creeks wanted to stay on their ancestral land, even though they would lose their government and be subject to the white government of Alabama. If the Jackson administration had honored its pledge to keep white intruders off the remaining Creek land, their situation "would not have been so desperate," remarks Grant Foreman, a leading expert on Indian removal.[36] But it didn't. Jackson wanted the Creeks to leave Alabama. Some Creeks never received the promised plots; others did, only to be evicted by whites. The intruders could "steal Creek property with impunity," Claudio Saunt writes, "since native people were not allowed to testify in Alabama state courts ... County sheriffs, accompanied by state militia and armed volunteers, arrested Creeks who fought back." The Creeks had decided to trust the US government. "Considering their previous experience in such matters, one wonders why," writes another leading authority. "The only apparent explanation is that the alternative to believing the unbelievable was to give up their hope of retaining their home ... For most Creeks, it was intolerable ... Homeless and hungry, many simply scattered into the woods to subsist on whatever they could find."[37] The Jackson administration continued to press the Creeks to leave Alabama. In December 1834, a first party of 630 Creeks left, under US supervision; 460 made it to Oklahoma, the others died *en route* or fled. Another party of 511 departed the following December; we don't know how many died during that trek. The great majority of the Creeks remained in Alabama, destitute because whites had stolen their plots. In May 1836, a group of Creeks rose in revolt. This was, for the Jackson administration, a godsend. The rebels were swiftly crushed by the army and the militia, and immediately deported, in chains, west of the Mississippi, together with their families. When the first group reached Montgomery at the beginning of their long trek, a local newspaper wrote, with surprising empathy, "The spectacle was ... truly melancholy. To see the remnants of a once mighty people fettered and chained together forced to depart from the land of their fathers into a country unknown to them, is of itself sufficient to move the stoutest heart."[38] But President Martin Van Buren (1837–41) seized the opportunity provided by the revolt to fulfill Jackson's vision of an Alabama peopled only by whites and their enslaved Blacks: he ordered that all the Creeks be deported to Oklahoma. By late 1837, only a few hundred Creeks were left in Alabama: some hid in swamps, the others worked on the farms of white masters as day laborers, sharecroppers or slaves.

The Supreme Court

Unlike the Creeks, the Cherokees could call on powerful white friends for assistance. Principal Chief John Ross corresponded with Jeremiah Evarts of the American Board about challenging Georgia's assertion of jurisdiction over the Cherokee nation. In December 1830, William Wirt, one of the country's most prominent constitutional lawyers, filed suit before the Supreme Court, *Cherokee Nation vs Georgia*, claiming that Georgia was violating the Cherokees' rights guaranteed by federal treaties.

In March 1831, the justices rendered their four to two verdict (the seventh justice was sick). Chief Justice John Marshall stated that "If Courts were permitted to indulge their sympathies, a case better calculated to excite them can scarcely be imagined." Marshall accepted Wirt's argument that the Cherokees were "a distinct political society, . . . capable of managing its own affairs and governing itself," but, he added, they were a "domestic dependent nation," not a sovereign state entitled to bring a suit before the court.[39] The court, therefore, refused to hear the case because it decided that the Cherokees had no standing—not because it rejected their argument that Georgia's action was unconstitutional. The eminent *North American Review* argued that by its words "The Court . . . intimate very strongly that their opinion on the merit of the case is in favor of the Indians."[40]

The Cherokees dared hope. The court might listen to their plight if they could reframe their case so that they had standing. In December 1830 just such an opportunity had arisen. In an attempt to target missionaries who were ardent opponents of removal, Georgia had enacted a law requiring whites living in Cherokee country to obtain a license from the state; those who violated the law would be sentenced to a minimum of four years hard labor. With the support of the American Board, two missionaries—Samuel Worcester and Elizur Butler—flouted the law in order to build a case against Georgia. They were arrested and sentenced to four years hard labor. They appealed to the Supreme Court. The court accepted the case and on March 3, 1832, Chief Justice Marshall issued the court's six to one decision. The Cherokees had "exclusive" authority over their territory, "which is not only protected but guaranteed by the United States." Georgia had no sovereignty over the Cherokees; therefore, the law under which the missionaries had been convicted was "void . . . The acts of Georgia," Marshall concluded, "are repugnant to the Constitution, laws, and treaties of the United States."[41]

"It is a glorious news," the editor of the *Cherokee Phoenix*, Elias Boudinot, exulted. "It is a great triumph."[42] But the victory was hollow. Georgia denied the Supreme Court's jurisdiction and refused to release the two missionaries. The Supreme Court had adjourned, and it would not reconvene until January 1833. What would happen then was very murky, a riddle. "General law governing federal judicial and executive power over the states was unclear," writes a knowledgeable scholar. As Wirt explained to the Cherokees and their supporters, the plaintiffs would have to obtain a contempt decree from the Supreme Court ordering the state to obey its order. If Georgia refused, the missionaries would have to petition the state's governor, Wilson Lumpkin, to release them. If Lumpkin refused, then the missionaries could call on the president of the United States to enforce the Supreme Court's judgment. Wirt himself was not sure whether the president was obligated to enforce the court's decision. If the president refused, the missionaries' only recourse would be to appeal to Congress, which could initiate impeachment proceedings against the president.[43] Meanwhile, it was likely that Jackson would win the November 1832 presidential elections and few believed that, if elected, he would force Georgia to obey the Supreme Court. In private, he referred to the ruling as "stillborn," but in public he said nothing, unwilling to give his political foes a potent issue.[44]

"The public is as fully appraised as it can ever be of our *grievances*," Boudinot lamented in August 1832, "and yet never was it more silent than at present."[45] For white Americans, including the National Republican opposition, there were more important issues, foremost Jackson's veto of the bill to recharter the Bank of the United States and the debate over the tariff. In July 1832, the US congress had approved a tariff that retained high import duties, over the vehement objections of South Carolina. In mid-November, after the presidential elections and before the Supreme Court reconvened, South Carolina nullified the tariff. At stake now, for white Americans, was much more than the welfare of a few thousand Indians: if further provoked, Georgia might support South Carolina, and other states from the lower South might follow suit. It was imperative to isolate South Carolina. Even the Cherokees' friends abandoned them: in late December, the American Board sent two letters: one, to Worcester and Butler, the two imprisoned missionaries, urging them to seek a pardon. And another to Principal Chief Ross, urging him to accept the inevitable—removal. The two missionaries did as requested, received a pardon, and instructed their lawyers to withdraw their case from the Supreme Court.[46] Georgia was appeased and South Carolina was isolated. The white men had resolved the crisis. The Cherokees had lost once again.

The Trail of Tears

In June 1830, following the enactment of the Removal Act, Georgia extended its laws over the Cherokees and confiscated their land, leaving each family only a small plot. Many Cherokees were then evicted from their homes by white invaders, robbed, and beaten. The Georgia Guard, a special militia created by the state to police the Cherokee territory, "seized every opportunity to steal or vandalize Cherokee property and insult or abuse Cherokee people."[47] As Chief Justice Marshall had ruled, Georgia's actions violated the US treaties with the Cherokees, but President Jackson refused to provide the federal protection the government owed the Cherokees, and he approved Georgia's illegal decision to extend its laws over Cherokee territory; he also halted the payment to the Cherokee General Council of the annuities due for earlier land cessions. Jackson's goal and Georgia's goal were the same: to make life impossible for the Cherokees so that they would "voluntarily" agree to removal; it would be their choice to self-deport.

On one point, all Cherokee leaders agreed: they could not fight the aggressors with arms because they would be crushed. What, then, should they do? Principal Chief John Ross, who enjoyed the support of an overwhelming majority of Cherokees, advocated passive resistance. He believed, Perdue and Green write, that "the goodwill of the American people and the institutions of the American government would ultimately join in the affirmation of Cherokee sovereignty."[48] Ross even proposed to Jackson that the Cherokees would cede most of their territory to Georgia, retaining only a strip where they would be allowed to live unmolested for a few more years; then they would dissolve their tribal government and become US citizens with full rights—that is, the rights of white people.[49] It was a nonstarter. The Georgians had no intention of accepting the Cherokees as equals. "The utmost of rights and privileges which public opinion would concede to Indians," Georgia's governor George Troup had explained, "would fix them in a middle station, between the negro and the white man." Inevitably, they "would gradually sink to the condition of the former—a point of degeneracy below which they could not fall."[50] For white Georgians, the problem was not the existence of an autonomous Cherokee nation in the territory they coveted, the problem was simply the presence of Indians in their midst. They wanted the Cherokees gone. And so did Jackson. They wanted ethnic cleansing.

A minority of Cherokees—the Treaty Party—disagreed with Ross because they had concluded, reluctantly, that passive resistance was futile and the nation had no alternative but to emigrate. Among them was Boudinot, the editor of the *Cherokee Phoenix*, who in the wake of the House approval of the Removal Bill in May 1830 had asked: "Who would trust his life and fortune to such a faithless nation?"[51] The Supreme Court's decision in March 1832 had given the Treaty Party a moment of hope, but with Worcester's and Butler's surrender, hope turned to despair. Over the next three years the leaders of the Treaty Party tried to convince Principal Chief Ross to negotiate a removal treaty on the best terms possible. Finally in December 1835, they colluded with the Jackson administration and signed the Treaty of New Echota, consenting to the removal of the Cherokee nation to Oklahoma.

This was treason. The leaders of the Treaty Party had acted against the will of the majority of the Cherokees who supported Ross, and behind the back of the Cherokee government. While some in the Treaty Party may have been motivated by animus toward Ross and the hope of gaining preferential treatment from the Americans, they all had accepted the reality that Ross and his followers refused to face: there was no future for the Cherokees in Georgia. Passive resistance can work if it is carried out by a great many, as in India against British rule; or if it can stir sympathy among the dominant group, or embarrass it internationally, as did the civil rights movement in the United States in the 1960s. But there were just a few thousand Cherokees, and white Americans of good will toward them—always a minority—were increasingly focused on other issues, notably the fight against slavery. Foreign countries paid no attention to the drama of the Cherokees; not even the British, who vied with the United States for moral superiority, expressed any interest. The British legation in Washington filed only two reports about the Removal Bill. While one report asserted that "the treatment of the Indians in the United States cannot be a matter of indifference to the British government,"[52] the evidence indicates that it was in fact a matter of supreme indifference for the legation, for the government in London, and for the British press. The London *Times'* critique of Jackson's Indian policy in his December 1829 message to Congress was a grand overture followed by silence. Both the congressional debate and the removal went unreported. Some Europeans who witnessed the plight of the Indians were critical—"if the American character may be judged by their conduct in this matter," wrote British novelist Frances Trollope, "they are most lamentably deficient in every feeling of honour and integrity." But these were isolated cries.[53]

The evidence that the Treaty of New Echota was fraudulent and that the men who had signed it represented only a small minority of the Cherokees, was overwhelming and well publicized, but the US Senate approved the treaty on May 16, 1836, with one vote more than the required two-thirds, and a week later, on May 23, Jackson signed it. The president had obtained what he wanted: he would claim that the Cherokees had freely agreed to removal. Henceforth any Cherokee who refused to emigrate would be violating a solemn treaty, and the US government would be justified in using force to make them comply.

The treaty stipulated that the Cherokees must leave within two years of ratification, that is by May 23, 1838. In those two years, about 2,000 Cherokees emigrated to Oklahoma with the leaders of the Treaty Party. In late May 1838, General Winfield Scott, who commanded the Eastern Department of the Army, with 7,000 soldiers, militia, and volunteers fell on the approximately 14,000 Cherokees who remained in Georgia. "These in general were taken just as they were found by the soldiers, without permission to stop either for friends or property," an eyewitness, the missionary Daniel Butrick, wrote in his diary. "Women absent from their families on visit, or for other purposes, were seized, and men far from their wives and children were not allowed to return and also children being forced from home were dragged off among strangers." The prisoners were herded into unsanitary stockades by soldiers using "the same language as if driving hogs," goading them forward "with their bayonets." White mobs seized everything that was left behind.[54] "Perhaps the most brutal aspect of the internment of the Cherokees," Ronald Satz remarks, "were the acts of rape, bestiality and murder committed by the 'lawless rabble' and some soldiers."[55] Then the trek of almost 1,000 miles to Oklahoma began, under army escort. As many as 4,000 of the 14,000 Cherokees died of malnutrition, exposure, cholera and other illnesses in the stockades as they awaited deportation and as they trudged along the "Trail of Tears." The suffering of the Cherokees was indescribable, a soldier who escorted them recalled. "The trail of the exiles was a trail of death ... Murder is murder and somebody must answer, somebody ... must explain the four thousand silent graves that mark the trail of the Cherokees to their exile."[56]

Black Hawk War

The more than 40,000 Native Americans who lived in the old Northwest contemplated the prospect of emigration to the trans-Mississippi west with despair. The 2,500 Indians in Ohio—fragments of once powerful tribes—were among the first to go, to Iowa or Kansas. Among them were Shawnees who lived in a small reservation at Wapakoneta in the northwest corner of Ohio. Geographically separated from the main body of the nation, they had chosen neutrality when the United States declared war on England in 1812. Told by US officials that if they remained neutral "they would be considered enemies of the United States," they had sent their young men to fight for the Americans. After the war they had sought to assure their white neighbors "that they could fit into American life." These efforts backfired. As they produced "growing harvests of corn and wheat or sold increased numbers of livestock at local and regional markets," white Ohians began to worry that they were "'fitting in too well'" and would never leave. The Removal Act settled the question. Jackson's envoys descended on Wapakoneta, warning the Shawnees that if they refused to leave they would get no legal protection and "might be beaten or killed by white men" with impunity. In August 1831, the Shawnees of Wapakoneta signed a removal treaty. The next year they were gone.[57]

The largest Indian group in the Northwest were the 6,000 Sauks and Foxes, two closely associated tribes living in Illinois. In 1804, General Harrison, Jefferson's governor of Indiana territory, had concluded a treaty with a delegation of five Sauk and Fox chiefs. In this treaty, the chiefs, who had not been authorized by their tribes to sell any land, ceded to the United States all their vast holdings east of the Mississippi, but with the proviso that the Sauks and Foxes did not have to vacate their land until the federal government decided white settlers needed it. In exchange, the Indians would receive $2,234.50 (c. $48,200) worth of goods on the spot and an annuity of $1,000 in perpetuity. Even by the standards of the Jefferson administration this was a particularly abusive treaty. It is likely, historian Anthony Wallace explains, that the chiefs had believed that the treaty was simply a formal gesture, as in "earlier French and British practice," that did not threaten the tribes' right of occupancy.[58]

It was not until the late 1820s that the US government opened the Sauk and Fox land to public purchase and the wave of white settlement swept over these northern Indians. It was time for them to leave, the Adams administration urged in 1828. Most did, settling in Iowa, but a Sauk chief, Black Hawk, balked. "You asked, 'Who I am,'" he told General Edmund Gaines, who commanded the US army's Western Department, and Illinois Governor John Reynolds in June 1831. "I am a Sauk; my fathers were great men and I wish to remain where the bones of my fathers are laid. I desire to be buried with my fathers. Why then should I leave their fields?"[59] The answer was clear: because of the power of the United States and the six companies of soldiers and 1,500 militiamen who accompanied Gaines and Reynolds. Very reluctantly, Black Hawk abandoned his homeland and emigrated to Iowa. But in April 1832, he led a band of about 1,000 Sauks and Foxes back across the Mississippi. They wanted to return to their land in northern Illinois. The band included approximately 500 women and children. Black Hawk did not seek war. He believed, wrongly, that if the Americans attacked, the other tribes of the region would come to his defense, and he believed, against all evidence, that the British would render assistance.

On May 14, the band encountered the first detachment of Illinois militia, several hundred men strong. Black Hawk sent three emissaries to invite the Americans to a parley. The militia took them prisoner and then attacked Black Hawk's encampment. The Indians fought back and the Americans fled—it was a "panic-stricken rout."[60] For several weeks, Black Hawk's band wandered in Illinois and Wisconsin, winning a few more skirmishes. Only the poor performance of the militia enabled them to survive that long; facing superior numbers and realizing that no one—neither Indians nor British—would come to their aid, Black Hawk and his people began to retreat toward the Mississippi and the relative safety of Iowa. Near the mouth of the Bad Axe River, on August 2, the remnants of the band—perhaps 150 warriors and 350 women and children—were attacked as they sought to cross the Mississippi. As many as 300 were killed. The militia scalped many of the Indians and tore strips of flesh off their backs to make razor straps. The survivors— those who were able to reach the Iowa shore—were killed or captured by the Dakotas (eastern or Santee Sioux), eager to settle old scores and please the mighty Americans.

The slaughter served as a warning to the other tribes of the Northwest to obey the War Department as it ordered them across the Mississippi. Thus, in September 1832, six weeks after the massacre of Bad Axe, the Ho-Chunks (also known as Winnebagos) were forced to trade their fertile land in Wisconsin for a tract in Iowa where they were surrounded by hostile tribes who saw them as intruders. "Father," a Ho-Chunk chief told an Indian agent, "you know better than we do that the land you gave us west of the Mississippi is occupied by the Sacs [Sauks] and Foxes, the Sioux and other tribes, and you know it [is] impossible for us to go and live there, because all these natives are jealous of us."[61] The Ho-Chunks were repeatedly relocated over the following years as the War Department sought to find a place for them that was free of hostile tribes and was not yet coveted by white settlers—a place, that is, where no one wanted to live, such as their reservation at Long Prairie, in central Minnesota, where, a government agent reported, the lands were "covered with swamps and almost impenetrable thickets." The shock of repeated dislocations and malnutrition sapped the strength of the Ho-Chunks. In 1860 they numbered 3,500, down from 5,000 before removal.[62]

Like the Ho-Chunks, the other tribes of the Northwest followed the orders of the War Department, abandoned their ancestral lands, emigrated to the Trans-Mississippi West, and were shunted around according to the whims of the US authorities and the demands of white settlers. Some Potawatomi Indians, however, dragged their feet after they had signed their removal treaty. In August 1838, the US army rounded them up. The Potawatomis offered no resistance. A journalist described their departure: "On September 4 they were lined up, some afoot, some on ponies followed by the wagons, and all heavily guarded with a lot of guards at the rear with bayonets, which were often used to keep the weak ones in the procession. Before starting the torch was applied to their village, so that they might see their homes destroyed and they would not want to return." Then "this gruesome procession, nearly three miles long, like a funeral procession, which in reality it was, started on its final journey."[63]

During the Jackson administration, almost 46,000 Indians were torn from their land and deported west of the Mississippi. Jackson's successors completed the task. In the South, where white planters wanted the Indians' lands for their lucrative cotton plantations built on chattel slavery, the ethnic cleansing was almost total. "The removal of Cherokees, Choctaws, Chickasaws, and Creeks was vital to King Cotton's rise," Ostler remarks.[64] In the North, however, several thousand Indians escaped deportation, mainly in the Upper Great Lakes region and in the Upper Mississippi Valley, where the white population was sparse and the land less valuable. Except for the Black Hawk War, the 1836 Creek revolt, and the Seminoles, the Indians mounted no armed resistance to this ethnic cleansing.

The Seminoles

The United States had annexed Spanish Florida in 1821. Five thousand Seminoles and several hundred Blacks lived in the fertile parts of the territory, particularly in the northeast, where they grew crops, raised cattle, and hunted. The land they inhabited, the new territorial governor, William DuVal declared, was too good for the Indians;

the Seminoles should be removed and the land given to white settlers.[65] The 1823 Treaty of Moultrie Creek stipulated that the Seminoles would be relocated to a reservation in central Florida where the land, DuVal wrote, "is by far the poorest and most miserable region I ever beheld"[66] [Map 7].

Moved into their new territory, the Seminoles became a nuisance to their white neighbors. The 1823 treaty had deprived them "of their cultivated fields and of a region of country fruitful of game," the Florida Legislative Council explained to the US Congress in 1832, confining them to "a wilderness, where the earth yields no corn, and where even the precarious advantages of the chase are in a great measure denied them. . . . They are thus left the wretched alternative of starving within their limits, or roaming among the whites, to prey upon their cattle. Many in the nation, it seems, annually die of starvation; but . . . the much greater proportion of those who are threatened with want, leave their boundaries in pursuit of the means of subsistence."[67] There were two possible solutions: the first, to grant the Seminoles fertile land, an idea that would never pass muster; the other, to remove them altogether, a solution that accorded with white American values and was what the Legislative Council demanded.

Removal was all the more necessary because escaped slaves were given refuge on the reservation. A January 1834 petition to President Jackson from white Floridians claimed that four-fifths of the more than 500 Blacks living with the Seminoles were runaways or their descendants. The Indians offered them sanctuary. As long as the Seminoles remained in Florida, the petitioners argued, "the owners of slaves . . . cannot for a moment, in anything like security, enjoy the possession of this description of property."[68]

The Removal Act solved the problem. In May 1832, President Jackson's representative forced the Treaty of Payne's Landing on a handful of Seminole chiefs who pledged that within three years of ratification the Seminoles would move to Oklahoma. The senate ratified the treaty in April 1834 and US officials began pressing the Seminoles to leave Florida without delay. When the Seminoles resisted, the whites in Florida—more than 20,000[69]—grew increasingly impatient, and US officials threatened to send in the army. In December 1835, after months of rising tension, the Seminoles struck back, annihilating a column of 109 US soldiers (only three survived) and attacking several plantations, burning crops, houses and—to the whites' horror—liberating several hundred slaves. The second Seminole War had begun.[70] (Jackson's invasion of Florida in 1818 was considered the first Seminole War.)

Niles' Weekly Register predicted that "the miserable creatures will be speedily swept from the face of the earth,"[71] but the fighting continued until 1842. It was a low intensity guerrilla war in which the Seminoles' only advantages were the topography—the swamps and hammocks of Florida—their knowledge of the terrain, their courage, and their fierce will to remain on their land. They were hunted by several thousand US soldiers, militia, and volunteers; at times the Navy helped. The regulars and the citizen soldiers regarded each other with contempt. In early 1841, the government decided to use only regular troops because the militia was ineffective and expensive. Almost half the US army— 5,000 soldiers—was sent to Florida. Most soldiers and officers hated the war because of the climate and the swamps of Florida; a few, because they considered it unjust.[72]

As groups of Seminoles were captured or surrendered, they were sent to detention camps and from there, deported to Oklahoma. By 1841, only a few hundred Seminoles remained in Florida; divided into small, mobile bands they continued to launch occasional attacks. To end the intractable conflict, US military commanders in the territory urged the government to allow the remaining Seminoles to stay in Florida. President Jackson and his successor Martin van Buren had been intransigent: they wanted every Seminole deported and every fugitive slave returned to the white masters. But white Americans had tired of the dirty war in the Florida swamps, which cost money and brought no glory. Finally, in 1842 a new president, John Tyler, relented: a reservation in southwestern Florida was set aside for the Seminoles.

And so the war ended. According to the government's official tally, it had cost the lives of 1,466 soldiers and sixty-nine sailors, three-quarters of whom succumbed to disease. Of the 30,000 citizen soldiers who served, fifty-six were killed in battle, and a much larger number died of disease. The number of dead Seminoles was not recorded. We know only that more than 3,000 were deported to Oklahoma and a few hundred were able to remain in Florida.

Looking back

The Indian tribes east of the Mississippi initially attempted to stay on their ancestral lands through armed resistance and acculturation. The Cherokees first fought the whites, but by the late eighteenth century they concluded, through bitter experience, that armed resistance was hopeless. They became the foremost proponents of acculturation. They did what the whites asked and more: they adapted to white culture, they became farmers, they created a written language, and they drafted a constitution. And when the whites, during the presidency of Jackson, decided to deport them, still they did not fight. They adopted passive resistance; they appealed to America's conscience.

In describing US-Indian relations, several historians, foremost among them Francis Prucha, focus on what US policymakers said, rather than what they did. The result is a soothing, but distorted picture of US Indian policy. Jackson's principal biographer, Robert Remini, argues that the president sincerely believed that removal was in the Indians' interest and that those Indian leaders who resisted him were greedy men who oppressed their people.[73]

Perhaps Jackson was sincere. Politicians have an uncanny ability to believe whatever is convenient for them. Whatever was in Jackson's heart, we must judge him by his actions. He violated the treaties concluded by the United States with the Indians: instead of protecting the Native Americans, he encouraged the states to trample on their rights. He dismissed the clear evidence that those Indian leaders who opposed removal represented the will of the great majority of their people, and he resorted to fraud and violence to impose removal treaties. He neither created the conditions that would allow the Indians to be safely deported to their new reservations, nor did he bother to protect those Creeks, Choctaws, and Chickasaws who, trusting in the guarantees offered by his administration, chose to remain in Alabama and Mississippi. As Perdue and Green write, "the removal policy ... caused unimaginable suffering, deaths in the thousands, and emotional pain that lingers to this day. The words 'oppressive, cruel, and unjust' do not capture its horror."[74]

And yet, Jackson did not invent the policy. Nor did he impose it on the unwitting white American people. The Washington, Adams, Jefferson, and Madison administrations had claimed that the goal of US Indian policy was to civilize the Indians so that they could assimilate with the American people. Some American leaders seem to have believed in this goal—for example, Madison's Secretary of War Crawford, who wanted the government to encourage intermarriage between whites and Indians.[75] But the policy had an obvious flaw: the Indians lived on land white Americans wanted. Pressured by land speculators and settlers, President Washington and his successors insisted that the Indians cede land at a fast pace, and they used fraud and force when necessary. This was the pillar of US Indian policy long before Jackson became president. With characteristic honesty, John Quincy Adams remarked in 1828, "we have scarcely given them [the Indians] time to build their wigwams before we are called upon by our own people to drive them out again. My own opinion is that the most benevolent course towards them would be to give them the rights and subject them to the duties of citizens, as a part of our own people. But even this the people of the States within which they are situated will not permit."[76] This was the cancer at the core of the United States' Indian policy: white Americans refused to accept Indians, however acculturated they might be, as equals. The Cherokees—who had traveled furthest along the road of acculturation—had to be deported not because they were uncivilized but because they were Indians. Removal had been the policy of the United States from the very beginning, despite the uplifting rhetoric of successive administrations and the good intentions of some US officials. Without Jackson ethnic cleansing east of the Mississippi might have taken a little longer, it might have been less brutal, but the policy would not have changed. It represented the will of white America.

Indian removal, John Quincy Adams wrote in his diary in 1841, "is among the heinous sins of this nation, for which, I believe, God will one day bring them to judgement. . . . [It is a] sickening mass of putrefaction."[77] It was not, however, the crime of a particular president. It was the crime of the American people, of their racism and their greed.

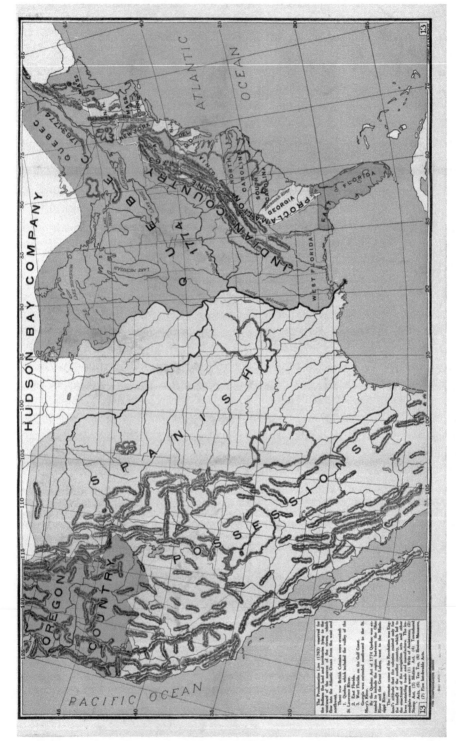

Map 1 North America at the Beginning of the American War of Independence.

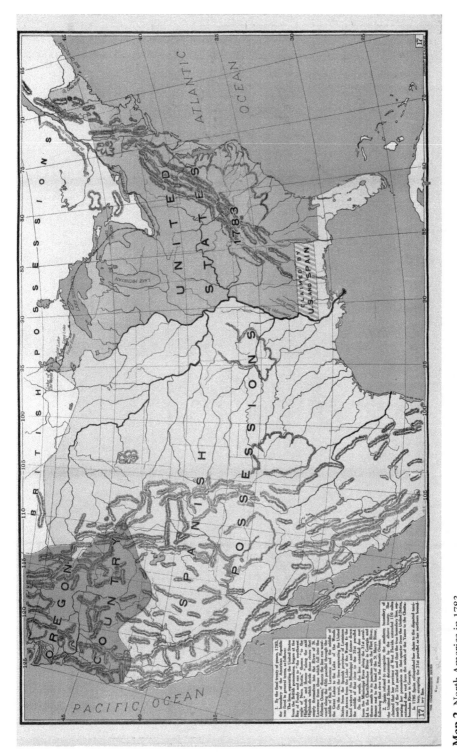

Map 2 North America in 1783.

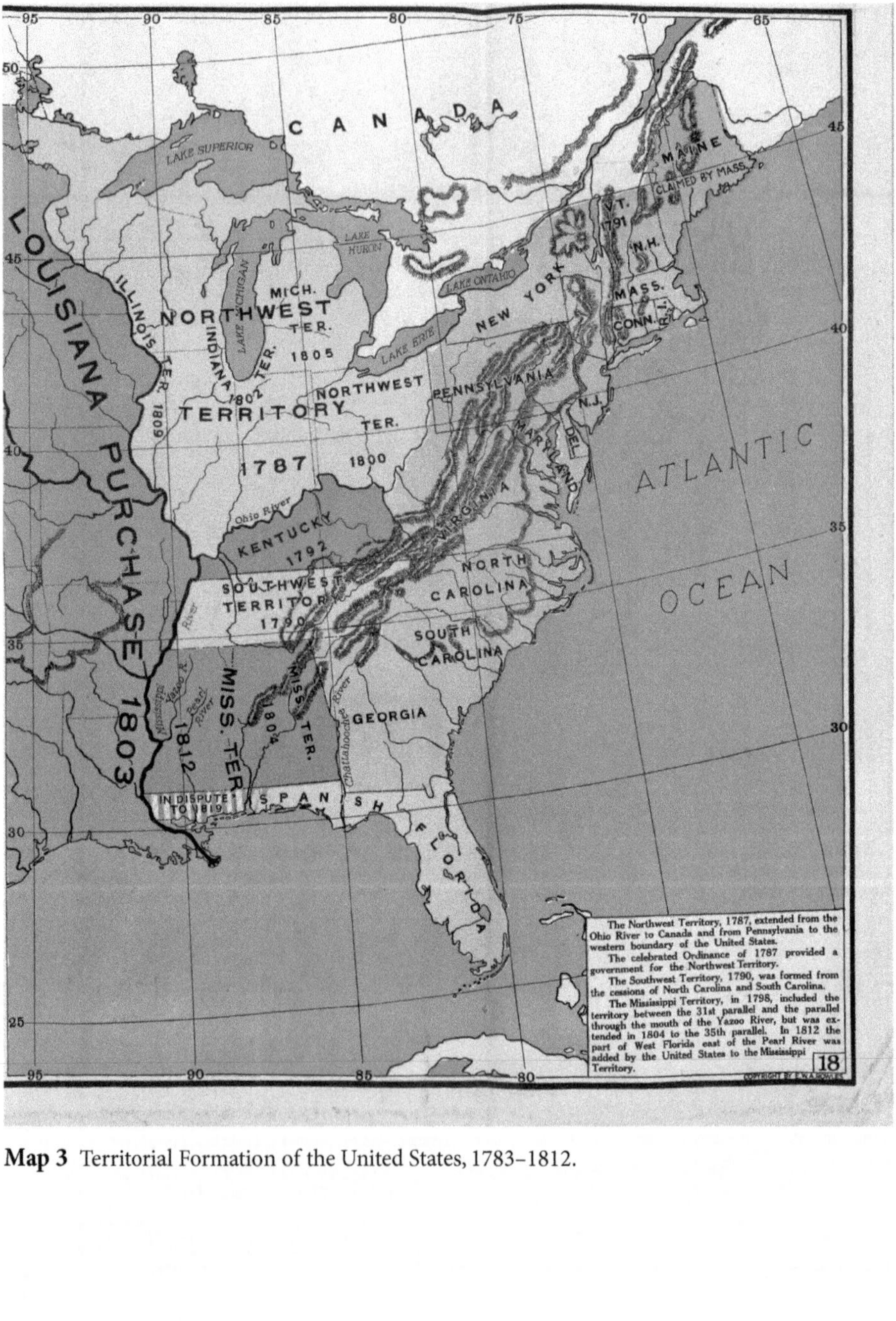
CANADA
LAKE SUPERIOR
LAKE MICHIGAN
LAKE HURON
LAKE ONTARIO
LAKE ERIE
MAINE
CLAIMED BY MASS.
VT. 1791
N.H.
MASS.
CONN.
R.I.
NEW YORK
PENNSYLVANIA
N.J.
DEL.
MARYLAND
VIRGINIA
NORTH CAROLINA
SOUTH CAROLINA
GEORGIA
KENTUCKY 1792
SOUTHWEST TERRITORY 1790
NORTHWEST TERRITORY 1787
MICH. TER. 1805
INDIANA TER. 1802
ILLINOIS TER. 1809
NORTHWEST TER. 1800
Ohio River
LOUISIANA PURCHASE 1803
MISS. TER.
MISS. TER. 1804
1812
Yazoo R.
Pearl River
Chattahoochee River
IN DISPUTE TO 1819
SPANISH FLORIDA
ATLANTIC OCEAN
The Northwest Territory, 1787, extended from the Ohio River to Canada and from Pennsylvania to the western boundary of the United States.
The celebrated Ordinance of 1787 provided a government for the Northwest Territory.
The Southwest Territory, 1790, was formed from the cessions of North Carolina and South Carolina.
The Mississippi Territory, in 1798, included the territory between the 31st parallel and the parallel through the mouth of the Yazoo River, but was extended in 1804 to the 35th parallel. In 1812 the part of West Florida east of the Pearl River was added by the United States to the Mississippi Territory.
18
COPYRIGHT BY E.W.A. ROWLES

Map 3 Territorial Formation of the United States, 1783–1812.

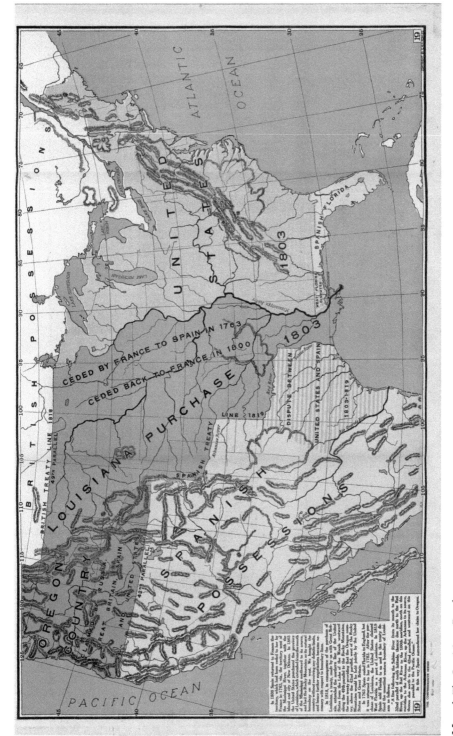

Map 4 The Louisiana Purchase.

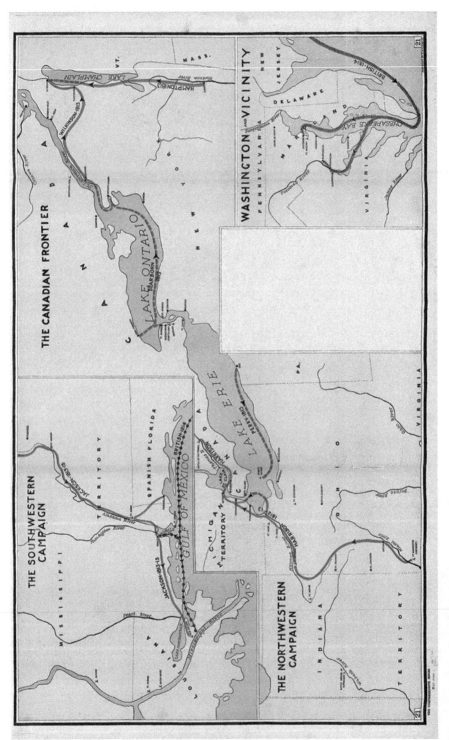

Map 5 The War of 1812—The Four Important Theaters.

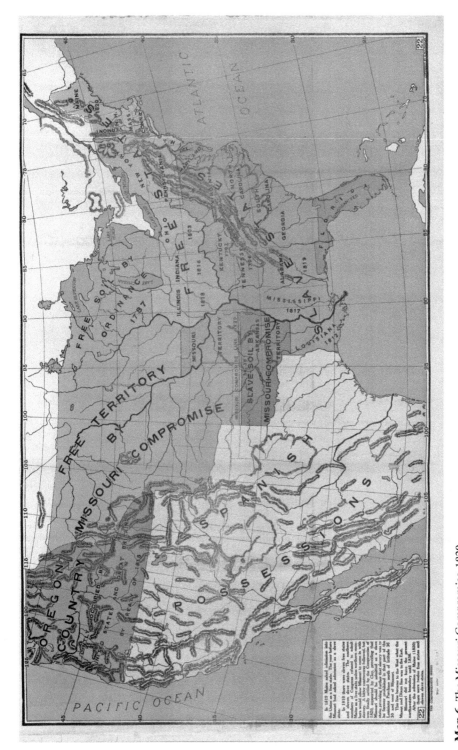

Map 6 The Missouri Compromise, 1820.

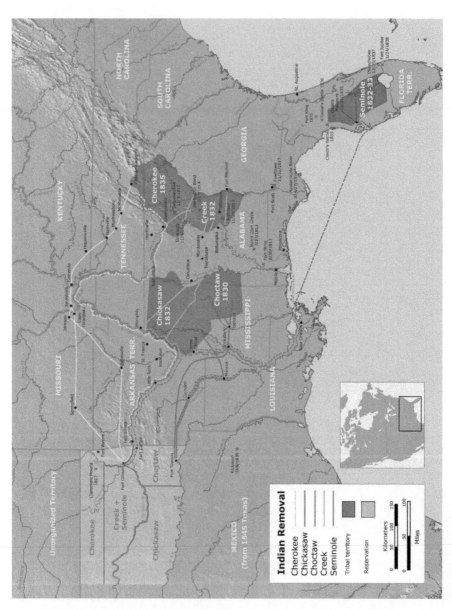

Map 7 Ethnic Cleansing East of the Mississippi.

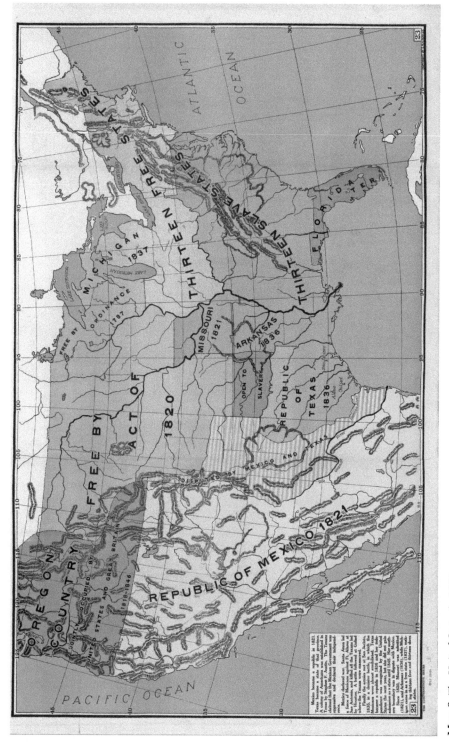

The following text appears within the map image:

PACIFIC OCEAN

ATLANTIC OCEAN

OREGON COUNTRY

JOINTLY OCCUPIED BY UNITED STATES AND GREAT BRITAIN 1818-1846

FREE BY ACT OF 1820

REPUBLIC OF MEXICO 1821

DISPUTED BY MEXICO AND TEXAS

REPUBLIC OF TEXAS 1836

OPEN TO SLAVERY

MISSOURI 1821

ARKANSAS 1836

FREE BY ORDINANCE 1787

MICHIGAN 1837

THIRTEEN FREE STATES

THIRTEEN SLAVE STATES

FLORIDA TER.

LAKE SUPERIOR
LAKE MICHIGAN
LAKE HURON

Map 8 The United States in 1837.

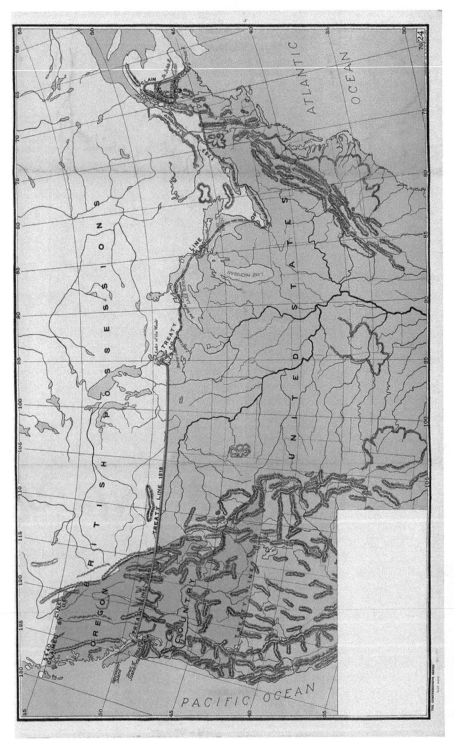

Map 9 Settlement of Northern Boundary Disputes.

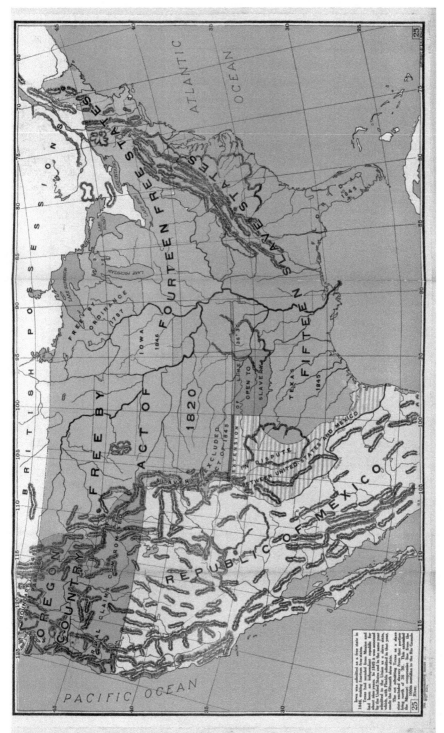

Map 10 The United States at Beginning of Mexican War, 1846.

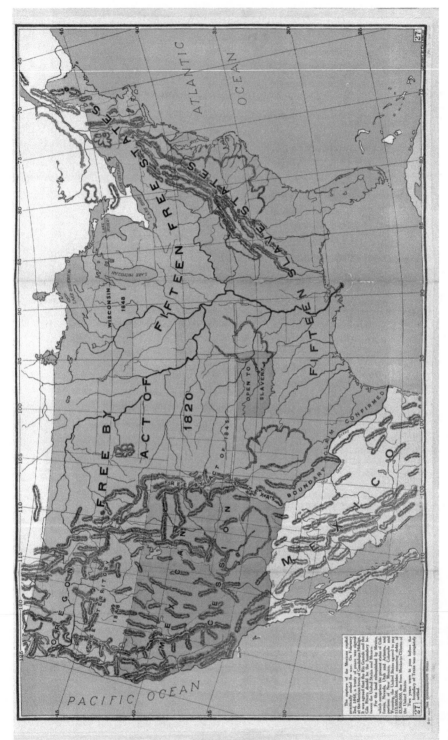

Map 11 Results of the Mexican War, 1848.

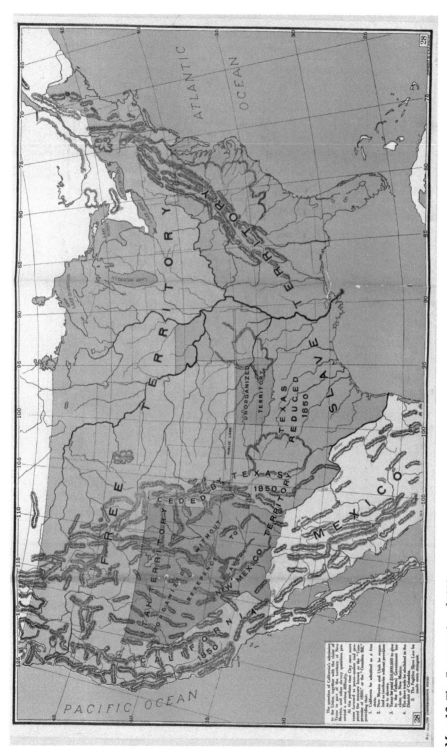

Map 12 The Compromise of 1850.

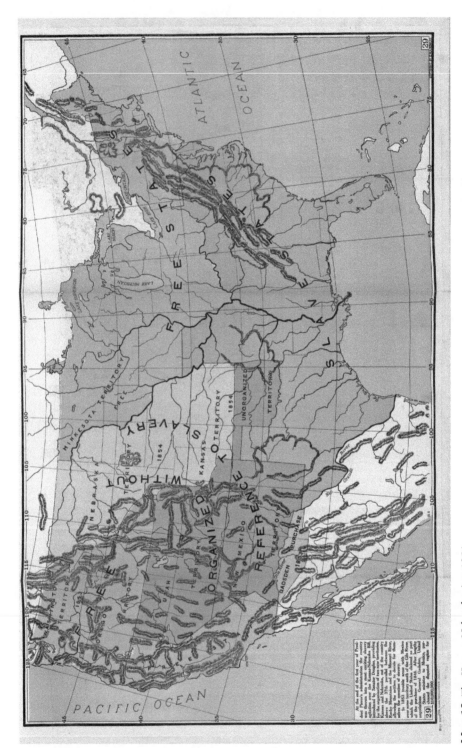

Map 13 The Kansas-Nebraska Act, 1854.

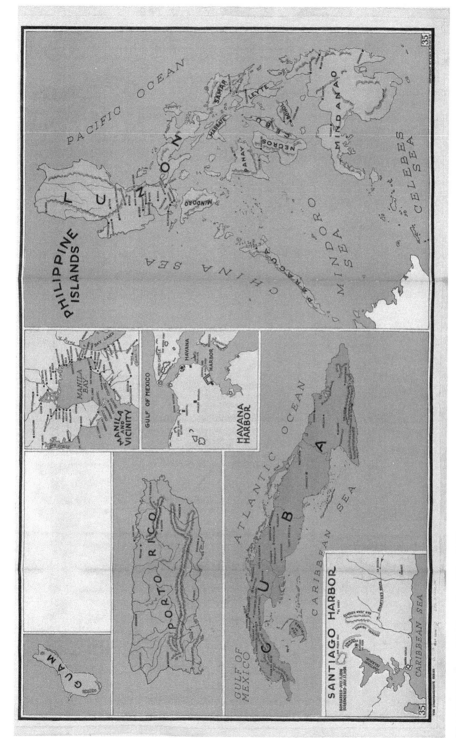

Map 14 The Spanish-American War, 1898.

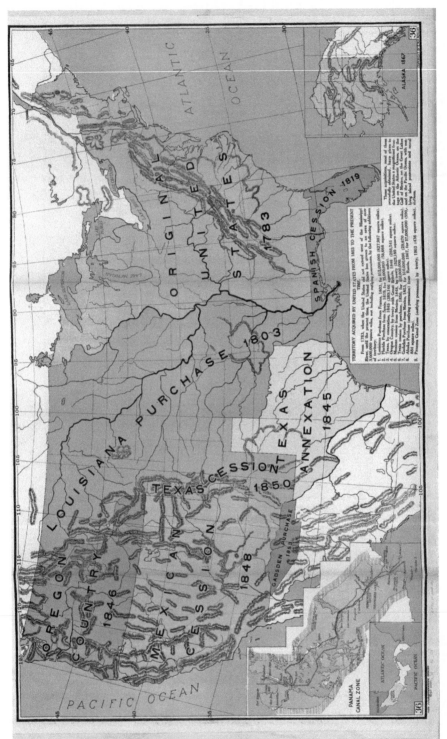

Map 15 The Territorial Growth of Continental United States.

CHAPTER 8
MANIFEST DESTINY

The war of 1812 led to the collapse of the Federalist Party, which had opposed the war. In the 1816 presidential elections, James Monroe sailed to victory, while the Federalist candidate carried only three states. In Congress, the Republicans enjoyed overwhelming majorities. For all practical purposes, the two-party system no longer existed. "The real or apparent moderation of party spirit has caused the present to be called 'the era of good feelings,'" *Niles' Weekly Register* noted in 1817.[1] Below the surface, there were strains— intraparty squabbles, as well as antipathy between the non-slave states and the South, where slavery was ever more entrenched due to the surge in the cultivation of cotton. By 1824, the good feelings had evaporated as the election of John Quincy Adams to the presidency triggered the frenzy over the "corrupt bargain" between Adams and Clay. For the next four years Andrew Jackson and his cohorts had one overriding goal: to render Adams a one-term president by opposing his policies, irrespective of their merits. They succeeded: John Quincy Adams, one of the most intelligent and intellectually honest presidents of the United States, was trounced by Jackson in 1828. In the process, a new party led by Andrew Jackson, soon to call itself the "Democratic Republican" or simply the Democratic Party, would be created.

Sectional antipathies and personal rivalries did not weaken the consensus on territorial expansion beyond the borders: all factions agreed about the desirability of acquiring Cuba, and President John Quincy Adams was as eager to purchase Texas from Mexico as his successor, Jackson, would be.

This consensus collapsed, however, in the 1830s, during the presidency of Jackson, as the rift between free and slave states deepened. The debate over Indian Removal exacerbated these sectional antipathies as did—to a greater degree—the fight over the tariff: the South favored low import duties, most free states wanted to raise them. Above all, however, was the problem of slavery.

Abroad, slavery was losing ground: the Spanish American countries were emancipating their enslaved people, as did Britain in 1833. At home, the white population of the free states was increasing faster than that of the South, widening the North's advantage in the House of Representatives. Suddenly, a threat to the South appeared: on January 1, 1831, the first issue of *The Liberator* heralded the arrival of militant abolitionism. "I will be as harsh as truth and as uncompromising as justice," the editor, William Lloyd Garrison, warned in his first editorial. "I will not equivocate—I will not excuse—I will not retreat a single inch—AND I WILL BE HEARD!"[2] Seven months later, a young enslaved preacher, Nat Turner, led a revolt in Southampton County, Virginia; fifty-seven whites were slain. Never before in the country's history had enslaved people killed so many whites. White southerners were certain that northern abolitionists had inspired Turner. Their fears deepened.

Against this tense backdrop, the American Anti-Slavery Society (AASS) was created in December 1833. It branded slaveowners as sinners. It urged the southern states to abolish slavery at once. It demanded that Congress prohibit slavery in the capital and in the territories, and outlaw the interstate slave trade.

Women were, historian Manisha Sinha writes, "abolition's most effective foot soldiers," and they played a key role in generating the antislavery petitions that flooded Congress. "The fact that women are denied the right of voting for members of Congress is but a poor reason why they *should also* be deprived of the right of petition," a leading abolitionist, Angelina Grimké, declared. White women had participated in the struggle against Indian Removal, and free black women joined the abolitionist crusade, some in prominent roles. Furthermore, women did more than draft petitions and collect signatures in support of abolition: they marched arm in arm, defying howling mobs; they spoke in public meetings; they organized women's branches (most of them interracial) of the AASS. In 1840, a woman was elected to the board of the AASS.[3]

In May 1835, the AASS embarked on what it called "the great postal campaign," inundating the South with abolitionist literature. It was "a pamphleteering effort of unprecedented proportions.... Hysteria swept through the South."[4] As the southerners' sense of insecurity grew, as they felt their grip over the national government slip, they sought refuge in the doctrine of state rights; therefore, in Congress, southern representatives began voting against federal money for internal improvements such as the construction of roads and canals, angering the Free States. And as the AASS petitioned Congress, in May 1836, southern congressmen pushed the Gag Rule through the House: henceforth anti-slavery petitions would be tabled without discussion or debate. It was counterproductive. Abolitionists were a tiny minority in the free states. Most white Americans north of the Mason-Dixon line feared that if the enslaved were freed they would rush north overwhelming their states. But the Gag Rule was a step too far: many white Americans in the free states believed that the South was attacking *their* right of petition. They resented what they increasingly saw as the South's attempt to dominate national politics.

Texas

This is the backdrop of the debate over Texas that roiled the United States in 1836. In the 1820s, Mexico had allowed American colonists (Anglos) into Texas, hoping they would become loyal Mexican citizens, help develop the territory, and protect its inhabitants from the powerful Comanches. By 1835, there were in Texas some 30,000 Anglos, as well as 15,000 Comanches, 5,000 Mexicans, and 5,000 enslaved Blacks owned by the Anglos. Mexico had abolished slavery in 1829, but it had let the decree lapse in 1831. However, the growing abolitionist sentiment in the Mexican Congress sowed insecurity among Anglo slaveowners who were building a prosperous cotton economy based on chattel slavery. (Slavery was definitively abolished in Mexico in 1837.)[5]

In the fall of 1835, some Anglos rose in revolt against Mexico in the name of freedom, including the freedom to own slaves. Had there been no outside interference, the Mexican army would have crushed the revolt. However, weapons and men poured in from the United States in flagrant violation of US neutrality laws. At the battle of San Jacinto, in April 1836, the rebels—most of whom were recent arrivals from the United States—defeated the Mexican army.[6] The overwhelming majority of Anglos wanted Texas to be part of the United States, and the provisional government they established sent two emissaries to Washington to offer annexation. Their request, however, was untimely. While the annexation of Texas had been a national project in the 1820s, by 1836 it appeared to many in the free states to be a southern ploy to annex a vast territory that would be carved into several slave states. No one exemplified this shift more than John Quincy Adams, who as president had sought to purchase Texas, but who as representative from Massachusetts told the House in 1836: "The war now raging in Texas is . . . a war for the re-establishment of slavery where it was abolished, . . . and every possible effort has been made to drive us into the war, on the side of slavery." Addressing Speaker James Polk, a Jackson protégé, Adams lashed out: "Do not you, an Anglo-Saxon, slave-holding exterminator of Indians, from the bottom of your soul hate the Mexican-Spaniard-Indian emancipator of slaves and abolisher of slavery? . . . And what will be your cause in such a war? Aggression, conquest, and the re-establishment of slavery where it has been abolished. In that war, Sir, the banners of freedom will be the banners of Mexico; and your banners, I blush to speak the word, will be the banners of slavery."[7]

As historian Leonard Richards writes, few people in the free states shared Adams' moral indignation, but his stand on Texas was popular. Annexation would mean "more southern Congressmen to vote against the tariff, against national banks, against internal improvements, against antislavery petitions."[8] Furthermore, by 1836 a new political party had emerged. The Whigs were a loose coalition that included the former National Republicans, and they were united by hostility to President Jackson. Like the Democrats, the Whigs, as a party, did not oppose slavery. Unlike the Democrats, most Whigs advocated a protective tariff and federally funded internal improvements and were cautious about territorial expansion. Their most popular leader, charismatic Henry Clay, spoke for most Whigs when he wrote, "I think it better to harmonize what we have, than to introduce a new element of discord into our political partnership, against the consent of existing members of the concern."[9] Like many other Whigs, Clay embraced the idea of "Sister Republics" and expected that Texas would become one, "settled by our race, who will carry there, undoubtedly, our laws, our language and our institutions."[10]

Whig opposition and sectional tensions forced Jackson's hand. When he stepped down in March 1837, his one great achievement in expanding the white American empire had been within the borders—the deportation of Native Americans west of the Mississippi. He had been unable to realize his other burning territorial ambition, the annexation of Texas. During Jackson's two terms, the borders of the United States did not change.

Beyond the acquisition of Texas, Jackson's foreign policy had focused on developing American trade through commercial treaties with governments in Europe, Asia, and Latin America. This policy, which Jackson conducted with skill and, when necessary, restraint, was largely successful. He also succeeded in negotiating with European governments the settlement of claims about the seizures of American ships during the Napoleonic wars.[11]

To the Rio Grande

Rebuffed by the United States, the Republic of Texas declared grandiose borders vis-à-vis Mexico: the Rio Grande from the mouth to the source. Texas and Mexico remained in a state of war, with occasional cross-border raids. Texas' one attempt to seize Santa Fe, on the upper Rio Grande, ended in disaster in 1841. Wisely, the Texans did not try to assert control over the lower course of the river; their reach barely extended beyond the western bank of the Nueces. Both banks of the Rio Grande remained Mexican [Map 8].

Some Tejanos (as Mexicans living in the Texas would be called) had joined the revolt against Mexico. They would soon rue it. For Anglos, Mexicans were, the US chargé reported, "stupid, mongrels, of Spanish, Indian, and Negro blood."[12] Tejanos became a despised and oppressed caste.

For several years, the Texas issue lay dormant in American politics. The economic crisis that engulfed the United States in 1837 doomed the presidency of Jackson's chosen successor, Martin Van Buren. In 1840, Van Buren was defeated by the Whig William Henry Harrison. But Harrison died a month after his inauguration. His successor, John Tyler, was a former Democrat who had clashed with Jackson, left the party and joined the Whigs. But once in the White House he quickly clashed with the Whig majority in Congress. His Whig cabinet resigned in September 1841 except for Secretary of State Daniel Webster, who remained at his post to negotiate a treaty with Britain which, he hoped, would add to his reputation and increase his chances to win the 1844 Whig presidential nomination.

Economic ties between Britain and the United States were very strong: each was the major trading partner of the other. But political relations, never very good, deteriorated sharply in the late 1830s as the long-standing boundary dispute between Maine and New Brunswick flared up. The Webster-Ashburton Treaty, in August 1842, determined that border on terms satisfactory to both countries. The treaty concluded, Webster resigned from the cabinet.

His resignation was welcomed by Tyler who was preparing to embark on a gambit for which Webster had no sympathy: secret negotiations with Texas for its incorporation into the Union. The president sprang a treaty of annexation on the Senate on April 22, 1844.

Tyler's justification was the foreign threat: not from bankrupt Mexico, but from England. London, he said, was trying to foist abolition on Texas and transform it into a British satellite.

The charge contained a grain of truth. Having concluded that Mexico lacked the strength to recover its lost province, British Foreign Secretary George Aberdeen had repeatedly urged the Mexicans to make peace with Texas. Ending the state of war with Mexico would render the Texans less eager to join the United States. An independent

Texas could become an alternate supplier of cotton for England and a buffer protecting Mexico from the United States—London had no wish to see the United States spread its tentacles over Latin America. Aberdeen also hoped that Texas might agree to abolish slavery as part of the peace agreement. This was the extent of the British threat.[13] Tyler may have believed the lurid tales of British plotting spun by his friend Duff Green, an ardent supporter of slavery whom he had sent as an unofficial agent to London, but the notion of a British threat was a most convenient prop to whip up support for the policy Tyler considered in the country's—and his—interest. A president without a party, he hoped that a major foreign policy success such as the annexation of Texas—Jackson's dream—might lead to the creation of a third party that would allow him to win the 1844 presidential election, or grateful Democrats might nominate him as their party's candidate; at a minimum, annexation would add "luster" to his presidency.[14]

The deep dislike most senators felt for Tyler, the fear of fanning the sectional conflict, and the Whigs' opposition to the annexation of Texas doomed the treaty. Its opponents dismissed the British threat as the ranting of a desperate politician. Defeated in the Senate, annexation was injected into the 1844 presidential election. The Democrats made annexing Texas their major foreign policy issue in the campaign. But at the Democratic National Convention, the delegations of Ohio and other states from the old Northwest demanded that the party platform also call for the annexation of the entire Oregon territory, which encompassed present-day British Columbia, Washington, Oregon, Idaho, and parts of Montana and Wyoming.[15] (Unable to agree on their conflicting claims to the territory, Britain and the United States had signed a ten-year treaty of joint occupation in 1818 and had renewed it indefinitely in 1827 [Map 9]. Negotiations between the Tyler administration and the British government had failed to break the impasse: the administration wanted to divide Oregon at the 49th parallel; Whitehall wanted the border to be the 49th parallel until it met the Columbia River, at which point the border would be the river, which would have left Vancouver and two-thirds of present-day Washington state in British hands.)

In the 1844 elections, Democrat James Polk, a dark-horse candidate from Tennessee who had been the choice of a deadlocked convention, narrowly defeated Clay, the Whig candidate. Polk was a protégé of Andrew Jackson and a fervent expansionist who had "few intellectual interests, little personal charm, and almost no sense of humor."[16] The Democratic Party was rent by internal discord and most Democratic leaders felt little personal loyalty toward the president-elect. But Polk was stubborn and strong-willed and would prove to be a strong chief executive who maintained "a firm grip on the reins of government ... never deviating from the path down which he wanted to lead the nation."[17]

One month after the elections, the lame duck 28th Congress reopened debate on the annexation of Texas. The Democrats closed ranks in favor of annexation, and a few southern Whigs joined them. After a lengthy debate, a joint resolution offering annexation to Texas cleared both houses of Congress and was signed by Tyler on March 1, 1845, just before he left office. Polk was inaugurated three days later, and on March 22 Mexico, which had repeatedly stated that annexation would mean war, broke diplomatic relations and warned that it would declare war if Texas agreed to annexation. The Texas Congress did just that on June 23, and the Texas constitutional convention ratified it on July 4. Immediately thereafter, US troops, led by General Zachary Taylor, entered Texas and set up camp near the hamlet of Corpus Christi, on the right bank of the Nueces, 130 miles from the Rio Grande. Mexico did not respond. "We officially threatened the Americans that we would declare war if they proposed annexation. They did, and we redoubled our threats but did not declare war," the influential Mexican daily *Siglo Diez y Nueve* lamented. "Then we said that we would declare war if Texas accepted annexation. It did, and then we said we would declare war if our territory was invaded by the US army. General Taylor has invaded it, and once again we have failed to declare war. Where will this end? . . . Impotence is no excuse."[18]

Mexico's President José Joaquín de Herrera knew that war with the United States would be suicidal. His country was bankrupt and torn by internal strife; several provinces—Sonora, Tabasco, Yucatan, and California—were effectively independent from the central government. *La Reforma* wrote, "California is the symbol of our misfortunes, of our backwardness ... of our utter lack of will to exploit the great advantages of our fertile soil, geography and the bounty of nature." What made the situation in California particularly dangerous was the fact that only a few thousand Mexicans lived there, that Americans were increasingly entering the province, and that the US desire to annex it was clear. What had happened in Texas was etched on the Mexicans' minds. "The US government," *El Monitor Constitucional* wrote, "will overrun Mexico and the entire continent step by step with this system of robbery and partial usurpations: today this has occurred in Texas; tomorrow it will do the same in California."[19]

The summer passed with a few hundred Mexican soldiers encamped at Matamoros on the right bank of the Rio Grande, and Taylor's troops at Corpus Christi. In late August, William Parrott, a confidential agent Polk had sent to Mexico to explore the possibility of restoring diplomatic relations, reported that "There is a desire, even publicly manifested, to receive a commissioner from the United States."[20] This desire was deepened by the Mexicans' growing awareness that they stood alone against the United States: Spain was too weak to help, France was not interested, and England had decided not to interfere. In September, the Mexican minister in London sought out Foreign Secretary Aberdeen. He "said that war was certain with the United States," Aberdeen reported to Prime Minister Robert Peel, and that Mexico lacked the means to defend California. "Under these circumstances, he was instructed to propose to me some arrangement by which it should be our interest to protect California from the invasion of the United States. He had no specifick [sic] proposal to make, but the Government would be ready to agree to any terms which should have the effect of excluding the United States." Aberdeen was eager "to keep the United States out of California if possible," but he did not believe that Britain should interfere, and Peel agreed with him.[21] The British were following the approach they had adopted since the end of the war of 1812: treating the United States as a strong regional power. US vital interests were in North America, while British vital interests lay in Europe and India. This explains British behavior toward both Texas and California.

The British preferred that neither territory become part of the United States, but it was not in their interest to launch a war to prevent it.

Ships in the night

By October 1845, Whitehall had made it clear to the Mexicans that it would provide no assistance beyond "useful suggestions" to avoid war at all costs. In a conflict with the United States, Foreign Secretary Aberdeen warned, "Mexico . . . could expect nothing but defeat and discomfiture."[22] It was under this cloud—painfully aware that all hope of British assistance was "illusory"[23]—that Mexican Foreign Minister Manuel de la Peña y Peña received a note on October 13 from John Black, the US consul in Mexico City, who had remained at his post in an unofficial capacity after the break in diplomatic relations, saying that Polk was willing to send "an envoy . . . entrusted with full power to adjust all the questions in dispute between the two governments." Two days later Peña y Peña replied, "My government is disposed to receive the commissioner of the United States, who may come to this capital, with full powers from his government to settle the present dispute in a peaceful and honorable manner."[24] The two notes were like ships passing in the night. For Polk, the annexation of Texas was a *fait accompli*, and the "questions" to adjust were the boundary between Mexico and the United States, and Mexico's failure to pay US citizens for losses suffered during the country's internal upheavals.[25] (In 1842, a joint commission had awarded these US claimants $2,007,000, that is, approximately $63.7 million. Bankrupt, Mexico had halted payments in 1844.) For Peña y Peña, "the present dispute" was the annexation of Texas; he was willing to receive a special envoy, not a minister because the latter would imply resumption of diplomatic relations. He understood that Texas was lost, even though his government was not yet ready to admit it publicly, and he expected that the United States would indemnify Mexico for the loss of the province; only after this "dispute" had been settled would diplomatic relations be restored, and other issues addressed.[26] Consul Black did not grasp—or conveniently overlooked—the difference between commissioner and minister.

The distinction was also ignored in Washington. Upon receiving Peña y Peña's reply, Polk sent Louisiana congressman John Slidell to Mexico as minister to negotiate the boundary and the financial issues. The logic of Polk's policy dictated that the negotiations include, from the outset, the claims of US citizens against Mexico. The claims were to be the lever for territorial concessions. Slidell's instructions stipulated that the territorial *sine qua non* was the Rio Grande boundary from the mouth to El Paso. But Polk wanted the boundary to extend northwest from El Paso to the source of the Rio Grande, giving the United States most of New Mexico, even though, as Secretary of State James Buchanan acknowledged, "The Texans never have conquered or taken possession of it." In return, the US government would assume Mexico's debts to American citizens. Mexico, which was "not now in a condition to satisfy these claims by the payment of money," would have to accept the Rio Grande border all the way to the source or face the collapse of the negotiations. Therefore, Buchanan told Slidell, "The two subjects [border and claims] must proceed hand in hand. They can never be separated."[27]

But what about California? Slidell's instructions made it clear that while the administration was eager to acquire the province, it was not a *sine qua non*. "If this cannot be effected," Buchanan told Slidell, "or if . . . you discover that the attempt to effect it would endanger your success in securing the one or the other of the two first objects mentioned in your instructions [the Rio Grande border from the mouth to El Paso and from El Paso to the source], then you are not to sacrifice these in the pursuit of what is unattainable."[28]

Arguably, this was fluff—words for the record. Did Polk purposely send Slidell with the wrong credentials because his real goal was the annexation of California, which he believed he could obtain only by war; or did he send Slidell in good faith, but when he finally understood his mistake, considered backing down humiliating? There is no conclusive answer. Polk's diary sheds very little light on the president's thinking. His papers are equally opaque. So, too, are the papers of his associates, for the simple reason, as Navy Secretary George Bancroft explained, that Polk kept "his own counsels most closely."[29] What we can do, however, is to analyze Polk's Mexican policy after he sent Slidell to discern its logic.

The Slidell Mission

Slidell reached Mexico just as the US Congress, in recess since March, convened on December 1, 1845. Americans were interested in what Polk would say about Mexico in his first annual message, on December 2, but they were even more eager to hear what he had to say about Oregon, because, unlike Mexico, Britain was a powerful country that could inflict grave damage on the United States.

During the presidential campaign Polk had embraced the demand for the entire Oregon territory. After declaring in his inaugural address that the US claim to Oregon was "clear and unquestionable," he had instructed Buchanan to offer the British a settlement in which Oregon would be divided along the 49th parallel. This would have meant that the southern tip of Vancouver Island would belong to the United States. However, Whitehall wanted the border to be the 49th parallel until it met the Columbia River, and from there the Columbia to the sea, leaving Vancouver and two-thirds of Washington state in British hands. By October, the United States was rife with rumors that Polk was going to embark on an aggressive policy toward Britain. His December 2 message did not clarify his intentions. He asked Congress to give the one-year notice required to abrogate the 1827 treaty of joint occupancy. "At the end of the year's notice . . . we shall have reached a period when the national rights in Oregon must either be abandoned or firmly maintained. That they can not be abandoned without a sacrifice of both national honor and interest is too clear to admit of doubt." Polk did not spell out whether these rights extended to the entire territory, but many in Congress and the press believed that this was what he meant, raising the question of what would happen if, at the end of the year's notice, Britain refused to bow to the US will.[30]

What Polk had to say about Mexico seemed less ominous: the Mexican government had agreed to resume diplomatic relations—which it had not done—and he had appointed "a distinguished citizen of Louisiana [Slidell] ... envoy extraordinary and minister plenipotentiary to Mexico, clothed with full powers to adjust and definitively settle all pending differences between the two countries."[31]

Three weeks later, on December 20, Peña y Peña informed Slidell that he had the wrong credentials: Mexico would receive him as an *ad hoc* commissioner, not as a minister, and would allow him "expressly and exclusively" to deal only with the Texas question.[32] Slidell rejected these "miserable sophistries" (as he wrote to Buchanan) and in a bombastic reply he accused the Mexicans of bad faith. "I hope that you will think that I have succeeded to throw all the responsibility, odium of the failure of the negotiations on the Mexican government," he wrote to Polk. The president told Slidell to remain in Mexico; he hoped that the new Mexican president, General Mariano Paredes, who had just overthrown Herrera, would be more amenable to US demands. Furthermore, he believed it was important to project an air of moderation, in order "that it may appear manifest to the people of the United States and to the world that a rupture could not be honorably avoided." And so Slidell waited. On March 1, 1846, he demanded again to be received. "No doubt the military superiority of the United States has inspired Mr. Slidell's threatening language," the Mexican Council of State noted. "But no matter how strong and powerful that government may be, no matter how easily it may steal new territories from us, it can never rob us of our honor. ... No one can dispute the right of the Mexican government to fix prudent, rational and dignified conditions with which it will receive the agents of another nation." On March 12, in polite terms, the Mexican government again refused to receive Slidell. On March 30, he boarded a US warship and returned to the United States.[33]

By then, the US army was on the Rio Grande. On January 13, after receiving the first dispatches indicating that it was likely that Slidell would not be received, Polk had ratcheted up the pressure on Mexico by ordering General Taylor to leave Corpus Christi and "occupy, with the troops under your command, positions on or near the east [left] bank of the Rio [Grande] del Norte."[34] It took three weeks for the order to reach Taylor and another month for the army to get ready to move. On March 28, the Americans reached the Rio Grande and set camp opposite Matamoros, where the Mexicans were still encamped. The two armies—fewer than 2,000 Mexicans against 3,500 Americans—were "within two or three hundred yards of each other," the New Orleans *Picayune* reported. A lull ensued. The Mexicans were awaiting their new commander, General Pedro de Ampudia, who arrived on April 11. The next day he sent an ultimatum to Taylor: "By explicit and definitive orders of my government ... I require you in all form and at the latest in the peremptory term of twenty-four hours, to break up your camp and retire to the other bank of the Nueces." If Taylor refused, "arms, and arms alone must decide the question." Taylor responded by ordering the US warships in the area to blockade the Rio Grande, cutting off the Mexican supply route.[35] The blockade was an act of war, but it was not the trigger that provoked the Mexicans to fight: the Mexican government had already decided that honor compelled them to try to repel the invaders. General Ampudia was simply waiting for reinforcements. As soon as they arrived, Mexican soldiers crossed the Rio Grande, and on April 25 they successfully ambushed a party of American dragoons.

By then, the Oregon dispute was headed toward an amicable settlement after a spirited debate in the US Congress and press about the notice of abrogation of the 1827 treaty of joint US-British occupation of the territory. One side argued that London should be told that the United States claimed all of Oregon; the other, fearing war, wanted to invite the British to negotiate a compromise. Polk had said nothing publically. He was in a difficult position: during the presidential campaign he had embraced the claim to all Oregon and anything less would disappoint Democrats in the old Northwest. But he did not want war with Britain. In February 1846, he quietly sketched the outlines of a compromise, telling the US minister in London that if Whitehall submitted a proposal dividing Oregon at the 49th parallel, but giving England the whole of Vancouver Island and temporary navigation rights on the Columbia River, he would submit the proposal to the Senate (throughout, Polk strove to shift the responsibility for compromise to the Senate). Maintaining his "inscrutability" in public, in private talks he "encouraged the moderates" in Congress to be flexible.[36] Finally, overcoming the opposition of the Democrats from the old Northwest, on April 23, the House and the Senate approved a notice of abrogation that included a preamble inviting both countries to negotiations for a settlement.

The administration turned next to Mexico. Polk had not learned of the clash on the Rio Grande when he convened his cabinet on Saturday morning, May 9, 1846. "I brought up the Mexican question," he wrote in his diary. "All agreed that if the Mexican forces at Matamoras [sic] committed any act of hostility on General Taylor's forces I should immediately send a message to Congress recommending an immediate declaration of war. . . . I said that in my opinion we had ample cause of war, and that it was impossible that we could stand in *statu quo*, or that I could remain silent much longer. . . . I then propounded the distinct question to the Cabinet . . . whether I should make a message to Congress on Tuesday, and whether in that message I should recommend a declaration of war against Mexico. . . . It was agreed that the message should be prepared and submitted to the Cabinet in their meeting on Tuesday." A few hours later, Polk received dispatches from Taylor reporting that Mexican troops had crossed the Rio Grande "and attacked and killed and captured two companies of dragoons of General Taylor's army consisting of 63 officers and men."[37] The following Monday, Polk told Congress that Mexico had "invaded our territory and shed American blood upon American soil." He demanded "the prompt action of Congress to recognize the existence of the war."[38]

Polk's war message provoked a fierce, albeit brief, debate in Congress and in the press. John Clayton (Whig-DE) spoke for many Whigs in the Senate when he said, "the whole conduct of the Executive . . . has been utterly unjustifiable. If the acts of the Executive do not amount to acts of war, they are acts which necessarily tended to provoke war, and to bring on war, and that without consulting Congress." And Garrett Davis (Whig-KY) spoke for many in the House when he concluded, "It is our own President who began this war. He has been carrying it on for months in a series of acts"[39] [Map 10].

Clayton and Davis were right: Polk had been pursuing a belligerent policy toward Mexico. But where had Clayton, Davis and the other members of Congress who expressed outrage in May 1846 been during the preceding months? Had they voiced their opposition while Polk had carried out the "series of acts" that, in Clayton's words, "necessarily tended to provoke war"? And what about those newspapers that harshly criticized Polk's war message?

Manifest Destiny and Mexico

Not warnings about impending war, but flowery words about the "manifest destiny" of the United States to "overspread the continent" had filled the pages of American newspapers and resonated in the halls of Congress as Taylor's army had marched to the Rio Grande.[40]

Manifest Destiny was a term coined in 1845 by the journalist John O'Sullivan, but it was not a new idea. It had inspired the first British colonists to North America, and had justified and propelled the territorial expansion of the United States. Jefferson's words are worth repeating: "However our present interests may restrain us within our own limits, it is impossible not to look forward to distant times when our rapid multiplication will expand itself beyond those limits, and cover the whole northern, if not the southern continent with a people speaking the same language, governed in similar forms, and by similar laws; nor can we contemplate with satisfaction either blot or mixture on that surface."[41]

In the two decades that followed the annexation of Florida in 1821, the borders of the United States had remained unchanged, but within the country the frontier of white settlement had constantly encroached on Indian territory. The ethnic cleansing initiated by Jackson in the early 1830s had forced almost 100,000 Indians west of the Mississippi. In the process, thousands had died. Then, in the election of 1844, the annexation of Texas and Oregon had become a major campaign issue. The Democrats had celebrated Polk's narrow victory as a mandate for expansion. Beyond Texas and Oregon loomed California, with its long coastline and natural harbors. American pioneers were already moving there.

The prospect of the acquisition of vast territories beyond the borders of the United States spurred a new, updated version of Manifest Destiny. Its proponents were politicians and journalists, Democrats and independents, and in particular the penny press—cheap and widely-read newspapers that were not aligned with any political party. The most influential of these papers was the *New York Herald*, which competed with the *Sun*, another New York penny paper, for the largest circulation in the United States.

While many Whigs still embraced the idea of "sister republics," the Democrats wanted more. The United States had successfully absorbed the immense Louisiana purchase, and technological advances—steamboats, railways, the telegraph—meant that vast distances were no longer forbidding. The Jacksonian Democrats, as they were called, shared Jefferson's vision of an America of yeoman farmers, where land would be cheap, and the ills of Europe—industrialization, a large servile population of factory workers, densely populated and congested cities—could be avoided. But whereas Jefferson had believed in 1801 that the territory of the United States offered "room enough for our descendants to the thousandth and thousandth generation,"[42] the Jacksonian Democrats were in a hurry.

The number of immigrants had skyrocketed during the 1820s and 1830s, from roughly 8,400 in 1820 to 84,000 in 1840, and 114,000 five years later. The extraordinary increase of the American population—which had grown from 8,638,453 in 1820 to 17,069,453 in 1840—created a sense of urgency.[43] Jefferson's grandchildren lusted for new lands beyond the borders of the United States.

Manifest Destiny was suffused with a sense of moral superiority and of American uniqueness. The United States, the *New York Herald* asserted, was "the only power which has never sought and never seeks to acquire a foot of territory by force of arms."[44] From the outset, this young nation of immigrants who lacked the bonds of history had felt the need to define itself by stressing its difference from those who stayed behind, the peoples of Europe. A key ingredient of the City on the Hill was the belief in American exceptionalism. "There are some things this nation will never do," wrote to the journalist O'Sullivan in late 1845, erasing the fate of the Indians. "It will never be the forcible subjugator of other countries; it will never despoil surrounding territories; it will never march through the blood of their unoffending inhabitants; it will never admit within its own Union those who do not freely desire the boon. The parallel of its territorial extensions will not be found in the history of the dismemberment of Poland or of the British conquests in India; and no patriots will ever rally upon their native hills to protect their own rights or their country's liberties from our rapacity."[45]

How, then, would the United States expand? Texas provided the answer. It was a vast land, sparsely inhabited by an "inferior race." Colonizers of good stock—whites—had arrived from the United States; they brought civilization. Their numbers increased steadily, they took over the government and proclaimed an independent republic. They asked for admission to the Temple of Freedom but were kept waiting. Finally, in 1845, they were admitted. Thus, the *Democratic Review* cheerfully predicted that Mexico was "destined to become an integral portion of these United States at some future period" in the same way: annexation would be carried out piece by piece over a long period of time "by the irresistible army of Anglo-Saxon emigration" that would pour over Mexico's borders—not by the US army. California would "next fall away" from Mexico's feeble grasp. The Polk administration's organ, the *Union*, agreed: "When California shall be like Texas, let her come in." It was not a question of greed. "It is our duty," the New York *Morning News* explained in November 1845, "whenever any contiguous territory, which is independent of all allegiance, asks the protection and benefits of our laws and institutions, to grant the application. Such is our glorious mission. . . . So has Texas been annexed; and so is California ripening to independence only to follow in the 'footsteps of her predecessor.'"[46] California "will be an independent State, and as a natural consequence will desire to be annexed to the United States in the same way that Texas did," the *New York Herald* predicted. "This appears to be the natural course of events; and it is only fulfilling the destiny which we were appointed to carry out. . . . piece by piece, the whole northern States of Mexico, with all the gold and the silver mines, will be finally absorbed in this great republic."[47]

For Mexicans, this was chilling. "The bold and insatiable Democracy of the North is growing more aggressive every day and taking off its mask to bare its expansionist plans in the full light of day," *Siglo Diez y Nueve* wrote. "The Americans are advocating and preparing a holy crusade like that which robbed us of Texas."[48]

But how could Americans think of annexing the whole of Mexico with its large non-white population? In 1801, Jefferson had warned against allowing "either blot or mixture" in the territories that would be peopled by American Anglo-Saxons, but he had not explained how this could be done. The new expansionists filled in the blanks. They were inspired by seven decades of US history. "There seems to be something in our laws and institutions," Representative Alexander Duncan (D-OH) explained in January 1845, "peculiarly adapted to our Anglo-Saxon-American race, under which they will thrive and prosper, but under which all others wilt and die. Where our laws and free institutions have been extended among the French and Spanish who have been on our continent, they have and are gradually disappearing; not that they move away, but they neither prosper nor multiply, but, on the contrary, dwindle. There is something mysterious about it; and, if accounted for, it can only be done on the principle that though they may be fitted for refined civilization, they are not fitted for liberal and equal laws, and equal institutions."[49]

If the French and Spaniards, who were white, dwindled in contact with the Anglo-Saxon-American race, what would happen to the swarthy inhabitants of Mexico and South America? The fate of the Mexicans, the *New York Herald* predicted, would be "similar to that of the Indians of this country—the race, before a century rolls over us, will become extinct."[50]

A lesson could also be drawn from the 1840 US census. It included data that had been falsified to prove that African Americans in the free states were far more susceptible than enslaved people in the South to physical and mental illnesses. This led many white Americans to conclude that the free black population would eventually wilt and die: "Public opinion at the North ... presents an insuperable barrier against its [free Blacks'] elevation in the social scale," explained Senator John Dix (D-NY). "A class thus degraded will not multiply ... It will not be reproduced; and in a few generations the process of extinction is performed. Nor is it the work of inhumanity or wrong. It is the slow but certain process of nature, working out her ends by laws so steady and yet so silent, that their operation is only seen in their results."[51] American Indians and free Blacks in the United States pointed to the fate that awaited the non-white people of Mexico and countries further south. No one could know how far the American Anglo-Saxon wave would reach, whether it would stop at the Isthmus of Darien or whether it would engulf South America, all the way to Patagonia.

This implied no contradiction with the pledge that the United States would not use force against its neighbors. The irresistible advance of the settlers would overwhelm every resistance. No patriots would fight on their native hills against US troops—they would have wilted and died, or they would have moved south to escape the imperial process.

This extreme language, describing the extinction of entire peoples, was the preserve of Democrats, but Whigs held similar views of Mexico: both parties agreed that it was helpless—"Mexico lies a victim-people, at our mercy," the *National Intelligencer*, the leading Whig paper, declared in November 1845. "We can inflict upon Mexico with impunity what we please." The virulent racism of the Democrats was shared by most Whig papers. The *American Review*, the preeminent Whig magazine, called the Mexicans "utterly ignorant, indolent and rapacious ... destitute of spirit, industry and courage, and perfectly incapable of the slightest emotions of ambition or the faintest pulsation of energy and enterprise." The Whigs had been ready to welcome Texas as a sister republic, and Oregon as well. But they wanted California to belong to the United States. With its famed natural harbors, that "vast and magnificent region" was the ideal springboard for the conquest of the markets of Asia. Recent events had enhanced its importance: in 1842, Britain had forced China to grant special privileges to British merchants; two years later, the Chinese had formally extended these concessions to the United States. "The natural progress of events will undoubtedly give us that province [California] just as it gave us Texas," the *American Review* asserted in January 1846. The Whigs did not advocate a war of aggression to seize California. The United States would try to purchase it. If Mexico refused to sell, "American emigrants ... shall dissolve the slight bonds that now link that province to Mexico, and prepare the way for its ultimate annexation to the United States."[52]

The British threat

It is striking how little attention Americans—Democrats and Whigs—paid to Mexico as their country hurtled toward war across the Rio Grande. The dominant foreign news was the Oregon dispute, which threatened war with mighty Britain. Mexico was a sideshow. In early March 1846, the US press reported that General Taylor had been ordered from Corpus Christi to the Rio Grande. For the next month, only brief and occasional reports of his advance toward the Rio Grande appeared. No paper bothered to comment on the significance of the decision or its possible impact on relations with Mexico. Finally, on April 20, the *New York Tribune* roused from its slumber to sound the alarm: "Can any man imagine for what purpose ... our Army ... has been ordered down from Corpus Christi to the Rio [Grande] del Norte? ... its advance has been through a region never belonging to the old provinces of Texas nor for a single moment subject to the rule of the recent Republic. ... Up to this time, both banks of the great River have been occupied by Mexican troops, we have dispossessed them of the Eastern [bank] by a display of a temporarily overwhelming force: can we expect them to remain quiet on the other?"[53]

These were obvious questions. It is stunning that it had taken the *Tribune* until April 20 to raise them, but its tocsin fell on deaf ears: even the *Tribune* continued to focus on Oregon. Its next editorial on relations with Mexico did not appear until May 8.

Why was the press silent? The answer must be found, first, in the obsessive focus on Oregon. Secondly, until his May 11 War Message, Polk had said little about Mexico, and the administration newspaper, the *Union*, had followed the president's lead. It had seemed unlikely that Polk would launch the country into a war with Mexico while the conflict with England festered. And it was difficult to imagine Mexico striking first, whatever the provocations, given its weakness and its isolation: it was clear that Britain, the one country that could help Mexico, would not come to its aid.

British newspapers had harsh words for the United States. *The Economist* called the annexation of Texas "the work of aggression and spoliation." *The Times* was scathing. The annexation of Texas was "one of the basest frauds and most unwarranted acts of spoliation ever perpetrated by any nation." But no redress was possible: "As a question of military strength and sound policy there can be no doubt that Mexico had better submit to this loss and this affront than expose herself to bear the brunt of that military and adventurous spirit which is now literally raging in many parts of the Anglo-American union."[54] Nothing could protect Mexico. "The Americans have already formed new and extensive designs of aggression," *The Economist* warned in August 1845. California would be next. Mexico was prostrate, unable to offer any resistance. "She is nodding and tottering to her fall," the *Morning Chronicle* wrote. *The Times* agreed: "unhappily the increasing decrepitude of the native government of Mexico seems to promise opportunities of spoliation as ample and immediate as the most insatiable aggressor could desire."[55] None of these papers suggested that Whitehall mediate between the United States and Mexico.

The message crossed the Atlantic. No US newspapers expressed any fear that England might intervene if war broke out between the United States and Mexico. A cartoon in the *New York Herald* in February 1846 epitomized this confidence. The cartoon "represents," the *Herald* explained, "Brother Jonathan [the United States] administering a little castigation [a whipping, to be precise] to our Mexican friends. He has borne for a long time their insolent and impotent threats; but, like an indulgent father, he corrects them as one would a wayward child. John Bull [England] is looking on, and appears not to like the operation, but has to keep his hands in his pockets." The drawing depicted Mexico, the Mexican *La Reforma* remarked bitterly, "as a half-witted and stupid kid."[56]

Therefore, the US press was complacent about events along the Rio Grande. It was possible that there would be no war: Mexico might realize the hopelessness of its situation and submit to the American demands. But, if war came—after the Oregon dispute had been settled—victory would be swift and easy.

US representatives and senators paid even less attention than did the US press to Mexico. Between December 1845, when the 29th Congress convened, and May 11, 1846, when Polk sent his war message to Congress, there was not one debate on relations with Mexico. On March 26, two days before General Taylor reached the Rio Grande, Rep. Abraham McIlvaine (Whig-PA) squarely challenged Polk: "Texas does not extend to the [Rio Grande] Del Norte, nor ever did. The President, in ordering the army to its banks, has invaded Mexico." It was the only open attack on Polk's Mexican policy and it was met by silence—no one rose to reply, in support or in opposition.[57] Pasted together, all the references to Mexico in the five months that preceded the war would fill, at most, four pages—out of more than 1,500 pages of debate.

In February 1845, former President Van Buren had written, "Too much care cannot be taken to save us from a war [with Mexico], in respect to which the opposition shall be able to charge us with plausibility, if not truth, that it is waged for the extension of slavery."[58] These wise words were soon forgotten. Through the entire year that preceded the outbreak of hostilities on the Rio Grande no member of Congress, no newspaper, no government official expressed anxiety that war with Mexico might exacerbate sectional strife in the United States by raising the question of whether the newly annexed territories would be slave or free. Not even South Carolina's Senator John Calhoun, who was the foremost exponent of southern sectionalism, mentioned this possibility. This is baffling. While the votes in Congress on the annexation of Texas had been largely along party lines, sectional strains had been present throughout. Sectional strains were also evident when the debate on Oregon began in December 1845, yet Polk's papers and diary indicate that the president, too, was blind to the sectional implications of war with Mexico, as were the members of his cabinet. Had Democratic or Whig leaders even an inkling of the bitter sectional clash that victory over Mexico would bring, they would have spoken up. As it was, they remained silent. The result was that in developing his Mexico policy, Polk was free from congressional pressure. When Polk, on May 11, 1846, announced that Mexico had invaded the United States and shed American blood on American soil, Congress readily did what the president wanted: on May 12, an overwhelming majority approved a bill appropriating $10 million ($342.4 million) and calling for 50,000 volunteers. The preamble stated that Mexico, by its actions, had started a war with the United States.

The burden of responsibility

Historians argue about whether Polk sought to provoke war with Mexico. The smoking gun used to prove this charge is Polk's own words: he told Secretary of the Navy Bancroft that "the acquisition of California" would be one of the "four great measures" of his administration. The only source for this statement, however, is Bancroft, or, more precisely, Bancroft's recollections forty years after the fact.[59] Furthermore, Polk may have believed that a combination of threats, financial inducements, and outright bribes could cow the Mexican leaders into surrendering California without war. "The wretched condition of the internal affairs of Mexico," Slidell's instructions read, and the absence of British support, "seem to render the present a propitious moment [to obtain the province]." And as late as March 28, 1846, two days before Slidell left Mexico, Polk deemed it possible that Mexican President Paredes might be bribed into selling California to the United States.[60] Moreover, purchase and war were not the only ways to acquire California: American colonists were moving in.

Therefore, in sending Slidell, Polk may have been following a two-track approach: offer Mexico the opportunity to submit peacefully to his non-negotiable territorial demands (the Rio Grande border); prepare for war should Mexico refuse.

Preparing for war did not mean military preparations—Mexico was too weak to require that. Nor did it mean gaining time in order to isolate Mexico diplomatically—this needed neither time nor effort. Pursuing its own national interest, London stood aside as Polk pushed Mexico to the brink. The evidence—Polk's diary, his correspondence, and the diplomatic record—suggests that the president never worried that England

OUR MEXICAN RELATIONS.

The above engraving represents Brother Jonathan administering a little castigation to our Mexican friends. He has borne for a long time their insolent and impotent threats; but, like an indulgent father, he accepts them as one would a wayward child. John Bull is looking on, and appears not to like the operation, but has to keep his hands in his pockets. Johnny Crapeau contents himself with viewing, through his glass, the proceedings of Brother Jonathan.

Figure 8.1 "Our Mexican Relatives." Cartoon. *New York Daily Herald*, February 15, 1846.

might come to the aid of Mexico. His correspondence with Louis McLane, the US minister in London, is revealing. Neither Polk nor Buchanan inquired about British intentions toward Mexico or California; McLane referred to the matter very infrequently, always expressing confidence that Britain would remain aloof. Foreign Secretary Aberdeen did not raise Mexico in his frequent conversations with Lane—he spoke only of Oregon; and Richard Pakenham, the British minister in Washington, was equally silent on the subject in his conversations with US officials and members of the US Congress.[61]

Preparing for war meant, for Polk, rallying US public opinion and the Congress. The United States had just swallowed an immense territory—Texas. It was on the verge of swallowing a large chunk of Oregon. The Whigs did not want war with Mexico and the Democrats were rent by factional strife. Moreover, as the editor of the Polk papers writes, "Polk commanded at best the second-hand loyalty of his party's discordant leadership."[62]

And so, Slidell's continuing saga proved useful to Polk. As the weeks passed, Oregon inched toward a peaceful compromise, eliminating a reason for caution in many congressmen's minds. Slidell's plight and the administration's forbearance—weren't the Mexicans reneging on their pledge to receive a US minister?—helped paint Mexico as the aggressor. The administration's keen awareness of the importance of shaping public opinion is evident in Buchanan's correspondence. He told Slidell on January 20, 1846: "You ought, in your language, so to conduct yourself as to throw the whole odium of the failure of the negotiation on the Mexican Government." And on March 12, he urged Slidell "not to leave [Mexico] ... until you should have made a formal demand to be received by the new Government ... [in order] to satisfy the American people that all had been done which ought to be done to avoid the necessity of resorting to hostilities. On your return to the United States, energetic measures against Mexico would at once be recommended by the President, and these might fail to obtain the support of Congress, if it could be asserted that the existing Government had not refused to receive our Minister."[63]

A young lieutenant in Taylor's army drew the appropriate conclusion: "I fear that Mr. Polk ... desires a war with Mexico," he wrote to his wife on April 21. Otherwise, "why should he insist on Mr. Slidell's being received as a Minister Plenipotentiary, when he was repeatedly assured by the Mexicans they would only receive a Commissioner? ... The requiring Mr. Slidell to insist on being received as Minister was a sad blunder of Mr. Polk's, if he desired peace; but my impression is he desires war."[64]

Polk may have begun with a two-track policy toward Mexico, but the moment came when he concluded that war was his only option. It is difficult to be sure of the turning point. Probably it was in the second week of April, after reading Slidell's dispatch stating that President Paredes had refused to receive him, and he was returning to the United States.[65] On May 9, Polk told the cabinet that the time had come to prepare a war message based on Mexico's unpaid claims and its refusal to receive Slidell. A few hours later news of clashes on the Rio Grande made justifying war much easier.

Polk had pushed Mexico to war in the midst of his dispute with England over Oregon. The evidence suggests that it was not bluster when he told Buchanan in August 1845 that he saw "no necessary connection" between the disputes with England and with Mexico, and that "the settlement of the one was not dependent on the other."[66] The evidence also indicates that, throughout, he was willing to compromise on the boundaries of Oregon and did not expect war with England.

England's desire to avoid a quarrel with the United States was starkly expressed by the anti-American London *Times* when it announced, on May 29, 1846, that war between the United States and Mexico had begun: it suggested not that the British government harden its stance on Oregon, but rather that it speed up the negotiations in case "we shall have to encounter a more intractable and more excited spirit on that question [Oregon] amongst the American people."[67] And this was, exactly, what Whitehall did. On June 6, Buchanan received Foreign Secretary Aberdeen's offer to divide Oregon along the lines that Polk had informally suggested: the 49th parallel except Vancouver Island which would be British, and the right of navigation on the Columbia River until 1859 [Map 9]. Polk immediately submitted the offer to the Senate which endorsed it by a thirty-eight to twelve vote on June 12. Six days later a formal treaty was ratified.

Polk had been able to provoke Mexico almost undisturbed because of his lucid assessment of British intentions and because of the flaccidity of those who opposed war—in Congress and in the US press. The silence of the opposition in the months that preceded the war was not for lack of information, nor because it was misled by a devious president. The information—about the Slidell mission and about Taylor's advance to the Rio Grande—was readily available. Polk could not have hoped for a more toothless opposition.

It was Polk's war message that rallied the opposition. Its timing—before the Oregon dispute had been settled—added to the outrage of his critics: they feared that England might respond by hardening its stance on Oregon. Furthermore, many had believed that the United States would be able to get Mexican territory—California—without war.

British minister Pakenham's indictment of Polk's Mexican policy also applies to its critics: it had "not been guided by an honest desire to preserve a state of peace with that ill-fated country," he told Aberdeen. "There has been, to say the least of it, I think, an indifference to war which cannot be considered otherwise than criminal."[68]

Does Mexico bear responsibility for the war? The Mexican ruling elites behaved in a thoroughly irresponsible manner after 1836: they refused to recognize the independence of Texas, and they refused to make the sacrifices necessary to try to recover the province. Precious resources were squandered in massive corruption and in uprisings that tore Mexico between 1836 and 1844. Money raised through taxes in the name of the recovery of Texas was stolen by Mexico's leaders—civilian and military.

It is very likely that Presidents Herrera and Paredes would have received Slidell had he arrived with the correct credentials. It can be argued that they should have received him anyway, and that they should have agreed to Polk's bottom line—the Rio Grande border—since Mexico was in no condition to fight, and they knew it. This might have avoided war and saved California. But for how long? Americans were moving in, and England was not going to intervene. A replay of Texas was in the offing. Arguably, by going to war, the Mexicans avoided the ignominy of surrendering their territory without a fight.

One fact is clear: Mexico bears no more responsibility for the war of 1846 than, say, Poland bears for its dismemberment at the hands of Russia, Prussia and Austria at the end of the eighteenth century. It bears the responsibility of not having kept its house in order and of not having prepared to fight. It bears the responsibility of the victim. The burden falls instead on the rapacity of its northern neighbor.

The onslaught

Approximately 27,000 US regulars and 59,000 volunteers served in the war against Mexico. Americans retained their mistrust of a standing army and looked down on the regulars as the dregs of society, men who accepted very low pay and harsh discipline because they could not find employment elsewhere. In 1845, 40 percent of the regulars were recently arrived immigrants, many not yet naturalized. By contrast, the volunteers who enlisted in 1846 for twelve months' service in specially created units were mostly native-born middle-class Americans. For the native-born Americans who stayed at home, these volunteers represented the true America. But they lacked the discipline and training of the regulars.[69]

The army continued to exclude African Americans from its ranks but it allowed officers to be accompanied by servants: four for major generals and one for junior officers. Southern officers brought their enslaved men; many northerners hired free Blacks. Slavery was illegal in Mexico and many slaves of US officers deserted their masters; some joined the Mexicans to fight against the Americans. For them, Mexico was the land of freedom.[70]

Given the vast US advantage in economic resources and weaponry, the outcome of the war was preordained. After defeating the Mexicans at Palo Alto and Resaca de la Palma, General Taylor crossed the Rio Grande and in September 1846 seized Monterrey, the largest city in northern Mexico. The following February at Buena Vista, with 5,000 soldiers, he defeated an army of 15,000 half-starved Mexicans (5,000 more had died, fallen ill, or deserted during their harrowing, three-week march from their base at San Luis Potosí—traversing more than 200 miles of semi desertic terrain). After the bloody battle, an act of humanity: upon learning that the Mexican army had left a large number of wounded at a nearby village, Taylor sent several wagons there loaded with food. "On reaching that place," wrote one of the soldiers who escorted the wagons, "the sight became sickening. The dead, dying and wounded were all crowded together." The food was unloaded and given to "those who were yet able to call for and masticate it."[71]

Contrary to Polk's expectations, Mexico did not sue for peace, and in March 1847, General Winfield Scott landed near Vera Cruz and forced the city to surrender after an indiscriminate bombardment that killed hundreds of civilians.[72] (To speed up the surrender, Scott rejected the pleas of the British, French, Prussian and Spanish consuls that he allow "foreigners, and women and children to leave the city."[73]) Scott then ably led the advance to Mexico City, which he occupied in September 1847, after repeated victorious encounters with the Mexican army.

The previous April, after the fall of Vera Cruz, Polk had sent a special envoy, Nicholas Trist, to offer the Mexicans a harsh peace: the *sine qua non* were the Rio Grande border to El Paso, New Mexico, and California. But the Mexican government rejected the *Diktat*, and many Democrats, including Treasury Secretary Robert Walker, as well as prominent newspaper editors, called for the United States to annex all of Mexico. What, then, would become of the millions of Mexicans who were not white? "I would treat them as we do our own Indians—give them agents and laws, and kindness, and education," Senate Foreign Relations Committee chairman Archibald Sevier (D-AK) explained. "They are a degraded race in Mexico. They could be made less so under our administration."[74]

"Make Heaven weep"

While US politicians spoke of uplifting the Mexicans, US soldiers were abusing them. The first US troops to cross the Rio Grande had been regular units of the army, and their treatment of the Mexican population was not particularly harsh. For years, the area south of the Rio Grande had been devastated by raids of the Comanches and their Kiowa allies who seized cattle, horses, and captives, and killed thousands of civilians. Mexico had been too weak to protect its population.[75] The arrival of the US troops, Peter Guardino writes, was followed by "a period of calm as the Mexican people of the Rio Grande Valley tried to make sense of what life under American occupation would be like." But in July 1846, the volunteers arrived. From Matamoros, Lt. Ulysses S. Grant wrote to his fiancée that the volunteers had murdered a "great many" Mexicans, and that "there seems to be but very weak means made use of to prevent frequent repetition."[76] The American journalists traveling with Taylor's army closed their eyes to the crimes committed by their countrymen, but the depredations were described in the letters soldiers wrote home. Some of these letters found their way into the press. On October 12, the Charleston *Mercury* printed a letter about "the murders, rapes, and robberies" perpetrated by the volunteers at Matamoros. After the fall of Monterrey, another letter in *Niles' National Register* reported that, "As at Matamoros, murder, robbery and rape were committed in the broad light of day ... It is thought that more than one hundred of the inhabitants were murdered in cold blood."[77] The veracity of these letters was confirmed by the senior commanders of the US army. "I deeply regret to report that many of the twelve months' volunteers ... have committed extensive depredations and outrages upon the peaceful inhabitants," General Taylor wrote. In Washington, General Scott told the secretary of war in January 1847, "our militia and volunteers, if a tenth of what is said be true, have committed atrocities—horrors—in Mexico sufficient to make Heaven weep and every American of Christian morals blush for his country. Murder, robbery and rape of mothers and daughters, in the presence of the tied up males of the families, have been common all along the Rio Grande."[78]

Violence begets violence. Soon guerrilla bands formed, spontaneously, without any encouragement or assistance from the Mexican government. A vicious cycle of atrocities began: Mexican guerrillas against US soldiers; US soldiers against guerrillas and civilians. After the war, a US officer lamented, "The smiling villages which welcomed our troops ... are now black and smouldering ruins, ... and the inhabitants ... have sought refuge in the mountains. The march of Attila was not more withering and destructive."[79]

General Scott understood that the volunteers' crimes in northern Mexico had transformed peaceful peasants into guerrillas, and after landing at Vera Cruz he made a concerted effort to restrain his troops. He had some success, but the guerrillas appeared nonetheless—a nationalist reaction to a foreign invader. Scott responded with extreme violence. He assigned the task of hunting down the guerrillas to volunteer units notorious for their hatred of Mexicans, such as the Texas volunteers; they terrorized the population, looted and burned villages, slaughtered civilians and engaged in mass rapes.

These atrocities fit a pattern. Throughout the nineteenth century, white nations fought two kinds of wars: one against other white nations, where the violence against civilians was generally contained; and another against nonwhites, where they indulged in acts of savagery. This was true of the British and the French, and it was true of the Americans. When Americans fought against the British in 1812 and the Spanish in 1898, they respected the basic rules of war. But against non-whites—Indians, Mexicans, and later Filipinos—the rules did not apply. The letters and diaries of US soldiers depicted non-white Mexicans as "a lesser form of human," like Indians or Blacks in the United States.[80]

The worst crimes were perpetrated by the volunteers, those nice, middle class boys of whom America was so proud. In the United States, most white Americans seem to have dismissed the reports of atrocities or deemed them rare exceptions that did not tarnish the heroism of the citizen-soldiers. Some, however, began to fear that the fighting was corroding the moral fiber of the nation, transforming young American men into murderers and rapists. Meanwhile, the war was becoming increasingly costly in both money and in American lives, and it was threatening the unity of the country.

The price of victory

On August 8, 1846, three months after the beginning of hostilities, Representative David Wilmot (D-PA) had introduced a resolution, the Wilmot Proviso, proscribing slavery in the territories to be acquired from Mexico. Many northerners, including Democrats, believed that the Polk administration had been favoring the South: Texas had been annexed but only half of Oregon; Congress had just approved a low tariff—the South's goal; and Polk had just vetoed a major internal improvements bill which the South opposed. It was time to draw the line. Hence the Wilmot Proviso. For southerners, the proviso was an abomination. Twice the House approved it; twice it failed in the Senate. This clash locked the slave and free states in such a bitter conflict that the prospect of victory over Mexico—and its territorial windfall—seemed to threaten the survival of the Union.[81]

Perhaps, without the low tariff and the compromise on Oregon, Wilmot would not have introduced his resolution and the sectional clash might have been delayed. But the low tariff was a central part of Polk's program and the alternative to compromise on Oregon was war. The sectional conflict could not have been averted: it was the poison in the acquisition of Mexican territory.

For Mexico, the Wilmot Proviso was a blessing, because the storm it unleashed set a limit to the victors' greed. While Polk dreamed of ever larger territorial gains and many Democrats talked of annexing all of Mexico, most Whigs opposed the annexation of any territory populated by many nonwhites and were even ready to forswear acquiring any Mexican territory in the hope of dampening the sectional conflict.

The Gordian knot was cut by Nicholas Trist, Polk's special envoy to Mexico, who on February 2, 1848, signed the Treaty of Guadalupe Hidalgo with the Mexican government. It granted the immense territorial cession that Polk had demanded when he had sent Trist to Mexico the previous April [Map 11]. By February 1848, Polk wanted more, but he had to face reality: Americans were tiring of war and the sectional conflict was tearing the country apart. In Congress, the Democrats retained a majority in the Senate but the House had fallen to the Whigs by a narrow margin (116 Whigs and 110 Democrats.)[82] Polk sent the treaty to the Senate which ratified it. The war was over. Twelve-and-a-half thousand American soldiers had died, almost 11,000 of disease, but the United States had acquired 525,000 square miles of Mexican territory for the paltry sum of $15 million (c. $494 million). About 75,000 Mexicans lived on this land and therefore fell under US rule. The peace treaty guaranteed them "all the rights of citizens of the United States," but this promise was not kept. California's very first constitution disenfranchised most Mexicans, stipulating that only those men who were white could vote. Many were robbed of their land through legal subterfuges and became a servile workforce for white settlers. "At best, Mexican-Americans became second-class citizens," an eminent historian writes. "At worst, they became victims of overt racial and ethnic prejudices."[83]

It was the first US war of aggression against a Latin American country, fulfilling Bolívar's prophesy that the United States was "destined by Providence to plague America with miseries in the name of liberty."[84]

CHAPTER 9
THE 1850s AND THE CIVIL WAR

In March 1848, Americans celebrated the news that the French had overthrown their king and proclaimed a republic. Other welcome news followed: in Germany, Italy, and the Austrian empire the population was rising up, demanding an end to despotism. The "springtime of people," as it would be called, had begun.

It did not last. In the summer of 1849, the last embers of revolt were snuffed out by Russian, Prussian, and Austrian bayonets, and thousands of political refugees fled to the United States, confirming white Americans' belief that the United States stood alone as the Temple of Freedom.

While white Americans celebrated their superiority over the Europeans, they were at each other's throats over how to govern the territory they had gained in the Mexican War. Before the war, the proponents of Manifest Destiny had believed the sectional divide would not hinder territorial expansion because in every newly acquired territory the settlers—white Americans—would decide whether to allow slavery, without interference from the US Congress. But in August 1846, the Wilmot Proviso—that Congress prohibit slavery in any territory acquired from Mexico—upended this expectation. The sectional conflict exploded. For the next fifteen years, until the guns roared at Fort Sumter, expansion and slavery would be inextricably intertwined.

Four men, two Whigs and two Democrats, occupied the White House in the 1850s: General Zachary Taylor, a hero of the Mexican War and a Whig, was elected in 1848 but died in July 1850. His vice president, Millard Fillmore, lost the Whig nomination in 1852 to General Winfield Scott, who was then defeated in the presidential election by Franklin Pierce, a northern Democrat who supported expansion and whose stance on sectional disputes over slavery was, a perceptive biographer writes, "flatly pro-southern."[1] His successor, Pennsylvanian James Buchanan (1857–61), was just as pro-southern, if not more so. One word, Kansas, epitomizes their two administrations. Pierce pushed through Congress a bill that created two territories, Kansas and Nebraska, that would be open to slavery, reversing a solemn pledge made by the US Congress in 1820; Buchanan aggressively supported the entry of Kansas as a slave state against the will of its inhabitants. With their foolhardy actions Pierce and Buchanan inflamed the sectional conflict, derailed their ambitious programs of territorial expansion, and spurred the extraordinary growth of the Republican Party. Republicans were not abolitionists, but they fiercely opposed the expansion of slavery beyond the states where it existed. In the 1856 presidential election, the Republican candidate gained 30 percent of the popular vote. In 1858, the Republicans displaced the Democrats as the largest party in the House. In the 1860 presidential election, the overriding issue was slavery, and the Republican candidate, Abraham Lincoln, won. His victory precipitated the secession of the South.

The Compromise of 1850

While southern and northern members of Congress brawled over slavery in the territories seized from Mexico, the 1848 discovery of gold in California meant that by late 1849 100,000 newcomers had settled there—a potpourri that included people from as far afield as China and Chile, but was mostly composed of US citizens. California needed law and order; it needed a government. The white settlers took matters into their own hands; with the encouragement of President Taylor, they drafted a constitution that barred slavery and petitioned for admission as a state. In Congress, southerners opposed the request, but slowly an agreement was forged: the Compromise of 1850 stipulated that in New Mexico (which included Arizona) and Utah (which included Nevada) the territorial legislatures would be free to decide whether slavery would be legal [Map 12]. Public slave auctions in the District of Columbia, which incurred the scorn of foreign diplomats and foreign visitors, were proscribed. To appease the South, the fugitive slave law of 1793 was tightened. But the key point was that California entered the Union as a free state. This was traumatic for many southerners: until then there had been an equal number of slave and free states in the Union, and therefore in the Senate; now parity was gone.

This sectional conflict intersected with filibustering, the attempt by groups of white Americans to conquer territories in Northern Mexico, Central America, and the Caribbean. Filibustering was a time-honored tradition in the United States: filibusters seeking to acquire territory for the United States had launched expeditions against Spanish Florida and Spanish Texas in the 1810s. But the filibusters of the 1850s were different. Some wanted to create independent states that they themselves would rule. They hoped, for example, to create a Republic of Lower California. Others sought to redress the balance between the South and the North by bringing another slave state into the Union. This meant, above all, Cuba.

Resurrecting old dreams[2]

Jefferson had lusted after Cuba, as had his successors, Madison and Monroe, but British opposition had rendered the acquisition of the island impossible. The Americans, therefore, waited. Let the island remain in the hands of feeble Spain until the United States was ready. Cuba disappeared from the concerns of US policymakers and from the public debate until 1847 when, inspired by the successful war against Mexico, many Americans began to look anew toward Cuba. This led President Polk to offer, in 1848, to buy the island from Spain; Madrid responded with a categorical refusal.

Spain's rebuff settled nothing. The Cuban issue flared up again in the early 1850s. In the free states a majority of citizens—Whigs and many Democrats—feared that the acquisition of Cuba would reignite the sectional conflict. The country "is like a house divided against itself on the slavery agitation," the *New York Herald* asserted. The *Herald* did not oppose the annexation of Cuba in principle, but believed the time was not ripe: "We are busy at home now, we can wait patiently." The New York *Journal of Commerce*, voice of the northern merchants, warned: "The possession of Cuba at this time would open anew the dangerous question relating to slavery and slave territory."[3]

In the South, Democrats and some Whigs were determined to redress the balance in the Senate lost in the Compromise of 1850. With its large population of 420,000 whites (as well as 435,000 enslaved people and 145,000 free people of color), Cuba "would in a short time make two powerful States," that is, four senators, a Democratic newspaper noted with enthusiasm.[4] Other southerners (mainly Whigs) thought that the Compromise had established a peace that was in the South's interest and ought not be disturbed. The annexation of Cuba "will probably reopen and embitter the sectional questions which have threatened and imperiled the existence of the Union," a Whig paper warned.[5]

Acquiring Cuba might also lead to war with Britain. Would London abandon its decades-long policy of support for Spanish rule and allow the United States to annex the island? And if war came would France join Britain? Alone, France was not strong enough to oppose US designs over Cuba, but the French government, led since late 1848 by President Louis-Napoleon Bonaparte (soon to be Napoleon III, emperor of the French), was intent on cultivating close relations with Britain and wanted Cuba to remain in Spanish hands.

Filibustering

There were three ways for the United States to acquire Cuba: US military invasion, purchase, or filibuster. Under the Whig administrations of presidents Taylor and Fillmore, the first two were out of the question because both men feared that the acquisition of the island would endanger the delicate sectional peace. Therefore, annexationists turned to filibustering. Two expeditions were launched from the United States to conquer Cuba. The first landed near the town of Cárdenas in May 1850, and the second at Bahía Honda in August 1851. The filibusters were overwhelmingly US citizens: the 605-man Cárdenas expedition included only five Cubans; the 435-man Bahía Honda expedition, only forty-nine. Both expeditions were led by Narciso López, a Venezuelan who had occupied senior positions in the Spanish administration in Cuba and, after falling out of favor, had begun to plot against Spanish rule; his plot discovered, he had fled to the United States.[6]

The filibusters planned to repeat the Texas precedent: they would take control of Cuba, proclaim its independence and, after a brief interval, demand annexation to the United States. Confronted with a *fait accompli* and fearful of provoking the South, the US Senate would not dare refuse.

To launch the filibustering expeditions with only a few hundred men signified contempt for Spain's military power as well as confidence that the Cubans were ready to revolt. But when the filibusters landed, no Cubans rallied to them. And the Spanish troops fought well; they proved, the London *Times* noted, "faithful, well conducted and resolute."[7] After landing near Cárdenas, López held the town for less than a day. Upon learning that 2,000 Spanish soldiers were approaching, the filibusters scurried back to their ship and steamed toward Key West. Their next attempt would end in disaster: many of the filibusters fell in battle, the others were captured, and many prisoners, including López, were executed.

These executions provoked a wave of outrage in the United States. The *Louisville Journal* noted that "extensive enlistments for a Cuba expedition are anticipated ... A spirit is aroused among our countrymen which ... nothing but Spanish blood can allay."[8] The paper, however, was mistaken. The annexationists might be bellicose, but they were not fools: few volunteered to face the Spanish troops in Cuba. The New York *Journal of Commerce* was closer to the temper of the people when it observed, "adventurers now see that ... to conquer Cuba without the cooperation of her own citizens, or a considerable portion of them, would require a large army."[9] There were no more expeditions. The filibusters intended to wait until their ranks had swelled to the thousands.

The election of 1852 gave the filibusters comfort: the Whigs were trounced, the Democrats won huge majorities in both houses of Congress, and President Pierce was a man to their liking. In his inaugural address Pierce averred: "the policy of my administration will not be controlled by any timid forebodings of evil from expansion."[10] The Democrats were eyeing Hawaii, a large slice of northern Mexico, and Samaná Bay in the Dominican Republic; they also wanted to expand US influence in Central America at Britain's expense. But the place of honor went to Cuba. "Cuba was understood by everyone to be the target of future U.S. expansion," a Pierce biographer writes. "In choosing the Senate's most outspoken advocate of Cuban annexation, Pierre Soulé, as minister to Madrid, Pierce signaled his future course."[11] Just a few weeks before Pierce's inauguration, in a speech in the Senate, Soulé had celebrated the filibusters and lambasted the Spanish government. "Let not Spain be deceived," he roared. "Cuba cannot long be hers." It would fall into "our mighty grasp."[12]

Soulé's instructions, written by Secretary of State William Marcy, were, however, remarkably restrained. They stated that a US attempt to purchase Cuba would be inopportune because "there is now no hope ... that ... [it] would be favorably received." Soulé was simply to ascertain "what arrangements have been made with Great Britain and France in regard with sustaining the present dominion of Spain over Cuba."[13] Until April 1854, this was the sum total of the instructions Soulé received about the issue.

This seems out of character with a president eager to acquire Cuba. US documents, including the papers of Pierce and other key officials, shed very little light on the administration's intentions toward the island. Historians, therefore, have speculated—in different directions. Pierce's biographer Peter Wallner argues that while the president's desire to annex Cuba was unambiguous, "how this was to be accomplished was unclear ... The Pierce administration had not decided on a policy with regard to Cuba and Spain." The lack of a plan of action, however, was not the only reason for Pierce's passivity. "Several circumstances," historian Basil Rauch writes, "suggest the possibility that the Pierce administration during its first year expected Cuba to be freed by a filibuster expedition."[14] This makes sense. The filibusters continued to organize, and they had a new, prestigious chief—former Mississippi governor John Quitman, who had served with Pierce in the Mexican War. Pierce hoped, biographer Roy Nichols concludes, "that the Cubans, aided by Americans, would revolt and, like Texas, seek admission to the Union as a state."[15]

Meanwhile, from Europe came rumblings of war. In 1853, Russia's policy toward Turkey grew increasingly threatening, and in October war broke out between them. Behind Turkey stood Britain, determined to halt the Russian advance toward the Mediterranean, and Napoleon III, who sought glory and British goodwill. The drift to a wider war was apparent to all. From Washington the British minister, John Crampton, warned that if Britain went to war against Russia, "we must expect to find renewed vitality given to all American 'doctrines,' pretensions, and aggressive schemes."[16] That is, if Britain were distracted by war against Russia, the US threat to Cuba would intensify. Aware of this danger, Spain embarked on a policy designed to curry London's favor.

The Africanization of Cuba

As the wave of independence swept Spanish America in the 1810s and 1820s, it was the upper class in almost every colony that led the struggle against Madrid. But not in Cuba. There, the upper class opposed independence because the island's burgeoning plantation economy required the massive importation of enslaved Africans. Cuba's slaveowners feared, above all, a slave revolt—like the one that had rocked Haiti in the 1790s. Independence was therefore a luxury the Cuban upper class could not afford. Their imperative was to maintain the status quo: to keep importing slaves to toil in the island's growing sugar plantations, and to avoid doing anything that might give the enslaved an opportunity to revolt.[17] The enslaved continued to arrive, by the tens of thousands, even though in 1818 Britain, which had embarked on a crusade to stamp out the slave trade, had imposed a treaty on Spain outlawing it. For the British, ending the slave trade became a question of honor, proof of their moral superiority as well as a demonstration of their power. After Brazil bowed to British pressure in 1850 and ended the slave trade, only Spain was left. Madrid's brazen violations of its treaty obligations exasperated British officials as well as British public opinion. In November 1852, the British chargé delivered a note to the Spanish foreign minister warning that Britain could not promise to protect Cuba if the Spanish persisted "in refusing their cordial cooperation with Her Majesty's Government for the total and final suppression of the slave trade to Cuba."[18]

Pierce, whose desire for Cuba was blatant, was elected at this juncture, heightening the pressure on Madrid. When the Spanish ambassador in London, Francisco Javier de Istúriz, approached the new British Foreign Secretary, Lord Clarendon, in March 1853 seeking assurances of support against the aggressive designs of the Pierce administration on Cuba, none were forthcoming. Instead, Istúriz reported, "as always whenever I talk about Cuba with these ministers, Lord Clarendon complains about the landings of slaves."[19]

Spanish officials resented Whitehall's constant impugning the honor of their government, but they needed British support. "The situation in Cuba," the Spanish foreign minister warned, "requires that we eliminate everything that could serve as a justification or pretext for Britain to ignore the conquest of the island by another power," that is, the United States.[20] On September 23, 1853, the government replaced Cuba's governor Valentín Cañedo, whom the British accused of conniving with the slave trade, with a man who had no sympathy for slavery, Juan de la Pezuela, and gave him unprecedented instructions: he must "prevent the entry of slaves in Cuba."[21]

Pezuela arrived in Cuba on December 2, 1853. He dismissed senior officials guilty of colluding with the slave traders, he ordered Spanish officials to search plantations for newly imported slaves, he instituted an annual registration of enslaved people, and he decreed that all enslaved people for whom the masters could not show registered titles would be freed. British officials penned missive after missive to express their "satisfaction for the honest efforts" made by Pezuela to suppress the trade.[22]

Pezuela did more. On May 24, 1854, he established a militia of free Blacks with white officers and black noncommissioned officers. Pezuela explained that the militia would help defend Cuba "if the extraordinary circumstances of the war in Europe" made it necessary.[23] His meaning was obvious: in March Britain and France had declared war on Russia, and Pezuela feared that the US government, or the filibusters, might take advantage of London's preoccupation to launch an attack on Cuba. In the United States, not even the *New York Tribune*, flagship of the antislavery Whigs, was comfortable with the idea of a black militia. It reported that "Every vagabond negro who presents itself is enlisted, and from that moment he is an important personage. . . . He is allowed to wear his side arms and to insult both women and men with impunity."[24] A wild charge, but for whites in the United States—even those who opposed slavery—the idea of a black militia was frightening.

Spain had embarked on a dangerous gamble: the measures it was taking to cultivate British support against US aggression were bound to increase the likelihood of that very aggression. Pezuela's policy gave new life to an old bugbear in the United States: the Africanization of Cuba. The fear was based on a simple scenario: the British, in a wily bid to prevent the United States from acquiring Cuba, would pressure feeble Spain to emancipate all the enslaved on the island, knowing full well that the United States would never want Cuba without slavery; Spain would acquiesce, preferring the ruin of the island to its cession to the United States. "It must end in the Africanization of Cuba," wrote to the Washington *Union*, the semiofficial newspaper of the Pierce administration, "the establishment upon that island of some form of barbarous or semi-barbarous negro government or anarchy."[25] A leading southern paper, the *Richmond Enquirer*, warned: "after the Captain General [Pezuela] has promulgated his decree of emancipation . . . it will be too late to talk about the annexation of Cuba. . . . The history of Haiti admonishes us of the difficulty of conquest under such circumstances."[26]

The Kansas-Nebraska Act

Pezuela's "Africanization" of Cuba occurred at a time when the United States was in the throes of sectional conflict triggered by the attempt, spearheaded by southern Democrats, to repeal the Missouri Compromise of 1820. That compromise had stipulated that in the vast expanse of the Louisiana Purchase slavery would be "forever prohibited" north of 36°30' [Map 6]. In January 1854, however, southern members of Congress convinced Pierce to support a measure that would create two territories that would be open to slavery—Kansas and Nebraska—north of the 36°30' line [Map 13]. The struggle that ensued for the following three-and-a-half months was, historian David Potter writes, "of unprecedented intensity." The Democrats controlled both the House and the Senate, but the Kansas-Nebraska Act ruptured the party along the sectional divide. Public opinion in the North was bitterly hostile to the measure, and the administration had to work hard, applying "whip and spur" on northern Democrats to garner votes. Finally, on March 4, 1854, the Senate approved the bill and the battle moved to the House, which followed suit, on May 22, by a vote of 113 to 100. All but two of the fifty-nine southern Democrats voted in favor, but half of the eighty-eight northern Democrats bolted. The Whigs also split along sectional lines.[27]

The Kansas-Nebraska Act exacerbated northerners' fears of southern power, while eviscerating their support for the administration. It also cast the issue of Cuba in a harsh sectional light. It hardened the northern Whigs' opposition to the acquisition of the island. Southern Whigs, too, opposed annexation because it would deepen the sectional conflict; furthermore, they asserted, there was "not the slightest evidence" that Spain intended to Africanize Cuba.[28]

When Pierce had been elected, the Democratic Party—North and South—had appeared united on the need to acquire Cuba. Even northern Democrats who feared that the island's annexation would rekindle the sectional conflict had rallied behind Pierce, whose desire to acquire Cuba was evident. "The Democrats of 1852 meant to resume where Polk had left off," David Potter concludes. They wanted Cuba.[29]

The battle over Kansas-Nebraska fractured this party unity. Northern Democrats looked askance at any attempt to acquire Cuba, leaving southern Democrats almost alone in demanding its annexation. The latter's demands were echoed by the Washington *Union*. This was significant because the *Union* usually spoke for the administration. On March 24, 1854, it noted: "The indications are daily multiplying that we are not long to enjoy uninterrupted peace with Spain. We feared as much when we saw Pezuela appointed captain-general [governor] of Cuba ... because of his known inveterate hostility to the United States and their institutions." The British government, the *Union* explained, had urged Spain to appoint Pezuela because "it had confidence that he could be employed under its dictation as an instrument to Africanize that beautiful island."[30] The British, the *Union* thundered, "would rather see the island sunk into the sea than it should pass into the hands of the American people; and Spain has united with France and Britain in attempting the next thing to that—that being to render Cuba both valueless to us as an acquisition and the citadel where the enemies of the American Union may safely concoct and consummate their plots."[31] Pierce and his aides may have been using the *Union* to intimidate Spain in the hope of forcing it to sell Cuba, but there is no doubt that they took the threat of Africanization seriously. Pierce, historian Robert May writes, "was nearly as worried" as were the southern Democrats "about Cuba's Africanization."[32]

The response of the US Government

On March 15, 1854, Secretary of State Marcy instructed a secret agent, Charles Davis, to go to Cuba to investigate whether Spain had embarked on the Africanization of the island. Davis reported on May 22: "The conclusion is irresistible that the emancipation of the slaves and consequent Africanization of the island is the true object had in view, and to which the march is as rapid as circumstances will allow."[33] Marcy received the same assessment from the US consul in Havana, Alexander Clayton, and from Clayton's successor, William Robertson.[34]

This added urgency to the administration's policy toward Cuba, which for more than a year had been simply to allow the filibusters to organize. On April 3, 1854, Marcy instructed Soulé in Madrid to try to buy Cuba for no more than $130 million (c. $4 billion). If purchase was not possible, Marcy wrote, Soulé should direct his efforts "to the next most desirable object, which is to detach the island from the Spanish dominion and from all dependence on any European power."[35]

What did Marcy mean by "detach"? According to two respected US historians, "by *detach* Marcy meant to say that the independence of Cuba was the object," not annexation.[36] This is splitting hairs: at the time, Americans believed that the island's independence would be an ephemeral way station on the road to annexation—as had been the case for Texas. Thus Soulé, that furious annexationist, had used "independence" and "annexation" interchangeably in his January 1853 Senate speech, when he had concluded that Cuba must belong to the United States. Cuba's independence would have violated the Pierce administration's goal of acquiring the island; it would have been an open slap to the South.

John Crampton, the very able British minister in Washington, understood that the administration was preparing to act. "There is, I fear, mischief brewing about Cuba." he wrote to Clarendon a few days before Marcy's dispatch to Soulé about acquiring the island. "The European war will not pass over without the question ... of whether we are to see Cuba become part of the United States, or to determine to prevent it by force, will be brought up for our decision. As they say here, 'we shall have to face the music' on that point before long."[37]

But the Pierce administration was hobbled by the uproar caused by the battle over Kansas-Nebraska. On May 25, 1854, Marcy wrote in a private letter to John Mason, the US minister in Paris: "The Nebraska bill ... will shortly become a law. From this which has proven a very troublesome matter we shall at once enter upon another still more embarrassing—the Cuban question ... The course to be pursued in this matter is not definitively settled, and I tell you is not one easily settled." The next day he wrote to Buchanan in London, "The Nebraska question being now disposed of, the most important matter to come up will be Cuba. It is under advisement, but the course to be taken, unsettled."[38]

The semi-official Washington *Union* argued that the best policy for the United States was to purchase Cuba from Spain. Should this fail, the only option was war. "The day may be near at hand," the *Union* warned in June 1854, "when ... we may have to present to the government of Madrid the purse in one hand and the sword in the other, and say to it Take Your Choice."[39]

The administration's hopes were fueled by turmoil in Spain. The country's deepening economic crisis led in July to massive street demonstrations, unrest in the army, and the establishment of a new government imposed by the rebellious generals. Soulé wrote to Marcy, "What a moment for taking in our own hands that question of Cuba, which it seems almost impossible we may hereafter be able to adjust in any other way than by force of arms!" Like Soulé, the US minister in Paris, John Mason, was optimistic that Spain would agree to sell, and Marcy's deputy, Dudley Mann, who was also in Paris, was ebullient: "I look upon it almost as good as accomplished," he wrote to Marcy on August 31, 1854. "Spain must have money or sink in a state of anarchy," he explained in a letter four days later. Britain and France, embroiled in war against Russia, had no money to spare. Spain would have to sell Cuba to the United States.[40]

Spain was bankrupt, indebted to foreign governments, riven by scandals and corruption, and torn by internal strife—but it was folly to expect that any Spanish government would sell Cuba. The new Spanish authorities were categorical: they would not sell Cuba—under any circumstance. After the high hopes of the summer, the Pierce administration was running out of options. Purchase was a fading hope and filibustering a receding mirage. The filibusters had promised much and delivered nothing. "For more than two years the filibusters have been announcing the departure of a new expedition" to seize Cuba, the Spanish minister reported from Washington in August 1854. "But the truth is that . . . they don't have the means or the confidence to carry out a major operation. The lesson of the tragic end of López's expedition has been seared into them." The British minister agreed: "Ever since the Lopez affair, I have expressed the opinion that no Filibusters' expedition against Cuba will leave the United States," he wrote to Clarendon on June 8, 1854.[41] By the summer of 1854 this was also the administration's conclusion.[42]

There was a third way: war.

War clouds over Cuba

On September 14, 1854, British and French troops landed in Crimea. For the next year, Britain's attention would be riveted on the bloody battles in that distant land. For the first time since Jefferson had eyed Cuba, the island seemed within America's grasp. The British complained that the Pierce administration was seeking to take advantage of the war. "Our relations with the U. States are clearly becoming more and more difficult every day," Prime Minister George Aberdeen noted a few days after the British troops had landed in Crimea. Crampton, the British minister in Washington, warned that the Pierce administration was "about as dangerous a one as we have ever had to deal with."[43]

Would Britain have intervened if the United States had invaded Cuba? British documents provide no answer. The Royal Navy could have repelled a US attack on Cuba, but war against the Yankees would have added a terrible burden—the loss of trade with the United States—to a Britain already straining under the weight of the Crimean War.

"Whatever may be the causes of transient differences between the Government of this country and that of the United States," *The Times* observed in August 1854, "these controversies and disputes bear no comparison to the enormous common interests of two great nations."[44] Palmerston, who replaced Aberdeen as prime minister in February 1855, believed that the only way to deal with "Vulgar minded Bullies, and such unfortunately the people of the United States are," was to be firm—but he also acknowledged that "a quarrel with the United States is at all times undesirable and is especially so when we are engaged in war with another power."[45] Furthermore, while the Crimean War would not have seriously diminished British naval capabilities in a conflict with the United States, it would have limited London's ability to defend Canada from a US invasion.

The clues suggest that if the United States had attacked Cuba the British would have been very reluctant to intervene. This created an opportunity for Washington. But Pierce was hamstrung by the battle over the Kansas-Nebraska Act. Denounced throughout the North as a tool of the southern slaveowners, Pierce could ill afford to provide his critics with additional fodder. "To tell you an unwelcome truth," Marcy wrote to the US minister in France in July 1854, "the Nebraska question has sadly shattered our party in all the Free States, and deprived it of that strength which was needed and would have been much more profitably used for the acquisition of Cuba."[46]

The administration was torn between its desire to annex Cuba and its need to quell the sectional conflict at home. And so, at Pierce's behest, Marcy turned to the three most senior US diplomats in Europe for counsel. On August 16, 1854, he instructed Soulé to meet with Buchanan and Mason, his colleagues in London and Paris, "to consult together … and to adopt measures for perfect concert of action in aid of your negotiations at Madrid [to buy Cuba]."[47] The three ministers met in Ostend, Belgium, on October 9 to prepare a secret report for the president, the notorious Ostend Manifesto. After noting that the United States "could not permit Cuba to be Africanized," they asserted that "The Union can never enjoy repose, nor possess reliable security, as long as Cuba is not embraced within its boundaries." They argued that the administration should make one final attempt to purchase Cuba; if Spain refused, the "law of self-preservation" demanded that the United States seize the island by force.[48]

The Ostend Manifesto has long occupied a special place in the history of nineteenth century US foreign policy. It was, a prominent historian asserts, "incredible."[49] Its language is bombastic, its spirit nakedly aggressive. Its recommendation, however, is consistent with Marcy's April 3, 1854, instructions to Soulé: if purchase proved impossible, then the United States must "detach" the island from Spain. It is also consonant with an important theme in US policy: the propensity to use force to grab territory from weaker neighbors. This had been the keynote of US relations with the Indian tribes. And with Spain as well, exemplified by the acquisition of the Floridas. President Polk's policy against Mexico was as aggressive as that proposed by the Ostend Manifesto against Spain.

The spirit of the Ostend Manifesto was, therefore, true to past US practice toward weak neighbors. But its timing was terrible: Buchanan, Mason and Soulé—the three authors of the Manifesto—took no account of the storm the Kansas-Nebraska Act had created in the United States. This was what made the manifesto a crass political blunder. To make matters worse, the Democrats suffered heavy losses in the free states in the fall 1854 mid-term elections, thereby losing control of the House of Representatives.

Under these circumstances, there was no way that Pierce could have followed the prescriptions of the Ostend Manifesto. It was a non-starter. Had it not been for the Kansas-Nebraska Act it is very likely that the Democrats, North and South, would have united to support the conquest of the island. Their attitude, when Pierce entered the White House, was aptly captured by the Spanish minister in Washington: "1. We resolve that the Saints will inherit the Earth; 2. We resolve that we are the Saints."[50] But the policy advocated in the Ostend Manifesto would have offered further proof to Pierce's critics that the administration had sold out to the southern slavocracy. This was made blatant when the Manifesto was leaked (probably by a garrulous Buchanan aide) to the *New York Herald*, which began publishing increasingly accurate reports of its contents in late October. A firestorm ensued. Confronted with a mounting wave of criticism in the North, Pierce ran for cover. On November 13, in a sharp letter to Soulé (soon shared with Congress), Marcy rejected the Manifesto as wholly inconsistent with the administration's peace-loving policy.[51]

Amidst this debacle, the administration could point to one piece of good news: Pezuela had been recalled on August 2, 1854. The threat of "Africanization" had passed. The generals who had seized power in Spain the previous month had close ties—personal and financial—with the great slaveowners and slave merchants of Cuba. Fear that Pezuela's policies might precipitate a US invasion had added to the reasons for his dismissal. "The United States had encouraged the removal of one of the few honest and progressive Spanish rulers that Cuba ever had," an eminent Cuban historian concluded.[52]

Spain's new rulers returned to the policies followed before Pezuela's tenure in Cuba: they loudly condemned the slave trade while fostering it *sotto voce*. Pezuela's measures against the slave trade were revoked and the black militia disbanded. Spain no longer needed to court British goodwill. The fracas over the Ostend Manifesto had reassured Madrid: Pierce had been defanged.

Mexico, again[53]

Pierce's one territorial acquisition was Mexican. He wanted to purchase territory in northern Mexico; he was willing to be flexible about the precise boundaries, but it must include land in what are today southern Arizona and southwestern New Mexico which, US officials believed, would provide the shortest and most practicable route for a southern transcontinental railway. In August 1853, Pierce's envoy, James Gadsden, informed Mexico's corrupt dictator, Antonio López de Santa Anna, of Pierce's intentions. Santa Anna needed money to put down revolts against his rule, and, above all, he feared antagonizing the United States. The Pierce administration claimed that part of the land it demanded had already been ceded by Mexico in the Treaty of Guadalupe Hidalgo. The

Mexican authorities knew from bitter experience how the United States could exploit a border dispute to manufacture a war, as Polk had done, and they were acutely aware that many in the United States shared Pierce's lust for more land in northern Mexico.

"Mexico was too weak to resist the attacks of the United States," Santa Anna told the British minister, Percy Doyle, "and must fall all into their power, unless they were supported by the Great Powers of Europe."[54] He turned to Britain, France, and Spain. Such was the power of France, his envoy pleaded with Napoleon's foreign minister in October 1853, "that the only thing Mexico would need to guarantee its security . . . would be a declaration that the French government would not countenance" the United States annexing any more Mexican territory. The French didn't even bother to reply. "We have not been able to advance a single inch in Paris," a Mexican official reported in April 1854.[55]

The news from London was equally dismal. The British were preoccupied with Russia, the Mexican minister, J.M. de Castillo y Lanzas, reported but even if they hadn't been, they would not help because their interests in Mexico "are minor." Britain might fight for Cuba, he insisted, but not for Mexico.[56] Santa Anna "must be well aware," Clarendon wrote to Doyle in Mexico City, that any British "interference . . . to protect Mexico from American aggression . . . would be regarded as a national offense" by the United States. All Britain did for Mexico was to urge Santa Anna to embark on a program of domestic reforms that might reinvigorate his country. "The difficulties in the way of success may be great," Clarendon added piously, "but so in proportion will be the glory of surmounting them."[57]

Knowing that Pierce wanted Cuba—and therefore threatened Spain—Santa Anna sought a defensive alliance with Madrid. It was a non-starter. "Sympathy and goodwill toward Mexico exist in Spain," the Mexican minister in Madrid reported, but that "cannot replace warships, soldiers and guns."[58]

There was an irony: Americans often complained about European interference in North America, but the Mexicans knew there would be no interference on their behalf, just as there had been none in 1846. "Our attempt to inspire the *active* goodwill of these great European powers," Castillo y Lanzas wrote from London, "has failed utterly."[59]

While Santa Anna sought European support, the US envoy, James Gadsden, pressed with Pierce's demands; fearing war, the Mexican dictator agreed to sell 45,000 square miles along the Mexican border for $15 million (c. $464 million). The Gadsden Treaty was signed on December 30, 1853.

Gadsden's timing—like that of the authors of the Ostend Manifesto—was unfortunate for the Pierce administration. In early 1854, the battle over Kansas-Nebraska erupted. Many free state senators feared that the Gadsden Purchase, like the desire to annex Cuba, was part of the southern plot to dominate the Union and they successfully amended it, returning 15,000 square miles to Mexico and slashing the purchase price by one third. The senate approved the revised treaty on April 25.

The Pierce administration also sought to annex Hawaii and acquire Samana Bay in the Dominican Republic but failed: its diplomacy was clumsy, it was constrained by the sectional struggle at home, and the British and French stiffened the opposition in both

Hawaii and the Dominican Republic. Neither issue attracted much attention in the United States and the administration itself was distracted by more weighty foreign policy issues: Cuba and Central America.

The saga of William Walker

Americans had paid little attention to Central America until the late 1840s, when three developments enhanced its importance: the annexation of Texas brought the United States geographically closer to the isthmus; the annexation of California opened the west coast; and the discovery of gold near Sacramento meant that many Americans would go there and it was easier to travel to California via the Caribbean and Central America than by covered wagons overland. There were two routes to cross the isthmus, both controlled by US citizens. In 1851, New York tycoon Cornelius Vanderbilt established the Accessory Transit Company through Nicaragua, and late that same year the Panama Railroad—the largest American direct foreign investment before the civil war—was partially opened. [60]

The British had been the dominant power in Central America, but they adapted to the new reality: in the Clayton-Bulwer Treaty of April 1850, London and Washington agreed to joint control and joint operation of any canal that might be built through the isthmus and pledged to abstain from acquiring territory in Central America. (The British already had a colony there, British Honduras, today's Belize; they controlled the Bay Islands, some thirty miles off the northern coast of Honduras; and they had a protectorate over the Indian Mosquito kingdom, on the Caribbean coast of present-day Nicaragua and Honduras.) In the United States, the Clayton-Bulwer Treaty was roundly condemned by the Democrats who were eager to control the region. Once they returned to power, with Pierce, they claimed that the treaty required Britain to abandon its possessions in Central America, while the British argued that the treaty was not retroactive. What the Democrats really wanted was exclusive US control of a future canal.[61]

It is against this backdrop that William Walker, the most famous filibuster of nineteenth century America, went to Nicaragua in June 1855 at the invitation of the ruling elite of the city of León, which was locked in a civil war against the ruling elite of Granada, the country's other major city. Walker led a group of fifty-eight well-armed American mercenaries.[62] Reinforced by hundreds of volunteers that kept arriving from the United States, attracted by the lure of riches and adventure, Walker defeated the rag-tag Granadan troops and established a puppet government under a pliant Nicaraguan. As his principal biographer, Michel Gobat, explains, Walker could not have succeeded without the support of two different groups of Nicaraguans: members of the elite who admired the United States and hoped that their country could join the Union as a state, and peasant leaders who hoped that the foreigners could relieve the oppression their people endured.

In July 1856, after a fraudulent election, Walker anointed himself president of the country. Unlike the filibustering expeditions organized against Cuba in the early 1850s with the goal of annexing the island to the United States, Walker wanted to create an empire that he would rule. He had a grandiose vision: his domain would eventually encompass all Central America.

Costa Rica, Nicaragua's southern neighbor, understood the threat he posed. President Juan Mora turned to the only European country that could help him, Britain. (French interests in Central America were, as a French report noted, "minimal,"[63] and Spain was too weak.) But the British responded with caution. Mora asked his consul general in London, Edward Wallerstein, "Is it possible that the European nations—which could so easily help us and at so little sacrifice to themselves—will in fact do nothing?"[64] In early 1856, London did agree to sell 2,000 muskets to Costa Rica, but the deal fell through, for reasons that are explained neither in the British nor the Costa Rican archives.[65] Whitehall complained about Walker to the US government and encouraged the Central Americans to resist; beyond this, it did nothing. The Admiralty ordered the British naval commanders along the Caribbean coast of Central America to use force only to defend British life and property "and to leave all other matters for the Diplomatists to settle as they best can."[66] Britain, Foreign Secretary Clarendon told Wallerstein, "could not assume the burden of defending every country in the world that is not strong enough to defend itself."[67]

Costa Rica, therefore, acted alone. In April 1856, an army of about 2,500 Costa Ricans, mostly peasants and urban artisans, invaded Nicaragua. After initial successes they were poised to attack Granada, where Walker had concentrated his remaining forces. "Panic seized his followers," Gobat writes. But cholera broke out among the Costa Ricans and forced them to return home. "For the filibusters the cholera outbreak was nothing short of a miracle that saved them from certain death."[68]

Walker sought to enlist the support of the US government and American public opinion by raising the usual bugaboo: Britain, he claimed, was seeking to assert hegemony over the region. President Pierce had given tacit support to the filibusters who sought to annex Cuba, but Walker was simply an adventurer eager to create a personal fiefdom; he complicated US relations with the countries of Latin America, as well as with Britain. Therefore, Pierce waffled. In December 1855, he refused to recognize Walker's puppet government, but the following May, as the Democratic presidential convention approached, he bowed to sentiment within his party and changed his stance. In August, having lost the nomination to Buchanan, he changed his stance again and refused to receive the minister sent by Walker. As Pierce zig-zagged, Secretary of State Marcy remained steadfast in opposition to Walker. Another powerful foe of Walker was Cornelius Vanderbilt: Walker had seized Vanderbilt's transit company in Nicaragua in February 1856.

Having failed to gain the assistance of the Pierce administration, Walker resorted to a desperate gamble: in September 1856 he reestablished slavery in Nicaragua. He was not motivated by sympathy for the institution—rather, his record indicates that he disliked it. He was simply an opportunist: since Pierce had rebuffed him, he would seek the support of southerners. He was impelled by an existential threat: Costa Rica, Guatemala,

El Salvador, and Honduras had united against him. Their troops had entered Nicaragua. It would be a rare and important moment of unity against foreign aggression in the tormented history of Central America.

In the fall of 1856, Walker had approximately 1,000 filibusters; they faced about 6,000 Central American soldiers, who fought with unexpected grit. Forced to evacuate Granada in late 1856, Walker decided to torch it as an object lesson to his enemies. "As the burning went on," he wrote, "the excitement . . . increased the thirst for liquor" of the filibusters, and the destruction proceeded amid scenes reminiscent "of a wild Bacchanalian revel."[69] The following May the US Navy evacuated Walker and his men, saving their lives.

Walker tried three times to return to Nicaragua. President Buchanan disapproved of his efforts, believing that they hindered the expansion of US influence in the region. Walker's first two attempts to return were frustrated by the US Navy; on his third try, in August 1860, he landed in Honduras with about 110 men and was captured by Honduran forces assisted by British marines. Sentenced to death by a Honduran court, he was executed on September 11. His death provoked little outcry in the United States: his repeated failures had undermined his mystique, and Americans were in any case focused on the fate of the Union.

Walker's exploits shaped Central American attitudes toward the United States. In the early 1850s, the region's elites had seen Americans as an antidote to the overbearing British. By the end of the decade, the roles were reversed: the Central Americans looked to Britain for protection from the Yankees. Walker's "liberal empire," as Gobat calls it, was unlike the United States because it replaced democracy for white men with one man's rule. But it was similar to the United States in its racism. Walker's weekly paper, *El Nicaraguense*, stated openly in its English section that Walker's empire would be led by US Anglo-Saxons, who were superior to the "half civilized races of Central America" and pointed out that the most ignorant white American had more natural intelligence than education could ever give to the "Indian or half-breed of Central America."[70] Perhaps Walker's rule would not have been worse for the Nicaraguan peasants than the life they endured under their native elites. But even this is open to question: Walker intended to bring tens of thousands of white Americans to Nicaragua and transform the country into a settler colony, and he intended to enforce vagrancy laws (forced labor) against the native population—*El Nicaraguense* estimated that about one third of Nicaragua's males would "fall under the effects" of the vagrancy laws and "another large proportion," laborers who violated their contracts with their employers, would be sentenced "to forced labor on the public works."[71]

Perhaps the best epitaph to Walker's saga was penned by the US minister to Nicaragua in 1858. "There is in all this country," he reported, "a deep-seated terror that, when the Americans are admitted into it, the natives will be thrust aside—their nationality lost, their religion destroyed—and the common classes be converted into hewers of wood and drawers of water."[72] Walker's deeds reverberated in South America. "Walker," wrote a prominent Chilean intellectual, "is the invasion, Walker is the conquest, Walker is the United States."[73]

Relations with Britain

British caution toward Central America was pragmatic: the British public had little interest in the region, and Whitehall had concluded that US dominance was inevitable: "Sooner or later these countries will be overrun and occupied just as in our own time have been Louisiana, Texas, and California added to the Union," Clarendon wrote in 1857. Prime Minister Palmerston agreed: "These Yankees ... are on the spot, strong, deeply interested in the matter, totally unscrupulous and dishonest and determined somehow or other to carry their point; we are far away, weak from distance, controlled by the indifference of the nation as to the question discussed, and by its strong commercial interest in maintaining peace with the United States."[74] Moreover, England faced more pressing issues. Having concluded the war with Russia in early 1856, it was engaged for the next four years in a colonial war against China, it faced a mutiny of Indian troops in 1857, and across the channel Napoleon III was plotting to make France the hegemon of continental Europe. And so the British stepped back from Central America: in the late 1850s they agreed to relinquish their protectorate over the Mosquito Kingdom, and they ceded the Bay Islands to Honduras. But they kept a toehold: they remained in British Honduras and retained the joint control over a future canal stipulated in the Clayton-Bulwer Treaty.

While British and Americans sparred over Central America, their relations in East Asia were congenial. Washington welcomed British aggression against China because Americans were able to share in the commercial concessions extorted from the Chinese, and for this same reason the British approved US warships in 1854 forcing Japan to open its ports. (US policy toward China and Japan is discussed in chapter 13.)

Closer to home, there was progress on the Canadian front. In 1854, London and Washington concluded a reciprocity treaty that permitted free trade between the United States and Canada (that is, Lower and Upper Canada) of most raw materials and agricultural products and gave each side access to the other's fisheries north of the 36th parallel (roughly north of North Carolina). It was a treaty that brought benefits to both sides.

Another positive note was struck by the strong economic ties between Britain and the United States. They continued to be each other's best customer; trade had received an additional boost when in 1846 Britain had abandoned protectionism and the United States had adopted a low tariff (and lowered it further in 1857); moreover, Britain was the United States' major source of foreign investment.

But despite these strong economic ties, the consonant policies in East Asia and the easing of tension over Canada, the attitude of US citizens toward Britain remained unfriendly. Some—following Hamilton's example—admired British institutions and culture, but the majority of white Americans followed Jefferson and bore a deep hostility to all things British, nurtured by the War of Independence, by the clashes over neutral rights and impressment during the wars of the French Revolution and the Napoleonic wars, and then by the War of 1812, when the British had allied with the Indians and armed runaway slaves. In the following decades, Americans continued to resent the condescension which the British elite displayed toward them, and they cursed Britain as the perennial obstacle to US expansion: in Texas, in Mexico, and more recently in Cuba and Central America. In the late 1840s, hundreds of thousands of Irish immigrants, fleeing the famine that devastated their country, a British possession, swelled the ranks of Anglophobes in the United States. During the Crimean War, white Americans sympathized with Russia—because it was fighting Britain.

For African Americans, however, Britain represented freedom—at least for those many, free or enslaved, who knew that Britain had abolished slavery in the 1830s and that Canada, a British colony, was a safe haven for escaped slaves. African Americans across the free states, writes historian Van Gosse, celebrated August 1, the day the British had emancipated West Indian enslaved peoples, "as their own vicarious Independence Day." A few went further. In 1856, a black pastor, William Newby, urged African Americans never to fight against England, even if it were at war against the United States: "England has done her duty toward us; she has abolished slavery in her colonies, and is doing what she can to destroy the system from the earth . . . her example, her influence is on the side of freedom. Would we, could we, do battle against England?"[75]

In the late 1850s, tensions over the international slave trade added to the strains between the United States and Britain. The United States insisted that it alone had the right to stop and search ships flying the American flag. In the Webster-Ashburton Treaty of 1842, the Tyler administration had pledged to maintain a naval squadron on the African coast to police its merchant marine, but because stopping the international slave trade was not a priority for the US government, the squadron was ineffectual, and the Star and Stripes became the refuge of slavers of all nationalities, to the mounting frustration of the British government. By the early 1850s Cuba was the only destination of slavers in the Western Hemisphere, and after the Crimean War Britain intensified its efforts to stamp out that trade. In the spring of 1858, British warships began searching vessels flying the US flag in the Caribbean. For Americans this was a reminder of the impressment of earlier times. Their reaction was immediate and violent. The press inveighed against Britain, the Senate unanimously approved a resolution denouncing British actions, and President Buchanan sent the navy to the Gulf of Mexico with orders to protect all vessels flying the Star and Stripes from the Royal Navy. At a time when the United States was torn by the sectional strife and "bleeding Kansas," southerners and northerners in a rare display of national unity applauded Buchanan's firm response. Even the *National Era*, flagship of the abolitionist press, joined the pack. It admitted that "the slaver seeks protection under the American flag," but this did not give the British the right to stop ships flying the Star and Stripes. "This state of things cannot be tolerated—it could not be continued without war."[76]

Britain blinked. On June 18, 1858, Whitehall declared that its legal advisers had concluded that it had "no right of search, no right of *visitation* whatever in time of peace." To avoid "the possibility of collision," the Admiralty would withdraw its ships from Cuban waters. "We have yielded all they have asked, and we were wise in doing so," the London *Times* approved. [77] Presciently, *The Times* also noted how before the end of the century the balance of power between Britain and the United States would change, because of "the immense growth of the Union. It is not that we shall decrease, but the States must increase. The stripling, now our equal, must one day be a giant."[78]

South America looks north

The expansionist fever in the United States aroused anxiety also in South America. "The strong feelings of hostility [of the Latin Americans] toward the United States were fully justified," a Peruvian historian writes. "US foreign policy was aggressive and arrogant."[79] The South Americans had heard the lurid language of Manifest Destiny, they had seen the United States annex Texas and go to war against Mexico, robbing it of one third of its territory (half, if Texas is included). They had read "the horrifying accounts" of the violence inflicted by the American Anglo-Saxons on Spanish Americans working in the California gold mines,[80] and they had seen the filibusters threaten Central America.

They had also begun to hear again about the Monroe Doctrine. In his first Annual Message in December 1845, Polk had referred to Monroe's statement to repeat that North America was closed to European colonization. "His invocation of the Monroe Doctrine," David Pletcher writes, was "the first important reference to it since 1823."[81] In the 1850s, it became part of the American credo. The Democrats brandished it to bludgeon the Whigs for betraying US interests in Central America with the Clayton-Bulwer Treaty. In London, the US minister during the Pierce administration, James Buchanan, invoked the Monroe Doctrine as he urged the British to surrender their possessions in Central America. But neither Britain nor any other country in the world recognized the Monroe Doctrine, which was simply a unilateral declaration of the United States without any basis in international law.[82]

As president, Buchanan had continued Pierce's aggressive policy, demanding a large slice of northern Mexico and coveting Cuba; if Spain refused to sell the island, he told Congress in words redolent of the Ostend Manifesto, the United States might have to take it by force, "under the imperative and overriding law of self-preservation."[83] His territorial ambitions, however, were derailed in the maelstrom of the sectional conflict. His gunboat diplomacy was more successful. In late 1858, he sent a fleet of eighteen warships and four supply vessels carrying 2,000 soldiers to intimidate the government of Paraguay. (Paraguayan soldiers had fired on a US warship that had intentionally sailed into restricted waters.) This was the largest naval expedition that had ever left the United States in peacetime; duly bullied, Paraguay apologized and paid an indemnity. It was "perhaps the most ludicrous assertion of American power" during Buchanan's presidency, one of his biographers writes.[84] Perhaps, but for the Latin Americans the message was clear. The southward advance of the United States had begun, Peru's foreign minister warned, and unless checked it would not cease until the New World was "only one nation," the United States.[85] But on April 12, 1861, rebel soldiers opened fire on Fort Sumter in Charleston harbor. The Civil War had begun, and the southward advance of the United States was halted, temporarily.

The Civil War

On April 15, the day after Fort Sumter surrendered, President Lincoln called upon the loyal states to raise 75,000 volunteers; on the 19th, he declared a blockade of the ports of the Confederacy. Most Northerners, cognizant of their region's superiority in manpower and industrial capacity, were confident that the conflict would be brief. Instead, it would be the longest and bloodiest war fought in the Western world in the interim between the Napoleonic Wars and the First World War. It cost the lives of approximately 750,000 soldiers out of a population of about 30 million in 1860—more than all those killed in all other wars ever fought by the United States.[86]

Abraham Lincoln, who led the Union with an increasingly sure hand through the Civil War, had not been the frontrunner for his party's presidential nomination when the Republican convention assembled in May 1860. That honor belonged to Senator William Seward (R-NY). However, whereas Seward was aggressively anti-slavery, Lincoln took a more moderate stance. Like Seward, he hated slavery and categorically opposed its extension to the territories, but he did not call for the end of slavery in the District of Columbia; he did not oppose the interstate slave trade; and his criticism of southerners was temperate, more in sorrow than anger. Acknowledging that the constitution protected slavery, he urged Northerners to respect the fugitive slave law. Seward, on the other hand, appealed to a "higher law" and asked Northerners to flout the fugitive slave law. And whereas Seward defended the right of African American men to vote, Lincoln stood squarely with most Republicans in opposition. (Black men were fully enfranchised only in five New England states.) Lincoln believed slavery could be ended only gradually and with the consent of the slaveowners, and unlike Seward he advocated the departure of Blacks from the United States. "What I would most desire," he explained in 1858, "would be the separation of the white and black races," with the voluntary departure of African Americans to the West Indies, Latin America, or Africa. He seemed, therefore, more electable than Seward, and the Republicans chose him as their candidate for the presidency. In his inaugural message, on March 4, 1861, Lincoln sought to reassure the South, pledging that he had "no purpose, directly or indirectly, to interfere with slavery in the states where it exists."[87]

But for the South any Republican president was unacceptable. Between December 1860 and May 1861, eleven southern states left the Union and founded the Confederacy, waving the banner of self-determination. Their real cause, however, was the defense of slavery. "Our new government," the Confederacy's Vice President Alexander Stephens said, "is founded ... upon the great truth that the Negro is not equal to the white man; that slavery ... is his natural and normal condition." The South had left the Union, the president of the Confederacy, Jefferson Davis, explained, "to save ourselves from a revolution" that threatened to make "property in slaves so insecure as to be comparatively worthless."[88]

The North went to war not to end slavery, but to maintain the Union. The vast majority of whites in the free states had contempt for Blacks. They wanted to restrain the power of the South and limit slavery to the states where it already existed, but they did not seek to eradicate it. However, as the war raged and Northern casualties mounted, public opinion shifted: many Republicans and a few Democrats began to favor ending slavery as a way to weaken the war-making potential of the Confederacy and to encourage the enslaved to help the advancing Union troops. "A year ago men might have faltered" at the thought of emancipating the slaves, a conservative Boston newspaper wrote in August 1862, but "[they are now] in great measure prepared for it."[89] This shift made possible Lincoln's Emancipation Proclamation of January 1863, which abolished slavery in the territory held by the Confederacy. Slavery throughout the United States would end only with the adoption of the 13th amendment in December 1865, but the decisive step was taken almost three years earlier.

A similar evolution occurred in white Northerners' attitudes toward Blacks in the military. Blacks were barred from the army and the militia, and they served in the Navy only in menial jobs (firemen, coal heavers, cooks, and stewards). Those African Americans in the free states who volunteered to join the army in 1861 were rejected on the principle that it was a "white man's war." But as the war continued, white men grew less eager to enlist and attitudes changed. In late 1862, the first black units began fighting for the Union. They performed well and in 1863 all restrictions on enlisting black soldiers, including recently emancipated men, were lifted. By the war's end more than 180,000 African Americans had fought in the Union armies, about 10 percent of the total Union force. They served in segregated units under white officers.

As Americans fought each other, the world watched. There were at the time five great powers. Prussia and Austria were sympathetic to the Union, but had no direct stakes in the conflict. Russia also wanted the Union to win—because a unified United States could serve as a powerful brake on Britain. Napoleon III, on the other hand, favored the South because he preferred a break-up of the United States. He was planning to transform Mexico, rent by civil war, into a French vassal state, and an independent Confederacy could provide a valuable buffer. But Napoleon would not interfere in the American civil war without the support of the British. Therefore, Britain's stance was decisive.

The Confederates went to war confident that King Cotton gave them a stranglehold over England. The textile industry dominated the British economy; the livelihood of millions of British workers and their families depended on it. Britain imported three-quarters of its cotton from the American South, and no alternative sources of supply were readily available. The Confederates were certain that the British people, desperate to keep their textile mills running, would demand that London break the Union's blockade of the southern ports and that Whitehall would comply. This proved to be a fallacy.

The traditional assessment of British public opinion during the US Civil War is that while most of the upper class sympathized with the Confederacy, most of the working class supported the Union because they appreciated the political freedoms the United States granted to all white men. (In Britain only about 20 percent of adult males could vote.) This class-based analysis has been challenged in recent years by scholars who argue that both working class sympathy for the North and upper-class sympathy for the South have been overstated. According to these scholars most Britons, rich and poor, disliked the Confederacy because they opposed slavery, but they also disliked the United

States because they considered Americans to be aggressive bullies. The threats Northern politicians and the Northern press hurled at Britain during the civil war, accusing it of supporting the Confederacy, confirmed their worst suspicions. *The Spectator,* an important London paper which supported the North because it abhorred slavery, expressed this viewpoint succinctly: "We have not the slightest sympathy with American ways or American foreign policy. They are collectively to us the most disagreeable of people."[90]

Despite their distaste for slavery, some Britons embraced the Confederacy because they wanted to see the Union weakened. The break-up of the United States would be the "riddance of a nightmare," *The Times,* by far the most influential British paper, noted in August 1862. "Indeed, people are breathing more freely, and talking more lightly of the United States, than they have done any time these thirty years. We don't now hear once a twelvemonth that England has complied with some ridiculous demand, or endured some high-flying specimen of American impudence, or allowed them to draw their boundary lines as they please."[91] One thing is certain, however: whatever their sympathies, the British—including the editors of *The Times*—did not want to see their country dragged into the conflict.

Given Britain's reluctance to fight against the United States, all President Lincoln needed to do was to do nothing that might drive Whitehall into a war it did not want. The only moment of real danger occurred in late 1861. On November 8, 1861, Navy Captain Charles Wilkes of the USS *San Jacinto* stopped the *Trent,* a British mail packet, on the high seas in order to forcibly remove and arrest two Confederate envoys, James Mason and John Slidell (Polk's man in Mexico), who were *en route* to Europe to take up their posts as unofficial ambassadors of the Confederacy in London and Paris.[92] This was a violation of international law. Adding insult to injury, Captain Wilkes was then lionized in the North, and the US House of Representatives voted a resolution thanking him. The British were outraged. Whitehall issued an ultimatum demanding the release of Slidell and Mason as well as an apology—but it also took pains to ease Lincoln's task: the ultimatum noted that London was "willing to believe" that Wilkes had acted without authority, and Foreign Secretary John Russell instructed the British minister in Washington, Lord Lyons, to first mention the ultimatum informally to Secretary of State Seward and wait "a day or two" before producing it, in order to give the Americans more time to reply. Russell also told Lyons that the British government would probably be "rather easy about the apology." But, he added, if the US government did not agree to release the prisoners within seven days of the official presentation of the ultimatum, Lyons and his entire staff should depart the United States. As a further sign that Britain meant business Whitehall ordered troops to Canada and strengthened the Western Atlantic Fleet. War with the United States was quite possible, Prime Minister Palmerston said, and it would "be an act of folly amounting to absolute imbecility to let those who may soon be our enemies" to continue acquiring in England "the means of war against us." Therefore, Britain prohibited the export of arms, ammunition, and military stores. The British government did not want war, but had Lincoln been obdurate it would have, at a minimum, broken diplomatic relations, maintained the embargo of war materiel, and forbidden raising war loans for the Union in British territory; it might also have refused to recognize the blockade. Wisely, Lincoln followed Seward's advice; he released Mason and Slidell and allowed them to continue their journey to Britain.[93]

The *Trent* affair fueled the Union's antipathy toward Britain. But no grievances burned as fiercely as those aroused by the *Florida* and the *Alabama*, two cruisers that a Confederate agent, James Bulloch, commissioned in the summer of 1861 from the Liverpool shipyards. Britain's Foreign Enlistment Act forbade the construction and arming of warships for a belligerent power in British territory. As work proceeded, Bulloch went to great efforts to conceal the fact that the ships were destined for the Confederacy, and he followed the advice of one of Liverpool's leading law firms, which asserted that a ship could be legally built for a belligerent as long as it was not armed in British territory.[94]

By early 1862, when the first cruiser, the *Oreto*, was nearing completion, the US legation in London had learned that it was destined for the Confederacy and urged the British authorities to detain it. But when the port authorities inspected the *Oreto* they found no weapons. They concluded that the law had not been violated and allowed the *Oreto* to depart Liverpool. Another vessel loaded with armament quietly followed the *Oreto*. In a deserted cay south of Nassau its munitions were transferred to the *Oreto*, which began its successful career as the *Florida*, capturing thirty-eight American merchant vessels before it was captured by a Union warship in October 1864.

In July 1862, the second cruiser, the *Alabama*, was being completed in Liverpool, and the US legation was again bombarding the Foreign Office with demands that the ship be seized. The British government eventually ordered that the ship be detained. Alerted by a Confederate sympathizer, the *Alabama* slipped out of Liverpool before the order was enforced and met in the Azores with a ship carrying its armament. The *Alabama* would be the most successful Confederate commerce raider, capturing sixty-four American merchant ships before being sunk in June 1864.

The *Florida* and the *Alabama* stoked Northerners' anger at Britain, but militarily they were no more than painful pinpricks. They did not loosen the Union's blockade of southern ports; and while they decimated the American merchant marine, they did not affect trade between the United States and England, which continued in British bottoms.

The late summer and early fall of 1862 was the only time that Whitehall seriously contemplated recognizing the Confederacy. The months between May and September 1862 marked the high tide of the southern war effort, carried forward by an uninterrupted series of victories. In the west, Confederate forces moved north into Kentucky, occupied Lexington, and established an ephemeral Confederate government in Frankfort, the state's capital. In the east, Stonewall Jackson won five battles in the Shenandoah Valley, and Robert E. Lee defeated the Union army at Bull Run in late August. "Less than a month earlier," James McPherson writes, the Union army had been only twenty miles from Richmond. "With half as many troops as his two main opponents," Lee was now twenty miles from Washington.[95] Meanwhile in England, the cotton famine was devastating the textile industry. Hundreds of thousands of workers lost their jobs as mills closed.

This was when the British government considered offering to mediate to end a war that it believed the North could not win and that was inflicting a heavy toll on British workers. A few days after the news of Bull Run reached London, Foreign Secretary Russell wrote to Prime Minister Palmerston: "The time is come for offering mediation to the United States government with a view to the recognition of the independence of the Confederates . . . In case of failure we ought ourselves to recognize the Southern States as an independent State."[96]

But what difference would British recognition make? As Lord Granville, head of the Privy Council, told Russell, it "would not by itself remove the blockade or supply us with cotton. It would give no physical strength to the South, but it would greatly stimulate the North and undoubtedly assist their government in raising men and money." Lord Derby, leader of the Conservative opposition, agreed: "recognition would merely irritate the North without advancing the cause of the South or procuring a single bale of cotton. . . . The recognition of the South could be of no benefit to England unless we meant to sweep away the blockade, which would be an act of hostility towards the North."[97]

Here was the Gordian knot: recognition without breaking the blockade would provoke the North to no practical end; breaking the blockade would be an act of war.

Perhaps—just perhaps—it might have been different if Bull Run had been followed by a string of southern victories, if Antietam, on September 17, 1862, had been a southern success, and Lee had smashed the Union army at Gettysburg, while the cotton famine continued. Perhaps in those circumstances the British government might have been tempted to lift the blockade even at the risk of war. But Antietam was a draw, and Gettysburg a Union victory; furthermore, the cotton famine slackened in the spring of 1863, when cotton from India and Egypt eased the crisis.

Assessing

The sectional conflict that had pulsed through American politics since the 1830s did not inhibit expansion within the country's borders, as evidenced by the ethnic cleansing that followed the 1830 Indian Removal Act. But the clash between slave and free states tended to restrain the expansionist impulse beyond the nation's borders. The sectional conflict delayed the annexation of Texas: the free states opposed its entry into the Union precisely because it meant another slave state. Likewise, it is likely that Polk would have insisted on an even larger territorial cession from Mexico than the one stipulated in the Treaty of Guadalupe Hidalgo, had not the raging sectional conflict stayed his hand.

The admission of California as a free state spurred southerners to push for the annexation of Cuba. And the opportunity seemed ripe because Britain was preoccupied by the Crimean War. But the sectional conflict cut both ways: it whetted the southerners' appetite for Cuba, but it also gave rise to the counterforce that defeated annexation: the free states fiercely opposed acquiring the island because it would have increased the number of slave states in the Union, and therefore the power of the South. These same considerations drove the free states to derail President Buchanan's plans to acquire Cuba and more Mexican territory.

Through these decades, the major economic partner and the major rival of the United States was Britain. But was there a British threat? After the War of 1812, the British abandoned all territorial ambitions in the United States and any thought of supporting the Indians who lived within the US borders. Did they try to stifle the expansion of the United States, as many Americans claimed? They urged Mexico to recognize the independence of Texas, but when in 1845 Mexico turned to Britain for help against the growing threat from the United States, all Whitehall did was urge the Mexicans to avoid war with the United States and abandon all hope of British assistance. It repeated this message in 1853 when Pierce prepared to extort more territory from Mexico. In Central America by the end of the 1850s, the British accepted US domination. Even in Cuba, the major brake on US expansion was not the Royal Navy but the sectional conflict.

The clash over slavery had caused the civil war, and abolition was the war's most important achievement. In the early stages of the conflict, Lincoln's approach to slavery was entirely pragmatic. "My paramount object in this struggle," he wrote in August 1862, "*is* to save the Union, and it is *not* either to save or to destroy slavery. If I could save the Union without freeing *any* slave I would do it, and if I could save it by freeing *all* the slaves I would do it, and if I could save it by freeing some and leaving others alone, I would also do that."[98] But the war broadened the president's horizon and that of many whites in the free states. The war for the Union became also a crusade against slavery. Had Lincoln not been assassinated in April 1865, at the beginning of his second term, he might have continued to lead Americans, white and Black, to a less imperfect Union. A few months after his death, the 13th amendment eradicated the cancer of slavery, but it could not eradicate the racism that ran deep in the American psyche.

CHAPTER 10
AFTER APPOMATTOX

In the two decades that preceded the Civil War the United States acquired Texas, one third of Mexico, and half of the immense Oregon territory; it clashed with Spain and Britain over Cuba and Central America. By contrast, the twenty-five years that followed Appomattox were "awkward years,"[1] when the United States turned to focus inside its borders. It was a period of great economic growth, rampant corruption, and concentration of wealth. It would be followed, in the 1890s, by an upsurge of foreign policy activism that would lead, at the end of the decade, to war with Spain and the acquisition of a colonial empire.

While the "awkward years" may not have been an exciting period in foreign policy, they were a time of great territorial expansion for the white American empire—expansion within the borders, despoiling the Indians of their land. This chapter will begin with white America's war on Native Americans and will end with the election in 1896 of William McKinley, the president who would lead the country to war against Spain.

The conquest of the West

When the Civil War was over, vast areas of the western plains remained the domain of the Indians, and white America was primed for the final onslaught. "The Indian in truth has no longer a country," General John Pope, commander of the army's department of the Missouri, wrote in August 1865. "His lands are everywhere pervaded by white men; his means of subsistence destroyed and the homes of his tribe violently taken from him; himself and his family reduced to starvation, or to the necessity of warring to the death upon the white man, whose inevitable and destructive progress threatens the total extermination of his race."[2] There are no reliable estimates of the Indian population of the trans-Mississippi West in 1865; the Department of the Interior suggested a figure of about 300,000, but this was only a guess.[3]

Many historians see similarities between the violence of the Union troops who invaded the South and the army's violence against the Native Americans. "The dominant view in the literature," Mark Grimsley remarks, "suggests that the last wars against the Plains Indians were principally an extension and amplification of the methods used against white Southerners." But there are key differences. Even in the final year of the Civil War, when the Union army employed its harshest methods against the rebels— General William Sherman's march to the sea, the destruction of Atlanta, the invasion of South Carolina—the Union troops killed very few non-combatants, Confederate soldiers who surrendered were spared, and rape seems to have been infrequent. When fighting against the Indians, however, the army often failed to distinguish between hostile and peaceful tribes; women and children were frequently killed, and rapes of Indian women were common. It was, in short, a different kind of warfare.[4] For most white Americans, the Indians were savages who had no place in the United States. Easterners sometimes expressed pity for the Indians, but they had already expelled them from their region, except for a few pockets. In the West, Grimsely notes, "'Indian hunting'—collective violence against native Americans by groups of white Americans—was common . . . and [it was] epidemic in California."[5] At Sand Creek in late 1864, Colonel John Chivington's Colorado volunteers attacked a peaceful village of Southern Cheyennes and Southern Arapahoes, killing more than 150, two-thirds of them women and children. The volunteers returned to Denver to a hero's welcome, "and scores of Cheyenne and Arapaho scalps were held up in theaters to cheering audiences or were hung as decorations on the mirrors behind the bars in Denver's saloons."[6]

The tribes that most fiercely resisted the whites' advance after the Civil War were the Lakotas (also known as Sioux) in the northern plains and the Apaches in the southwest. The last stand of the Lakotas occurred in June 1876, at the battle of Little Bighorn. The Lakotas were fighting to defend their beloved Black Hills, 6,000 square miles in South Dakota that had been guaranteed them by the US government in treaties of 1851 and 1868. President Ulysses S. Grant, who in 1850 had written to his wife that "the whole [Indian] race would be harmless and peaceable if they were not put upon by the whites,"[7] was that rare American military leader who felt some empathy for the Native Americans. Upon becoming president he announced that he would adopt a more humane policy toward them, a policy that would eschew violence and teach the Indians the white man's civilization. He may have been sincere, but when gold was discovered in the Black Hills, and whites demanded the expulsion of the Indians, Grant leaned on the Lakotas to sell the land. When they refused, he jettisoned his country's solemn pledges and chose war. The Lakotas fought back, stunning white America. Led by Sitting Bull and Crazy Horse, and joined by their Cheyenne allies, they annihilated Lt. Colonel George Custer's column, killing an estimated 268 soldiers. White America responded with fury. Hunted by thousands of US troops, their food supplies exhausted, the Lakotas bowed to the inevitable. Before the end of 1877 Crazy Horse was dead, Sitting Bull had led a thousand followers to refuge in Canada, and cowed chiefs had ceded the Black Hills to the US government. Never again would the Lakotas fight against the United States.[8]

A manmade ecological disaster helped the United States subdue the Indian tribes. The Indian economy rested on the buffalo, which provided the meat they ate and the leather for their clothes. But in the years after the Civil War white hunters invaded the Plains, decimating the immense herds, slaughtering the bison for their hides, much sought after in the eastern United States and Europe. As Pekka Hämäläinen remarks in his path-breaking study of the Comanches, "their defeat was not a military but an economic one." Understanding that the destruction of the bison would cripple the Comanches, the army encouraged the hunters and supplied them with equipment and ammunition—"all you could use, all you wanted, more than you needed," one hunter marveled. The bison disappeared from the southern plains. All that was left were skinned, rotting carcasses, and Comanches starved. In late 1874, they surrendered to the US army. A few bands held out until the spring of 1875, when they trudged to Fort Sill, in Indian Territory (Oklahoma), "where they were processed for a new life. They were stripped of their horses, weapons, and remaining possessions. Women and children were removed from their husbands and fathers and placed in separate camps. Men accused of particular crimes were put in irons to await trial and expulsion to Florida. The rest of the warriors ... were locked in a roofless and windowless icehouse.... In the morning they received their first rations when the soldiers threw chunks of raw meat over the wall."[9]

It was inevitable that the federal government would want the territory of the western Indians, immense tracts of land that were thinly populated. Most Indian chiefs understood this and were willing to cede part of their domain for modest compensation. But the failure of the federal government to honor the treaties it signed rendered peaceful coexistence impossible. Treachery was compounded by greed and callousness: not only did the federal government confine the Indians to ever smaller reservations, but all too often these were miserable tracts of land. "Many of the Indian reservations," anthropologist George Bird Grinnell wrote in 1899, "consist of the most arid and barren lands that the sun ever shone on—a waterless, desolate, soul-withering region ... regions where white farmers could not possibly make a living."[10] When the Indians received a reservation with good land, however, another problem arose: white settlers demanded that the Indians be moved elsewhere. The settlers were citizens and voters. The Indians were neither. Indian Territory (Oklahoma), where the great southern tribes had been deported in the 1830s, became a dumping ground for western tribes expelled from their homelands.

As the years passed, white control over life in the reservations tightened. Each reservation had an Indian agent, appointed by the Bureau of Indian Affairs, an agency that was notoriously corrupt. The agent—usually a political appointee with no qualifications for the job—had under his control a native police force. He could order this police force to arrest, fine, or confine to hard labor Indians in his reservation. The Indians, who had roamed over the vast expanses of the West, needed the permission of the agent to travel outside their reservations. "An Indian agent has absolute control of affairs on his reservation," anthropologist Grinnell wrote. "The courts protect citizens but the Indian is not a citizen and nothing protects him."[11]

The conquest of the West became part of American lore: the virile cowboys, the courageous settlers, and the cavalry chasing marauding Indians. The slaughter was particularly intense in California. When the first US troops arrived in 1846 about 150,000 Native Americans lived there—far more than in any state or territory of the Union. They were fragmented in many small tribes, lacking warlike traditions. Under Spanish and then Mexican rule, the policy had been to exploit the Indians as a servile work force, not to exterminate them (though many were killed in the process). Most Indians, however, had been left alone. The tribes were spread through the entire territory, and the non-Indian population of California in 1846 was only 10,000–14,000 people.

Beginning in 1848, the American newcomers came by the hundreds of thousands. Many Native Americans were spared to work as slaves or serfs; others were herded into barren reservations where many died of malnutrition and exposure. ("Confinement to federal reservations was a death sentence for many of the state's Indian people," writes

Benjamin Madley, the foremost expert on American-Indian relations in California during the first twenty-five years of US rule.) Through the early 1870s, the policy of California's authorities was, with the strong support of the local white people and the press, to exterminate the Indian population. The federal government did not encourage this, but it did nothing to stop it and at times provided troops to help hunt the Native Americans. "The direct and deliberate killing of Indians in California," Madley concludes, "was more lethal and sustained than anywhere else in the United States." By the time the violence abated, in the early 1870s, only 30,000 Indians were left in California.[12]

The Apaches, who roamed between Mexico and Arizona, were the last Indians to give up the struggle. In September 1886, Geronimo and his remaining followers—about forty men, women and children—surrendered to General Nelson Miles, who had been hunting them with 5,000 troops, almost one-fifth of the entire US army, and 500 Indian scouts. They were loaded onto a train and sent to be imprisoned in Florida, together with many of the scouts who had helped the Americans track them—they, too, were Apaches and the government did not trust them.[13] White America had triumphed. The Indian wars were over.

Four years later there was a tragic epilogue: the massacre of Wounded Knee. The backdrop of the massacre is admirably described by Jeffrey Ostler, a leading historian of the Lakotas. "Life on the reservation was hard from the start," he writes, "but conditions worsened in the late 1880s." Responding to the demands of white settlers and land speculators, in 1888 the Cleveland administration decided to buy half of the Lakotas' reservation. Congress had abolished treaty making with the Indians in 1871—it would enact laws to govern them, and their consent would not be necessary. But the US government still wanted the Indians' formal consent before taking their land—even Jackson had forced the Indians to "freely" sign removal treaties before deporting them. Accordingly, Cleveland sent a commission to negotiate with the Lakotas, and when they resisted, his successor, Benjamin Harrison, sent a second commission, which used a very persuasive argument: if the Lakotas resisted, the government would use force, their land would be confiscated, and they would be shipped far away, to the dreaded Indian Territory in Oklahoma. And so the Lakotas gave up, ceding half of their land; the Harrison administration divided what remained into six separate reservations. Meanwhile, the Lakotas' living conditions were deteriorating. Successive droughts withered the crops on which they depended to supplement the inadequate rations they received from the government as payment for previous land cessions. Poor diet and social stress contributed to an increase in tuberculosis and other illnesses brought by the white man. Then in late 1889, soon after surrendering half of their land, the Lakotas learned that the government would cut their beef rations by 20–25 percent.[14]

In happier times, the Lakotas might have fought, but now they were powerless. In their despair, they turned instead to the message of hope of a new religion preached by a Paiute Indian holy man in Nevada. His religion, or rather the version that reached the Lakotas, said that if the Indians returned to their traditional way of life and performed a new dance—the Ghost Dance—an apocalyptic event would usher in a new world in which all white people would be washed away from the Indians' lands. The federal agents on the reservations ordered the Lakotas not to join the movement, but between one-fourth and one-third of the Lakotas embraced the Ghost Dance; the others stood aside, skeptical or fearful of the white man's punishment.

They were right to be afraid. In November 1890, President Harrison ordered the army to enter the Lakota reservations, put an end to the Ghost Dance, and arrest the ringleaders. Nine thousand soldiers, "fully a third of the U.S. army," poured into the reservations and the lands between them.[15] At Wounded Knee Creek, on December 29, the soldiers attacked a group of 400 Lakotas—men, women, and children—many of them Ghost Dancers, who had fled in fear and wanted to surrender. The soldiers killed between 270 and 300 Indians; of these 170 to 200 were women and children. When asked why so many women had been killed, the soldiers resorted to the time-honored explanation, "We could not discern the distinction between bucks and squaws."[16] (In any case, the *New York Tribune* pointed out, "A Sioux squaw is as bad an enemy as a man ... The little boys, too, can shoot quite as well as their fathers."[17]) Twenty soldiers who participated in the massacre were awarded the Congressional Medal of Honor.

A few years after Wounded Knee, as the century drew to a close, a prominent American historian saluted what for him, and most of his white countrymen, was a key facet of America's greatness: "How the country ... has carried itself in turn towards Indian, African and Asiatic is matter of history," Charles Francis Adams wrote in 1899. "And yet it is equally matter of history that this carriage, term it what you will—unchristian, brutal, exterminating—has been the salvation of the race. It has saved the Anglo-Saxon stock from being a nation of half-breeds.... The Canadian half-breed, the Mexican, the mulatto ... are not virile or enduring races; and that the Anglo-Saxon ... is essentially virile and enduring, is due to the fact that the less developed races perished before him."[18]

France and Mexico

Napoleon III, emperor of the French, had many dreams. The greatest, the most obsessive, was to transform France into the hegemonic power of continental Europe. But he also dreamed of a colonial empire—in Africa, in Asia, and in Latin America. Mexico, which was bankrupt after three years of Civil War, tempted him. When President Benito Juárez suspended the payment of the foreign debt in July 1861, France, Britain, and Spain agreed that all three would send troops to occupy Vera Cruz, seize the customs houses, and force Mexico to pay up. Once in Vera Cruz, however, the British and Spaniards understood that Napoleon had a secret agenda: convinced that he could rely on the support of the Mexican conservative elites, who loathed President Juárez, Napoleon hoped to transform Mexico into a French satellite. The American Civil War offered an opportunity: "[it] has made it impossible for the United States to get involved," Napoleon told his ambassador in London.[19]

After lingering a few weeks in Vera Cruz, the British and the Spaniards withdrew, unwilling to be Napoleon's accomplices, and the French troops began their slow advance toward Mexico City, which they occupied in June 1863, a few days before the Battle of

Gettysburg. The following year, the man Napoleon had chosen as his puppet, Maximilian, a brother of the Austrian emperor, was installed on the throne of the newly created Mexican empire. But the French were unable to pacify the vast country. Juárez led the resistance.

The Lincoln administration continued to recognize Juárez as Mexico's president; however, fearing Napoleon's wrath, it refrained from providing him any assistance. This provoked vehement criticism in the United States from Lincoln's political enemies, the Democrats and radical Republicans, who accused him of betraying that hallowed principle, the Monroe Doctrine. "All this politicking," Jay Sexton writes, "fueled an unprecedented public discussion regarding the Monroe Doctrine. Though the phrase had gained popularity in the preceding decade, it became a nationalistic symbol, a permanent feature of the political and diplomatic landscape during the Civil War."[20]

After General Robert E. Lee surrendered at Appomattox in April 1865, the Civil War ended and the Union troops marched to the Rio Grande. While the US Congress and the press loudly demanded that the French leave Mexico, General Grant, the army's commander-in-chief, and other senior officers helped Juárez's supporters acquire weapons surrendered by Confederate forces in Texas. Grant urged President Andrew Johnson to give military aid to the Juaristas and even invade Mexico to drive the French out. Secretary of State Seward, however, preferred diplomacy: the United States was exhausted after five years of civil war, and overt threats or acts of war might only harden French resistance. He persuaded President Johnson that discreet pressure would be effective. In late 1865, Johnson sent Napoleon a secret message warning that "it would be impossible for the administration to withstand the pressure of public opinion in America for the expulsion of these [French] troops if their withdrawal were postponed much longer."[21]

In early 1866, Napoleon decided to gradually withdraw his army from Mexico. (The last troops left in March 1867.) US pressure had merely accelerated the inevitable outcome. For Napoleon, the Mexican adventure had backfired. Instead of being a source of income, it was a heavy burden on the French treasury; French public opinion, never enthusiastic about the war, had turned against it, as had the business community; in Mexico, the population supported Juárez, miring the French in an unwinnable guerrilla war. Above all, Napoleon needed his troops at home. The French army was based on long-term service and had no trained reserves; that is, it could not expand quickly. The quality of the troops was uneven, with many soldiers in their fifties and sixties who were good only for garrison duty. The 30,000 French soldiers in Mexico included some of the army's best units. When the Mexican adventure had begun, in 1861, Europe had been quiet; but the Prussian victory over Austria in the summer of 1866 meant that the danger of German unification—a French nightmare—was imminent.

As the French left Mexico, the American press boasted that it was "the Monroe Doctrine that prompted France's ignominious withdrawal."[22] Mexicans knew better: they had saved themselves. Juárez, who had longed for US help when he was being hunted by French troops, summed up the role of the United States: "I know that the rich and powerful nations neither feel nor even less seek remedies for the misfortunes of others." Of US relations with France he said, "Wolves do not bite each other."[23]

Reconstruction

Americans had little time to celebrate the departure of the French from Mexico. Their own country was in turmoil. In 1866, the Republican Party, which controlled Congress, had rejected President Johnson's lenient policy toward the defeated Confederates. (The president would be impeached in early 1868.)

In determining how to treat the defeated South, the victorious Northerners faced a moral challenge: the fate of four million African Americans just released from bondage. For the formerly enslaved, these were years of drama, hope, and pain. For a time, the men could vote; they even elected a handful of black representatives and two black senators to the US Congress. But the white backlash was swift and violent. The freed slaves never received the land they had been promised, and despite the concerted efforts of the Freedman's Bureau they left the plantations with only the clothes on their backs. By the late 1870s, thousands of the formerly enslaved had been murdered and the South was returning to what white southerners and, increasingly, northern whites considered normalcy: white supremacy, with the Blacks as serfs.[24]

While Americans failed to rise to the moral challenge of Reconstruction, the 1870s and the 1880s were years of extraordinary economic growth, with a widening gulf between rich and poor. The completion of the transcontinental railroads linked the heartland of the United States to the bustling seaports of the eastern and western coasts, and thence to international markets. (Railroads, Richard White notes, were also "a means of national and racial conquest," making it possible for the army to concentrate troops "quickly and effectively" against Native Americans.[25]) American exports—mainly foodstuffs and raw materials—increased from $471 million in 1870 to $858 million in 1890. The bulk went to Europe: $381 million in 1870, $684 million in 1890.[26]

Expansion beyond the borders

In the wake of the Civil War, the American public and the US Congress had little interest in territorial expansion beyond their borders. The white American empire was expanding internally with the conquest of the West, without facing international complications and without requiring a large army. Americans were recovering from the trauma of civil war, and they wanted to lower the government's expenses. The army was cut to the bone: from 54,302 in 1866 to 27,447 in 1876, and the powerful Union Navy from about 700 ships to fifty-two. By European standards, most of the ships were obsolete because they were made of wood and powered by sails.[27]

In the three decades that followed the Civil War, the United States annexed no foreign lands beyond Russian America (Alaska) and tiny Midway, both in 1867. The purchase of Alaska for $7,200,000 (c. 126.5 million) was largely the handiwork of Secretary of State Seward and, on the Russian side, of Grand Duke Constantine, who convinced his brother, the Tsar, that the colony was a fiscal burden and a strategic liability. In case of war with Britain, Russia's potential adversary, it could not be defended. Furthermore, the Russian minister in Washington insisted that sooner or later the United States would decide to annex the territory; he "was haunted by the image of Americans swarming to a Russian Alaska."[28]

The US Senate overwhelmingly ratified the purchase. For Seward, and many senators, Alaska was attractive not only for its strategic and economic value, but also because in US hands it would hem in British Columbia, a struggling British colony of 10,000 people, and hasten its annexation to the United States. Eventually, all of British North America might follow. This was an old American dream that had acquired new urgency after the Civil War when many in the United States wanted to punish Britain for its alleged support for the Confederacy. After Appomattox, thousands of unemployed Union veterans joined the US branch of the Fenian Brotherhood, an association dedicated to Irish independence from Britain, which in 1866 launched several raids into British North America. The threat from the United States provided a powerful impulse for Upper and Lower Canada to unite with Nova Scotia and New Brunswick in 1867 to create a Canadian confederation. Over the next six years, British Columbia, Manitoba, and Prince Edward Island joined the confederation, which became "a new creation," a British dominion—neither a colony nor an independent nation.[29]

The same US Senate that welcomed the acquisition of Alaska, a vast territory with only a handful of nonwhites, recoiled from annexing the Dominican Republic.[30] In the late 1860s, the Dominican president, Buenaventura Báez, his shaky rule threatened by rebels, offered his country to the United States. American businessmen with investments in the Dominican Republic became his lobbyists. President Grant was an enthusiastic supporter of annexation, seeing the Dominican Republic as a valuable strategic and economic asset. A treaty was concluded in late 1869; it stipulated that the Dominicans would become US citizens and their country would join the Union as a territory that could eventually become a state. Grant lobbied the Senate hard: "Favors, promises, persuasion, he tried everything," the French minister in Washington reported.[31] Nevertheless, on June 30, 1870, the Senate defied the president and rejected the treaty by a vote of twenty-eight to twenty-eight, well short of the required two-thirds. There were several reasons for the senators' opposition, but racism was paramount. The Dominican Republic was a mixed-race country, and the thought that black Dominican senators and representatives might sit someday in the US Congress was unacceptable.

Ten years later, the United States launched its first foray into South America since Buchanan's bout of gunboat diplomacy against Paraguay in 1858. Beginning in 1879, Chile had been at war with Peru and Bolivia over control of the rich deposits of nitrate along the coast of southern Peru and Bolivia. By the time President James Garfield took office in March 1881, Chile had knocked Bolivia out of the war, smashed the Peruvian Navy, occupied the whole nitrate-producing region, and captured Lima. For Garfield's Secretary of State James Blaine, Chile was Britain's stalking horse: "It is a perfect mistake to speak of this as a Chilean war on Peru," Blaine said. "It is an English war on Peru with Chile as the instrument." Britain, he believed, was using Chile to gain control of the nitrates of Peru and Bolivia. This foolhardy conclusion, shared by Garfield, reflected both the administration's ignorance and its Anglophobia: neither British capitalists nor Whitehall had any interest in the war between Santiago and Lima.[32]

Seeking to strongarm Chile to forswear territorial acquisitions, Blaine intimated that refusal could lead to war against the United States. He was playing with a very weak hand: the Chilean Navy was stronger than the American, and the American people had no stomach for war with Chile. After the death of Garfield in September 1891 the charade ended: President Chester Arthur abandoned Blaine's minatory policy toward Chile. The war dragged on until late 1883 when the Peruvians accepted Chile's territorial demands; a few months later Bolivia followed suit, surrendering its seacoast.

Blaine's attempt to interfere in the conflict had brought the United States a self-inflicted humiliation, exposing it as a weak and inept bully. For many Americans, the crisis illustrated the need for a strong navy. "We Cannot Fight the Chilean Navy," was the title of an article in the *Army and Navy Journal*, lamenting the weakness of the US fleet.[33] In March 1883, Congress allocated funds for the construction of three steel cruisers and a dispatch boat. It was the first step toward the creation of a blue water navy.

Except for the Chilean fiasco, the 1870s and 1880s were a period of calm in US relations with Latin America. Instead of hankering after Mexican territory, Americans began investing in Mexican railroads and mines. US foreign investment worldwide was still modest; the bulk went to Mexico. The only other Latin American country with significant US investment was Cuba. But interest in Central America was growing. It was in Costa Rica that the extraordinary saga of twenty-three-year-old New Yorker Minor Keith began. The Costa Rican government was eager to facilitate the export of coffee, the country's major crop, to Europe. This required building a railroad from the central plateau, where the coffee was grown, to Puerto Limón on the Caribbean coast, across mountains, steep canyons and almost impassable swamps. In the 1870s, foreign entrepreneurs contracted by the Costa Rican government built disconnected sections of track; further progress was hindered by lack of funds. In 1884, the government turned to Keith, who owned extensive banana plantations in Costa Rica, and offered him a ninety-nine-year lease of the railroad once he had completed it, and 800,000 acres of land, which would make him the country's largest landowner. Keith completed the line in 1890, after raising the necessary funds in Britain. Meanwhile, other American entrepreneurs were building railways in Guatemala to bring that country's coffee from inland plantations to the Pacific coast. Unlike the railway in Costa Rica, these were built largely with American capital.[34]

While US foreign trade grew dramatically between 1870 and 1890, Americans failed to expand their share of the Latin American market. On average, no more than 11 percent of US exports went to the region in those decades.[35] The growth of exports was hampered by the Republicans' high tariff policies, by the Democrats' opposition to reciprocity treaties (they preferred broad tariff reductions), and by the stinginess of the US Congress. In 1884, for example, after lengthy and sustained pressure, mercantile interests from the Midwest were able to wring from a reluctant Congress an appropriation for a Presidential Commission that would travel through Latin America to explore trade possibilities. The Commissioners visited several Spanish American countries, but when they arrived in Argentina they received instructions from the new Cleveland administration to wind up their tour and return to the United States. As a result, they spent only forty-eight hours in Buenos Aires. "The people of the United States know little about us and care no more," an Argentine journalist wrote. "They have a vague notion that we are a cross between Indians, whites and wild horses.... So long as Europe comes here with its millions and Americans come here with itinerating commissions, the business supremacy of Europe in this country will be seen."[36] Americans lacked not only the products but also the knowledge—including linguistic skills—to conquer the Latin American markets. The British continued to dominate the trade of Latin America, and this fed the Anglophobia of many US citizens who believed that those markets were rightfully theirs.

There were, however, no attempts by Britain or other European powers to extend their political influence in Latin America after the collapse of Napoleon's Mexican adventure, or to interfere with US policy in the region. Therefore, US relations with the European countries were focused on trade. Europe absorbed on average 80 percent of total American exports, and Britain was by far the major market. (In 1890, total US exports were $858 million, $448 of which went to Britain.)[37]

US relations with Asia were minor and will be discussed in a later chapter. Economic relations with Africa were minimal. The value of US exports to that continent had been $3 million in 1870 and had grown to $5 million by 1890.[38] What little trade existed was concentrated in South Africa.[39]

An important number of Americans—almost 15 percent in 1880—came from Africa or were descendants of Africans, but they wielded no influence over US foreign policy. Their ties with their homelands had been severed by the Middle Passage, and their political power had been crushed by brutal oppression in the United States. The very small black elite—church leaders, editors of black newspapers, businessmen—may have felt a blood tie with Africa but also, all too often, looked down on Africans as savages who had to be rescued. While white missionaries went to almost every part of the nonwhite world in the century before the First World War, black missionaries—men and women— went only to Africa. Some were sent by black churches, especially the African Methodist Episcopal Church; others were sent by white missionary boards to serve as assistants to white missionaries. In Africa, many became courageous defenders of the native population against the violence of the colonizers.[40]

The United States did not participate in the scramble for Africa—the partition of the continent among European nations that began in the 1870s—but it had a *de facto* protectorate, Liberia. The origins of Liberia are intertwined with the history of the American Colonization Society (ACS).[41] Created in 1816, the ACS professed a lofty goal: many slaveowners, it argued, wished to emancipate their enslaved people but were loath to increase the number of free Blacks in the United States—free Blacks, most white Americans, north and south, agreed, were a scourge. Therefore, the ACS would purchase land in Africa to settle both African Americans who were freed on condition that they leave the United States, and free Blacks who wanted to emigrate. The ACS would help them start a new life. The Monroe administration was sympathetic to the project, and eager to help. It was the captain of a US warship who convinced a local African king, at gunpoint, to sell the ACS its first tract of land, near Monrovia in 1821.

By 1830, 1,353 African Americans, including 479 formerly enslaved people, had been brought to the settlements established by the ACS. As the number of immigrants grew, the settlements expanded. In 1847, they became the independent Republic of Liberia. The United States did not recognize the new republic until 1862 because southern congressmen feared that recognition would undermine the principle that Blacks lacked the capacity for self-government. President Lincoln, who was an eager supporter of colonization, saw Liberia as a possible home for African Americans, and this hope lingered among some white racists long after Lincoln's death. "I have been influenced by such opinions in the moral support of the Republic of Liberia," Senator John Morgan (D-AL), a rabid racist, wrote in 1903.[42] But most southerners at that time did not share Morgan's views. "The Southern planters highly value the negro as a laborer," Washington's *Evening Star* wrote. "Should he leave who would take his place? The Chinaman? The Japanese? The South would not for a moment seriously consider any such exchange."[43] It was better that African Americans remain in the South, as a ready supply of cheap labor.

The roaring 1890s

In the late 1890s, the United States embarked on a wave of territorial expansion beyond its borders: after waging war on Spain, it imposed its control over Cuba and annexed the Philippines, Guam, and Puerto Rico. Trying to explain this surge, historians have noted that a widespread social malaise had "plunged Americans into a state of anxiety and gloom in the late eighties and early nineties."[44] This malaise was spurred by dramatic demographic changes: the population had grown from 39 million in 1870 to 63 million in 1890; and the waves of immigrants that reached the United States—half a million a year in the 1880s—were no longer coming from what a senior official called the "sturdy, peace-loving people from the north of Europe," but instead from the "objectionable class": Italy, Austro-Hungary, Russia.[45] For the Anglo-Saxon elite that had dominated the United States since its creation, this was unsettling. America's racial stock was being diluted, and its major cities were becoming home to what they saw as hordes of illiterate foreigners with un-American customs and alien tongues. The nation's economy, too, was changing, with the proliferation of the robber barons, who ruled over giant corporations and huge banking houses, and with the rising number and militancy of labor unions.

A new generation of leaders was emerging, troubled by the changes at home and scornful of what they deemed their country's feckless foreign policy since Appomattox. Their fathers had proved their manhood in the Civil War and the time had come for Americans to prove themselves again.[46] They were inspired by the great colonial expansion of the European powers that had been underway since the 1870s. At home, the conquest of the West had concluded with the surrender of Geronimo. The Superintendent of the 1890 census had announced that the frontier had closed. Historian Frederick Jackson Turner explained what this meant "in perhaps the most influential essay ever written in American history":[47] the frontier experience had molded America's national character. "And now," Turner warned, "four centuries from the discovery of America, at the end of a hundred of years of life under the Constitution, the frontier has gone, and with its going has closed the first period of American history."[48] For this new generation of leaders the end of the frontier heightened the need for a virile foreign policy. The yellow press—cheap, mass circulation newspapers reminiscent of the penny press of the 1840s—supported their quest. "We have brushed aside 275,000 Indians," the jurist Theodore Marburg wrote in 1890, "and in place of them have this population of 70,000,000 of what we regard as the highest type of modern man . . . we have done more than any other race to conquer the world for civilization . . . and we will probably . . . go on with our conquests."[49]

The stock-market crash of May 1893 ushered in four years of harrowing economic crisis and social unrest, punctured by strikes that were violently repressed. "Quite simply," a historian writes, "the leaders of both [the Democratic and the Republican] parties were impervious to the cries of farmers and workingmen."[50] Among them, Grover Cleveland (1885–8 and 1893–97), the only Democrat to serve in the White House between 1861, when Buchanan stepped down and 1913, when Wilson was inaugurated. A man of great personal probity he was also, as historian George Herring points out, stubborn and unimaginative.[51]

The economic distress strengthened the conviction of many Americans that the country needed to increase its exports to escape overproduction. In the words of a US senator from Minnesota, "We will be compelled to seek new markets for the surplus or close our factories and let a portion of our harvests rot upon the ground."[52] The search for foreign markets reinforced the argument that the United States needed a strong fleet.

While the spirit of jingoism grew through the decade, the debate on expansion beyond the borders did not begin in earnest until 1897. Before then, public attention had focused on domestic politics even though there were some foreign policy squalls. The first had erupted in 1888 over the Samoan Islands. Three powers held sway in that remote South Pacific archipelago: Britain, the United States, and Germany. In the late 1880s, German Chancellor Otto von Bismarck sought to transform his country's commercial preponderance in the archipelago into political control. This led the foolhardy German consul there to ask German marines to land and clash with the natives; the consul then declared martial law. This provoked an explosion of anti-German feeling in the US press and the Congress. Bismarck, who faced a difficult situation in Europe, was determined to avoid a major crisis with the United States. At a hastily-called conference in Berlin in April 1889, Germans, British, and Americans agreed to establish a tripartite protectorate over the islands. A British delegate aptly summed up the German attitude: "The Samoan question has been decided . . . with an obvious wish on the part of the German government to propitiate the Americans. . . . The Chancellor, I believe, sees war looming in the future [in Europe] . . . 'We cannot risk any quarrel with the U.S.,' Baron [Friedrich von] Holstein said to me.'"[53] The United States was not a military power, but it was an economic colossus, and this imposed respect in a Europe increasingly fragmented by enmities and suspicions.

The "Baltimore" Affair[54]

The quarrel over Samoa reflected the emerging, more aggressive mood of American public opinion toward foreign policy. Two years later, the United States indulged in successful gunboat diplomacy against Chile. Americans were disliked in this South American nation. The antipathy hailed back from the 1850s, when thousands of Chileans had gone to work in California's gold rush. Most were mestizos, and in California they had experienced the violence and contempt that white Americans reserved for what they called lesser breeds.[55] Other incidents in the following decades had kept the antipathy alive, most recently US sympathy for Chilean President José Balmaceda during the civil war that had bloodied the country between January and September 1891.

On October 16, 1891, less than a month after Balmaceda's ouster, 117 sailors from the USS *Baltimore*, which was docked in the Chilean port of Valparaiso, received shore leave. That evening a scuffle between two sailors from the *Baltimore* and a Chilean escalated, and street fights ensued between American sailors and Chileans. Two Americans were killed, several were wounded, and the police arrested thirty-six Americans and ten Chileans. The *Baltimore*'s Board of Inquiry swiftly determined that the US sailors had been blameless and that the Chilean police, instead of protecting them, had joined the anti-American mob. The Chilean judicial inquiry, on the other hand, concluded that the incident had been a drunken brawl and that the police had acted properly. The Chilean foreign minister and Secretary of State James Blaine agreed to arbitration. The Chileans, Blaine told the French minister in Washington, were "an insignificant people, who are very vain. We know that they are weak ... and we are willing to be patient."[56] The crisis seemed headed to a peaceful settlement when President Harrison intervened. On his orders, on January 21, 1892, Blaine sent an ultimatum to Chile, demanding that Santiago apologize and pay reparations or the United States would break diplomatic relations. Four days later, without waiting for Chile's reply, Harrison upped the ante: he sent a special message to Congress stressing that the demands he had made must be enforced lest "the dignity as well as the prestige and influence of the United States ... be wholly sacrificed."[57] He was threatening war—a war without glory, the French minister in Washington remarked.[58]

Several factors explain Harrison's behavior. Blaine had not consulted him before agreeing to arbitration, and the president resented his secretary of state, whom he saw as a rival for the Republican presidential nomination in 1892. Harrison's hardline intervention in the crisis—humiliating Blaine—would make it clear that he was in charge of foreign policy. Furthermore, it suited his own temperament. Harrison was not willing to tolerate insults from lesser powers: he had dealt brusquely with Italy when that country had complained too insistently about the lynching of eleven Italians in New Orleans in March 1891. And he would not allow the Chileans to insult the United States by behaving as though they were America's equal. He was encouraged in his bellicosity by his closest advisers, Navy Secretary Benjamin Tracy and his friend John Foster, and by the knowledge that if war came, the United States would win easily.

Chile was desperately alone. European public opinion was sympathetic, but the British, German, and French governments made it clear that they would provide no assistance whatsoever and urged Chile to avoid war at all costs. The US Navy had grown significantly since 1881 and was stronger than the Chilean. Chile was exhausted by the recent civil war, and the Chilean government rightly feared that in case of war Argentina would help the Americans in the hope of annexing territory in southern Chile. The government in Santiago capitulated. It offered the apology demanded by Harrison and pledged to pay reparations in an amount to be set by the Supreme Court of the United States or any other body Harrison might choose.

The *Baltimore* affair spurred jingoism in the United States: the president had taught a lesson to a half-savage (nonwhite) country that had refused to acknowledge US superiority. The fact that Chile was deemed a British protégé added to the Americans' pleasure. Support for the Navy grew.

Having proven their mettle, Americans returned to their domestic concerns until, in 1893, a debate about Hawaii erupted.

Hawaii[59]

Hawaii had been sliding into the US sphere of influence ever since the first American missionaries had landed there in 1820. Seventy years later, the 2,000 Americans who lived in the archipelago owned most of the sugar plantations that were the basis of the islands' economy; the United States monopolized the kingdom's foreign trade, providing three-fourths of its imports and taking 99 percent of its exports, and it had negotiated the sole right to use Pearl Harbor as a coaling and naval station. In January 1893, with the help of marines from the cruiser USS *Boston* who intervened at the request of the US minister to the kingdom, John Stevens, the American residents and other whites overthrew the Hawaiian queen. They established a provisional government (fourteen of its eighteen members were Americans, two were British and two were German[60]) and asked Washington to annex the island chain. President Harrison, a Republican, was strongly in favor and a treaty of annexation was signed on February 14, 1893. But Harrison had been defeated for reelection by the Democrat, Grover Cleveland. Cleveland withdrew the treaty from the Senate, "for the purpose of reexamination."[61] He then sent a special commissioner, James Blount, to Hawaii to ascertain "all the facts you can learn" about the political situation in the archipelago, the causes of the uprising, and the attitude of the population toward union with the United States.[62]

In the United States, the proponents of annexation spoke of the strategic and economic benefits of acquiring Hawaii, and warned of Britain's designs on the islands. A few Americans opposed annexation on moral grounds, condemning the role of minister Stevens in the overthrow of the queen, but most critics argued that annexation was both unnecessary and dangerous. Unnecessary because the United States already had "all practical benefits of a protectorate"; dangerous because a large majority of Hawaii's 90,000 people were nonwhite. "It would be a curious thing indeed," a *New York Herald* correspondent wrote, "to some day have a close election for President of the United States settled by the votes of semi-barbaric Sandwich [Hawaii] islanders, whose grandfathers were cannibals."[63]

In July, Blount sent his report to Secretary of State Walter Gresham. He asserted that Stevens and the marines had played a decisive role in the coup and that the native Hawaiians were overwhelmingly opposed to annexation. After much deliberation, on December 18, Cleveland sent a special message to Congress declaring that "the Provisional Government owes its existence to an armed invasion by the United States." He asked Congress to decide on a policy "consistent with American honor, integrity, and morality."[64] In effect, after determining that annexation was inadvisable, the president, historian Julius Pratt has remarked, "washed his hands of the affair."[65]

Cleveland's rejection of annexation was based on idealistic considerations very unusual in any country's foreign policy. Idealism was buttressed, however, by pragmatism: Cleveland and Gresham believed that a territory so distant would represent a strategic liability and an economic burden for the United States, requiring a strong navy to protect it; they also believed that the nonwhite population of Hawaii would add to the racial problems that beset the United States.

After months of wrangling, the closest Congress came to suggesting a policy was when the Senate approved, on May 31, 1894, a resolution that declared that the United States should not interfere in the internal affairs of Hawaii. This meant that it should accept the *status quo*—the white minority government imposed by the US minister. Cleveland reluctantly complied. The resolution also warned foreign governments not to intervene in Hawaiian affairs. The warning was unnecessary: at no moment, throughout the crisis, did any European power attempt to interfere. In the words of the British minister in Washington, they all recognized "the exceptional interests that the government of the United States had in the islands."[66]

Humbling Britannia

In the United States, the economic crisis triggered by the crash of 1893 continued, relentlessly. In the mid-term elections of 1894, the Republicans achieved a slim plurality in the Senate and crushed the Democrats in the House, where they gained a two to one majority. In the wake of this debacle, the administration faced the first major foreign policy crisis of the decade. For years, Britain and Venezuela had bickered over Venezuela's border with British Guiana. In late 1894, a pamphlet suggestively titled *British Aggressions in Venezuela: Or the Monroe Doctrine on Trial*, was published in the United States. The author, William Scruggs, was a former US diplomat on the payroll of the Venezuelan government. His accusations that Venezuela, and the Monroe Doctrine, were under British attack fell on fertile soil.

For over a century, since the early 1770s, Britain had been the country most disliked by Americans. The US Civil War had heightened American hostility: Southerners felt betrayed by Britain's failure to help them; Northerners were furious over what they deemed to be Britain's brazen support for the Confederacy and they held London responsible for the depredations of the *Alabama* and the *Florida*, which had been built in Liverpudlian shipyards. In 1871, the two countries had finally agreed to arbitration, which the following year awarded the United States $15 million (*c.* $320 million) as restitution for the actions of the *Alabama* and the *Florida*. While disagreeing with the verdict, Whitehall promptly paid, closing a turbulent chapter in relations between the two countries. But among Americans antipathy and suspicion persisted and deepened in the early 1890s.

As the depression ravaged the United States and the need for foreign markets became a national credo, Americans increasingly resented British domination of Latin American trade. Recent developments in Latin America fueled the feeling that Britain sought to assert hegemony over the region that—US citizens believed—rightly belonged to the United States. In late 1893 many Americans had mistakenly seen British connivance behind a naval revolt in Brazil.[67] Then, in April 1895, the British occupied the Nicaraguan port of Corinto to force the government to pay an indemnity for the detention of eleven British subjects. They left two weeks later after Nicaragua had agreed to pay. The occupation of Corinto, however fleeting, provoked outrage in the United States. Republican newspapers attacked the "imbecile diplomacy" and "cowardly feebleness" of the Cleveland administration for failing to respond. In their indignation Americans overlooked the fact that Britain had just agreed to the full incorporation into Nicaragua of its former protectorate, the Mosquito Kingdom, surrendering what residual influence it might still have there—not exactly the behavior of a power bent on extending its influence in the region.[68]

The urge to increase US exports to Latin America; resentment at British commercial dominance in the region; British alleged transgressions in Brazil and Nicaragua; the more aggressive mood of American public opinion evidenced in the 1891 Chilean affair; and the desire of Republicans to weaponize Americans' Anglophobia against the Cleveland administration were the backdrop to the Venezuelan crisis of 1895. The Republicans sounded the alarm. "All that England has done has been a direct violation of the Monroe Doctrine," Senator Henry Cabot Lodge (R-MA) wrote in June 1895. "The supremacy of the Monroe Doctrine should be established at once—peacefully if we can, forcibly if we must." If Cleveland failed to act, "It will be the duty and the privilege of the next Congress to see that this is done."[69]

For an increasingly unpopular president, bashing Britain was tempting and, given public opinion, necessary. On July 20, 1895, Secretary of State Richard Olney sent a bombastic note to the British government. "Today the United States is practically sovereign on this continent," it said. The British-Venezuelan boundary dispute fell within the purview of the Monroe Doctrine, and the United States demanded to know whether Britain was willing to submit the dispute to arbitration.[70]

It took four months—until November 26—for the British to reply. Their note said, quite correctly, that the Monroe Doctrine had no standing in international law, and it added that a boundary dispute between Britain and Venezuela was "a controversy with which the United States have no apparent practical concern."[71] Cleveland sent a special message to Congress on December 17. He asserted that the British rejection of arbitration was a serious threat to the Monroe Doctrine, and he asked Congress to approve funds for a US Investigating Commission that would determine the border between British Guiana and Venezuela. If the president found the commissioners' decision satisfactory, the United States would enforce it.[72] Congress unanimously appropriated $100,000 for the Commission. This was the only time, a biographer notes, that Cleveland "enjoyed the support of even his most intractable critics in Congress." The American press, the French ambassador reported, celebrated the opportunity "to settle old scores with Britain."[73]

Historians disagree about the president's motivations. The most likely explanation is that he perceived the British response, and its tardiness, as an affront to the honor of the United States, a threat to the Monroe Doctrine, and a personal insult. Anything but a strong reply would add fuel to the Republicans' attacks a time when the November 1896 presidential elections were approaching. But while the words of Cleveland's special message were "as bold as any jingo's,"[74] he had left himself room to maneuver: he would need time to select the commissioners, the commissioners would need time to reach a conclusion, and he would need time to decide if he approved their findings. More time would then be needed to negotiate with the British over the disputed boundary. But would the British remain obdurate through this entire process, risking war with the United States?

They didn't. The first reaction of Prime Minister Robert Salisbury was to stand his ground. But when the cabinet met in London on January 11, 1896, only one minister supported him; the others wanted to appease the Americans, as did the British press. "The English, with characteristic pragmatism, have immediately understood how dangerous this war ... would be for them," the French ambassador reported from London. "While they would be willing to fight for some causes, it would not be to defend a border with Venezuela."[75] The timing was propitious for the Americans. Britain's relations with France and Russia—which had concluded an alliance in 1894—were strained over matters that affected major British interests in Africa, the Ottoman Empire, China and on the frontiers of India. Germany was increasingly unfriendly. Why clash with the Americans over a trifle? The British threw in the towel. They accepted arbitration and the right of the United States to participate in the resolution of their boundary dispute with Venezuela. It was a turning point in US-British relations. In its aftermath, the mantra of a "Special Relationship" between the two countries was adopted by the British government, the British press, and British public opinion. Their embrace was motivated by their sense of weakness: Britain faced powerful enemies in Europe and its resources were overstretched; it was time to cultivate the rich Americans. In this relationship—which endures to this day—the British were the suitors, and they were willing to entice the Americans with one-sided concessions. The courtship would blossom as the United States prepared to fight Spain over Cuba.[76]

CHAPTER 11
CUBA AND THE PHILIPPINES

In Cuba, José Martí had launched the revolt against Spain in February 1895. He sought independence and social reform. Like Bolívar, he was deeply suspicious of the United States. "What I have done, and shall continue to do," he wrote in May 1895, "is to . . . block with our blood . . . the annexation of the peoples of America to the turbulent and brutal North that despises them. . . . I lived in the monster [the United States] and know its entrails—and my sling is that of David." The next day he was killed on the battlefield.[1]

Despite Martí's death, the Cuban revolt grew, as did the violence of Spanish repression. Americans sympathized with the rebels, but policy toward Cuba played no role in the 1896 US presidential elections. In fact, foreign policy was virtually ignored during the campaign. The United States was in the throes of recession and social unrest, and the Democratic Party had been taken over by charismatic William Jennings Bryan, whose battle cry was free coinage of silver. Free silver, Bryan promised, would break the thrall of the eastern financiers and create a more just society. For the Republicans and conservative Democrats, Bryan was a wild-eyed agitator who led a ragtag army of "Anarchists, Socialists, and destructives in society."[2]

The Republican candidate, William McKinley, defeated Bryan at the polls. It was only after McKinley's inauguration, in 1897, that the debate over foreign policy began in earnest.

As he entered the White House, McKinley could boast of a long, illustrious career. In 1861, at age eighteen, he had joined the Union Army as a private, and had left, when the war ended, as a brevet major. He had then served in the House of Representatives and as governor of his home state, Ohio, becoming a leader of the Republican Party and its foremost spokesperson on the tariff. Urbane, a good listener, he was widely admired for his devotion to his ailing wife (who suffered from epilepsy), was popular among the party's rank and file, and was respected by business leaders as a man of sound principles. A strong personality, his *modus operandi* was, in the words of a biographer, "to keep his own counsel, write down very little, and let others think that they were doing much of the steering."[3] Throughout his career, foreign policy had not been his focus, but it would dominate his presidency, first the war against Spain and then the war against the Philippine Republic.

In 1897, McKinley's first year in the White House, the US economy began to improve. Americans celebrated the "signs of returning prosperity"[4] but Republicans and conservative Democrats warned that danger still lurked: the silverites—Bryan's Democrats—had been beaten but not crushed, and the recovery was fragile. In Cuba, the insurrection against Spanish rule continued, and in late 1897 another foreign policy crisis confronted the McKinley administration: China, facing a new round of demands by the European powers, seemed in danger of imminent partition. American businessmen shuddered at the prospect of losing the promise of the China market.

But China was far away. What attracted the attention of most Americans was Cuba where the insurgents had brought the war to a virtual stalemate; Spanish troops controlled the cities, but much of the countryside was in rebel hands. In the United States, an influential group which included leading Republican politicians such as Senator Henry Cabot Lodge, senior administration officials like Navy Assistant Secretary Theodore Roosevelt, and prominent strategists like Navy Captain Alfred Mahan, advocated war against Spain to assert American manhood, gain control of Cuba, and take the first step toward transforming the Caribbean into an American lake. They were joined by an important sector of the press, particularly the "yellow press" which sought to inflame public opinion (and sell papers) by printing lurid articles about Spanish atrocities—real and fake. But these war hawks encountered strong opposition. This was unlike 1846, in the months prior to war against Mexico. Then, everyone had agreed that Mexico was defenseless, so there had been no debate. But in early 1898, many Americans feared war with Spain, even though the United States was an economic giant of 74 million people and Spain a nation of 17 million, backward and bankrupt. The argument of those who opposed war hinged on two points: the costs would be high and the benefits low.

The costs

The pro-war press clamored that defeating Spain would be child's play—"a tap with one finger" would suffice "to prostrate her,"[5]—but many Americans, including some prominent war hawks, had their doubts. They worried about the Spanish Navy: "The Spaniards have assembled a fleet of seagoing armorclads almost equal in point of strength to our own," Theodore Roosevelt wrote two weeks before hostilities began, "and they have torpedo destroyers, while we have none."[6] Most naval experts, on both sides of the Atlantic, believed that the two fleets were roughly equal.

It is striking, in hindsight, how unaware these experts were of the plight of the Spanish Navy. "It is the general opinion of French officers with whom I have talked on the subject," the US naval attaché in Paris, the well-respected William Sims, wrote in March 1898, "that the ships of the Spanish Navy are kept in good condition, and crews well drilled; and from information that I have been able [to] collect, I am of the same opinion."[7] In fact, the Spanish warships were in poor condition and their ordnance in disrepair, as the fleet's senior admiral reminded his government with despair in the months before the war.[8]

Many Americans also worried about the Spanish army. Since February 1895, Madrid had sent more than 200,000 soldiers to Cuba. Their ranks had been piteously thinned— by disease more than by enemy fire—and the British estimate that only 80,000 were still fit for duty was probably accurate.[9] But the entire US army was only 27,532 strong and in Cuba it would confront not only the Spanish but also yellow fever. It would be "extremely hazardous, and I think . . . injudicious," General Nelson Miles, the commander of the US army, warned in April 1898, "to put an army on that island [Cuba] at this season of the year, as it would be undoubtedly decimated by the deadly disease."[10]

Americans did not doubt that the United States would defeat Spain. But at what price? The Spanish Navy could "resort to a guerrilla warfare on sea," targeting American merchant ships, the Boston *Herald* warned. The very nature of the Spanish people—the alleged irrationality typical of the Latin races—boded ill. The Spanish are "vindictive to the last degree," the Richmond *Dispatch* explained. They might continue fighting even after they had been defeated by all rational standards.[11] A protracted war could derail America's fragile economic recovery. US investments in Cuba were worth about $50 million (*c.* $1.5 billion) and US exports to the island in 1894, before the outbreak of the revolt had cut them in half, had been worth $20 million, out of total exports of $892 million;[12] for the American business community, this was peanuts, compared to the possible cost of war with Spain. "Heavy as has been the loss inflicted upon the commerce of the United States by the long-continued Cuban insurrection," *Bankers' Magazine* noted, "a war between Spain and the United States would incalculably increase the loss to business interests."[13]

The lack of spoils

Victory over Spain would give the United States Cuba, but many Americans feared that it would be a poisoned fruit. Why? Racism. While the war hawks claimed that the revolt was led by upper class white Cubans, some of them "of blonde, Saxon type," antiwar papers reminded their readers that the Cubans were "more than half negroes," and that "men of color" held "high places of command" in Cuba's rebel army.[14] African American men, who had gained the right to vote after the Civil War, had not yet been fully disenfranchised in the US South; therefore, many white Americans feared that if the island was annexed black Cuban men would be able to vote. Annexation, the *New York Herald* warned with bitter irony, would add to the Union "new Congo-creole constituencies, over whose electoral enlightenment we may rejoice as we do over the [largely black] Red River parishes of Louisiana or the Sea Islands of South Carolina."[15]

What, then, would be the rewards of victory? Before the outbreak of the war no one in the US press, Congress, or the White House, even hinted—with the sole exception of a remark in the *New York Herald* that "The Philippines would give us a potent voice in that mighty drama of the East now pressing to a consummation"—that the United States should acquire the archipelago or any part of it. The decision to attack the feeble Spanish flotilla there harked back to a 1896 war plan; it was "intended only to support operations against the prime objective," Cuba, and it expressed no interest in acquiring any part of the archipelago.[16] The idea that the Philippines would be a vital stepping stone toward asserting US rights in the fabled China market arose only after Commodore George Dewey had destroyed Spain's Asiatic squadron at Manila Bay.[17]

The anti-war position was a balance sheet in which the potential costs—in money and American lives—greatly outweighed the potential benefits. War would be "pure waste and folly," the *Commercial Advertiser* warned.[18] Therefore, a majority of the business community opposed the war, exciting the wrath of the pro-war press that was itching for a fight. The New York *Journal* lambasted "the eminently respectable porcine citizens who wallow for dollars in the money-grubbing sty," the Omaha *World-Herald* inveighed against "the wretched spirit of commercialism" that opposed war on Spain, and the Chicago *Tribune* depicted Minerva, sword in one hand and the American flag in the other, saying, "Let the men whose loyalty is to the dollar stand aside while the men whose loyalty is to the flag come to the front."[19]

The shift

In late January 1898, the administration had sent the USS battleship *Maine* on a visit to Havana. The Cuban capital had been torn by riots and the *Maine*'s task was to be on hand to protect US lives and property. However unwelcome the battleship's arrival may have been, the Spanish authorities received the visitors with courtesy. Suddenly, on February 15, the *Maine* blew up in Havana harbor. The explosion killed 268 US sailors and provoked fierce outrage in the United States. The tragedy of the *Maine* swelled the pro-war ranks. The new converts included prominent newspaper editors and members of the business community; fear of William Jennings Bryan and the silverites motivated them.

"Intervention in Cuba, peacefully if we can, forcibly if we must, is immediately inevitable," asserted the Chicago *Times-Herald* on March 4, reversing its previous opposition to war against Spain. If McKinley failed to avenge the *Maine*, Bryan and his followers would seize the issue "and who dare doubt that 'war for Cuban liberty' will be the crown of thorns the free silver democrats and populists will adopt at the [congressional] elections this fall? And who can doubt that by that sign, held aloft and proclaimed by such magnetic orators as William J. Bryan, they will sweep this country like a cyclone?" The *Times-Herald* was blunt: "Between war and free silver, the Times-

Figure 11.1 "The Cart Before the Horse." Cartoon. Chicago: *Inter Ocean*, February 22, 1898.

Herald is for war." Spain would "inflict much damage" and the war would cost the United States an "enormous sum" of money, but there was no choice.[20] On March 21, the Navy's Board of Inquiry announced that the disaster had been caused by a submarine mine placed under the *Maine* by persons unknown. The public, led by the yellow press, drew the obvious conclusion: Spain was to blame. This heightened the war frenzy in the United States. (A far more accurate report, seven decades later, concluded that "in all probability the *Maine* was destroyed by an accident which occurred inside the ship." There had been no mine and no Spanish perfidy.[21])

The sinking of the *Maine* affected McKinley's policy. Between March 27 and April 10, the United States presented Madrid with a series of demands that amounted to an ultimatum: Spain must conclude an armistice with the Cuban rebels at once and enter into negotiations with them "through friendly offices of President United States"; and it must pledge that, "if terms of peace not satisfactorily settled by Oct. first, President of the United States to be final arbiter between Spain and insurgents."[22] Would McKinley have agreed to Cuba's independence or would he have sought to foist a US protectorate on Cuba if Spain had submitted to his demands? There is no evidence. But no Spanish government could have accepted such humiliating terms, and war was inevitable. On April 11, McKinley sent his long-awaited message to Congress: announcing that his efforts to reach a peaceful settlement with Madrid had failed, he asked Congress to empower him to use force "to secure a full and final termination of hostilities between the government of Spain and the people of Cuba."[23] Congress's joint resolution, on April 20, authorized the president to use the army and the navy to eject Spain from Cuba. It also included an amendment proposed by Senator Henry Teller (R-CO) which declared that the United States "hereby disclaims any disposition or intention to exercise sovereignty, jurisdiction, or control over said island except for pacification thereof, and asserts its determination, when that is accomplished, to leave the government and control of the island to its people."[24] The Teller Amendment made it possible for those who opposed the annexation of Cuba for a variety of reasons—racist, economic or moral—to vote for war.

McKinley did not confide his thoughts to his aides or to paper, and his policy toward Spain remains subject to conflicting interpretations.[25] The evidence suggests that through 1897 he believed that Spain might be able to restore order if it granted the Cubans considerable autonomy; he also worried that if Spain failed to quell the rebellion it could precipitate a Spanish-American war, an outcome he hoped to avoid. By early February 1898, before the *Maine* blew up, McKinley had grown increasingly pessimistic about Madrid's ability to resolve the crisis and, like many Americans, was dismayed by the suffering of the island's population. It is quite possible that in 1898, McKinley would have chosen war even if the *Maine* had never docked in Havana harbor because of the growing pressure of American public opinion and Republican leaders. On the other hand, worries about the cost of war—in money and in American lives—and the opposition of the business community might have restrained him. Both interpretations are plausible because the evidence is slight. Perhaps much would have hinged on McKinley's assessment of Spain's ability to inflict pain on the United States, and this assessment we do not know. He was aware, however, that Spain was desperately alone: while the governments of continental Europe were sympathetic to Spain, their sympathy was trumped by far more pressing foreign policy concerns and by the deep hostilities that divided them. Britain, the only power that could have spearheaded a European coalition in support of Spain, showed warm sympathy to the United States, in the name of the "special relationship" and, above all, because it sought the benefits of American friendship.[26]

By late March, had McKinley resisted war, he would have risked a revolt within his own party and opened the door to a Democratic victory in the fall. Since the Democrats in Congress were by then solidly in favor of war—and many Republicans had joined them—there was a real danger that Congress would defy the president and vote for armed intervention. "I can no longer hold back action by the Senate," Vice President Garret Hobart warned McKinley; "they will act without you if you do not act at once."[27] The president was under great pressure. "Whatever happens next," France's ambassador reported from Washington on April 4, "one must respect a president who has resisted, for as long as he has, the blind passions of this country."[28]

As the United States prepared for war, US journalists and politicians boasted about the generosity of the American purpose—its war against Spain would be "the most honorable single war in all history," Senator George Hoar (R-MA) asserted. "It is a war in which there does not enter the slightest thought or desire of foreign conquest, or of national gain, or advantage."[29] European diplomats and journalists were not impressed. "These high-minded claims fool no one," the Paris Le Temps concluded.[30] Americans scoffed at the Europeans' cynicism. The Teller Amendment was proof of the purity of their intentions.

The amendment calmed Cuban misgivings. General Calixto García, who commanded the rebels in eastern Cuba, where the US troops landed and fought, placed his forces at the Americans' disposal. "They have recognized our right to be free and independent," he declared, "and that is enough for me."[31] José Martí would have been less trusting, but Martí had been killed in a skirmish with Spanish troops in May 1895.

The test of war

Defeating Spain turned out to be extremely easy [Map 14]. The US Navy effortlessly sank the dilapidated Spanish Far Eastern flotilla at Manila Bay on May 1 and the main Spanish fleet off Santiago on July 3. But what about the Spanish army? The American troops had landed in Oriente, Cuba's easternmost province, on June 22. Their objective was Santiago, the country's second largest city. The Cuban rebels dominated the vast province, penning the Spanish troops into a few towns. "All communications were cut off, forests, roads, and mountains," a Spanish officer wrote. "Everything was infested by the Cubans."[32] The Americans fought only two battles of any significance: near Santiago, at El Caney and at San Juan Hill, both on July 1. The Spaniards, who were outnumbered more than twelve to one, resisted for several hours, and their losses were less than half the

Americans': 215 Spanish soldiers were killed, 376 wounded and two taken prisoner (a total of 593) against 205 Americans killed and 1,180 wounded (a total of 1385).[33]

While the Spaniards celebrated "our heroic soldiers," and the Europeans praised "the stubborn tenacity of the Spanish defence," the Americans worried. From the battlefield, Theodore Roosevelt, who led a regiment of volunteers, wrote to Senator Lodge: "We are within measurable distance of a terrible military disaster." The French ambassador reported from Washington, "The attack ... was considered by everyone here a bloody failure."[34]

There was no reason to worry: Madrid did not intend to continue fighting. The Spanish government had entered the war certain that Spain would be defeated but persuaded that the alternative—to surrender Cuba without a fight—would precipitate a revolt in the army or even a revolution. The US minister in Madrid had captured this mood well: "they prefer the chances of war," he wrote to McKinley in February 1898, "to the overthrow of the dynasty."[35] And no one in Madrid anticipated that defeat would spell the loss of the Philippines, an understandable error, since no one in the United States had voiced any interest in that Spanish colony.

"Even after the loss of ... the fleet and all the communications by sea," the British military attaché in Cuba reported, the Spanish troops could have resisted for several months.[36] But why prolong the agony? The navy had sunk with dignity—its ill-fated sailors had gone obediently to the slaughter aboard their useless ships—and the army had fought well: Spanish honor had been saved. On August 12, Spain signed the armistice. For the US troops in Cuba, Madrid's decision was timely. Malaria and yellow fever were felling their first American victims. On August 3, the senior officers commanding the American units near Santiago stated that "the army is disabled by malarial fever to the extent that its efficiency is destroyed."[37]

A month before the armistice, on July 6, Congress had approved a joint resolution annexing Hawaii. The debate had been brief. McKinley supported the measure. The anti-annexationists had raised again the specter of race—"Are we to have a Mongolian state in this Union?" representative John Fitzgerald (D-MA) had asked the House[38]—but their objections had been overwhelmed by the wave of jingoism unleashed by what the future Secretary of State, John Hay, famously called the "splendid little war" against Spain.[39] Hawaii became a territory of the United States, with the possibility, however distant, of statehood.

The Platt Amendment

As the Europeans had expected, the Americans did not keep their promise pledged in the Teller Amendment; instead, as a condition of withdrawing their occupying troops, they forced the Cubans to include the Platt Amendment in their constitution. The amendment granted Washington the right to send troops to the island whenever it deemed necessary and to establish naval bases on Cuban soil. In other words, Cuba became a protectorate of the United States. This was a flagrant violation of the Teller Amendment, yet few

Americans, in Congress or the press, expressed any qualms about the reversal. Instead, any Cuban who dared oppose the Platt amendment and demand that Cuba be independent was denounced as ungrateful and chastised as an errant child. Americans believed that they—not the Cubans—had won Cuba's independence. Senator Albert Beveridge (R-IN) asserted in a much-admired article in the *North American Review*: "Cuba was not able to expel Spain. . . . The United States ejected [the] Spanish government from that island."[40]

This was a cruel distortion of the truth. The Cuban guerrillas fought valiantly under able commanders. In 1898, after more than three years of fierce Cuban insurgency, Spain was bankrupt, its population desperately tired of war, its army decimated. The evidence indicates that had the United States not entered the war, the Spaniards would have been able to hold onto Cuba for a while longer—one year or possibly two—before exhaustion and the rebels' resilience would have forced them out.[41] The US intervention hastened Spain's departure and robbed the Cubans of their independence. It was as if France, having intervened in the American war of independence, had demanded a naval base at Norfolk and the right to land troops in the United States whenever it deemed necessary. What is striking is that so many Americans still believe that the United States fought for Cuba's independence and kept its promise. As US historian Nancy Mitchell has pointed out, "Our selective recall not only serves a purpose; it also has repercussions. It creates a chasm between us and the Cubans: we share a past, but we have no shared memories."[42]

There had not been a strong independence movement in Puerto Rico, Spain's only other Caribbean colony, and no revolt against Spain. Before April 1898, the US press and US officials had paid almost no attention to the island. However, soon after the war began McKinley decided that because the island had strategic value, particularly after the Teller amendment precluded the annexation of Cuba, the United States should annex it. In late July, US troops invaded Puerto Rico meeting almost no resistance from the weak Spanish garrison. In the months that followed, the fate of Puerto Rico did not engender much discussion in the United States; its annexation was taken as a given. But what, exactly, would the island's status be? US officials knew very little about Puerto Rico. McKinley, therefore, sent a special commissioner to the island to investigate. A key finding of his report was that 64 percent of Puerto Rico's roughly 890,000 people were white.[43] This led some senators to advocate annexing the island as a territory, with the possibility of statehood at a later stage—how long that stage would last could be determined much later; after all, New Mexico and Arizona, annexed as territories in 1848, were still waiting for statehood half a century later.[44] But other senators were skeptical about the whiteness of Puerto Ricans and urged caution. Their view prevailed without much opposition or debate—the key issue confronting the Senate, and the American people, was the future status of the Philippines. Puerto Rico was annexed without territorial status; those Puerto Ricans who hoped for integration into the United States first as a territory and then as a state, "just like California or Nebraska," were rebuffed, and the Foraker Act of April 1900 turned the island into a US colony.[45]

The Philippines

The debate about Cuba's future, which had roiled American politics since 1895, ended as soon as the United States entered the war against Spain. It was only then that the debate about the Philippines began.

After receiving news of Dewey's victory in Manila Bay, McKinley decided to send several thousand soldiers to the Philippines to seize Manila, increase the pressure on Spain and accelerate the end of the war. Spain's control over the archipelago was shaky. A year-long insurrection had ended in December 1897 with an uneasy truce; its leader, Emilio Aguinaldo, had gone into exile in Hong Kong. But the following March scattered fighting had erupted in Luzon, the largest island and home to half the country's population; encouraged by the outbreak of the war between the United States and Spain, and then by Dewey's victory over the Spanish fleet, the revolt grew. Meanwhile, US Navy officers met with Aguinaldo, offering him weapons and and promising to help him return to Luzon. They apparently made no promises about the future status of the archipelago. Aguinaldo was wary, but he had little choice: at home, the insurgents fighting the Spaniards would welcome the Americans' offer of help. On May 19, he returned to Luzon aboard a US ship and took command of the guerrillas, whose ranks were augmented by thousands of Filipino soldiers deserting the Spanish army. By the time the first US troops arrived in late June, a rebel army led by Aguinaldo was besieging Manila. Aguinaldo, who had just declared the independence of the Philippines "under the protection of the Mighty and Humanitarian North American nation," agreed to evacuate some of his guerrillas' trenches surrounding the capital to make room for the US troops.[46]

The Americans wanted to take Manila without allowing the Filipino rebels to share in the victory; they were helped in this by the Spanish authorities in the city, who considered resistance hopeless, and wanted to surrender Manila to the Americans while keeping the guerrillas out. Therefore, American and Spanish commanders reached a secret agreement behind Aguinaldo's back: after a mock battle (to save their honor), the Spaniards would surrender the city to the Americans, who would keep the rebels out. Accordingly, on August 13, the Spanish in Manila surrendered, and when Filipino troops attempted to enter the city, they were stopped by US soldiers.[47] A few weeks later, bowing to pressure from the commanding US general, Elwell Otis, Aguinaldo ordered his soldiers to evacuate the Manila suburbs they had occupied on August 13.

The US capture of Manila added fuel to the debate about the Philippines that had begun to rage in the United States, arraying those who wanted to annex the archipelago—the imperialists—against the anti-imperialists, who opposed annexation. The case for annexation was eloquently presented in October 1898 by prominent journalist Mayo Hazeltine. The cost of annexation, he argued, would be remarkably low. There would be no resistance: the seven million Filipinos "are an industrious people, docile and easily managed by an administration at once firm and just." Annexation would entail no economic burden for the American people: the islands were rich. Not only were the Philippines important as a source of raw materials and as a "capacious market" for American goods, they were the key to the China market: "Such is their strategic relation to China that our possession of them would give us an influence at Peking second only to that of Russia and Great Britain."[48]

The anti-imperialists argued that the annexation of the Philippines would require the creation of a much larger and more expensive military establishment to defend the colony against foreign powers. But their warnings rang hollow because none of the great powers expressed any objection to the United States annexing the Philippines, not even Germany, which would have liked to buy the archipelago from Spain but did not want to pick a quarrel with the United States. As for the British, they encouraged McKinley to claim the Philippines, hoping that a US presence there would foster British-American cooperation in China, where both powers supported free trade.

Therefore, the anti-imperialists' argument that the Philippines might become a strategic liability to the United States gained little traction. Andrew Carnegie sounded the tocsin: "Just consider her [the United States'] position [without the Philippines], solid, compact, impregnable ... all the powers in the world would be impotent to injure her seriously."[49] His words fell on deaf ears.

There were Americans who opposed the annexation of the Philippines on moral grounds, asserting that acquiring a colony would violate the anti-imperialist tradition of the United States and, some added, the rights of the Filipinos. Racism was central to the debate. Many anti-imperialists feared that annexation would be the back door through which hordes of "Malays and other unspeakable Asiatics" would swamp the United States, as former Senator Carl Schurz warned;[50] worse, one day American reformers might crusade to make them citizens.

The imperialists spoke of American manhood, of glory and of commercial gain, and also of the duty to uplift the savage races. Americans, they said, were particularly suited to this task. "Our experience has been a school in the arts of conquering savages without exterminating them by war," explained a former senator from Kansas in the *North American Review*. The United States would bring civilization to the Filipinos, "a semi-barbarous people ... Developing, constructing, trading, improving, are our special lines of work."[51] Famed British author and imperialist Rudyard Kipling urged Americans to take up the "White Man's burden,"[52] while the *Colored American*, a leading black newspaper, unpacked the real meaning of that burden:

> With all due respect for the alleged genius of one Rudyard Kipling, his latest conglomeration of rot about the "white man's burden" makes us very, very tired. It has ever been the dark races who have born the world's burdens both in the heat of the day and the travail of the night. The white man has never had a burden that was not self-imposed, sometimes through a temporary wave of indignation or charity, but more frequently through greed of gold and territory. Might has been made to pose for right and the weak and untutored people have had burdens forced upon them at the mouth of the cannon or point of the bayonet. The white man's burden is a myth. The black man's burden is a crushing, grinding reality. Let us have done with cant and hypocrisy.[53]

McKinley's decision

While pundits and politicians debated the merits of annexing the Philippines, jingoism swept through the United States. Many white Americans believed that since the Star and Stripes had been raised in the Philippines, it would be unmanly to haul it down. However, after taking Manila the United States had not attempted to expand its control of the archipelago. When the peace treaty with Spain was signed in December 1898, the United States held only Manila and its bay. The rest of Luzon was controlled by Aguinaldo, and many of the other islands supported him. "America is in actual possession at this time of one hundred and forty-three square miles of territory, with a population of three hundred thousand," Aguinaldo's special envoy wrote to the US Senate in January 1899.[54] As Richard Welch, an authority on the war, points out, if the United States had decided to withdraw from the Philippines, "few flags would have been lowered."[55]

It is impossible to establish with any certainty how McKinley's views about the Philippines evolved in the months that followed Dewey's victory. When the US commissioners set off for Paris in late September 1898 to negotiate peace with Spain, the president gave them no definite instructions about the archipelago. But then, on October 11, McKinley set off on a ten-day speaking tour of the Midwest, and whenever he mentioned annexing the Philippines the crowds applauded enthusiastically. Upon his return to Washington, on October 25 he instructed the US commissioners in Paris to demand the entire archipelago. Spain was in no condition to resist. The Filipinos were excluded from the negotiations, as were the Cubans, who had fought alone against Spain for more than three years. On December 10, 1898, the two white powers signed the peace treaty. Spain ceded to the United States the Philippines (receiving in exchange $20 million [c. $620 million]), the island of Guam in the Pacific, and Puerto Rico; and it relinquished all claims of sovereignty over Cuba. (The distinction indicated that Cuba was not expected to be a US colony.) Two months later, on February 6, 1899, the US Senate ratified the treaty in a fifty-seven to twenty-seven vote. Had McKinley waited until the next session of Congress, the majority would have been larger, because the Republicans gained six senate seats in the November 1898 mid-term elections.

If the United States had left the Philippines in Spanish hands, the most likely outcome is that Madrid, bankrupt, without a Navy and with an exhausted army, would have been unable to pacify the islands and would have sold them to Germany, which wanted them. But the United States did not have to annex the Philippines in order to avoid their sale to Germany. There was another option: Aguinaldo was ready to accept a US protectorate. He formally offered it in December 1898 in a letter to McKinley, in which he proposed that a commission of Americans and Filipinos be appointed "to determine the period of protectorate."[56] He received no reply. He reiterated the offer when his representatives held six meetings in January 1899 with US officers chosen by General Otis.[57] If the United States had established a protectorate, the Germans might have grumbled, but they would have acquiesced. The Kaiser spoke loudly, but he was cautious; the German Navy was still weak, and in Europe Berlin faced a formidable enemy in the alliance between

France and Russia. The Germans had no intention of risking a conflict with the United States.[58] Whereas the establishment of the US protectorate in Cuba was the betrayal of a solemn pledge and could not be justified by a foreign threat—no European power sought to dominate Cuba—in the Philippines, where a real European challenge existed, a protectorate made sense and would have avoided war. But the McKinley administration had no interest in it. Nor did the Republican majority in Congress. They wanted a colony.

This meant war. After August 1898, when the Spaniards had surrendered Manila, two armies had faced one another: the all-white US army, penned inside the city; and, outside, the makeshift Army of Liberation of the Philippines. For most US soldiers, the brown-skinned Filipinos were simply "niggers." The white American boys, used to submissive Blacks at home, were now surrounded by armed dark-skinned rebels. The Americans' racial world was up-ended and their manhood challenged. As weeks stretched into months their outrage grew. The racism in their letters home hardened. There was also, as a leading historian of the war, Paul Kramer, notes, "a crisis of martial masculinity." The American soldiers, eager for glory, had been deprived of a battle against the Spaniards, so they itched for confrontation with the Filipinos.[59] "If they would turn the boys loose," a Nebraska volunteer wrote to his parents, "there wouldint [sic] be a nigger left in Manila twelve hours after." The American soldiers "were determined to prove their manhood by 'shooting niggers,'" another authority, Richard Welch, concludes.[60]

On the night of February 4, 1899, the stalemate was broken. General Otis exploited an incident between US sentries and a Filipino patrol on the edges of Manila to launch a general offensive against the rebel army surrounding the city. For the outmatched Filipinos, it was a rout. Aguinaldo tried to negotiate, but he was told that only unconditional surrender would be accepted. He refused.

The fighting had been underway for several months when in July 1899 the first black troops began arriving in Manila.

African Americans

In 1898 there were in the United States almost 9 million African Americans out of a population of 74 million. In the North, they were subject to virulent racism. In the South, where the great majority lived, the promises of Reconstruction had been squelched.[61]

At no moment, while white Americans had debated on the merits of a possible war with Spain, did black Americans lose sight of what was, for them, the overriding question: how would the war affect their oppression at home? Ever since the Civil War the US army had included black soldiers in segregated units, under white officers—2,000 in early 1898. If war with Spain came, should African Americans volunteer or should they hold back, in dignified protest? "The colored man is in a quandary," a reader wrote to the *Colored American.* "Why should he desire to take up arms against any foreign government, when the United States, his adopted country, offers him such little protection?"[62] For most black papers the answer was clear: African Americans must show their patriotism in the hope that this might ease white racism. "We fight as brethren of one blood, and under one flag. We are all American citizens, bound inseparably by a common cause," the *Colored American* wrote in April 1898. "Thousands of valiant colored men are only waiting for Uncle Sam to say 'come on boys,' and a howling response will be forthcoming," another black paper, the *Washington Bee*, asserted.[63]

When war came African Americans rushed to enlist, and black soldiers in segregated units participated with great distinction in both of the important battles fought by the US army against Spain, at San Juan Hill and El Caney. "We [white] officers of the Tenth [black] Cavalry could have taken our black heroes in our arms," wrote Lieutenant John Pershing, the future commander of the American Expeditionary Forces on the Western Front in 1917–18. "They had again fought their way into our affections." The valor of the black soldiers went beyond the battlefield. The dedication with which they tended the sick white soldiers in the yellow fever hospitals in Oriente stood in stark contrast to the refusal of eight white regiments to join them. It was, a white officer noted, "the crucial test of the mettle of men."[64]

It made no difference. "It would seem," the Richmond *Planet*, a black paper, remarked in July 1898, "that the war . . . would tend to allay race prejudice and bring closer together the races in the South. It has had an opposite tendency, for the number of lynchings has been steadily on the increase."[65] The reason was simple: white Americans resented and feared the sight of Blacks with weapons. And African American soldiers had a disquieting tendency to insist on their civil rights. Aware that the sight of black troops could alarm whites, the US army had stationed its four black regiments in the western plains. When the war with Spain began, however, black troops, both regulars and volunteers, gathered in the South for possible embarkation to Cuba. They were not welcome. Violence erupted. There were murders and beatings. Most of the victims were black; and, more often than not, white soldiers from the North sided with their southern brethren against Blacks. The old scars of the Civil War faded as white boys, northern and southern, sat around the canteen in military camps, forging white unity while otherizing Blacks.

After the armistice with Spain was signed in August 1898, the campaign for the November mid-term elections began in earnest. The major national issue was the fate of the Philippines, but in the few southern states where African Americans retained some political rights, race was also important. It was paramount in North Carolina, where black officials were, the New Orleans *Picayune* lamented, "as plenty as blackberries."[66] More accurately, African Americans were slightly more than one-third of North Carolina's population and held less than 7 percent of the seats in the state legislature and a handful of local offices. By southern—and northern—standards this was impressive.

North Carolina's leading white newspaper, the *News and Observer*, boldly proclaimed, "the question has resolved itself into a simple one, 'Shall the white man or the black man rule in North Carolina?'" The *Washington Post*, which provided extensive coverage of the mid-term campaign in North Carolina, reported that white violence was filling "the negroes' souls with fear."[67] The intimidation was successful: the great majority of African Americans in North Carolina did not go to the polls, and the white supremacists—Democrats—swept the state.

For some of North Carolina's white citizens, victory only whetted their appetite for more: Blacks needed to be convinced that their situation was hopeless. Where better for that lesson than Wilmington, the state's largest city, and the place where African Americans enjoyed more influence than in any other southern city? On November 10, two days after the elections, a pogrom took place in Wilmington. Armed whites hunted down African Americans with the assistance of local members of the North Carolina State Guard. Estimates of the number of Blacks killed range from a low of twenty to thirty to well over one hundred; three whites were wounded. All black office holders were ejected from their posts and replaced by white Democrats. The local and national white press reported it as a black riot.[68]

The McKinley administration did nothing. The president and white America were celebrating the return of harmony between whites, North and South, brought on by the victory over Spain. In December, McKinley embarked on a week-long tour of Georgia and Alabama. "Sectional lines no longer mar the map of the United States," he told the Georgia legislature. "Under a hostile fire on a foreign soil, fighting in a common cause, the memory of old disagreements has faded into history."[69] In Atlanta, Montgomery, Selma, and Savannah, white crowds responded enthusiastically. McKinley rallied support for the most controversial provision of the peace treaty with Spain, the annexation of the Philippines. His rousing appeals—"Who will haul ... [the US flag] down? Answer me, ye men of the South. Who is there in Dixie who will haul it down?"[70]—were matched by what the *Washington Post* called his "delicate tact ... in dealing with the negro question." The *News and Observer* explained this tact: "Mr. McKinley has come and gone and not a word has he said about the rights of the 'down-trodden' blacks."[71] The federal government was not interested in the fate of Blacks.

This would be demonstrated a few months later with the lynching of Sam Hose in Georgia. The lynching was advertised several hours in advance and "a special train was engaged as an excursion train to take people to the burning.... After this special moved out, another was made up to accommodate the late comers and those who were at church."[72] For half an hour, the *New York Times* wrote, Hose was mutilated with knives—first his ears, then his fingers were cut off one by one. Then he was burned alive. "The crowd fought for places about the smoldering tree, and with knives secured such pieces of his carcass as had not crumbled away."[73] The Attorney General of the United States hastened to declare that the lynching had not violated any federal law and "the government would take no action whatever."[74]

This was the context in which black Americans had to decide whether or not to support the war in the Philippines. The African American press expressed empathy for the plight of the Filipinos. At a time when African Americans were "butchered like hogs,"[75] robbed of the vote, and discriminated against in every sphere of life, it was impossible to deny that "there is some analogy between the struggle which is now going on among the colored people for constitutional liberty and that of a similar race in the Orient and hence a bond of sympathy naturally springs up."[76] A few African American newspapers dared go further: "our sympathies, which are as broad as the universe, are with the Filipinos," the *Broad Ax* wrote, "and it is perfectly clear to our minds that the war upon them is contrary and antagonistic to the fundamental principles of liberty and justice."[77] But pragmatism prevailed. African Americans could not afford to be considered "half-hearted and cold" in their patriotism, the *Freeman* warned.[78] Most black papers endorsed the conquest of the Philippines.

War

Through the first months of the war against the Filipinos, the major US military effort was in Luzon, where Aguinaldo's army fought a conventional war, suffering one defeat after another. Finally, in November 1899, Aguinaldo turned to guerrilla warfare. This complicated the task of the American troops, operating, as an American captain noted, "in a country thoroughly in sympathy" with the rebels.[79] The guerrillas' hit-and-run tactics, and their ability to blend into the population, "infuriated" the US soldiers, writes historian Brian Linn.[80] Senior commanders urged their officers to redouble their efforts. "I want you to take the most aggressive stance against the natives," Col. Robert Howze ordered in August 1900. "Clear up that situation [in the area of Badoc] even if you have to kill off a large part of the malcontents; do some terrorizing yourself."[81] The troops responded with alacrity. The diaries and letters of white American soldiers, Richard Welch writes, reflected "a growing conviction that all Filipinos were their enemies, deserving of any form of punishment that would assure surrender."[82] This included torture such as water boarding. The white American GIs despised the rebels as "niggers," cowards, and savages, who, as Private John Brown told his mother, did not "stand up for a square fight."[83] Private Al Miller wrote to a friend that six men of his company had been killed in an ambush. The "reinforcements arrived . . . only in time to see them lying around dead. The men just went wild, and scattering in every direction they killed every negro [Filipino] they ran across. Then they burned their shacks and killed all their stock and chickens. They tied one negro to a rice stack and then set fire to it. I'll tell you he hollered some."[84]

In the United States, pro-administration newspapers demanded more draconian measures. "The American people are plainly tired of the Philippines war," warned the *New York Times* in January 1901; "why does it take such an unconscionably long time" to teach the Filipinos "reason and obedience?" The correspondent of the New York *Post* reported from Manila that "officers and men who know the situation and the natives are all agreed that the Filipino hates us as he never hated the Spaniard; that every Filipino is an insurrecto; and that the present guerrilla warfare will continue for years unless some strong policy be inaugurated. Fear is the only force that the Tagal [Filipino] savage recognizes."[85] It was "a mistake" to believe that the Filipinos "have a moral sense," the US general in charge of the war in northwestern Luzon noted in December 1900. "If the majority of them ever had a moral sense, it has been carefully eliminated. The Spaniards and other European nations who have had dealings with this kind of people have learned this and treat rebellious subjects in the way they appreciate and do not accord them the same treatment as is given civilized races."[86]

Like the American rebel leaders during the US War of Independence, the Filipino rebel leaders belonged, with rare exceptions, to their country's upper class. As had been true for the American rebel leaders, theirs was a political—not a social—revolution. Just as the Americans had refrained from addressing the most important social question they faced—slavery—and had spurned the support of tens of thousands of enslaved men in the South, so the Filipino rebel leaders avoided the most pressing social question of their country—agrarian reform—and thereby forfeited the peasant support that reform would have garnered them. But whereas the American rebel leaders received decisive foreign aid, the Filipinos were desperately alone. No foreign country offered any assistance, and virtually no weapons reached them from abroad.

Given the Americans' massive superiority in weapons and training, the outcome of the war was predictable. The 1900 presidential elections in the United States—a resounding Republican victory returning McKinley to office—deprived the rebels of any hope of a change in US policy. In the spring of 1901, the US troops finally suppressed the guerrillas in the Ilocano provinces, a stronghold of the rebellion. "It will take years to remove impressions of American civilization as taught by the outrageous conduct of many American soldiers," Colonel William McCaskey, the US commander in Ilocos Norte, wrote in March 1901.[87] By the fall of 1901, the only strong guerrilla units still in the field were in the province of Batangas (in southwestern Luzon) and in the island of Samar. Within the next few months they were crushed.

Parallel with the repression, the army was engaged in an effort to demonstrate to the Filipinos the benefits of US rule if they were submissive. In areas that had been pacified, the US military authorities undertook, sometimes very successfully, civic projects such as sanitation, education, and local government. Increasing numbers of the local elite concluded that it was pointless to resist American power, and the US authorities ensured their cooption by eschewing the social reforms the Filipino masses desperately needed. Over the years, the partnership between the Americans and the Filipino upper class blossomed. When the Americans departed the archipelago in July 1946, the conservative oligarchy that they had nurtured took their place. Eager to maintain its immense privileges, this oligarchy readily granted the Americans the military bases they sought.[88]

War crimes?

The issue of American atrocities in the Philippines remains controversial. A compelling case that massive war crimes were committed is made by Stuart Miller in "*Benevolent Assimilation*": *The American Conquest of the Philippines*. Miller's evidence has been challenged by other US scholars. Thus John Gates, an expert on the war, has argued that "Miller builds his case largely on soldiers' letters, the truth of which was often denied by the authors at the time of investigation, and newspaper accounts from an era in which editors and reporters were notorious for their sensationalism and partisanship."[89] Gates seems to overlook the fact that it was in the soldiers' interest to recant if the army threatened them with court martial. Furthermore, many documents in the US archives, as well as the 1902 Congressional hearings on the Philippines, contain clear evidence of the extent of American war crimes.[90]

In order to understand the behavior of the white American troops it is important to understand their mindset. The vast majority of white soldiers had two frames of reference: the treatment of Blacks in the United States and "injun warfare" against Native Americans. "The country [Philippines] won't be pacified," a Kansas volunteer told a reporter, "until the niggers are killed off like the Indians"[91] Almost every member of the US high command in the Philippines had his formative experience in the wars against Indians. Secretary of War Elihu Root urged them to use the "methods that have proved successful in our Indian campaigns in the West."[92] Back home only a "small minority" of Americans expressed "deep concern" over the reports of atrocities perpetrated by the US troops in the Philippines, Richard Welch writes. Most Americans dismissed them as "infrequent and exceptional."[93]

The letters and diaries of the soldiers reveal that many crimes committed by the troops against the Filipinos were not reported. "Most senior officers preferred a policy of 'don't ask, don't tell,'" Linn writes.[94] When crimes were reported, the perpetrators were rarely punished. The most notorious prosecution was the May 1902 court martial of General Jacob Smith, who had ordered his troops to "kill and burn" and turn the island of Samar into a "howling wilderness." The evidence against him was overwhelming, but the court found him guilty only of "conduct to the prejudice of good order and military discipline" and he was retired from the army. Most Americans believed that his court martial was proof of the rigor of American justice, but some dissented. Senator Hoar addressed the Senate in May 1902 about the behavior of the US troops in the Philippines: "We are talking about torture, torture—cold-blooded, deliberate, calculated torture ... You make the American flag in the eyes of a numerous people the emblem of sacrilege in Christian churches, and of the burning of human dwellings, and of the horror of the water torture."[95] Some US soldiers expressed remorse—"we left desolation in our trail," a private wrote after participating in an expedition in the island of Marinduque, near Luzon; "talk about American liberty and humanity, it makes me sick."[96]

White Americans fought in the Philippines in ways similar to those the Europeans used in their colonial wars in Africa and Asia: the lives of non-whites were devalued. Race became "a sanction for exterminist war," Paul Kramer writes, "the means by which earlier distinctions between combatants and noncombatants—already fragile—eroded or collapsed entirely."[97]

Black soldiers treated the Filipinos far better than did their white comrades. The difference, a Filipino explained, was that they did not "connect race hatred with duty."[98] By all accounts, black soldiers fought well, but they also recognized the Filipinos' humanity. The correspondence of black soldiers, Willard Gatewood writes, "revealed that they were continually plagued by misgivings about their role in the Philippines."[99]

"Victory"

President McKinley was assassinated in September 1901 and Vice President Theodore Roosevelt, a man of intelligence, charisma, and willpower, took over. A fervent expansionist and believer in the need for Americans to assert their manhood, Roosevelt had eagerly hoped for war against Spain. With the help of his close friend and ally Senator Lodge he had been appointed Assistant Secretary of the Navy in April 1897 by McKinley. As soon as the war began, he resigned to enlist in the army. At the head of a regiment of volunteers, he fought gallantly in Cuba. Celebrated as a hero in the United States, he was elected governor of New York in November 1898 and was chosen as McKinley's running mate in 1900. At age thirty-nine, in September 1901, he became president of the United States. An ardent proponent of the annexation of the Philippines, he endorsed the military effort to crush the rebels and was eager to tell the American people before the 1902 elections that the insurrection had been defeated. Fortified by the success of the bloody campaigns against the remaining guerrilla strongholds in Batangas and Samar, on July 4, 1902, he announced that the war was over. This was, Paul Kramer writes, "a beleaguered fiction":[100] until 1913, resistance continued to flare up. The Filipinos paid a heavy price. Between February 1899 and the official end of the war, in July 1902, the US army killed between 16,000 and 20,000 insurgents. No one knows the number of war-related civilian deaths. The American troops had conducted what a careful scholar has deemed "incineration campaigns" in areas where the guerrillas operated, destroying crops and burning villages in order to deprive the rebels of food and punish the population; many expeditions "took on an apocalyptic quality."[101] The population suffered terribly, and an untold number died. In some areas the army forcibly relocated the people into so-called protected zones where "many"—that number, too, is unrecorded—"died of malnutrition and sickness."[102] Serious estimates range from a minimum of 100,000 to more than 200,000 war-related Filipino civilian deaths.[103]

American losses were far fewer. By July 4, 1902, 4,165 US soldiers had died, 1,004 of whom had been killed in action or of wounds sustained in combat;[104] 126,468 US soldiers had served in the Philippines, including approximately 6,000 African Americans.

Imperialism

There were several debates over war and imperialism at the turn of the century. One was among African Americans, which was virtually ignored by whites and is often overlooked by historians of US foreign policy. This debate tells a poignant story—the story of how oppressed people deal with their oppression, torn as they are between the desire to lash out and the need to court the goodwill of their tormentors. It is a story that is repeated again and again, in many countries—and in the United States. In the 1960s, Malcolm X could turn to the outside world, to the newly independent African countries, to relieve the sense of being desperately alone and outnumbered. But in the 1890s, Africa lay in chains and Europe was indifferent. The African Americans' best hope, therefore, was to appeal to the conscience of white Americans. In October 1898, the *Washington Bee* wrote: "There is an American conscience. It needs only to be awakened to see its duty and to act."[105] The American conscience, however, was slumbering, and African Americans could not awaken it.

Was there a distinctive women's position on the Philippines? Many women joined the male-dominated Anti-Imperialist League where they were excluded from leadership—in part to avoid giving fodder to the imperialists who mocked those who opposed annexing the Philippines as "old aunties."[106] The country's two most important women's organizations— the Woman's Christian Temperance Union (WCTU) and the much smaller National American Woman Suffrage Association (NAWSA)—did not take a stance on the annexation of the Philippines. Both were led by middle- and upper-class white Protestant women and in both black women were marginalized. They focused on domestic goals— prohibition for the WCTU and suffrage for the NAWSA. The WCTU's weekly organ, the *Union Signal,* included letters and articles expressing a spectrum of viewpoints about the war, but the only position the organization took was to exhort the government to protect the American soldiers in the Philippines from the twin evils of alcohol and prostitutes. "Our boys are being debauched," a WCTU leader lamented. NAWSA's white leaders had something in common with African Americans: they, too, when addressing the issue of imperialism, asked themselves, first and foremost, what stance could best advance their cause: support for the administration's policy, or support for the Anti-Imperialist League? The answers of members differed and the leadership took no position.[107]

The debate on imperialism that has captured the attention of most historians of US foreign policy was that among white men, that is, the Americans who controlled the vote and the US congress.

In the 1890s, the fear of overproduction gripped Americans. There was, as Walter LaFeber, a leading diplomatic historian, has written, "a wide and strongly held opinion that the United States needed additional markets for its prosperity."[108] The economic crisis that tore the country apart between 1893 and 1897 deepened this conviction. However, the search for markets was not the engine behind the support for territorial expansion. American business leaders had opposed war with Spain because they feared it would hurt the economic recovery and bring no benefits; their opposition weakened only after the sinking of the USS *Maine* because they worried that failure to intervene would lead to a Democratic victory at the polls.

While the business community supported the annexation of the Philippines, the careful analysis of Richard Welch shows that it was not the driving force behind the policy: "A majority of the representatives and spokesmen of business who offered an opinion concerning McKinley's Philippine policy indicated a belief in its propriety," Welch writes. "Few expressed any great interest in that policy, however, or in the Philippine-American War. The Philippines was an issue of major concern for only a few representatives of the business community, and the initial flurry of excitement respecting the economic advantages of the islands was not long sustained."[109]

The driving forces behind both the war with Spain and the annexation of the Philippines were the supporters of the "large policy"—politicians, intellectuals, and military leaders who sought to establish the United States as one of the world's great powers and to reinvigorate through martial deeds the manhood of the American people, threatened, as Frederick Jackson Turner warned, by the closing of the frontier. They swept the country into war against Spaniards and Filipinos on a wave of jingoism.

Until Dewey's victory at Manila Bay, the demands of the expansionists of the 1890s had run along traditional lines, except for their insistence on a strong navy. Senator Lodge is considered the Senate's "point man for American imperialism,"[110] but the "large policy" he advocated was not new: he wanted Cuba, which Americans had desired since Jefferson. He wanted Canada, which Americans had desired since the War of Independence. He wanted Hawaii, which President Pierce had sought to annex. He wanted sole control of a canal through Central America, which Presidents Pierce and Buchanan had sought.[111] Before May 1898, Lodge did not mention the Philippines. The desire to acquire the archipelago was a sudden impulse inspired by Dewey's victory.

Was the annexation of the Philippines a rupture in American foreign policy? Was the United States embarking on an imperialist path—or had it been imperialist all along? In two ways the annexation of the Philippines was a departure. First, never before had the United States annexed territories beyond the Western Hemisphere, except for tiny Midway and, in August 1898, Hawaii. Furthermore, before 1898, the United States had always annexed territories with the expectation that they would one day become states of the Union, even when it was not intended that all their inhabitants would become citizens. However, in every other way the annexation of the Philippines was consistent with American history. Since its creation, the American empire had expanded: the constant advance of the white frontier within the borders of the United States had been accompanied by spurts of expansion beyond the borders. The acquisition of Spanish Florida in 1821 had been followed by two decades of expansion within the borders, followed by the annexation of Texas in 1845, the violent acquisition of a third of Mexico's remaining territory in 1848, and the Gadsden Purchase in 1854 [Map 15]. After the Civil War, the United States had embarked on a long period of expansion within the borders— the conquest of the West—and then, in the late 1890s, a new surge of expansion beyond the borders had followed. Senator Lodge put it well in a speech he delivered in 1900: "The record of American expansions ... has been a long one and today we do but continue the same movement."[112] What had changed by the late 1890s was that the United States had become more powerful and Britain had embraced the "special relationship."

Contrary to what the anti-imperialists claimed, the annexation of the Philippines did not represent the first time that the United States would rule over subject peoples. White Americans had ruled over millions of slaves, and after the failure of Reconstruction most African Americans resembled colonial subjects. Likewise, the Native Americans. According to the 1890 census, most of the 248,000 Indians in the United States[113] lived on reservations, where they were treated as colonial wards. If the anti-imperialists were right in considering the annexation of the Philippines immoral, Lodge argued, "then our whole past record of expansion is a crime."[114]

CHAPTER 12

CONQUERING THE BACKYARD: THE LATIN AMERICAN POLICY OF ROOSEVELT, TAFT, AND WILSON

The occupation of the Philippines did not open a period of US territorial expansion in Asia. The major focus of America's imperial energy remained where it had always been, in the Western Hemisphere. Latin America was where the United States could strive to exercise hegemony, elbowing the Europeans out. During the presidencies of Theodore Roosevelt, William Taft, and Woodrow Wilson, the United States established a sphere of influence over Latin America and consolidated its rule over the backyard—Central America, the Caribbean, and to a lesser degree Mexico.[1]

Through its first decades as an independent nation, Mexico, convulsed by internal strife, had been the object of US land hunger, losing half its original expanse to its northern neighbor. But after the departure of the French in 1867 it entered a period of relative peace, and in the 1880s the dictatorship of Porfirio Díaz brought stability. Mexico became a lucrative field for American investment, particularly railroads and mines, and the major market for American exports to Latin America. As historian Paolo Riguzzi writes, the "peaceful conquest" of Mexico had begun.[2] By the early 1890s, when public opinion in the United States began to favor, once again, a more aggressive foreign policy, Mexico was a stable neighbor, friendly to American investment.

US vistas ranged beyond Mexico. James Blaine was again secretary of state when the first pan-American conference since Bolívar's botched Panama Congress of 1826 convened in Washington in 1889. Blaine hoped to create a pan-American trading bloc that would give the United States a privileged position over its European rivals, but the Latin Americans' mistrust of the Yankees, and their desire to maintain their strong economic and cultural ties with Europe, frustrated his grand design.[3]

Latin American mistrust was justified. In 1891–2, President Harrison humiliated Chile. Then in the Venezuelan crisis of 1895–6, Caracas was not consulted as Washington and London discussed the modalities of arbitration. In October 1899, the arbitration tribunal handed Britain nine-tenths of the disputed territory, confirming the Latin Americans' suspicion that the Yankees had intervened not to protect Venezuela but simply to assert their hegemony over the hemisphere.

When the United States declared war on Spain in April 1898, the Latin American governments hastened to proclaim their neutrality. As historian Bradford Burns notes, Brazil, which had enjoyed a friendly relationship with the United States after the overthrow of the monarchy in 1889, was "the only Latin American nation sympathetic to the United States" during the war.[4] Elsewhere, public opinion, which had previously supported the Cuban rebels, swung in favor of Spain—because of antipathy for the

United States and fear of the repercussions of US victory. The Spanish Americans "are afraid," the French consul wrote from Costa Rica in April 1898, "that bit by bit this overpowering neighbor will swallow them all." The French chargé reported from Mexico City that the Mexican government was observing "religiously the strictest neutrality," but "the people, both the upper and the lower classes, are entirely in favor of Spain."[5]

The war led to US rule over Cuba and Puerto Rico. It also hardened the conviction of a growing number of Americans that the United States had to build a canal through Central America and exercise complete control over it so that US warships could move swiftly from one ocean to the other—the USS *Oregon* had needed sixty-eight days to steam from San Francisco to Florida by way of the Magellan Strait. And once the canal was opened, it would have to be protected. "The inevitable effect of our building the canal must be to require us to police the surrounding premises," Roosevelt's future secretary of state Elihu Root wrote.[6]

But protection from whom? The French were busy with dreams of revanche against Germany and colonial conquests in Africa and Asia. Russia had no interest in Latin America. This left two potential adversaries, Britain and Germany.

The British threat?

The British had bowed to the United States in 1896 during the Venezuelan crisis, and they had displayed their new-found affection for their Yankee cousins during the Spanish-American war. The next step of their courtship was to renounce the Clayton-Bulwer Treaty, which stipulated that a canal through the isthmus would be under joint British and US control. "The canal will certainly be made by the U.S.," the British ambassador, Julian Pauncefote, warned from Washington, urging his government to accept the inevitable. The new treaty signed in February 1900 by Secretary of State Hay and Pauncefote allowed the United States to build a strictly American canal but stipulated that it should not be fortified, arousing a storm of protest in the US Congress. Therefore, Hay went back to the drawing board: in November 1901 the second Hay-Pauncefote Treaty allowed the United States to fortify the canal.[7]

As the strength of the German Navy grew, so did British interest in the "special relationship" with the United States. In the two decades that followed the Venezuelan crisis, Britain never openly criticized or opposed any US action in Latin America. Prime Minister Arthur Balfour set the tone in a 1903 speech: "The Monroe Doctrine has no enemies in this country that I know of. We welcome any increase of the influence of the United States of America upon the great Western Hemisphere."[8]

The German threat?

We are left with Germany. Before the creation of the German empire in 1871, US "points of contact" with Prussia, the most important German state, had been "few, and points of friction virtually nonexistent."[9] Prussia had been sympathetic to the rebels during the American War of Independence and had voiced support for the Union during the Civil War. During the 1870–1 war between France and Prussia, the Grant administration and American public opinion had been sympathetic to Berlin.

But in the 1880s and 1890s, the United States and Germany became increasingly embroiled in bitter trade disputes. Antipathy grew on both sides and burst into the open in the sudden clash over Samoa in 1888. A decade later, German sympathy for Spain confirmed in American eyes the image on an unfriendly Reich just as German foreign and military policy underwent a dramatic change. Under Chancellor Otto von Bismarck (1871–90), the German empire had been the most peaceful great power in modern history: Bismarck was opposed to building a strong navy; he was opposed to acquiring colonies; and he was opposed to annexing any additional territory in Europe. By the final years of Bismarck's tenure, many Germans had tired of his restraint. "If Germany had wanted to play only a modest role in the world," the influential *Kölnische Volkszeitung* complained in August 1886, "then the German people should have been spared the high cost in blood and treasure needed to build the German empire."[10] In 1897–8 the young emperor William II launched a new policy: Germany would build a great navy and embark on a world policy, *Weltpolitik*. "The days when Germany would yield the earth to one neighbor, and the sea to another, reserving for itself only the sky . . . those times are over," the emperor's foreign minister told the German parliament in his maiden speech in December 1897. "We don't want to force anyone into the shadow, but we demand our place in the sun."[11]

A place in the sun . . . where? By the time Germany embarked on *Weltpolitk* Africa had been carved up and in Asia only China was left, a giant prey already surrounded by a pack of predators. And so the Kaiser, naval officers, prominent politicians and journalists began talking loudly about acquiring territory in Latin America. According to John Röhl, a prominent biographer of the Kaiser, "recent historical research has established beyond doubt that the Americans' 'concern' about German intentions was no figment of their imagination": the threat to Latin America was real.[12] However, this exciting notion has been pulverized by historian Nancy Mitchell in a book aptly titled *The Danger of Dreams*. Yes, she explains, Germans had dreams—but the historians' mistake has been to confuse dreams for reality.[13]

The notion that there was a German threat to Latin America meant that there was a German threat to the United States, the champion of the Monroe Doctrine. When a scholar, researching in the German archives in 1971, discovered the Reich's war plans against the United States, first drafted in the 1890s, the story made the front page of the *New York Times*.[14] A constant and reasonable assumption of these plans was that the German Navy would defeat the US Navy, because of the superiority of German training and readiness. But then what? When Vice-Admiral Otto von Diederichs, who headed the war planning branch of the German Navy, asked the army in May 1900 to provide the second phase of the war plans, the army failed to respond for almost a year, and when it finally did, in March 1901, it dismissed the whole enterprise: Germany would need 100,000 men to take Boston and many more to take New York—and this was impossible.

Diederichs decided that conferring with the army was "'hopeless,'" Mitchell writes. "He continued to tinker with the plan but he never again consulted the army. The Kaiser maintained a 'hands off' policy." The plan, Mitchell concludes, was "toothless."[15]

The Navy's war plan was predicated on a chimera. "The necessary precondition for a German war against the United States," wrote Diederichs' successor, Vice Admiral Wilhelm Büchsel, in March 1903, "is a political situation in Europe that gives the German Reich a completely free hand abroad. Any insecurity in Europe would exclude the successful conduct of a war against the USA."[16] But beginning in 1894, Germany had been caught in a pincer by the military alliance between its two powerful neighbors, France and Russia; in 1904 France and Britain, which had been on the brink of war over colonial matters, settled their differences and drew close together—against Germany; as did, in 1907, Britain and Russia. Under such circumstances, war against the United States would have been folly. In May 1906, Admiral Büchsel ordered that "detailed preparatory work for a war against the United States be terminated."[17]

If Germany had aggressive plans in the hemisphere (as opposed to dreams), southern Brazil, home of the largest German community in Latin America, would have been the most tempting target. By the turn of the century, between 250,000 and 500,000 German immigrants (depending on whether one included second-, third-, or even fourth-generation Germans) lived in Brazil. They were concentrated in the country's three southernmost states: Rio Grande do Sul, Santa Catarina, and Paraná. The overthrow of the Brazilian monarchy in 1889 was followed by a decade of political unrest, and even though political stability returned with the new century, conservative German newspapers expressed the hope that the three southern states would break away from Rio, seek German protection, and become German protectorates or even colonies—a hope that was shared by the Kaiser and many German officials.[18]

Biographer Röhl writes that "when his trusted friend, Karl Georg von Treutler, was appointed minister to Brazil in 1901, William II instructed him . . . to focus above all on the German immigrants in southern Brazil."[19] Sounds ominous, but there was no German fifth column in Brazil: "this purported vanguard of the fatherland in the Southern Hemisphere had no desire, was in fact averse to returning to its protection," Mitchell explains. This was also the conclusion of the Brazilian government, and of both the US and the German embassies in Rio. US Minister David Thompson told Secretary of State Hay in 1903 that "Brazil [not Germany] is their country, first, last and always." In disgust, the Kaiser's confidant, Minister Treutler, lamented in 1906, "The longer I am here [in Brazil], the more I am convinced that the sacrifices we make for them [the Germans in Brazil] are deserved only in a very few cases." But what sacrifices was the Reich making? The Germans in Brazil were proud of their German culture and wanted to retain it. However, the subsidies Berlin doled out for German teachers and German schools were "risible"; therefore, the schools had to charge tuition, and only a few German parents enrolled their children in German schools—in Florianopolis, with a community of 10,000 German immigrants, the German school had only fifty students. What else did the Reich do for the German community in Brazil? As Mitchell's exhaustive research demonstrates, the answer is: virtually nothing.[20]

The "height of the German challenge" to the United States, Mitchell writes tongue-in-cheek, occurred in December 1902, when Germany and Britain, with Italy in tow, imposed a naval blockade on Venezuela to force that country's dictator, Cipriano Castro, to pay the debts he owed their citizens. London and Berlin had agreed, before imposing the blockade, that neither would back out unilaterally. It was a rare instance of cooperation between the two powers—their relations had frayed, largely because of the growth of the German Navy. The German chargé in Caracas expressed the hope that the blockade would allow Germany to establish "something of a permanent administrative nature" over Venezuela. The historians who promote the idea of a German threat have pounced on this phrase as evidence of the nefarious intentions of the German empire. In fact, the Reich's intentions were simply to force Castro to honor his debts. "Under no circumstances," German Ambassador Theodor von Holleben told US Secretary of State Hay, did Germany intend "the acquisition or the permanent occupation of Venezuelan territory." Hay raised no objections to the blockade.[21] Roosevelt himself, in his first annual message to Congress, had said, "We do not guarantee any [American] state against punishment if it misconducts itself, provided that punishment does not take the form of the acquisition of territory by any non-American power."[22]

But when the blockade began and the British and Germans captured the few antiquated vessels of the Venezuelan navy and shelled two Venezuelan forts at Puerto Cabello, American public opinion was outraged and Roosevelt asked London and Berlin to agree to arbitration. The British press, which had approved the blockade, turned, with virtual unanimity, against the operation as soon as public opinion in the United States erupted against it. America's goodwill was, the *Manchester Guardian* wrote, "one of the cardinal principles of our foreign policy." It was crazy to risk it just to collect a paltry debt from Venezuela and to fulfill a pledge to Germany, the Americans' bête noire. In parliament, even supporters of Prime Minister Balfour joined in the criticism. The German ambassador in London cabled Berlin: "Reluctantly, I must express my opinion that the sooner we get out of this business with honor, together with England, the better." Therefore, the Kaiser agreed to arbitration. (In 1916, Roosevelt claimed that Berlin had capitulated only after he had threatened to unleash the US fleet against the German ships blockading Venezuela. Some naive historians have believed this canard, but Mitchell has debunked it. The withdrawal of British support, not Roosevelt's imaginary "big stick," convinced the Kaiser to agree to arbitration.)[23]

This second Venezuelan crisis demonstrated how important US friendship was to the British. It also exposed how cautious and timid was the Reich's policy toward Latin America.

But how aware were Americans of the hollowness of the German threat to the hemisphere? Anyone with a passing knowledge of international affairs and some common sense should have understood that Germany was increasingly constrained in Europe. This fact, however, escaped the leaders of the US Navy. Occasionally, there were some glimmers of sanity. Rear Admiral S.A. Staunton, a member of the General Board of the Navy (high-ranking naval officers who advised the president), wrote in 1912, "Although probably somewhat impatient at the maintenance of the Monroe Doctrine in

Central and South America, there is not a chance in a thousand that she [Germany] would, under present political and naval conditions carry, in any contingency, her disapproval of that doctrine to the test of war."[24] But his was an isolated voice. As Mitchell remarks, "The detailed minutes of the meetings of the General Board [of the Navy] reveal how separate war planning was from diplomacy and even current events."[25] Self-interest fueled the admirals' obtuseness: "A fading of the German threat would have deprived the General Board of its most effective argument for the expansion of the American fleet."[26]

Unlike the Navy, the White House and the State Department assessed the German threat realistically—until Woodrow Wilson was president. Roosevelt's correspondence is sprinkled with references to the Kaiser's dangerous proclivities, but his behavior tells a different story. He expressed no alarm when he learned that the Reich, together with Britain, would blockade Venezuela and, the navy's dire warnings notwithstanding, the evidence reveals that he was not worried about the alleged German designs on Brazil. "The absence of any record of a discussion in Washington—at the White House or at the State Department—about a German threat to Brazil is absolute," Mitchell writes.[27] Roosevelt did not trust the Kaiser, but he understood that if Germany presented a threat, it was not to the Western Hemisphere: Berlin faced powerful enemies in Europe and could not afford the luxury of war with the United States. At the end of his presidency, Roosevelt told the secretary of state designate, Philander Knox: "I do not believe that Germany has any designs that would bring her in conflict with the Monroe Doctrine."[28] President Taft and Knox agreed. Given Germany's straits in Europe, any other conclusion would have been folly.

Roosevelt, Taft, and the backyard

The absence of a European threat is the backdrop of the Latin American policy of the Roosevelt, Taft, and Wilson administrations. The British had passed the baton to their Yankee cousins, and the Germans were in no position to challenge the Americans. The United States moved to assert control over its backyard.

The tightening of the US grip included the growth of private American investment in the region, paralleling the growth of US investment globally. The United States was still a net importer of capital (Europe was the source) but US direct investment abroad swelled from an estimated $635 million (c. $19.9 billion) in 1897 to $2.6 billion (c. $67.6 billion) in 1914. Over one-third went to Latin America.[29] For the region, and particularly the backyard, this was the era of Dollar Diplomacy, a term associated with Taft but that actually spanned all three presidencies: the US government vigorously supported the expansion of US capital investment to help US businessmen, strengthen US influence and, at least in theory, uplift the benighted countries in the backyard.[30]

A few weeks after Roosevelt became president, the British had accepted, in the second Hay-Pauncefote Treaty, that the United States would build and fortify a canal through the isthmus. Roosevelt and the US Congress determined that the best route was through

Panama, a province of Colombia. However, in August 1903 the Colombian senate decisively rejected the canal treaty negotiated by Secretary Hay with the Colombian chargé in Washington.

The Colombians wanted better terms, but Roosevelt had no intention of haggling with those "contemptible little creatures," as he called them.[31] While contemplating force to seize the land needed for the canal, he learned that a revolt was being hatched in Panama, where secessionist sentiment was strong and Colombian authority weak. It is unclear exactly what Roosevelt promised the plotters, but it is very likely that it was his promise of support that gave them the confidence, on November 3, 1903, to seize power in Panama City in a bloodless coup. The US Navy had dispatched warships to the province's two ports, Colón and Panama City, landing US marines and bluejackets in Colón while the US government informed Bogotá that it would not permit the landing of Colombian troops in the province. The few hundred Colombian soldiers already in Colón were intimidated by the US show of force, and those in Panama City were bought off by the rebel leaders.

Less than three weeks after the coup, Secretary Hay and Philippe Bunau-Varilla, an adventurer who represented the Panamanian junta, signed a treaty that gave the United States the perpetual grant of a ten-mile-wide strip of land traversing the isthmus, where the United States would have "all rights, power and authority" as if it were "the sovereign of the territory," in exchange for a modest payment. The terms were so draconian that the Panamanian junta protested, in vain. The Colombians seethed, impotent. In 1906, the US minister in Bogotá wrote to Secretary of State Root that "you could not realize how strong still was the feeling, amounting almost to intense hatred, among the people of Colombia against the United States."[32]

After midwifing the Panamanian Republic, Roosevelt announced that Washington would no longer allow the Europeans to resort to gunboat diplomacy to recover their debts from Latin American countries, however justified their claims. This meant, he wrote to Root in June 1904, that "sooner or later we must keep order ourselves."[33] In his December 1904 State of the Union address, Roosevelt asserted that "Chronic wrongdoing ... may in America, as elsewhere, ultimately require intervention by some civilized nation, and in the Western Hemisphere the adherence of the United States to the Monroe Doctrine may force the United States, however reluctantly, in flagrant cases of such wrongdoing or impotence, to the exercise of an international police power."[34] The Roosevelt Corollary to the Monroe Doctrine was born. Because the United States would not allow European powers to use force to recover debts from Latin American countries, it would intervene on their behalf. In April 1905, the Dominican government, which owed money to several European countries, agreed to the establishment of the US receivership of the Dominican customs, despite strong domestic opposition. The presence of two US warships in the harbor of Santo Domingo throughout the negotiations had, a US official noted, "a powerful moral effect on the rash and ignorant elements," that is, on the Dominican masses.[35]

The next major step was taken by President Taft. US officials accused Nicaragua's dictator José Santos Zelaya of meddling in the internal affairs of his neighbors, but his real sin, in the Americans' eyes, was his nationalism, totally inappropriate for the ruler of a country in the US backyard. In December 1909 Secretary of State Knox issued Zelaya what amounted to an ultimatum to step down; the dictator complied, to forestall a US invasion. But US marines landed anyway, and Washington continued to threaten Zelaya's anointed successor until he resigned. The United States then installed its own puppets as president, first Juan Estrada and then Adolfo Díaz. More than 2,000 marines occupied the country. In October 1912, they crushed a band of courageous Nicaraguans who had rebelled against the US-dominated government. They then departed, leaving behind a "legation guard" of 130 marines as a reminder of US power. Nicaragua became the model protectorate, with a docile government agreeing to whatever the United States demanded, and granting control of the country's economy to US bankers.[36]

Like Nicaragua, Cuba was a model protectorate. True, there were troubles on the island, inter-elite squabbles that spurred Roosevelt to dispatch the marines and impose direct US rule from 1906 to 1909. The marines met no resistance. A British official noted aptly: "Though independent in name the island is in the position of a lap-dog whose owner keeps a tight hold on the string."[37] Meanwhile, American investment blossomed. The US government used its privileged position to foster American economic interests at the expense of its European rivals, as the British learned painfully. In 1900, Cuba had been Britain's best customer in the region, ranking ahead even of Mexico, but from 1902 to 1906 US officials torpedoed Britain's attempt to negotiate a commercial treaty with the island. The British minister in Havana and the chambers of commerce of several British cities repeatedly complained to the Foreign Office about US interference in the negotiations, but Foreign Secretary Henry Lansdowne and his successor Edward Grey were wary of ruffling the Americans' feathers. They expressed, historian Warren Kneer concludes, "fatalism as to the inevitability of American commercial inroads on British interests and fear that any real defense of those interests would lead to trouble with the United States."[38] Their deference to the United States owed to the German threat: the British were fixated on the ominous growth of the German Navy and were building alliances in Europe to counter it; they also bowed to the reality that the United States had become an economic giant. In other words, there was a German threat, but it was directed against Britain, not the United States or Latin America, and it helped US expansion.

South America

Roosevelt's aggressive policies in the Caribbean and Central America had deepened the South Americans' distrust of the United States. Throughout Spanish America, historian Joseph Smith writes, "there was widespread concern about the apparently unquenchable American appetite for expansion."[39] Fear was spiked with resentment for "the arrogant and contemptuous bearing of Americans," Roosevelt's Secretary of State Elihu Root noted.[40] "The South Americans now hate us," he told Senator Benjamin Tillman in December 1905, "largely because they think we despise them and try to bully them."[41] The following year he attended the third pan-American conference in Rio, the first time that a sitting US secretary of state had traveled abroad. Root may have thought of the Latin Americans as "Dagos," two historians write, but he hid his feelings and treated them with respect.[42] Root's courtesy, however, brought a change of tone rather than substance, and even that was fleeting. The Taft administration's disdain for Latin Americans was clear; its aggressive support for American business in the region surpassed the practice of its predecessor, fostering more resentment.

Brazil's attitude toward the United States stood in sharp contrast to its neighbors. Surrounded by Spanish American countries he neither liked nor trusted, Rio's foreign minister, the Baron of Rio Branco, sought to strengthen relations with the United States. Rio Branco "definitively shifted," in the words of two Brazilian historians, "the axis of Brazilian diplomacy from London to Washington"; he hoped US friendship would help Brazil become the leading South American power, foster the settlement of several border disputes, and assure free access to the US market.[43]

Brazil's embrace of the United States disturbed Argentina, which had entered a period of extraordinary economic development in the 1880s spurred by waves of immigration from Europe and the massive inflow of European, mainly British, capital. The Argentine leaders thought of their country as the only great white nation of South America, aspired to the leadership of the subcontinent, saw Brazil as a rival, and mistrusted the United States. "The Monroe Doctrine appears to be made of rubber," an eminent Argentine statesman said, "adaptable to the exclusive interest of the interventions which the United States itself generates." The doctrine sought to separate Latin America from Europe, the Argentine foreign minister warned in 1906, and ran against "the natural Argentine tendency to tighten the bonds with the European nations to which we owe the labor and the capital . . . which is our pride and the astonishment of the world."[44]

By the time Taft stepped down, in March 1913, the United States was the dominant economic power in the Caribbean, Central America, and Mexico. In South America, however, it still lagged behind Britain and also the upstart, Germany. And while the value of US exports to Latin America almost tripled from $132 million in 1900 to $348 million in 1913, it remained a small share of total US exports ($1,394 million in 1900 and $2,466 million in 1913), most of which went to Europe.[45] It was the upheaval of the First World War, which disrupted European trade, that would finally give the United States the largest share of the South American market.

Wilsonian idealism and Mexico

Woodrow Wilson assumed the presidency of the United States in March 1913. He was the first Democrat to occupy the White House since Cleveland had stepped down in 1897, and the first southerner since Taylor's death in 1850. A moderate reformer at home, Wilson was as keen as Roosevelt and Taft had been to expand his country's economic stake in the Western Hemisphere and to assert US hegemony over the region. Unlike his two predecessors, however, Wilson was considered an idealist who would introduce a moral dimension in US foreign policy. He said little about foreign affairs during the presidential campaign—his focus was on domestic reform—but his election generated a wave of hope in Latin America. His selection of William Jennings Bryan, who was considered a leading anti-imperialist, as secretary of state reinforced the Latin Americans' hope that US policy would become less aggressive.

Wilson's first year as president brought great successes for his domestic agenda, with Congress' approval of tariff reform and the Federal Reserve bank, but in foreign policy he faced a crisis in Mexico.

In 1911, more than 40,000 Americans lived in Mexico, a country of 15 million people. More than 20 percent of American direct investment abroad was in Mexico: $587 million (c. $15.3 billion) out of $2.6 billion. Americans were the leading investors in the country, and they dominated its foreign trade.[46] By the early 1900s, the extent of US influence had begun to worry President Porfirio Díaz. He had no intention of challenging the United States but he sought, gently, to lessen American economic dominance by seeking European investment; in 1906 he even sought German military instructors to train the Mexican army, but Berlin declined, fearful of angering the United States.[47]

Advancing age weakened Díaz's ability to retain control, and in May 1911 he was forced to resign by a disparate coalition, united only by the desire to end a dictatorship that had lasted more than thirty years. The following November, Francisco Madero, scion of one of the country's wealthiest families, was elected president. Madero believed in political democracy but did not grasp the urgency of social reform or hear the desperate cries of millions of dispossessed peasants for land. After fumbling for fourteen months, he was overthrown, on February 19, 1913, by General Victoriano Huerta, who commanded the garrison of the capital. Three days later, Madero was executed, most likely on Huerta's orders. Cowed, the Mexican Congress elected Huerta president of the republic.

The US ambassador, Henry Lane Wilson, who had been a fierce critic of Madero, had supported the coup and had refused to intervene to save Madero's life. He urged Washington to recognize Huerta, but Taft, who would be president until March, wanted to use recognition as a lever to pry Mexico's concessions on a few outstanding issues. Huerta was still unrecognized when Wilson assumed the presidency.[48]

Neither Wilson nor Bryan had focused on foreign policy, and they knew little about Mexico. Wilson reacted with genuine revulsion to Madero's assassination; he also questioned Huerta's staying power: within days of the coup, rebels were challenging the general. Civil war erupted, and it also became a social revolution as peasants fought for land. Wilson despised Huerta as a treasonous murderer, and he wanted Mexico to hold free elections. The problem was that he had no idea how to make this happen. He did not object when bankers from France, Belgium, Britain, and the United States raised a loan for Huerta in June 1913, even though the loan would strengthen the dictator. Wilson and Bryan, Alan Knight writes, "were still uncertain and malleable."[49]

"The trouble," Wilson told a press conference in July, "is that we don't know what is going on in Mexico."[50] Because he did not trust Ambassador Lane Wilson, he sent confidential agents to Mexico City, first the journalist William Bayard Hale and then former Minnesota governor John Lind. Their reports damned Huerta as a traitor, and stressed that he would not be able to restore order. Therefore, morality and realpolitik demanded that he be replaced.[51]

While Wilson groped for a policy, he understood the balance of power. First, Europe was split into two hostile blocs, led by England and Germany, and neither side wanted to add to their troubles by quarreling with the United States, the strongest economic power in the world. Second, the United States was the paramount foreign power in Mexico, and the European governments would follow his lead. On August 8, 1913, the day before Lind landed in Vera Cruz, Wilson sent a note to the European powers, asking that their representatives in Mexico urge Huerta to give "very serious consideration to any suggestions this government [Lind] may make." The problem, Nancy Mitchell remarks, is that Wilson did not "grace the Europeans with a description of the suggestions. 'The contents of this communication [that Lind would deliver to Huerta] will be made known to you when it is ready,' the note informed the startled foreign ministers of the great powers." The Germans fumed at Washington's arrogance, but they obliged, as did the British.[52]

Finally, on November 24, 1913, Wilson penned a circular note to fifteen European powers, Brazil and Japan clarifying US policy toward Mexico: his administration intended "to isolate General Huerta entirely; to cut him off from foreign sympathy and aid and from domestic credit ... and so to force him out. It hopes and believes that isolation will accomplish this end.... If [not] ... it will become the duty of the United States to use less peaceful means to put him out."[53] Wilson's policy was informed by moralism and by imperial hubris—the conviction that the United States had the right, even the duty, to shape the Mexican government—and also by realpolitik: Huerta could not provide the stability US interests required.

Seeking to please the United States, the Germans refrained from providing any assistance to Huerta, even though they considered Wilson's policy foolhardy and arrogant. They earned unusual American praise. "The German government has occupied a most dignified position in the matter," Wilson told a press conference in March 1914. "It hasn't gone around with a chip on its shoulder."[54]

Like the Germans, the British considered Wilson's Mexican policy misguided, but they were too keen on solidifying the "special relationship" to reject Washington's lead. "I do not dispute the inconvenience and untoward results of United States policy," Foreign Secretary Grey wrote to the British minister in Mexico, "but ... His Majesty's government cannot with any prospect of success embark upon an active counter-policy to that of the United States or constitute themselves the champions of Mexico."[55]

Huerta, however, would not capitulate, and Wilson upped the ante. The precipitating event occurred on April 9, 1914, when a group of American sailors who had wandered into a restricted military zone in the port of Tampico, were arrested—and immediately released, with apologies. Wilson, however, demanded a formal apology, severe punishment of the officer responsible, and a 21-gun salute to the American flag. Huerta refused. Wilson seized on this to justify occupying Mexico's major port, Vera Cruz, to intercept the *Ypiranga*, a German commercial ship carrying weapons for Huerta. Wilson believed that, confronted by the superior power of the US Navy, the Mexicans would not dare resist the occupation. He was wrong. It took almost two days of street fighting and a naval bombardment before the city was in American hands, on April 22. Nineteen Americans and at least 200 Mexicans had been killed. Outrage swept across Mexico.[56]

US officials occupying Vera Cruz ordered the *Ypiranga* not to unload the weapons, and the ship eventually steamed away—not back to Hamburg, as Washington expected, but southward, to Puerto Mexico. There, it unloaded the weapons.

The US press lashed out at the German government, and the specter of the fiendish Reich reappeared. But Berlin was innocent. The weapons of the *Ypiranga* came from American, French and British manufacturers; the German government had nothing to do with the shipment; and the decision to unload the weapons at Puerto Mexico had been taken by the ship's captain without consulting Berlin, in the mistaken belief that the United States would not object.[57] As Mitchell remarks, German policy toward Mexico had been "remarkably consistent and restrained.... Germany both resented its fate—being bested by the Americans in Mexico—and bowed to it."[58]

By late March 1914, even before the occupation of Vera Cruz, the fortunes of the civil war had turned against Huerta. Powerful rebel columns were advancing on Mexico City. Huerta fled the country in July, but his departure did not bring peace. Mexico was in the throes of social revolution, and the leaders who had defeated Huerta fought each other. In Washington, Wilson strove clumsily to shape Mexico's future, even sending, in July 1914, "a detailed set of instructions of proper behavior" to Venustiano Carranza, the most powerful of the men vying to replace Huerta.[59] For over a year Wilson tried, as he said, "to guide what is taking place there [in Mexico],"[60] applying pressure on Carranza, who was winning battle after battle against his major rival, Pancho Villa. But Carranza stubbornly rejected Wilson's right to interfere in Mexican affairs. Bowing to the reality of the battlefield, in October 1915 Wilson extended *de facto* recognition to Carranza, but relations remained acrimonious, and Carranza still had to bring the entire country under his control.

Suddenly, on March 9, 1916, Pancho Villa attacked the small town of Columbus, New Mexico, about three miles across the border, killing seventeen Americans. Villa calculated that given Washington's preoccupation with the Great War in Europe, which had been raging for almost two years, its response to the raid would be a limited incursion. He expected this to put Carranza in a bind: either fight the US forces or lose the respect of the Mexican people.[61]

In the United States, the clamor for a full-scale invasion of Mexico was ferocious, but Mexico was not a small Caribbean country that could be subdued with a battalion of marines. In March 1916, the US War College estimated that an invasion of Mexico would require 387,000 soldiers for the first three months, and then 557,280 for a period of pacification of undetermined length.[62] This was unacceptable at a time when the United States might be dragged into the inferno that consumed Europe: "It begins to look as if war with Germany is inevitable," Wilson told his private secretary Joseph Tumulty in June 1916. "If it should come—I pray to God it may not—I do not wish America's energies and forces divided, for we will need every ounce of reserve we have to lick Germany."[63] Resisting the calls for a full-scale invasion, Wilson sent instead a punitive expedition to hunt down Villa: six days after the Columbus raid, General John Pershing led the first US troops across the border into the state of Chihuahua, Villa's stronghold—their number would peak at 10,000. For the first few months they wandered around the state, searching for their elusive quarry; then, facing the growing hostility of the Carranza government and of the local population, they retreated to northern Chihuahua. Wilson had given up hope that they would capture Villa, but he wanted to use their presence on Mexican soil to force Carranza to grant the United States the right to send troops into Mexico whenever the Mexican government proved unable "to afford full and adequate protection to the lives and properties of citizens of the United States." Such a clause, Friedrich Katz remarks, "would have converted Mexico into a U.S. protectorate."[64]

Carranza refused to surrender his country's sovereignty and insisted on the unconditional withdrawal of the US troops. It was Wilson, not Carranza, who was cornered: facing the likelihood of entering the European war against Germany, he folded in Mexico. The last US soldiers left Mexico on February 5, 1917. Four days earlier, Germany had launched a campaign of unrestricted submarine warfare. The German government had also sent a cable to its minister in Mexico—the notorious Zimmermann telegram, which the British promptly decoded—offering Carranza Texas, New Mexico and Arizona if he joined Germany in war against the United States. The telegram, branded proof of German perfidy, was a foolhardy and defensive gesture: defensive, because the offer would apply only if the Americans declared war on Germany; foolhardy, because no Mexican government would declare war on the United States when Germany, blockaded by the British fleet, could offer no assistance.

Mexico was the most important challenge Wilson faced in Latin America. Over time, his attitude had evolved from disgust at Huerta's murder of Madero to a desire to shape Mexico's future. His lofty words bore little relationship to his actions. "We must respect the sovereignty of Mexico," he declared in 1916 while he was trying to turn Mexico into a US protectorate.[65] He failed to realize that he was in no position to teach Mexicans democracy. In many parts of the United States, and particularly in Texas, Mexican Americans were disenfranchised and discriminated against, and lynched with impunity. As an eminent historian notes, on rare occasions, in the tormented history of the US Southwest, Mexican Americans responded with violence to Anglo oppression.[66] One such occasion occurred on Wilson's watch. In July 1915, armed bands, largely of Mexican Americans (Tejanos), with the participation of Mexicans from south of the border, began raiding the Lower Rio Grande Valley, killing dozens of Anglo farmers, attacking ranches and burning railroad bridges. The rebels were inspired by the Mexican Revolution, with its promise of freeing Mexico of its corrupt leaders. The Texas Rangers and bands of vigilantes responded to the raids—which lasted only a few months—with a wave of terror against the Tejano population; estimates of the number killed vary from the low thousands down to the official US Army estimate of 300.[67] There is irony in Wilson browbeating the Mexicans for the murder of Americans in the midst of a revolution, while many more Mexicans and Tejanos were being slaughtered in south Texas. While this wave of repression abated in 1916, the lynchings continued. After two Mexicans had been lynched in Pueblo, Colorado, on September 13, 1919, the *New York Globe* noted,

America's Road to Empire

"When two Americans are killed in Mexico . . . a roar for intervention goes up throughout this country. When two Mexicans are killed in a civilized American city by a mob it is regrettable to be sure; but, after all, they look somewhat like Negroes, and everyone knows what we do with the latter."[68]

Wilson and the Caribbean

The outbreak of the First World War offered the United States the chance to become the major commercial partner of the South American states, and the Wilson administration moved eagerly to seize it. During the war, from 1914 to 1918, the value of US exports to South America doubled.[69] While US trade and influence in South America were growing, the administration was also tightening its control over Central America and the Caribbean.

Nicaragua continued to be the model protectorate, with corrupt governments, an economy controlled by US bankers, and two presidential elections (1916 and 1920) in which Washington intervened to ensure the victory of its candidate. The marines remained until 1925, but they did not have to fire a shot. The Nicaraguans were cowed.[70] The other Central American republics had learned the lesson: they were at the mercy of the United States. With only slight exaggeration, the US chargé in Guatemala wrote in his memoirs, "In those days of 'Dollar Diplomacy' and in those regions, the voice of the United States was the voice of Jove."[71]

There were only two independent countries in the Caribbean when Wilson entered the White House: Haiti and the Dominican Republic. By the time he stepped down, both were under US military occupation. How this came to pass under the president who is considered an exemplar of idealism is a revealing episode in the history of US foreign policy.

The most navigable passage to the Panama Canal lay between Cuba and Haiti. "The Haitians hope to reap great benefits from the opening of the canal," the German minister in Port-au-Prince reported in May 1912. Haiti would become, the Haitian minister of agriculture mused, "an international market, where merchant ships from around the world could buy provisions."[72] Woodrow Wilson, however, had a darker vision. "Anxiety about the role of foreign powers shaped a considerable part of Wilson's early Haitian policy," writes historian Brenda Plummer, a leading authority on the subject.[73] A wave of instability had engulfed the country, with one *coup d'état* after another, and Wilson feared that the chaos opened the door to European—German—encroachment. "The United States cannot consent to stand by and permit revolutionary conditions constantly to exist there," he told Bryan in January 1915.[74]

The administration's anxiety was heightened by the presence in Haiti of two vibrant and economically powerful European communities: French and, particularly worrisome, German. More than 200 Germans lived in Haiti and many were proficient in both French and Creole; like the French, they intermingled socially with the Haitian elite and German men married upper class Haitian women. In 1912, the German community established a school in Port-au-Prince where German-Haitian pupils received a German education.[75] But in August 1914, when war erupted in Europe, Haitian public opinion quickly sided with France. The German minister in Port-au-Prince complained bitterly that "the spineless elite, who have already forgotten the French whip, do not hide their sympathy for France." Neither did the Haitian press, nor the population at large. "Because of their hostile attitude," he added, "the Haitians have lost the Germans' goodwill, even of those who are married to Haitian ladies." The Germans in Haiti "felt they were living in enemy territory."[76]

Unlike the French and Germans, the small American expatriate community—about fifty strong in 1914—rigidly enforced the color line and did not mix socially with Haitians. Their linguistic skills were limited to English, and they complained that Haitian law discriminated against them. Every Haitian constitution since 1820 had stipulated that foreigners could not own real property. This was, a Haitian wrote, "the bedrock of our freedom."[77] It was possible to get around this prohibition by marrying Haitian women, as Germans and French did, but white Americans could not bring themselves to stoop so low. Therefore, the only remedy was to change the constitution, and this could be done only if the United States ruled the country.

At first sight it seems absurd that economic considerations could have influenced Wilson's policy toward Haiti: US direct investment there was only $4 million (c. $103 million), compared to $587 million in Mexico and $220 million in Cuba, and the Haitian market absorbed only four-tenths of 1 percent of total American exports. The major American investment was the National Railroad of Haiti, owned by a New York syndicate that included National City Bank. The syndicate had been contracted by the Haitian government to build a railway between Port-au-Prince and Cap Haitien. Construction had begun in 1910, but the Haitian government stopped payment in 1914, for good cause. Instead of building a continuous railway from Port-au-Prince to Cap Haitien, the company had built three disconnected sections, with two gaps, one of thirty and the other of forty miles, where the tracks would have traversed mountains. It was, the former US minister to Haiti remarked, "a criminally poorly constructed railway." The Wilson administration, however, supported the company in its dispute with the Haitian government.[78]

Every Haitian government, aware of both the country's precarious position in a white world and of the mounting US threat, had met its foreign debt obligations. Nevertheless, President Wilson demanded that Haiti accept an American financial adviser and US control of its customhouses. The Haitians' refusal angered Wilson, a man little inclined to brook dissent from white Americans, let alone Blacks in a puny, bankrupt country.

The administration's policies were shaped by its racism. Wilson intensified segregation in the federal bureaucracy and drastically curtailed the number of African Americans in the relatively senior positions informally reserved for them: by 1916, only eight of the thirty-one highest "Negro" offices of 1912 were held by Blacks.[79] Among the positions reclaimed for the white man was that of minister to Haiti, which had been occupied since 1895 by a Harvard-educated black physician, Henry Furniss. Furniss, who had become an expert on Haiti, was replaced by a white former congressman and then by

Arthur Bailly-Blanchard, a white career diplomat whom Secretary of State Bryan soon deemed incompetent.[80] As a result, Bryan turned to a man who was eager to provide information and counsel on Haitian affairs, Roger Farnham, a vice president of National City Bank and the President of the National Railroad of Haiti—a man, in short, who had a vested interest in the US takeover of the country. Farnham was also a close friend of Boaz Long, the chief of the State Department's Latin American division. "Farnham and his representatives in Haiti," Plummer writes, "acted as a shadow diplomatic and consular agency."[81] He dangled the German threat to spur Bryan to take action. It was an impressive performance, particularly since Berlin, engulfed in a major war in Europe, could not, as the German minister in Port-au-Prince remarked, "pay any attention to Haiti."[82] Nevertheless, in March 1915, after a briefing from Farnham, Bryan told Wilson: "There seems to be some sympathetic cooperation between the French and German interests in Haiti. There are some indications that their plans include taking advantage of Mole St. Nicholas [which had a deep harbor well suited for a naval base]." Wilson was alarmed: "The whole matter has a most sinister appearance," he responded.[83]

There is no rational explanation for this extraordinary exchange: Germans and French were slaughtering one another in Europe. Many historians have dealt with this embarrassing nonsense mercifully: they have ignored it—the roster includes prominent scholars.[84] At most, grasping at straws, one can point to the context: the administration was eager to intervene, and an invasion would entail no costs because the Haitian army was a rabble and neither white Americans nor the European powers would condemn the assault on a black country in the US backyard. The only downside was Wilson's qualms about openly violating international law. He needed a pretext.

That was provided by the overthrow of Haitian president Vilbrun Guillaume Sam on July 27, 1915. It was a bloody and chaotic scene: following the execution of 167 prisoners, an enraged mob—believing Sam responsible—violated the French legation, where the president had sought refuge, hauled him into the street and murdered him, an eyewitness, the French minister, reported. "The corpse was dragged through the town until it was reduced to almost nothing."[85]

Although lynchings were common in the United States, Wilson issued no public condemnation of them until July 26, 1918.[86] The murder of the Haitian president, on the other hand, evoked outrage and an immediate response. On July 28, the first 330 US marines and sailors invaded Port-au-Prince. They met no resistance. The administration presented the invasion as a humanitarian intervention to protect the lives of Americans and other foreigners (although none had been hurt), and of Haitians as well. It wanted a free hand. Admiral William Caperton, who commanded the occupation forces, had told the captains of French and British warships near Port-au-Prince not to land troops, "because he was in charge of the situation." Predictably, both French and British obeyed, while the French foreign minister complained bitterly that the Americans would soon close the economy to foreign competition, as they had done in Cuba.[87]

To preserve appearances, Admiral Caperton coopted pliant locals to enforce his orders. He identified a Haitian, Senator Philippe Dartiguenave, who was willing to serve as the puppet president. After Dartiguenave was duly elected by a subdued National

Assembly, the Americans presented him with the draft of a treaty that robbed Haiti of its independence: US officials would control the country's finances and customs, and the Haitian army and police would be replaced by a constabulary (gendarmerie) officered by Americans. Cornered, the National Assembly ratified the treaty. The United States continued to maintain a diplomatic mission in Port-au-Prince, but real power was in the hands of the senior US officer who commanded the marine brigade stationed in Haiti. Hundreds of American technical advisers arrived in the wake of the marines, their exorbitant salaries paid by the Haitian treasury. "The American Agricultural Engineer," a US consul noted, received "an amount equal to the salaries of 159 rural school teachers."[88] US marines who served as officers in the gendarmerie received a hefty raise paid by the Haitian state. The problem, the British Legation reported, was that they were "not suited for the job." The gendarmerie became notorious for its brutality. "This Legation," the report said, "has had to interfere several times on behalf of British West Indian subjects who have been unnecessarily beaten."[89]

In the Dominican Republic, too, the Wilson administration unearthed a German threat: General Desiderio Arias, who in early 1916 was emerging as the country's strongman, was deemed pro-German by the State Department. More exactly, as the French foreign ministry noted, he "embodied the spirit of independence."[90] But the foreign threat—in the Dominican Republic as in Haiti—was the United States, not Germany. Between 1911 and 1916 US officials had "intervened in Dominican affairs more and more frequently, often on a daily basis, and with increasing belligerence," writes Bruce Calder, author of the authoritative study of the US occupation of the Dominican Republic.[91] As a result, anti-Americanism deepened. The German minister did not exaggerate when he wrote about the "fury" and "hatred" of the Dominicans against the United States. US Admiral Caperton agreed. "I have never seen such hatred displayed by one people for another as I notice and feel here," he reported from Santo Domingo in June 1916. "We positively have not a friend in the land."[92]

Caperton was in command of the US marines that had landed in the Dominican Republic the previous May to prevent General Arias from taking power. In November 1916, having failed to establish a puppet Dominican government, the Wilson Administration resorted to direct military rule. The United States, the State Department announced, was "acting for and on behalf" of the Dominican government, "in a sense as a trustee."[93] Except that the "trustee" eviscerated the government. In place of a Dominican president, there was a US military governor, Navy Captain (later Rear Admiral) Harry Knapp, who presided over a cabinet of ministers, all of whom were US naval and marine officers.

Since there were no costs for Americans, the invasions of Haiti and the Dominican Republic stirred very little debate in the United States. With rare exceptions, white American journalists expressed only contempt for Haitians and Dominicans—they were "'coons,' 'mongrels,' 'unwholesome,' child-like, ignorant, lazy, savage, and superstitious," or, simply, "'a horde of naked niggers.'"[94] The editor of *The Nation*, Oswald Garrison Villard, aptly summed up the response of the white press: "If the desideratum is a watchful, well-informed, intelligent, and independent press, bent upon preserving the liberties of ourselves and our neighbors, then truly are our newspapers sorely lacking."[95] The response of African American newspapers was muted: perhaps they feared that criticism would be branded as lack of patriotism; perhaps they were wary of being associated with the despised Haitians; or perhaps some believed with Booker T. Washington that Haiti needed a "firm hand" that only the United States could provide. A rare exception was provided by *The Crisis*, organ of the National Association for the Advancement of Colored People. "A portion of Hayti's leaders have robbed her shamefully," the editor, W.E.B. DuBois, wrote. "Let us help Haiti rid herself of thieves and not try to fasten American thieves on her."[96]

US colonial rule in Haiti and the Dominican Republic

Assessing the occupation of the Dominican Republic, which lasted until 1924, a respected American political scientist, Abraham Lowenthal, wrote: "For eight years American military and civilian personnel ruled the Dominican Republic directly, taking over every branch of public administration. American troops attempted to impose order, American officers trained and commanded a Dominican constabulary, American revenue agents collected taxes, American engineers built roads and bridges, American bureaucrats set up a civil service system and revamped the post office, and American educators revamped the Dominican Republic's schools."[97] What Lowenthal writes is largely true, although he overstates the achievements in education and public health.[98] The problem is what Lowenthal overlooks.

If President Wilson intended to bring democracy to the Dominican people, he chose the oddest route: a US military dictatorship that suspended the Dominican Congress and postponed elections indefinitely. It instituted censorship "more rigid than any the country had ever seen in the darkest days of dictatorship, and which has continued to the present day," a prominent US lawyer reported to the State Department in December 1919. He added that Dominican newspapers were forbidden to comment on any act of the military government, or to use such terms as "national," "freedom of thought," or "freedom of speech."[99] In their cells, journalists and writers had time to contemplate Wilsonian democracy. They had been convicted by military courts composed of US officers ignorant not only of the laws of the country but also of the Spanish language. These courts were "unjust, oppressive and cruel."[100]

In Haiti, too, censorship under US rule was "formidable,"[101] but the façade of democracy was better preserved: a Haitian, Dartiguenave, continued to serve as puppet president and, for a while, the National Assembly survived. Dutifully, the Haitian government paid in full the claims of the American-owned National Railroad.[102] Under strict US supervision, it drafted a new constitution that allowed foreigners to own real property and presented it to the National Assembly for ratification. "It is imperative that recommendations made by [State] Department be adopted," Secretary of State Robert Lansing urged Minister Bailly-Blanchard, who in turn told the puppet government that "the United States can only accept a constitution permitting foreign ownership of land."[103] The Haitian foreign minister responded, Bailly-Blanchard reported, that "foreign ownership of Haitian land was such a vital question ... that the government could not, to use his words, 'count upon its own brother' in a vote upon it; it is out of the government's control, in other words."[104]

As a Haitian scholar explains, "public opinion was so strenuously opposed to granting property ownership to foreigners" that in June 1917 the assembly unanimously rejected the draft constitution.[105] In response, the occupation authorities ordered Dartiguenave to dissolve the Assembly, and Marine Lt. Colonel Smedley Butler, who doubled as the commanding general of the gendarmerie, executed the order "in three minutes" with two squads of gendarmes who used, Butler told a friend, "genuinely Marine Corps methods" to eject the legislators.[106] US officials then submitted the constitution to a plebiscite, ordering the gendarmerie to arrest anyone who criticized it. When the vote was held, in June 1918, the gendarmerie handed the voters a white ballot signifying approval of the new constitution. Those who wanted to vote "no" had to request a different color ballot. According to the official count, the document was approved by 98,294 votes in favor and 769 opposed.[107] Wilsonian democracy at work.

Several American companies acquired land in Haiti after the promulgation of the new constitution, but it was the Dominican Republic that felt the full brunt of American investment. American entrepreneurs had begun acquiring large sugar estates in the country in the decade before the US invasion, and during the occupation the military authorities overhauled the republic's rural title system. They proceeded with particular vigor in the east, where the land was well suited to sugar cane plantations. Dominican peasants who did not possess the necessary legal documents were thrown off their land. "The period of the military government," Bruce Calder writes, "was a fruitful one for the sugar interests." On key issues, "especially ... laws affecting the ability of the sugar companies to swallow up large portions of the country's arable land, the military government completely capitulated to foreign interests." When the US troops withdrew in 1924, US sugar companies owned 355,854 acres of the most fertile Dominican land. This was, by some estimates, more than one fifth of the country's arable land.[108]

From the very beginning of the Dominican occupation, the marines behaved, in the words of the acting head of the French consulate, "with the greatest brutality."[109] The "American police," another French report noted in late 1917, were "notorious for the violence of their operations, detentions, executions, and looting of suspects' houses," even when they met no armed resistance.[110] When a guerrilla movement arose, the Americans' repression intensified. US atrocities in the Dominican Republic fit the pattern of US wars against Native Americans, Mexicans, Filipinos, and Haitians. As Calder remarks, US racism "found a fertile field in the Dominican Republic, 'a country whose people,' Military Governor Harry Knapp noted, 'are almost all touched with the tarbrush.'" The commander of marine operations in the east, Colonel George Thorpe, referred to the guerrillas as "'the black savage enemy.' ... In a more philosophical mood he noted 'the instinctive antagonism between the white and colored races,' adding that 'no white nationality has less sympathy with colored races than the American; ie, the American goes further than any other people in its race prejudice.'"[111]

As in the Dominican Republic, so too there was a budding guerrilla movement in Haiti. A brief uprising in the wake of the US invasion ended in November 1915 with the marine victory at the battle of Fort Rivière, in which fifty-one rebels were killed (no prisoners were taken), while one marine was "hit in the face with a rock" and lost two teeth.[112] Guerrilla war flared up again in 1918. "The risings dragged on until 1919," the British Legation reported, "and were only finally put down by severe and drastic measures such as aeroplane bombing etc."[113] In September 1919, Marine Corps Commander George Barnett noted that "practically indiscriminate killing of natives had gone on for some time." In September 1920, he reported that since the beginning of the occupation the rebels had killed thirteen marines. The marines and the gendarmerie, on the other hand, had killed 3,250 "armed Haitian bandits";[114] the noncombatant death toll is unrecorded.

By the end of the Wilson administration, US officials considered the Dominicans subdued and the marines, therefore, were no longer necessary to assure US political and economic domination over the country. The last American troops left in September 1924. The occupation of Haiti, however, continued. The Haitians had not yet learned to submit. The Haitians are "anti-American, owing to the treatment meted out to them," noted the British Legation in Port-au-Prince. Even the British, racist as they were, were shocked by the racism of the Americans in Haiti and the brutality of the US officered gendarmerie. The Americans had improved public health and sanitation in Haiti, the Legation noted, but their "moral behavior has lowered the prestige of the white race in the eyes of the natives."[115] The marines remained until 1934.

Before the US invasion, political power had rested in Haitian hands. The Americans violently wrested authority from them. Instead of democracy, Woodrow Wilson brought American racism to Haiti. "The color-line is justifiable in so far as it protects against intermingling of blood, characteristics, and habits," remarked a white American writer after visiting Haiti in 1919, "but there is a point beyond which it becomes d----d foolishness, and that point is sometimes passed by our officers." Educated Haitians, he urged, "should be treated more like human beings."[116]

Protective imperialism?

White Americans considered themselves superior to all Latin Americans, but particularly to the peoples of Central America and the Caribbean whom they thought of as less civilized than those of the southern cone and Brazil. Furthermore Argentina, Brazil, and even Chile (despite the humiliation it suffered at US hands in 1892) were protected by geography—their distance from the United States—their relative political stability, and their ability to inflict pain on the aggressor. Therefore, the United States dealt with them more subtly than it did with the small republics in the backyard; by 1914 they were within the US sphere of influence, but they were not US pawns.

Mexico had the misfortune of having a common border with the United States, and Yankee contempt for Mexicans was long ingrained. But US arrogance and violence were tempered by Mexico's size and by the fierce nationalism of its people. As the US military told Wilson, it would not be easy to subdue the Mexicans.

The United States behaved like an armed bully toward the Central American and Caribbean countries. In many ways, the story of the US takeover of its backyard requires no explanation. A great power, which had been constantly expanding, with an aggressive and racist history, had recovered from the trauma of civil war and reconstruction. Eliminating one obstacle (Spain) and reconciling with another (Britain), it moved to take control of its neighborhood. The weakness of the victims, the fact that they were not white, as well as the indifference of the American people, made this takeover all the more unremarkable. But we are talking of the United States, the city on the hill, and explanations that might be appropriate for a European power, cannot suffice here. And so historians dwell on a nonexistent German threat. And they wax eloquent about Wilson's missionary impulse, although any analysis of US actions in the region—as opposed to rhetoric—reveals that there was no effort to "spread democracy," just the arrogance of a powerful president towards small, non-white countries. US policy toward the backyard under Roosevelt, Taft, and Wilson was defined by imperial hubris, racism, greed, and the search for absolute security at virtually no cost.

CHAPTER 13
THE FAR EAST

By the early twentieth century, the idea that there was a special relationship between the United States and China was etched in the American mind, and it would persist for many decades. "Americans held to the reassuring myth of a golden age of friendship engendered by altruistic American aid and rewarded by ample Chinese gratitude," writes Michael Hunt, a leading historian of Sino-American relations.[1]

The myth contained a kernel of truth: the United States was the least aggressive of the predators that tormented China: it did not wage war on China, did not occupy Chinese territory, did not establish a formal sphere of influence in China. There was, however, a dark side: Americans treated the Chinese in the United States with appalling contempt. In 1905, the first major boycott in Chinese history directed against foreigners targeted Americans, not Europeans. Stunned by such ingratitude—wasn't the United States China's friend and protector?—some Americans claimed the boycott was due to the manipulations by an unfriendly power, usually Germany, Russia, or Japan. Others, like the influential magazine *Review of Reviews*, understood it for what it was: the Chinese response "to the barbarity to which we have been subjecting them."[2]

US-Japanese relations followed a similar pattern. The United States was the least violent of the nations threatening Japan in the second half of the nineteenth century, and it was the most aggressive in its treatment of Japanese immigrants on its own soil. American racism affected relations with both China and Japan, but there was a difference: China was militarily impotent, while victory over Russia in 1904–5 vaulted Japan to the first rank of the great powers. This mattered: Japan could respond to racist insults by striking the United States.

Early relations with China

In 1784, the first American ship—the *Empress of China*—reached Canton, China's only port open to the West. For the next half century, a modest level of US-Chinese trade developed, in the shadow of British-Chinese trade. The major export to China of both British and Americans was opium, which they sold with the connivance of corrupt Chinese officials.

The United States watched as Britain waged a war of aggression against China from 1839–42 and imposed a victor's peace that demanded the cession of Hong Kong, an indemnity, the opening of more Chinese ports to trade, tariff concessions, and extraterritoriality (Britons accused of crimes would be tried in their own consular courts). A second war of aggression by England and France imposed still heavier penalties on China in 1860. The United States was, again, a spectator, but it shared in the privileges the victors extorted through the most-favored-nation clause, which had been included in the treaty of Wanghia, signed by the Tyler administration with China in 1844, in the wake of the British victory. "The lion roared and made the kill," the eminent historian Warren Cohen writes; "the jackal smiled and picked the bones."[3]

But neither President Tyler nor his successors had much time for China. In the decade and half that followed the Treaty of Wanghia the United States was focused on territorial expansion in North America and hegemony in the Caribbean and Central America. American trade with China was just $22 million (c. $690 million) in 1860, out of a total trade of $688.[4] This did not change after the US Civil War. The diplomatic and consular staff in China, David Pletcher writes, was "inadequate ... miserably neglected by a parsimonious, semi-isolationist Congress."[5] When Americans paid attention to China, their focus was on the Chinese immigrants in their midst. Unlike the European powers, the United States received hundreds of thousands of Asian immigrants. Its response illuminates the nature of the City on the Hill.

This wave of immigration began a few years after the Treaty of Wanghia, as thousands of Chinese rushed to California after gold was discovered near Sacramento in 1848. They encountered intense hostility and discrimination. In 1854, the California Supreme Court ruled that the Chinese could not testify in court against whites. "With this sort of 'justice' being dispensed from the highest bench in the state," a scholar remarks, "it is understandable that the phrase 'a Chinaman's chance' meant no chance at all."[6] Nevertheless, due to the dire poverty of southern China, Chinese kept arriving. And they made a signal contribution to the economic development of the United States. In 1863, the Central Pacific Railroad (CP) began building the western half of what would become the first transcontinental railway of the United States, but the company had difficulty attracting white workers, particularly when the tracks approached the forbidding Sierra Nevada. Between 1866 and 1869, more than 10,000 Chinese comprised the vast bulk of the workforce, performing both unskilled and highly skilled tasks. When the tracks of the CP met those of the Union Pacific in May 1869, the CP's senior engineer acknowledged that "the early completion" of the railroad was "in large measure due to that poor, despised class of laborers called the Chinese."[7]

Secretary of State Seward wanted to assure a continuing supply of cheap labor to foster the development of the West and in 1868 the Burlingame Treaty allowed unrestricted Chinese emigration to the United States "for purposes of curiosity, of trade, or as permanent residents."[8] This alarmed white Americans in the West, who were intensely hostile to the Chinese on economic grounds—accusing them of lowering wages and acting as scabs—and on racial grounds. "Like blacks, the Chinese were described as heathen, morally inferior, savage, childlike and lustful," writes Ronald Takaki. "Like blacks ... [they] were viewed as threats to white racial purity."[9] The economic hardships that followed the Panic of 1873 added to the tension. By the late 1870s, Republicans and Democrats in California vied with each other to promote the most vile anti-Chinese resolutions, and the US Congress paid heed.

Enshrined in the American mind as proof of the country's generosity, the Statue of Liberty welcomes "the huddled masses yearning to be free." But the statue looks eastward, toward white Europe. Bowing to intense congressional pressure, in 1880 the Hayes administration concluded the Angell Treaty with China, which allowed the United States to "regulate, limit or suspend" but not "absolutely prohibit" the entry of Chinese laborers in the United States; teachers, students, merchants, and tourists were exempt. This was the first treaty in US history limiting immigration. There were at the time 105,000 Chinese in the United States, mostly in the West.[10]

The US Senate promptly ratified the treaty, and then violated it: the 1882 Exclusion Act prohibited the immigration of *all* Chinese laborers for ten years. The Act also barred all Chinese from naturalized citizenship. This was consistent with US law. In 1790, Congress had restricted naturalization to whites; after the Civil War, in 1870, it had included "persons of African descent," but—with the Chinese in mind—the legislators had refused to make the statute color blind. (Second generation Chinese were considered US citizens.)

The Exclusion Act did not temper the violence against the Chinese who lived in the United States. For many white Americans in the West, it was not enough to halt the immigration of Chinese: they wanted to expel those who were already in the country.[11] "No one can ever know how many Chinese were murdered and brutalized," Roger Daniels writes.[12] The violence spread from California to other Western states and territories. The worst massacre occurred in the mining town of Rock Springs, in Wyoming territory, in September 1885, when a white mob invaded Chinatown. They killed, looted, and set fire to the houses. The Chinese fled "like a flock of frightened sheep," the Rock Springs *Independent* reported. Fifty-one Chinese immigrants died, many murdered by the mob or burned alive in the dwellings where they had hidden; others perished from exposure or were killed by wolves in the woods where they had sought refuge. In the days that followed, sixteen whites were arrested, charged with arson, murder, and robbery, and immediately freed on bail. "Any attempted trial or punishment of the men who murdered the Chinese," an army officer predicted, "will prove a burlesque and farce." And so it was. A grand jury was impaneled, no Chinese was allowed to testify, and the jurors returned no indictments.[13]

Inspired by the Rock Springs massacre, mobs attacked Chinese immigrants in eight Western states and territories, from Alaska to New Mexico. In some cases, the Chinese were forced to leave and robbed of their possessions; in others, they were murdered.[14] The violence and the impunity provoked outrage in China. From Beijing, the US minister, Charles Denby, warned Secretary of State Thomas Bayard in 1886 that "hostility to the United States confronts me at every point—in diplomatic circles and in private life."[15]

Impervious to the repeated complaints of the Chinese minister in Washington, President Cleveland flatly refused to offer any apology or accept any responsibility for the massacre. Finally, at Bayard's urging, he asked Congress in March 1886 to appropriate money for the survivors of Rock Springs—"with the distinct understanding that such action . . . is wholly gratuitous and is resorted to in a spirit of pure generosity."[16] It took almost a year for Congress to appropriate $148,000 (*c.* $4 million). But this exceptional gesture of "generosity" was not repeated when thirty-one Chinese miners were killed near Snake River, Oregon, in June 1887, nor were the murderers punished. "I guess if they

Figure 13.1 George F. Keller, "The First Blow at the Chinese Question." Cartoon. *San Francisco Wasp*, December 8, 1877.

had killed 31 white men something would have been done about it," remarked a white rancher after the acquittal of the only three killers who stood trial, "but none of the jury knew the Chinamen or cared much about it, so they turned the men loose."[17]

The irony was cutting: extraterritoriality in China was justified by the inadequacies of the Chinese legal system. But it was the Chinese who should have enjoyed extraterritoriality in the United States because US laws and the American sense of justice were utterly inadequate when it came to protect the rights of nonwhite people.

The Chinese government wanted a new treaty that would guarantee better treatment for the Chinese already in the United States. The negotiations dragged until early 1894 when, facing the growing threat of war with Japan, Beijing wanted to court US goodwill. In March 1894, the Gresham-Yang Treaty prohibited, for ten more years, the migration of all Chinese laborers to the United States without any of the changes China had demanded. Four months later, the Sino-Japanese war began.

The "model pupil"

Americans were proud of their policy toward Japan. It was an American, Commodore Matthew Perry, who had brought the country out of its self-imposed isolation by entering Tokyo Bay with nine warships in February 1854 and compelling Japan to sign a treaty opening two ports for the provisioning of American ships.[18]

Imposing more onerous conditions on the Japanese would be the accomplishment of Townsend Harris, the first US consul in Japan, who in July 1858 forced his hosts to sign a treaty that included the twin evils that Western powers foisted on weak non-white countries: extraterritoriality and loss of tariff autonomy, setting Japanese import and export duties at low levels to favor American trade. This treaty—in which the Japanese conceded much and received nothing—was made possible by the threat of violence from the United States and the other Western powers which, Harris argued, were ready to pounce on Japan. The Japanese "have yielded nothing except from *fear*," Harris noted as the negotiations proceeded, "and any future ameliorations of our intercourse will only take place after a demonstration of force on our part."[19]

The Europeans were already circling the wounded prey. The British led the pack. They had welcomed Perry's mission, which occurred as they prepared for war against Russia. It was "better to leave it to the Government of the United States to make the experiment [of opening Japan]," Foreign Secretary James Malmesbury had mused; "and if that experiment is successful, Her Majesty's government can take advantage of its success."[20] In 1858, one month after Townsend Harris' victory, a British naval squadron entered Tokyo Bay to demand, at gunpoint, the same concessions for Britain. Russia, France, and the Netherlands followed.[21] The door had been broken down.

A debate roiled through the Japanese elite: how should they respond to this foreign aggression? Armed resistance was impossible: the gunboat diplomacy of the foreigners was too effective. In August 1863, a British squadron destroyed the city of Kagoshima, and in September 1864 a combined flotilla of sixteen British, Dutch, and French warships prepared to attack the forts of Shimonoseki.

The British had invited the Americans to participate in the attack on Shimonoseki, and Secretary of State Seward, eager to show "the semi-barbarians of Japan" that the United States remained powerful despite the Civil War, wanted the US Navy to join. But the only American vessel in Japanese waters was a sailing ship, the USS *Jamestown*, that could not have kept up with the Europeans' warships, which were steamers. Relations between Britain and the United States had been strained over Latin America before the Civil War, and during the war they were frayed by alleged British bias in favor of the Confederacy, but in the Far East, where the United States had no hope of supplanting Britain, there was cooperation. The British offered to tow the *Jamestown* to battle, but the Americans found a more dignified solution: they chartered a small merchant steamer and transferred a gun and a crew from the *Jamestown* to carry the US flag into battle. A British diplomat observed that in so doing, the Americans had abandoned "the affectation of acting on different lines from the 'effete monarchies of Europe.'" The forts of Shimonoseki were demolished.[22]

By the early 1870s, the Japanese had learned their lesson. Rather than dream of resisting, Japan would modernize and build powerful armed forces to safeguard its independence and break free of the unequal treaties. Unable to finance the country's industrialization through customs revenues because of the artificially low tariffs, the Japanese government had to impose oppressively high taxes, and the heaviest burden fell on the country's small farmers.

Americans watched "with amazement," William Neumann writes, "the speed with which Japan was able to adopt and refine Western technology."[23] Unlike China, Japan was eager to learn from the West. It invited hundreds of Western experts, among them many Americans, and sent thousands of students to Western countries. In the 1870s, most went to the United States rather than England or other European countries.[24] Americans were flattered, the image of Japan as the "model pupil" took hold, and US policy toward Japan softened. In 1878, the Hayes administration concluded a treaty with Tokyo that restored the country's tariff autonomy. But US goodwill had limits: the treaty would be implemented only after the other Western predators made the same concession.[25]

Carving up China?

Japan demonstrated its military prowess in 1894–5, when it crushed the Chinese on land and at sea, expelling them from Korea. The Western powers were impressed, but their admiration was tempered by the fact that the Japanese victory was over a non-white country, and one that was obviously weak. China's vulnerability excited the lust of the pack. Acting on the pretext of the murder of two German missionaries in November 1897, Germany extorted from Beijing the lease of the bay of Kiaochow, in Shandong, as well as valuable mining and railway concessions. In rapid succession, the other European predators struck: the Russians forced China to grant them a twenty-five-year leasehold of the strategic Liaotung Peninsula, which included the naval base of Port Arthur; the British claimed the harbor of Weihaiwei in northern Shandong; and the French obtained special rights in three southern provinces. This scramble for concessions seemed to presage a scramble to carve up China, repeating what the European powers had done in Africa over the previous two decades. American business newspapers responded with horror. US exports to China had grown in the mid 1890s, even though they were still puny—$12 million in 1897 (c. $374 million) out of total exports of $1,051 million.[26] Stressing that only through increasing exports "can we find employment for our teeming new population," the *Journal of Commerce* pointed to the potential of China: "If we can gain access to that vast source of consumption, the serious problem—where can we find markets for our prospective surplus of manufacture?—would be in no small measure solved." The *Commercial Advertiser* agreed, and urged a forceful response to "the descent of confederated vultures upon the spoil of China." The Boston *Herald* asserted in March 1898 that "We have ten times as much reason for defending our great interests in the east as we have of fighting a sentimental war with Spain over which class of people shall misrule Cuba."[27]

But the backwardness of the country meant that the 400 million Chinese bought only a limited amount of foreign goods.[28] This explains why, despite occasional flights of rhetoric, the US government, Congress, and the press had paid little attention to the China market. The acquisition of the Philippines brought the United States closer to China and modestly increased public interest in that country. American businessmen might call for a forceful policy to protect their interests in China from the Europeans, but US public opinion had no stomach for it. Nimbly, Secretary of State Hay crafted a policy that sounded ambitious but required no actual US commitment: the Open Door notes, sent in the fall of 1899, asked Britain, Germany, Russia, France, Italy, and Japan to respect equal trading opportunities for all powers within their spheres of influence in China.[29] The secretary had not consulted Beijing before sending the notes, and for good reason: the notes did not challenge the unequal treaties. As Warren Cohen remarks, they "were intended to serve the interests of the United States, and their value to China was incidental."[30]

Some of the recipients, notably Britain and Germany, were in favor of the Open Door.[31] Others, like Russia, weren't, but none wanted to offend the United States, and they all replied with varying degrees of approval that committed them to nothing. Hay proclaimed it a success for US policy and Americans applauded. And this was the true significance of the 1899 Open Door notes: to demonstrate the administration's resolve without committing it to any concrete action.

The Boxer Revolt

The European onslaught, Jonathan Spence writes, made some Chinese fear "that their country was about to be 'carved up like a melon.'" The sense that they were facing an overwhelming threat gave rise to anxiety, resentment and, ultimately, nationalism.[32] An early manifestation of this budding nationalism was the Boxer uprising—a brutal, disorganized revolt fueled by drought and famine that began in Shandong province and spread across northern China by the early months of 1900. The Boxers lacked a clear leader and were poorly armed. Unlike previous rebels, they did not direct their ire against the dynasty but against the Western powers. They threatened and manhandled the Western missionaries and killed Chinese Christians, whom they damned as a fifth column.

In the spring of 1900, the first groups of Boxers entered Beijing. Until then the imperial court had equivocated, assuring foreign governments that it would suppress the Boxers but doing almost nothing. In June, an international force of approximately 1,000 men, mainly British, Japanese, and Russians, seized the strategic Dagu Forts—the gateway to Beijing. Facing the growing strength of the Boxers in Beijing on the one hand and, on the other, the escalating threat from the foreigners, the Empress Dowager was forced to choose sides. "Today China is extremely weak," she told princes and senior officials on June 17. "We have only the people's hearts and minds to depend upon. If we cast them aside and lose the people's heart, what can we use to sustain the country?"[33] Four days later, the imperial government issued a declaration of war against the Western powers and Japan, explaining that "the foreigners have . . . infringed upon our territorial integrity, trampled our people under their feet, and taken our property by force."[34] This was accurate, but foolhardy, given China's impotence. Chinese troops then joined the Boxers besieging the legation quarter in Beijing, where the diplomatic community and other foreigners huddled.

Hastily assembled, an international force of some 19,000 soldiers began advancing from the port of Tianjin toward Beijing on August 4. It included 8,000 Japanese (who had the advantage of proximity), 4,500 Russians, 3,000 British, 2,500 Americans (rushed in from the Philippines), 800 French, and a smattering of Italians and Austrians. (7,000 German soldiers were *en route*, but they arrived after the fall of Beijing.)[35]

Chinese troops sought to halt the column as soon as it left Tianjin, but they were defeated in two hard-fought battles on August 5 and 6. Thereafter, the invaders met no resistance, but this did not temper their savagery: they torched villages and killed tens of thousands of civilians as they marched toward the capital. In their wake, they left "a picture of destruction that it would take a volume to describe," a journalist wrote. Two other journalists reported, "The feature . . . of all the villages on the line of march . . . was the number of dead bodies everywhere."[36] On August 14, as the empress and the court fled west to the city of Xian, the invaders entered Beijing and indulged in what a newspaper called a "carnival of loot."[37] They also engaged in "indiscriminate and generally unprovoked shooting of Chinese. It is safe to say," the commanding general of the US contingent noted, "that where one real Boxer has been killed since the capture of Pekin, fifty harmless coolies or laborers on farms, including not a few women and children, have been slain."[38] The US troops, while perpetrating "a fair number of individual abuses," proved more restrained than the Europeans toward the city's civilian population.[39]

After the fall of Beijing, the United States returned to being the least violent member of the pack, and when discussing the indemnity to impose on China, the McKinley administration sought, unsuccessfully, to persuade the other powers to scale back their demands. The indemnity was set at the staggering sum of four times China's annual income in 1900. The Chinese government had to accept it, and other harsh demands that further constrained China's independence, as the price of peace. The US government took its share of the indemnity, but later used part of it to fund scholarships for Chinese students in the United States and to establish an American college in Beijing.[40]

In July 1900, as the international expedition prepared to advance on Beijing, Hay had sent what became known as his second Open Door note: a circular letter to the powers calling for the preservation of China's "territorial and administrative entity." McKinley and Hay understood, Warren Cohen explains, that the American public's interest in China was "neither broad enough nor deep enough for the government to be able to muster the support it would need to become involved in power politics on the Asian mainland." It was best, therefore, that China should not be carved up.[41] This dovetailed with the policies of Japan and the great powers of Europe, with one exception, Russia, which coveted Manchuria, the vast and rich province in China's far northeast.

Turning against the Tsar

Until the late nineteenth century, relations between the United States and Russia were good, but not close. There were no areas where their interests clashed, and they shared a common enemy, England. But by the turn of the century the "special relationship" was replacing the old enmity between London and Washington. This led Americans to take a more objective view of the Tsarist regime. Its growing anti-Semitism and the pogroms that ensued tarnished Russia's image in the United States, despite the fact that the persecution of minorities was a trait the two countries shared. The Russian ambassador, Arthur Cassini, remarked that Americans had "less moral right than any other people" to advocate on behalf of the Jews, "whose situation in Russia was far better than that of the blacks in the United States";[42] he could also have pointed to American mistreatment of the Chinese, Tejanos, and Indians. But Tsarist violence against Jews directly affected the United States: Russian Jews were emigrating in increasing numbers to the United States. For the Anglo-Saxon caste that governed the United States and for most white Americans, Jews were at the bottom of the Caucasian race. In the words of Secretary of State Gresham, the Russian persecution of Jews, "necessarily driving to our shores large numbers of degraded and undesirable persons ... cannot be regarded as consistent with the friendship which the Russian government has long professed for the United States."[43]

Furthermore, the Russians were encroaching on Manchuria. In 1896, they had forced Beijing to grant them a concession to build a railroad across Manchuria to their port at Vladivostok; in 1898, they had seized Port Arthur. During the Boxer revolt they occupied the entire province of Manchuria and stationed troops there. The bulk of US exports to China, while modest, went to northern China and, increasingly, to Manchuria. "Essentially America's involvement with Manchuria was future oriented," writes Michael Hunt. "American exporters hoped to build their promising start in this virgin market into a booming trade."[44] They feared that Russian control would mean their exclusion. And Russia, Norman Saul observes, "was indeed doing what some Americans feared most: consolidating an exclusive trade zone."[45] In April 1902, Russia promised to withdraw its troops from Manchuria but then reneged. Secretary of State Hay wrote to Roosevelt, "Dealing with a government with whom mendacity is a science is an extremely difficult and delicate matter."[46]

Roosevelt and Hay knew that neither Congress nor American public opinion would support a military confrontation with Russia over Manchuria. Therefore, they welcomed Japan's challenge to Russian power. For Tokyo, the Russians represented an existential threat: not content with Manchuria, they were extending their influence into Korea. "If Russia is left alone, she will go on to take complete possession of Manchuria, and after that would invade Korea, and eventually threaten Japan," warned Ito Hirobumi, a leading Japanese statesman who sought—in vain—to convince Russia to compromise: remaining in Manchuria but leaving Korea to Japan.[47] As the two countries drifted toward war, the US press cheered Japan, seen as a champion of the Open Door. "American and Japanese commercial interests are one," wrote the New York weekly *Outlook*, while the *New York Times* warned, "mankind will sympathize with any nation which undertakes to bring this hardened national perjurer [Russia] to her senses … [We] hope that Japan will give Russia a lesson that at least the present generation of Russian 'statesmen' and 'diplomatists' will not forget."[48] In late December 1903, the Russian ambassador reported from Washington: "Public opinion here at this critical moment favors Japan because of the incessant insinuations of the Anglo-Jewish press." A few days later he added, "I am forced to conclude that the attitude toward us of the USA becomes every day more negative and distrustful."[49]

The Russo-Japanese War

In the early hours of February 9, 1904, Japanese destroyers launched a successful attack on the Russian fleet at Port Arthur, Manchuria. Japan is "playing our game," Roosevelt wrote to his son.[50] He expected a Japanese victory, but not what happened: stunning the world, the Japanese defeated the Russians on land and annihilated their fleet. In July 1905, they conquered the large Russian island of Sakhalin. The Tsar's plight was compounded by a wave of riots and strikes at home that began in June 1905. The US ambassador in St. Petersburg warned Roosevelt on July 3, "I have believed heretofore that revolution in Russia is impossible, but events of the past week have altered conditions and aspects."[51]

As Japan replaced Russia as the strongest power in northeast Asia, Americans' goodwill toward their model pupil waned. On August 18, 1905, the *New York Times* noted that "Japan must be prepared to see in the Western World a marked, if gradual, change of attitude and sentiment toward her achievements, her aspirations, and herself." The *New York Herald* worried: "Japan now sees the opportunity not only to end the Russian advance on the Pacific, but of becoming master of the East."[52] Roosevelt had hoped that Japan would win, "but not too overwhelmingly," because a balance of power in the Far East was in the interest of the United States.[53] When Japanese and Russian negotiators met at Portsmouth, New Hampshire, in August 1905, Roosevelt played an impartial and positive role, helping to convince the Tsar to cede southern Sakhalin to Japan, making peace possible. The success of the conference garnered Roosevelt high praise at home and abroad, as well as the Nobel Peace Prize. Its success, however, was made possible by the concessions of the Japanese government, and by the conviction of the head of the Russian delegation, Sergei Witte, that Russia, wracked by internal strife, needed peace. Signed on September 5, 1905, the Treaty of Portsmouth stipulated that Russia recognized Japan's control of Korea and transferred its rights in southern Manchuria to Japan. Russia remained the dominant power in northern Manchuria.[54]

The war's impact

The military success of Japan, a non-white nation, inspired oppressed races of the world. Jawaharlal Nehru, the first prime minister of independent India, who was then fourteen years old, wrote in his autobiography: "Japanese victories stirred up my enthusiasm and I waited eagerly for the papers for fresh news daily. I invested in a large number of books on Japan … Nationalist ideas filled my mind. I mused of Indian freedom and Asiatic freedom from the thraldom of Europe."[55] In the United States, many African Americans celebrated. "The brown men continue to trash the white men in the East," the Indianapolis *Freeman*, a black-owned newspaper, explained in February 1905. The Japanese victories, the *Colored American Magazine* wrote, had destroyed the claims of white superiority and were a beacon of hope for "other dark and accursed races." In the New York *Age*, Archibald Grimké, a leading black intellectual who had been enslaved, rhapsodized, "Across the seas, across the continents, across the ages," the samurai had come as "the avenger of God." His sword would not be stayed "until liberty and justice descend from on high … to make men, brown men and white men and black men brothers again."[56]

In 1914, a prominent Chinese academic explained the importance of the Japanese victory: "For the first time a European power in carrying out her unrestrained aggression in Asia was obliged to own defeat at the hands of an Asiatic power. The event was too instructive not have its effect upon China."[57] Japan's triumph "sent shockwaves running through every level of Chinese society," a Chinese historian noted recently.[58] It emboldened the Chinese to strike—against the United States.

When the war between Japan and Russia had begun, Washington and Beijing had been locked in a bitter dispute. At issue was the renewal of the 1894 immigration treaty which was due to expire in December 1904. The Roosevelt administration wanted to extend it for ten more years, but Beijing demanded a new treaty that would include a "bill of rights"[59] to protect the Chinese who lived in the United States; it did not ask for a change in the exclusion policy, knowing that this was unattainable given the racism of white Americans, but it sought an end to the humiliating treatment inflicted on members of the "exempt classes" (merchants, students, teachers, and tourists) when they arrived in the United States. Immigration officers, Michael Hunt writes, subjected these Chinese to "intimidating, arbitrary, and abusive" treatment.[60] The officers' superiors, historian Erika Lee adds, stressed "that Chinese are an undesirable addition to our society; that their presence is a disturbing element that tends only to evil and corruption, and that every presumption, every technicality and every intendment should be held against their admission and their testimony should have little or no weight when standing alone." Interrogations were stymied by the absence of qualified interpreters. The immigration service was loath to hire Chinese as interpreters—"I suppose we want an honest Chinaman for interpreter and if so I reckon we would have to go Heaven to find him and I doubt whether there are any there or not," a senior immigration officer mused. Instead, white men were hired; more important than their linguistic ability was their antipathy for the Chinese.[61]

San Francisco was the port of entry for most Chinese. Those who aroused any suspicion of immigration inspectors were detained in a two-story wooden building at the end of Pier 40 known as The Shed; investigations could take weeks, even months. In December 1904, a report by the secretary of commerce, who supervised the Bureau of Immigration, noted:

> The requirements of the various acts of Congress applying to aliens of the Chinese race are so much more stringent than those applied to other aliens that prolonged detention is frequently necessary in order that the right of the applicants to lawful entry may be thoroughly investigated ... The accommodations available [in San Francisco] are of such a character that it would be discreditable in the extreme for the Government to continue the use of them. The sanitary conditions are so poor that not only is the health and physical welfare of the detained persons constantly subjected to serious menace, but the danger to the Government employees and others who are compelled to transact official business at the detention quarters is a matter of grave consequence.[62]

The plight of the Chinese was not over even if they were admitted into the United States. The regulations of the Bureau of Immigration stipulated that "An inspector with the slightest suspicion might with impunity stop, interrogate, insult and even detain a Chinese, whether American citizen, Chinese official, student, businessman, or plain traveler" anywhere in the United States.[63]

The Chinese press carried articles describing the indignities inflicted on Chinese in the United States. Cartoons "pictured in detail Chinese being driven into the detention shed ... and subjected to violence and insults in the street."[64] Letters from Chinese living in the United States denounced the treatment they endured. These indignities were nothing new—what was new was the spirit of nationalism emerging in China. "A wrong is needlessly being inflicted," a senior Chinese official warned in the *North American Review* in 1904, "which, unless checked, is sure to lead to retaliation and to drive China's great trade into more friendly hands."[65] This was language American businessmen could understand. The American Asiatic Association, which represented virtually every firm active in the China trade, pleaded with Roosevelt to improve the treatment of Chinese in the United States. American missionaries added their voices. They had never before challenged US policy toward China; on the contrary they had argued that the best way of dealing with the Chinese was the gunboat, and they had asserted that "the heathens"— that is, virtually all the Chinese—were "prone to covetousness, lust and deceit." But a new generation of missionaries was emerging, more sensitive to the dignity of the Chinese and aware that humiliating them made evangelizing more difficult.[66]

Deaf to Beijing's complaints, and to the warnings of businessmen and missionaries, in April 1904, Congress extended the Chinese Exclusion Act with no time limit (it lasted until 1943); meanwhile, the Japanese were defeating the Russians on land and at sea, proving, a Chinese journal asserted, that "We yellow people can defend ourselves and stand up with pride."[67] Finally, the Chinese reacted: in May 1905, the Shanghai Chamber of Commerce proposed a boycott of American goods. The boycott spread the length of China, from Canton to Beijing, and into the central Yangtze Valley. It was spearheaded by merchants, intellectuals, and students. Chinese in the United States applauded the boycott and raised money to support it.[68]

Until 1905, Roosevelt had paid no heed, beyond occasional lip service, to the bitter complaints of the Chinese legation. However, the boycott got his attention, and he ordered immigration officers to refrain from their "very oppressive conduct" toward the Chinese.[69] At the same time, he told the US minister in Beijing to demand that the Chinese authorities suppress the boycott and punish its leaders; the United States would hold Beijing responsible for losses suffered by American merchants.

In late 1905, Roosevelt ordered the navy and the army to develop a plan for a military intervention in China. They proposed landing 5,000 troops in Canton, the nerve center of the boycott. "As with many of Roosevelt's schemes, there is always some uncertainty about the President's commitment to it," Richard Challener writes. "He certainly seemed serious about action in the early weeks of 1906, but he may have expected that the threat to use force would be sufficient to achieve his purpose."[70]

Whatever the president's intentions may have been, by early 1906 the use of force was no longer necessary: the boycott was collapsing. The Chinese merchants abandoned it as too costly; the Chinese authorities turned against it under US pressure and in fear that it could spawn forces that would threaten the dynasty. As the boycott ended, Roosevelt again lost interest in improving the treatment of the Chinese in America.

The Japanese threat

It was inevitable that the Japanese victory over Russia would provoke uneasiness in the United States: Americans were accustomed to seeing Japan as a pupil, not an equal. Suddenly, Japan was a great power—the first nonwhite great power in two centuries— bent on asserting hegemony in Northeast Asia.

In late 1906, Roosevelt ordered the navy and the army to develop a war plan against Japan. The General Board of the Navy, which drew up War Plan Orange, concluded that while the United States had two possible enemies, Germany and Japan, Germany was the more dangerous. The German Navy was stronger than the American, and the Japanese fleet was weaker; furthermore, members of Congress from the eastern and Gulf states were unwilling "to permit the western states to share in the pot of gold of naval expenditures," and their arguments were bolstered by the dearth of shipyards on the Pacific seaboard.[71] If war broke out, the fact that the US fleet was concentrated on the Atlantic Coast meant that the Japanese Navy would enjoy a virtually free hand in the Pacific for the first three months.

At the turn of the century, during the debate over the annexation of the Philippines, there were people like Andrew Carnegie who had warned that the far away archipelago would become a strategic liability for the United States, but their counsel had been dismissed because most Americans could not imagine that any power would threaten US control of the Philippines—certainly not Japan, the "model pupil." In 1900, at the time of the Boxer rebellion, the Philippines had been a strategic asset: the US troops sent to join the international force that conquered Beijing had come from the archipelago, a far shorter distance than if they had had to travel from California. However, by 1906, Japan was a great power and potential enemy, and the prophesy of the Cassandras of 1898 had come true: the archipelago was no longer a strategic asset. "The possession of the Philippines renders us vulnerable in Asia," Theodore Roosevelt lamented in August 1907. "The Philippines form our heel of Achilles."[72]

There were many revisions of War Plan Orange before the US entry in the First World War. They all posited that Japan would be able to overrun the Philippines as well as Guam while the US fleet was still steaming toward the Pacific. However, once the American warships reached the combat zone the momentum would shift. The US Navy would bypass Luzon if too strongly defended by the Japanese, and seize instead smaller islands that would serve as advance bases for the troops that would follow. Their final objective would be the Ryukius, a chain immediately south of Japan, that would serve as the base for a naval blockade that would cut off all imports to Japan. War Plan Orange consistently anticipated that honor would force the Japanese fleet to seek battle and the US Navy would defeat it. All drafts agreed that the United States would not attempt to invade Japan, because it would require too many soldiers and cost too many American lives. "If the American nation does not weary, Japan will be reduced by exhaustion," the Navy's foremost strategist, Alfred Mahan, remarked. How long would it take? The Japanese "have tremendous national feeling, a great deal of endurance and determination, and probably could stand this condition for, say, two years or even more," warned Admiral Bradley Fiske, a senior member of the General Board of the Navy.[73]

It was not Japan's military power, however, that poisoned relations between Tokyo and Washington in late 1906: it was American racism.

The first Japanese immigrants had arrived in the United States in the 1870s. There were 148 in 1880; 2,039 in 1890, and then the flow increased. By 1900, there were 24,326. They were concentrated on the Pacific coast, especially in California. They started as migrant workers on the farms and railroads. Most had been farmers in Japan, eking a meager living on plots that were too small to sustain a family. Their dream was to become farmers in America, not field laborers, and by the late 1890s many were succeeding. The men sent money to Japan so their wives could join them, or they chose picture brides. They created families; they became settlers. As their numbers grew and their circumstances improved, so did the hostility they encountered from whites on the West Coast. The American Federation of Labor (AFL), the largest labor union in the United States, argued that Japanese workers lacked the capacity to become "union men": they could not be taught the fundamentals of unionism and could not be counted "to stand shoulder to shoulder with faithful workers."[74]

The Oxnard strike[75]

In early 1903, the Western Agricultural Contracting Company (WACC), which hired the sugar beet workers of Oxnard, California, lowered their wages. In response, 500 Japanese and 200 Mexicans who worked on the sugar beet farms created the Japanese-Mexican Labor Association (JMLA). The JMLA had a Japanese president, a secretary of the Japanese branch, and a secretary of the Mexican branch.

By early March 1903, the JMLA had more than 1,300 members (90 percent of the sugar beet workers in Oxnard); they went on strike. "Japs and Mexicans Combined to Defeat American Contractors," ran the front page headline of the Oxnard *Courier* on March 7.[76] After three weeks, the WACC settled, agreeing to wages that were significantly higher than those the workers earned before the pay cut. On behalf of the victorious union, the secretary of the Mexican branch of the JMLA, J.M. Lizarras, applied to AFL president Samuel Gompers for membership. Gompers agreed, on one condition: "Your union will under no circumstance accept membership of any Chinese or Japanese." Lizarras' reply was a lesson in dignity:

In the past we have counseled, fought and lived on very short rations with our Japanese brothers and toiled with them in the fields, and they have been uniformly kind and considerate. We would be false to them and to ourselves and to the cause of unionism if we now accepted privileges for ourselves which are not accorded to them. We are going to stand by men who stood by us in the long, hard fight which ended in a victory over the enemy. We therefore respectfully petition the A.F. of L. to grant us a charter under which we can unite all the sugar beet and field laborers in Oxnard, without regard to their color or race. We will refuse any other kind of charter, except one which will wipe out race prejudices and recognize our fellow workers as being as good as ourselves.[77]

As Ronald Takaki writes, "tragically for the American labor movement, Gompers had drawn a color line for Asians." For Gompers, as for white Californians, the Japanese were even more dangerous than the Chinese. They were "especially feared," Erika Lee remarks, "because of their great success in agriculture."[78] Moreover, unlike the Chinese workers, the Japanese were allowed to bring their wives and start families in the United States. The

San Francisco Chronicle, the most influential newspaper on the Pacific coast, explained: "The Chinese were faithful laborers and did not buy land. The Japanese are unfaithful laborers and do buy land . . . They are driving their stakes in our fruit-growing districts, where they intend to stay and possess the land. The people of California are determined that they shall do neither."[79] Japan's victory over Russia increased the danger: unlike the Chinese, Japanese immigrants had a powerful country behind them. The *San Francisco Examiner* printed a cartoon showing a Japanese soldier casting his shadow across the Pacific into California:[80] Japanese immigration was considered an existential threat.

White San Francisco strikes

On October 11, 1906, the San Francisco Board of Education ordered that all Japanese schoolchildren must forthwith attend the city's "Oriental school," a segregated school for all Chinese students. There were only ninety-three Japanese students in a total school population of 29,000:[81] the real aim of the order was to force the federal government to end Japanese immigration to the United States.

The school board's decision—the first discriminatory act by a local authority against the Japanese—was "particularly ungracious," the *Outlook* remarked, because after the earthquake and fire that had ravaged San Francisco the previous April the Japanese government and the Japanese branch of the Red Cross had contributed $246,000 for the relief fund, more than all the other foreign donors combined.[82] The school board's decision provoked, the *Literary Digest* reported, a "storm of popular indignation" in Japan, where some newspapers called for war or at least a boycott of American goods. These were isolated voices, but on one point the Japanese press agreed: the School Board's decision had to be revoked. The Japanese government was eager to maintain good relations with the United States, but it was also sensitive to public opinion and to insults to the nation's honor. It forcefully complained to Washington. From Tokyo the US ambassador warned, "It should not be forgotten that the Japanese are an emotional, proud people, who just at this time have a very considerable opinion of themselves, and who are neither as phlegmatic nor as long-suffering as the Chinese."[83]

Many Americans dismissed the risk of war. Others were not so sure. "The Japanese, flushed by success in one of the world's notable wars . . . cannot be expected to sit by calmly and see their subjects treated with contumely," the *Nation* wrote. Roosevelt believed that war was unlikely, but he, too, was not certain. He wrote to his son Kermit, "The infernal fools in California, and especially in San Francisco, insult the Japanese recklessly, and in the event of war it will be the Nation as a whole which will pay the consequences. However, I hope to keep things straight."[84] But the Californians, from the governor to the legislature to the white citizen in the street, stood firmly behind the school board's decision. They enjoyed the support of fellow whites in the West and the South, while public opinion in the Midwest was divided. Only in the East was white public opinion strongly against the Californians.[85] As for African Americans, Marc Gallicchio writes, "the feeling of kinship they felt [with the Japanese] as a result of the

[Russo-Japanese] war only increased" as they sympathized with "the plight of the Japanese in America."[86]

Roosevelt chose to finesse the issue. He promised the Californians that he would negotiate a treaty with Tokyo prohibiting the emigration of Japanese laborers to the United States. Reassured, the San Francisco Board of Education rescinded the segregation order against Japanese children in March 1907. Then, through laborious negotiations that lasted until February 1908, the American and Japanese governments completed the "Gentlemen's Agreement." The key stipulation was that Tokyo promised to forbid the emigration to the United States of laborers, skilled or unskilled, allowing only the emigration of parents, wives, and children of laborers who were already in the United States.[87] The Californians' strategy—to create an incident and force Washington's hand—had worked.

While Roosevelt was busy defusing the crisis created by the San Francisco School Board, American racism provoked yet another potential flare up with Japan, this time about naturalization. In 1870, Congress had limited naturalization to "white people and persons of African descent." As the debate had made clear, the legislators' intent had been to prevent the naturalization of Chinese. No one had mentioned the Japanese, which was understandable, given that there were only fifty-five Japanese in the United States (and 63,000 Chinese). Over the next thirty-five years some lower federal courts issued naturalization papers to Japanese immigrants—420 in all. But in June 1906, Congress standardized naturalization requirements and procedures, confirming that only whites and people of African descent were eligible for naturalization. In conjunction with this act, the US Attorney General ordered federal courts to cease issuing naturalization papers to Japanese immigrants.[88] Roosevelt pushed back. In December, he urged Congress to pass an act "specifically providing for the naturalization of Japanese who come here intending to become American citizens."[89] However, he did not follow through. He did not lobby Congress to pass the act, nor did he ever propose it again. Perhaps he was deterred by the obvious lack of support in Congress and the press for what would have been, by US standards, a revolutionary change. (The ban was not lifted until 1952.) Or, more likely, his proposal had been simply a gesture to assuage sensitivities in Japan.[90] And for the time being it worked. Japanese officials and public opinion were focused on the immigration issue; the ban on naturalization, however offensive, seemed a far less pressing problem—there were no press reports about Japanese immigrants being denied naturalization or suffering additional hardship because of the ban.

Roosevelt's Far Eastern policy was predicated on the fact that the dominant power in northeast Asia was Japan; that the most important issue in US-Japanese relations was the Gentlemen's Agreement curtailing Japanese immigration; and that US economic and strategic interests in China were minimal. (In his final year as president, American exports to China were $14 million, slightly over 1 percent of total US exports.)[91] Roosevelt complained to Tokyo when he felt that the Japanese were violating the open door in southern Manchuria, but he accepted the reality that it was within Japan's sphere of influence. He summed up his policy in a December 1910 letter to his successor, William Howard Taft: "Our vital interest is to keep the Japanese out of our country . . . The vital interest of the Japanese, on the other hand, is in Manchuria and Korea. It is therefore peculiarly our interest not to take any steps as regards Manchuria which will give the Japanese cause to feel . . . that we are hostile to them . . . Our interests in Manchuria are really unimportant, and not such that the American people would be content to run the slightest risk of collision about them."[92]

During last two years of Roosevelt's term, there were no further assaults on Japanese pride by US local or state authorities. This, as well as Roosevelt's respect of Tokyo's interests in the Far East, was appreciated by the Japanese. When the US fleet visited Japan in October 1908, it was welcomed by enthusiastic crowds. In the United States, "flurries of appreciation of the reception and Japanese cordiality were heard from coast to coast."[93] It seemed that relations between the two peoples were finally improving when the Californians struck again.

In January 1909, at the very end of Roosevelt's presidency, the California legislature began considering a bill barring aliens ineligible for citizenship from owning land. The bill targeted the Japanese; the Chinese owned very little land. Roosevelt went into high gear; pressuring and cajoling, he was able to derail the measure, as well as the anti-Japanese bills and resolutions that were introduced in solidarity with California in the legislatures of Nevada, Oregon, Washington, Montana, and Nebraska.[94]

Taft and Japan

Taft was Roosevelt's hand-picked successor. In Latin America, he followed in Roosevelt's footsteps, but in East Asia he veered abruptly from Roosevelt's policy. Taft and his secretary of state, Philander Knox, believed that it was imperative that the United States increase its exports, that China and Latin America were "the regions of greatest potential for foreign commerce," and that they were, "geographically, by tradition and by common consent two fields preeminently adapted for American enterprise."[95]

With Taft's blessing, Knox launched an aggressive policy to promote American economic interests in China. He was convinced that the long-term growth of American trade was closely tied to US investment in China, and he therefore urged a reluctant Wall Street to pump dollars into that vast country.

The second prong of the administration's Far Eastern policy targeted Japan. Taft and Knox believed that Roosevelt had greatly exaggerated the power of Japan. Tokyo was too dependent on the British and American financial markets to resist the combined pressure of Washington and London. The administration would enlist the British to loosen Japan's hold on southern Manchuria. Manchuria, historian Michael Hunt writes, "continued to preoccupy Americans, principally as a symbol of their China dreams; events there were for them an omen for the future of all China."[96]

Taft and Knox overestimated American bankers' willingness to incur the risks of investment in China when so many opportunities for surer profits beckoned elsewhere; by the time Taft left office in March 1913, American investment in China was slightly less than $50 million (c. $1.3 billion), that is, approximately 3 percent of total foreign investment—behind Britain ($607 million), Russia ($269 million), Germany ($263 million), Japan

($219 million), and France ($171 million).[97] As for American exports to China, they were $19 million when Taft entered the White House and $21 million when he left.[98] US exports did not stagnate because of unfair competition from the Europeans and the Japanese, but because Americans did not aggressively pursue the Chinese market: they "sent goods for which the Chinese had little or no use," Warren Cohen explains. "They packaged their goods badly. Unlike their British and Japanese competitors, few Americans kept agents in China. They provided no credit facilities or sales organization."[99]

The administration's belief that Whitehall would support its half-baked schemes against Japan in southern Manchuria was naive. The British were willing to accommodate Washington whenever reasonably possible, but since 1902 Japan was their ally. Furthermore, the China Association (which represented virtually all the British firms trading with China), as well as British officials in China and Japan, repeatedly confirmed that the Japanese were respecting the open door for trade in Manchuria.[100]

The best that can be said of Taft's Far Eastern policy is that, while ill-conceived and clumsily executed, it caused no lasting damage to the United States. The administration resented the British failure to curb Japan, but the relationship between the two countries was based on far more important considerations. The strains Taft and Knox provoked in the US relationship with Japan were minor, largely because they were unable to seriously threaten Tokyo's interests. By early 1911 the administration had abandoned its attempts to undermine Japan in southern Manchuria.

Enter Woodrow Wilson

When Taft stepped down, China was no longer an empire. Facing a growing revolt, the emperor had abdicated in February 1912, and a republic had been proclaimed. "I feel so keenly the desire to help China," President Wilson told his cabinet shortly after his inauguration "that I prefer to err in the line of helping that country than otherwise."[101] Not keenly enough, however, to consider renouncing extraterritoriality and the other privileges acquired through the policy of the jackal, or to attempt to improve the treatment of the Chinese in the United States.

Meanwhile, relations with Japan were becoming tense again. The cause was, once more, American racism and in particular those "infernal fools" in California, as Roosevelt had deemed them.

In May 1913, a few weeks after Wilson's inauguration, the legislature in Sacramento made good on the threat Roosevelt had defused four years earlier: it approved a bill that declared unlawful the ownership of "real property" by "aliens ineligible to citizenship."[102] This meant that the ban on naturalization of Japanese could have severe economic consequences.

The law sparked street demonstrations throughout Japan. The Japanese ambassador in Washington lodged an "urgent and official protest": the measure was "unfair and discriminatory . . . against my countrymen . . . and opposed to the spirit and fundamental principles of amity and good understanding."[103]

The Japanese reaction unnerved the military brass in the United States. Admiral Fiske warned the secretary of the Navy that "a war is possible, and even probable." He wrote that the United States, "by refusing citizenship to the Japanese, and by such state laws as are now pending on the West Coast, hit the Japanese in their tenderest spots: their sense of honor; their pride of race and their patriotism."[104] Wilson maintained his sang-froid, he did not believe that war was likely. Through the next year, the State Department and the Japanese government engaged in fruitless negotiations. "Pathetically eager for a settlement that would save face," Tokyo "would have been satisfied by almost any positive action by the Washington government," Arthur Link, Wilson's preeminent biographer, writes, but Wilson offered nothing beyond protestations of friendship. Perhaps, Link muses, the president's failure to find some compromise formula was influenced by the fact that he was sympathetic to the position of the Californians. "Whatever the causes of the failure," Link concludes, "the consequences embittered Japanese-American relations for years to come."[105] A draft of War Plan Orange noted in 1915, "the trend of events promises to make Japan an enemy.... The persistent refusal of Blue [the United States] to admit the Asiatic on terms of equality and citizenship wounds the pride and self-love of a sensitive people and closes the door to a land of gold and opportunity."[106]

Looking back

The China market was not important for American business—not even in the 1890s, when fear of overproduction was rampant—except as a dream of future riches. Nor did China have strategic value for US officials. At times, Beijing looked at the United States as the least violent of its aggressors and hoped to enlist its support. At other times, Beijing considered Americans as bad as the others. The most important bilateral issue was the treatment of Chinese in the United States, and on that the US record was dismal.

Japan, too, was not an important economic partner. American exports to Japan were less than $10 million a year until 1897, when they jumped to $13 million. Thereafter, they rose steadily to $51 million in 1914—a little more than 2 percent of total US exports.[107] Once they stopped resisting their Western aggressors, the Japanese enjoyed American goodwill as the "model pupil." But at the beginning of the twentieth century, two developments rocked the relationship: Japan's victory over Russia and the racist treatment of the Japanese in the United States. Japan had proven its military prowess, and Americans feared that it might retaliate against the treatment of its citizens. Moreover, many Americans believed that the Japanese, a non-white race, were unpredictable. What dark schemes might lurk behind their smiles? Some feared Tokyo's "nefarious projects" in the Western Hemisphere, and in 1912 transformed the desire of a Japanese fishing syndicate to acquire land in Baja California into Tokyo's scheme to establish a naval base.[108] Books and newspaper articles about the Japanese peril became common fare. In *The Valor of Ignorance*, published in 1909, Homer Lea warned that Japan was powerful enough to overrun the Philippines and the other US possessions in the Pacific, and land hundreds of thousands of soldiers on the West Coast. Large parts of the American West would fall into Japanese hands. "A story which every American would do well to ponder," advised the *Literary Digest* in its review. The book, which had a glowing introduction by General Adna Chaffee, a former chief of staff of the US army, was a best seller. Readers focused on the Japanese threat, not on Lea's point that "the American people and not Japan are responsible for this approaching conflict" because they treated the Japanese as "racial lepers."[109]

CHAPTER 14
THE WHITE CITY ON THE HILL

The belief in American exceptionalism is the keynote of the political culture of white America. It resonates in the constant boasting that the United States is "the greatest democracy in the world," a claim that was made even when millions of African Americans were enslaved and, after the Civil War, disenfranchised. When John Kennedy strode to the dais on January 20, 1961, to speak on behalf of liberty, he was the leader of a country in which citizens were not allowed to vote because of the color of their skin. It was only in 1965, with Lyndon Johnson's Voting Rights Act, that the United States became a full-fledged member of the community of Western democracies.

What *is* exceptional is white Americans' stubborn belief in American exceptionalism. Many countries may suffer from a similar delusion, but the strength of the white consensus that has surrounded the myth and the poverty of the domestic debate about it makes the United States, indeed, exceptional.

Many African Americans and other minorities may believe today, and may have believed in the past, in American exceptionalism, but it is impossible, when looking at the first 150 years of US foreign policy, to talk about "America." There were white Americans and there were the others: African Americans, Native Americans, Mexican Americans, Asians … the pariahs. The experiences of these others were dramatically different from those of white Americans. For the white majority, and the white US government, African Americans and Native Americans were not part of the nation. The American melting pot excluded them—indeed, fear of miscegenation was another keynote of white America. (Or, rather, there were two kinds of miscegenation: the one that was considered repulsive, involving white women and black men; and the one that was politely ignored, white men raping black women.) Mexican Americans and people of Asian descent were also outside the nation, as defined by white Americans, although the chasm was not as extreme as for African Americans and Indians.

From the outset, white America, this young nation of immigrants who lacked the bonds of common roots, defined itself by stressing its difference from those who stayed behind, the peoples of Europe. What helped the white melting pot melt? The belief in American exceptionalism, in the City on the Hill. The strength of the consensus around this belief, and its persistence through American history, are notable. In Western Europe, powerful groups—socialist and communist parties, for example—have questioned the very nature of their countries' society and challenged the foundations of their domestic systems and their foreign policies. In the United States, however, the political debate has dealt very rarely with the essential nature of American society. Those few who have probed deeper have been marginalized. The United States' economic and military successes have reinforced the belief in American exceptionalism—power has been equated to virtue—and the keynote has remained: America may make mistakes, but its intentions have always been pure. America is the City on the Hill.

In 1901, twelve years before he became president, Woodrow Wilson observed that in its foreign policy America was not exceptional. "When issues of our own interest arose, we have not been unselfish," he wrote. "We have shown ourselves kin to all the world, when it came to pushing an advantage. Our action against Spain in the Floridas, and against Mexico on the coasts of the Pacific; our attitude toward first the Spaniards, and then the French, with regard to the control of the Mississippi; the unpitying force with which we thrust the Indians to the wall wherever they stood in our way, have suited our professions of peacefulness and justice and liberality no better than the aggressions of other nations."[1]

This sobering statement, voiced by one of the nation's great "idealists," is realistic. In the century-and- a-half examined in this book, the United States has been "kin to all the world" even on the one occasion when it fought a war for the ostensible purpose of freeing another country—in 1898, against Spain. Before entering the war, the US Congress had solemnly pledged that Cuba would be independent, but after Spain's defeat it transformed the island into a US protectorate, granting the president the right to send troops whenever deemed necessary. The Europeans were unfazed; they had expected no better. Americans too were unfazed. Judging by their press and their elected representatives, they weren't even aware that the pledge had been violated and that by robbing the Cubans of the independence for which they had strenuously fought the United States was proving itself "kin to all the world."

The anti-colonial tradition of the United States

A pillar of the white City on the Hill is the claim that the United States is a nation born in revolution against the colonial power, and that it remained opposed to colonial adventures until the aberration of the annexation of the Philippines. The United States, the *New York Herald* asserted in 1845, was "the only power which has never sought and never seeks to acquire a foot of territory by force of arms."[2] To maintain this myth, US policy toward Native Americans has routinely been erased from the history of US foreign relations, with the explanation that the tribes were not independent nations. But if US Indian policy is not foreign policy in the sense of relations among recognized independent states, then it is colonial policy—and it is therefore an integral part of the history of the American empire. At its birth, in 1776–83, the United States fought two wars: a war of independence against Britain and a colonial war against Native Americans. Thereafter, the white American empire constantly expanded. At times it was expansion beyond the borders: the Floridas, Louisiana, half of Mexico, Alaska, Midway, Hawaii, Cuba, Puerto Rico, Guam, the Philippines, Samoa, Panama, Nicaragua, Haiti, the Dominican Republic, and the Virgin Islands (bought from Denmark in 1917 under the threat of force). At other times—almost without pause—it was expansion within the borders, taking the land of the Indians. With good reason, Senator Lodge argued in 1900 that if the anti-imperialists were right in considering the annexation of the Philippines immoral, "then our whole past record of expansion is a crime."[3]

There are two types of colonialism: one where the colonial power sends its administrators and its troops to the subject country, but very few of its citizens follow the flag. This was the case of the British in India. But there is another form of colonialism, even more pernicious for the subject peoples: when large numbers of citizens move from the metropole into the conquered lands.

Settler colonialism ranges over a wide arc. On one extreme, Algeria during the French occupation: hundreds of thousands of French and other Europeans settled there; they wanted the land of the natives and they wanted their labor. On the other extreme, Australia, where the white settlers sought to eliminate the natives. As a British official wrote in 1883, white Australians regarded the natives "as vermin, to be cleared off the face of the earth ... I heard men of culture and refinement ... talk not only of the wholesale butchery, but of the individual murder of natives, exactly as they would talk of a day's sport, of having to kill some troublesome animal."[4] In other words, genocide.

Like the French in Algeria, white Americans wanted the land of the natives. Unlike the French, however, they did not want to keep the natives as a servile work force. Unlike white Australians, they usually did not embark on a deliberate extermination policy—they simply wanted to push the Indians out of their way. Their goal was ethnic cleansing. Indians might die by the thousands while being deported or confined in barren reservations, but this was collateral damage, not the goal.

As they conquered the continent, white Americans treated the Indians with brutality, greed, and racism. The best epitaph of US Indian policy was provided by John Quincy Adams when he called the removal policy a "sickening mass of putrefaction."[5] There is no reason to believe that any of the European colonial powers would have behaved any better. The point is not that the United States was worse than its European counterparts; the point is that it was no better, that, to paraphrase Wilson, it was "kin to all the world."

Race and the empire of liberty

From the beginning, even when the Founding Fathers were unsure whether the United States would continue as one united country, they were confident that white Anglo-Saxon Americans would expand over the continent. In Jefferson's words, "However our present interests may restrain us within our own limits, it is impossible not to look forward to distant times when our rapid multiplication will expand itself beyond those limits, and cover the whole northern, if not the southern continent with a people speaking the same language, governed in similar forms, and by similar laws; nor can we contemplate with satisfaction either blot or mixture on that surface."[6]

Jefferson's "empire of liberty" was for white people; this great slaveowner wanted neither "blot" nor "mixture." (Enslaved people were chattel, not considered part of the expanding empire and, if they were freed, Jefferson hoped that they would leave the United States.) Through the period covered in this book—and beyond—the United

States was a white man's country, governed by an Anglo-Saxon Protestant elite that believed that the American divine mission was to regenerate the land for the profit of the white race. Racism was integral to the City on the Hill. Racism explains why Indians, even when they no longer represented a military threat, had to be deported. Political scientist David Hendrickson writes that the Cherokees had a choice: "When shoved aside by Jackson in the 1830s, they were given the choice between assimilation and removal."[7] This is a common and colossal error: the Cherokees were not offered assimilation, the choice given them was between leaving Georgia or staying behind and being treated as free Blacks. And even this does not reflect reality: Georgians did not want the Cherokees to stay under any conditions, they wanted to expel them because they were Indians.

Likewise, the vast majority of white Americans despised Mexicans. "[They] look upon us ... as inferiors," Mexico's first minister reported from Washington in 1822; the Mexicans "want nothing but tails to be more brutes than apes," Stephen Austin wrote from Mexico a few months later.[8] Whigs and Democrats in the 1840s disagreed about expansion—the Democrats were more aggressive—but with rare exceptions they shared contempt for Mexicans and they believed that God had given the United States the right, or perhaps the mission, to grab Mexican territory. California, the *American Review*, the preeminent Whig magazine, explained in January 1846, was destined to belong to the United States: "the Omnipotent Lawgiver" could not allow "this vast and magnificent region" to continue to be held by a degenerate race "utterly ignorant, indolent and rapacious ... destitute of spirit, industry and courage, and perfectly incapable of the slightest emotions of ambition or the faintest pulsation of energy and enterprise."[9]

Racism also infected the Europeans, as they amply demonstrated in Africa and Asia. Was there anything distinctive in the racism of white Americans, that set them apart from the Europeans? The answer is both yes and no. The United States alone, among white states, had a significant number of nonwhites living in its metropolitan territory. This heightened whites' fears and intensified their racism. One need only look at the case of African Americans. The abolition of slavery in 1865 allowed the United States to join the ranks of more civilized nations, but after the bloody parenthesis of Reconstruction the nightmare of Jim Crow began.

While only a handful of Chinese and Japanese lived in European countries, in the western United States they were a statistically significant number and they were subjected to indignities which they did not have to endure in Europe—lynchings, beatings, exclusion laws, segregation. North of the US border, British Columbia, which also had a statistically significant number of Chinese and Japanese, indulged in similarly savage behavior.

Because white powers dominated the world, American racism from independence through the First World War complicated US foreign policy only slightly. The treatment of African Americans only began to affect US foreign relations in 1960, when during the Cold War sixteen black African countries became independent. Discrimination and violence were the norm for Mexican-Americans and Mexicans in the United States, but no Mexican government dared retaliate. The 1905 Chinese boycott against American goods was the only time, through the period covered in this book, that Americans had to pay a price for their mistreatment of the Chinese, and the price was low: the boycott collapsed within a few months. In Latin America, in the words of Roosevelt's secretary of state, "the arrogant and contemptuous bearing of Americans,"[10] and fear of US imperialism, fueled antipathy against the Yankees—to the point that when the United States declared war on Spain in April 1898, Spanish American public opinion, which had previously supported the Cuban rebels, swung in favor of Spain. But this was of little consequence. If until the First World War US trade with South America lagged behind British and Germans, it was because British and Germans were better merchants, not because of Latins' anti-Americanism.

Even in relations with Japan, the one non-white country that was powerful, the cost of American racism was modest: beginning in late 1906, fear that the Japanese might respond militarily to American racist outrages unnerved many US citizens, including senior officials, but the Japanese government issued only polite complaints.

The white American empire

Is there anything in the history of US foreign relations that is truly distinctive? Of course there is. The very birth of the United States owed to a set of circumstances unique in modern history: beginning in 1765 with the response to the Stamp Act, the colonists were able to organize freely against the metropole; for a decade it was more dangerous to be a loyal subject of the Crown than a Son of Liberty. Then, in 1776, France offered the rebels aid even before they had requested it; and two years later, it entered the war on behalf of American independence. Compare this with the revolution that erupted a few years later in Haiti: the Haitians fought alone against the world's greatest powers, first the British and then Napoleon's France. Compare it with the great wars of independence of the twentieth century: no foreign power waged war on France to help the Algerians and the Vietnamese achieve their freedom.

During the first decades of independence, the United States was involved in serious disputes with two powerful European states, Britain, foremost, and also France. This was the only period before the Second World War when the country was vulnerable to foreign threats. In 1795, President Washington, ably advised by Hamilton, reached a *modus vivendi* with Britain and with the Jay Treaty avoided a naval war that would have gravely hurt the infant nation. Granted, the collateral effect of the Jay Treaty was naval war with France in the late 1790s, but France was far weaker than Britain at sea and therefore could inflict far less damage. Napoleon's acquisition of Louisiana might have become a threat to US security but the Haitian "cannibals," as Jefferson called them,[11] and the Royal Navy forced Napoleon to abandon his dream of a Western Empire.

When the United States went to war against Britain in 1812, it was woefully unprepared, but it chose the moment well: Britain was on the ropes in Europe and could devote very little attention to the United States. After Napoleon's defeat, new dangers in Europe—including the possibility of war with Russia—further distracted the British.

After the peace settlement with Britain in 1815, the United States no longer faced a foreign threat. Henceforth, the British would treat the United States as a strong regional power. They would fight, if their vital interests were threatened. But British vital interests were in Europe and India; those of the United States, in North America. This asymmetry would define the relationship between the two countries.

This gave the US government a much freer hand. Because it was clear that Britain would not interfere, President Monroe was able to annex what was left of Spanish Florida. Andrew Jackson and James Polk presided over a wave of territorial aggrandizement. Expansion within the borders under Jackson, who unleashed the massive deportation of Native Americans living east of the Mississippi. Expansion beyond the borders with Polk, who understood that London would not intervene when he engineered a war of aggression that netted the United States one-third of Mexico.

Americans continued to bandy about the notion of the British threat; it rallied the populace and justified expansion. But after the War of 1812, there was no British threat. London did not interfere when Texas proclaimed its independence in 1836. The British would have liked Texas to abolish slavery, but they applied no pressure; they would have liked California to remain Mexican, but they raised not a finger to restrain the United States. They spurned Santa Anna's plea for help when President Pierce demanded additional Mexican territory, and they watched passively as the filibuster, Walker, wreaked havoc on Nicaragua in the 1850s. Then they relinquished most of their possessions in Central America to appease the Americans.

The Union was in danger during the Civil War, but not because of a foreign threat. Napoleon III would have liked to help the Confederacy, but he did not dare to act without Britain, and Britain had no intention of risking a war with the United States. As a result, foreign—British—intervention could have been possible only in response to an egregious US provocation. That possibility arose early when the *Trent* incident challenged British national honor. President Lincoln handled the crisis adroitly, his task made easier by London's moderation: the British did not want to humiliate the US government.

Before the end of the century, the London *Times* predicted in 1858, the balance of power between Britain and the United States would change, because of "the immense growth of the Union. It is not that we shall decrease, but the States must increase. The stripling, now our equal, must one day be a giant."[12] The *Times* was right. In the 1895–96 Venezuelan crisis, Britain bowed to the United States and embraced the "special relationship," acknowledging US primacy in the Western Hemisphere and courting the friendship of the United States with unilateral concessions.

Could any other foreign power pose a threat to the United States before 1917? Not France after the fall of Napoleon Bonaparte. Napoleon III's foolhardy attempt to establish a vassal state in Mexico was bound to fail because of the Mexicans' resistance and the growing power of Prussia, which meant that the French troops had to return home. The German threat to Latin America was a figment of American imagination. Japan could have threatened only a distant US colony—the Philippines—but Tokyo had no intention of waging war on the United States, despite the Americans' racist provocations.

Through the century-and-half considered in this book, the great European powers had to live in uneasy proximity with each other. Geography ensured that none could aspire to more than relative security. But the United States developed as an island nation—the Atlantic separated it from Europe and a sea of racism separated it from Latin America and Asia. Americans came to believe, Nancy Mitchell writes, "that they deserve absolute security, the security geography blessed them with and ruthlessness secured . . . because they are the last best hope for humankind, the bastion of freedom."[13] This had costs: it fostered intolerance and fueled the tendency to exaggerate threats and then to confront them with violence. Perhaps this helps explain, insofar as any explanation is possible, how in 1915 President Wilson could entertain the absurd notion that the Germans and the French might be cooperating in Haiti.

Empire on the cheap

Not only was there no foreign threat, but white Americans faced neighbors who could not defend themselves, with the exception of the British in Canada.

This points to another mainspring of American exceptionalism: the very low cost of expansion. Native Americans were too few and too divided to effectively challenge the growing colossus. In the early 1790s, they tenaciously resisted the American advance into the Ohio Valley and during the War of 1812 they helped save Upper Canada for the British, who then betrayed them. But after 1815 the imbalance of power—in numbers, weapons and technology—was so crushing that US wars against Native Americans were little more than police actions. In November 1791, the Shawnees and their allies had inflicted a devastating defeat on the US army, killing more than 600 Americans, but after 1815 the Indians' greatest victory was the annihilation of Custer's column of 268 men in 1877. Custer's defeat stunned Americans because in the preceding decades Indian victories had been rare and US casualties light. White America celebrated the conquest of the West as an epic tale of heroic feats, but given the imbalance of power the true heroes were the defeated, the Indians.

The Mexicans' resistance meant that Polk's war lasted one-and-a-half years—rather than the weeks Americans expected—but at no moment was there any doubt about the outcome. Twelve-and-a-half thousand American soldiers died, almost 11,000 of disease—but the United States acquired one-third of Mexico.

In 1898, the United States faced Spain, exhausted by three years of fighting against the Cubans. In the only two land battles of any significance, at El Caney and San Juan Hill, the Spanish inflicted heavy losses on the Americans. The commander of the US army, General Nelson Miles, later wrote, "it is impossible to describe the condition of anxiety that existed in Washington at that time."[14] The Spanish troops could have continued to make the Americans pay a heavy price, but the Spanish government was eager to surrender. The conquest of the Philippines was a one-sided conflict that followed the pattern of European colonial wars. The first time—after 1815—that the United States fought a powerful enemy was in 1918, when the American Expeditionary Force met the German army in France.

Land and racism

What explains US expansion? As Jefferson, the champion of the yeoman farmers, stressed, foreign markets were indispensable for the United States. As the US population grew the yeoman farmers would export their surplus abroad and import the industrial goods they needed, avoiding the ills of manufacturing and urbanization and the class conflicts that scarred Europe.

But the search for markets was not the engine driving the territorial expansion of the United States. In 1784, the *Empress of China* carried the flag of the fledgling United States to mysterious Canton; in 1844 the Treaty of Wanghia opened more Chinese ports to American merchants while the great natural harbors of California—soon to be American—could serve as springboards to the fabled China market. But US trade with China remained minuscule, and the federal government did very little to foster it. As David Pletcher reminds us, until the 1880s, the US consular staff in China was "inadequate ... miserably neglected by a parsimonious, semi-isolationist Congress."[15] Likewise, through the nineteenth century, the US government did very little to spur trade with South America.

The great American market was and remained in Europe, which on average absorbed about 70 percent of American exports in the decades before the Civil War and over 80 percent from 1870 to 1890.[16] Trade with Europe had brought Americans great profits and also dangers during the wars of the French Revolution and the Napoleonic wars, but after 1815 the Atlantic became a majestic and safe highway for American exports, with reliable customers awaiting in Europe. There were at times trade wars with European powers, often provoked by the high tariff walls of the United States, but at no moment was there even a remote hint that the United States or any of its European partners might resort to force to resolve these disputes. Gunboat diplomacy was reserved for the countries of Asia and Latin America.

The settlers who moved into Texas, into California or onto the Indian lands were not pursuing foreign markets. They sought land. The factors fueling US territorial expansion were the growing population; the government eager to acquire land and natural resources for this population; and racism. White Americans felt that they had a right to these lands inhabited by inferior peoples, and their hunger for land faced no sustained, effective resistance. Therefore, it would have been surprising if the United States had not expanded. Bolívar had been prophetic: "There is at the head of this great continent," he warned in 1822, "a very powerful country, very rich, very warlike, and capable of anything."[17] Only when facing a neighbor that could defend itself—Britain's Canada—did the American juggernaut stop. The US Civil War saved Mexico from further amputation: by the time Americans began looking outward again, the Mexican state had consolidated, and the US desire for Mexico's land had been replaced by the search for its commerce and investment opportunities.

A majority of the American business community had opposed war against Spain because it feared that it would be very costly and affect the country's economic recovery. Many shifted after the *Maine* blew up not because they sought new markets but because of domestic politics: they had concluded that continuing opposition to war would lead to a Democratic victory at the polls. But they were reluctant warriors. "It is well known," *Bradstreet's*, a leading business journal, noted on April 23, 1898, "that the representatives of the business interests of the country, mindful of the havoc and destruction and economic derangement which follow in the wake of war, have earnestly hoped for an adjustment of the difficulty which would be compatible with the maintenance of peace."[18]

Victory over Spain led to the conquest of the Philippines. The business community supported the annexation of the archipelago, but the driving forces behind the policy were the supporters of the "large policy"—politicians, intellectuals and military leaders who sought to establish the United States as one of the world's great powers and to reinvigorate the manhood of Americans through martial deeds.

The annexation of the Philippines was no aberration, no sudden fall from anticolonial grace, but part of the continuum that had begun with the arrival of the first settlers in North America. Senator Lodge put it well in a speech about the Philippines: "The record of American expansions . . . has been a long one and today we do but continue the same movement."[19]

In the wake of the war in the Philippines, the United States proceeded to tighten its control over the backyard. US actions were driven by imperial hubris, racism, greed, and by the search for absolute security at virtually no cost. The policy peaked with Wilson's invasions of Haiti and the Dominican Republic. With rare exceptions white Americans approved his actions. Why would they object? The occupations entailed almost no cost in blood or treasure, and they were justified—it was alleged—on humanitarian and strategic grounds: they rescued the hapless black natives from their savagery and protected them, and the United States, from the (nonexistent) German threat. White Americans had been outraged by the Germans' invasion of white, tidy Belgium, declaring it a crime, but Haiti and the Dominican Republic? Here, too, Americans were kin to all the world.

There have been in American history eloquent voices that have decried imperialism. Former president John Quincy Adams warned the House of Representatives in 1836 about war against Mexico: "And what will be your cause in such a war? Aggression, conquest, and the re-establishment of slavery where it has been abolished. In that war . . . the banners of freedom will be the banners of Mexico; and your banners, I blush to speak the word, will be the banners of slavery."[20] Senator George Hoar (R-MA) lashed out at the crimes of the US troops in the Philippines: "We are talking about torture, torture—cold-blooded, deliberate, calculated torture . . . You make the American flag in the eyes of a numerous people the emblem of sacrilege in Christian churches, and of the burning of human dwellings, and of the horror of the water torture."[21] Representative Luther Severance (W-ME), one of the fourteen members of the House who in May 1846 had voted against a war of aggression against Mexico, wrote to the Washington *National Intelligencer*: "I believe the Mexicans upon the Rio Grande have been acting strictly in self-defence, and, if they have made a manly resistance to Gen. Taylor, they are to be honored and applauded for doing so.... The war has not been commenced by Mexico but by the President of the United States, without the authority of Congress and without any necessity."[22] These voices expressed the best of white America. But they fell on deaf ears.

The pariahs

The foreign policy views of the black, brown, or yellow people who inhabited the United States were not relevant to policymakers. But, of course, these views existed. Like American whites, African Americans applauded Japan's victories over Russia, but for different reasons: white Americans saw Japan as the instrument to break the Russian hold over Manchuria and protect the markets of northern China from Russian rapacity; African Americans celebrated the victory of a non-white people over a great white power. But whereas African Americans were united in welcoming Japan's feats, they had sharply disagreed a few years earlier about wars in Cuba and the Philippines. This had been the most vigorous foreign policy debate among African Americans in the period considered in this book. On one side were those who stressed that African Americans should show their loyalty to the United States, in the hope that their eagerness to enlist would soften white racism. On the other side was the minority view, expressed by a black clergyman in August 1899. "There's no place in this infernal country for manly Negroes," Bishop Henry Turner declared, before, the *Colored American* reported, "he strode across the platform shaking his massive head and incubating a sentence which he hurled at 'Old Glory,' saying of it the stars on you belong to the white man, the stripes to the Negro."[23]

But if the views of non-whites were irrelevant to white Americans, race played a key role in US expansion. Racism added an essential moral justification to the wresting of North America from Native Americans and Mexicans. In the years before the Civil War, the clash between free and slave states restrained US expansion beyond its borders. It delayed the annexation of Texas: the free states opposed its entry into the Union because it meant another slave state. It forced Polk to content himself with only one third of Mexico. It stymied the efforts of southerners to push for the annexation of Cuba as a slave state. It derailed President Buchanan's plans to acquire Cuba and more Mexican territory.

Wilsonian idealism

The gap between white Americans' idealized perception of US foreign policy during the country's first 150 years and the reality is evident when one focuses on two pillars of the City on the Hill, Thomas Jefferson and Woodrow Wilson. Generations of Americans have learned in school about the clash in foreign policy between Jeffersonian idealism and Hamiltonian realism. But if we focus on the policy, rather than the rhetoric, where is Jefferson's idealism? Jefferson warmly endorsed Napoleon's plan to crush the fledgling

Haitian state because he feared that Haiti's successful revolt would set an example for the enslaved people of the US South. His lofty words of sympathy for the Native Americans masked his relentless pursuit of their land, acquired through fraud and violence. In order to wrest the Floridas from Spain he was willing to resort to war, bribery and threats. His clashes with Alexander Hamilton over relations with France and England were motivated not by idealism but by his intransigent assertion of US neutral rights, his belief that the United States had the right "to fatten on the folly" of the Old World,[24] and his dogged antipathy to Britain. The embargo revealed his disregard for civil liberties.

Jefferson's idealism resides in his words. He had the gift of enveloping his actions in uplifting rhetoric. Generations of Americans have overlooked Jefferson's policies and remembered his words. This—judge me by what I say, not by what I do—would be Jefferson's greatest contribution to the myth of the City on the Hill.

But what about Woodrow Wilson, the other icon of American idealism in foreign policy? His claim to the mantle of idealism rests on his soaring wartime speeches, his role at Versailles, and the League of Nations.

Wilson went to Versailles bent on creating a new international order in which no nation would seek to dominate another. He offered the Monroe Doctrine as a model. "I am proposing, as it were," he said, "that the nations should with one accord adopt the doctrine of President Monroe as the doctrine of the world; that no nation should seek to extend its polity over any other nation or people." (Mexico, Henry Kissinger writes, "was probably astonished to learn that the president of the country which had seized a third of its territory in the nineteenth century [half, with Texas] ... was now presenting the Monroe Doctrine as a guarantee for the territorial integrity of sister nations and as a classic example of international cooperation.")[25] Wilson's words indicated both his profound myopia about the violent role that the United States had played in inter-American relations, and his belief that the United States, as the richest and the wisest country on earth, should "serve mankind from a position of political and economic preponderance."[26]

But however blurred Wilson's idea about the equality of nations may have been, he did long for a world without war, one in which aggressors would be resisted and punished by the community of nations—hence the League of Nations. The League expressed a noble ideal, tarnished by the fact that it protected the *status quo* established by the victors and by the refusal of Wilson and other white leaders to include in the covenant the statement on racial equality proposed by Japan.[27]

Nevertheless, Wilson's speeches aroused a wave of enthusiasm not only among white Europeans, who longed for peace, but also among the colonial peoples of Africa and Asia. His statements in favor of self-determination stirred deep hopes among the great many who hungered for freedom from foreign rule. As historian Erez Manela writes, Wilson became "for millions worldwide the ... most prominent exponent of the vision ... of a just international order based on the principle of self-determination."[28]

The hope was misplaced. Wilson, himself the president of a colonial power, was a deeply racist man who presided over one of the most racist US administrations since the end of the Civil War. While he spoke of peace in Paris, US marines were hunting guerrillas in Haiti and the Dominican Republic, and white Americans lynched black and brown people in the United States with impunity.

What, then, can we say about Wilsonian idealism? We have his generous dream of a world without war and his violence in the backyard, his soaring speeches and his lack of empathy for nonwhite people, at home and abroad. He was, at best, a very flawed idealist.

The Two Faces of the City on the Hill

If one takes nonwhite people out of the equation, US foreign policy before the First World War appears peaceful, except for the 1812 war against Britain and the brief clash with Spain in 1898. The United States did not seek even an acre of land in Europe, nor did it foist unequal treaties on the European states. Instead, it offered the people of Europe the example of its democracy—the white City on the Hill. It had strong economic ties with European countries, but did not meddle in their internal affairs, and demanded only that they not interfere in the ever-expanding US backyard in Latin America.

But if one includes the nonwhite people in the equation, another side of the United States is exposed. It is the black, brown, yellow, and red peoples who paid the heavy price for the creation of the white City on the Hill. They have inspired this book.

NOTES

1 Independence

Page 1

1. Fred Anderson, *Crucible*; Dziembowski, *La guerre*. Also Havard and Vidal, *Histoire*.

Page 2

2. Benjamin Franklin to William Franklin, Aug. 28, 1767, *PBF*, 14: 244. For a survey of the period covered in this chapter see Middlekauff, *Glorious*; Taylor, *Revolutions*; Dull, *Miracle*.

3. Wells, "Population," 39–41.

4. Burner, *Empire*, 17.

5. On the British regiments, Greene, "War" and Shy, *Toward Lexington*; on the Indian revolt, Fred Anderson, *Crucible*, 535–71, 617–37.

Page 3

6. Quoted by Freeman, *Washington*, 3: 123.

7. Quotations from Morgan and Morgan, *Stamp Act*, 207 and Draper, *Struggle*, 258.

8. Morgan and Morgan, *Stamp Act*, 187–8, 137. The best accounts of the social tensions of the day are Nash, *Unknown* and Taylor, *Revolutions*.

9. Crane, "Dependence," 257.

Page 4

10. Thomas, *Townshend Duties*.

11. Zobel, *Massacre*; Hinderhaker, *Massacre*.

12. Tucker and Hendrickson, *Fall of the British Empire*, 306 quoted; Burner, *Empire*, 50–161.

13. Nash, *Unknown*, 130.

14. Chernow, *Washington*, 107.

Page 5

15. Burner, *Empire*, 188.

16. Carp, *Defiance*; Labaree, *Tea Party*.

17. Labaree, *Tea Party*, 143.

18. Quoted by Valentine, *North*, 1: 322.

19. Quoted by Draper, *Struggle*, 278.

Page 6

20. Middlekauff, *Glorious*, 264–5.

21. "A Proclamation by the King for Suppressing Rebellion and Sedition," Aug. 23, 1775, in Commager, *Documents*, 1: 96.

22. O'Shaughnessy, *Empire*.

23. Rutledge to Izard, Dec. 8, 1775, in Izard, ed., *Correspondence*, 165 quoted; Alan Gilbert, *Black*, 15–45; Selby, *Revolution*, 55–79; Holton, *Forced*, 133–63; Schama, *Rough*, 59–88.

24. Samuel Johnson, *Works*, 14: 144.

25. The Committee of Secret Correspondence: Instructions to Silas Deane, March 3, 1776, *PBF*, 22: 369–74.

Page 7

26. Véri, *Journal*, 1: 113. The best biographies of Louis XVI are Petitfils, *Louis XVI*, and Hardman, *Life*.

27. Vergennes to Louis XVI, "Exposé Succint de la Situation Politique de l'Europe," Dec. 8, 1774, AAE, M&D, vol. 584. The best biographies of Vergennes are Labourdette, *Vergennes*, and Murphy, *Vergennes*.

28. Vergennes, "Mémoire pour servir d'instructions au Sieur baron de Breteuil . . .," Dec. 28, 1774, in Sorel, *Recueil*, 1: 478.

29. Vergennes to Garnier, Jan. 15, 1775, AAE, CP, Angleterre, vol. 508.

30. Vergennes to Guines, Aug. 7, 1775, AAE, CP, Angleterre, vol. 511.

31. Bonvouloir to Guines, Dec. 28, 1775, in Doniol, *Histoire*, 1: 287–92.

32. Dull, *French Navy*, 31. This is the best book on the Franco-American minuet discussed in this chapter.

Page 8

33. Vergennes to Grimaldi, March 1, 1776, in Doniol, *Histoire*, 1: 370; Vergennes to Louis XVI, "Considérations," March 12, 1776, AAE, CP, Angleterre, supplement, vol. 18; Véri, *Journal*, March 12, 1776, 1: 428.

34. Petitfils, *Louis XVI*, 369, 339, 372; Louis XVI, quoted by Soulavie, *Mémoires*, 3: 348.

35. "Réflexions redigées à l'occasion d'un mémoire remis par de Vergennes au Roi . . .," April 6, 1776, in Schelle, ed., *Oeuvres*, 5: 384–420, quotes 406 and 419.

36. Grimaldi to Vergennes, March 14, 1776, AAE, CP, Espagne, vol. 579. On Spain and American independence see Yela Utrilla, *España*; Konetzke, *Politik*; Chávez, *Spain*.

37. Hardman and Price, eds., *Louis XVI*, 41; Vergennes to Louis XVI, May 2, 1776, ibid, 227. In this book all conversions to 2021 dollars are based on the US Inflation Calculator, Department of Labor.

Page 9

38. For the Model Treaty, see Ford, ed., *Journals*, 5: 568–78; "Instructions to the Agent," Sept. 24, 1776, ibid., 813–17. On US diplomacy during the war Felix Gilbert, *Farewell*; Dull, *Diplomatic History*; Hutson, *John Adams*; Stinchcombe, *American*; Hoffman and Albert, eds., *Diplomacy*.

39. Herring, *Colony*, 17.

40. Franklin, Deane, and Lee to Vergennes, Jan. 5, 1777, *PBF*, 23: 122–4.

Page 10

41. Deane to Vergennes, March 18, 1777, ibid., 503–5.

42. Franklin to Aranda, April 7, 1777, ibid., 562–3.

43. Felix Gilbert, *Farewell*, 67.

44. Vergennes to Aranda, April 10, 1777, AAE, CP, Espagne, vol. 584.

45. "The American Commissioners: Receipt for Money from the French Treasury," Jan. 17, 1777, *PBF*, 23: 198–9.

Page 11

46. Dull, *French Navy*, 75–83; Fowler, *Rebels*, 127–48.

47. Herring, *Colony*, 21.

48. Diesbach, *Necker*, 163–4; Labourdette, *Vergennes*, 151.

49. Véri, *Journal*, Fall 1777, 1: 522–3.

50. Louis XVI to Vergennes, Dec. 6, 1777, in Vergennes to Montmorin, Dec. 11, 1777, AAE, CP, Espagne, vol. 587.

51. Konetzke, *Politik*, 146.

52. Montmorin to Vergennes, Dec. 23, 1777, AAE, CP, Espagne, vol. 587.

53. "Lû au Roi le 7 janv 1778 et envoyé en Espagne le lendemain," AAE, CP, Espagne, vol. 588.

54. Dull, "France and the American Revolution Seen as Tragedy," in Hoffman and Albert, eds., *Diplomacy*, 94.

55. Quoted by Rulhière, *Portrait*, 64.

Page 12

56. Vergennes to Montmorin, Dec. 13, 1777, AAE, CP, Espagne, vol. 587.

57. Hardman and Price, eds., *Louis XVI*, 59.

58. Hardman, *Life*, 125.

59. The treaties are printed in *PBF*, 25: 585–626.

Page 13

60. Dull, "France," 94–5.

61. Vergennes, "Réflexions," [April 1776], AAE, CP, Angleterre, Supplement, vol.18.

62. Bemis, *Diplomacy*, 255. On the war Mackesy, *War*; Higginbotham, *War*; Shy, *A People*; Ferling, *Miracle*. For a French perspective, Chaline et al., eds., *La France*.

63. Starkey, *European*, 113. For the number of native Americans Ostler, *Surviving*, 190.

64. White, *Middle Ground*, 384.

Page 14

65. Shy, "American Society," 82.

66. Higginbotham, "Reflections," 16.

67. Men of "the middling sort" is from Ellis, *Excellency*, 113.

68. In recent years several excellent books on the African Americans' role in the war have appeared, among them Alan Gilbert, *Black*; Nash, *Forgotten*; Schama, *Rough*; Frey, *Water*; Pybus, *Epic*; Egerton, ed., *Death*. Quarle's pathbreaking *Negro* is still valuable.

69. Quotations from Chernow, *Washington*, 333 and Laurens to Washington, May 19, 1782, in Massey, *John Laurens*, 208. Also Wienchek, *Imperfect*, 197–205, 218–36.

Page 15

70. Higginbotham, "American Militia," 93.

71. Kaplan and Kaplan, *Black*, 64–9; Nash, *Unknown*, 228–31; Morgan and O'Shaugnessy, "Slaves."

72. Lanning, *African Americans*, 130–52.

73. For the text of the proclamation, ibid., 209.

74. Bemis, *Diplomacy*, 93; *PBF*, 37: 633–5 and 39: 301–2 (loans only).

Page 16

75. Mackesy, *War*, 381–2, 388–94; Dull, *French Navy*, 224–6.

76. Ketchum, *Victory*, 228–9.

77. Washington to Morris, Sept. 6, 1781, in Wharton, ed., *Revolutionary*, 4: 699; also Brant, *Madison*, 2: 163–4.

78. Flexner, *Washington*, 2: 454 quoted; Bourgerie and Lesouef, *Yorktown*; Chernow, *Washington*, 398–422; Mackesy, *War*, 420–7.

79. Quoted by Acomb, ed., *Revolutionary*, 92.

80. Quoted by Parkinson, *Common*, 517.

81. Schama, *Rough*, 123 quoted; Pybus, *Epic*, 52–5; Taylor, *Enemy*, 28; Nash, *Forgotten*, 38.

82. Alan Gilbert, *Black*, 260 n. 1.

Page 17

83. Lanning, *African Americans*, 166–72, 197–8; Zilversmit, *First*.

84. "Instructions to the Commissioners for Peace," June 15, 1781, in Wharton, ed., *Revolutionary*, 4: 504–5.

85. Hoffman and Albert, eds., *Peace*; Harlow, *Founding*, 1: 223–407.

86. Quoted by Calloway, *American Revolution*, 174.

87. Downes, *Council Fires*, 276 quoted; White, *Middle Ground*, 366–412; Dowd, *Spirited*, 65–89; Graymont, *Iroquois*.

Page 18

88. Vergennes to Luzerne, Dec. 19, 1872, AAE, CP, États-Unis, vol. 22.

89. Franklin to Morris, Dec. 23, 1782, *PBF*, 38: 488.

90. Wood, *Americanization*, 171, 180.

91. Dull, *Franklin*, 91.

92. Burt, *United States*, 59 quoted; Ritcheson, *Aftermath*, 3–32.

Page 19

93. Ritcheson, *Aftermath*, 36–7.

94. Jasanoff, *Exiles*, 351–8.

95. Chernow, *Washington*, 442 quoted; Wienchek, *Imperfect*, 253–9; Pybus, *Epic*, 57–72; Frey, *Water*, 172–205; Alan Gilbert, *Black*, 177–206; Schama, *Rough*, 127–56.

96. Willig, *Restoring*, 11–30; Allen, *Allies*, 56–71. For the list of the posts, Bemis, *Treaty*, 3.

97. Adams to Jay, Feb. 14, 1788, in Charles Francis Adams, ed., *Works*, 8: 476.

98. Scott Jackson, "Impressment," 59.

99. Adams to Jefferson, Oct. 3, 1785, *PTJ*, 8: 577.

Page 20

100. Ferling, *First*.

101. Quotations from Ellis, *Excellency*, 35, 74. On Washington's generalship, Freeman, *Washington*, vols. 3–5; Flexner, *Washington*; Higginbotham, *Washington*; Lengel, *Washington*.

102. Cunliffe, "Washington," 10.

103. Higginbotham, *War*, 88.

104. Chernow, *Washington*, 404.

Page 21

105. Ellis, *Excellency*, 146; Washington quoted in ibid.

2 The Federalist Era

Page 23

1. Taylor, *American Revolutions*, 358.

2. US Department of Commerce, *Historical*, 1: 14, 33, 36; Berlin, *Slaves*, 46. The Virginia statistic includes West Virginia.

3. Hinderaker, *Elusive*, 267.

4. Montesquieu, *Spirit*, 120.

5. "Farewell Address," Sept. 17, 1796, in James Richardson, ed., *Compilation*, 1: 216.

6. Horsman, "On to," 8.

Page 24

7. Malone, *Jefferson*, 2: 473. Even though biased in favor of his subject, Malone's six volume biography, *Jefferson and His Time*, is indispensable; see also Peterson, *Jefferson*; Onuf, *Empire*; Ellis, *Sphinx*. Other key works on Jefferson will be cited in this and the next two chapters.

8. Quotations from Miller, *Federalist*, 111, 112.

Page 25

9. Jefferson, *Notes*, 164–5.

10. For an excellent discussion of Jeffersonian views about political economy, see McCoy, *Elusive*, 127 quoted.

11. Gordon-Reed and Onuf, *"Blessed,"* 129.

Page 26

12. Quoted by Nash, *Forgotten*, 104.

13. Berlin, *Slaves*, 46; US Department of Commerce, *Historical*, 1: 36.

14. Jefferson, *Notes*, 162.

15. Davis, *Problem*, 174.

16. Elkins and McKitrick, *Age*, 198. This is the best study of US foreign policy in the 1790s.
17. Finkelman, "Jefferson," 204.
18. McCullough, *Adams*, 319.
19. Elkins and McKitrick, *Age*, 72–3.
20. Henriques, *Realistic*, 127.

Page 27

21. The best biography of Hamilton is Chernow, *Hamilton*.

Page 28

22. Combs, *Treaty*, 103.
23. Jefferson to Lafayette, June 16, 1792, *PTJ*, 24:85; Jefferson to Short, Jan. 3, 1793, *PTJ*, 25: 14–15.
24. Miller, *Federalist*, 127.
25. Jefferson to Hammond, May 29, 1792, *PTJ*, 23: 551–614. Also Elkins and McKitrick, *Age*, 244–56; Ritcheson, *Aftermath*, 141–4.

Page 29

26. Calloway, *Victory*, 32–3 quoted; White, *Middle Ground*, 413–68. Until 1792, when it became a state, Kentucky was a county of Virginia.
27. Pickering to Washington, Dec. 4, 1790, PGW: PS, 7: 28; St. Clair to Knox, Jan. 27, 1788, quoted by White, *Middle Ground*, 418.
28. Washington to Duane, Sept. 7, 1783, in Fitzpatrick, ed, *Writings*, 27: 139–40. The best book on Washington's Indian policy is Calloway, *World*. For an excellent essay, Sheehan, "Problem."
29. Pickering to Washington, March 21, 1792, enclosed in Pickering to Hamilton, May 8, 1792, *PAH*, 11:377, emphasis in original.
30. Knox to St. Clair, Sept. 14, 1790, in William Smith, ed., *Papers*, 2: 181.
31. The best accounts of these campaigns are Calloway, *Victory*; Sugden, *Blue Jacket*; Sword, *President*, 79–195; Kohn, *Eagle*, 73–116.

Page 30

32. Willig, *Restoring*, 11–58; Allen, *Allies*, 56–86. There are several good biographies of senior members of the Indian department. The best is Horsman, *Elliott*. Also by Horsman two excellent articles on the British Indian Department (see bibliography).
33. Millett, Maskowski and Feis, *For*, 84–6.
34. Elkins and McKitrick, *Age*, 336–41 (339 quoting Hamilton); Chernow, *Hamilton*, 431–7; Washington, "A Proclamation," April 22, 1793, in Commager, *Documents*, 1: 163.

Page 31

35. Jefferson to Madison, June 23, 1793 (emphasis in original) and Aug. 11, 1793, *PTJ*, 26: 346, 652. Also Ammon, *Genet*.
36. Scott Jackson, "Impressment," 1 quoted. For the Royal Navy's manpower needs, Rodger, *Command*, 442–4.
37. Jefferson to Rutledge, July 4, 1790, PTJ, 16: 601.
38. Grenville to Hammond, March 12, 1793, TNA, FO 115/2.

Page 32

39. "Report on Commerce," Dec. 16, 1793, *PTJ*, 27: 532–78.

40. Elkins and McKitrick, *Age*, 375–88.

41. Cunningham, *Republicans*, 67–76; Martis, *Atlas*, 72.

42. "From Lord Dorchester to the Seven Nations of Lower Canada," Feb. 10, 1794, in Cruikshank, ed., *Correspondence*, 2: 149–50.

43. Elkins and McKitrick, *Age*, 393–5.

44. Chernow, *Hamilton*, 459.

Page 33

45. Until 1893 the United States did not have ambassadors, considering the title too ostentatious and aristocratic. The highest rank was minister. In 1893, Congress authorized the appointment of ambassadors. That same year ambassadors were exchanged first with Britain and then also with France, Germany and Italy, Before the First World War, ambassadors were also exchanged with seven more of the nearly fifty countries with which the United States entertained diplomatic relations: Russia, Austria, Spain, Turkey, Japan, Mexico and Brazil (Plischke, *U.S.*, 211–12).

46. Madison to Jefferson, May 11, 1794, *PTJ*, 28: 73.

47. The best studies of the Jay Treaty are Combs, *Treaty* and Bemis, *Treaty*. For an excellent synopsis Trautsch, *Genesis*, 71–106.

48. Ritcheson, *Aftermath*, 326 quoted; Ehrman, *Pitt*. 2: 511–16.

Page 34

49. Perkins, *First*, 73.

50. US Department of Commerce, *Historical*, 2: 905.

51. Jefferson to Giles, Apr. 27, 1795, *PTJ*, 28: 337.

52. On the French Navy in the 1790s see Réné, *Histoire*, 173–235; Monaque, *Une histoire*, 218–55; Dull, *Age*, 118–60; Acerra and Meyer, *Marines*.

Page 35

53. Allen, *Allies*, 83 quoted; Sugden, *Blue Jacket*, 128–207; Hogeland, *Autumn*.

54. Sword, *President*, 324.

55. Monroe to Madison, Dec. 18, 1794, *PJMO*, 3: 187–8.

56. See the relevant letters in Johnston, ed., *Correspondence*, 4: 26–144.

57. Flexner, *Washington*, 4: 207.

58. Ehrman, *Pitt*, 2: 515 n.2.

Page 36

59. *Aurora* (Philadelphia), July 4, 1795, 2.

60. Madison, Apr. 15, 1796, *Annals*, 4th Cong., 1st sess., 977.

61. Jefferson to Rutledge, Nov. 30, 1795, *PTJ*, 28: 542.

62. For the public debate about the treaty, see Estes, *Debate*.

63. Camillus [Hamilton], "The Defence," no. 7, Aug. 12, 1795, *PAH*, 19: 123.

64. Camillus, "The Defence." no. 2, July 25, 1795, *PAH*, 18: 498, 499.

65. Jefferson to Madison, Sept. 21, 1795, *PTJ*, 28: 475–6.

Page 37

66. Jefferson to Mazzei, Apr. 24, 1796, *PTJ*, 29: 81–3.

67. Jefferson to Madison, Aug. 3, 1797, *PTJ*, 29: 490.

68. Cunningham, *Republicans*, 76–88; Martis, *Atlas*, 73.

69. Feldman, *Three*, 402.

70. Madison, Apr. 15, 1796, *Annals*, 4th Cong., 1st sess., 976–87.

Page 38

71. Bécker, *Historia política*, 81 quoted; Whitaker, *Frontier*, 185–222; Bemis, *Pinckney's Treaty*.

72. Wood, *Empire*, 201.

73. Quoted by Cunningham, *Republicans*, 97.

74. Washington, "Farewell Address," in James Richardson, ed., *Compilation*, 1: 221–3.

75. Ibid., 222.

Page 39

76. Bowman, *Struggle*, 228–61.

77. *Aurora*, Oct. 11, 1796, 3.

78. Portius, *Aurora*, Oct. 11, 1796, 2.

79. *Gazette of the United States*, Nov. 16, 1796, 3. For Adet's two broadsides, see *Aurora*, Oct. 31, 1796, 3 and *Claypoole's American Daily Advertiser* (Philadelphia), Nov. 19, 1796, 3.

80. *Aurora*, March 4, 1797, 3.

81. Ellis, *Excellency*, 226. Other key biographies of Washington are Chernow, *Washington*; Ferling, *First*; Flexner, *Washington*; Freeman, *Washington*; Henriques, *Realistic*.

82. Chernow, *Washington*, 770.

Page 40

83. Ibid., 758, 490.

84. See Ferling, *Adams*; McCullough, *Adams*; DeConde, *Quasi-War*; Bowman, *Struggle*; Perkins, *First*; Palmer, *War*; Trautsch, *Genesis*, 107–67; Bonnell, *La France*, 48–116.

85. Adams, May 16, 1797, in James Richardson, ed., *Compilation*, 1: 233–9.

86. On US military policy in the 1790s see Toll, *Six*, 5–143; Kohn, *Eagle*; Smelser, *Congress*. On the instructions to the envoys, Bowman, *Struggle*, 286–7.

Page 41

87. Létombe to foreign minister Delacroix, June 7, 1797, AAE, CP, États-Unis, vol. 47; Jefferson to Randolph, Jan. 11, 1798, *PTJ*, 30: 25.

88. Pallain, ed., *Le ministère*, 309.

89. The most detailed account of the mission is Stinchcombe, *XYZ*. Also Poniatowski, *Talleyrand et le Directoire*, 540–80 and Waresquiel, *Talleyrand*, 287–92.

90. Quoted by Elkins and McKitrick, *Age*, 585.

91. Adams, March 19, 1798, in James Richardson, ed., *Compilation*, 1: 264–5.

92. Jefferson to Madison, March 21, 1798, *PTJ*, 30: 189.

93. Jefferson to Madison, April 6, 1798, *PTJ*, 30: 251.

Page 42

94. Jefferson to Eppes, April 11, 1798, *PTJ*, 30: 263.

95. Jefferson to Madison, April 6, 1798, *PTJ*, 30: 250 quoted; Jefferson to Eppes, April 11, 1798, ibid., 263; Jefferson to Carr, April 12, 1798, ibid., 267; Jefferson to Randolph, April 12, 1798, ibid., 269.

96. Jefferson to Madison, March 21 and 29, 1978, *PTJ*, 30: 190, 227.

97. Palmer, *War*, 6, 74.

98. DeConde, *Quasi-War*, 126–7 quoted; Smelser, *Congress*, 160–77.

Page 43

99. McCullough, *Adams*, 501–2; Abigail Adams to Mary Cranch, July 9, 1798, in Stewart Mitchell, ed., *New*, 201.

100. Ferling, *Adams*, 370.

101. Perkins, *First*, 96.

102. Palmer, *War*, 141 quoted; Demerliac, *La marine*, 288–308.

103. See for example Réné, *Histoire*; Monaque, *Une histoire*; Acerra and Meyer, *Marines*.

104. See John Adams to Abigail, Feb. 25, 1799, in Hogan and Taylor, eds., *My*, 463–4.

105. Adams, Feb. 18, 1799, in James Richardson, ed., *Compilation*, 1: 282–3.

106. Palmer, *War*, 130; DeConde, *Quasi-War*, 130.

Page 44

107. Adams, Feb. 18, 1799, in James Richardson, ed., *Compilation*, 1: 282–3.

108. Bonnel, *La France*, 114; Palmer, *War*, 192–232.

Page 45

109. US Department of Commerce, *Historical*, 1: 14; Berlin, *Slaves*, 45.

110. Freehling, *Road*, 147.

111. *Mercury and New-England Palladium* (Boston), Jan. 20, 1801, 2.

3 The Louisiana Purchase

Page 47

1. Peterson, *Jefferson*, 687.

2. Jefferson, March 4, 1801, in James Richardson, ed., *Compilation*, 1: 323.

3. The best biography of Madison is Brant's multi-volume (and sympathetic) *Madison*, but see also Rakove, *Madison*; Ralph Ketcham, *Madison*; Rutland, *Madison*. On Gallatin, Gregory May, *Jefferson's Treasure*.

4. Martis, *Atlas*, 76.

5. The best overviews of Jefferson's foreign policy are Cogliano's sympathetic *Emperor* and Tucker's and Hendrickson's critical *Empire*.

6. See Lambert, *Wars*; Toll, *Frigates*, 164–263; Reid, *Derne*; Ellsworth, *Marines*, 157–9.

Page 48

7. Jefferson to Adams, July 11, 1786, *PTJ*, 10: 123.

8. Cogliano, *Emperor*, 170.

Page 49

9. DeConde, *Affair*; LaFeber, *American Age*, 53; Cogliano, *Emperor*, 203.

10. Lentz, *Consulat*, 479.

Page 50

11. DeConde, *Affair*, 98.

12. The best books on the Haitian revolution are Girard, *Toussaint*; Pluchon, *Toussaint*; Geggus, *Slavery*; Fick, *Making*; James' classic *Black*. For the background, Gliech, *Saint-Domingue*.

Page 51

13. Otto to Talleyrand, Oct. 23, 1801, AAE, CP, Angleterre, vol. 597.

14. *The Times* (London), Oct. 26, 1801, 2; *Cobbett's Annual Register* (London), Jan. 16, 1802, 42–4; *Morning Post and Gazetteer* (London), Oct. 24, 1801, 2. For a representative sample see Gleijeses, "Napoleon," 249, n. 12.

15. Toussaint to Adams, Nov. 6, 1798, NA, RG 59, DOS, Consular Despatches, Cap Haitien, vol. 1, no. 168.

16. Quotations from Pickering to Mayer, June 27, 1798, ibid., no. 0011 and Nov. 30, 1798, ibid., no. 0024. The best book on the Adams administration and Haiti is Ronald Johnson, *Diplomacy*.

17. Jefferson to Madison, Jan. 30 and Feb. 12, 1799, *PTJ*, 30: 665 and 31: 29.

Page 52

18. Pichon to Talleyrand, July 22, 1801, AAE, CP, États-Unis, vol. 53.

19. Peterson, *Jefferson*, 749; Malone, *Jefferson*, 4: 252.

20. Jefferson to Randolph, May 14, 1801, *PTJ*, 34:111; Jefferson to Monroe, May 26, 1801, ibid., 186. For the diplomats' reports, Humphreys to Madison, March 23, 1801, *PJM: SSS*, 1: 36; King to Madison, March 29, 1801, ibid., 55–6.

21. Jefferson, *Notes*, 163; Miller, *Wolf*, 126; Jefferson to Holmes, April 22, 1820, in Paul Leicester Ford, ed., *Works*, 12: 159.

22. Jefferson to Burr, Feb. 11, 1799, *PTJ*, 31: 22.

23. Jefferson to Madison, Feb. 12, 1799, ibid., 30; Monroe to Jefferson, Sept. 15, 1800, ibid., 32: 144.

24. John Randolph to Nicholson, Sept. 26, 1800, quoted by Kirk, *Randolph*, 162. The figure of twenty-five is from Nicholls, *Whispers*, 156–8.

25. Jefferson to King, July 13, 1802, *PTJ*, 38: 54.

Page 53

26. Pichon to Talleyrand, July 22, 1801, AAE, CP, États-Unis, vol. 53.

27. King to Madison, Nov. 20, 1801, *PJM: SSS*, 2: 254. Livingston to King, Dec. 30, 1801, quoted, in *American State Papers, 1789–1828: Foreign Relations*, 2: 512.

28. Madison to Pinckney, May 11, 1802, *PJM: SSS*, 3: 215.

29. DeConde, *Affair*, 101; LaFeber, *American Age*, 53 and 66 n.30. At the end of a long paragraph that discusses inter alia the administration's alleged aid to the Haitians, LaFeber lists three sources: DeConde's *Affair*; Lyon, *Louisiana*; and a January 18, 1803 letter from Madison to Livingston. Neither Lyon nor Madison refer to any assistance to the Haitians.

30. Gordon Brown, *Clause*, 205–6, 214–17; Auguste and Auguste, *L'expédition*, 47–8.

31. Madison to Livingston, 28 Sept. 1801, in *PJM: SSS*, 2: 145.

32. In 1791, the future federal city was named Washington, and the district in which it would be located the Territory of Columbia. For simplicity, in the notes I consistently refer to Washington DC.

Page 54

33. Jefferson to Livingston, April 18, 1802, *PTJ*, 37: 263–6.

34. Tucker and Hendrickson, *Empire*, 114.

35. Lord Hawkesbury's speech is printed in *The Times*, May 14, 1802, 2–4, 3 quoted.

36. *The Times*, May 13, 1802, 3 (edit.).

37. Whitworth to Hawkesbury, Feb. 7, 1803, in Browning, ed., *England*, 60.

38. Pichon to Talleyrand, Jan. 2, 1802, AAE, CP, États-Unis, vol. 54.

39. Poniatowski, *Talleyrand et le Consulat*, 631–2.

Page 55

40. Girard, *Slaves*, 76.

41. Livingston to Madison, Aug. 16, 1802, *PJM: SSS*, 3: 492.

42. Livingston to Madison, Feb. 18, 1803, ibid., 4: 328.

43. Poniatowski, *Talleyrand et le Consulat*, 636–7; DeConde, *Affair*, 165–7; Garnier, *Bonaparte*, 135.

44. Quotations from the *Columbian Centinel* (Boston), Feb. 17, 1802, 2 and the *Gazette of the United States* (Philadelphia), Feb. 17, 1802, 3.

45. *National Intelligencer*, Dec. 31, 1802, 3.

46. *National Intelligencer*, March 14, 1803, 3 and March 16, 1803, 3.

47. *Aurora* (Philadelphia), Feb. 15, 1803, 2.

48. *Gazette of the United States*, Dec. 21, 1802, 3.

Page 56

49. Jefferson to Randolph, Jan. 17, 1803, *PTJ*, 39: 341.

50. Mary Adams, "Reaction," 174, 176, [178].

51. Jefferson to Harrison, Feb. 27, 1803, *PTJ*, 39: 591 quoted; Jefferson to Dearborn, Dec. 29, 1802, ibid., 231–3; Jefferson to Dearborn, Feb. 15, 1803, ibid., 529; Jefferson to Clairborne, May 24, 1803, ibid., 40: 422–4.

Indiana Territory was the old Northwest Territory minus Ohio, which became a separate territory in 1800, and the country's 17th state in 1803.

52. Crackel, *Army*, 36–45; Malone, *Jefferson*, 4: 249 quoted.

Page 57

53. Madison to Livingston and Monroe, April 18, 1803, *PJM: SSS*, 4: 527–32, 530 quoted.

54. DeConde, *Affair*, 144.

55. Lyon, *Louisiana*, 135; Tucker and Hendrickson, *Empire*, 121.

56. Barbé-Marbois, *Histoire*, 201.

57. "Les Consuls de la République aux habitants de Saint-Domingue," Nov. 8, 1801, in Roussier, ed., *Lettres*, 62–3.

58. Mézière and Jourquin, 'Le général," 27. The 19,500 figure in the text includes 3,600 soldiers who arrived in late March and early April (Girard, *Slaves*, 114).

Page 58

59. Leclerc to Napoleon, Aug. 6, 1802, in Roussier, ed. *Lettres*, 202; Leclerc to Decrès, Aug. 9, 1802, ibid., 206.

60. Leclerc to Decrès, Aug. 25, 1802, ibid., 219.

61. Auguste and Auguste, *L'expédition*, 312.

62. Lacroix, *Mémoires*, 2: 171.

63. Ott, *Revolution*, 178 quoted; Fleming, *Louisiana*, 152; Tucker and Hendrickson, *Empire*, 130; Scherr, *Policy*, 269, n. 71.

64. Admiral Latouche-Tréville to Admiral Villaret, April 25, 1803, quoted by Monaque, *Latouche-Tréville*, 529.

Page 59

65. Rochambeau, quoted by Branda and Lentz, eds., *Napoléon*, 330.

66. Girard, *Slaves*, 244.

67. Rochambeau, quoted by Auguste and Auguste, *L'expédition*, 272.

68. La Gravière, *Souvenirs*, 2: 78–110.

69. [Sansay,] *Secret*, 34.

70. Girard, *Slaves*, 343; Monaque, *Latouche-Tréville*, 510–11.

71. Peyre-Ferry, *Journal*, 237.

72. Napoleon to Rochambeau, no. 7460, Feb. 4, 1803, in Napoléon Bonaparte, *Correspondance générale. IV*, 44–5.

73. Napoleon to Decrès, no. 7528, March 18, 1803, ibid., 77.

74. Tulard, *Empire*, 63.

75. Poniatowski, *Talleyrand et le Consulat*, 576.

76. Whitworth to Hawkesbury, Feb. 21, 1803, in Browning, ed., *England*, 78–85, 82 quoted.

Page 60

77. Lentz, *Consulat*, 464.

78. Poniatowski, *Talleyrand et le Consulat*, 631–2; Barbé-Marbois, *Histoire*, 301.

79. Barbé-Marbois, *Histoire*, 285–7.

80. Branda, *Le prix*, 255–8.

81. DeConde, *Affair*, 169.

Page 61

82. Monroe to Madison, April 19, 1803, *PJM: SSS*, 4: 538.

83. Livingston and Monroe to Madison, June 7, 1803, ibid., 5: 69.

84. Lentz, *Napoléon*, 215.

Page 62

85. "Secret Instructions for the Captain-General of Louisiana, Approved by the First Consul," Nov. 26, 1802, in Robertson, ed., *Louisiana*, 1: 371.

86. Barbé-Marbois, *Histoire*, 219; Tulard, *Empire*, 61.

87. Jefferson to Stuart, Jan. 25, 1786, *PTJ*, 9: 218; Monroe to Jefferson, June 15, 1801, *PTJ*, 34: 344–6; Jefferson to Monroe, Nov. 24, 1801, *PTJ*, 35: 719–20.

88. Jefferson to Clark, Dec. 25, 1780, *PTJ*, 4: 237.

89. Jefferson to Priestly, Jan. 29, 1804, *PTJ*, 42: 369; Jefferson, March 4, 1805, in James Richardson, ed., *Compilation*, 1: 379.

Page 63

90. Tucker and Hendrickson, *Empire*, 312–13.

91. Peterson, *Jefferson*, 789.

92. Foster to his mother, Dec. 30, 1804, in Parr, "Foster," 97.

93. Bradford Perkins, *Prologue*, 37.

94. Martis, *Atlas*, 78.

Page 64

95. Hamilton to Jay, March 14, 1779, *PAH*, 2: 18.

96. Hamilton, "Purchase of Louisiana," July 5, 1803, *PAH*, 26: 130.

97. Chernow, *Hamilton*, 4.

4 Jefferson's Second Term

Page 66

1. Jefferson to Madison, July 5, 1804, *PJM: SSS*, 7: 421.

2. Malone, *Jefferson*, 4: 309.

3. Livingston to Madison: Apr. 24, 1802, *PJM: SSS*, 3: 156; Sept. 1, ibid., 3: 536; Nov. 2, ibid., 4: 79; Nov. 11, ibid, 115; Dec. 20, ibid., 204; Feb. 18, 1803, ibid., 330; March 3, ibid., 385; Apr. 11, ibid., 500–1; May 12, ibid., 591–2; May 20, ibid., 5: 18–20.

4. Monroe to Madison: May 18, 1803, ibid., 5: 12–13, and May 23, 1803, ibid., 24–5.

5. Pinckney to Madison: March 20, 1802, ibid., 3: 54; April 20, ibid., 143, 145; May 24, ibid., 249, 254; July 1, ibid., 354–5; Nov. 6, ibid., 4: 88; May 4, 1803, ibid., 571.

6. Malone, *Jefferson*, 4: 309.

Page 67

7. Monroe to Madison, April 19, 1803, *PJM: SSS*, 4: 538.

8. Franco-Spanish convention, Jan. 4, 1805, in Davenport and Paullin, eds., *Treaties*, 4: 189.

9. Jefferson to Bowdoin, April 27, 1805, in Ford, ed., *Works*, 10: 140. For an authoritative Spanish view of Jefferson and Spain, see Bécker, *Historia de las relaciones*, 1: 110–43.

10. Jefferson to Madison, Aug. 4 and 27, 1805, *PJM: SSS*, 10: 166–7, 247 (emphasis in original).

11. See the correspondence of Monroe and Pinckney with Spanish Foreign Minister Cevallos in February–May 1805 in *PJMO*, vol. 5.

12. Madison to Jefferson, Sept. 30, 1805, *PJM: SSS*, 10: 387; Jefferson to Madison, Aug. 27, 1805, ibid., 247.

13. Gallatin to Jefferson, Sept. 12, 1805, in Henry Adams, ed., *Writings*, 1: 241–54.

14. Jefferson to Madison, Oct. 11, 1805, *PJM: SSS*, 10: 421. Emphasis in original. On relations with France see Egan, *Neither* and Peter Hill, *Troublesome*.

Page 68

15. Armstrong to Madison, Sept. 10, 1805, *PJM: SSS*, 10: 313–14; Jefferson to Madison, Oct. 23, 1805, ibid., 461 quoted.

16. Jefferson, "Confidential message on Spain," Dec. 6, 1805, in Ford, ed., *Works*, 10: 198–205, 205 quoted.

17. Peterson, *Jefferson*, 686, 690.

18. House, Jan. 11, 1806, *Annals*, 9th Congress, 1st sess., Supplementary Journal, 1120–3; Senate, Feb. 13, 1806, ibid., 1226–7. See also the exchange of letters between Gallatin and Jefferson, Dec. 3–7, 1805, in Henry Adams, ed., *Writings*, 1: 275–82.

19. Eppes, Feb. 24, 1806, *Annals*, House, 9th Cong., 1st sess. (Washington DC: Gales and Seaton, 1852), col. 499; Pickering to Jefferson, Feb. 24, 1806, emphasis in original, in Hickey, "Pickering," 158, 160.

Page 69

20. Quotations from Madison to Armstrong and Bowdoin, March 13, 1806, *PJM: SSS*, 11: 382, 380.

21. Jefferson to William Short, July 8, 1806, *Founders Online*, www.founders.archives.gov.

22. Jefferson to Bowdoin, April 2, 1807, in Washington, ed., *Writings*, 5: 64.

23. Prucha, *Great*, 49. On Jefferson's Indian policy Sheehan, *Seeds* and Wallace, *Jefferson*. Two excellent overviews of US Indian policy since independence are Horsman, *Expansion*; Ostler, *Surviving*.

Page 70

24. Jefferson to the Delawares, Dec. 1808, in Esarey, ed., *Messages*, 334.

25. Ostler, *Surviving*, 134 quoted; Sugden, *Tecumseh*, 106 quoted.

26. Jefferson, Dec. 2, 1806, in James Richardson, ed., *Compilation*, 1: 407; Jefferson, Nov. 8, 1808, ibid., 454.

27. Jefferson to Secretary of War Dearborn, Aug. 28, 1807, in Lipscomb, ed., *Writings*, 11: 342–6, 345 quoted; Ostler, *Surviving*, 145.

28. The best work on impressment is Scott Jackson, "Impressment"; the runner-up is Zimmerman, *Impressment*.

29. Monroe to Madison, July 1, 1804, *PJM: SSS*, 7: 403.

Page 71

30. US Department of Commerce, *Historical*, 2: 905; Nettels, *Emergence*, 396.

31. Bradford Perkins, *Prologue*, 77. Perkins' *Prologue* and Horsman's *Causes* are excellent on Anglo-American relations during Jefferson's presidency.

32. Hickey, "Treaty," 74 quoted.

33. Madison to Monroe and Pinkney, May 17, 1806, *PJM: SSS*, 11: 576–90.

Page 72

34. Monroe to Jefferson, Jan. 11, 1807, in Hamilton, ed., *Monroe*, 5: 2.

35. Quoted by Horsman, *Causes*, 89.

36. Holland and Auckland to Monroe and Pinkney, Nov. 8, 1806, NA, RG 59, Dispatches from U.S. Ministers to Great Britain, 1791–1906, M-30, roll 10.

37. Jefferson, entry of Feb. 2, 1807, in Sawvel, ed., *Anas*, 251.

38. Madison to Monroe and Pinkney, May 20, 1807, *PJMO*, 5: 609.

39. Gilje, *Free*, 178.

40. Jefferson, entry of April 3, 1807, in Sawvel, ed., *Anas*, 254.

41. Gallatin to Jefferson, April 13 and 16, 1807, in Henry Adams, ed., *Writings*, 1: 332, 336; Jefferson to Madison, April 21, 1807, in James Morton Smith, *Republic*, 3: 1469.

Page 73

42. Madison to Monroe and Pinkney, May 20, 1807, *PJMO*, 5: 621.

43. Erskine to Canning, Oct. 5, 1807, TNA, FO 5/52.

44. Spencer Tucker and Reuter, *Injured,* is the best study of the incident. For the two exceptions mentioned in the text, see ibid., 65–7.

45. Jefferson to Smith, Sept. 3, 1807, in Ford, ed., *Works,* 10: 492.

46. Jefferson to Page, July 9, 1807, *Founders Online*, www.founders.archives.gov; Gallatin to Jefferson, Sept. 12, 1805, in Henry Adams, ed., *Writings*, 1: 252–53.

Page 74

47. Spencer Tucker, *Gunboat*, esp. 1–35.

48. Crackel, *Army*, 44.

49. Jefferson to Claiborne, April 26, 1806, in Ford, ed., *Writings*, 8: 442.

50. Jefferson, entry of July 26, 1807, in Sawvel, ed., *Anas*, 255–7.

51. Jefferson to Madison, Aug. 16, 1807, in James Morton Smith, *Republic*, 3: 1486; Turreau to French foreign minister Talleyrand, July 18, 1807, AAE, CP, États-Unis, vol. 60.

52. Spencer Tucker and Reuter, *Injured*, 114–15.

53. Madison to Monroe, July 6, 1807, *PJMO*, 5: 625–8.

54. Gallatin to Jefferson, Oct. 21, 1807, in Henry Adams, ed, *Writings*, 1: 360.

55. Dearborn to Crowninshield, Dec. 2, 1807, quoted by Brant, *Madison*, 4: 392.

Page 75

56. Jefferson to Randolph, Oct. 26, 1807, *Founders Online*, www.founders.archives.gov.

57. Turreau to foreign minister Champagny, Sept. 4, 1807, AAE, CP, États-Unis, vol. 60.

58. Malone, *Jefferson*, 5: 475–9.

59. US Department of Commerce, *Historical*, 2: 905; Nettels, *Emergence*, 396.

60. Jefferson to the Senate and House of Representatives of the United States, Dec. 18, 1807, in James Richardson, ed., *Compilation*, 1: 433; Gallatin to Jefferson, Dec. 18, 1807, in Henry Adams, ed., *Writings*, 1: 368. The best study of the embargo is Spivak, *Crisis*. Also Walter Jennings, *Embargo*; Bradford Perkins, *Prologue*, 140–83.

61. Senate, Dec. 18, 1807, *Annals*, 10th Cong., 1st sess., Dec. 1807, 50–1; House, Dec. 21, 1806, ibid., 1217–22.

Page 76

62. Jefferson to Rush, Jan. 3, 1808, in Washington, ed., *Writings*, 5: 226; Jefferson to Thomson, Jan. 11, 1808, in Ford, ed., *Works*, 11: 7.

63. Erney, *Dearborn*, 231.

64. Jefferson to Gallatin, May 6, 1808 in Henry Adams, ed., *Writings*, 1: 385.

65. Jefferson, entry of July 6, 1808, in Sawvel, ed., *ANAS*, 266; Madison to Pinkney, July 18, 1808, NA, RG 59, Diplomatic Instructions of the Department of State, 1801–1906, All Countries, M 77, roll 2; Madison to Armstrong, July 22, 1808, ibid.

66. Frankel, "Embargo"; Walter Jennings, *Embargo*, 70–93.

67. Gallatin to Jefferson, Dec. 2, 1807, in Henry Adams, ed., *Writings*, 1: 367.

68. Wood, *Empire*, 650.

Page 77

69. Jefferson to Madison, March 11, 1808, in James Morton Smith, *Republic*, 3: 1514–15.

70. Peterson, *Jefferson*, 886; Malone, *Jefferson*, 5: 576

71. Dolley Madison to Anna Cutts, Aug. 28, 1808, in Mattern and Shulman, eds., *Letters*, 87.

72. Gallatin to Jefferson, July 29, 1808, in Henry Adams, ed, *Writings*, 1: 398; Jefferson to Gallatin, Aug. 11, 1808, in Ford, ed., *Works*, 11: 41, emphasis in original.

73. Levy, *Jefferson*, 138–9.

Page 78

74. Cogliano, *Emperor*, 241. On the economic impact of the embargo see esp. Jennings, *Embargo*, 166–231; also Sears, *Embargo*, 142–252.

75. Gallatin to Jefferson, Aug. 6, 1808, in Henry Adams, ed, *Writings*, 1: 402.

76. Jefferson, Nov. 8, 1808, in James Richardson, ed., *Compilation*, 1: 452–53; Gallatin to Jefferson, Nov. 15, 1808, in Henry Adams, ed., *Writings*, 1: 428

77. Jefferson to Lincoln, Nov. 13, 1808, in Ford, ed., *Works*, 11: 74–5; Boles, *Jefferson*, 421.

78. Jefferson to Randolph, Feb. 7, 1809, in Ford, ed., *Works*, 11: 96–7. Emphasis added.

79. Wood, *Empire*, 651 quoted; Gregory May, *Jefferson's Treasure*.

5 The War of 1812

Page 81

1. US Department of Commerce, *Historical*, 1: 32–6.

2. "Campbell's Report," Nov. 1808, in Henry Adams, ed., *Writings*, 1: 443–4.

3. Macon's Bill no. 2, May 1, 1810, in Commager, *Documents*, 1: 204.

Page 82

4. On French relations with the United States, Peter Hill, *Troublesome*, 93 quoted; Egan, *Neither*.

5. Peter Hill, *Troublesome*, 109.

6. Whitaker, *United States*, 52–5.

7. Quotations from Sérurier to French foreign minister, May 4 and May 27, 1812, AAE, CP, États-Unis, vol. 67.

8. The best books on the origins of the War of 1812 are Horsman, *Causes*; Bradford Perkins, *Prologue*; Roger Brown, *Republic*; Stagg, *Madison's War*, 3–176.

Page 83

9. Harrison to Secretary of War, Aug. 7, 1811, in Esarey, ed., *Messages*, 1: 549.

10. Sugden, *Tecumseh*, 185. This is the best biography of Tecumseh.

11. Horsman, *Elliott*, 172 quoted; Willig, *Restoring*, 197–242; Allen, *Allies*, 88–122; Dowd, *Spirited*, 116–47.

12. Sugden, *Tecumseh*, 260–1.

13. Grundy, quoted by Brant, *Madison*, 5: 392–3.

14. For troops' strength Hitsman, *Incredible*, 295. Population figures from Bercuson et al., *Colonies*, 201, 227, 240 and from US Department of Commerce, *Historical*, 1: 14.

Page 84

15. Prevost to Liverpool, May 18, 1812, TNA, CO 42/146.

16. Jefferson to Duane, Aug. 4, 1812, *PTJ: RS*, 5: 293.

17. Bradford Perkins, *Prologue*, 290. For the number of Americans impressed, ibid., 91–3; Scott Jackson, "Impressment," 52–3; Zimmerman, *Impressment*, 259–75; Hickey, *Don't*, 21; Wolf, "'Misfortune,'" 61.

18. Horsman, *Causes*, 195.

Page 85

19. Millett et al, *For*, 95; Dull, *Naval*, 55. For Madison's messages of Nov. 5, 1811 and June 1, 1812, see James Richardson, ed., *Compilation*, 1: 491–6 and 499–505.

20. *National Intelligencer* (Washington DC), Apr. 14, 1812, 3 (edit.).

21. Hickey, *War*, 44.

22. Scholars don't agree on the exact number of Federalists and Republicans in Congress. I follow here Leland Johnson, "Suspense."

23. *The Times* (London), June 24, 1812, 2–3.

24. Bradford Perkins, *Prologue*, 321.

25. Hickey, *War*, 39 quoted; Bradford Perkins, *Prologue*, 421; Horsman, *Causes*, 244.

Page 86

26. The best books on the war are Hickey, *War*; Taylor, *War*; Stagg, *War*. For the Canadian perspective, Hitsman, *Incredible*. Scholars have given short shrift to the British perspective, but see Bickham, *Weight* and Black, *War*. For the Indians' role, in addition to the sources listed in nn. 10 and 11, see Benn, ed., *Mohawk*. An excellent, wide-ranging collection of essays is Hickey and Clark, eds., *Routledge*.

27. Allen, *Allies*, 140.

28. Malcomson, *Capital*; Benn, *Battle*, 45–51.

29. Quotations from Horsman, *War*, 114 and Brock to Liverpool, Aug. 29, 1812, in Cruikshank, ed., *Documents*, 192. Also Sugden, *Last Stand* and Skaggs, *Harrison*, 187–217.

Page 87

30. Kert, *Privateering*, 86.

31. *The Times*, Sept. 29, 1814, 2.

32. Bathurst to Prevost, June 3, 1814, and Bathurst to Prevost, Aug. 22, 1814, quoted, both TNA, CO 43/23.

33. The best discussions of the operation are Graves, *Glory*, 139–203; Everest, *War*, 141–205; Grodzinski, *Defender*, 145–242.

Page 88

34. Bathurst to Beckwith, March 18, 1813, TNA, CO 42/23.

35. Cochrane to Bathurst, July 14, 1814, TNA, WO 1/141.

36. Sérurier to Foreign Minister Talleyrand, Aug. 22 [sic], 1814, AAE, CP, États-Unis, vol. 71.

37. Ralph Ketcham, *Madison*, 576.

38. Cochrane to Cockburn, Aug. 22, 1814, in Crawford, ed., *War*, 3: 197.

39. Sérurier to Talleyrand, Aug. 22 [sic], 1814, AAE, CP, États-Unis, vol. 71; Margaret Smith to Jane Kirkpatrick, Aug. 1814, in Gaillard Hunt, ed., *Years*, 101.

Page 89

40. Ross to Bathurst, Aug. 30, 1814, *The Times*, Sept. 28, 1814, 2.

41. Ross, quoted by Latimer, *War*, 318 (emphasis in original); Paul Jennings, *Reminiscences*, 8.

42. Gaillard Hunt, ed., *Years*, 112.

43. Hickey, *War*, 208.

44. Black, *War*, 174.

45. Sérurier to Talleyrand, Sept. 8, 1814, AAE, CP, États-Unis, vol. 71.

Page 90

46. The best source on African Americans and the War of 1812 is Taylor's masterful *Enemy*, 325 quoted; also Gene Allen Smith, *Gamble*, 135–41 and Altoff, *Best*.

47. Shomette, *Flotilla*, 59.

48. Paul Jennings, *Reminiscences*, 7–8.

49. *The Times*, Sept. 27, 1814, 3; Sérurier to Talleyrand, Aug. 22 [sic], 1814, AAE, CP, États-Unis, vol. 71.

50. Ball, *Slavery*, 404.

51. Quoted by Taylor, *Enemy*, 141.

Page 91

52. Bathurst to Beckwith, March 18, 1813, TNA, CO 42/23.

53. Cockburn to Cochrane, May 10, 1814, LOC, Manuscript Division, Sir George Cockburn Papers, box 10; Captain Ross to Cockburn, May 29, 1814, TNA, Adm 1/507.

54. Cockburn to Cochrane, Aug. 27, 1814, TNA, Adm. 1/507.

Page 92

55. Quoted by Owsley, *Struggle*, 128.

56. The best study of the revolt is Paquette, "Brigands?"

57. Bassett, ed., *Correspondence*, 2: 58, 119.

58. The best account is Hickey, *Glorious*.

59. "Events of the War: Glorious from New-Orleans," *NWR*, Feb. 11, 1815, 372.

Page 93

60. Taylor, *Enemy*, 327–31; Pack, *The Man*, 209–13; Roger Morris, *Cockburn*, 114–18.

61. Quotations from Liverpool to Castlereagh, Sept. 25, 1814 and Liverpool to Canning, Dec. 28, 1814, in Yonge, *Life*, 2: 31, 75.

Page 94

62. Quoted by Allen, *Allies*, 174.

63. Quoted by Armstrong, ed., *Spoken*, 49–50.

64. Owsley, *Struggle*; Braund, ed., *Tohopeka*.

65. Remini, *Jackson*, 1: 303.

66. Ibid., 304.

Page 95

67. Bathurst to Hadio, Sept. 21, 1815, TNA, FO 5/140 quoted; Nicholls to Goulburn: Jan. 15, 1816; Sept. 24; Oct. 8; Jan. 7, 1817 (all in TNA, WO 1/144); Goulburn to Hamilton, May 17, 1816, TNA, FO 5/118.

68. Nicholls to Goulburn, Sept. 23, 1817, TNA, WO 1/144; Hamilton to Crocker, Sept. 15, 1818, TNA, FO 5/140, quoted; Owsley, *Struggle*, 181–3.

69. Hickey, *War*, 305.

70. Taylor, *Enemy*, 322.

71. *Richmond Enquirer*, Feb. 18, 1815, quoted by Taylor, *Enemy*, 335; Cambreleng (N.Y.), April 20, 1826, in *Register of Debates*, 19th Cong., 1st Sess., Part II of Vol. II, 1825–1826, 2441.

Page 96

72. The best biographies of Monroe are Ammon, *Monroe*, and McGrath, *Monroe*.

73. Taylor, *Enemy*, 345, 347; Hickey, *Don't*, 179.

74. Bemis, *Foundations*, 231. On US foreign policy in the aftermath of the war, see also Bradford Perkins, *Castlereagh*.

75. Taylor, *Enemy*, 441–2, 429–33.

76. Brooks, *Diplomacy*.

Page 97

77. Crawford to Hawkins, Oct. 16, 1815, quoted by Heidler and Heidler, *War*, 59.

78. Calhoun to Jackson, in Moser et al., eds., *Papers*, 4: 163; Calhoun to Bibb (governor of Alabama), quoted by Benton, *Thirty*, 1: 170.

79. Remini, *Jackson*, 1: 353.

80. Monroe to Jackson, Dec. 28, 1817, quoted in ibid., 349.

Page 98

81. Weeks, *Empire*, 109.

82. Ministro de Estado to Onís, April 25, 1818, quoted by Bécker, *Historia de las relaciones*, 1: 465.

83. Duke of San Carlos to Pizarro, Aug. 1, 1818, quoted by Weeks, *Empire*, 131.

84. Adams, entry of April 13, 1820, in *Memoirs*, edited by Charles Francis Adams, 5: 69.

85. Bécker, *Historia de las relaciones*, 1: 463–82, 478 quoted.

86. Mateo de la Serna to foreign minister, Dec. 24, 1819, ibid., 479.

87. US Department of Commerce, *Historical*, 1: 14.

Page 99

88. North, *Growth*, 53.

89. Jefferson to Eppes, June 30, 1820, *Founders Online*, www.founders.archives.gov.

6 The Limits of Sympathy: The United States and the Independence of Spanish America

Page 101

1. On the Spanish American Wars of Independence, see Lynch, *Revolutions*; Guerra Vilaboy, *El dilema*; Rodríguez O., *Independence*.

Page 102

2. This section is based on Verna, *Pétion*; Gleijeses, "Contribution."

3. Bolívar to Pétion, Jan. 29, 1816, in Sociedad Bolivariana de Venezuela, ed., *Escritos*, 9: 9. At the time Haiti was divided into two states, one under Pétion, the other under Henry Christophe. Since the latter played no role in the events considered here, I refer to Pétion's state as Haiti.

4. Bolívar to Wellesley, May 27, 1815, in Lecuna, ed., *Cartas*, 1: 152–3.

5. Bolívar to Hyslop, Oct. 30, 1815, ibid., 217

Page 103

6. Bolívar to Pétion, Sept, 4, 1816, in Sociedad Bolivariana de Venezuela, ed., *Escritos*, 9: 340.

7. Bolívar to Pétion, Oct. 9, 1816, in Lecuna, ed., *Cartas*, 1: 255; Bolívar to Pétion, Sept. 4, 1816, in Sociedad Bolivariana de Venezuela, ed., *Escritos*, 9: 346.

8. On the United States and the independence of Spanish America see John Johnson, *Hemisphere*; James Lewis, *Union*; Sexton, *Doctrine*, 37–84; Whitaker, *United States*; Gleijeses, "Limits." On British policy, Kaufmann, *British*; Temperley, *Canning*; Webster, *Castlereagh*; Jiménez Codinach, *La Gran Bretaña*.

9. Fitz, *Republics*,115, 5, 128.

Page 104

10. Ibid., 4, 11.

11. John Johnson, *Hemisphere*, 82.

12. Whitaker, *United States*, 197–8.

13. Gleijeses, "Limits," 481–2. Also Pappas, *United States*; Santelli, *Greek*.

14. Griffin, "Privateering," 2 quoted; Head, *Privateers*.

15. Bolívar to White, May 1, 1820, in Lecuna, ed., *Cartas*, 2: 157.

16. Hasbrouck, *Legionaries*, 106.

Page 105

17. Humphreys, "Merchants."

18. The communiqué, dated June 25, 1821, was reprinted in *NWR*, Sept. 1, 1821, 15.

19. Encina, *Historia*, 7: 416–31, 569–84 and 8: 5–32, 67–87, 254–78.

20. Bemis, *Policy*, 47.

Page 106

21. Polignac to Chateaubriand, Oct. 1 and Oct. 3 (quoted) 1823, AAE, CP, Angleterre, vol. 617.

22. "Memorandum of a Conversation between the Prince de Polignac and Mr. Canning, begun Thursday, October 9th, and Concluded Sunday, October 12, 1823," in Webster, ed., *Britain*, 2: 118.

23. Jefferson to Monroe, Oct. 24, 1823, in Lipscomb, ed., *Writings*, 15: 477–80.

24. Adams, entry of Nov. 7, 1823, in *Memoirs*, edited by Charles Francis Adams, 6: 177–8.

25. Adams, entries of Nov. 25 and Nov. 26, 1823, ibid., 201, 208 (quoted).

26. Monroe, Dec. 2, 1823, in James Richardson, ed., *Compilation*, 2: 218.

27. For a discussion of the Latin American response, Whitaker, *United States*, 534–8

28. *The Times* (London), Jan. 6, 1824, 2; *Morning Chronicle* (London), Jan. 14, 1824, 2.

29. Dexter Perkins, *Hands Off*, 61; Jaramillo, *Bolívar*, 124.

Page 107

30. Van Alstyne, *Empire*, 98–9.

31. Quoted by Carcovich, *Portales*, 5, n. 1.

32. Bolívar to Santander, July 23, 1826, in Lecuna, ed., *Cartas*, 5: 366.

33. Bolívar to Santander, June 28, 1825, ibid., 13.

34. Bolívar to Santander, Dec. 23, 1822, ibid., 3: 126.

35. José Manuel Zozaya to the Foreign Minister of Mexico, Dec. 26, 1822, in Mexico, Secretaría de Relaciones Exteriores, *La diplomacia*, 1: 103.

Page 108

36. Jefferson to Madison, April 27, 1809, in James Morton Smith, *Republic*, 3: 1586

37. Adams to Nelson, April 28, 1823, in Worthington Ford, ed., *Writings*, 7: 372.

38. Ibid., 373.

39. Guerra Vilaboy, *América*, 15–67; Roig de Leuchsenring, *Bolívar*; Jaramillo, *Bolívar*, 304–13.

40. Clay to Middleton, May 10, 1825, in Manning, ed., *Independence*, 1: 248.

Page 109

41. Morales Padrón, "Conspiraciones"; Garrigó, *Historia*, 1: 145–250, 2: 117–259.

42. See Clay to Everett, April 27, 1825 and April 13, 1826, in Manning, ed., *Independence*, 1: 242–3 and 271–3; Clay to King, May 11 and Oct. 17, 1825, ibid., 250–1 and 254–60; Clay to Middleton, Dec. 26, 1825 and April 21, 1826, ibid., 265–6 and 273–4; Canning to King: Aug. 7, Aug. 25, Sept. 8, 1825 in Webster, ed., *Britain*, 2: 520–8. For more, Gleijeses, "Limits," 492–3.

43. Clay to Richard Anderson and John Sergeant, May 8, 1826, *PHC*, 5: 335. See also Clay to Salazar, Dec. 20, 1825 and April 11, 1826, in Manning, ed., *Independence*, 1: 263–4 and 270–1; Clay to Obregón, Dec. 20, 1825, ibid., 263 n.3. For more, Gleijeses, "Limits," 493.

44. "Address to the People of the Congressional District," March 26, 1825, *PHC*, 4: 144–5.

45. Clay to Blair, Jan. 29, 1825, ibid., 47.

Page 110

46. Andrew Jackson to Swartwout, Feb. 23, 1825, *NWR*, March 12, 1825, 21.

47. Remini, *Jackson*, 2: 105.

48. Quotations from Robert Hayne (S-SC), March 1826, ibid., part 1, 175 and Joseph Hemphill (H-PA), Apr. 13, 1826, ibid, pt 2, 2237–8.

49. Hayne, March 1826, ibid., part 1, 175.

50. Daniel Webster (H-MA), Feb. 2, 1826, ibid., pt. 1, 1,242.

51. William Brent (H-LA), April 6, 1826, ibid., pt 2, 2,064.

52. John Berrien (S-GA), March 1826, ibid., pt 1, 284.

53. Hugh White (S-TN), March 1826, ibid., pt 1, 214.

54. John Forsyth (H-GA), Apr. 21, 1826, ibid., pt 2, 2,057; Edward Livingston (H-LA), April 21, 1826, ibid.

Page 111

55. Brown to Clay, May 29, 1826, *PHC*, 5: 404.

56. Bemis, *Adams*, 77.

57. Bolívar to Campbell, Aug. 5, 1829, in Lecuna, ed., *Obras*, 2: 737.

58. R.A.C. Sperling, minute on Spring Rice to Gray, June 13, 1916, TNA, FO 371.

7 Indian Removal: A "Sickening Mass of Putrefaction"

Page 113

1. McLoughlin, *Renascence*, 203.

2. Calhoun to the House, Dec. 5, 1818, *American State Papers: Indian Affairs*, 2: 183.

3. Monroe to Congress, Jan. 27, 1825, in James Richardson, ed., *Compilation*, 2: 280–3.

4. Thomas McKenney (Dept. of War, Office of Indian Affairs) to Calhoun, Jan. 10, 1825, enclosed in Calhoun to Monroe, Jan. 24, 1825, in *Register of Debates*, 18th Congress, 2nd sess., 1824–5 (Washington: Gales and Seaton, 1825), vol. 1, Appendix, 57–63.

5. Wilms, "Cherokee," 7.

6. Ostler, *Surviving*, 187–91.

Page 114

7. Adams, entry of March 26, 1824, in Charles Francis Adams, ed., *Memoirs*, 6: 268.

8. I rely on the excellent discussion in Green, *Politics*, 69–139, 95 quoted.

9. Andrew Jackson, Dec. 8, 1829, in James Richardson, ed., *Compilation*, 2: 459. The best biography of Jackson is Remini, *Jackson*. Also Meacham, *Lion*; Wilentz, *Jackson*; Opal, *Avenging*.

Page 115

10. *The Times* (London), Jan. 9, 1830, 2.

11. Hershberger, "Mobilizing," 26–7 quoting the "Circular"; Beecher, *Reminiscences*, 63 quoted; Portnoy, *Their*.

12. Perdue and Green, *Cherokee*, 66. The best overviews of US Indian policy in the 1820s and 1830s are Satz, *American*; Ostler, *Surviving*; Saunt, *Unworthy*.

Page 116

13. McLoughlin, *Renascence*, 3–21, 20 quoted; Perdue and Green, *Cherokee*, 1–19; Boulware, *Deconstructing*, 164 quoting the headman.

14. On Cherokee participation in the war see McLoughlin, *Renascence*, 186–211, 192 quoted, and Abram, "Cherokees."

15. Meigs, quoted by McLoughlin, *Renascence*, 195.

16. *National Intelligencer* (Washington DC), Feb. 21, 1816, 2.

17. This paragraph and the next are based on Thurman Wilkins, *Tragedy*, 81–96 and McLoughlin, *Renascence*, 194–205.

18. McLoughlin, *Renascence*, 196.

Page 117

19. *Cherokee Phoenix* (New Echota), June 18, 1828, 2, emphasis in original.

20. McLoughlin, *Renascence*, 329.

21. Ibid., 352–3.

22. Wilms, "Cherokee," 7.

Page 118

23. McLoughlin, *Missionaries*, 102–49.

24. *NWR*, July 9, 1825, 298, emphasis in original.

25. McLoughlin, *Renascence*, 396–401, 408–9.

26. Adams, entry of March 27, 1824, in Charles Francis Adams, ed., *Memoirs*, 6: 272.

Page 119

27. *Cherokee Phoenix*: June 11, 1828, 2; July 30, 1828, 1; Nov. 26, 1828, 1. In February 1829, the paper was renamed *Cherokee Phoenix and Indians' Advocate* to indicate that it spoke on behalf of all native Americans against the federal government's policies.

28. *Cherokee Phoenix*, Feb. 24, 1830, 2, emphasis in original.

Page 120

29. Frelinghuysen resolution, April 24, 1830, in *Register of Debates*, 21st Cong., 1st sess., Senate, 381.

30. *Connecticut Observer*, quoted in *Cherokee Phoenix*, May 29, 1830, 4; *American Spectator* (Washington DC), May 8, 1830, 2, emphasis in original.

31. Cole, *Presidency*, 72–4.

Page 121

32. Saunt, *Unworthy*, 82, 121.

33. Gibson, *Chickasaws*, 193. The best accounts of the deportation of the Indian tribes that followed Congress' approval of the Removal bill are Ostler, *Surviving*, 247–373; Grant Foreman, *Removal* and *Last Trek*; Bowes, *Land*.

34. Saunt, *Unworthy*, 88 quoted; Ackers, *Living*, 1–20, 87–94; Carson, "Native."

35. This account of ethnic cleansing in Alabama is based on Grant Foreman, *Removal*, 107–8 quoted; Green, *Politics*, 171 quoted; Haveman, *Rivers*.

Page 122

36. Grant Foreman, *Removal*, 112.

37. Saunt, *Unworthy*, 174; Green, *Politics*, 173, 183.

38. *Advertiser* (Montgomery), quoted by Grant Foreman, *Removal*, 154.

Page 123

39. "The Cherokee Nation v. The State of Georgia, 30 U.S. (5 Peters) 1 (1831)," in Norgreen, *Cases*, 165–9.

40. *NAR*, "Cherokee," 142.

41. "Samuel A. Worcester v. The State of Georgia, 31 U.S. (6 Pet.) 515 (1832)," in Norgreen, *Cases*, 170–86.

42. Boudinot to Stand Watie, March 7, 1832, University of Oklahoma, Western History Collection, Cherokee Nation Papers, box 117.

43. I rely on Garrison, *Legal*, 169–97 and on Norgreen, *Cases*, 123 quoted.

44. Jackson to Coffee, April 7, 1832, in Bassett, ed., *Correspondence*, 4: 430.

45. Boudinot to Ross, Aug. 1, 1832, in Moulton, ed., *Papers*, 1: 246. Emphasis in original.

Page 124

46. McLoughlin, *Missionaries*, 297–9.

47. Perdue, *Editor*, 22.

48. Perdue and Green, *Cherokee*, 98.

49. Ross et al. to Jackson, March 28, 1834, in Moulton, ed., *Papers*, 1: 282–4.

50. Troup to Calhoun, Feb. 28, 1824, in *American State Papers: Indian Affairs*, 2: 475–6.

Page 125

51. *Cherokee Phoenix*, June 19, 1830, 3.

52. Vaughan to Aberdeen, May 28, 1830, TNA, FO 5/259 and Vaughan to Aberdeen, June 27, 1830 (quoted), TNA., FO 5/260.

53. Trollope, *Domestic*, 133 quoted; Tocqueville, *Democracy*, 307–25; Featherstonhaug, *Canoe*, 2: 192–246.

Page 126

54. Butrick, *Removal*, 1–2.

55. Satz, *American*, 101.

56. John Burnett, "Removal," 181, 185.

57. Stephen Warren, "Ohio."

Page 127

58. This paragraph and the next two rely on Wallace, *Prelude*, 21 quoted; Hall, *Uncommon*; Jung, *War*.

59. Wallace, *Prelude*, 42.

60. Jung, *War*, 88.

Page 128

61. Kellogg, "Removal," 28, quoting from the notes of the Indian agent.

62. Government agent assigned to the Ho-Chunks, quoted by Ostler, *Surviving*, 310; Hagan, *Indians*, 65–8.

63. Stuart, "Transportation," 261. Also Bowes, *Land*, 149–81.

64. Ostler, *Surviving*, 287.

Page 129

65. Governor William DuVal to Secretary of War, Sept. 22, 1822, in Carter, ed., *Territorial*, 22: 533–4.

66. DuVal to McKenney, Feb. 22, 1826, ibid., 23: 417.

67. Legislative Council, Memorial to Congress, Feb. 1832, ibid., 24: 667.

68. Quoted by Clavin, "'It is,'" 193.

69. US Department of Commerce, *Historical*, 1: 26.

70. Laumer, *Dade's*. On the war see Monaco, *War*; Missall and Missall, *Wars*; Mahon, *History*.

71. *NWR*, Jan. 9, 1836, 313.

72. Particularly valuable are the memoirs of Capt. John Sprague, *Origin*, and army surgeon Jacob Rhett Motte, *Journey*.

Page 130

73. Remini, *Wars*. For Prucha, see esp. his *Great Father*.

Page 131

74. Perdue and Green, *Cherokee*, 43.

75. Crawford, "Trade and Intercourse," March 13, 1815, *American State Papers: Indian Affairs*, 2: 28.

76. Adams, entry of Jan. 23, 1828, in Charles Francis Adams, ed., *Memoirs*, 7: 411.

77. Adams, entry of June 30, 1841, ibid., 10: 492.

8 Manifest Destiny

Page 147

1. *NWR*, Nov. 8, 1817, 163.

2. *The Liberator* (Boston), Jan. 1, 1831, 1, uppercase in original.

Page 148

3. Sinha, *Cause*, 266 quoted; Grimké, *Letters*, 112 quoted (emphasis in original); Portnoy, *Their*.

4. Stewart, *Warriors*, 69–70.

5. Torget, *Seeds*, 97–176. On slavery and the independence of Texas, also Baumgartner, *South*, 61–121.

Page 149

6. For contrasting views on Jackson's role, Remini, *Jackson*, 3: 352–68; Vázquez, ed., *Rebelión*, 20; Belohlavek, "*Let*," 230–8; Robert May, *Manifest*, 9.

7. Adams, May 25, 1836, *Register of Debates*, vol. 12, pt 4, 4041–2.

8. Richards, *Life*, 159.

9. Clay to Porter, Jan. 26, 1838, in *PHC*, 9: 135.

10. Clay to Crittenden, Dec. 5, 1843, ibid., 897–9. The most authoritative work on the Whig party is Holt, *Rise*. The best discussion of the Whigs and Texas is Michael Morrison, "Westward."

Page 150

11. On Jackson's foreign policy see Belohlavek, "*Let!*" For overviews of US foreign policy in the 1830s and 1840s, see Howe, *What* (also excellent on domestic politics); Pletcher, *Diplomacy of Annexation*; Haynes, *Unfinished*. For overviews of US-British relations, also Dykstra, *Shifting*; Rakestraw and Jones, *Prologue*; Bourne, *Britain*.

12. Joseph Eve (US chargé in Texas) to John White, Dec. 29, 1841, in Nance, ed., "Letter," 218.

Page 151

13. Pletcher, *Diplomacy of Annexation*; Vázquez, ed., *Gran Bretaña*; Roeckell, "Bonds."

14. Leahy, *Life*, 300 quoted; Crapol, *Tyler*; Merk, *Slavery*.

15. Miles, "Fifty-four," 293–6.

16. Pletcher, *Diplomacy of Annexation*, 230.

17. Haynes, *Polk*, 193.

Page 152

18. *Siglo Diez y Nueve* (Mexico City), Nov. 30, 1845, 4 (edit.).

19. *La Reforma* (Mexico City), Feb. 10, 1846, 96 (edit.); *Monitor Constitucional* (Mexico City), May 10, 1845, 4.

20. Parrott to Buchanan, Aug. 26, 1845, in Manning, ed., *Affairs*, 8: 747.

21. Aberdeen to Peel, Sept. 23, 1845, quoted, Peel Papers, v. 275, British Museum, Additional Manuscripts; Peel to Aberdeen, Sept. 23, 1845, ibid.; Aberdeen to Peel, Sept. 25, 1845, ibid.

Page 153

22. Aberdeen to Bankhead, Oct. 1, 1845, TNA, FO 50/183.

23. Bankhead to Aberdeen, Nov. 29, 1845, TNA, FO 50/187.

24. Quotations from Black to Peña y Peña, Oct. 13, 1845, in Manning, ed., *Affairs*, 8: 762; Peña y Peña to Black, Oct. 15, 1845, ibid., 763.

25. On Polk's Mexican policy, Pletcher, *Diplomacy of Annexation*; Sellers, *Polk*; Merry, *A Country*; Gleijeses, "A Brush."

26. Peña y Peña to Bankhead, Oct. 15, 1845, TNA, FO 50/187; Bankhead to Aberdeen, Nov. 29, 1845, ibid.

27. Buchanan to Slidell, Nov. 10, 1845, in Manning, ed., *Affairs*, 8: 179, 176; Buchanan to Slidell, Jan. 20, 1846, ibid., 186.

Page 154

28. Buchanan to Slidell, Nov. 10, 1845, ibid., 180–1; Buchanan to Slidell, Dec. 17, 1845, ibid., 184 quoted.

29. Bancroft to E.D. Bancroft, Feb. 15, 1845, in DeWolfe Howe, *Life*, 1: 259.

30. Polk, Dec. 2, 1845, in James Richardson, ed., *Compilation*, 5: 2247. On Polk and Oregon, see Sellers, *Polk*, 235–58, 357–97, 405–15; Merk, *Oregon*, 216–417; Pletcher, *Diplomacy of Annexation*, 236–52, 291–351, 402–17; Dykstra, *Shifting*, 69–147; Bourne, *Britain*, 120–69.

Page 155

31. Polk, Dec. 2, 1845, in James Richardson, ed., *Compilation*, 5: 2241.

32. Peña y Peña to Slidell, Dec. 20, 1845, in Manning, ed., *Affairs*, 8: 789.

33. Quotations from Slidell to Buchanan, Dec. 27, 1845, ibid., 801; Slidell to Polk, Dec. 29, 1845, LOC, Manuscript Division, Papers of James Polk, Ser. 11, reel 66; Buchanan to Slidell, Jan. 28, 1846, in Manning, ed., *Affairs*, 8: 188; Mexican Council of State to Mexican foreign minister, Mar. 6, 1846, *La Reforma*, Mar. 23, 1846, 1.

34. Marcy to Taylor, Jan. 13, 1846, NA, RG 94, Office of the Adjutant General, Letters Sent, roll 14.

35. New Orleans *Picayune*, Apr. 9, 1846, 2; Ampudia to Taylor, Apr. 12, 1846, enclosed in Taylor to Adjutant General of the Army, Apr. 15, 1846, NA, RG 94, Office of the Adjutant General, Letters Received, roll 327.

Page 156

36. Pletcher, *Diplomacy of Annexation*, 348.

37. Polk, entry of May 9, 1846, emphasis in original, in Quaife, ed., *Diary*, 1: 384–6.

38. Polk, May 11, 1846, in Commager, ed., *Documents*, 1: 310–11.

39. Clayton, May 11, 1846, *CG*, 29th Cong., 1st sess., 786; Davis, May 11, 1846, ibid., 794.

Page 157

40. [O'Sullivan], "Annexation," *Democratic Review* (Washington DC), July–Aug. 1845, 5 quoted. The best books on Manifest Destiny are Hietala, *Manifest* and Horsman, *Race*. See also Weinberg, *Manifest*; Merk, *Destiny*; Greenberg, *Manifest*; Stephanson, *Manifest*.

41. Jefferson to Monroe, Nov. 24, 1801, *PTJ*, 35: 719–20.

42. Jefferson's First Inaugural Address, March 4, 1801, in James Richardson, ed., *Compilation*, 1: 323.

Page 158

43. US Department of Commerce, *Historical*, 1: 14, 106.

44. *NYH*, Dec. 14, 1845, 2

45. *Morning News* (New York), Nov. 15, 1845, 2 (edit.).

46. *Democratic Review*, Oct. 1845, 243; *Union* (Washington DC), Oct. 25, 1845, 602; *Morning News*, Nov. 15, 1845, 2 (edit.).

47. *NYH*, Apr. 30, 1846, 2 (edit.) and May 2, 2 (edit.).

Page 159

48. *Siglo Diez y Nueve*, Sept. 24, 1845, 1 and Oct. 8, 4.

49. Duncan, Jan. 29, 1845, *CG*, 28th Cong., 2nd sess, appendix, 178

50. *NYH*, June 5, 1846, quoted by Hietala, *Manifest*, 155.

51. Dix, July 26, 1848, quoted by Gardiner, *Great*, 163.

Page 160

52. *National Intelligencer*, Nov. 6, 1845, 3 (edit.); *American Review* (New York), Jan. 1846, 82–7.

53. *New York Tribune*, April 20, 1846, 2 (edit.). On the US press and Mexico in the months before the war, Gleijeses, "A Brush," 233–42.

Page 161

54. *The Economist* (London), Aug. 30, 1845, 813; *The Times*, Aug. 12, 1845, 4 (edit.) and Sept. 1, 4 (edit.).

55. *The Economist*, Aug. 30, 1845, 815; *Morning Chronicle* (London), Feb. 16, 1846, 2; *The Times*, Jan. 15, 1846, 4 (edit.).

56. *NYH*, Feb. 15, 1846, 1; *La Reforma*, Apr. 8, 1846, 3.

57. McIlvaine, March 26, 1846, *CG*, 29th Cong., 1st sess., Appendix, 580; Gleijeses, "A Brush," 242–4.

58. Van Buren to Bancroft, quoted by Chaplain Morrison, *Democratic*, 14

Page 162

59. Pletcher, *Diplomacy of Annexation*, 230–1.

60. Buchanan to Slidell, Nov. 10, 1845, ibid., 172; Quaife, ed., *Diary*, entry of March 28, 1846, 1: 305–8.

Page 163

61. See McLane to Buchanan, Sept. 18 and 26, 1845, and May 18, 1846, NA, RG 59, Despatches from US Ministers to Great Britain, M30, Roll 52. Also LOC, Manuscript Division, Papers of Louis McLane, esp. boxes 2–3.

62. Cutler, ed., *Correspondence*, 9: ix.

Page 164

63. Quotations from Buchanan to Slidell, Jan. 20, 1846, in Manning, ed., *Affairs*, 8: 186 and Buchanan to Slidell, Mar. 12, 1846, ibid., 190.

64. Lt. George Meade to Mrs. Meade, Apr. 21, 1846, in Meade, ed., *Life*, 1: 65.

65. Quaife, ed., *Diary*, entry of Apr. 21, 1846, 1: 343.

66. Ibid., entry of Aug. 4, 1845, 1: 4.

67. *The Times*, May 30, 1846, 4 (edit.).

Page 165

68. Pakenham to Aberdeen, May 13, 1846, TNA, FO 115/92.

69. On the war see Guardino, *Dead*; Greenberg, *War*; Vázquez, ed., *México*; Foos, *Killing*.

Page 166

70. Ernest May, "Invisible"; Baumgartner, *South*, 152.

71. Buhoup, *Narrative*, 132.

72. According to the official report of the deputy commander of the Mexican garrison, at least 400 civilians were killed by the bombardment (Olavarría y Ferrari, *México*, 4: 650).

73. Joint note of the French, British, Spanish and Prussian consuls in Vera Cruz to Scott, enclosed in Gloux to "Mon cher commandant," Vera Cruz, April 1, 1847, AAE, CP, Méxique, vol. 35.

74. Sevier, Jan. 4, 1848, *CG*, 30th Cong., 1st sess., 1848, Appendix, 261.

Page 167

75. DeLay, *War*, 129–38; Hämäläinen, *Comanche*, 219–32.

76. Guardino, *Dead*, 124; Ulysses S. Grant to Julia Dent, July 25, 1846, in Simon, ed., *Papers*, 1: 102.

77. *Mercury* (Charleston), Oct. 12, 1846, 2; *Niles' National Register*, Nov. 21, 1846, 180.

78. Taylor to the Adjutant General, US Army, June 16, 1847, *CG*, 30th Cong., 1st sess., "Mexican War Correspondence," Executive Document no. 60, 1178; Scott to Marcy, Jan. 16, 1847, LOC, Manuscript Division, William L. Marcy Papers, box 12. The most authoritative discussions of the behavior of the US troops are Foos, *Killing*, 113–37 and Guardino, *Dead*, 101–12, 123–33, 223–5, 294–300.

79. Capt. Hughes, "Memoir Descriptive of the March of a Division of the United States Army Under the Command of Brigadier General John E. Wool," 1846, in US Senate, Report of the Secretary of War, *CG*, 31st Cong., 1st sess., 1849, Ex Doc. no. 32, 43–4.

80. McCaffrey, *Army*, 68.

Page 168

81. Chaplain Morrison, *Democratic*.

82. Quaife, ed., *Diary*, 3: 343–51; Martis, *Atlas*, 101.

Page 169

83. Weber, ed., *Foreigners*, 143 quoted; Rana, *Faces*, 114–20.

84. Bolívar to [Patricio] Campbell, Aug. 5, 1829, in Lecuna, ed., *Obras*, 2: 737.

9 The 1850s and the Civil War

Page 171

1. Holt, *Pierce*, 17.

Page 172

2. On the United States and Cuba in the 1850s Rauch, *American*; Chaffin, *Fatal*; Robert May, *Quitman*; Robert May, *Underworld*; Jerónimo Bécker, *Historia de las relaciones*, 2: 159–79, 217–27; Gleijeses, "Clashing."

Page 173

3. *NYH*, July 3, 1850, 2 and April 9, 2; *Journal of Commerce* (New York), Aug. 23, 1851, 2.

4. *Delta* (New Orleans), Nov. 6, 1850, 2.

5. *Crescent* (New Orleans), July 27, 1851, 2.

6. For the overall number of participants in the two expeditions, Chaffin, *Fatal*, 127, 200. For the number of Cubans, Guerra, *Manual*, 477; Morales y Morales, *Iniciadores*, 2: 132; *Journal of Commerce*, Sept. 11, 1851, 2.

7. *The Times* (London), Sept. 27, 1851, 5.

Page 174

8. *Louisville Journal*, Aug. 28, 1851, 3.

9. *Journal of Commerce*, Sept. 11, 1851, 2.

10. Pierce, March 4, 1853, in James Richardson (ed.), *Compilation*, 5: 198–9.

11. Wallner, *Pierce*, 133. The best studies of the Pierce administration are Wallner's sympathetic volume and Nichols's *Pierce*.

12. Soulé, Jan. 25, 1853, *CG*, 32d Cong., 2nd sess., Appendix, 119–23, 123 quoted.

13. Marcy to Soulé, July 23, 1853, in Manning, ed., *Affairs*, 11: 163.

14. Wallner, *Pierce*, 134–5; Rauch, *American*, 262.

Page 175

15. Nichols, *Pierce*, 267.

16. Crampton to Clarendon, Nov. 20, 1853, Oxford, Bodleian Library (hereafter Bodl), Clarendon Papers, container (hereafter c.) 11.

17. Rodríguez, *Cuba*, 1: 4–88; Ferrer, *Mirror*.

18. Otway to Beltrán de Lis, Nov. 7, 1852, AHN, Estado, leg. 8046, exp. 3, no. 6.

19. Istúriz to Primer Secretario de Estado, March 22, 1853, AHN, Estado, leg. 8046, exp. 3, no. 27.

Page 176

20. Ministro de Estado to Presidente del Consejo de Ministros, Feb. 11, 1853, AHN, Ultramar, leg. 3548, exp. 4, no. 13.

21. Estorch, *Apuntes*, 6.

22. Clarendon to Howden, April 1, 1854, TNA, FO 84/933.

23. Decree of May 24, 1854 in *Gaceta de la Habana*, May 25, 1854, 1.

24. *New York Tribune*, Aug. 4, 1854, 5.

25. *Union* (Washington DC), Aug. 23, 1853, 2.

26. *Richmond Enquirer*, May 16, 1854, 2.

Page 177

27. Potter, *Crisis*, 165–6 quoted.

28. *Louisville Journal*, May 29, 1854, 2.

29. Potter, *Crisis*, 181.

30. *Union*, March 24, 1854, 3.

31. *Union*, May 16, 1854, 2.

32. Robert May, *Slavery*, 115.

Page 178

33. Marcy to Davis, March 15, 1854, in Manning, ed., *Affairs*, 11: 170–3; Davis to Marcy, May 22, 1854, ibid, 789 quoted.

34. Clayton to Marcy, no. 3, Dec. 5, 1853, NA, DOS, Dispatches from U.S. Consuls in Havana, M899, roll 26; Robertson to Marcy, no. 21, Jan. 27, 1854, ibid., roll 27; Robertson to Marcy, March 20, 1854, in Manning, ed., *Affairs*, 11: 748–9.

35. Marcy to Soulé, April 3, 1854, in Manning, ed., *Affairs*, 11: 175–8, 177 quoted.

36. Klein, *Buchanan*, 238 quoted, emphasis in original; Nichols, *Pierce*, 370–1.

37. Crampton to Clarendon, March 26, 1854, Bodl, Clarendon Papers, c. 24.

38. Marcy to Mason, May 25, 1854, LOC, Manuscript Division, William L. Marcy Papers, 1806–1930, box 80 (hereafter Marcy Papers); Marcy to Buchanan, May 26, 1854, ibid.

Page 179

39. *Union*, June 23, 1854, 2.

40. Soulé to Marcy, no. 28, July 18, 1854, NA, DOS, Dispatches from U.S. Ministers to Spain, M31, Roll 38; Mason to Marcy, July 5, 1854, Marcy Papers, box 50; Mann to Marcy, Aug. 31 and Sept. 4, 1854, ibid., box 52.

41. Cueto to Calderón de la Barca, Aug. 22, 1854, AHN, Ultramar, leg. 4645, exp. 47, no. 3; Crampton to Clarendon, June 8, 1854, Bodl, Clarendon Papers, c. 24.

42. Robert May, *Quitman*, 284.

43. Aberdeen to Clarendon, Sept. 25, 1854, British Library, London, Western Manuscripts, Add MS 43189, Correspondence of the Prime Minister, Lord Aberdeen, with the Foreign Sec., Lord Clarendon: March 1854–November 1859, v. CLI; Crampton to Clarendon, Sept. 10, 1854, Bodl, Clarendon Papers, c. 25.

Page 180

44. *The Times*, Aug. 17, 1854, 6.

45. Palmerston, "Mem[orandum] on a Draft of Despatch from Ld. Clarendon to Mr. Crampton at Washington," Sept. 2, 1854, University of Southampton, Hartley Library, MS 62 Palmerston Papers, PP/MM/US/11/1.

46. Marcy to Mason, July 23, 1854, Marcy Papers, box 80.

47. Marcy to Soulé, Aug. 16, 1854, in Manning, ed., *Affairs*, 11: 193.

48. Buchanan to Marcy, Oct. 18, 1854, in Moore, ed., *Works*, 9: 260–6.

49. Robert May, *Southern*, 68.

Page 181

50. Calderón de la Barca to Presidente del Consejo, Feb. 12, 1853, AHN, Ultramar, leg. 4645, exp. 25, no. 1.

51. Marcy to Soulé, Nov. 13, 1854, in Manning, ed., *Affairs*, 11: 196–201.

52. Portell Vilá, *Historia*, 2: 95.

53. This section relies on Garber, *Treaty*; Terrazas y Basante, *Inversiones*, 15–97; Devine, *Slavery*; and on my research in the Mexican, French, and British archives.

Page 182

54. Doyle to Clarendon, Dec. 3, 1853, TNA 50/261.

55. Quotations from Pacheco to French foreign minister Drouyn de Lhuys, Oct. 24, 1853, AAE, CP, Mexique, vol. 41 and Esteva, memorandum, April 2, 1854, MAH, 6-1-8.

56. Castillo y Lanzas to Mexican foreign minister, Jan. 20, 1854, MAH, 6-1-8; Esteva, memorandum, April 2, 1854, ibid.

57. Clarendon to Doyle, Jan. 16, 1954, TNA, FO 50/265.

58. Buenaventura Vivó to Mexican foreign minister, Jan. 21, 1854 and April 23 (quoted), MAH, 6-1-8.

59. Castillo y Lanzas to Mexican foreign minister, Jan. 20, 1854, emphasis in original, MAH, 6-1-8.

Page 183

60. McGuinness, *Path*; Mira Wilkins, *Emergence*, 22–7.

61. The most important works for this section are Robert May, *Underworld* and Gobat, *Empire*. Gobat's book contains new information and valuable insights, but his assertion that Walker sought to create a "liberal empire" is contradicted by his own evidence. See also Acuña Ortega, ed., *Filibusterismo*; Greenberg, *Manifest Manhood*; Martelle, *Wars*; Beer, *Transnational*.

62. Different authors give different numbers. I rely on Walker's memoirs, *War*, 32.

Page 184

63. Gizolme to French Secretary of the Navy and Colonies, June 6, 1856, AAE, CP, Amérique Centrale, vol. 15.

64. Mora to Wallerstein, Feb. 10, 1856, AN, MRREE, 17960.

65. Wallerstein to Clarendon, Jan. 12, 1856, AN, MRREE, 27124; Wallerstein to Clarendon, April 30, 1856, ibid.; Clarendon, May 19, 1856, *Hansard's Parliamentary Debates*, House of Lords (London: Cornelius Buck, 1856), 3rd ser, vol. CXLII, 311–12; Dallas to Marcy, May 23, 1856, in Manning, ed., *Affairs*, 7: 645–7.

66. Bourne, *Britain*, 198, quoting Foreign Office to Admiralty, June 9, 1856.

67. Wallerstein to Calvo, Jan. 16, 1856, AN, MRREE, 17976.

68. Gobat, *Empire*, 71, 73.

Page 185

69. Walker, *War*, 314

70. Gobat, *Empire*, 152, quoting *El Nicaraguense*.

71. Ibid., 242–3, quoting *El Nicaraguense*.

72. Lamar to Cass, Feb. 26, 1858, in Manning, ed., *Affairs*, 4: 660.

73. Francisco Bilbao, quoted by Sater, *Chile*, 22.

Page 186

74. Clarendon to Cowley, May 26, 1857, TNA, FO 519/175; Palmerston to Clarendon, Dec. 31, 1857, in Bourne, "Treaty," 290.

Page 187

75. Gosse, "As," 1026.

76. *National Era* (Washington DC), May 27, 1858, 82. The most useful discussion of this crisis is Soulsby, *Right*, 118–76.

77. *The Times*, June 19, 1858, 8 (edit.), emphasis in original.

Page 188

78. *The Times*, June 3, 1858, 8 (edit.).

79. Garibaldi, *Política*, 253.

80. Gobat, "Invention," 1354.

81. Pletcher, *Diplomacy of Annexation*, 307.

82. Sexton, *Doctrine*, 123–37.

83. Buchanan, Second Annual Message, Dec. 6, 1858, in James Richardson, ed., *Compilation*, 5: 510–11.

84. Baker, *Buchanan*, 111.

85. Foreign minister Castillo, quoted by Gobart, "Invention," 1360.

Page 189

86. Hacker, "Count."

87. Lincoln, July 17, 1858, in Basler, ed., *Works*, 2: 521; Lincoln, March 4, 1861, ibid., 4: 263. See esp. Foner, *Trial*.

88. McPherson, *Battle*, 244–5 quoted, is the best account of the Civil War. On the foreign relations of the conflict, see also Mahin, *One*; Owsley, *King*; Duncan Campbell, *English*; Amanda Foreman, *World*; Blackett, *Divided*; Myers, *Caution*.

Page 190

89. *Boston Advertiser*, Aug. 20, 1862, quoted by Foner, *Trial*, 209.

Page 191

90. *Spectator*, Aug. 16, 1862, quoted by Duncan Campbell, *English*, 111.

91. *The Times*, Aug. 15, 1862, 6 (edit.).

92. On the *Trent* affair see Ferris, *Trent*, and Gordon Warren, *Fountain*.

Page 192

93. Russell to Lyons, Nov. 30, 1961, TNA, FO 5/758 and Dec.1, 1861 (quoted), TNA, Russell Papers, 30/22/96; Ferris, *Trent*, 63 quoting Palmerston to Granville, Nov. 29, 1961. For the prohibition to export arms, ammunition, and military stores, Royal Proclamation, Dec. 4, 1861, in *British and Foreign State Papers* (London: Foreign Office, 1868), 51: 171–2.

94. On the *Florida* and the *Alabama* see Fox, *Wolf*; Owsley, *Florida*; Luraghi, *History*.

95. McPherson, *Battle*, 454–545, 532 quoted.

Page 193

96. Russell to Palmerston, Sept. 17, 1862, quoted by Walpole, *Life*, 2: 349.

97. Granville to Russell, Sept. 27, 1862, quoted by Fitzmaurice, *Life*, 1: 442–3; Derby, quoted in Clarendon to Palmerston, Oct. 16, 1862, in Ephraim Adams, *Great Britain*, 2: 51–2.

Page 194

98. Lincoln to Horace Greeley, Aug. 22, 1862, in Basler, ed., *Works*, 5: 388–9, emphasis in original.

10 After Appomattox

Page 195

1. I borrow the expression from Pletcher, *The Awkward Years*.

2. General Pope to Col. Sawyer, Aug. 1, 1865, quoted by Olson, *Red Cloud*, 3–4.

3. US Department of the Interior, *Are the Indians Dying? Indian Civilization and Education* (Washington DC: GPO, 1877), 10.

Page 196

4. For an insightful analysis of these differences, see Grimsley, "'Rebels,'" 138 quoted. For the "dominant view," see Janda, "Shutting"; Weigley, *American*, 153–63.

5. Grimsley, "'Rebels,'" 153.

6. Josephy, *War*, 312 quoted; West, *Contested*, 271–316.

7. Quoted by Calhoun, *Presidency*, 263.

8. See Hämäläinen, *Lakota*; Ostler, *Sioux* and *Lakotas*; Olson, *Red Cloud*; Utley, *Lance*.

Page 197

   9. Hämäläinen, *Comanche*, 336, 339, 341.

  10. Grinnell, "Indian," 259.

  11. Ibid., 256, 260.

Page 198

  12. Madley, *Genocide*, 306, 358 quoted. Also Lindsay, *Murder*.

  13. Cozzens, ed., *Eyewitnesses*, esp. 343–648; Debo, *Geronimo*; Sweeney, *From*.

  14. My discussion in this and the next two paragraphs is based on Ostler, *Lakotas*, 111–24, 117 quoted; Louis Warren, *Red*; Heather Richardson, *Wounded Knee*; Andersson, *Lakota*.

Page 199

  15. Heather Richardson, *Wounded Knee*, 217.

  16. Ostler, *Sioux*, 345.

  17. *New York Tribune*, Jan. 6, 1891, 1, quoted by Heather Richardson, *Wounded Knee*, 287–8.

  18. Charles Francis Adams, "*Imperialism*," 5.

  19. Napoleon III to Flahaut, Oct. 14, 1861, quoted by Gouttman, *La guerre*, 88–9.

Page 200

  20. Sexton, *Doctrine*, 153.

  21. Foulke, *Life*, 1: 457. On US policy, Schoonover, *Dollars* and *Mexican*; Hardy, "South"; Chernow, *Grant*, 554–7; Case and Spencer, *United States*, 516–55.

  22. Sexton, *Doctrine*, 157.

  23. Juárez, quoted by Schoonover, *Dollars*, 209.

Page 201

  24. Foner, *Reconstruction*; Downs, *After*.

  25. White, "American," 207.

  26. US Department of Commerce, *Historical*, 2: 904.

  27. Millett, Maskowski and Feis, *For*, 219

Page 202

  28. Saul, *Distant*, 390.

  29. Azzi, *Reconcilable*, 54.

  30. This paragraph and the next rely on Love, *Race*, 27–72; Calhoun, *Presidency*, 199–261; Tansill, *United States*, 338–464. Also Conde, *Historia*, 1: 545–643.

  31. Berthemy to French Foreign Minister Gramont, July 4, 1870, AAE, CP, Étas-Unis, vol. 147.

  32. Healy, *Blaine*, 55–99, 63 quoted; Sater, *Tragedy*.

Page 203

  33. *Army and Navy Journal*, Aug. 1, 1885, 2.

  34. Colby, *Business*; Stewart, *Keith*; O'Brien, *Century*, 3–23.

  35. US Department of Commerce, *Historical*, 2: 904.

Page 204

36. *Herald* (Buenos Aires), Nov. 21, 1885, 1, quoted by Schoultz, *Best*,18; Joseph Smith, "Commission." A good overview of US trade with Latin America in this period is Pletcher, *Diplomacy of Trade.*

37. US Department of Commerce, *Historical*, 2: 904.

38. Ibid.

39. See Noer, *Briton*, 3–43.

40. On African Americans and Africa Jacobs, *Nexus* and "Give"; Skinner, *African Americans*; Campbell, *Middle Passage*; Tyrrell, *Reforming.*

41. This paragraph and the next rely on Burin, *Slavery*; Mills, "United States"; Clegg, *Price.*

Page 205

42. Senator Morgan, letter printed in the *Evening Star* (Washington DC), Jan. 28, 1903, 7.

43. *Evening Star*, Dec. 16, 1902, 4.

44. Beisner, *Old*, 73.

45. Austin, "Immigration?" 564, 563.

46. For an excellent discussion of the importance of the idea of manhood to these leaders see Hoganson, *Fighting.*

Page 206

47. LaFeber, *American Age*, 175.

48. Turner, *Frontier*, 13.

49. Quoted by Rosenberg, *Spreading*, 41,

50. Graff, *Cleveland*, 117.

51. Herring, *Colony*, 278.

52. William Washburn (R-MN), April 23, 1894, quoted by Schoultz, *Best*, 18.

53. Kennedy, *Samoan*, 1–97, 95 quoted. On the European context, ibid., 78–82; Canis, *Aussenpolitk*, 231–353; Hildebrand, *Das*, 100–46.

Page 207

54. See Healy, *Blaine*, 205–34; Barros Franco, "El Caso"; Sanz, *El caso*; Goldberg, "*Baltimore*".

55. Sater, *Chile*, 20–1; Monahan, *Chile*, 152–70; Beilharz and López, *We.*

56. Blaine quoted in Desprez to French foreign minister Ribot, Oct. 29, 1891, AAE, CP, États-Unis, vol. 168.

57. Harrison to Congress, Jan. 25, 1892, in James Richardson, ed., *Compilation*, 9: 215–26, 225 quoted.

58. Patenôtre to Ribot, Jan. 27, 1892, AAE, CP, États-Unis, vol. 169.

Page 208

59. See Calhoun, *Gilded Cato*, 145–61; Love, *Race*, 73–158; Russ, *Hawaiian*; Pratt, *Expansionists.*

60. Russ, *Hawaiian*, 90.

61. Cleveland to the Senate, March 9, 1893, in James Richardson, ed., *Compilation*, 9: 393.

62. Gresham to Blount, March 11, 1893, quoted by Russ, *Hawaiian*, 169.

Page 209

63. *NYH*, Feb. 23, 1898, 6.

64. Cleveland, Special Message to Congress, Dec. 18, 1893, in James Richardson, ed., *Compilation*, 9: 460–72, 469 and 472 quoted.

65. Pratt, *Expansionists*, 143.

66. Pauncefote to Gresham, March 16, 1893, quoted by Pratt, *Expansionists*, 126

Page 210

67. Joseph Smith, *Unequal*, 19–25; Joseph Smith, "Britain."

68. Pletcher, *Diplomacy of Trade*, 294 quoted; Mary Williams, *Anglo-American*, 288–99; Tansill, *Bayard*, 665–90; Dozier, *Mosquito*, 141–56.

69. Lodge, "England," 657–8.

70. Olney to Bayard, July 20, 1895, *FRUS*, 1895, 1: 542–76. On the crisis see Eggert, *Olney*, 189–253, 206 quoted; Tansill, *Bayard*, 650–65, 690–781; Roberts, *Salisbury*, 601–33.

71. Salisbury to Pauncefote, no. 15, Nov. 26, 1895, in *British Parliamentary Papers*, vol. 15: *United States of America* (Shannon: Irish University Press, 1971), 877.

Page 211

72. Cleveland, Special Message to Congress, Dec. 17, 1895, in James Richardson, ed., *Compilation*, 9: 655–8.

73. Brodsky, *Cleveland*, 366; Patenôtre to foreign minister Berthelot, Jan. 8, 1896, AAE, CP, États-Unis, vol. 174.

74. Eggert, *Olney*, 222.

75. Geoffray to foreign minister Berthelot, Dec. 30, 1895, AAE, CP, Angleterre, vol. 910.

76. On the "Special Relationship" see Stuart Anderson, *Race*; Kramer, "Empire."

11 Cuba and the Philippines

Page 213

1. Martí to Manuel Mercado, May 18, 1895, in Martí, *Epistolario*, 5: 250. On Cuba's war of independence see Rodríguez, *Cuba*, vol. 3; Pérez, *Empires*; Stucki, *Aufstand*.

2. Chandler and Quincy, "Issues," 181 quoted. Also Hal Williams, *Realigning*; Lodge, "The Meaning;" Bryan, "Has?"

3. Phillips, *McKinley*, 110. See also Morgan, *McKinley*; Ernest May, *Imperial*; Gould, *Presidency*; Merry, *President*.

4. *Bankers' Magazine* (New York), Sept. 1897, 335.

Page 214

5. *Tribune* (Chicago), Feb. 25, 1898, 6 (edit.). For a detailed discussion of the press in the months before the war, based on forty-one US papers and twelve foreign papers (British, French, German, and Spanish) see Gleijeses, "1898."

6. Roosevelt to Root, April 5, 1898, in Morison, *Letters*, 2: 813.

7. Sims to Roosevelt, March 25, 1898, NA, RG 38, E 90, vol. 12.

8. Cervera, ed., *Colección*. Also Gleijeses, "1898," 686–94.

9. "The Military Forces of Spain. Compiled in the Intelligence Division, War Office, and Corrected to April 1898," [end April 1898], TNA, FO 881/7016.

10. Miles to Secretary of War, April 13, 1898, U.S. War Department, U.S. Adjutant-general's office, *Correspondence Relating to the War with Spain*, vol. 1 (Washington DC: GPO, 1902): 8.

Page 215

11. *Herald* (Boston), March 14, 1898, 6 (edit.); *Dispatch* (Richmond), April 21, 1898, 4 (edit.).

12. US Department of Commerce, *Historical*, 2: 903–4.

13. *Bankers' Magazine*, March 1898, 358. On the business community and the war, Gleijeses, "1898."

14. Flint, *Marching*, 52; *Chronicle* (Chicago), Feb. 4, 1898, 6 (edit.); *Harper's Weekly* (New York), March 26, 1898, 291.

15. *NYH*, April 20, 1898, 12 (edit.).

16. Quotations from *NYH*, April 2, 1898, 8 (edit.) and Trask, *War*, 78.

17. Gleijeses, "1898," 705–6.

18. *Commercial Advertiser* (New York), March 28, 1898, 6 (edit.).

Page 216

19. *Journal* (New York), Feb. 24, 1898, 6 (edit.); *World-Herald* (Omaha), April 17, 1898, 4 (edit.); *Tribune* (Chicago), March 26, 1898, 3.

Page 217

20. *Times-Herald* (Chicago): March 4, 1898, 6 (edit.); March 7, 6 (edit.); April 4, 6 (edit.); April 17, 6 (edit.).

21. Rickover, *How*, 104.

22. Day to Woodford, March 27, 1898 (quoted); Woodford to Day, March 28; Day to Woodford, March 29; Day to Woodford, March 30. All in LOC, Manuscript Division, William Rufus Day Papers, c. 35.

23. McKinley to Congress, in James Richardson, ed., *Compilation*, 10: 139–50, 150 quoted.

24. Commager, ed., *Documents*, 2: 5.

25. See LaFeber, *Empire*, 326–417; Pratt, *Expansionists*, 230–78; Pérez, *War*; Trask, *War*, 1–59; Offner, *War*; Hoganson, *Fighting*; Pletcher, *Diplomacy of Trade*, 325–56.

Page 218

26. On the great powers and the US wars against Spain and the Filipino Republic, de la Torre, *Inglaterra*; Havemann, *Spanien*, 338–92; Hilton and Ickringill, eds., *Perceptions*; Tom Lewis, "Politique"; Girón Garrado, ed., *España*; Álvarez Gutiérrez, "Los imperios." Also Bruti Liberati, *Santa Sede*.

27. Magie, *Life*, 174.

28. Cambon to French Foreign Minister Hanotaux, April 4, 1898, Ministère des Affaires Étrangères, *Documents Diplomatiques Français (1871–1914), 1re Série (1871–1900)*, Paris, 1957, 14: 215. (Hereafter MAE, *Documents*).

29. Gillett, *Hoar*, 203.

30. *Le Temps* (Paris), Apr. 14, 1898, 1 (edit.).

31. Quoted by Pérez, *Cuba*, 96.

32. Captain Víctor Concas, quoted by Trask, *War*, 209.

Page 219

33. Trask, *War*, 244–5. Another authority, Graham Cosmas, gives Spanish losses at about 650 and American losses at 1,520 ("San Juan Hill and El Caney," 144).

34. *El Imparcial* (Madrid), July 8, 1898, 1; *Times*, July 4, 1898, 11 (edit.); Roosevelt to Lodge, July 3, 1898, in Morison, *Letters*, 2: 846; Ambassador Cambon to Foreign Minister Delcassé, July 8, 1898, MAE, *Documents*, 372.

35. Woodford to McKinley, Feb. 26, 1898, LOC, Manuscript Division, John Bassett Moore Papers, box 185. On Spain's perspective, see Robles Muñoz, *1898*, 5–144; Núñez Florencio, *Militarismo*, 215–329; Varela Ortega, "Otra vez!"; Companys, *España*; Rubio, *El Tránsito*, vol. 1; Fusi and Niño, eds., *Antes*.

36. Major G.F. Leverson, "Report of the Military Attaché with the Spanish Forces in Cuba," Nov. 8, 1898, TNA, WO 33/155.

37. Major-General Kent et al. to General Shafter, Aug. 3, 1898, in Morison, *Letters*, 2: 865–6.

38. Quoted by Stuart Miller, "*Benevolent*," 15.

39. Hay to Roosevelt, July 27, 1898, in Thayer, ed., *Life*, 2: 337.

Page 220

40. Beveridge, "Cuba," 541. Also Pérez, "Incurring."

41. My estimate is consistent with the conclusions of recent Spanish scholarship. See, for example, Ruiz-Manjón and Langa, eds., *Significados*; Elorza and Hernández Sandoica, *La guerra*; Pan-Montojo, ed., *Más*; Marimon, *Crisis*; Maluquer de Motes, *España*.

42. Nancy Mitchell, "Remember the Myth," *News and Observer* (Raleigh), Nov. 1, 1998, G5.

43. Carroll, *Report*, 10–11.

44. Maass, *Picky*, 192.

45. Go, "Anti-imperialism," 40 quoted; Burnett and Marshall, *Foreign*; Erman, *Almost*; Cabán, *Constructing*; Lanny Thompson, *Imperial*.

Page 221

46. Trask, *War*, 391–410; Spector, *Admiral*, 83–93; Agoncillo, *Malolos*, 225 quoted.

47. The best account is Trask, *War*, 411–22.

Page 222

48. Hazeltine, "What?" For the debate on the annexation of the Philippines, Hilfrich, *Debating*; Beisner, *Twelve*; Tompkins, *Anti-Imperialism*; Walter Williams, "United States"; Lasch, "Anti-Imperialists"; Welch, *Response*.

49. Carnegie, "Americanism," 9.

50. Schurz, "Thoughts," 784.

51. Peffer, "A Republic," 320.

52. Kipling, "The White Man's Burden," *McClure's Magazine*, Feb. 1899, 4.

53. *Colored American* (Washington DC), March 18, 1899, 4 (edit.).

Page 223

54. Felipe Agoncillo, "Memorial to the Senate of the United States" [January 1899], printed in Agoncillo, *Malolos*, 362–8.

55. Welch, *Response*, 7.

56. The letter, of which only the draft remains, was probably written in early December 1898 and is quoted in Agoncillo, *Malolos*, 357–8.

57. US Senate, Committee on the Philippines, *Affairs in the Philippine Islands*, vol. 3 (Washington DC: GPO, 1902): 2709–51; Agoncillo, *Malolos*, 437–49.

Page 224

58. See Havemann, *Spanien*, 378–92; Kaikkonen, *Deutschland*, 93–110, 149–56.

59. Kramer, *Blood*, 103.

60. Private Frank Johnson to his parents, Jan. 31, 1899, quoted by Thiessen, "Fighting," 234; Welch, "Atrocities," 241. The literature on the US war in the Philippines is rich and expresses conflicting viewpoints. See Kramer, *Blood*; Welch, *Response*; Miller, *"Benevolent"*; Glenn May, *Battle*; Scott, *Ilocano*. Other important books are Linn, *War*; Agoncillo, *Malolos*; Ileto, *Pasyon*; Velasco Shaw and Francia, eds., *War*; Tan, *War*; Guerrero, *Luzon*.

61. This section is based on Gleijeses, "African Americans"; Gatewood, *Black* and *"Smoked"*; also Morey, *Fagen*; Marasigan, "Between."

62. Letter by X-Ray, *Colored American*, March 12, 1898, 4.

Page 225

63. *Colored American*, April 9, 1898, 4; *Washington Bee*, April 23, 1898, 4.

64. Quotations from Trask, *War*, 247; Gatewood, *Black*, 103.

65. *Planet* (Richmond), July 2, 1898, 3.

66. *Picayune* (New Orleans) quoted by *Literary Digest*, Nov. 5, 1898, 540.

67. *News and Observer*, Oct. 19, 1898, 4; *Washington Post*, Nov. 1, 1898, 1.

Page 226

68. 1898 Wilmington Race Riot Commission, "1898 Wilmington Race Riot Report," May 31, 2006, https://www.ncdcr.gov/learn/history-and-archives-education; Prather, *Wilmington*; Cecelski and Tyson, eds., *Wilmington*.

69. *NYT*, Dec. 15, 1898, 1 and Dec. 16, 1.

70. *Washington Post*, Dec. 16, 1898, 1.

71. *Washington Post*, Dec. 19, 1898, 1; *News and Observer*, Dec. 20, 1898, 4.

72. *Planet*, Oct. 14, 1899, 1, quoting the report of a white detective hired by a group of African Americans from Chicago to investigate the lynching. Also Mathews, *Lynching*, 139–77.

73. *NYT*, April 24, 1899, 2.

74. *NYT*, April 25, 1899, 2

75. *Colored American*, March 18, 1899, 4.

76. *Washington Bee*, March 11, 1899, 4.

Page 227

77. *Broad Ax* (Salt Lake City), April 25, 1899, 2.

78. *Freeman* (Indianapolis), May 6, 1899, 4.

79. Sibert, "Military," 408.

80. Linn, *War*, 170.

81. Howze, Aug. 16, 1900, NA, RG 395, no. 4043.

82. Welch, *Response*, 34.

83. Private John Clifford Brown to his mother, July 5, 1900, in McCallus, ed., *Gentleman*, 230.

84. The letter, written on March 5, 1900, was printed, "by permission of Mr. Miller's mother," in the Omaha *World Herald*, May 13, 1900, 21.

85. *NYT*, Jan. 2, 1901, 6; New York *Post* quoted by *Public Opinion*, Jan. 31, 1901, 137.

86. General Samuel Young, Dec. 11, 1900, NA, RG 395, no. 2150.

Page 228

87. Col. McCaskey, March 25, 1901, ibid., no. 4053.

88. Birtle, *Counterinsurgency*, 108–46; Go, *Patterns*; Ileto, *Knowledge*; Kramer, *Blood*.

89. Gates's review of "*Benevolent Assimilation,*" *Military Affairs*, v. 48 (July 1984): 160.

90. See US Senate, Committee on the Philippines, *Affairs in the Philippine Islands*, 3 vols. (Washington DC: GPO, 1902).

Page 229

91. Miller, "*Benevolent,*" 179.

92. Root to Secretary of State, Nov. 2, 1900, quoted by Linn, *U.S. Army*, 23.

93. Welch, "Atrocities," 249. For a brilliant analysis, Kramer, *Blood*, 145–51.

94. Linn, *War*, 224. Like Gates, Linn reduces the massive evidence of US atrocities to the acts of "individual Americans" (*War*, 196).

95. Hoar, *CR*, Senate, May 22, 1902, 5788–98, 5795 quoted.

96. Ralph Bitting to his mother (late 1900), quoted by Birtle, "Pacification," 264.

97. Kramer, "Race-Making," 201.

98. John Galloway to the editor of the Richmond *Planet*, Nov. 16, 1899, in Gatewood, "*Smoked,*" 253.

99. Gatewood, *Black*, 285.

Page 230

100. Kramer, *Blood*, 154. On President Roosevelt: Morris, *Theodore*; Nathan Miller, *Theodore*; Cooper, *Warrior*; Beale, *Theodore*. Lammersdorf, *Anfänge*, is particularly good for relations with Europe.

101. Quotations from Birtle, *Counterinsurgency*, 129 and Birtle, "Pacification," 268.

102. Linn, *U.S. Army*, 27.

103. Gates, "War-Related Deaths"; Graff, ed., *American*, xiv; Glenn May, "150,000"; Kramer, *Blood*, 157.

104. Millett, Maskowski and Feis, *For*, 681.

105. *Washington Bee*, Oct. 29, 1898, 4.

Page 231

106. Hoganson, *Fighting*, 176–9.

107. Ella Thatcher, quoted by Rogers, "'Noble-Hearted,'" 53. Also Sneider, *Suffragists*, 87–116; Hoganson, "As"; Andolsen, *"Daughters."*

108. LaFeber, *Empire*, 250.

109. Welch, *Response*, 76.

Page 232

110. Immerman, *Empire*, 141.

111. Lodge, "Blundering."

112. Lodge, March 7, 1900, quoted by Walter Williams, "United States," 817.

113. United States, Department of the Interior, *Report*, 24–5.

114. Lodge, March 7, 1900, quoted by Walter Williams, "United States," 820.

12 Conquering the Backyard: The Latin American Policy of Roosevelt, Taft, and Wilson

Page 233

1. The best overview of US policy toward the region in this period is Schoultz, *Beneath*, 152–252.

2. Riguzzi, "México," 370.

3. See Healy, *Blaine*, 138–60.

4. Burns, *Alliance*, 61.

Page 234

5. Quotations from Emile Joré, French consul in Costa Rica, to Foreign Minister Hanotaux, April 24, 1898, AAE, 152 CPCOM–2 and Hugues Boulard-Pouqueville, French chargé in Mexico, to Foreign Minister Delcassé, June 30, 1898, AAE, 181 CPCOM–18. Also Quijada, "Latinos" and Uribe Salas et al., eds., *México*.

6. Root to Flagler, Jan. 3, 1905, quoted by Jessup, *Root*, 1: 471.

7. Charles Campbell, *Anglo-American*, 186–239; Pauncefote to Salisbury, Jan. 19, 1900, ibid., 190.

8. *The Times* (London), Feb. 14, 1903, 9.

Page 235

9. Jonas, *United States*, 17.

10. Ullrich, *Die nervöse*, 106–7.

11. Bülow, Dec. 6, 1897, quoted by Mommsen, *Grossmachtstellung*, 149. On Bismarck in 1871–90 see Gall, *Bismarck*; Canis, *Aussenpolitk*; Hildebrand, *Das*, 13–146.

12. Röhl, *Wilhelm II*, 249. See also Fiebig-von Hase, *Lateinamerika*; Herwig, *Vision*; Katz, *Secret*.

13. Mitchell, *Danger*. This is by far the best discussion of German policy in Latin America and of the clash between US and German imperialism in the region.

14. *NYT*, April 24, 1971, 1.

Page 236

15. The best analysis of the German war plans is Mitchell, *Danger*, 42–63, 48 and 50 quoted.

16. Quoted by Herwig and Trask, "Naval," 56.

17. Mitchell, *Danger*, 48.

18. This paragraph and the next rely on Mitchell, *Danger*, 108–59.

19. Röhl, *Wilhelm II.*, 253.

20. Mitchell, *Danger*, 123, 126, 145 and 143 quoted.

Page 237

21. The best account of this second Venezuelan crisis is Mitchell, *Danger*, 64–107, quotations from 65, 79, 98.

22. Roosevelt, Dec. 3, 1901, https://millercenter.org/the-presidency/presidential-speeches/december-3-1901.

23. Mitchell, *Danger*, 91, 97 quoted. The naive historians include Frederick Marks, *Velvet*, 37–88; Ricard, *Théodore Roosevelt*, 279–94; Morris, "Few."

Page 238

24. Staunton, memorandum, June 26, 1912, quoted by Bäcker, "Das deutsche Feindbild," 70.

25. Mitchell, *Danger*, 220.

26. Bäcker, "Das deutsche Feindbild," 76.

27. Mitchell, *Danger*, 132.

28. Roosevelt to Knox, Feb. 8, 1909, in Morison, ed., *Letters*, 6: 1511.

29. The most authoritative source for US direct foreign investment in 1914 (1879 figures in parenthesis) suggests: Canada $618 million ($160 million); Mexico $587m ($200m); Caribbean Islands and Central America $371m ($60m); South America $323m ($38m); Europe $573m ($131m); Asia $120m ($23m); Africa $13m ($1m); Oceania $17m ($2m) (Mira Wilkins, *Emergence*, 110, 153n, 201)

30. Colby, *Business*; Mira Wilkins, *Emergence*; Rosenberg, *Financial*; Rosenberg, *Spreading*; O'Brien, *Century*, 25–56.

Page 239

31. Roosevelt to Hay, July 14, 1903, quoted by Schoultz, *Beneath*, 164. The best account of Roosevelt's Panama policy is McCullough, *The Path*, 329–86.

32. John Barrett to Root, May 23, 1906, quoted by Schoultz, *Beneath*, 172.

33. Roosevelt to Root, June 7, 1904, in Morison, *Letters*, 4: 821.

34. Roosevelt, Dec. 6, 1904, https://www.presidency.ucsb.edu/documents/fourth-annual-message-15.

35. US minister to the Dominican Republic Thomas Dawson, quoted by Healy, *Drive*, 120.

Page 240

36. Schoonover, *United States*, 130–48; Stansifer, "Zelaya"; Gobat, *Confronting*.

37. Stephen Leech, "General Report on Cuba for 1909," Jan. 26, 1910, TNA, FO 277/169.

38. Kneer, *Great Britain*, 93 (ibid., 69 for the importance of the Cuban market).

39. Smith, *Unequal*, 35.

40. Root, "The causes of War," Feb. 26, 1909, quoted by Schoultz, *Beneath*, 204.

41. Root to Tillman, Dec. 13, 1905, quoted by Jessup, *Root*, 1: 469.

Page 241

42. Scholes and Scholes, *Foreign*, 12.

43. Cervo and Bueno, *História*, 135–213, 162 quoted; Bandeira, *Presença*, 229–94; Burns, *Unwritten*.

44. McGann and Handlin, *Argentina*, 230, 235–6 quoted; Cisneros et al., eds., *Historia*, 8: 61–112 and 10: 175–216; Morgenfeld, *Vecinos*.

45. US Department of Commerce, *Historical*, 2: 903. The principal markets for US exports in the hemisphere were Canada ($415 million), followed by Cuba ($71 million), and Mexico ($54 million).

Page 242

46. Mira Wilkins, *Emergence*,113–34; also Table V.2, ibid., 110.

47. Nancy Mitchell, *Danger*, 163

48. Alan Knight's masterful *Mexican Revolution* has profound insights on Wilson's policy toward Mexico, as does Mitchell's *Danger*, 160–215. Valuable studies include Larry Hill, *Emissaries*; Robert Freeman Smith, *United States*; Ulloa, *Revolución*.

49. Alan Knight, *Mexican Revolution*, 2: 71.

50. Wilson, "Remarks at a Press Conference," July 17, 1913, *WWP*, 28: 37.

Page 243

51. Larry Hill, *Emissaries*, 21–39, 60–89.

52. Mitchell, *Danger*, 178; "A Circular Note to the Powers," Aug. 8, 1913, *WWP*, 28: 130.

53. "International Note: 'Our Purpose in Mexico,'" enclosed in Wilson to Bryan, Nov. 23, 1913, *WWP*, 28: 585–6.

54. Wilson, Press conference, March 9, 1914, *WWP*, 50: 406.

55. Grey to Carden, Oct. 17, 1913, TNA, FO 371/1676.

Page 244

56. Quirk, *Affair*.

57. Bäcker, *Mexikopolitik*, 174–87; Mitchell, *Danger*, 195–208.

58. Mitchell, *Danger*, 210.

59. Robert Freeman Smith, *United States*, 36

60. Wilson to Lansing. June 17, 1915, *PWW*, 33: 414.

61. The most insightful discussion is Katz, *Life*, 545–614.

62. War College Division, "The Military Strength for Armed Intervention in Mexico," [March 1916,] NA, RG 165, War Dept. General and Special Staffs, Correspondence of War College Division and Related Gen. Staff Offices 1903–19, M1024, Roll 86.

63. Tumulty, *Wilson*, 159.

Page 245

64. Katz, *Life*, 611. For the text of the US note, Haley, *Revolution*, 235–6.

65. Wilson, July 10, 1916 speech, quoted by Haley, *Revolution*, 224.

66. Weber, ed., *Foreigners*, 204.

67. See Benjamin Johnson, *Revolution*; Harris and Sadler, *The Plan*; Muñoz Martinez, *Injustice*, 76–119.

Page 246

68. *New York Globe*, Sept. 16, 1919 (edit.), quoted by Carrigan and Webb, *Forgotten*, 275 n.65.

69. US Department of Commerce, *Historical*, 2: 903; Gilderhus, *Visions*; Kaufman, "Trade"; Rosenberg, *Spreading*, 63–86.

70. Gobat, *Confronting*, 123–202.

71. Hugh Wilson, *Education*, 46.

72. Perl to German chancellor, May 14, 1912, BA, R 901/77360.

73. Plummer, *Haiti*, 191.

74. Wilson to Bryan, Jan. 13, 1915, *PWW*, 32: 62.

Page 247

75. Bernard, *Histoire*; Plummer, "Metropolitan"; "D'Confidential Tentative Plan for Employment of Naval Forces Stationed in Haitian Ports–Port-au-Prince," c. July 1914, NA, RG 45, WA-7, box 631.

76. Quotations from Perl to Bethman Hollweg, Aug. 5, 1914 and Aug. 11, BA, R 901/86715.

77. Delva, *Considérations*, 6. Between 1806 and 1820 the constitution of the northern part of Haiti, ruled by Henri Christophe, had omitted this prohibition.

78. Perl to Bethman Hollweg, Jan. 8, 1915 (quoting former US minister Henry Furniss), PA AA, R 16806; Schmidt, *United States*, 32–42, 60; Plummer, *Haiti*, 181–2.

79. Sosna, "Saddle," 34.

Page 248

80. See Bryan to Bailly-Blanchard, March 25, 1915 and Bryan to Wilson, April 3, 1915, *PWW*, 32: 437 n.2 and 471.

81. Plummer, *Haiti*, 198–9 quoted; Healy, *Gunboat*, 124.

82. Perl to Bethman Hollweg, Aug. 20, 1914, BA, R 901/86715.

83. Bryan to Wilson, March 27, 1915, *PWW*, 32: 439–40; Wilson to Bryan, March 31, 1915, ibid., 458.

84. LaFeber, *American Age*, 267; Cooper, *Wilson*, 248–9; Schoultz, *Beneath*, 231–2; Link, *Wilson*, 101–2.

85. Girard to foreign minister Delcassé, July 31, 1915, AAE, Nouvelle Série, Haïti, vol. 15.

86. Blumenthal, "Wilson," 10–11.

87. Girard to French foreign ministry, quoting Caperton, July 29, 1915, AAE, Nouvelle Série, Haïti, vol. 15; Delcassé to Girard, Aug. 6, 1915, ibid.

Page 249

88. Damon Woods (US consul at Cap Haitien), "Some observations and suggestions relative to the work of the American occupation in Haiti," Oct. 31, 1923, NA, RG 59, SDDF, 838.00/1961.

89. British Legation Port-au-Prince, Jan. 18, 1927, TNA, FO 420/345.

90. French Foreign Ministry, Direction des Affaires Politiques et Commerciales, "République Dominicaine," April 9, 1919, AAE, 16 CPCOM–2.

91. Calder, *Impact*, 5. Three other important studies are Melvin Knight, *Americans*; Conde, *Historia*, 2: 473–642; Munro, *Intervention*, 269–325.

92. Perl to Bethman Hollweg, July 20 and July 6, 1916, PA AA, R 17004; Caperton to Admiral Benson, June 15, 1916, LOC, Manuscript Division, William B. Caperton Papers, box 1.

93. Memorandum of the Solicitor of the State Department, July 10, 1918, *FRUS*, 1918, 389.

94. Blassingame, "The Press," 29.

Page 250

95. "The Press and the International Situation," *The Nation*, Mar. 21, 1918, 315.

96. Washington, quoted by *New York Age*, Aug. 19, 1915, 1; *The Crisis*, Sept. 1915, 232. Also Plummer, "Response"; Byrd, *Black*, 196–238.

97. Lowenthal, *Intervention*, 9.

98. See the careful assessment in Calder, *Impact*, 32–66.

99. Otto Schoenrich, "Suggestions for actions to be taken in Santo Domingo," enclosed in Schoenrich to Rowe, Dec. 11, 1919, NA, RG 59, SDDF 839.00/2247.

100. Ibid.

101. Healy, *Gunboat*, 203.

102. Millspaugh, *Haiti*, 119–23; Montague, *Haiti*, 245.

Page 251

103. Lansing to Bailly-Blanchard, June 10, 1917, NA, RG 59, SDDF 838.011/69; Bailly-Blanchard to SecState, June 15, 1917, ibid., 838.011/10.

104. Bailly-Blanchard to SecState, June 14, 1917, ibid., 838.011/22.

105. Moïse, *Constitutions*, 2: 60.

106. Quotations from Bailly-Blanchard to SecState, June 21, 1917, NA, RG 59, SDDF 838.011/23; Butler to McIlhenny, June 23, 1917, in Venzon, *Butler*, 194. For a detailed account, Gaillard, *Les blancs*, 4: 237–55.

107. Schmidt, *United States*, 98–9; Moïse, *Constitutions*, 2: 62–5. For the official results, *Moniteur* (Port-au-Prince), June 19, 1918, quoted in ibid., 2: 65.

108. Calder, *Impact*, 91–114, 100 quoted; Melvin Knight, *Americans*, 129–48; Frost to SecState, Aug. 6, 1927, NA, RG 59, Records of the Department of State Relating to Internal Affairs of the Dominican Republic, 1910–1929, M626, Roll 68.

109. Delage, vice consul in charge of the French consulate in Santo Domingo, to French foreign minister Briand, Oct. 29, 1916, AAE, 193 CPCOM–7.

110. French Ministry of Foreign Affairs, "Notes sur l'intervention des États-Unis en République dominicaine," [late 1917,] AAE, 16 CPCOM–2.

111. Calder, "Some Aspects," 153–4. On the guerrilla war, also Ducoudray, "Gavilleros"; Conde, *Historia*, 2: 527–38, 559–60.

Page 252

112. Schmidt, *Maverick*, 81 quoted; for a detailed account, Gaillard, *Les Blancs*, 3: 183–9.

113. British Legation Port-au-Prince, Jan. 18, 1927, TNA, FO 420/345.

114. General Barnett to Col. Russell, Sept. 2, 1919, *NYT*, Oct. 14, 1920, 1; Barnett's report to Navy Secretary Daniels, Sept. 18, 1920, ibid., 3.

115. British Legation Port-au-Prince, Jan. 18, 1927, TNA, FO 420/345.

116. Franck, *Roaming*, 118.

13 The Far East

Page 255

1. Michael Hunt, *Making*, 299. The best overviews of Sino-American relations in the period covered in this book are Hunt, *Making*; Warren Cohen, *Response*; Chang, *Fateful*; Dong Wang, *United States*.

2. *Review of Reviews*, Aug. 1905, 143.

Page 256

3. Warren Cohen, *Response*, 20.

4. US Department of Commerce, *Historical*, 2: 904, 907.

5. Pletcher, *Diplomacy of Involvement*, 118.

6. Daniels, *Asian America*, 34.

7. Chang and Fishkin, eds., *Chinese*, 18 quoted; Karuka, *Tracks*, 82–103.

8. Foner and Rosenberg, eds., *Racism*, 22.

9. Takaki, *Strangers*, 101.

Page 257

10. Abstract of the Fourteenth Census of the United State, quoted by Lee, *Gates*, 238.

11. Pfaelzer, *Driven Out*; Lew-Williams, *Chinese*.

12. Daniels, *Asian America*, 58.

13. This paragraph is based on Storti, *Incident*, 115, 141 quoted.

14. Ibid., 159–66.

15. Denby to Bayard, Aug. 10, 1886, NA, RG 59, Despatches from U.S. Minister to China, M 92, Roll 79. Also Tansill, *Bayard*, 137–49.

16. US Congress, House, Committee on Foreign Relations, Report no. 2044, 49th Cong., 1st sess., 1885–1886, 3.

Page 259

17. Stratton, "Snake River," 125 quoted.

18. See Wiley, *Yankees*. The best overview of US-Japanese relations for the period covered in this book remains Neumann, *America*; see also LaFeber, *Clash*.

19. Cosenza, ed., *Complete*, 357–8 quoted (emphasis in original); Dennett, *Americans*, 347–66.

20. Quoted by Beasley, *Great Britain*, 93.

21. Ibid., 168–93.

Page 260

22. Seward quoted by Paolino, *Foundations*, 175; Satow, *Diplomat*, 141–56, 143 quoted; Dennett, *Americans*, 393–406.

23. Neumann, *America*, 66.

24. Jansen, *The Making*, 361.

25. Dennett, *Americans*, 515–20.

Page 261

26. US Department of Commerce, *Historical*, 2: 903.

27. *Journal of Commerce* (New York), Dec. 28, 1897, 6 (edit.); *Commercial Advertiser* (New York), Dec. 30, 1897 (edit.); *Herald* (Boston), Mar. 27, 1898, 12 (edit.).

28. See Varg's excellent essay, "Myth."

29. Charles Campbell, *Anglo-American*, 150–69.

30. Warren Cohen, *Response*, 46.

31. See Schrecker, *Imperialism*.

32. Spence, *Search*, 231.

Page 262

33. Ibid., 233. On the Boxer uprising see Silbey, *Boxer*; Paul Cohen, *History*; Bickers and Tiedemann, eds., *Boxers*.

34. Quoted by Ch'ên, "Nature," 293.

35. Kelly, *Forgotten*,

36. Chamberlin, *Ordered*, 127; Sharf and Harrington, *Boxer*, 28.

37. James Hevia, "Looting and Its Discontents," in Bickers and Tiedemann, eds., *Boxers*, 94.

38. General Chaffee to Adjutant General, US Army, Nov. 30, 1900, quoted by Roger Thompson, "Military," 313.

39. Silbey, *Boxer*, 216 quoted; Michael Hunt, "Forgotten."

Page 263

40. Kelly, *Forgotten*; Michael Hunt, "Remission."

41. Hay's Circular Letter of July 3, 1900, in Commager, ed., *Documents*, 2: 9; Warren Cohen, *Response*, 53.

42. Cassini to Lamsdorf, June 3, 1903, in Iakovleva, ed., *Rossia*, 285.

43. Gresham to White, Aug. 28, 1893, quoted by Saul, *Concord*, 397–8.

Page 264

44. Michael Hunt, *Frontier*, 21. On the growth of US trade with Manchuria Hosie, *Manchuria*, 254–7.

45. Saul, *Concord*, 469.

46. Hay to Roosevelt, May 12, 1903, LOC, Manuscript Division, John Hay Papers, reel 4, box 1.

47. Ito Hirrobumi, Feb. 4, 1904, quoted by Warner and Warner, *Tide*, 175.

48. *Outlook* (New York), Jan. 23, 1904, 205; *NYT*, Oct. 13, 1903, 8 (edit.).

49. Cassini to Foreign Ministry, Jan. 11, 1904, in Iakovleva, ed., *Rossia*, 49; Cassini to Lamsdorf, Jan. 27, 1904, ibid., 51–2.

50. Roosevelt to Theodore Roosevelt Jr., Feb. 10, 1904, in Morison, ed., *Letters*, 4: 724.

51. Meyer to Root, July 3, 1905, NA, RG 59, Despatches from U.S. Ministers to Russia, 1808–1906, M-35, Roll 63.

52. *NYT*, Aug. 18, 1905, 6 (edit.); *NYH*, Aug. 9, 1905, 4.

Page 265

53. Roosevelt, quoted in Hay Diary, Dec. 6, 1904, LOC, Manuscript Division, Hay Papers, reel 1, box 1.

54. On the Portsmouth conference see Esthus, *Double*.

55. Nehru, *Toward*, 29–30.

56. *Freeman* (Indianapolis), Feb. 18, 1905; *Colored American Magazine* (Boston), July 1905, 348; Grimké, *Age* (New York), July 13, 1905. All quoted by Kearney, *African American*, 35, 19, 29.

57. Ung Bing Li, *Outlines*, 617.

58. Anshan Li, "Miscellany," 2: 503.

59. I borrow the expression from McKee, *Chinese Exclusion*, 96.

Page 266

60. Michael Hunt, *Making*, 228.

61. Lee, *Gates*, 64, 58–9 quoted.

62. V.H. Metcalf, "Letter from the Secretary of Commerce and Labor, Transmitting a Report of an Investigation of the Conditions of the Immigrant Service at San Francisco, Cal.," Dec. 30, 1904, House of Representatives, 58 Cong., 3rd sess., doc. #166, 2.

63. Michael Hunt, *Making*, 229.

64. Coolidge, *Chinese*, 469.

65. Wong, "Menace," 414.

Page 267

66. Varg, *Missionaries*, 18 quoted; Fairbank, ed., *Missionary*; Hunter, *Gospel*; Chang, *Fateful*, 52–67.

67. *Dongfang Zazhi*, quoted by Anshan Li, "Miscellany," 498.

68. Ts'ai, "Reaction"; Chen, *Chinese*, 148–61; John Thompson, *Great Power*, 93–119; Guanhua Wang, *Justice*.

69. Roosevelt to Metcalf, June 19, 1905, in Morison, ed., *Letters*, 4: 1240.

70. Challener, *Admirals*, 217.

Page 268

71. Ibid., 249.

72. Roosevelt to Taft, in Morison, ed., Letters, 5: 761–2.

73. Mahan quoted by Seager, *Mahan*, 487; Fiske to Secretary of the Navy, May 13, 1913, in Cronon, ed., *Cabinet*, 57. The best source on War Plan Orange is Edward Miller, *War Plan*. See also Challener, *Admirals*, 225–64; Vlahos, "Naval"; Bönker, *Militarism*, 52–7, 92–3, 131–7.

Page 269

74. Takaki, *Strangers*, 177–201 (200 quoted); Daniels, *Politics*, 16–30; Azuma, *Between*, 3–85.

75. Almaguer, "Racial"; Street, *Beasts*, 197–200.

76. *Courier* (Oxnard), quoted by Fukuyama, "Japanese," 7.

77. Quoted by Almaguer, "Racial," 346–7.

78. Takaki, *Strangers*, 200; Lee, *Gate*, 52.

Page 270

79. *San Francisco Chronicle*, March 6, 1905, 6 (edit.).

80. Daniels, *Politics*, 70.

81. Metcalf Report, 17–18; McClain, ed., *Japanese*, 181.

82. *Outlook* (New York), Nov. 3, 1906, 538; for the amount, Report of San Francisco Relief and Red Cross Funds, quoted by George Kennan, "The Japanese in the San Francisco Schools," *Outlook*, June 1, 1907, 246.

83. Quotations from *Literary Digest* 33 (Nov. 3, 1906): 621 and Wright to Root, Oct. 22, 1906, NA, RG 59, Numerical and Minor Files of the Department of State, 1906–1910, M862. Also Bailey, *Roosevelt*, 46–56; Neu, *Uncertain*, 29–38.

84. *Nation*, Nov. 1, 1906, 364; Roosevelt to Kermit Roosevelt, Oct. 27, 1906, in Morison, ed., *Letters*, 6:475.

85. Tupper and McReynolds, *Japan*, 29–32, 38–9; Bailey, *Roosevelt*, 67–79.

Page 271

86. Gallicchio, *African American*, 14–15.

87. Neu, *Uncertain*, 51–88, 123–80; Bailey, *Roosevelt*, 112–92.

88. Ichioka, *Issei*, 210–26; McClain, ed., *Japanese*, 125.

89. Roosevelt, Dec. 3, 1906, https://www.presidency.ucsb.edu/documents/sixth-annual-message-4

90. John Thompson, *Great Power*, 122–9; Kawakami, "Naturalization."

91. US Department of Commerce, *Historical*, 2: 903.

Page 272

92. Roosevelt to Taft, Dec. 22, 1910, in Morison, ed., *Letters*, 7: 189–90.

93. Tupper and McReynolds, *Japan*, 44.

94. Ibid., 45–9; Neu, *Uncertain*, 291–305; Bailey, *Roosevelt*, 304–21; John Thompson, *Great Power*, 144–7.

95. Knox to Huntington Wilson, undated [1909,] quoted by Challener, *Admirals*, 267.

96. The best analysis of Taft's Far Eastern policy is Michael Hunt, *Frontier*, 53 quoted; for a wealth of details Scholes and Scholes, *Taft*, 109–248. On the Taft presidency, Gould, *Taft*.

Page 273

97. Remer, *Foreign*, 76.

98. US Department of Commerce, *Historical*, 2: 903.

99. Warren Cohen, *Response*, 61–2 quoted; Varg, "Myth," 753–4.

100. Parlett, *Brief*, 19–21; Michael Hunt, *Frontier*, 107–13. Also Matsusaka, *Making*, 60–148.

101. Daniels, entry of May 28, 1913, in Cronon, ed., *Cabinet*, 17.

102. McClain, ed., *Japanese*, esp. 59–83, 104–27, 145–87.

103. Chinda to Bryan, May 9, 1913, *FRUS*, 1913, 629.

Page 274

104. Fiske to Secretary of Navy, May 14, 1913, in Cronon, ed., *Cabinet*, 60–1.

105. Link, *Wilson*, 303, 304.

106. General Board of the Navy, "Black War Plan," 1915, NA, RG 80, War Portfolios, 1902–1923, Box 10.

107. US Department of Commerce, *Historical*, 2: 903–4.

108. Dexter Perkins, *Hands Off*, 271 quoted; Bailey, "Lodge Corollary."

Page 275

109. Lea, *Valor*, 153, 179; *Literary Digest*, quoted by Neumann, *America*, 128.

14 The White City on the Hill

Page 278

1. Woodrow Wilson, "Democracy and Efficiency," *Atlantic Monthly*, March 1901, 293.

2. *NYH*, Dec. 14, 1845, 2.

Page 279

3. Lodge, March 7, 1900, quoted by Walter Williams, "United States," 820.

4. Tatz, "Genocide", 324.

5. Adams, entry of June 30, 1841, in *Memoirs*, edited by Charles Francis Adams, 10: 492.

6. Jefferson to Monroe, Nov. 24, 1801, *PTJ*, 35: 719–20.

Page 280

7. Hendrickson, *Union*, 269.

8. José Manuel Zozaya to the Foreign Minister of Mexico, Dec. 26, 1822, in Mexico, Secretaría de Relaciones Exteriores, *La diplomacia*, 1: 103; Stephen Austin to J.E.B. Austin, June 13, 1823, in Barker, ed., *Papers*, 1: 671.

9. *American Review*, Jan. 1846, 85–7.

Page 281

10. Root, "The causes of War," Feb. 26, 1909, quoted by Schoultz, *Beneath*, 204.

11. Jefferson to Burr, Feb. 11, 1799, *PTJ*, 31: 22.

Page 282

12. *The Times* (London), June 3, 1858, 8 (edit.).

Page 283

13. Mitchell, *Danger*, 224.

14. Miles, "War," 750.

Page 284

15. Pletcher, *Diplomacy of Involvement*, 118.

16. US Department of Commerce, *Historical*, 2: 903–5.

17. Bolívar to Santander, Dec. 23, 1822, in Lecuna, ed., *Cartas*, 3: 126.

Page 285

18. *Bradstreet's*, April 23, 1898, 257.

19. Lodge, March 7, 1900, quoted by Walter Williams, "United States," 817.

20. Adams, May 25, 1836, *Register of Debates*, vol. 12, pt 4, 4041–2.

21. Hoar, *CR*, Senate, May 22, 1902, 5795.

Page 286

22. Luther Severance (W-ME), May 12, 1846, *National Intelligencer* (Washington DC), May 13, 1846, 3.

23. *Colored American* (Washington DC), Sept. 2, 1899, 6.

Page 287

24. Jefferson to Rutledge, July 4, 1790, PTJ, 16: 601.

25. Kissinger, *Diplomacy*, 224; Wilson quoted in ibid.

26. Levin, *Wilson*, 7.

27. Shmazu, *Japan*.

28. Manela, *Wilsonian*, 6.

BIBLIOGRAPHY

Archives

Costa Rica
Archivo Nacional, Ministerio de Relaciones Exteriores, San José

France
Archive des affaires étrangères, Paris

Germany
Bundesarchiv, Auswärtiges Amt, Berlin

Mexico
Archivo Histórico Genaro Estrada de la Secretaría de Relaciones Exteriores, Mexico City

Spain
Archivo del Ministerio de Asuntos Exteriores, Madrid

United Kingdom
Bodleian Library, Oxford
British Library, London
The National Archives, Kew, Surrey
University of Southampton, Hartley Library, Southampton

United States
Library of Congress, Manuscript Division, Washington DC
National Archives, College Park, MD
University of Oklahoma, Western History Collection, Cherokee Nation Papers, Norman, OK

Works cited

Abram, Susan. "Cherokees in the Creek War," in Kathryn Braund, ed., *Tohopeka: Rethinking the Creek War and the War of 1812* (Tuscalosa: University of Alabama Press, 2012), 122–45.
Acerra, Martine and Jean Meyer. *Marines et Révolution* (Caen: Éditions Ouest-France, 1988).
Ackers, Donna. *Living in the Land of Death: The Choctaw Nation, 1830–1860* (East Lansing: Michigan State University Press, 2004).
Acomb, Evelyn, ed. *The Revolutionary Journal of Baron Ludwig von Closen, 1780–1783* (Chapel Hill: University of North Carolina Press, 1958).
Acuña Ortega, Víctor, ed. *Filibusterismo y Destino Manifiesto en las Américas* (Alajuela, C.R.: Museo Histórico Cultural Juan Santamaría, 2010).
Adams, Charles Francis. *"Imperialism" and "The Tracks of our Forefathers"* (Middletown, DE: Valde Books, 2009 [1899]).

Bibliography

Adams, Charles Francis. ed. *Memoirs of John Quincy Adams*, 12 vols. (Philadelphia: Lippincott, 1874–7).

Adams, Charles Francis. ed. *The Works of John Adams, Second President of the United States*, 10 vols. (Boston, MA: Little, Brown and Co., 1850–6).

Adams, Ephraim. *Great Britain and the American Civil War*, 2 vols. (London: Longmans, Green and Co., 1925).

Adams, Henry, ed. *The Writings of Albert Gallatin*, 3 vols. (Philadelphia: Lippincott, 1879).

Adams, Mary. "Jefferson's Reaction to the Treaty of San Ildefonso," *Journal of Southern History*, 21 (May 1955): 173–88.

Agoncillo, Teodoro. *Malolos: The Crisis of the Republic* (Quezon City: University of the Philippines, 1960).

Allen, Robert. *His Majesty's Indian Allies: British Indian Policy in the Defence of Canada, 1774–1815* (Toronto: Dundurn Press, 1993).

Almaguer, Tomás. "Racial Domination and Class Conflict in Capitalist Agriculture: The Oxnard Sugar Beet Workers' Strike of 1903," *Labor History*, 25 (1984): 325–50.

Altoff, Gerard. *Amongst My Best Men: African-Americans and the War of 1812* (Put-in-Bay, OH: The Perry Group, 1996).

Álvarez Gutiérrez, Luis. "Los imperios centrales ante el progresivo deterioro de las relaciones entre España y los Estados Unidos," *Hispania*, 57/2 (May–Aug. 1997): 435–78.

American State Papers: Foreign Relations, 1789–1827, 6 vols., *American State Papers: Documents, Legislative and Executive of the Congress of the United States*, 38 vols. (Washington DC: Gales and Seaton, 1832–61).

American State Papers: Indian Affairs, 1789–1828, 2 vols., *American State Papers: Documents, Legislative and Executive of the Congress of the United States*, 38 vols. (Washington DC: Gales and Seaton, 1832–61).

Ammon, Harry. *The Genet Mission* (New York: Norton, 1973).

Ammon, Harry. *James Monroe: The Quest for National Identity* (Charlottesville: University Press of Virginia, 1990).

Anderson, Fred. *Crucible of War: The Seven Years' War and the Fate of Empire in British North America, 1754–1766* (New York: Vintage Books, 2001).

Anderson, Stuart. *Race and Rapprochement: Anglo-Saxonism and Anglo-American Relations, 1895–1904* (Rutherford, NJ: Fairleigh Dickinson University, 1981).

Andersson, Rani-Henrik. *The Lakota Ghost Dance of 1890* (Lincoln: University of Nebraska Press, 2008).

Andolsen, Barbara. *"Daughters of Jefferson, Daughters of Bootblacks": Racism and American Feminism* (Macon, GA: Mercer University Press, 1986).

Armstrong, Virginia, ed. *I Have Spoken: American History Through the Voices of the Indians* (Chicago: Swallow Press, 1971).

Auguste, Claude and Marcel Auguste. *L'expédition Leclerc 1801–1803* (Port-au-Prince: Henri Deschamps, 1985).

Austin, O.P. "Is The New Immigration Dangerous to the Country?" *NAR*, 178 (April 1904): 558–70.

Azuma, Elichiro. *Between Two Empires: Race, History, and Transnationalism in Japanese America* (New York: Oxford University Press, 2005).

Azzi, Stephen. *Reconcilable Differences: A History of Canada-US Relations* (Don Mills, Ontario: Oxford University Press, 2015).

Bäcker, Thomas. *Die deutsche Mexikopolitik 1913/14* (Berlin: Colloquium Verlag, 1971).

Bäcker, Thomas. "Das deutsche Feindbild in der amerikanischen Marine 1900–1914," *Marine-Rundschau*, 70, no. 2 (1973): 65–84.

Bailey, Thomas. "The Lodge Corollary to the Monroe Doctrine," *Political Science Quarterly*, 48 (June 1933): 220–38.

Bailey, Thomas. *Theodore Roosevelt and the Japanese-American Crises* (Gloucester, MA: Peter Smith, 1964 [1934]).

Baker, Jean. *James Buchanan* (New York: Henry Holt, 2004).

Ball, Charles, *Slavery in the United States: A Narrative of the Life and Adventures of Charles Ball, a Black Man* (Pittsburgh, PA: J.T. Shryock, 1853).

Bandeira, Moniz. *Presença dos Estados Unidos no Brazil* (Rio de Janeiro: Civilização Brasileira, 1973).

Barbé-Marbois, François. *Histoire de la Louisiane et de la cession de cette colonie par la France aux États-Unis de l'Amérique Septentrionale* (Paris: Imprimerie de Firmin Didot, 1829).

Barker, Eugene, ed. *The Austin Papers*, 2 vols. (Washington DC: GPO, 1924, 1928).

Barros Franco, José. "El Caso del 'Baltimore'. Apuntes para la historia diplomatica de Chile" (Ph.D. Diss., Universidad de Chile, 1950).

Basler, Roy, ed. *The Collected Works of Abraham Lincoln*, 9 vols. (New Brunswick, NJ: Rutgers University Press, 1953–5).

Bassett, John, ed. *Correspondence of Andrew Jackson*, 7 vols. (Washington DC: Carnegie Institute, 1926–35).

Baumgartner, Alice. *South to Freedom: Runaway Slaves to Mexico and the Road to the Civil War* (New York: Basic Books, 2020).

Beale, Howard. *Theodore Roosevelt and the Rise of America to World Power* (Baltimore, MD: Johns Hopkins University Press, 1956).

Beasley, W.G. *Great Britain and the Opening of Japan, 1834–1858* (London: Luzac, 1951).

Bécker, Jerónimo. *Historia política y diplomática desde la independencia de los Estados Unidos hasta nuestros días (1776–1895)* (Madrid: Antonino Romero, 1897).

Bécker, Jerónimo. *Historia de las relaciones exteriores de España durante el siglo XIX*, 3 vols. (Madrid: J. Ratés, 1924–6).

Beecher, Catharine. *Educational Reminiscences and Suggestions* (New York: Ford and Co., 1864).

Beer, Andreas. *A Transnational Analysis of Representations of the US Filibusters in Nicaragua, 1855–1857* (London: Palgrave Macmillan, 2016).

Beilharz, Edwin and Carlos López. *We Were 49ers! Chilean Accounts of the California Gold Rush* (Pasadena, CA: Ward Ritchie Press, 1976).

Beisner, Robert. *Twelve Against Empire: The Anti-Imperialists, 1898–1900* (New York: McGraw-Hill, 1968).

Beisner, Robert. *From the Old Diplomacy to the New, 1865–1900* (Arlington Heights, IL: Harlan Davidson, 1975).

Belohlavek, John. *"Let the Eagle Soar!" The Foreign Policy of Andrew Jackson* (Lincoln: University of Nebraska Press, 1985).

Bemis, Samuel Flagg. *John Quincy Adams and the Foundations of American Foreign Policy* (New York: Knopf, 1949).

Bemis, Samuel Flagg. *John Quincy Adams and the Union* (New York: Knopf, 1956).

Bemis, Samuel Flagg. *Pinckney's Treaty: America's Advantage from Europe's Distress, 1783–1800* (rev. ed., New Haven, CT: Yale University Press, 1960).

Bemis, Samuel Flagg. *Jay's Treaty: A Study in Commerce and Diplomacy* (rev. ed., New Haven, CT: Yale University Press, 1962).

Bemis, Samuel Flagg. *The Diplomacy of the American Revolution* (Bloomington: Indiana University Press, 1967 [1935]).

Bemis, Samuel Flagg. *The Latin American Policy of the United States* (New York: Norton, 1967 [1943]).

Benn, Carl. *The Battle of York* (Belleville, Ontario: Mike Publishing Co., 1984).

Benn, Carl, ed. *A Mohawk Memoir from the War of 1812: John Norton-Teyoninhokarawen* (Toronto: University of Toronto Press, 2019).

Benton, Thomas Hart. *Thirty Years' View*, 2 vols. (New York: D. Appleton, 1854).

Bibliography

Bercuson, David et al. *Colonies: Canada to 1867* (Toronto: McGraw-Hill, 1992).

Berlin, Ira. *Slaves without Masters: The Free Negro in the Antebellum South* (New York: The New Press, 1974).

Bernard, Joseph. *Histoire de la colonie allemande d'Haïti. Geschichte der deutschen Kolonie Haitis* (rev. ed., Port-au-Prince, 2011).

Beveridge, Albert. "Cuba and Congress," *NAR*, 172 (Apr. 1901): 535–50.

Bickham, Roy. *The Weight of Vengeance: The United States, the British Empire, and the War of 1812* (New York: Oxford University Press, 2012).

Bickers, Robert and R.G. Tiedemann, eds. *The Boxers, China, and the World* (Lanham, MD: Rowman and Littlefield, 2007).

Birtle, Andrew. "The U.S. Army's Pacification of Marinduque, Philippine Islands, April 1900–April 1901," *Journal of Military History* 61 (April 1987): 255–82.

Birtle, Andrew. *U.S. Army Counterinsurgency and Contingency Operations Doctrine 1860–1941* (Washington DC: Center of Military History, United States Army, 2009).

Black, Jeremy. *The War of 1812 in the Age of Napoleon* (London: Continuum, 2009).

Blackett, R.J.M. *Divided Hearts: Britain and the American Civil War* (Baton Rouge: Louisiana State University Press, 2001).

Blassingame, John. "The Press and the American Intervention in Haiti and the Dominican Republic, 1914–1920," *Caribbean Studies*, 9 (July 1969): 27–43.

Blumenthal, Henry. "Woodrow Wilson and the Race Question," *JNH*, 48 no. 1 (Jan. 1963): 1–21.

Boles, John. *Jefferson: Architect of American Liberty* (New York: Basic Books, 2017).

Bönker, Dirk. *Militarism in a Global Age: Naval Ambitions in Germany and the United States before World War I* (Ithaca, NY: Cornell University Press, 2012).

Bonnell, Ulane. *La France, les États-Unis et la guerre de course* (Paris: Nouvelles Editions Latines, 1961).

Boulware, Tyler. *Deconstructing the Cherokee Nation: Town, Region, and Nation among Eighteenth-Century Cherokees* (Gainesville: University Press of Florida, 2011).

Bourne, Kenneth. "The Clayton-Bulwer Treaty and the Decline of British Opposition to the Territorial Expansion of the United States, 1857–60," *Journal of Modern History* 33 (Sept. 1961): 287–91.

Bourne, Kenneth. *Britain and the Balance of Power in North America, 1815–1908* (Berkeley: University of California Press, 1967).

Bourgerie, Raymond and Pierre Lesouef, *Yorktown (1781): La France offre l'indépendance à l'Amérique* (Paris: Economica, 1992).

Bowes, John. *Land Too Good for Indians: Northern Indian Removal* (Norman: University of Oklahoma Press, 2016).

Bowman, Albert. *The Struggle for Neutrality: Franco-American Diplomacy During the Federalist Era* (Knoxville: University of Tennessee Press, 1974).

Branda, Pierre. *Le prix de la gloire: Napoléon et l'argent* (Paris: Fayard, 2007).

Branda, Pierre and Thierry Lentz, eds. *Napoléon, l'esclavage et les colonies* (Paris: Fayard, 2006).

Brant, Irving. *James Madison*, 6 vols. (Indianapolis: Bobbs-Merrill, 1941–61).

Braund, Kathryn, ed. *Tohopeka: Rethinking the Creek War and the War of 1812* (Tuscaloosa: University of Alabama Press, 2012).

Brodsky, Alyn, *Grover Cleveland: A Study in Character* (New York: St. Martin's Press, 2000).

Brooks, Philip. *Diplomacy and the Borderlands: The Adams-Onís Treaty of 1819* (New York: Routledge, 2020 [1939]).

Brown, Gordon. *Toussaint's Clause: The Founding Fathers and the Haitian Revolution* (Jackson, MS: University Press of Mississippi, 2005).

Brown, Roger. *The Republic in Peril: 1812* (New York: Norton, 1971 [1964]).

Browning, Oscar, ed. *England and Napoleon in 1803: Being the DoF of Lord Whitworth* (London: Longmans, Green, and Co., 1887).

Bruti Liberati, Luigi. *La Santa Sede e le origini dell'impero americano: la guerra del 1898* (Milano: Unicopli, 1984).

Bryan, William Jennings. "Has the Election Settled the Money Question?" *NAR*, 169 (Dec. 1896): 703–10.

Buhoup, Jonathan. *Narrative of the Central Division, or Army of Chihuahua, Commanded by Brigadier General Wool* (London: Forgotten Book, 2015 [1847]).

Burin, Eric. *Slavery and the Peculiar Institution: A History of the American Colonization Society* (Gainesville: University Press of Florida, 2005).

Burner, Nick. *An Empire on the Edge: How Britain Came to Fight America* (New York: Vintage Books, 2014).

Burnett, John. "The Cherokee Removal through the Eyes of a Private Soldier," *Journal of Cherokee Studies*, 3 (Summer 1978): 181–5.

Burnett, Christina and Burke Marshall, eds. *Foreign in a Domestic Sense: Puerto Rico, American Expansion, and the Constitution* (Durham, NC: Duke University Press, 2001).

Burns, Bradford: *The Unwritten Alliance: Rio-Branco and Brazilian-American Relations* (New York: Columbia University Press, 1966).

Burt, A.L. *The United States, Great Britain, and British North America from the Revolution to the Establishment of Peace after the War of 1812* (New Haven, CT: Yale University Press, 1940).

Butrick, Daniel. *Cherokee Removal: The Journal of Rev. Daniel S. Butrick, May 19, 1838–April 1, 1839* (Park Hill, OK: The Trail of Tears Association, Oklahoma Chapter, 1998).

Byrd, Brandon. *The Black Republic: African Americans and the Fate of Haiti* (Philadelphia: University of Pennsylvania Press, 2020).

Cabán, Pedro. *Constructing a Colonial People: Puerto Rico and the United Sttaes, 1898–1932* (Boulder, CO: Westview, 1999).

Calder, Bruce. "Some Aspects of the United States Occupation of the Dominican Republic, 1916–1924," Ph.D. Diss., University of Texas at Austin, 1974.

Calder, Bruce. *The Impact of Intervention: The Dominican Republic during the U.S. Occupation of 1916–1924* (Austin: University of Texas Press, 1984).

Calhoun, Charles. *The Presidency of Ulysses S. Grant* (Lawrence: University Press of Kansas, 2017).

Calhoun, Charles. *Gilded Age Cato: The Life of Walter Q. Gresham* (Lexington: University Press of Kentucky, 1988).

Calloway, Colin. *The American Revolution in Indian Country* (Cambridge, UK: Cambridge University Press, 1995).

Calloway, Colin. *The Victory With No Name: The Native American Defeat of the First American Army* (New York: Oxford University Press, 2015).

Calloway, Colin. *The Indian World of George Washington* (New York: Oxford University Press, 2018).

Campbell, Charles. *Anglo-American Understanding, 1898–1903* (Westport, CT: Greenwood, 1980 [1957]).

Campbell, Duncan. *English Public Opinion and the American Civil War* (Woodbridge, UK: Boydell Press, 2003).

Campbell, James. *Middle Passages: African-American Journeys to Africa, 1787–2005* (New York: Penguin, 2006).

Canis, Konrad. *Bismarcks Aussenpolitk 1870–1890* (Paderborn: Schöningh, 2008).

Carcovich, Luis. *Portales y la política internacional hispano-americana* (Santiago, Chile: Imprenta Universitaria, 1937).

Carnegie, Andrew. "Americanism *versus* Imperialism," *NAR*, 168 (Jan. 1899): 1–13.

Carp, Benjamin. *Defiance of the Patriots: The Boston Tea Party and the Making of America* (New Haven, CT: Yale University Press, 2011).

Carrigan, William and Clive Webb, *Forgotten Dead: Mob Violence against Mexicans in the United States, 1848–1928* (New York: Oxford University Press, 2013).

Bibliography

Carroll, Henry. *Report on the Island of Porto Rico* (Washington DC: GPO, 1899).

Carson, James, "Native Americans, the Market Revolution and Culture Change," in Greg O'Brien, ed., *Pre-Removal Choctaw History* (Norman: University of Oklahoma Press, 2002), 183–99.

Carter, Clarence, ed., *The Territorial Papers of the United States*, 28 vols. (Washington DC: GPO, 1934–75).

Case, Lynn and Warren Spencer, *The United States and France: Civil War Diplomacy* (Philadelphia: University of Pennsylvania Press, 1970).

Cecelski, David and Timothy Tyson, eds. *Democracy Betrayed: The Wilmington Race Riot of 1898 and Its Legacy* (Chapel Hill: University of North Carolina Press, 1998).

Cervera, Pascual, ed. *Colección de documentos referentes a la escuadra de operaciones de las Antillas* (Madrid: Editorial Naval, 1986 [1899]).

Cervo, Amado and Clodoaldo Bueno. *História da política exterior do Brazil* (San Paolo: Ática, 1992).

Chaffin, Tom. *Fatal Glory: Narciso López and the First Clandestine U.S. War against Cuba* (Charlottesville: University Press of Virginia, 1996).

Chaline, Olivier et al., eds. *La France et l'indépendance américaine* (Paris: Presses de l'Université Paris-Sorbonne, 2008).

Challener, Richard. *Admirals, Generals, and American Foreign Policy, 1898–1914* (Princeton, NJ: Princeton University Press, 1973).

Chamberlin, Wilbur. *Ordered to China: Letters Written from China While Under Commission from the New York Sun During the Boxer Uprising of 1900* (London: Forgotten Books, 2012 [1904]).

Chandler, William and Josiah Quincy. "Issues and Prospects of the Campaign," *NAR*, 163 (Aug. 1896): 175–94.

Chang, Gordon. *Fateful Ties: A History of America's Preoccupation with China* (Cambridge, MA: Harvard University Press, 2015).

Chang, Gordon and Shelley Fishkin, eds. *The Chinese and the Iron Road: Building the Transcontinental Railroad* (Stanford, CA: Stanford University Press, 2019).

Chávez, Thomas. *Spain and the Independence of the United States: An Intrinsic Gift* (Albuquerque: University of New Mexico Press, 2002).

Ch'ên, Jerome. "The Nature and Characteristics of the Boxer Movement," *Bulletin of the School of Oriental and African Studies*, 23 (1960): 287–308.

Chen, Yong. *Chinese San Francisco, 1850–1943: A Trans-Pacific Community* (Stanford, CA: Stanford University Press, 2000).

Chernow, Ron. *Alexander Hamilton* (New York: Penguin Press, 2004).

Chernow, Ron. *Washington: A Life* (New York: Penguin Books, 2010).

Chernow, Ron. *Grant* (New York: Penguin Press, 2017).

Cisneros, Andrés, et al., eds. *Historia general de las relaciones exteriores de la República Argentina*, 16 vols. (Buenos Aires: Grupo Editor Latinoamericano, 1998–2003).

Clavin, Matthew. "'It is a Negro, not an Indian War,'" in William Belko, ed., *America's Hundred Years' War: U.S. Expansion to the Gulf Coast and the Fate of the Seminoles, 1763–1858* (Gainesville: University Press of Florida, 2011), 181–208.

Clegg, Claude. *The Price of Liberty: African Americans and the Making of Liberia* (Chapel Hill: University of North Carolina Press, 2004).

Coffman, Tom. *Nation Within: The History of the American Occupation of Hawai'i* (Durham NC: Duke University Press 2016).

Cogliano, Francis. *Emperor of Liberty: Thomas Jefferson's Foreign Policy* (New Haven, CT: Yale University Press, 2014).

Cohen, Paul. *History in Three Keys: The Boxers as Event, Experience, and Myth* (New York: Columbia University Press, 1997).

Cohen, Warren. *America's Response to China: A History of Sino-American Relations* (5th rev. ed., New York: Columbia University Press, 2010).

Colby, Jason. *The Business of Empire: United Fruit, Race, and U.S. Expansion in Central America* (Ithaca, NY: Cornell University Press, 2011).

Cole, Donald. *The Presidency of Andrew Jackson* (Lawrence: University Press of Kansas, 1993).

Combs, Jerald. *The Jay Treaty: Political Battleground of the Founding Fathers* (Berkeley: University of California Press, 1970).

Commager, Henry. *Documents of American History*, 2 vols. (Englewood Cliffs, NJ: Prentice-Hall, 1973).

Companys, Julián. *España en 1898: entre la diplomacia y la guerra* (Madrid: Ministerio de Asuntos Exteriores, 1991).

Conde, Leonardo. *Historia de la Nación Dominicana*, 2 vols. (Santo Domingo, DR: np, 2016 and 2017).

Coolidge, Mary. *Chinese Immigration* (New York: Henry Holt, 1909).

Cooper, John. *The Warrior and the Priest: Woodrow Wilson and Theodore Roosevelt* (Cambridge, MA: Harvard University Press, 1983).

Cooper, John. *Woodrow Wilson: A Biography* (New York: Knopf, 2009).

Cosenza, Mario, ed. *The Complete Journal of Townsend Harris, First American Consul in Japan* (London: Forgotten Books, 2015 [1930]).

Cosmas, Graham, "San Juan Hill and El Caney," in Charles Heller and William Stoff, eds., *America's First Battles, 1776–1965* (Lawrence: University Press of Kansas, 1986), 109–48.

Cozzens, Peter, ed. *Eyewitnesses to Indian Wars, 1865–1890: The Struggle for Apacheria* (Mechanicsburg, PA: Stackpole Books, 2001).

Crackel, Theodore. *Mr. Jefferson's Army: Political and Social Reform of the Military Establishment, 1801–1809* (New York: New York University Press, 1987).

Crane, Elaine. "Dependence in the Era of Independence," in Jack Greene, ed., *The American Revolution: Its Character and Limits* (New York: New York University Press, 1987), 253–75.

Crapol, Edward. *John Tyler: The Accidental President* (Chapel Hill: University of North Carolina Press, 2006).

Crawford, Michael, ed. *The Naval War of 1812: A Documentary History*, 3 vols. (Washington: DC: Naval Historical Center, Department of the Navy, 2002).

Cronon, David, ed. *The Cabinet Diaries of Josephus Daniels, 1913–1921* (Lincoln: University of Nebraska Press, 1963).

Cruikshank, Ernest. *Documents relating to the invasion of Canada and the Surrender of Detroit, 1812* (Ottawa: Government Printing Bureau, 1913).

Cruikshank, Ernest, ed. *The Correspondence of Lieut. Governor John Graves Simcoe*, 3 vols. (Toronto: Ontario Historical Society, 1924).

Cunliffe, Marcus. "George Washington: George Washington's Generalship," in George Billias, ed., *George Washington's Generals and Opponents* (New York: Da Capo Press, 1994), 3–21.

Cunningham, Noble. *The Jeffersonian Republicans: The Formation of Party Organization, 1789–1801* (Chapel Hill: University of North Carolina Press, 1957).

Cutler, Wayne, ed. *Correspondence of James K. Polk*, 13 vols. (Knoxville: University of Tennessee Press, 1969–2009).

Daniels, Roger. *The Politics of Prejudice: The Anti-Japanese Movement in California and the Struggle for Japanese Exclusion* (Berkeley: University of California, 1977).

Daniels, Roger. *Asian America: Chinese and Japanese in the United States since 1850* (Seattle: University of Washington Press, 1988).

Davenport, Frances and Charles Paullin, eds. *European Treaties Bearing on the History of the United States and its Dependencies*, 4 vols. (Washington DC: Carnegie Institution, 1917–37).

Davis, David Brion. *The Problem of Slavery in the Age of Revolution, 1770–1823* (Ithaca, NY: Cornell University Press, 1975).

Debo, Angie. *Geronimo: The Man, His Time, His Place* (Norman: University of Oklahoma Press, 1976).

Bibliography

DeConde, *The Quasi-War: The Politics and Diplomacy of the Undeclared War with France, 1797–1801* (New York: Charles Scribner's Sons, 1966).

DeConde, Alexander. *This Affair of Louisiana* (New York: Charles Scribner's Sons, 1976).

De la Torre, Rosario. *Inglaterra y España en 1898* (Madrid: EUDEMA, 1988).

DeLay, Brian. *War of a Thousand Deserts: Indians Raids and the U.S.-Mexican War* (New Haven, CT: Yale University Press, 2008).

Delva, Alexandre. *Considérations sur l'article 7 de la Constitution d'Haïti* (Paris: Librarie Générale, 1873).

Demerliac, Alain. *La marine de la révolution. Nomenclature des navires français de 1792 à 1799* (Nice: Editions OMEGA, 1999).

Dennett, Tyler. *Americans in Eastern Asia* (New York: Barnes and Noble, 1941).

Devine, David. *Slavery, Scandals, and Steel Rails* (New York: Universe, 2004).

DeWolfe Howe, Mark. *The Life and Letters of George Bancroft*, 2 vols. (New York: Charles Scribner's Sons, 1908).

Diesbach, Ghislain de. *Necker ou la faillite de la vertu* (Paris: Perrin, 1978).

Doniol, Henry. *Histoire de la participation de la France à l'établissement des États-Unis d'Amérique*, 5 vols. (Paris: Imprimerie Nationale, 1886–92).

Dowd, Gregory. *A Spirited Resistance: The North American Struggle for Unity, 1745–1815* (Baltimore, MD: Johns Hopkins University Press, 1992).

Downes, Randolph. *Council Fires on the Upper Ohio: A Narrative of Indian Affairs in the Upper Ohio Valley until 1795* (Pittsburgh, PA: University of Pittsburgh Press, 1989 [1940]).

Downs, Gregory. *After Appomattox: Military Occupation and the Ends of War* (Cambridge, MA: Harvard University Press, 2015).

Dozier, Craig. *Nicaragua's Mosquito Shore* (Tuscaloosa: University of Alabama Press, 1985) Draper, Theodore. *A Struggle for Power: The American Revolution* (New York: Times Books, 1996).

Ducoudray, Félix Servio. *Los "gavilleros" del Este: una epopeya calumniada* (Santo Domingo, DR: Universidad Autónoma de Santo Domingo, 1976).

Dull, Jonathan, *The French Navy and American Independence* (Princeton, NJ: Princeton University Press, 1975).

Dull, Jonathan, "France and the American Revolution Seen as Tragedy," in Ronald Hoffman and Peter Albert, eds., *Diplomacy and Revolution: The Franco-American Alliance of 1778* (Charlottesville: University Press of Virginia, 1981), 73–106.

Dull, Jonathan, *A Diplomatic History of the American Revolution* (New Haven, CT: Yale University Press, 1985).

Dull, Jonathan, *The Age of the Ship of the Line: The British and French Navies, 1650–1815* (Lincoln: University of Nebraska Press, 2009).

Dull, Jonathan, *Benjamin Franklin and the American Revolution* (Lincoln: University of Nebraska Press, 2010).

Dull, Jonathan, *American Naval History, 1607–1865: Overcoming the Colonial Legacy* (Lincoln: University of Nebraska Press, 2012).

Dull, Jonathan, *The Miracle of American Independence: Twenty Ways Things Could Have Turned Out Differently* (Lincoln, NE: Potomac, 2015).

Dykstra, David. *The Shifting Balance of Power: American-British Diplomacy in North America, 1842–1848* (Lanham, MD: University Press of America, 1999).

Dziembowski, Edmond. *La guerre de Sept Ans, 1756–1763* (Paris: Perrin, 2018).

Egan, Clifford. *Neither Peace Nor War: Franco-American Relations, 1803–1812* (Baton Rouge: Louisiana State University Press, 1983).

Egerton, Douglas, ed. *Death or Liberty: African Americans and Revolutionary America* (New York: Oxford University Press, 2008).

Eggert, Gerald. *Richard Olney: Evolution of a Statesman* (University Park: Pennsylvania State University Press, 1974).

Ehrman, John. *The Younger Pitt*, 2 vols. (London: Constable, 1983, 1986).

Elkins, Stanley and Eric McKitrick, *The Age of Federalism: The Early American Republic, 1788–1800* (New York: Oxford University Press, 1993).

Ellis, Joseph. *American Sphinx: The Character of Thomas Jefferson* (New York: Vintage Books, 1998).

Ellis, Joseph. *His Excellency George Washington* (New York: Vintage Books, 2005).

Ellsworth, Harry. *One Hundred Eighty Landings of United States Marines, 1800–1934* (Washington DC: U.S. Marine Corps, 1974).

Elorza, Antonio and Elena Hernández Sandoica. *La guerra de Cuba (1895–1898): Historia política de una derrota colonial* (Madrid: Alianza Editorial, 1998).

Encina, Francisco. *Historia de Chile*. 20 vols (Santiago, Chile: Editorial Nascimento, 1945–52).

Erman, Sam. *Almost Citizens: Puerto Rico, the U.S. Constitution, and Empire* (New York: Cambridge University Press, 2019).

Erney, Richard. *The Public Life of Henry Dearborn* (New York: Arno Press, 1979).

Esarey, Logan, ed. *Messages and Letters of William Henry Harrison* (New York: Arno Press, 1975 [1922]).

Estes, Todd. *The Jay Treaty Debate, Public Opinion, and the Evolution of Early American Political Culture* (Amherst: University of Massachusetts Press, 2006).

Esthus, Raymond. *Double Eagle and Rising Sun: The Russians and Japanese at Portsmouth in 1905* (Durham, NC: Duke University Press, 1988).

Estorch, Miguel. *Apuntes para la historia sobre la administración del marqués de la Pezuela en la isla de Cuba* (Madrid: Manuel Galiano, 1856).

Everest, Allan. *The War of 1812 in the Champlain Valley* (Syracuse, NY: Syracuse University Press, 1981).

Fairbank, John, ed. *The Missionary Enterprise in China and America* (Cambridge, MA: Harvard University Press, 1974).

Featherstonhaug, George. *A Canoe Voyage Up the Minnay Sotor*, 2 vols. (St. Paul: Minnesota Historical Society, 1970 [1847]).

Feldman, Noah. *The Three Lives of James Madison: Genius, Partisan, President* (New York: Random House, 2017).

Ferling, John. *The First of Men: A Life of George Washington* (New York: Oxford University Press, 1988).

Ferling, John. *John Adams: A Life* (New York: Oxford University Press, 1992).

Ferling, John. *Almost a Miracle: The American Victory in the War of Independence* (New York: Oxford University Press, 2007).

Ferrer, Ada. *Freedom's Mirror: Cuba and Haiti in the Age of Revolution* (New York: Cambridge University Press, 2014).

Ferris, Norman. *The Trent Affair: A Diplomatic Crisis* (Knoxville: University of Tennessee Press, 1977).

Fick, Carolyn. *The Making of Haiti: The Saint Domingue Revolution from Below* (Knoxville: University of Tennessee Press, 1990).

Fiebig-von Hase, Ragnhild. *Lateinamerika als Konfliktherd der deutsch-amerikanischen Beziehungen 1890–1903*, 2 vols. (Göttingen: Vandenhoek und Ruprecht, 1986).

Finkelman, Paul. "Jefferson and Slavery: 'Treason Against the Hopes of the World,'" in Peter Onuf, ed., *Jeffersonian Legacies* (Charlottesville: University Press of Virginia, 1993), 181–221.

Fitz, Caitlin. *Our Sister Republics: The United States in an Age of American Revolutions* (New York: Norton, 2016).

Fitzmaurice, Edmund. *The Life of Granville George Leveson Gower, Second Earl Granville*, 2 vols. (London: Longmans, Green and Co., 1905).

Fitzpatrick, John. *The Writings of George Washington from the Original Manuscript Sources*, 39 vols. (Washington DC: GPO, 1931–44).

Bibliography

Flexner, James. *George Washington*, 4 vols. (Boston, MA: Little, Brown and Co., 1967–72).

Fleming, Thomas. *The Louisiana Purchase* (New York: Wiley, 2003).

Flint, Grover. *Marching with Gomez: A War Correspondent's Field Note-Book Kept During Four Months with the Cuban Army* (Boston: Lamson, Wolffe and Co., 1898).

Foner, Eric. *The Fiery Trial: Abraham Lincoln and American Slavery* (rev. ed., New York: Norton, 2010).

Foner, Eric. *Reconstruction: America's Unfinished Revolution, 1863–1877* (rev. ed., New York: Harper and Row, 2014).

Foner, Philip and Daniel Rosenberg, eds. *Racism, Dissent, and Asian-Americans from 1850 to the Present: A Documentary History* (Westport, CT: Greenwood, 1993).

Foos, Paul. *A Short, Offhand, Killing Affair: Soldiers and Social Conflict during the Mexican-American War* (Chapel Hill: University of North Carolina Press, 2002).

Ford, Paul Leicester, ed. *The Works of Thomas Jefferson*, 12 vols. (New York: G.P. Putnam's Sons, 1904–5).

Ford, Worthington, ed. *Journals of the Continental Congress, 1774–1789*, 34 vols. (Washington DC: GPO, 1904–37).

Ford, Worthington ed., *The Writings of John Quincy Adams*, 7 vols. (New York: Macmillan, 1913–1917.

Foreman, Amanda. *A World on Fire: Britain's Crucial Role in the American Civil War* (New York: Random House, 2010).

Foreman, Grant. *Indian Removal: The Emigration of the Five Civilized Tribes of Indians* (Norman: University of Oklahoma Press, 1932).

Foreman, Grant. *The Last Trek of the Indians* (Chicago: University of Chicago Press, 1946).

Foulke, William. *Life of Oliver P. Morton*, 2 vols. (Indianapolis, IN: Bowen-Merrill, 1899)

Fowler, William, *Rebels under Sail: The American Navy during the Revolution* (New York: Charles Scribner's Sons, 1976).

Fox, Stephen. *Wolf of the Deep: Rafael Semmes and the Notorious Confederate Raider CSS Alabama* (New York: Knopf, 2007).

Franck, Harry. *Roaming through the West Indies* (New York: The Century Co., 1920).

Frankel, Jeffrey. "The 1807–1809 Embargo Against Great Britain," *Journal of Economic History* (June 1982): 291–308.

Freehling, William. *The Road to Disunion: Secessionists at Bay, 1776–1854* (New York: Oxford University Press, 1990).

Freeman, Douglas. *George Washington: A Biography*, 7 vols. (New York: Charles Scribner's Sons, 1948–57).

Frey, Sylvia. *Water From the Rock: Black Resistance in a Revolutionary Age* (Princeton, NJ: Princeton University Press, 1991).

Fukuyama, Yoshio. "The Japanese in Oxnard, California, 1898–1945," *Ventura County Historical Society Quarterly*, 39 (1994): 3–31.

Fusi, Juan Pablo and Antonio Niño, eds. *Antes del "Desastre": Orígenes y antecedentes de la crisis del 98* (Madrid: Universidad Complutense, 1996).

Gaillard, Roger. *Les blancs débarquent*, 7 vols. (Port-au-Prince: Le Natal, 1973).

Gall, Lothar. *Bismarck. Der weisse Revolutionär* (Frankfurt: Ullstein, 1980).

Gallicchio, Marc. *The African American Encounter with Japan and China: Black Internationalism in Asia, 1895–1945* (Chapel Hill: University of North Carolina Press, 2000).

Garber, Paul. *The Gadsden Treaty* (Gloucester, MA: Peter Smith, 1959).

Gardiner, Oliver. *The Great Issue or the Three Presidential Candidates* (Westport, CT: Negro University Press, 1970 [1848]).

Garibaldi, Rosa. *La Política exterior del Perú en la era de Ramón Castilla: Defensa hemisférica y defensa de la jurisdicción nacional* (Lima: Academia Diplomática del Perú, 2003)

Garnier, Michaël. *Bonaparte et la Louisiane* (Paris: S.P.M., 1992).

Garrigó, Roque. *Historia documentada de la conspiración de los Soles y Rayos de Bolívar*, 2 vols. (Havana: El Siglo XX, 1929).

Garrison, Tim. *The Legal Ideology of Removal: The Southern Judiciary and the Sovereignty of Native American Nations* (Athens: University of Georgia Press, 2002).

Gates, John. "War-Related Deaths in the Philippines, 1898–1902," *PHR* (Aug. 1984): 367–78.

Gatewood, Willard. *Black Americans and the White Man's Burden, 1898–1903* (Urbana: University of Illinois Press, 1975).

Gatewood, Willard. *"Smoked Yankees" and the Struggle for Empire: Letters from Negro Soldiers 1898–1902* (Fayetteville: University of Arkansas Press, 1987).

Geggus, David. *Slavery, War, and Revolution: The British Occupation of St. Domingue, 1793–1798* (Oxford, UK: Clarendon Press, 1982).

Gibson, Arrell. *The Chickasaws* (Norman: University of Oklahoma Press, 1971).

Gilbert, Alan. *Black Patriots and Loyalists: Fighting for Emancipation in the War of Independence* (Chicago, IL: University of Chicago Press, 2012).

Gilbert, Felix. *To the Farewell Address: Ideas of Early American Foreign Policy* (Princeton, NJ: Princeton University Press, 1961).

Gilderhus, Mark. *Pan American Visions: Woodrow Wilson in the Western Hemisphere, 1913–1921* (Tucson: University of Arizona Press, 1986).

Gilje, Paul. *Free Trade and Sailors' Rights in the War of 1812* (New York: Cambridge University Press, 2013).

Gillett, Frederick. *George Frisbie Hoar* (Boston, MA: Houghton Mifflin, 1934).

Girard, Philippe, *The Slaves Who Defeated Napoléon: Toussaint Louverture and the Haitian War of Independence, 1801–1804* (Tuscaloosa: University of Alabama Press, 2011).

Girard, Philippe, *Toussaint Louverture: A Revolutionary Life* (New York: Basic Books, 2016).

Girón Garrado, José, ed. *España y Estados Unidos en 1898. La guerra a través de la prensa europea* (Oviedo: Universidad de Oviedo, 2018).

Gleijeses, Piero. "Haiti's Contribution to the Independence of Spanish America," *Revista/Review Interamericana*, 9 (Winter 1980): 511–28.

Gleijeses, Piero. "The Limits of Sympathy: The United States and the Independence of Latin America," *JLAS*, 24 (Oct. 1992): 481–505.

Gleijeses, Piero. "African Americans and the War against Spain," *North Carolina Historical Review*, 73 (April 1996): 184–214.

Gleijeses, Piero. "1898: The Opposition to the Spanish-American War," *JLAS*, 35 (Nov. 2003): 681–719.

Gleijeses, Piero. "A Brush with Mexico," *Diplomatic History*, 29 (April 2005): 223–54.

Gleijeses, Piero. "Napoleon, Jefferson, and the Louisiana Purchase," *International History Review*, 39 (April 2017): 233–55.

Gleijeses, Piero. "Clashing over Cuba: The United States, Spain and Britain, 1853–55," *JLAS*, 49 (May 2017): 215–41.

Gliech, Oliver. *Saint-Domingue und die Französiche Revolution: Das Ende der weissen Herrschaft in einer karibischen Plantagenwirtschaft* (Cologne, GE: Böhlau Verlag, 2011).

Go, Julian. "Anti-imperialism in the U.S. Territories after 1898," in Ian Tyrrell and Jay Sexton, eds., *Empire's Twins: U.S. Anti-imperialism from the Founding Era to the Age of Terrorism* (Ithaca, NY: Cornell University Press, 2015).

Go, Julian. *Patterns of Empire: The British and American Empires, 1688 to the Present* (New York: Cambridge University Press, 2011).

Gobat, Michel. *Confronting the American Dream: Nicaragua Under U.S. Imperial Rule* (Durham, NC: Duke University Press, 2005).

Gobat, Michel. "The Invention of Latin America: A Transnational History of Anti-Imperialism, Democracy, and Race," *AHR*, 118 (2013): 1345–75.

Gobat, Michel. *Empire by Invitation: William Walker and Manifest Destiny in Central America* (Cambridge, MA: Harvard University Press, 2018).

Bibliography

Goldberg, Joyce. *The "Baltimore" Affair* (Lincoln: University of Nebraska Press, 1986).

Gordon-Reed, Annette and Peter Onuf, *"Most Blessed of the Patriarchs": Thomas Jefferson and the Empire of the Imagination* (New York: Norton, 2016).

Gosse, Van. "'As a Nation, the English Are Our Friends': The Emergence of African American Politics in the British Atlantic World, 1772–1861," *AHR*, 113 (Oct. 2008): 1003–28.

Gould, Lewis. *The Presidency of William McKinley* (Lawrence: University Press of Kansas, 1980).

Gould, Lewis. *The William Howard Taft Presidency* (Lawrence: University Press of Kansas, 2009).

Gouttman, Alain. *La guerre du Mexique, 1862–1867: Le mirage américain de Napoléon III* (Paris: Perrin, 2008).

Graff, Henry, ed. *American Imperialism and the Philippine Insurrection* (Boston, MA: Little, Brown and Co., 1969).

Graff, Henry. *Grover Cleveland* (New York: Times Books, 2002).

Graves, Donald. "Why the White House Was Burned," *Journal of Military History*, 76 (Oct. 2012): 1095–127.

Graves, Donald. *And All Their Glory Past: Fort Erie, Plattsburgh and the Final Battles of the North, 1814* (Toronto: Robin Brass, 2013).

Graymont, Barbara. *The Iroquois in the American Revolution* (Syracuse, NY: Syracuse University Press, 1972).

Green, Michael. *The Politics of Indian Removal: Creek Government and Society in Crisis* (Lincoln: University of Nebraska Press, 1982).

Greenberg, Amy. *Manifest Manhood and the Antebellum American Empire* (New York: Cambridge University Press, 2005).

Greenberg, Amy. *A Wicked War: Polk, Clay, Lincoln and the 1846 U.S. Invasion of Mexico* (New York: Vintage Books, 2013).

Greene, Jack. "The Seven Years' War and the American Revolution," in Peter Marshall and Glyn Williams, eds., *The British Atlantic Empire before the American Revolution* (London: Frank Cass, 1980), 85–105.

Griffin, Charles. "Privateering from Baltimore during the Spanish American Wars of Independence," *Maryland Historical Magazine*, 35 (March 1940): 1–25.

Grimké, Angelina. *Letters to Catherine E. Beecher* (Boston, MA: Isaac Knapp, 1838).

Grimsley, Mark. "'Rebels' and 'Redskins': U.S. Military Conduct toward White Southerners and Native Americans in Comparative Perspective," in Mark Grimsley and Clifford Rogers, eds., *Civilians in the Path of War* (Lincoln: University of Nebraska Press, 2002), 137–61.

Grinnell, George Bird. "The Indian on the Reservation," *Atlantic Monthly*, 83 (Feb 1899): 255–67.

Grodzinski, John. *Defender of Canada: Sir George Prevost and the War of 1812* (Norman: University of Oklahoma Press, 2013).

Guardino, Peter. *The Dead March: A History of the Mexican-American War* (Cambridge, MA: Harvard University Press, 2017).

Guerra, Ramiro. *Manual de historia de Cuba* (Havana: Ciencias Sociales, 1980).

Guerra Vilaboy, Sergio. *El dilema de la independencia: las luchas sociales en la emancipación latinoamericana (1790–1826)* (Havana: Editorial Universitaria, 1993).

Guerra Vilaboy, Sergio. *América Latina y la independencia de Cuba* (Caracas: Ediciones Ko'eyú, 1999).

Guerrero, Milagros. *Luzon at War: Contradictions in Philippine Society, 1899–1902* (Mandaluyong City, Phil.: Anvil, 2015).

Hacker, David. "A Census-Based Count of the Civil War Dead," *Civil War History*, 57 (Dec. 2011): 307–48.

Hagan, William. *American Indians* (4th ed., revised by Daniel Cobb, Chicago: University of Chicago Press, 2013).

Haley, Edward. *Revolution and Intervention: The Diplomacy of Taft and Wilson with Mexico, 1910–1917* (Cambridge, MA: MIT Press, 1970).

Hall, George. *Uncommon Defense: Indian Allies in the Black Hawk War* (Cambridge, MA: Harvard University Press, 2009).

Hämäläinen, Pekka. *Comanche Empire* (New Haven: Yale University Press, 2008).

Hämäläinen, Pekka. *Lakota America: A New History of Indigenous Power* (New Have, CT: Yale University Press, 2019).

Hamilton, Stanislaus Murray, ed. *The Writings of James Monroe*, 7 vols. (New York: G.P. Putnam's Sons, 1898–1903).

Harlow, Vincent. *The Founding of the Second British Empire, 1763–1793*, 2 vols. (London: Longmans, Green and Co., 1952).

Hardman, John. *The Life of Louis XVI* (New Haven, CT: Yale University Press, 2016).

Hardman, John and Munro Price, eds. *Louis XVI and the Comte de Vergennes: Correspondence 1774–1787* (Oxford, UK: Voltaire Foundation, 1988).

Harris, Charles and Louis Sadler. *The Plan de San Diego: Tejano Rebellion, Mexican Intrigue* (Lincoln: University of Nebraska Press, 2013).

Hardy, William. "South of the Border: Ulysses S. Grant and the French Intervention," *Civil War History*, v. 54, no. 1 (March 2008): 63–86.

Hasbrouck, Alfred. *Foreign Legionaries in the Liberation of Spanish South America* (New York: Columbia University Press, 1928).

Havard, Gilles and Cécile Vidal. *Histoire de l'Amérique française* (rev. ed, Paris: Flammarion, 2019).

Haveman, Christopher. *Rivers of Sand: Creek Indian Emigration, Relocation, and Ethnic Cleansing in the American South* (Lincoln: University of Nebraska Press, 2016).

Havemann, Nils. *Spanien im Kalkül der deutschen Aussenpolitik von den letzten Jahren der Ära Bismarck bis zum Beginn der Wilheminischen Weltpolitik (1883–1899)* (Berlin: Dunker und Humblot, 1997).

Haynes, Sam. *James K. Polk and the Expansionist Impulse* (New York: Longman, 1997).

Haynes, Sam. *Unfinished Revolution: The Early American Republic in a British World* (Charlottesville: University of Virginia Press, 2010).

Hazeltine, Mayo. "What Shall Be Done About the Philippines?" *NAR*, 167 (Oct. 1898): 385–92.

Head, David. *Privateers of the Americas* (Athens: University of Georgia Press, 2015).

Healy, David. *Gunboat Diplomacy in the Wilson Era: The U.S. Navy in Haiti, 1915–1916* (Madison: University of Wisconsin Press, 1976).

Healy, David. *Drive to Hegemony: The United States in the Caribbean, 1898–1917* (Madison: University of Wisconsin Press, 1988).

Healy, David. *James G. Blaine and Latin America* (Columbia: University of Missouri Press, 2001).

Heidler, David and Jeanne Heidler. *Old Hickory's War: Andrew Jackson and the Quest for Empire* (Mechanicsburg, PA: Stackpole Books, 1996).

Hendrickson, David. *Union, Nation, or Empire: The American Debate Over International Relations, 1789–1941* (Lawrence: University Press of Kansas, 2009).

Henriques, Peter. *Realistic Visionary: A Portrait of George Washington* (Charlottesville: University of Virginia Press, 2006).

Herring, George. *From Colony to Superpower: U.S. Foreign Relations since 1776* (New York: Oxford University Press, 2008).

Hershberger, Mary. "Mobilizing Women, Anticipating Abolition: The Struggle against Indian Removal in the 1830s," *JAH*, 86 (1999): 15–40.

Herwig, Holger. *Germany's Vision of Empire in Venezuela, 1871–1914* (Princeton, NJ: Princeton University Press, 1986).

Herwig, Holger and Donald Trask, "Naval Operations Plans between Germany and the USA, 1898–1913," in Paul Kennedy, ed., *The War Plans of the Great Powers, 1880–1914* (Boston, MA: Allen and Unwin, 1979), 39–74.

Hickey, Donald. *Glorious Victory: Andrew Jackson and the Battle of New Orleans* (Baltimore, MD: Johns Hopkins University Press, 2015).

Bibliography

Hickey, Donald. "Timothy Pickering and the Haitian Slave Revolt," *Essex Institute Historical Collections*, 120 (July 1984): 149–63.

Hickey, Donald. "The Monroe-Pinkney Treaty of 1806: A Reappraisal," *WMQ* (Jan. 1987): 65–88.

Hickey, Donald. *Don't Give Up the Ship! Myths of the War of 1812* (Urbana: University of Illinois Press, 2006).

Hickey, Donald. *The War of 1812: A Forgotten Conflict* (rev. ed., Urbana: University of Illinois Press, 2012).

Hickey, Donald and Connie Clark, eds. *The Routledge Handbook of the War of 1812* (New York: Routledge, 2016).

Hietala, Thomas. *Manifest Design: American Exceptionalism and Empire* (rev. ed., Ithaca, NY: Cornell University Press, 2003).

Higginbotham, Don. *The War of American Independence* (New York: Macmillan, 1971).

Higginbotham, Don. "The American Militia," in Don Higginbotham, ed., *Reconsiderations on the Revolutionary War: Selected Essays* (Westport, CT: Greenwood, 1978), 83–103.

Higginbotham, Don. "Reflections on the War of Independence, Modern Guerrilla Warfare, and the War in Vietnam," in Ronald Hoffman and Peter Albert, eds., *Arms and Independence: The Military Character of the American Revolution* (Charlottesville: University Press of Virginia, 1984), 1–24.

Higginbotham, Don. *George Washington and the American Military Tradition* (Athens: University of Georgia Press, 1985).

Hildebrand, Klaus. *Das vergangene Reich. Deutsche Aussenpolitik von Bismarck bis Hitler* (Stuttgart: Deutsche Verlags-Anstalt, 1995).

Hilfrich, Fabian. *Debating American Exceptionalism: Empire and Democracy in the Wake of the Spanish-American War* (New York: Palgrave Macmillan, 2012).

Hill, Larry. *Emissaries to a Revolution: Woodrow Wilson's Executive Agents in Mexico* (Baton Rouge: Louisiana State University Press, 1973).

Hill, Peter. *Napoleon's Troublesome Americans: Franco-American Relations, 1804–1815* (Washington DC: Potomac, 2005).

Hilton, Sylvia and Steve Ickringill, eds. *European Perceptions of the Spanish-American War of 1898* (Bern: Peter Lang, 1999).

Hinderaker, Eric. *Elusive Empires: Constructing Colonialism in the Ohio Valley, 1763–1800* (New York: Cambridge University Press, 1997).

Hinderaker, Eric. *Boston's Massacre* (Cambridge, MA: Belknap Press, 2017).

Hitsman, Mackay, updated by Donald Graves. *The Incredible War of 1812: A Military History* (Toronto: Robin Brass, 1999).

Hoffman, Ronald and Peter Albert, eds. *Diplomacy and Revolution: The Franco-American Alliance of 1778* (Charlottesville: University Press of Virginia, 1981).

Hoffman, Ronald and Peter Albert, eds. *Peace and the Peacemakers: The Treaty of 1783* (Charlottesville: University Press of Virginia, 1986).

Hogan, Margaret and James Taylor, eds. *My Dearest Friend: Letters of Abigail and John Adams* (Cambridge, MA: Belknap Press, 2007).

Hoganson, Kristin. *Fighting for American Manhood: How Gender Politics Provoked the Spanish-American and the Philippine-American Wars* (New Haven, CT: Yale University Press, 1998).

Hoganson, Kristin. "'As Badly Off as the Filipinos': U.S. Women's Suffragists and the Imperial Issue at the Turn of the Twentieth Century," *Journal of Women's History*, 13 (Summer 2001): 9–33.

Hogeland, William. *Autumn of the Black Snake: George Washington, Mad Anthony Wayne, and the Invasion That Opened the West* (New York: Farrar, Strauss and Giroux, 2017).

Holt, Michael. *The Rise and Fall of the American Whig Party: Jacksonian Politics and the Onset of the Civil War* (New York: Oxford University Press, 1999).

Holt, Michael. *Franklin Pierce* (New York: Henry Holt, 2010).

Holton, Woody. *Forced Founders: Indians, Debtors, Slaves and the Making of the American Revolution in Virginia* (Chapel Hill: University of North Carolina Press, 1999).

Horsman, Reginald. "The British Indian Department and the Abortive Treaty of Lower Sandusky, 1793," *Ohio Historical Quarterly* 70 (July 1961): 189–213.

Horsman, Reginald. "The British Indian Department and the Resistance to General Anthony Wayne, 1793–95," *Mississippi Valley Historical Review* 49 (Sept. 1962): 269–90.

Horsman, Reginald. *The Causes of the War of 1812* (New York: Perpetua, 1962).

Horsman, Reginald. *Matthew Elliott, British Indian Agent* (Detroit: Wayne State University Press, 1964).

Horsman, Reginald. *The War of 1812* (London: Eyre and Spottiswoode, 1969).

Horsman, Reginald. *Race and Manifest Destiny: The Origins of American Racial Anglo-Saxonism* (Cambridge, MA: Harvard University Press, 1981).

Horsman, Reginald. "On to Canada: Manifest Destiny and United States Strategy in the War of 1812," *Michigan Historical Review*, 13 (Fall 1987): 1–24.

Horsman, Reginald. *Expansion and American Indian Policy, 1783–1812* (Norman: University of Oklahoma Press, 1992 [1967]).

Hosie, Alexander. *Manchuria: Its People, Resources and Recent History* (London: Methuen, 1904).

Howe, Daniel. *What Hath God Wrought: The Transformation of America, 1815–1848* (New York: Oxford University Press, 2007).

Humphreys, R.A. "British Merchants and South American Independence," *Proceedings of the British Academy*, 51 (1966): 151–74.

Hunt, Gaillard, ed. *The First Forty Years of Washington Society* (London: Forgotten Books, 2015 [1906]).

Hunt, Michael. "The American Remission of the Boxer Indemnity: A Reappraisal," *Journal of Asian Studies* 31 (May 1972): 539–59.

Hunt, Michael. *Frontier Defense and the Open Door: Manchuria in Chinese-American Relations, 1895–1911* (New Haven, CT: Yale University Press, 1973).

Hunt, Michael. "The Forgotten Occupation: Peking 1900–1901," *PHR*, 48 (Nov. 1979): 501–29.

Hunt, Michael. *The Making of a Special Relationship: The United States and China to 1914* (New York: Columbia University Press, 1983).

Hunter, Jane. *The Gospel of Gentility: American Women Missionaries in Turn-of-the Century China* (New Haven, CT: Yale University Press, 1984).

Hutson, James. *John Adams and the Diplomacy of the American Revolution* (Lexington: University Press of Kentucky, 1980).

Iakovleva, A.N., ed. *Rossia i SHA: diplomaticheskie otnoshenia, 1900–1917* (Moscow: Mejdunarodnii Fond "Demokratia," 1999).

Ichioka, Yuji. *The Issei: The World of the First Generation Japanese Immigrants, 1885–1924* (New York: The Free Press, 1988).

Ileto, Reynaldo. *Pasyon and Revolution: Popular Movements in the Philippines, 1840–1910* (Quezon City: Ateneo de Manila University Press, 1979).

Ileto, Reynaldo. *Knowledge and Pacification: On the U.S. Conquest and the Writing of Philippine History* (Quezon City: Ateneo de Manila University Press, 2017).

Immerman, Richard. *Empire for Liberty: A History of American Imperialism from Benjamin Franklin to Paul Wolfowitz* (Princeton, NJ: Princeton University Press, 2010).

Izard, Ralph, ed. *Correspondence of Mr. Ralph Izard of South Carolina* (New York: Charles S. Francis, 1844).

Jacobs, Sylvia. *The African Nexus: Black American Perspectives on the European Partitioning of Africa, 1880–1920* (Westport, CT: Greenwood, 1981).

Jacobs, Sylvia. "Give a Thought to Africa," in Nupur Chaudhuri and Margaret Strobel, eds., *Western Women and Imperialism* (Bloomington: Indiana University Press, 1992), 207–29.

Bibliography

Jackson, Scott. "Impressment and Anglo-American Discord, 1787–1818," Ph.D. Diss., University of Michigan, 1976.

James, C.L.R. *The Black Jacobins: Toussaint L'Ouverture and the San Domingo Revolution* (rev. ed., New York: Vintage Books, 1963).

Janda, Lance. "Shutting the Gates of Mercy: The American Origins of the Total War, 1860–1880," *Journal of Military History*, 59 (Jan. 1995): 7–26.

Jansen, Marius. *The Making of Modern Japan* (Cambridge, MA: Harvard University Press, 2000).

Jaramillo, Juan. *Bolívar y Canning, 1822–1827* (Bogota: Banco de la República, 1983).

Jasanoff, Maya. *Liberty's Exiles: American Loyalists in the Revolutionary World* (New York: Vintage Books, 2011).

Jefferson, Thomas. *Notes on the State of Virginia*, edited by William Pedeu (New York: Norton, 1972).

Jennings, Paul. *A Colored Man's Reminiscences of James Madison* (Brooklyn: George C. Beadle, 1865).

Jennings, Walter. *The American Embargo 1807–1809* (Iowa City: University of Iowa, 1921).

Jessup, Philip. *Elihu Root*, 2 vols. (New York: Dodd, Mead and Co., 1938).

Jiménez Codinach, Guadalupe. *La Gran Bretaña y la independencia de México, 1808–1821* (Mexico City: Fondo de Cultura Económica, 1991).

Johnson, Benjamin. *Revolution in Texas: How a Forgotten Rebellion and Its Bloody Suppression Turned Mexicans into Americans* (New Haven, CT: Yale University Press, 2003).

Johnson, John. *A Hemisphere Apart: The Foundations of United States Policy toward Latin America* (Baltimore, MD: Johns Hopkins University Press, 1990).

Johnson, Leland. "The Suspense Was Hell: The Senate Vote for War in 1812," *Indiana Magazine of History*, 65 (Dec. 1969): 247–67.

Johnson, Ronald. *Diplomacy in Black and White: John Adams, Toussaint Louverture, and Their Atlantic World Alliance* (Athens: University of Georgia Press, 2014).

Johnson, Samuel. *The Works of Samuel Johnson*, vol. 14 (Troy, NY: Pafraets Book Co., 1905).

Johnston, Henry, ed. *The Correspondence and Public Papers of John Jay*, 4 vols. (New York: Burt Franklin, 1970 [1890]).

Jonas, Manfred. *The United States and Germany: A Diplomatic History* (Ithaca, NY: Cornell University Press, 1984).

Josephy, Alvin. *The Civil War in the American West* (New York: Vintage Books, 1991).

Jung, Patrick. *The Black Hawk War of 1832* (Norman: University of Oklahoma Press, 2007).

Kaikkonen, Olli. *Deutschland und die Expansionspolitik der USA in den 90er Jahren des 19. Jahrhunderts* (Jiväskylä, Finland: Jiväskylän Yliopisto, 1980).

Kaplan, Sidney and Emma Kaplan. *The Black Presence in the Era of the American Revolution* (rev. ed., Amherst: The University of Massachusetts Press, 1989).

Karuka, Manu. *Empire's Tracks: Indigenous Nations, Chinese Workers, and the Transcontinental Railroad* (Oakland: University of California Press, 2019).

Katz, Friedrich. *The Secret War in Mexico: Europe, the United States and the Mexican Revolution* (Chicago, IL: University of Chicago Press, 1981).

Katz, Friedrich. *The Life and Times of Pancho Villa* (Stanford, CA: Stanford University Press, 1998).

Kaufman, Burton. "United States Trade and Latin America: The Wilson Years," *JAH*, 58 (Sept. 1971): 342–63.

Kaufmann, William. *British Policy and the Independence of Latin America, 1804–1828* (New Haven, CT: Yale University Press, 1951).

Kawakami, K.K. "The Naturalization of Japanese," *NAR*, 185 (June 1907): 394–402.

Kearney, Reginald. *African American Views of the Japanese: Solidarity or Sedition?* (Albany: State University of New York Press, 1998).

Kellogg, Louise Phelps. "The Removal of the Winnebago," *Transactions of the Wisconsin Academy of Science, Arts and Letters*, 21 (1929): 23–9.

Kelly, John. *A Forgotten Conference: The Negotiations at Peking, 1900–1901* (Geneva: Droz, 1963).

Kennedy, Paul. *The Samoan Tangle: A Study in Anglo-German-American Relations, 1878–1900* (St Lucia, Australia: University of Queensland Press, 1974).

Kert, Faye. *Privateering: Patriots and Profits in the War of 1812* (Baltimore, MD: Johns Hopkins University Press, 2015).

Ketcham, Ralph. *James Madison: A Biography* (Charlottesville: University Press of Virginia, 1990).

Ketchum, Richard. *Victory at Yorktown: The Campaign That Won the Revolution* (New York: Henry Holt, 2004).

Kirk, Russell. *John Randolph of Roanoke: A Study in American Politics* (Indianapolis, IN: Liberty Fund, 1997 [1953]).

Kissinger, Henry. *Diplomacy* (New York: Simon and Schuster, 1994).

Klein, Philip. *President James Buchanan: A Biography* (University Park: Pennsylvania State University, 1962).

Kneer, Warren. *Great Britain and the Caribbean, 1901–1913: A Study in Anglo-American Relations* (East Lansing: Michigan State University Press, 1975).

Knight, Alan. *The Mexican Revolution*, 2 vols. (New York: Cambridge University Press, 1986).

Knight, Melvin. *The Americans in Santo Domingo* (New York: Vanguard Press, 1928).

Kohn, Richard. *Eagle and Sword: The Federalists and the Creation of the Military Establishment in America, 1783–1802* (New York: Free Press, 1975).

Konetzke, Richard. *Die Politik des Grafen Aranda* (Berlin: Emil Ebering, 1929).

Kramer, Paul. "Empires, Exceptions, and Anglo-Saxons: Race and Rule between the British and United States Empires, 1880–1910," *JAH*, 88 (March 2002): 1315–53.

Kramer, Paul. *The Blood of Government: Race, Empire, the United States & the Philippines* (Chapel Hill: University of North Carolina Press, 2006).

Kramer, Paul. "Race-Making and Colonial Violence in the U.S. Empire: The Philippine-American War as Race War," Diplomatic History, 30 (April 2006): 169–210.

Labaree, Benjamin. *The Boston Tea Party* (Boston, MA: Northeastern University Press, 1979 [1964]).

Labourdette, Jean-François. *Vergennes, ministre principal de Louis XVI* (Paris: Éditions Desjonquères, 1990).

Lacroix, Pamphile. *Mémoires pour servir à l'histoire de la révolution de Saint-Domingue* 2 vols. (Paris: Pillet Ainé, 1819).

LaFeber, *The New Empire: An Interpretation of American Expansion 1860–1898* (Ithaca, NY: Cornell University Press, 1963).

LaFeber, *The American Age: United States Foreign Policy at Home and Abroad since 1750* (New York: Norton, 1989).

LaFeber, Walter. *The Clash: U.S.-Japanese Relations Throughout History* (New York: Norton, 1997).

La Gravière, Pierre Jurien de. *Souvenirs d'un admiral*, 2 vols. (Paris: L'Hachette, 1860).

Lambert, Frank. *The Barbary Wars: American Independence in the Atlantic World* (New York: Hill and Wang, 2005).

Lammersdorf, Raimund. *Anfänge einer Weltmacht. Theodore Roosevelt und die transatlantischen Beziehungen der USA, 1901–1909* (Berlin: Akademie Verlag, 1994).

Lanning, Michael. *African Americans in the Revolutionary War* (New York: Citadel Press, 2000).

Lasch, Christopher. "The Anti-Imperialists, the Philippines, and the Inequality of Man," *Journal of Southern History* 24 (Aug. 1958): 319–31.

Latimer, Jon. *War with America* (Cambridge, MA: Harvard University Press, 2007).

Laumer, Frank. *Dade's Last Command* (Gainesville: University Press of Florida, 1995).

Lea, Homer. *The Valor of Ignorance, With Specially Prepared Maps* (New York: Harper and Brothers, 1909).

Leahy, Christopher. *President Without a Party: The Life of John Tyler* (Baton Rouge: Louisiana State University Press, 2020).

Bibliography

Lecuna, Vicente. *Cartas del Libertador*, 11 vols. (Caracas: Lit. y Tip. del Comercio, 1929–48).

Lecuna, Vicente, ed. *Obras Completas*, 3 vols. (Havana: Editorial Lex, 1947).

Lee, Erika. *At America's Gates: Chinese Immigration During the Exclusion Era, 1882–1943* (Chapel Hill: University of North Carolina Press, 2003).

Lee, Erika and Judy Yung. *Angel Island: Immigrant Gateway to America* (New York: Oxford University Press, 2010).

Lengel, Edward. *General George Washington: A Military Life* (New York: Random House, 2005).

Lentz, Thierry. *Le Grand Consulat, 1799–1804* (Paris: Fayard, 1999).

Lentz, Thierry. *Napoléon Diplomate* (Paris: CNRS, 2012).

Levin, Gordon. *Woodrow Wilson and World Politics* (New York: Oxford University Press, 1968).

Levy, Leonard, *Jefferson and Civil Liberties: The Darker Side* (New York: Quadrangle Paperback, 1973).

Lewis, James. *The American Union and the Problem of Neighborhood: The United States and the Collapse of the Spanish Empire, 1783–1829* (Chapel Hill: University of North Carolina Press, 1998).

Lewis, Tom. "La politique étrangère de la France face à la guerre hispano-américaine," *Travaux de Recherches*, University of Metz, 1974, 37–57.

Lew-Williams, Beth. *The Chinese Must Go: Violence, Exclusion, and the Making of the Alien in America* (Cambridge, MA: Harvard University Press, 2018).

Li, Anshan. "The Miscellany and Mixed: The War and Chinese Nationalism," in David Wolff et al., eds., *The Russo-Japanese War in Global Perspective*, vol. 2 (Leiden: Brill, 2007), 491–512.

Li, Ung Bing. *Outlines of Chinese History* (Shanghai: Commercial Press, 1914).

Lindsay, Brenda. *Murder State: California's Native American Genocide, 1846–1873* (Lincoln: University of Nebraska Press, 2012).

Link, Arthur. *Woodrow Wilson and the Progressive Era, 1910–1917* (New York: Harper and Row, 1954).

Link, Arthur. *Wilson: The New Freedom* (Princeton, NJ: Princeton University Press, 1956).

Linn, Brian. *The U.S. Army and Counterinsurgency in the Philippine War, 1899–1902* (Chapel Hill: University of North Carolina Press, 1989).

Linn, Brian. *The Philippine War, 1899–1902* (Lawrence: University Press of Kansas, 2000).

Lipscomb, Andrew, ed. *The Writings of Thomas Jefferson*, 20 vols. (Washington DC: Thomas Jefferson Memorial Association of the United States, 1904–5).

Lodge, Henry Cabot. "Our Blundering Foreign Policy," *Forum*, 19 (March 1895): 8–17.

Lodge, Henry Cabot. "England, Venezuela, and the Monroe Doctrine," *NAR*, 160 (June 1895): 651–8.

Lodge, Henry Cabot. "The Meaning of the Votes," *NAR*, 164 (Jan. 1897): 1–11.

Love, Eric. *Race over Empire: Racism and U.S. Imperialism, 1865–1900* (Chapel Hill: University of North Carolina Press, 2004).

Lowenthal, Abraham. *The Dominican Intervention* (2d ed., Baltimore, MD: Johns Hopkins University Press, 1994).

Luraghi, Raimondo. *A History of the Confederate Navy* (Annapolis, MD: Naval Institute Press, 1996).

Lynch, John. *The Spanish American Revolutions 1808–1826* (2nd rev. ed., New York: Norton, 1986).

Lyon, Wilson. *Louisiana in French Diplomacy, 1759–1804* (Norman: University of Oklahoma Press, 1974).

McCaffrey, James. *Army of Manifest Destiny: The American Soldier in the Mexican War 1846–1848* (New York: New York University Press, 1992).

McCallus, Joseph, ed. *Gentleman Soldier: John Clifford Brown and the Philippine-American War* (College Station: Texas A&M University Press, 2004).

McClain, Charles, ed. *Japanese Immigrants and American Law: The Alien Land Laws and Other Issues* (London: Routledge, 2019).

McCoy, Drew. *The Elusive Republic: Political Economy in Jeffersonian America* (Chapel Hill: University of North Carolina Press, 1980).

McCullough, David. *The Path Between the Seas: The Creation of the Panama Canal, 1870–1914* (New York: Touchstone, 1977).

McCullough, David. *John Adams* (New York: Simon and Schuster, 2001).

McGann, Thomas and Oscar Handlin. *Argentina, the United States, and the Inter-American System, 1880–1914* (Cambridge, MA: Harvard University Press, 1957).

McGrath, Tim. *James Monroe: A Life* (New York: Dutton, 2020).

McGuinness, Aims. *Path of Empire: Panama and the California Gold Rush* (Ithaca, NY: Cornell University Press, 2008).

McKee, Delber. *Chinese Exclusion versus the Open Door: 1900–1906* (Detroit: Wayne State University Press, 1977).

McLoughlin, William. *Cherokees and Missionaries, 1789–1839* (Norman: University of Oklahoma Press, 1984).

McLoughlin, William. *Cherokee Renascence in the New Republic* (Princeton, NJ: Princeton University Press, 1986).

McPherson, James. *Battle Cry of Freedom: The Civil War Era* (New York: Oxford University Press, 1988).

Maass, Richard. *The Picky Eagle: How Democracy and Xenophobia Limited U.S. Territorial Expansion* (Ithaca, NY: Cornell University Press, 2020).

Mackesy, Piers. *The War for America 1775–1783* (Cambridge, MA: Harvard University Press, 1964).

Madley, Benjamin. *An American Genocide: The United States and the California Indian Catastrophe, 1846–1873* (New Haven, CT: Yale University Press, 2016).

Magie, David. *Life of Garret Augustus Hobart* (New York: G.P. Putnam's Sons, 1910).

Mahin, Dean. *One War at a Time: The International Dimensions of the American Civil War.* (Washington DC: Brassey's, 1999).

Mahon, John. *History of the Second Seminole War, 1835–1842* (rev. ed., Gainesville: University of Florida Press, 1991).

Malcomson, Robert. *Capital in Flames: The American Attack on York, 1813* (Montreal: Robin Brass, 2008).

Malone, Dumas. *Jefferson and His Time*, 6 vols. (Boston, MA: Little, Brown and Co., 1948–81).

Maluquer de Motes, Jordi. *España en la crisis de 1898* (Barcelona: Ediciones Peninsula, 1999).

Manela, Erez. *The Wilsonian Moment: Self-Determination and the International Origins of Anticolonial Nationalism* (New York: Oxford University Press, 2007).

Manning, William. *Diplomatic Correspondence of the United States Concerning the Independence of the Latin American Nations*, 3 vols. (New York: Oxford University Press, 1925).

Manning, William, ed. *Diplomatic Correspondence of the United States: Inter-American Affairs, 1831–1860*, 12 vols. (Washington: Carnegie Endowment for International Peace, 1932–9).

Marasigan, Cynthia. "'Between the Devil and the Deep Sea': Ambivalence, Violence, and African American Soldiers in the Philippine-American War," Ph.D. Diss., University of Michigan, 2010.

Marimon, Antoni. *La crisis de 1898* (Barcelona: Ariel, 1998).

Marks, Frederick. *Velvet on Iron: The Diplomacy of Theodore Roosevelt* (Lincoln: University of Nebraska Press, 1979).

Martelle, Scott. *William Walker's Wars* (Chicago, IL: Chicago Review Press, 2019).

Martí, José. *Epistolario*, 5 vols. (Havana: Editorial de Ciencia Sociales, 1993).

Martis, Kenneth. *The Historical Atlas of Political Parties in the United States Congress, 1789–1989* (New York: Macmillan, 1989).

Massey, Gregory. *John Laurens and the American Revolution* (Columbia: University of South Carolina Press, 2015).

Bibliography

Mathews, Donald. *At the Altar of Lynching: Burning Sam Hose in the American South* (New York: Cambridge University Press, 2018).

Matsusaka, Yoshihisa Tak. *The Making of Japanese Manchuria, 1904–1932* (Cambridge, MA: Harvard University Press, 2001).

Mattern, David and Holly Shulman, eds. *The Selected Letters of Dolley Payne Madison* (Charlottesville: University of Virginia Press, 2003).

May, Ernest. *Imperial Democracy: The Emergence of America as a Great Power* (New York: Harcourt, Brace and World, 1961).

May, Glenn. *Battle for Batangas: A Philippine Province at War* (New Haven, CT: Yale University Press, 1991).

May, Glenn. "150,000 Missing Filipinos: A Demographic Crisis in Batangas, 1897–1903," *Annales de Démographie Historique* (1985): 215–43.

May, Robert. *The Southern Dream of a Caribbean Empire, 1854–1861* (Baton Rouge: Louisiana State University Press, 1973).

May, Robert. *John A. Quitman: Old South Crusader* (Baton Rouge: Louisiana State University Press, 1985).

May, Robert. "Invisible Men: Blacks and the U.S. Army in the Mexican War," *The Historian* (Aug. 1987): 463–76.

May, Robert. *Manifest Destiny's Underworld: Filibustering in Antebellum America* (Chapel Hill: University of North Carolina Press, 2002).

May, Robert. *Slavery, Race, and Conquest in the Tropics: Lincoln, Douglas, and the Future of Latin America* (New York: Cambridge University Press, 2013).

May, Gregory. *Jefferson's Treasure: How Albert Gallatin Saved the New Nation from Debt* (Washington DC: Regnery, 2018).

Meacham, Jon. *American Lion: Andrew Jackson in the White House* (New York: Random House, 2008).

Meade, George, ed. *The Life and Letters of George Gordon Meade*, 2 vols. (New York: Charles Scribner's Sons, 1913).

Merk, Frederick. *Manifest Destiny and Mission in American History* (New York: Vintage Books, 1966).

Merk, Frederick. *The Oregon Question: Essays in Anglo-American Diplomacy and Politics* (Cambridge, MA: Harvard University Press, 1967).

Merk, Frederick. *Slavery and the Annexation of Texas* (New York: Knopf, 1972).

Merry, Robert. *A Country of Vast Designs: James K. Polk, the Mexican War, and the Conquest of the American Continent* (New York: Simon and Schuster, 2009).

Merry, Robert. *President McKinley: Architect of the American Century* (New York: Simon and Schuster, 2017).

Mexico, Secretaría de Relaciones Exteriores. *La diplomacia mexicana*, vol. 1 (Mexico City: Tipografía "Artistica," 1910).

Mézière, Henri and Jacques Jourquin, 'Le général Leclerc à Saint-Domingue,' *Revue du Souvenir Napoléonien*, no. 440 (April–May 2002): 22–38.

Middlekauff, Robert. *The Glorious Cause: The American Revolution, 1763–1789* (rev. ed., New York: Oxford University Press, 2005).

Miles, Edwin. "'Fifty-four Forty or Fight'—An American Political Legend," *Mississippi Valley Historical Review*, 44 (Sept. 1957): 291–309.

Miles, Nelson. "The War with Spain," *NAR*, 168 (June 1899): 749–60.

Miller, Edward. *War Plan Orange: The U.S. Strategy to Defeat Japan, 1897–1945* (Annapolis, MD: Naval Institute Press, 1991).

Miller, John. *The Federalist Era, 1789–1801* (New York: Harper and Row, 1960).

Miller, John. *The Wolf by the Ears: Thomas Jefferson and Slavery* (New York: Free Press, 1977).

Miller, Nathan. *Theodore Roosevelt: A Life* (New York: William Morrow, 1992).

Miller, Stuart. *"Benevolent Assimilation": The American Conquest of the Philippines, 1899–1903* (New Haven, CT: Yale University Press, 1982).

Millett Allan, Peter Maskowski, and William Feis. *For the Common Defense: A Military History of the United States from 1607 to 2012* (rev. ed., New York: Free Press, 2012).

Mills, Brandon. "'The United States of Africa:' Liberian Independence and the Contested Meaning of a Black Republic," *JER*, 34 (Spring 2014): 79–107.

Millspaugh, Arthur. *Haiti under American Control, 1915–1930* (Boston, MA: World Peace Foundation, 1931).

Missall, John and Mary Lou Missall. *The Seminole Wars: America's Longest Indian Conflict* (Gainesville: University Press of Florida, 2004).

Mitchell, Nancy. *The Danger of Dreams: German and American Imperialism in Latin America* (Chapel Hill: University of North Carolina Press, 1999).

Mitchell, Stewart, ed. *New Letters of Abigail Adams, 1788–1801* (Boston, MA: Houghton Mifflin, 1947).

Moïse, Claude. *Constitutions et luttes de pouvoir en Haïti (1804–1987)*, 2 vols. (Québec: CIDIHCA, 1990).

Mommsen, Wolfgang. *Grossmachtstellung und Weltpolitik: Die Aussenpolitik des deutschen Reichs, 1870 bis 1914* (Berlin: Ullstein, 1993).

Monaco, C.S. *The Second Seminole War and the Limits of American Aggression* (Baltimore, MD: Johns Hopkins University Press, 2018).

Monahan, Jay. *Chile, Peru, and the California Gold Rush of 1849* (Berkeley: University of California Press, 1973).

Monaque, Rémi. *Latouche-Tréville, 1745–1804. L'amiral qui défiait Nelson* (Paris: SPM, 2000).

Monaque, Rémi. *Une histoire de la marine de guerre française* (Paris: Perrin, 2016).

Montague, Ludwell. *Haiti and the United States, 1714–1938* (Durham, NC: Duke University Press, 1940).

Montesquieu, Charles de Secondat. *The Spirit of the Laws* (Amherst, NY: Prometheus Books, 2002).

Moore, John Bassett, ed. *The Works of James Buchanan*, 12 vols. (Philadelphia, PA: J.B. Lippincott, 1908–11).

Morales Padrón, Francisco, "Conspiraciones y masonería en Cuba (1810–1826)," *Anuario de Estudios Americanos*, 29 (1972): 343–77.

Morales y Morales, Vidal. *Iniciadores y primeros martires de la revolución cubana*, 2 vols. (Havana: Moderna Poesia, 1931).

Morey, Michael. *Fagen: An African American Renegade in the Philippine-American War* (Madison: University of Wisconsin Press, 2019).

Morgan, Edmund and Helen Morgan, *The Stamp Act Crisis: Prologue to Revolution* (Chapel Hill: University of North Carolina Press, 1995 [1953]).

Morgan, Philip and Andrew O' Shaughnessy. "Arming Slaves in the American Revolution," in *Arming Slaves.* edited by Christopher Brown and Philip Morgan (New Haven, CT: Yale University Press, 2006), 180–208.

Morgan, Wayne. *William McKinley and His America* (Syracuse, NY: Syracuse University Press, 1963).

Morgenfeld, Leandro. *Vecinos en conflicto: Argentina y Estados Unidos en las conferencias panamericanas* (Buenos Aires: Peña Lillo, 2011).

Morison, Elting, ed. *The Letters of Theodore Roosevelt*, 8 vols. (Cambridge, MA: Harvard University Press, 1951–4).

Morris, Edmund. "'A Few Pregnant Days': Theodore Roosevelt and the Venezuelan Crisis of 1902," *Theodore Roosevelt Association Journal*, 15 (Winter 1989), 2–13.

Morris, Edmund. *Theodore Rex* (New York: Random House, 2002).

Morris, Roger. *Cockburn and the British Navy in Transition: Admiral Sir George Cockburn* (Columbia: University of South Carolina Press, 1997).

Bibliography

Morrison, Chaplain. *Democratic Politics and Sectionalism: The Wilmot Proviso Controversy* (Chapel Hill: University of North Carolina Press 1967).

Morrison, Michael. "Westward the Curse of Empire: Texas Annexation and the American Whig Party," *JER* (Summer 1990): 221–49.

Moser, Harold et al., eds. *The Papers of Andrew Jackson*, 11 vols. to date (Knoxville: University of Tennessee Press, 1989).

Motte, Jacob Rhett. *Journey into the Wilderness: An Army Surgeon's Account of Life in Camp and Field during the Creek and Seminole Wars, 1836–1838*, edited by James Sunderman (Gainesville: University Press of Florida, 1953).

Moulton, Gary, ed. *The Papers of Chief John Ross*, 2 vols. (Norman: University of Oklahoma Press, 1985).

Muñoz Martinez, Monia. *The Injustice Never Leaves You: Anti-Mexican Violence in Texas* (Cambridge, MA: Harvard University Press, 2018).

Munro, Dana. *Intervention and Dollar Diplomacy in the Caribbean, 1900–1921* (Princeton, NJ: Princeton University Press, 1964).

Myers, Phillip. *Caution and Cooperation: The American Civil War in British-American Relations* (Kent, OH: Kent State University Press, 2008).

Murphy, Orville. *Charles Gravier, Comte de Vergennes* (Albany, NY: SUNY, 1982).

Napoléon Bonaparte. *Correspondance générale. IV: Rupture et fondation 1803–1804*, ed. François Houdecek et al. (Paris: Fayard, 2007).

Nance, Joseph, ed. "A Letter Book of Joseph Eve, United States Chargé d'Affaires to Texas," *Southwestern Historical Quarterly*, 43 (Oct. 1939): 196–221.

Nash, Gary. *The Unknown American Revolution: The Unruly Birth of Democracy and the Struggle to Create America* (New York: Viking, 2005).

Nash, Gary. *The Forgotten Fifth: African Americans in the Age of Revolution* (Cambridge, MA: Harvard University Press, 2006).

Nehru, Jawaharlal. *Toward Freedom: The Autobiography of Jawaharlal Nehru* (Boston, MA: Beacon Press, 1963 [1941]).

Nettels, Curtis. *The Emergence of a National Economy, 1775–1815* (Armonk, NY: M.E. Sharpe, 1962).

Neu, Charles. *An Uncertain Friendship: Theodore Roosevelt and Japan, 1906–1909* (Cambridge, MA: Harvard University Press, 1967).

Neumann, William. *America Encounters Japan: From Perry to MacArthur* (Baltimore, MD: Johns Hopkins University Press, 1963).

Nicholls, Michael. *Whispers of Rebellion: Narrating Gabriel's Conspiracy* (Charlottesville: University of Virginia Press, 2012).

Nichols, Roy. *Franklin Pierce: Young Hickory of the Granite Hills* (rev. ed., Newton, CT: American Political Biography Press, 1998).

Noer, Thomas. *Briton, Boer and Yankee: The United States and South Africa, 1870–1934* (Kent, OH: Kent State University Press, 1978).

Norgreen, Jill. *The Cherokee Cases: Two Landmark Federal Decisions in the Fight for Sovereignty* (Norman: University of Oklahoma Press, 2004).

North, Douglass. *The Economic Growth of the United States, 1790–1860* (New York: Norton, 1966).

North American Review, "The Cherokee Case," 33 (July 1831): 136–53.

Núñez Florencio, Rafael. *Militarismo y Antimilitarismo en España (1888–1906)* (Madrid: Consejo Superior de Investigaciones Científicas, 1990).

O'Brien, Thomas. *The Century of U.S. Capitalism in Latin America* (Albuquerque: University of New Mexico Press, 1999).

O'Shaughnessy, Andrew. *An Empire Divided: The American Revolution and the British Caribbean* (Philadelphia: University of Pennsylvania Press, 2000).

Offner, John. *An Unwanted War: The Diplomacy of the United States and Spain over Cuba, 1895–1898* (Chapel Hill: University of North Carolina Press, 1992).

Olavarría y Ferrari, Enrique. *México a través de los siglos, vol. 4: México independiente, 1821–1855* (Barcelona: Espasa, 188X).

Olson, James. *Red Cloud and the Sioux Problem* (Lincoln: University of Nebraska Press, 1965).

Onuf, Peter. *Jefferson's Empire: The Language of America Nationhood* (Charlottesville: University Press of Virginia, 2000).

Opal, J.M. *Avenging the People: Andrew Jackson, the Rule of Law, and the American Nation* (New York: Oxford University Press, 2017).

Ostler, Jeffrey, *The Plains Sioux and U.S. Colonialism from Lewis and Clark to Wounded Knee* (New York: Cambridge University Press, 2004).

Ostler, Jeffrey, *The Lakotas and the Black Hills: The Struggle for Sacred Ground* (New York: Penguin Books, 2010).

Ostler, Jeffrey, *Surviving Genocide: Native Nations and the United States from the American Revolution to Bleeding Kansas* (New Haven, CT: Yale University Press, 2019).

Ott, Thomas. *The Haitian Revolution, 1789–1804* (Knoxville: University of Tennessee Press, 1973).

Owsley, Frank. *Struggle for the Gulf Borderlands: The Creek War and the Battle of New Orleans, 1812–1815* (Tuscaloosa: University of Alabama Press, 1981).

Owsley, Frank. *The C.S.S. Florida: Her Building and Operations* (Tuscaloosa: University of Alabama Press, 1987 [1965]).

Owsley, Frank. *King Cotton Diplomacy: Foreign Relations of the Confederate States of America* (rev. ed., Tuscaloosa: University of Alabama Press, 2008 [1931]).

Pack, James. *The Man Who Burned the White House: Admiral Sir George Cockbur* (Ensworth, UK: Kenneth Mason, 1987).

Pallain, Georges, ed. *Le ministère de Talleyand sous le Directoire: Correspondance diplomatique de Talleyrand* (Paris: Plon, 1891).

Palmer, Michael. *Stoddert's War: Naval Operations during the Quasi-War with France, 1798–1801* (Annapolis, MD: Naval Institute Press, 2000 [1983]).

Paolino, Ernest. *The Foundations of the American Empire: William Henry Seward and U.S. Foreign Policy* (Ithaca, NY: Cornell University Press, 1973).

Pan-Montojo, Juan, ed. *Más se perdió en Cuba. España, 1898, y la crisis de fin de siglo* (Madrid: Alianza Editorial, 1998).

Pappas, Paul. *The United States and the Greek War for Independence, 1821–1828* (New York: Columbia University Press, 1985).

Paquette, Robert. "'Horde of Brigands?' The Great Louisiana Slave Revolt of 1811 Reconsidered," *Historical Reflections*, 35 (Spring 2009): 72–96.

Parkinson, Robert. *The Common Cause: Creating Race and Nation in the American Revolution* (Chapel Hill: University of North Carolina Press, 2016).

Parlett, Harold. *A Brief Account of Diplomatic Events in Manchuria* (London: Oxford University Press, 1929).

Parr, Marilyn. "Augustus John Foster and the 'Washington Wilderness': Personal Letter of a British Diplomat," Ph.D. Diss., George Washington University, 1987.

Peffer, W.A. "A Republic in the Philippines," *NAR*, 168 (March 1899), 310–20.

Perdue, Theda and Michael Green, *The Cherokee Nation and the Trail of Tears* (New York: Penguin, 2007).

Perdue, Theda. *Cherokee Editor: The Writings of Elias Boudinot* (Athens: University of Georgia Press, 1996).

Pérez, Louis. *Cuba Between Empires, 1878–1902* (Pittsburgh, PA: University of Pittsburgh Press, 1983).

Pérez, Louis. *Cuba and the United States: Ties of Singular Intimacy* (Athens: University of Georgia Press, 1990).

Bibliography

Pérez, Louis. *The War of 1898: The United States and Cuba in History and Historiography* (Chapel Hill: University of North Carolina Press, 1998).

Pérez, Louis. "Incurring a Debt of Gratitude: 1898 and the Moral Sources of United States Hegemony in Cuba," *AHR*, 104 (April 1999): 356–98.

Perkins, Bradford. *Prologue to War: England and the United States, 1805–1812* (Berkeley: University of California Press, 1961).

Perkins, Bradford. *Castlereagh and Adams: England and the United States, 1812–1823* (Berkeley: University of California Press, 1964).

Perkins, Bradford. *The First Rapprochement: England and the United States 1795–1805* (Berkeley: University of California Press, 1967).

Perkins, Dexter. *Hands Off: A History of the Monroe Doctrine* (Boston, MA: Little, Brown and Co., 1943).

Peterson, Merrill. *Thomas Jefferson and the New Nation: A Biography* (New York: Oxford University Press, 1970).

Petitfils, Jean-Christian. *Louis XVI* (Paris: Perrin, 2005).

Peyre-Ferry, Joseph Élysée. *Journal des opérations militaires de l'armée française à Saint-Domingue, 1802–1803* (Paris: Les Éditions de Paris, 2006).

Pfaelzer, Jean. *Driven Out: The Forgotten War Against Chinese Americans* (New York: Random House, 2007).

Phillips, Kevin. *William McKinley* (New York: Henry Holt, 2003).

Pletcher, David. *The Awkward Years: American Foreign Relations Under Garfield and Arthur* (Columbia: University of Missouri Press, 1962).

Pletcher, David. *The Diplomacy of Annexation: Texas, Oregon, and the Mexican War* (Columbia: University of Missouri Press, 1973).

Pletcher, David. *The Diplomacy of Trade and Investment: American Economic Expansion in the Hemisphere, 1865–1900* (Columbia: University of Missouri Press, 1998).

Pletcher, David. *The Diplomacy of Involvement: American Economic Expansion across the Pacific, 1784–1900* (Columbia: University of Missouri Press, 2001).

Plischke, Elmer. *U.S. Department of State: A Reference Book* (Westport, CT: Greenwood, 1999).

Pluchon, Pierre. *Toussaint Louverture. Un révolutionnaire noir d'Ancien Régime* (Paris: Fayard, 1989).

Plummer, Brenda. "The Afro-American Response to the Occupation of Haiti, 1915–1934," *Phylon*, 43 (June 1982): 125–41.

Plummer, Brenda. "The Metropolitan Connection: Foreign and Semiforeign Elites in Haiti, 1900–1915," *Latin American Research Review*, 19 (1984): 119–42.

Plummer, Brenda. *Haiti and the Great Powers, 1902–1915* (Baton Rouge: Louisiana State University Press, 1988).

Poniatowski, Michel. *Talleyrand et le Directoire* (Paris: Perrin, 1982).

Poniatowski, Michel. *Talleyrand et le Consulat* (Paris: Perrin, 1986).

Portell Vilá, Herminio. *Historia de Cuba en sus relaciones con los Estados Unidos y España*, 3 vols. (Havana: Jesús Montero, 1938).

Portnoy, Alisse. *Their Right to Speak: Women's Activism in the Indian and Slave Debates* (Cambridge, MA: Harvard University Press, 2005).

Potter, David. *The Impending Crisis 1848–1861* (New York: Harper, 1976).

Prather, Leon. *We Have Taken a City: Wilmington Racial Massacre and Coup of 1898* (Cranbury, NJ: Associated University Presses, 1984).

Pratt, Julius. *Expansionists of 1898: The Acquisition of Hawaii and the Spanish Islands* (Gloucester, MA: Peter Smith, 1959 [1936]).

Prucha, Francis. *The Great Father: The United States Government and the American Indians* (Lincoln: University of Nebraska Press, 1984).

Pybus, Cassandra. *Epic Journeys of Freedom: Runaway Slaves of the American Revolution and Their Global Quest for Liberty* (Boston, MA: Boston Press, 2006).

Quaife, Milo, ed. *The Diary of James K. Polk During His Presidency, 1845 to 1849*, 4 vols. (Chicago: McClurg, 1910).

Quarles, Benjamin. *The Negro in the American Revolution* (New York: Norton, 1973 [1961]).

Quijada, Mónica. "Latinos y anglosajones. El 98 en el fin de siglo sudamericano," *Hispania*, 57 (1997): 589–609.

Quirk, Robert. *An Affair of Honor: Woodrow Wilson and the Occupation of Veracruz* (New York: Norton, 1967).

Rakestraw, Donald and Howard Jones. *Prologue to Manifest Destiny: Anglo-American Relations in the 1840s* (Wilmington, DE: SR Books, 1997).

Rakove, Jack. *James Madison and the Creation of the American Republic* (New York: Pearson Longman 2007).

Rana, Aziz. *The Two Faces of American Freedom* (Cambridge, MA: Harvard University Press, 2010).

Rauch, Basil. *American Interest in Cuba: 1848–1855* (New York: Columbia University Press, 1974).

Reid, Chipp. *To the Walls of Derne: William Eaton, the Tripoli Coup and the End of the First Barbary War* (Annapolis, MD: Naval Institute Press, 2017).

Remer, C.F. *Foreign Investment in China* ((New York: MacMillan, 1933).

Remini, Robert. *Andrew Jackson*, 3 vols. (New York: Harper and Row, 1977–84).

Remini, Robert. *Andrew Jackson and his Indian Wars* (New York: Penguin, 2001).

Réné, Jouan. *Histoire de la marine française* (Paris: Payot, 1950).

Ricard, Serge. *Théodore Roosevelt: Principes et pratique d'une politique étrangère* (Aix-en-Provence: Université de Provence, 1991).

Richards, Leonard. *The Life and Times of Congressman John Quincy Adams* (New York: Oxford University Press, 1986).

Richardson, Heather. *Wounded Knee: Party Politics and the Road to an American Massacre* (New York: Basic Books, 2010).

Richardson, James, ed. *A Compilation of the Messages and Papers of the Presidents*, 10 vols. (Washington: GPO, 1896–9).

Rickover, Hyman. *How the Battleship Maine Was Destroyed* (Washington DC: Department of the Navy, 1976).

Riguzzi, Paolo. "México, Estados Unidos y Gran Bretaña, 1867–1910: Una difícil relación triangular," *Historia Mexicana*, 41 (1992): 365–436.

Ritcheson, Charles. *Aftermath of Revolution: British Policy Toward the United States, 1783–1795* (New York: Norton, 1969).

Roberts, Andrew. *Salisbury: Victorian Titan* (London: Weidenfeld and Nicholson, 1999).

Robertson, James, ed. *Louisiana under the Rule of Spain, France, and the United States, 1785–1807*, 2 vols. (Cleveland, OH: Arthur R. Clark, 1911).

Robles Muñoz, Cristóbal. *1898: Diplomacia y opinión* (Madrid: Consejo Superior de Investigaciones Científicas, 1991).

Rodger, N.A.M. *The Command of the Ocean: A Naval History of Britain, 1649–1815* (London: Allen Lane, 2004).

Rodríguez, Rolando. *Cuba: La forja de una nación*. 3 vols. (Havana: Editorial de Ciencias Sociales, 2005).

Rodríguez O., Jaime. *The Independence of Spanish America* (New York: Cambridge University Press, 1998).

Roeckell, Leila. "Bonds over Bondage: British Opposition to the Annexation of Texas," *JER* (Summer 1999): 257–78.

Rogers, Kathryn. "'Noble-Hearted Ladies': Women's Response to the Spanish-American and Philippine-American Wars, 1898–1905," MA Thesis, University of New Brunswick, 2008.

Röhl, John. *Wilhelm II: Der Weg in den Abgrund, 1900–1941* (Munich: Beck, 2009).

Roig de Leuchsenring, Emilio. *Bolívar, el Congreso Interamericano de Panamá, en 1826, y la independencia de Cuba y Puerto Rico* (Havana: Oficina del Historiador de la Ciudad, 1956).

Rosenberg, Emily. *Spreading the American Dream: American Economic and Cultural Expansion, 1890–1945* (New York: Hill and Wang, 1982).

Rosenberg, Emily. *Financial Missionaries to the World: The Politics and Culture of Dollar Diplomacy, 1900–1930* (Durham, NC: Duke University Press, 2003).

Roussier, Paul, ed. *Lettres du général Leclerc* (Paris: Ernest Leroux, 1937).

Rubio, Javier. *El Tránsito del siglo XIX al XX. Del Desastre de 1898 al principio del reinado de Alfonso XIII* (Madrid: Ministerio de Asuntos Exteriores y de Cooperación, 2011).

Ruiz-Manjón, Octavio and Alicia Langa, eds. *Los significados del 98: La sociedad española en la génesis del siglo xx* (Madrid: Universidad Complutense, 1999).

Russ, William. *The Hawaiian Revolution (1893–94)* (Selinsgrove, PA: Susquehanna University Press, 1959).

Rutland, Robert. *The Presidency of James Madison* (Lawrence: University Press of Kansas, 1990).

Rulhière, Claude Carloman de. *Portrait du Comte de Vergennes, Ministre et Secrétaire d'État au département des Affaires étrangères* (np, 1788).

[Sansay, Leonora.] *Secret History: Written by a Lady at Cape Francois to Colonel Burr* (Freeport, NY: Books for Libraries Press, 1971).

Santelli, Maureen. *The Greek Fire: American-Ottoman Relations and Democratic Fervor in the Age of Revolutions* (Ithaca, NY: Cornell University Press, 2020).

Sanz, Luis. *El caso Baltimore. Una contribución al esclarecimiento de la actitud argentina* (Buenos Aires: Instituto de Publicaciones Navales, 1998).

Sater, William. *Chile and the United States: Empires in Conflict* (Athens: University of Georgia Press, 1990).

Sater, William. *Andean Tragedy: Fighting the War of the Pacific, 1879–1884* (Lincoln: University of Nebraska Press, 2007).

Satow, Ernest. *A Diplomat in Japan* (London: Seeley, Service, 1921).

Satz, Ronald. *American Indian Policy in the Jacksonian Era* (Norman: University of Oklahoma Press, 2002 [1975]).

Saul, Norman. *Distant Friends: The United States and Russia, 1763–1867* (Lawrence: University Press of Kansas, 1991).

Saul, Norman. *Concord and Conflict: The United States and Russia, 1867–1914* (Lawrence: University Press of Kansas, 1996).

Saunt, Claudio. *Unworthy Republic: The Dispossession of Native Americans and the Road to Indian Territory* (New York: Norton, 2020).

Sawvel, Franklin, ed. *The Complete Anas of Thomas Jefferson* (New York: Leopold Classic Library [1903]).

Schama, Simon. *Rough Crossings: Britain, the Slaves, and the American Revolution* (New York: HarperCollins, 2005).

Schelle, Gustave, ed. *Oeuvres de Turgot et documents le concernant*, 5 vols. (Paris: Félix Alcan, 1913–23).

Scherr, Arthur. *Thomas Jefferson's Haitian Policy: Myths and Realities* (Lanham, MD: Rowman and Littlefield, 2011).

Schmidt, Hans. *The United States Occupation of Haiti, 1915–1934* (New Brunswick, NJ: Rutgers University Press, 1971).

Schmidt, Hans. *Maverick Marine: General Smedley D. Butler and the Contradictions of American Military History* (Lexington: University Press of Kentucky, 1987).

Scholes, Walter and Marie Scholes. *The Foreign Policies of the Taft Administration* (Columbia: University of Missouri Press, 1970).

Schoonover, Thomas. *Dollars over Dominion: The Triumph of Liberalism in Mexican-United States Relations, 1861–1867* (Baton Rouge: Louisiana State University Press, 1978).

Schoonover, Thomas. *Mexican Lobby: Matías Romero in Washington, 1861–1867* (Lexington: University Press of Kentucky, 1986).

Schoonover, Thomas. *The United States in Central America, 1860–1911: Episodes of Social Imperialism and Imperial Rivalry in the World System* (Durham, NC: Duke University Press, 1991).

Schoultz, Lars. *Beneath the United States: A History of U.S. Policy Toward Latin America* (Cambridge, MA: Harvard University Press, 1998).

Schoultz, Lars. *In Their Own Best Interest: A History of the U.S. Effort to Improve Latin Americans* (Cambridge, MA: Harvard University Press, 2018).

Schrecker, John. *Imperialism and Chinese Nationalism: Germany in Shantung* (Cambridge, MA: Harvard University Press, 1971).

Schurz, Carl. "Thoughts on American Imperialism," *Century Illustrated Magazine*, 56 (Sept. 1898): 781–88.

Scott, William. *Ilocano Responses to American Aggression, 1900–1901* (Quezon City, Philippines: New Day Publishers, 1986).

Seager, Robert. *Alfred Thayer Mahan: The Man and His Letters* (Annapolis, MD: Naval Institute Press, 1977).

Sears, Louis. *Jefferson and the Embargo* (New York: Octagon Books, 1966 [1927]).

Selby, John. *The Revolution in Virginia, 1775–1783* (Charlottesville: University Press of Virginia, 1988).

Sellers, Charles. *James K. Polk, Continentalist: 1843–1846* (Princeton, NJ: Princeton University Press, 1966).

Sexton, Ray. *The Monroe Doctrine: Empire and Nation in Nineteenth-Century America* (New York: Hill and Wang, 2012).

Sharf, Frederic and Peter Harrington. *The Boxer Rebellion, China, 1900: The Artists' Perspective* (London: Greenhill Books, 2000).

Sheehan, Bernard. *Seeds of Extinction: Jeffersonian Philanthropy and the American Indian* (Chapel Hill: University of North Carolina Press, 1973).

Sheehan, Bernard. "The Indian Problem in the Northwest: From Conquest to Philanthropy," in Ronald Hoffman and Peter Albert, eds. *Launching the "Extended Republic": The Federalist Era* (Charlottesville: University Press of Virginia, 1996), 190–222.

Shmazu, Naoko. *Japan, Race and Equality: The Racial Equality Proposal of 1919* (New York: Routledge, 1988).

Shomette, Donald. *Flotilla: The Patuxent Naval Campaign in the War of 1812* (Baltimore, MD: Johns Hopkins University Press, 2009).

Shy, John. *Toward Lexington: The Role of the British Army in the Coming of the American Revolution* (Princeton, NJ: Princeton University Press, 1965).

Shy, John. "American Society and Its War for Independence," in Don Higginbotham, ed., *Reconsiderations on the Revolutionary War: Selected Essays* (Westport, CT: Greenwood, 1978), 72–82.

Shy, John. *A People Numerous and Armed: Reflections on the Military Struggle for American Independence* (rev. ed., Ann Arbor: University of Michigan Press, 1990).

Sibert, W.L. "Military Occupation of Northern Luzon," *Journal of the Military Service Institution of the United States*, 30 (1902): 404–8.

Silbey, David. *The Boxer Rebellion and the Great Game in China* (New York: Hill and Wang, 2012).

Simon, John, ed. *The Papers of Ulysses S. Grant*, 32 vols. (Carbondale: Southern Illinois University Press, 1967–2012).

Sinha, Manisha, *The Slave's Cause: A History of Abolition* (New Haven: Yale University Press, 2016).

Skaggs, David. *William Henry Harrison and the Conquest of the Ohio Country* (Baltimore, MD: Johns Hopkins University Press, 2014).

Skinner, Elliott. *African Americans and U.S. Policy Toward Africa, 1850–1924* (Washington DC: Howard University Press, 1992).

Bibliography

Smelser, Marshall. *The Congress Founds the Navy, 1787–1798* (Notre Dame, IN: University of Notre Dame Press, 1959).

Smith, Gene. *The Slaves' Gamble: Choosing Sides in the War of 1812* (New York: Palgrave MacMillan, 2013).

Smith, James Morton. *The Republic of Letters: The Correspondence between Thomas Jefferson and James Madison 1776–1826*, 3 vols. (New York: Norton, 1995).

Smith, Joseph. "Britain and the Brazilian Naval Revolt of 1893–94," *JLAS*, 2 (Nov. 1970): 175–98.

Smith, Joseph. "The Latin American Trade Commission of 1884–5," *Inter-American Economic Affairs* 24 (Spring 1971): 3–24.

Smith, Joseph. *Unequal Giants: Diplomatic Relations Between the United States and Brazil, 1889–1930* (Pittsburgh, PA: University of Pittsburgh Press, 1991).

Smith, Robert Freeman. *The United States and Revolutionary Nationalism in Mexico, 1916–1932* (Chicago: University of Chicago Press, 1972).

Smith, William, ed. *The St. Clair Papers: The Life and Public Services of Arthur St. Clair*, 2 vols. (Cincinnati, OH: Robert Clarke, 1882).

Sneider, Allison. *Suffragists in an Imperial Age: US Expansion and the Woman Question, 1870–1929* (Oxford, UK: Oxford University Press, 2008).

Sociedad Bolivariana de Venezuela. *Escritos del Libertador*, 12 vols. (Caracas: Editorial Arte, 1964–76).

Sorel, Albert. *Recueil des instructions données aux ambassadeurs et ministres de la France depuis les Traités de Westphalia jusqu'à la Révolution Française*, 30 vols. (Paris: Félix Alcan, 1884).

Sosna, Morton. "The South in the Saddle: Racial Politics During the Wilson Years," *Wisconsin Magazine of History*, 54 (Autumn 1970): 30–49.

Soulavie, Jean-Louis. *Mémoires historiques et politiques du règne de Louis XVI*, 6 vols. (Paris: Treuttel et Würtz, 1801).

Soulsby, Hugh. *The Right of Search and the Slave Trade in Anglo-American Relations. 1814–1862* (Baltimore, MD: Johns Hopkins University Press, 1935).

Spector, Ronald. *Admiral of the New Empire: The Life and Career of George Dewey* (Columbia: University of South Carolina Press, 1988 [1974]).

Spence, Jonathan. *The Search for Modern China* (New York: Norton, 1990).

Spivak, Burton. *Jefferson's English Crisis: Commerce, Embargo, and the Republican Revolution* (Charlottesville: University Press of Virginia, 1979).

Sprague, John. *The Origin, Progress, and Conclusion of the Florida War* (London: Forgotten Books, 2015 [1848]).

Stagg, J.C.A. *Mr. Madison's War: Politics, Diplomacy, and Warfare in the Early American Republic 1783–1830* (Princeton, NJ: Princeton University Press, 1983).

Stagg, J.C.A. *The War of 1812: Conflict for a Continent* (New York: Cambridge University Press, 2012).

Stansifer, Charles. "José Santos Zelaya: A New Look at Nicaragua's 'Liberal' Dictator," *Revista/Review Interamericana*, 7 (Sept. 1978): 468–83.

Starkey, Armstrong. *European and Native American Warfare, 1675–1815* (Norman: University of Oklahoma Press, 1998).

Stephanson, Anders. *Manifest Destiny: American Expansionism and the Empire of Right* (New York: Hill and Wang, 1995).

Stewart, James. *Holy Warriors: The Abolitionists and American Slavery* (New York: Hill and Wang, 1976).

Stewart, Watt. *Keith and Costa Rica: A Biographical Study of Minor Cooper Keith* (Albuquerque: University of New Mexico Press, 1964).

Stinchcombe, William. *The American Revolution and the French Alliance* (Syracuse, NY: Syracuse University Press, 1969).

Stinchcombe, William. *The XYZ Affair* (Westport, CT: Greenwood, 1980).

Storti, Craig. *Incident at Bitter Creek: The Story of the Rock Springs Chinese Massacre* (Ames: Iowa State University Press, 1991).

Stratton, David. "The Snake River Massacre of Chinese Miners, 1887," in Duane Smith, ed., *A Taste of the West* (Boulder, CO: Pruett, 1983), 109–29.

Street, Richard. *Beasts of the Field: A Narrative History of California Farmworkers, 1769-1911* (Stanford, CA: Stanford University Press, 2004).

Stuart, Benjamin. "Transportation of Pottawattomies: The Deportation of Menominee and His Tribe of the Pottawattomie Indians," *Indiana Magazine of History*, 18 (Sept. 1922): 255–65.

Stucki, Andreas. *Aufstand und Zwangsumsiedlung. Die kubanischen Unabhängigkeitskriege* (Hamburg: Hamburger Edition, 2012).

Sugden, John. *Tecumseh's Last Stand* (Norman: University of Oklahoma Press, 1985).

Sugden, John. *Tecumseh: A Life* (New York: Henry Holt, 1998).

Sugden, John. *Blue Jacket: Warrior of the Shawnees* (Lincoln: University of Nebraska Press, 2000).

Sweeney, Edwin. *From Cochise to Geronimo: The Chiricahua Apaches, 1874-1886* (Norman: University of Oklahoma Press, 2010).

Sword, Wiley. *President Washington's Indian War: The Struggle for the Old Northwest, 1790-1795* (Norman: University of Oklahoma Press, 1985).

Takaki, Ronald. *Strangers From A Different Shore: A History of Asian Americans* (New York: Penguin Books, 1989).

Tan, Samuel. *The Filipino-American War, 1899-1913* (Quezon City: University of the Philippines Press, 2002).

Tansill, Charles. *The Foreign Policy of Thomas F. Bayard, 1885-1897* (New York: Fordham University Press, 1940).

Tansill, Charles. *The United States and Santo Domingo, 1798-1873* (Gloucester, MA: Peter Smith, 1967 [1938]).

Tatz, Colin. "Genocide in Australia," *Journal of Genocide Research*, v.1, no. 3 (1999): 315–52.

Taylor, Alan. *The Internal Enemy: Slavery and War in Virginia 1772-1832* (New York: Norton,

Taylor, Alan. *The Civil War of 1812: American Citizens, British Subjects, Irish Rebels and Indian Allies* (New York: Knopf, 2010).

Taylor, Alan. *American Revolutions: A Continental History, 1750-1804* (New York: Norton, 2016).

Terrazas y Basante, Manuela. *Inversiones, especulación y diplomacia: Las relaciones entre México y los Estados Unidos durante la dictadura Santannista* (Mexico City: Universidad Nacional Autónoma de México, 2000).

Thayer, William. *The Life and Letters of John Hay*, 2 vols. (Boston, MA: Houghton Mifflin, 1914).

Temperley, Harold. *The Foreign Policy of Canning, 1822-1827* (London: Frank Cass, 1966).

Thiessen, Thomas. "The Fighting First Nebraska: Nebraska's Imperial Adventure in the Philippines, 1898-99," *Nebraska History*, 70 (1989): 210–72.

Thomas, P.D.G. *The Townshend Duties Crisis: The Second Phase of the American Revolution, 1767-1773* (Oxford, UK: Clarendon Press, 1987).

Thompson, John. *Great Power Rising: Theodore Roosevelt and the Politics of U.S. Foreign Policy* (New York: Oxford University Press, 2019).

Thompson, Lanny. *Imperial Archipelago: Representation and Rules in the Insular Territories under U.S. Dominion after 1898* (Honolulu: University of Hawaii Press, 2010).

Thompson, Roger. "Military Dimensions of the 'Boxer Uprising,' Shanxi, 1898-1901," in Hans van de Ven, ed. *Warfare in Chinese History* (Leiden: Brill, 2000).

Tocqueville, Alexis de. *Democracy in America*, edited by Harvey Mansfield and Delba Winthrop (Chicago, IL, 2000 [1833]).

Toll, Ian. *Six Frigates: The Epic Story of the Founding of the U.S. Navy* (New York: Norton, 2006).

Tompkins, Berkeley. *Anti-Imperialism in the United States: The Great Debate, 1890-1920* (Philadelphia: University of Pennsylvania Press, 1972).

Bibliography

Torget, Andrew. *Seeds of Empire: Cotton, Slavery, and the Transformation of the Texas Borderlands, 1800–1850* (Chapel Hill: University of North Carolina Press, 2015).

Trask, David. *The War with Spain in 1898* (New York: Macmillan, 1981).

Trautsch, Jasper. *The Genesis of America: U.S. Foreign Policy and the Formation of National Identity, 1793–1815* (New York: Cambridge University Press, 2018).

Trollope, Frances. *Domestic Manners of the Americans* (Mineola, NY: Dover Publications, 2003 [1832]).

Ts'ai, Shih-shan. "Reaction to Exclusion: The Boycott of 1905 and Chinese National Awakening," *The Historian*, 39 (1976): 95–110.

Tucker, Robert and David Hendrickson. *Empire of Liberty: The Statecraft of Thomas Jefferson* (New York: Oxford University Press, 1990).

Tucker, Robert and David Hendrickson. *The Fall of the First British Empire: Origins of the War of American Independence* (Baltimore, MD: Johns Hopkins University Press, 1982).

Tucker, Spencer. *The Jeffersonian Gunboat Navy* (Columbia: University of South Carolina Press, 1993).

Tucker, Spencer and Frank Reuter, *Injured Honor: The Chesapeake-Leopard Affair* (Annapolis, MD: Naval Institute Press, 1996).

Tulard, Jean. *Le Grand Empire, 1804–1815* (Paris: Albin Michel, 2009).

Tumulty, Joseph. *Woodrow Wilson As I Know Him* (Garden City, NY: Doubleday, 1921).

Tupper, Eleanor and George McReynolds, *Japan in American Public Opinion* (New York: Macmillan, 1937).

Turner, Frederick Jackson, *The Frontier in American History* (n.p.: Okitoks Press, 2017).

Tyrrell, Ian. *Reforming the World: The Creation of America's Moral Empire* (Princeton, NJ: Princeton University Press, 2010).

Ulloa, Berta. *La revolución intervenida: Relaciones diplomáticas entre México y Estados Unidos, 1910–1914* (Mexico City: El Colegio de México, 1971).

Ullrich, Volker. *Die nervöse Grossmacht 1871–1918: Aufstieg und Untergang des deutschen Kaiserreichs* (Frankfurt am Main: Fischer, 1999).

United States. *American State Papers, Foreign Relations*, vol. 2 (Washington DC: Gales and Seaton, 1832).

United States, Department of Commerce, Bureau of the Census, *Historical Statistics of the United States*, 2 vols. (Washington DC: GPO, 1975).

United States, Department of the Interior. *Report on Indians Taxed and Indians Not Taxed in the United States (Except Alaska) at the Eleventh Census: 1890* (Washington DC: GPO, 1894).

United States, Department of the Interior. *Are the Indians Dying? Indian Civilization and Education* (Washington DC: GPO, 1877).

Uribe Salas, José et al., eds. *México frente al desenlace del 98. La guerra hispanonorteamericana* (Michoacán: Universidad Michoacana, 1999).

Utley, Robert. *The Lance and the Shield: The Life and Times of Sitting Bull* (New York: Henry Holt, 1993).

Valentine, Alan. *Lord North*, 2 vols. (Norman: University of Oklahoma Press, 1967).

Van Alstyne, Richard. *The Rising American Empire* (New York: Quadrangle Books, 1965).

Varela Ortega, José. "Otra vez el 98!" in Manuel Moreno Franginals et al., eds., *Cien años de historia de Cuba (1898–1898)* (Madrid: Editorial Verbum, 2000), 99–151.

Varg, Paul. *Missionaries, Chinese, and Diplomats: The American Protestant Missionary Movement in China, 1890–1952* (Princeton, NJ: Princeton University Press, 1958).

Varg, Paul. "The Myth of the China Market, 1890–1914," *AHR*, 73 (Feb. 1968): 742–58.

Vázquez, Josefina, ed. *De la rebelión de Texas a la guerra del 47* (Mexico City: Nueva Imagen, 1994).

Vázquez, Josefina, *México al tiempo de su guerra con Estados Unidos (1846–1848)* (Mexico City: Secretaría de Relaciones Exteriores, 1997).

Vázquez, Josefina, ed. *La Gran Bretaña frente al México amenazado 1835–1848* (Mexico City: Secretaría de Relaciones Exteriores, 2002).

Velasco Shaw, Angel and Luis Francia, eds. *The Philippine-American War and the Aftermath of an Imperial Dream, 1899–1999* (New York: New York University Press, 2002).

Venzon, Anne Cipriano. *General Smedley Darlington Butler: The Letters of a Leatherneck, 1898–1931* (Westport, CT: Praeger, 1992).

Véri, Joseph-Alphone abbé de. *Journal de l'abbé de Véri*, edited by Philippe Haudrère, 2 vols. (Geneva: Droz, 2016).

Verna, Paul. *Petión y Bolívar* (rev. ed., Caracas: Presidencia de la República, 1980).

Vlahos, Michael. "The Naval War College and the Origins of War-Planning Against Japan," *Naval War College Review* (July–August 1980): 23–45.

Walker, William. *The War in Nicaragua* (Mobile: S.H. Goetzel, 1860).

Wallace, Anthony. *Prelude to Disaster: The Course of Indian-White Relations Which Led to the Black Hawk War of 1832* (Springfield: Illinois Historical Library, 1970).

Wallace, Anthony. *Jefferson and the Indians: The Tragic Fate of the First Americans* (Cambridge, MA: Belknap Press, 1999).

Wallner, Peter. *Franklin Pierce: Martyr for the Union* (Concord, NH: Plaidswede, 2007).

Walpole, Spencer. *The Life of Lord John Russell*, 2 vols. (New York: Greenwood, 1968 [1889]).

Wang, Dong. *The United States and China: A History from the Eighteenth Century to the Present* (Lanham, MD: Rowman and Littlefield, 2013).

Wang, Guanhua, *In Search of Justice: The 1905–1906 Chinese Anti-American Boycott* (Cambridge, MA: Harvard University Pres, 2001).

Waresquiel, Emmanuel de. *Talleyrand. Le prince immobile* (rev. ed, Paris: Tallandier, 2015).

Warner, Dennis and Peggy Warner, *The Tide at Sunrise: A History of the Russo-Japanese War, 1904–1905* (New York: Charter House, 1974).

Warren, Gordon. *Fountain of Discontent: The Trent Affair and Freedom of the Seas* (Boston, MA: Northeastern University Press, 1981).

Warren, Louis. *God's Red Son: The Ghost Dance Religion and the Making of Modern America* (New York: Basic Books, 2017).

Warren, Stephen. "The Ohio Shawnees' Struggle Against Removal," in David Edmunds, ed., *Enduring Nations: Native Americans in the Midwest* (Urbana: University of Illinois Press, 2008), 72–93.

Washington, H.A. *The Writings of Thomas Jefferson*, 9 vols. (Washington DC: Taylor and Maury, 1853–54).

Weber, David, ed. *Foreigners in their Native Land: Historical Roots of the Mexican Americans* (Albuquerque: University of New Mexico Press, 2003 [1973]).

Webster, Charles. *The Foreign Policy of Castlereagh, 1815–1822* (London: Bell, 1925).

Webster, Charles, ed., *Britain and the Independence of Latin America, 1812–1830: Select Documents from the Foreign Office Archives*, 2 vols. (New York: Octagon Books, 1970 [1938]).

Weeks, William. *John Quincy Adams & American Global Empire* (Lexington: University Press of Kentucky, 1992).

Weigley, Russell. *The American Way of War: A History of United States Military Strategy and Policy* (Bloomington: Indiana University Press, 1973).

Weinberg, Albert. *Manifest Destiny: A Study of Nationalist Expansionism in American History* (Chicago: Quadrangle Books, 1963 [1935]).

Welch, Richard. "American Atrocities in the Philippines: The Indictment and the Response," *PHR* 43 (1974): 233–53.

Welch, Richard. *Response to Imperialism: The United States and the Philippine-American War, 1899–1902* (Chapel Hill: University of North Carolina Press, 1979).

Wells, Robert. "Population and Family in Early America," in Jack Greene and J.R. Pole, eds., *A Companion to the American Revolution* (Oxford, UK: Blackwell, 2000), 39–50.

West, Elliott. *The Contested Plains: Indians, Goldseekers, and the Rush to Colorado* (Lawrence: University Press of Kansas, 1998).

Bibliography

Wharton, Francis, ed. *Revolutionary Diplomatic Correspondence of the United States*, 6 vols. (Washington DC: GPO, 1889).

Whitaker, Arthur. *The United States and the Independence of Latin America, 1800–1830* (New York: Norton, 1964 [1941]).

Whitaker, Arthur. *The Spanish-American Frontier: 1783–1795* (Lincoln: University of Nebraska Press, 1969 [1927]).

White, Richard. "The American West and American Empire," in *Manifest Destinies and Indigenous People*, ed. David Maybury-Lewis et al. (Cambridge, MA: Harvard University Press, 2009), 203–24.

White, Richard. *The Middle Ground: Indians, Empires, and Republic in the Great Lakes Region, 1680–1815* (New York: Cambridge University Press, 2011).

Wiencheck. Henry. *An Imperfect God: George Washington, His Slaves, and the Creation of America* (New York: Farrar, Straus and Giroux, 2003).

Wilentz, Sean. *Andrew Jackson* (New York: Times Books, 2005).

Wiley, Peter. *Yankees in the Land of the Gods: Commodore Perry and the Opening of Japan* (New York: Viking, 1990).

Wilkins, Mira. *The Emergence of Multinational Enterprise: American Business Abroad from the Colonial Era to 1914* (Cambridge, MA: Harvard University Press, 1970).

Wilkins, Thurman. *Cherokee Tragedy: The Ridge Family and the Decimation of a People* (2nd rev. ed., Norman: University of Oklahoma Press, 1986).

Williams, Hal. *Realigning America: McKinley, Bryan, and the Remarkable Election of 1896* (Lawrence: University Press of Kansas, 2010).

Williams, Mary. *Anglo-American Isthmian Diplomacy, 1815–1915* (London: Forgotten Books, 2018 [1916]).

Williams, Walter. "United States Indian Policy and the Debate over Philippine Annexation: Implications for the Origins of American Imperialism," *JAH*, 66 no. 4 (March 1980): 810–31.

Willig, Timothy. *Restoring the Chain of Friendship: British Policy and the Indians of the Great Lakes, 1783–1815* (Lincoln: University of Nebraska Press, 2008).

Wilms, Douglas. "Cherokee Land Use in Georgia before Removal," in William Anderson, ed., *Cherokee Removal: Before and After* (Athens: University of Georgia Press, 1991).

Wilson, Hugh. *The Education of a Diplomat* (London: Longmans, Green and Co, 1938).

Wolf, Joshua. "'The Misfortune to Get Pressed': The Impressment of American Seamen and the Ramifications on the United States, 1793–1812," Ph.D. Dissertation, Temple University, 2015.

Wong, Kai Kah, "A Menace to America's Oriental Trade," *NAR*, 178 (March 1904): 414–24.

Wood, Gordon. *The Americanization of Benjamin Franklin* (New York: Penguin Press, 2004).

Wood, Gordon. *Empire of Liberty: A History of the Early Republic, 1789–1815* (New York: Oxford University Press, 2009).

Yela Utrilla, Juan-Francisco. *España ante la independencia de los Estados Unidos* (Madrid: Istmo, 1988 [1925]).

Yonge, Charles. *The Life and Administration of Robert Banks, Second Earl of Liverpool*, 3 vols. (London: Forgotten Books, 2015 [1868]).

Zilversmit, Arthur. *The First Emancipation: The Abolition of Slavery in the North* (Chicago, IL: University of Chicago Press, 1967).

Zimmerman, James. *Impressment of American Seamen* (New York: Columbia University Press, 1925).

Zobel, Hiller. *The Boston Massacre* (New York: Norton, 1970).

INDEX

Index

Index